International Journal on Advances in Intelligent Systems

IARIA

2016 vol. 9 nr. 1&2

Printed from e-media with permission by:

Curran Associates, Inc.
57 Morehouse Lane
Red Hook, NY 12571

Some format issues inherent in the e-media version may also appear in this print version.

Printed by Curran Associates, Inc. (2018)

International Academy, Research, and Industry Association (IARIA)
412 Derby Way
Wilmington, DE 19810

Phone: (408) 893-6407
Fax: (408) 527-6351

petre@iaria.org

Additional copies of this publication are available from:

Curran Associates, Inc.
57 Morehouse Lane
Red Hook, NY 12571 USA
Phone: 845-758-0400
Fax: 845-758-2634
Email: curran@proceedings.com
Web: www.proceedings.com

The *International Journal on Advances in Intelligent Systems* is Published by IARIA.
ISSN: 1942-2679
journals site: http://www.iariajournals.org
contact: petre@iaria.org

Reference should mention:

> *International Journal on Advances in Intelligent Systems, issn 1942-2679*
> *vol. 9, no. 1 & 2, year 2016, http://www.iariajournals.org/intelligent_systems/*

Reference to an article in the journal is as follows:

> *<Author list>, "<Article title>"*
> *International Journal on Advances in Intelligent Systems, issn 1942-2679*
> *vol. 9, no. 1 & 2, year 2016, <start page>:<end page> , http://www.iariajournals.org/intelligent_systems/*

IARIA journals are made available for free, proving the appropriate references are made when their content is used.

Sponsored by IARIA
www.iaria.org

International Journal on Advances in Intelligent Systems
Volume 9, Number 1 & 2, 2016

Roland Dodd, CQUniversity, Australia
Suzana Dragicevic, Simon Fraser University- Burnaby, Canada
Mauro Dragone, University College Dublin (UCD), Ireland
Marek J. Druzdzel, University of Pittsburgh, USA
Carlos Duarte, University of Lisbon, Portugal
Raimund K. Ege, Northern Illinois University, USA
Jorge Ejarque, Barcelona Supercomputing Center, Spain
Larbi Esmahi, Athabasca University, Canada
Simon G. Fabri, University of Malta, Malta
Umar Farooq, Amazon.com, USA
Mehdi Farshbaf-Sahih-Sorkhabi, Azad University - Tehran / Fanavaran co., Tehran, Iran
Anna Fensel, Semantic Technology Institute (STI) Innsbruck and FTW Forschungszentrum Telekommunikation Wien, Austria
Stenio Fernandes, Federal University of Pernambuco (CIn/UFPE), Brazil
Oscar Ferrandez Escamez, University of Utah, USA
Agata Filipowska, Poznan University of Economics, Poland
Ziny Flikop, Scientist, USA
Adina Magda Florea, University "Politehnica" of Bucharest, Romania
Francesco Fontanella, University of Cassino and Southern Lazio, Italy
Panagiotis Fotaris, University of Macedonia, Greece
Enrico Francesconi, ITTIG - CNR / Institute of Legal Information Theory and Techniques / Italian National Research Council, Italy
Rita Francese, Università di Salerno - Fisciano, Italy
Bernhard Freudenthaler, Software Competence Center Hagenberg GmbH, Austria
Sören Frey, Daimler TSS GmbH, Germany
Steffen Fries, Siemens AG, Corporate Technology - Munich, Germany
Somchart Fugkeaw, Thai Digital ID Co., Ltd., Thailand
Naoki Fukuta, Shizuoka University, Japan
Mathias Funk, Eindhoven University of Technology, The Netherlands
Adam M. Gadomski, Università degli Studi di Roma La Sapienza, Italy
Alex Galis, University College London (UCL), UK
Crescenzio Gallo, Department of Clinical and Experimental Medicine - University of Foggia, Italy
Matjaz Gams, Jozef Stefan Institute-Ljubljana, Slovenia
Raúl García Castro, Universidad Politécnica de Madrid, Spain
Fabio Gasparetti, Roma Tre University - Artificial Intelligence Lab, Italy
Joseph A. Giampapa, Carnegie Mellon University, USA
George Giannakopoulos, NCSR Demokritos, Greece
David Gil, University of Alicante, Spain
Harald Gjermundrod, University of Nicosia, Cyprus
Angelantonio Gnazzo, Telecom Italia - Torino, Italy
Luis Gomes, Universidade Nova Lisboa, Portugal
Nan-Wei Gong, MIT Media Laboratory, USA
Francisco Alejandro Gonzale-Horta, National Institute for Astrophysics, Optics, and Electronics (INAOE), Mexico
Sotirios K. Goudos, Aristotle University of Thessaloniki, Greece
Victor Govindaswamy, Concordia University - Chicago, USA
Gregor Grambow, University of Ulm, Germany
Fabio Grandi, University of Bologna, Italy
Andrina Granić, University of Split, Croatia
Carmine Gravino, Università degli Studi di Salerno, Italy
Michael Grottke, University of Erlangen-Nuremberg, Germany
Maik Günther, Stadtwerke München GmbH, Germany
Francesco Guerra, University of Modena and Reggio Emilia, Italy
Alessio Gugliotta, Innova SPA, Italy

Fakri Othman, Cardiff Metropolitan University, UK
Enn Õunapuu, Tallinn University of Technology, Estonia
Jeffrey Junfeng Pan, Facebook Inc., USA
Hervé Panetto, University of Lorraine, France
Malgorzata Pankowska, University of Economics, Poland
Harris Papadopoulos, Frederick University, Cyprus
Laura Papaleo, ICT Department - Province of Genoa & University of Genoa, Italy
Agis Papantoniou, National Technical University of Athens, Greece
Thanasis G. Papaioannou, École Polytechnique Fédérale de Lausanne (EPFL), Switzerland
Andreas Papasalouros, University of the Aegean, Greece
Eric Paquet, National Research Council / University of Ottawa, Canada
Kunal Patel, Ingenuity Systems, USA
Carlos Pedrinaci, Knowledge Media Institute, The Open University, UK
Yoseba Penya, University of Deusto - DeustoTech (Basque Country), Spain
Cathryn Peoples, Queen Mary University of London, UK
Asier Perallos, University of Deusto, Spain
Christian Percebois, Université Paul Sabatier - IRIT, France
Andrea Perego, European Commission, Joint Research Centre, Italy
Mark Perry, University of Western Ontario/Faculty of Law/ Faculty of Science - London, Canada
Willy Picard, Poznań University of Economics, Poland
Agostino Poggi, Università degli Studi di Parma, Italy
R. Ponnusamy, Madha Engineering College-Anna University, India
Stefan Poslad, Queen Mary University of London, UK
Wendy Powley, Queen's University, Canada
Jerzy Prekurat, Canadian Bank Note Co. Ltd., Canada
Didier Puzenat, Université des Antilles et de la Guyane, France
Sita Ramakrishnan, Monash University, Australia
Elmano Ramalho Cavalcanti, Federal University of Campina Grande, Brazil
Juwel Rana, Luleå University of Technology, Sweden
Martin Randles, School of Computing and Mathematical Sciences, Liverpool John Moores University, UK
Christoph Rasche, University of Paderborn, Germany
Ann Reddipogu, ManyWorlds UK Ltd, UK
Ramana Reddy, West Virginia University, USA
René Reiners, Fraunhofer FIT - Sankt Augustin, Germany
Paolo Remagnino, Kingston University - Surrey, UK
Sebastian Rieger, University of Applied Sciences Fulda, Germany
Andreas Riener, Johannes Kepler University Linz, Austria
Ivan Rodero, NSF Center for Autonomic Computing, Rutgers University - Piscataway, USA
Alejandro Rodríguez González, University Carlos III of Madrid, Spain
Paolo Romano, INESC-ID Lisbon, Portugal
Agostinho Rosa, Instituto de Sistemas e Robótica, Portugal
José Rouillard, University of Lille, France
Paweł Różycki, University of Information Technology and Management (UITM) in Rzeszów, Poland
Igor Ruiz-Agundez, DeustoTech, University of Deusto, Spain
Michele Ruta, Politecnico di Bari, Italy
Melike Sah, Trinity College Dublin, Ireland
Francesc Saigi Rubió, Universitat Oberta de Catalunya, Spain
Abdel-Badeeh M. Salem, Ain Shams University, Egypt
Yacine Sam, Université François-Rabelais Tours, France
Ismael Sanz, Universitat Jaume I, Spain
Ricardo Sanz, Universidad Politecnica de Madrid, Spain
Marcello Sarini, Università degli Studi Milano-Bicocca - Milano, Italy
Munehiko Sasajima, I.S.I.R., Osaka University, Japan

Minoru Sasaki, Ibaraki University, Japan
Hiroyuki Sato, University of Tokyo, Japan
Jürgen Sauer, Universität Oldenburg, Germany
Patrick Sayd, CEA List, France
Dominique Scapin, INRIA - Le Chesnay, France
Kenneth Scerri, University of Malta, Malta
Rainer Schmidt, Austrian Institute of Technology, Austria
Bruno Schulze, National Laboratory for Scientific Computing - LNCC, Brazil
Ingo Schwab, University of Applied Sciences Karlsruhe, Germany
Wieland Schwinger, Johannes Kepler University Linz, Austria
Hans-Werner Sehring, Namics AG, Germany
Paulo Jorge Sequeira Gonçalves, Polytechnic Institute of Castelo Branco, Portugal
Sandra Sendra Compte, Polytechnic University of Valencia, Spain
Kewei Sha, Oklahoma City University, USA
Roman Y. Shtykh, Rakuten, Inc., Japan
Robin JS Sloan, University of Abertay Dundee, UK
Vasco N. G. J. Soares, Instituto de Telecomunicações / University of Beira Interior / Polytechnic Institute of Castelo Branco, Portugal
Don Sofge, Naval Research Laboratory, USA
Christoph Sondermann-Woelke, Universitaet Paderborn, Germany
George Spanoudakis, City University London, UK
Vladimir Stantchev, SRH University Berlin, Germany
Claudius Stern, University of Paderborn, Germany
Mari Carmen Suárez-Figueroa, Universidad Politécnica de Madrid (UPM), Spain
Kåre Synnes, Luleå University of Technology, Sweden
Ryszard Tadeusiewicz, AGH University of Science and Technology, Poland
Yehia Taher, ERISS - Tilburg University, The Netherlands
Yutaka Takahashi, Senshu University, Japan
Dan Tamir, Texas State University, USA
Jinhui Tang, Nanjing University of Science and Technology, P.R. China
Yi Tang, Chinese Academy of Sciences, China
John Terzakis, Intel, USA
Sotirios Terzis, University of Strathclyde, UK
Vagan Terziyan, University of Jyvaskyla, Finland
Lucio Tommaso De Paolis, Department of Innovation Engineering - University of Salento, Italy
Davide Tosi, Università degli Studi dell'Insubria, Italy
Raquel Trillo Lado, University of Zaragoza, Spain
Tuan Anh Trinh, Budapest University of Technology and Economics, Hungary
Simon Tsang, Applied Communication Sciences, USA
Theodore Tsiligiridis, Agricultural University of Athens, Greece
Antonios Tsourdos, Cranfield University, UK
José Valente de Oliveira, University of Algarve, Portugal
Eugen Volk, University of Stuttgart, Germany
Mihaela Vranić, University of Zagreb, Croatia
Chieh-Yih Wan, Intel Labs, Intel Corporation, USA
Jue Wang, Washington University in St. Louis, USA
Shenghui Wang, OCLC Leiden, The Netherlands
Zhonglei Wang, Karlsruhe Institute of Technology (KIT), Germany
Laurent Wendling, University Descartes (Paris 5), France
Maarten Weyn, University of Antwerp, Belgium
Nancy Wiegand, University of Wisconsin-Madison, USA
Alexander Wijesinha, Towson University, USA
Eric B. Wolf, US Geological Survey, Center for Excellence in GIScience, USA

International Journal on Advances in Intelligent Systems
Volume 9, Numbers 1 & 2, 2016

CONTENTS

Reliable Document-centric Processing and Choreography Policy in a Loosely Coupled Email-based System

Magdalena Godlewska
University of Gdansk
Faculty of Mathematics, Physics and Informatics
Institute of Informatics
Gdansk, Poland
Email: maggod@inf.ug.edu.pl

***Abstract*—Email is a simple way to exchange digital documents of any kind. The Mobile INteractive Document architecture (MIND) enables self-coordination and self-steering of document agent systems based on commonly available email services. In this paper, a mechanism for providing integrity and reliability of such an email based agent system is proposed to cope with message soft or hard bounces, user interrupts, and other unexpected events. This mechanism consists of a system acting as a "ground control" for migrating documents and a set of protocols that improve the implementation of document coordination patterns. It allows for an estimation of the global state of a distributed loosely coupled agent system and making top-down decisions in unforeseen situations. In complex human organizations, it is important to determine who can make decisions and what is their scope in the process. The choreography policy allows for defining communication tactics and assigning permissions of workflow editing to participants of the process.**

***Keywords*–multi-agent systems; collaborative work; electronic documents; email-based systems; knowledge-based organization; choreography**

I. Introduction

This paper extends the previous work describing "ground control" service to ensure reliability of workflow processes in a loosely coupled email system [1].

A knowledge-based organization is a management idea, describing an organization in which cooperating people use knowledge resources to achieve organizational goals. People are the key intellectual resource but only collaboration with other workers in accordance with the organizational procedures enables converting knowledge of individuals to knowledge of organization [2]. Section II outlines main features of the knowledge-based organization from the perspective of the knowledge resources and the interaction between them. This section is new from the previous paper [1] and presents the motivation for the work of the MIND architecture.

Knowledge workers communicate through the exchange of documents constituting units of information. Nowadays, email has a dominant position in the computer mediated communication and document exchange in the workplace [3]. Email messaging provides an easy to use simple textual form and allows to disseminate attachments in any format to one or multiple recipients.

The MIND architecture [4] is a proposition of a document-centric uniform interface to provide both effective communication of content and coordination of activities performed on documents. MIND is a solution that augments email messaging with proactive documents, capable of initiating process activities, interacting with individual workers on their personal devices and migrating on their own between collaborators. Thus, each MIND document is a mobile agent. Document-agents have built-in migration policy to control their own workflow and services to proper processing contained information. Section III contains a more detailed overview of the MIND architecture.

The migration path of the document-agent contains all information and status of the workflow process to perform it locally on users' devices. An email client installed on each worker's device participating in the process needs to be extended with functionality to activate the document-agents and switch documents between the activity and transition phases of the workflow. This special email client with workflow enactment capability has been implemented as a Local Workflow Engine (LWE) [5]. All LWEs participating in the process and performing independently form together both a loosely-coupled agent system and a distributed workflow enactment service. Section IV outlines generic functionality of LWE and the idea of distributed workflow enactment service.

In the LWE-based MIND system, individual knowledge workers perform activities on documents independently, using their personal devices, and yet collaborate on achieving a common goal. This is possible owing to the migration policy embedded in each document. This policy defines for each document a workflow process composed of specific document-flow patterns that provide process wide coordination. The document-flow patterns [5] are the result of analysis of the coordination patterns proposed by van der Aaalst [6] under the assumption that email is the transport layer for document migration. The work of van der Aaalst shows that a relatively small and well defined set of collaboration patterns contains building blocks of arbitrary complex workflow processes in real organizations. Thus, the document-flow patterns that directly follow the collaborations patterns for the proposed MIND architecture enable modeling and coordination of any workflow process.

The crucial services for MIND implementation are executability and mobility. The former involves activating document-agents to enable their autonomous execution, while the latter involves transporting them between users' devices in accordance with the migration policy. These services have already been implemented and described before [4][5]. In the prototype system, mobility has been implemented based on email as the transport layer.

In most cases, these mentioned services are sufficient to properly perform the MIND agent system. However, in human organizations, some situations unforeseen by the designer of the process may occur and the reliable system should be able to cope with them. For a distributed loosely coupled and interactive system it is impossible to determine a global state of all document-agents. Consequently, it is not possible to determine where all documents are located at a specific time. A document may be lost and it often remains beyond the knowledge of the authors, who have edited it earlier. There are various reasons why documents may be lost: a problem with a transport layer, an error of a local environment or an unexpected user behavior. The initial workflow process definition makes it possible to search for documents in the specified places. However, the process may be modified during its execution. Therefore, a document may take a path that was not originally designed and a document originator has not information about its definition.

Thus, the *reliability* of the MIND agent system is a service that makes the system more useful and trustworthy than the typical email-based communication. It allows for an estimation of the global state of a distributed loosely coupled system, taking into account transport layer errors, unforeseen actions of users and process modifications.

Thus, Section V identifies problems associated with distributed workflow execution. Section V-A focuses on the problems associated with email as the transport layer for the MIND documents, while Section V-B presents problems that may occur in specific document-flow patterns. In particular, it is interesting the canceling pattern due to the loosely-coupling principle at operating of the MIND agent system.

Section VI presents a concept of a "ground control" service, which introduces the ability to track document-agents globally and solve some of the problems associated with the documents flow. The service is designed to receive signals containing the status of the document from the LWE clients and send control signals to LWEs that resolve situations incompatible with the designed workflow. The proposed syntax of a notification sending to the "ground control" service is adapted to document-flow patterns. Further, this section outlines two pilot implementations of the "ground control" service – one using the Handle System [7], and another based on an email-based notification system. It also presents assumptions for tracing tool and its possible implementation.

The "ground control" service enables a global monitoring of the process and extends communication by message-based interactions among the participants. But it would be very impractical if the whole complex process of the organization was tracked only by one worker. Thus, there are important questions: which workers can monitor or change workflow process and how should be specified messaging behavior of the workflow participants. The impact of many workers on the process execution, interaction and communication between them from a global perspective is defined by a concept called a choreography [8]. The choreography policy allows for defining communication tactics and editing workflow strategy. It can be added to the MIND architecture as a new policy, which is presented in Section VII. This section is new from the previous paper [1].

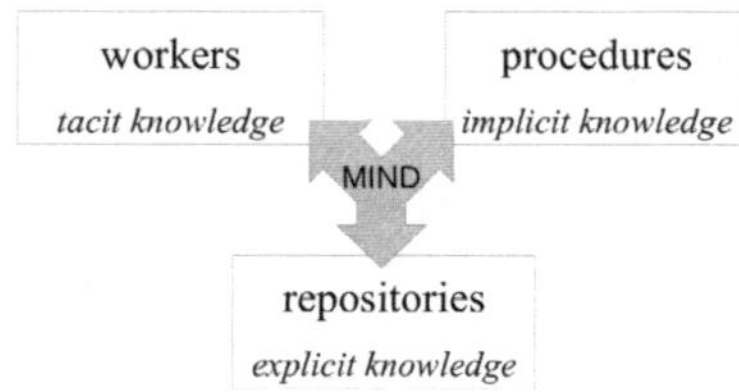

Figure 1. The knowledge resources in the knowledge-based organization.

Section VIII presents real use-cases based on business scenarios. Section IX surveys previous work related to a document-centric processing and a reliability of workflow enactment in distributed loosely-coupled systems.

II. A KNOWLEDGE-BASED ORGANIZATION

Data are defined as symbols that represent properties of objects, events and their environment. They are the products of some "observation". But are of no use until they are in a relevant form. Information can be defined as ordering and interpretation of data based on some patterns. The set of patterns in a certain context creates knowledge. Knowledge is know-how, and is what makes possible the transformation of information into instructions. New knowledge is built through the creation of new patterns [9].

Knowledge-based organizations focus on processes based on collection, transfer and use of knowledge. Such processes are called knowledge processes. Knowledge workers play an important role in the knowledge process. They generate new knowledge based on current information, their own knowledge and knowledge transferred by other workers mostly through the documents. The purpose of the knowledge-based organization is to implement the knowledge process, in which the human mind is an important element [2][4].

The literature on knowledge management distinguishes three types of knowledge: explicit, implicit and tacit [10]. These terms reflect the knowledge resources use in the knowledge process and presented in Figure 1.

- *repositories* with explicit knowledge that has been articulated, encoded mostly in documents and organized in a form enabling accessibility, such as databases, libraries or knowledge bases.
- *procedures* are mostly implicit knowledge that is not written down yet but locked in processes, products, culture, routines, artifacts, or structures and not dependent on an individuals context. It is known also as embedded or procedural knowledge.
- *workers* with their tacit knowledge, i.e., the knowledge in their heads that is made up from personal learning and experience. It is not written down and is often hard or impossible to articulate.

These knowledge resources and the interaction between them are essential in processes of the knowledge-based organization. Workers are the key knowledge resource of an organization and there are some interfaces enable them to access the three types of knowledge resources mentioned above. These interfaces are often independent of each other and they push most of the work on workers, i.e., workers

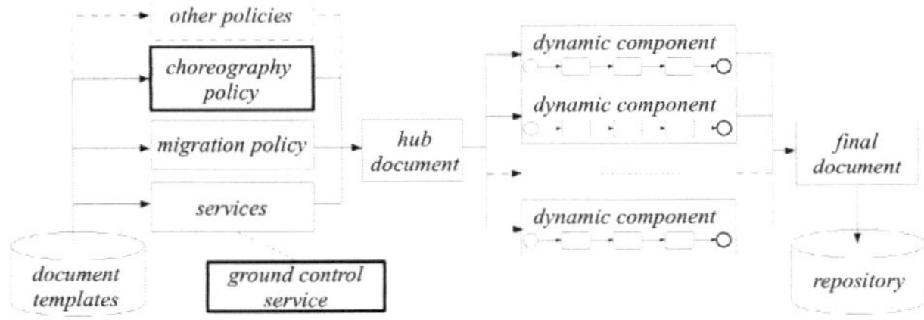

Figure 2. The MIND document lifecycle.

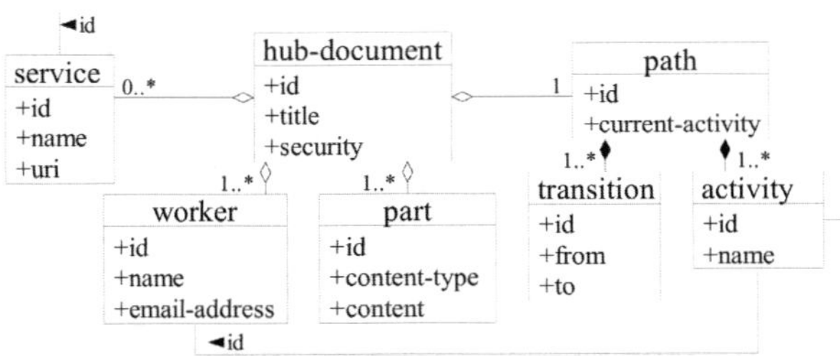

Figure 3. Dynamic form of the MIND architecture [5].

can query repositories, workers often must know procedures or sometimes they are supported by workflow tools, and workers initiate communication with coworkers. Thus, people do simultaneously: creative work, which is their goal, and bureaucratic work, which can be largely automated.

The MIND architecture, outlined in the next section, enables to direct the attention of workers to their creative work, through the coordination of process activities and simplification of interaction with the knowledge resources.

III. THE MIND ARCHITECTURE

The MIND architecture enables the new agent-based distributed processing model. Traditionally, electronic documents have been static objects downloaded from a server or sent by email. MIND allows static documents to be converted into a set of dynamic components that can migrate between collaborative workers according to their migration policy.

The concept of the MIND document life cycle is illustrated in Figure 2. At the beginning of the knowledge process, some originator forms a *hub document* based on document templates that includes *migration policy*, which specifies the steps of the process and services that will be performed on different parts of the document during the process. The hub document is changing to mobile components that meet their mission in the distributed agent system. Each component performs its migration policy and interacts with workers of the organization.

The MIND architecture makes possible a radical shift from *data-centric* distributed systems, with hard-coded functionality, to flexible *document-centric* ones, where specialized functionality is embedded in migrating document components and some generic or supporting services are provided by local devices or external servers. The essence of the MIND architecture is that the documents have capability of self-organization and self-steering during the process execution.

Figure 3 outlines the dynamic form of the MIND architecture. It includes five components: *hub-document* is the main component and it contains basic information about all MIND document and is common to all other components, *worker* component contains data about workers who participate in the process, *part* component defines parts of the document, *service* component contains information about services that can be performed on different parts of the document during the process, and *path* component defines migration policy of each part of the document. It specifies the steps of the process and activities that should be performed at each step of the process.

The service objects provide document functionality that makes it proactive. Three types of services are possible: *embedded* that are transferred together with the document, *local*, which may be acquired by the document components from local worker's device, and *external*, called on the remote hosts by the worker's system at the request of arriving document.

The components of the MIND dynamic form reflect the knowledge resources presented in Section II. The worker component defines the participants of the process, who bring to the organization their tacit knowledge. The part component defines parts of whole MIND document, each of which contains a constituent document migrates independently between the participants in the process. The constituent document is a specific document with a specified format, structure and purpose, e.g., an Excel document with attendance list. Thus, parts reflect explicit knowledge. They are created based on templates available in organization, accumulate knowledge obtained from workers during the process, and finally, they are archived in repository for future use. The path component is an implementation of organizational procedures. The path component may be modified during the process, thus knowledge remains implicit in general. The service component, which activates the MIND document, allows interaction between other components.

The MIND architecture can be considered as a knowledge organization system in its general definition. Generally, the term *knowledge organization systems (KOSs)* is intended to encompass all types of schemes for organizing information and promoting knowledge management [11]. Originally, KOSs were used in digital libraries, but they are mechanisms for organizing information, so the term may be used in the context of knowledge management systems in all knowledge-based organizations. Especially, MIND has the following characteristics of the KOS [11]:

- in the static form, MIND is a set of schemes for organizing information, promoting knowledge management and defining migration policy of the documents.
- serves as a bridge between the users information need and a document contained this information. User are able to receive a relevant document without prior knowledge of its existence.
- adapts to the requirements of a particular organization through the ability to add services and editing workflow.
- adapts to the specific case, using the same document templates in a variety of ways.
- does not impose a fixed structure, but supports the knowledge of users, adapting to their requirements.

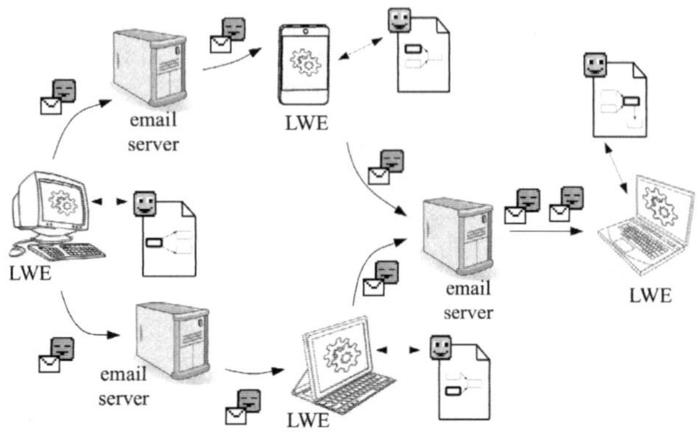

Figure 4. Distributed workflow enactment service based on LWE clients and email transport layer (LWEs are symbolized as gear wheels).

– supports knowledge workers with their creative work, through the coordination of process activities and simplification of interaction with the knowledge resources. In this manner, it facilitates the generation of new knowledge of organization.

The MIND architecture may be extended with new services and politics. The bold line rectangles in Figure 2 depict additional functions, which are not necessary to properly perform the MIND agent system, but allow for improving it and adapting to the characteristics of human organization. The *ground control service* makes system more reliable by tracing documents globally. It is also used in new *choreography policy* that enables enhanced workflow management by knowledge workers.

IV. Distributed workflow enactment

A key feature of the MIND architecture is physical distribution of business process activities, performed dynamically on a system of independent personal devices. MIND documents have built-in process definition and functionality (the respective path and embedding service components mentioned in the previous section). This makes them agents, which are autonomous and mobile. Especially, they are independent of any particular platform supporting workflow enactment and they are capable of launching individual activities onto various workers' devices, which maintain process coordination across the organization.

Workflow enactment service interprets the process description and control sequencing of activities through one or more cooperating workflow engines [12]. Even if the workflow engines are distributed, workflow enactment is centralized in most of the implementations, because the control data must be available for all engines. In the MIND architecture, all data needed for workflow enactment are embedded in documents [5]. This allows for implementation of distributed workflow enactment service consisting of LWEs.

The idea of the distributed workflow enactment service built on top of LWE clients and email transport layer is illustrated in Figure 4. In the prototype system, LWE was implemented as lightweight email client installed on personal devices of each worker. Each LWE is independent of other LWEs, so it can be implemented in any technology and adapted

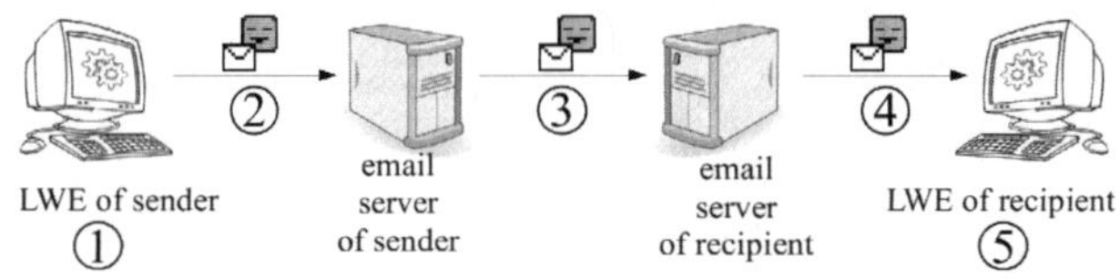

Figure 5. LWE to LWE connection. The numbers indicate points, where some problems with the transport of the document may occur.

to requirements of particular devices, especially mobile devices such as tablets and smartphones. Also, it may be implemented as a plug-in to existing email clients.

States of the LWE correspond to the phases of a document lifetime and the initial state is when a message with a document is received, i.e., noticed by LWE in the worker's mailbox. The LWE downloads the document on the local device and activates it, which means launching its embedded functionality. The activated document may interact with the knowledge worker, his/her local system and some external services. The interaction begins with obtaining the document path component and determining the current activity that should be performed in this particular step of the process. If the next activity is intended for another worker, the document is serialized, packed and sent as an attachment to the next worker's email address.

LWE is capable of recognizing and executing all document-flow patterns contained in the path component. More details about the document-flow patterns are in Section V-B, which presents a discussion about their execution in a loosely-coupled distributed system consisting of the LWE clients.

V. Problems of reliable workflow execution

MIND and LWE clients form a distributed workflow enactment system, in which the coordination of activities is based on control data contained in the documents. In most cases, it ensures that the documents arrive at a specific location at a specific time. Nevertheless, some situations unforeseen by the designer of the process may occur in loosely-coupled system.

First of all, the document may be lost: during the transfer by email, due to failure of the local system, accidentally deleted by the user. The transfer of the document may also be delayed to miss the designed deadline. The knowledge worker may also make a decision unforeseen by the workflow, e.g., cancel some document flow or modify the workflow path, which is just not possible in typical message passing via email.

Figure 5 shows the path of the document from a sender to a recipient and indicates points where some problems may occur. Points ②–④ are associated with several well known email transport layer problems briefly described in Section V-A, while points ① and ⑤ indicate problems with document-flow patterns execution by LWE clients, detailed in Section V-B.

A. Email transport layer problems

Email message is a simple textual form combined with attachments in any format. It can be sent to one or multiple recipients and supports asynchronous work. Email mechanisms have a reputation of being robust and trustworthy since its invention a few decades ago, as email messages reach their recipients in most cases without problems. Nevertheless, there is a list of problems associated with the delivery of messages.

The first step in the email processing model is to submit email message by an email client (Mail User Agent – MUA) to a sender Simple Mail Transfer Protocol (SMTP) server (Mail Transfer Agent – MTA) [13]. Figure 5 indicates it as point ②. This step may fail due to the lack of network connection, incorrect SMTP server configuration or SMTP server failure. The message usually remains in the sender outbox and the email client tries to send it again. Configuration of SMTP server for LWE client does not differ from the configuration of other email clients and does not require any special functionality. Temporary lack of network connection is a typical situation for mobile devices. SMTP server failure is a rather transient situation that can be solved by resending the email message.

In the next step, sender MTA transfers messages to the receiver MTA mostly by SMTP protocol (point ③ in Figure 5). SMTP server should deliver the message or notify about any problem [13]. The SMTP reply consists of a three digit number often followed by some text for the human user. The message may be rejected, however, in a transient or permanent way. In transient situations, the SMTP client should try to send the message again. In the case of permanent errors, the SMTP client should not repeat the exact request. After a failed attempt to send a message, the sender SMTP agent sends a notification message to the mail user agent. This notification message is known as a Delivery Status Notification (DSN) or email bounce [14].

Nevertheless, receiving of email bounces does not necessarily mean that the message has not been delivered and, conversely, the lack of notice does not necessarily mean that a message has arrived to the recipient. For instance, the receiver SMTP server may silently drop message to protect themselves from attacks [13]. Many SMTP servers are configured to block messages categorized as spam based on DNS blacklists or anti-spam filters [15].

Receiving a message by the SMTP server and placing it in a user's mailbox does not imply that the user will read it. Point ④ in Figure 5 indicates the problem of the recipient's email server – email client communication. Firstly, some messages may be marked as spam and placed in the spam folder in user's mailbox. In this case, the frameworks to build mail applications (like Java Mail [16] and IMAP – Internet Message Access Protocol [17] used in the LWE implementation) often enable access to the spam folder. In fact, also the email client may have its own spam filters and other solutions to manage received messages automatically, like the automatic responses software (e.g., "out of office" message) [18].

Next to email bounces and automatic responses there is one more type of notifications, the Message Disposition Notifications (MDNs) [19]. These notifications are intended to report of the disposition of a message after it successfully reaches a recipient's mailbox. The MDN can be used to notify the sender of any of several conditions that may occur after successful delivery such as display, printing or deletion of the message. Allow mail user agents to keep track of the message (only) in its subsequent step of the flow. The sending of the response depends on the functionality of recipient email client and often on the decision of the recipient.

Message tracking is also possible through email tracking services like ReadNotify [20] or WhoReadMe [21]. These services add to the message some hidden information: picture, or pieces of HyperText Markup Language (HTML) code (like IFRAMEs). Tracking is hidden from the recipient and not too elegant.

There is yet another reason for which the message may not reach the mail user agent - the human action. The recipient may accidentally or intentionally delete the message from his/her mailbox, move it to a different folder or mark it as a spam. Also, his/her email client or a local system may fail.

B. Document-flow patterns execution

In mailing systems, notification mechanisms can provide the status of messages in their the next step of flow, but never any further. It can be said that the email message can store history of its own flow, inform about its next step, but does not "know" its future flow. The MIND document has an embedded workflow path, thus it has information about whole its flow and about flow of other documents in the process. However, a worker that finished his activity has no control on further flow of document – this knowledge is built in document, which has left his device.

In some cases, the location of the document may be required for the proper execution of the workflow process, especially in unexpected situations, like a lost document. LWE temporarily stores copy of documents in the worker's mailbox, in case the process has to be recreated from a certain place. Searching for a document in all places indicated by a workflow is possible but often time-consuming and costly, and may not take into account the modification of the path during the process execution.

This paper proposes a "ground control" external service for receiving and storing notifications from LWEs about status of documents. Each notification from LWEs contains information about: process id, document id, current activity id, and sender of the notification. This section presents what other information about the document should be included in the notifications for reliable coordination of all document-flow patterns.

Based on the work of van der Aaalst [6] and the result of previous research [5], three categories of document-flow patters have been identified: distributed state patterns, coupled state patterns, and embedded state patterns.

1) Distributed state patterns: These patterns describe situations in which the next activity or activities can be determined solely on the state of the current activity. Four patterns of this type have been distinguished: sequencer, splitter, merger, and iterator.

a) Document sequencer: This pattern involves a knowledge worker sending a document to another worker. The document may be sent in its entirety in one message or it may be partitioned into several messages. In this basic situation, the following problems may occur: a sender may receive bounce notifications from each sent message and recipient may not receive all messages. However, a bounce notification does not always mean that the recipient has not received the message in a timely manner. In this pattern, the notification should contain one of the three route-status: sent (sends from sender's LWE after sending the document), received (sends from recipient's LWE - after receiving the document) or bounced (sends from sender's LWE - after receiving the bounce notification). It is possible that some notification does not reach to the "ground control" service or arrives in the wrong order. Thus, in all patterns, the *received* status and the subsequent *sent* status are considered to more important then previous *bounced* and *received*.

b) Document splitter: This pattern creates identical copies of the document or partitions it into separate fragments. The resulting documents are next sent to the respective knowledge workers specified in the migration policy. These documents, either copies or fragments, get new document IDs. The parent document is considered to be delivered if all its child documents have been delivered. Thus, the *sent* route-status is given to each parent and child documents. The parent document has also assigned a *splitted* document-status and references to the child documents are indicated. Each arrived child document gets the *received* status individually. Once all the child documents have the *received* status (or the subsequent *sent* status), the "ground control" service gives automatically the *received* status to the parent document. The child documents are determined by the references. The *bounced* status is also assigned to each child document separately.

c) Document merger: This pattern complementing the document splitter pattern merges all received documents in one. Of course, this pattern may involve various document functionality, depending on whether the preceding splitter has been cloning or decomposing. But before merging, all the expected documents must be delivered. The LWE client on the basis of path component of the first received document determines the number of expected documents that have to be merged. Each of the arrived document gets the *received* status. When all documents are collected, they are merged and a new document gets the *received* route-status and constitutes documents get the *merged* document-status and reference to this new merged document. The document merger fails when at least one child document has been not received. In exceptional situations, decision about completing merger before receiving all child document may be made.

d) Document iterator: This pattern enables repeated execution of some sequence of activities controlled by a condition specified in the respective document migration policy. The route-status is assigned as in document sequencer, but the activities can be performed several times and notification may be received by "ground control" service in incorrect order. Thus, the activity id and route-status is not enough to determine where the document resides. To solve this problem, some basic partial ordering mechanism, like Lamport's timestamps [22], has been used. The path component of the document has a timestamp attribute that is incremented by LWE. When the documents are merged, the new one gets a maximum value of all merged documents' timestamps plus 1. Thus, each notification contains also a timestamp value.

2) Coupled state patterns: Sometimes completion of an activity performed by one worker may require a notification on a state of some activity performed by another worker somewhere in the organization. That involves the notion of asynchronous signals, sent between different parts of the workflow process. Three document-flow patterns of this kind have been distinguished: deferred choice, milestone and cancel activity.

a) Deferred choice and milestone: These patterns are used to deal with situations when the current activity of one worker has to be blocked until a signal notifying on some external event has been received from another worker. Both patterns require a proactive document to provide a worker's device with a semaphore and embedded functionality to handle it. Initial value of the semaphore is closed, so if the signal from another worker has not been received, the current activity is blocked. Upon receiving a signal, the waiting activity is resumed. Deferred choice is used when sending a given document has to be postponed until the worker gets information to whom it should be sent. Milestone just blocks some activity of one worker by another. The problem appears, if the signal does not arrive within the specified time and the received document activity can not be proceed. In this case, the route-status of the document is *received* but the signal-status is *waiting*.

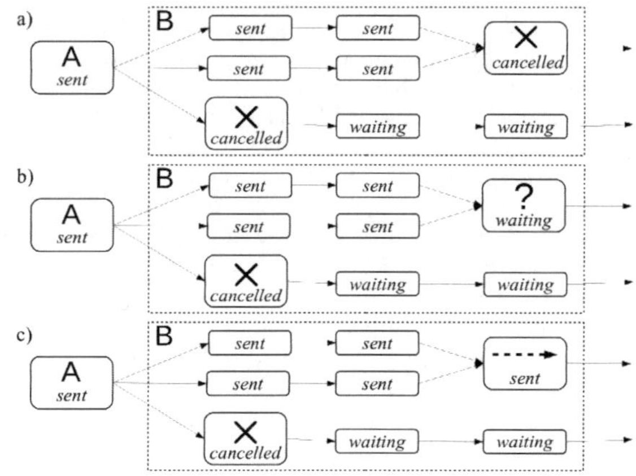

Figure 6. Cancellation of the document.

b) Cancelling pattern: Implementation of this pattern depends on what exactly should be cancelled. If a particular activity should be cancelled, a cancellation signal is sent only to the LWE client responsible for its performance. The decision on canceling the activity is immediate for the receiving device or does not make sense any more if the document has been sent to another worker.

More problematic situation is to cancel the document, because it requires the designation of its location. It is possible to search for a document in all places indicated by the workflow, but the "ground control" service can significantly reduce this set of places. If the route-status of document is *received*, the cancellation signal is sent only to the sender of that notification. After a successful cancellation, LWE sends the *cancelled* route-status.

If instead the *cancelled* route-status, the "ground control" service receives the *sent* status, it can start chasing the document. This situation is shown in Figure 6. To increase the chance of success, a cancellation signal is sent to, say, three subsequent activities for each possible path of the document flow. The three cases are possible for each activity: an activity was finished, an activity is currently being preformed or waiting for a document. Figure 6a) shows successful cancellation, i.e., the "ground control" service received a *cancelled* notification from all possible paths of the document. Figure 6b) shows cancellation potentially successful but not yet completed. While Figure 6c) shows the failed cancellation - the cancelling process should be continued for the subsequent

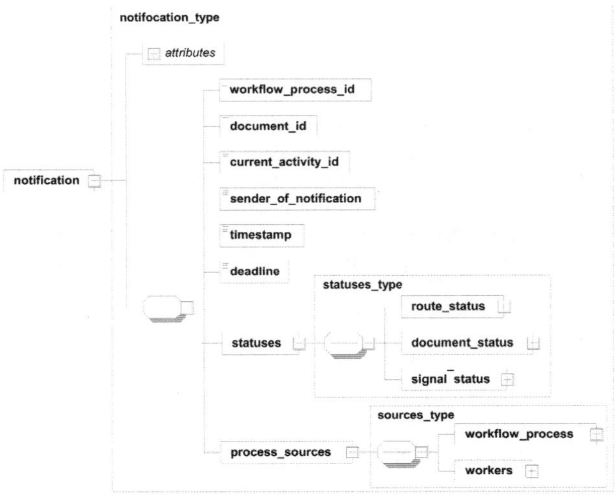

Figure 7. Schema of notification.

TABLE I. RELIABILITY OF PATTERNS EXECUTION

PATTERN	PROBLEMS TO SOLVE
Sequencer	Check whether the document has reached the recipient. Route-status: sent, received, bounced.
Splitter	Check whether all constituents of the splitted document have reached the recipients. Route-status: sent, received, bounced. Document-status: splitted (for splitted document + references to constituents).
Merger	Check whether all documents that should be merged into one have reached the recipient. Route-status: sent, received, bounced. Document-status: merged (for merged documents + references to new document).
Iterator	Check whether the document has reached the recipient as many times as it has been established in the loop. Route-status: sent, received, bounced. Timestamp to determine the order of the activities.
Deffered choice Milestone	Check whether both the document and the signal have reached the recipient. Route-status: sent, received, bounced. Signal-status: waiting (or indefinite).
Cancelling	Check whether the document has been cancelled. Route-status: cancelled (when it succeeded).
Internal subprocess	Track a subprocess added during the workflow process execution. Attach subprocess sources to the notification.
External subprocess	This pattern is not tracked by the "ground control" service.

activities on this particular path.

It is worth mentioning that the rate of the document flow is measured in minutes or hours, even days, rather than seconds. For example, the Intel's Email Service Level Agreement defines the acceptable time frame for replying to emails to 24 hours [23]. Thus, chasing the document will not be so much demanding as it might appear to be.

3) Embedded state patterns: Performing an activity by some worker may require a subprocess delegated to someone else, with activities not specified originally in the migration policy of the arriving document. States of such a subprocess are embedded in the state of the current activity enabling that.

a) Internal subprocess: If the current worker is authorized to extend the original migration policy of a document with new activities, they constitute an internal subprocess. Neither the structure of the internal subflow nor identity of added workers have to be known earlier to the workflow designer. The notification from the subflow activities are the same like from other activities, but the "ground control" service has only the structure of the designed workflow. Thus, for reliable coordination of subflow, its structure and identity of added workers must be sent to the "ground control" service. If the "ground control" does not have the current data of the subprocesses, tracing a document, and in particular, the cancellation may not be possible.

b) External subprocess: The performed activity may call some external subprocess, which structure are unknown for both, workflow designer and the performer of the current activity. The external subprocess is often performed outside of the organization, thus, it is not traced by the "ground control" service. Only the lack of received notification at the end of the subprocess within the specified time may indicate troubles.

The document-flow patterns analysis allowed for formulating the syntax of notifications, which schema is presented in Figure 7. The route-status type should be one of the: sent, received, bounced, cancelled and finished, the optional document-status can be one of the: splitted or merged. The signal-status can be waiting or just indefinite. Each notification

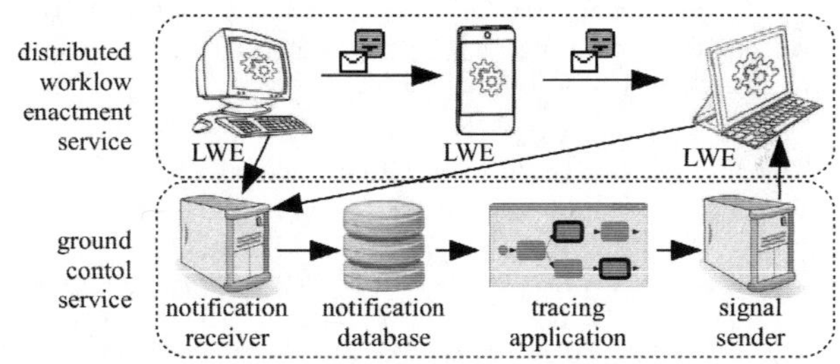

Figure 8. The *Ground control* service architecture.

contains also timestamp value. LWE performed a first activity adds to the notification a migration path and information about workers. If it notices a modification of the path component by adding a subprocess, it also sends definition of subprocess and information about new workers to provide the most recent data of the process. Table I summarizes the problems associated with the reliable execution of presented patterns.

VI. GROUND CONTROL SERVICE

This is an external service intended for a central document tracing to ensure the reliability of distributed workflow execution. The workflow enactment remains distributed and may be still performed without it, however. The intention of the "ground control" service is to collect notifications from LWEs in order to determine the approximate global state of the distributed document flow and to make top-down decisions in some unforeseen cases. The document policy component decides whether the notification has to be sent or not.

Figure 8 presents the concept of this service. It constitutes a notification receiver, i.e., a service receiving notifications from the LWEs via the particular transport layer. Then, the notifications are parsed and placed in the database. The notification database has some functionality, e.g., trigger that gives automatically the *received* status to the splitted document, after all its child documents have also got this status.

A tracing application visualizes the workflow process and marks the currently executing activities, designated on the basis of the notifications. It is also an interface for some users allows for monitoring the process and/or makes some top-down decisions. Some decisions may require sending the notification signal to the particular LWE. Signals are generated by the tracing application and transfered by the signal sender service.

A. Implementation

Two possible implementations of transferring and storing notifications were taken into account. The former uses the Handle System, while the latter uses an email-based notification system.

1) Handle System [7]: is a solution for assigning, managing, storing and resolving persistent identifiers for digital objects on the Internet. It includes a set of protocols enabling a distributed computer system to store identifiers of digital resources and resolve those identifiers into the information necessary to locate and access the resources. This information can be changed to reflect the current state of the identified resource without changing the identifier. The most popular system based on Handle System is DOI (Digital Object Identifier) [24] used for persistent citations in scholarly materials, research datasets or European Union official publications.

The Handle System defines a hierarchical service model. The top level consists of a single handle service, known as the Global Handle Registry. The lower level consists of all other handle services, known as Local Handle Services. The Handle System provides the Java-based Handle Server and a set of tools needed for the Local Handle Service installation. The Global Handle Registry is used to manage any handle namespace and provides the service used to manage naming authorities. The Local Handle Service and its responsible set of local handle namespaces must be registered with the Global Handle Registry and gets a unique prefix.

The Handle System provides unique persistent identifiers called handles for digital objects, such as the MIND document. The handle is a character string that consists of two parts: its naming authority and a local name separated by the ASCII (American Standard Code for Information Interchange) character "/". Each handle may have a set of values assigned to it. A handle value may be thought as a record that consists of a group of data fields. Every handle value must have a data type. The Handle System predefines a set of data types and allows for defining another.

Thus, the "ground control" service can use the Handle System to create an unique handle for each migrating document (see Figure 9). Each handle has a set of values corresponding to the syntax of the LWE notifications. The LWE modifies it at each change of document status.

Nevertheless, this solution has some disadvantages. Modifications of handles occur frequently, and each time they require a connection with Global Handle Registry. Besides, the Local Handle Service administration requires additional skills and needs control of other than email transport layer. The Handle System indicates the current location of the document. However, extraction of the list of all the documents in given process requires additional functionality. The Handle System tracks each document separately.

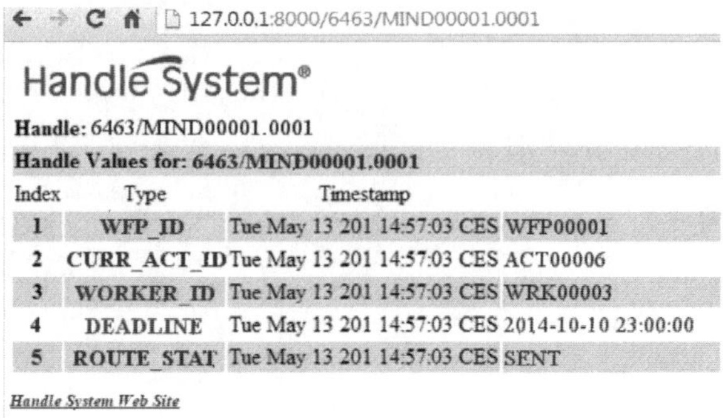
127.0.0.1:8000/6463/MIND00001.0001

Handle System®

Handle: 6463/MIND00001.0001

Handle Values for: 6463/MIND00001.0001

Index	Type	Timestamp	
1	WFP_ID	Tue May 13 201 14:57:03 CES	WFP00001
2	CURR_ACT_ID	Tue May 13 201 14:57:03 CES	ACT00006
3	WORKER_ID	Tue May 13 201 14:57:03 CES	WRK00003
4	DEADLINE	Tue May 13 201 14:57:03 CES	2014-10-10 23:00:00
5	ROUTE_STAT	Tue May 13 201 14:57:03 CES	SENT

Handle System Web Site

Figure 9. A handle for the MIND document.

2) Email-based notification system: The "ground control" service has been also implemented as the email-based notification system on basis of email transport layer. Email is intended for frequent passing of messages so that it can easily receive multiple notifications and does not require any additional users skills in the installation, configuration and operation. It does not require unlocking new ports for the transport layer, which affects the security of the organization.

The LWE notifications are sent to one or more email addresses. The notification receiver services run on some organizational server check dedicated mailboxes frequently, parse attached LWE notifications and insert new records to a database.

There are three main tables in the database: Notifications, Documents, and WorkflowProcesses. Each new notification is inserted into the Notifications table. The new notification is distinguished by the address of the mailbox and email's Unique Identifier (UID - a unique number referencing an email in a mailbox). Only those notifications are inserted to the Documents table, which have higher value of logical timestamp than the already registered. The last record for each document ID refers to the current state of this document.

When a notification for a new process appears or process was modified, a new record is inserted to the Workflow-Processes table. This table stores workflow process IDs, the migration path files and workers data files.

Thus, the WorkflowProcesses table stores structure of the process, while the Documents table stores the states of documents flow. The tracing application selects only the most recent records from Documents and WorkflowProcesses tables and constructs a current workflow process structure with its approximate global state.

In contrast to the LWE, which has been implemented in Java, the "ground control" service has been implemented based on PHP (Personal Home Page) and Postgresql database [25]. PHP technology has been chosen in order to test it for email messaging and XML (Extensible Markup Language) manipulating. PHP provides classes to access mailbox, e.g., by IMAP protocol and functions to XML manipulation. PiBX (XML-Data-Binding framework for PHP) is similar to JAXB (Java Architecture for XML Binding), but it is in the alpha-state at the moment. PHP technology has been good enough for the rapid implementation of the "ground control" service, but many other technologies could be used for this purpose.

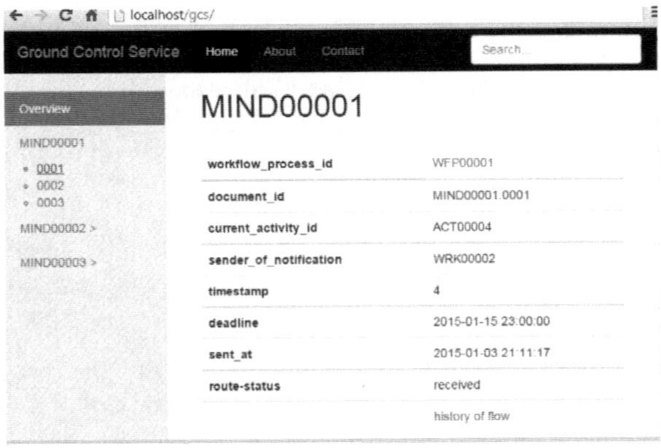

Figure 10. GUI of the email based "ground control" service.

In fact, the syntax of notifications is essential for the "ground control" service, since implementation does not require any new or advanced technology.

Figure 10 shows information about one MIND document selected from the database. An interface allows the user to view all documents related to the process and to view a history of document flow.

During the experiments, emails were received from the dedicated mailbox every minute (for this purpose, the "Cron" software was used). So, emails often appear in mailbox in the different order than they were sent. First sent notification provides a workflow process resources (process definitions, data about workers) to the "ground control" service. However, sometimes this notification is received later then subsequent notifications. In such a situation, only worflow process ID is inserted to the WorkflowProcesses table and the table is updated at a later time.

Emails with notifications generally were delivered to the inbox without any problems. However, the service does not require to deliver all notifications. There was a problem during testing that emails have been received from mailbox and deleted, but the service crashed while writing data to the database. To prevent such situations, emails are stored in the inbox for a month.

VII. THE CHOREOGRAPHY POLICY

Orchestration and choreography terms are used most frequently in the context of web services composition and collaboration [8] [26]. In this paper, they are meant more generally as strategies for business processes enactment in a knowledge-based organization. *Orchestration* addresses the situation when the business process is controlled by one of the workers/services and another workers/services just perform their activities. Similarly as in an orchestra, where the conductor manages played music, while the musicians perform their parts. *Choreography* is more collaborative in nature, where workers involved in the process perform their activities but also may manage some part of the process and interact with another workers. As in dance, the choreographer writes the descriptions down and gives it to the dancers and works with them to make sure they learn their parts, but he/she is not on the stage when it is happening. The dancers are co-responsible for the execution of the choreography and they must communicate with each other to achieve a success [27].

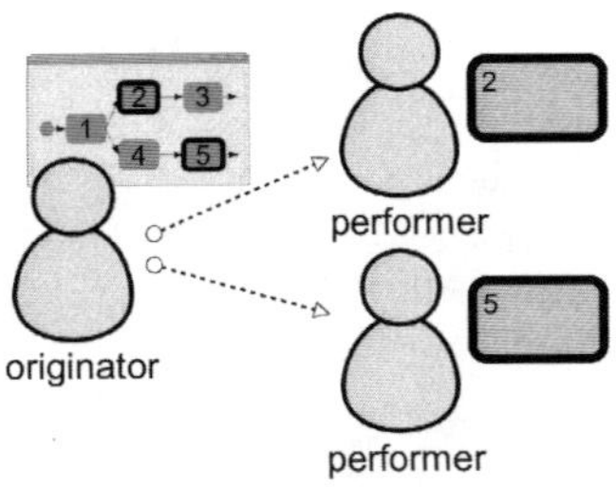

Figure 11. The orchestration of MIND.

In the MIND architecture, the path component (see Figure 3) is implemented as a XML Process Definition Language (XPDL) [28] file. It is an XML-based orchestration language from the Workflow Management Coalition (WfMC), which is executable and enables task sharing for a distributed collaboration [29]. There are three main roles that can be assigned to workers in XPDL:

- Author – name of the author of this process definition. The one who put it into the repository.
- Responsible(s) – participant, who is responsible for the process. It is assumed that the responsible is the supervisor during execution of the process.
- Performer(s) – the particular resource (not necessarily refer to a human), which can be assigned to perform a specific activity.

In a knowledge-based organization, an author is a document designer. He/She combines the knowledge of the procedural steps, required documents and participants or services, thus creating a MIND document template. This template can be used many times in the organization, and every time it is customized to the specific situation. The designer does not have to participate in the process execution.

A special and important role in the process execution has participant called a document originator. He/She forms a hub document based on document templates (see Figure 2) and is responsible for the execution of the main (root) process. In simple processes, it is sufficient that the originator is the only person responsible for the process execution. Other participants or services only perform their activities defined in the migration path. Figure 11 shows the orchestration of the MIND document flow applicable in such simple processes. The originator, like a conductor in orchestra, tracks the entire process, e.g., using "ground control" service and makes some top-down decisions by sending signals to performers. Performers fulfill their tasks in interaction with the document and sometimes receives signals from the originator. The possible interaction between workers and possible directions of that interaction are indicated by the dashed arrows The flow of documents is indicated by the solid arrows and can be tracked by the "ground control" service.

However, in real organizations, such simple processes are a rarity. In complex processes, it is very impractical, when one person is responsible for each step in the entire process. In XPDL, for each WorkflowProcess element, there can be

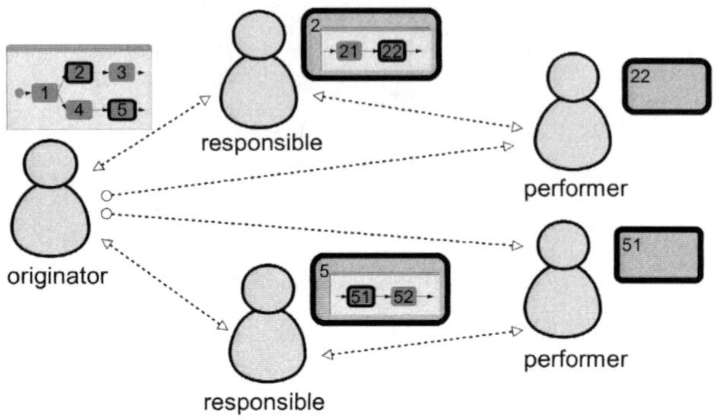

Figure 12. The choreography of MIND.

specified the participant (or participants) responsible for its execution [28]. The WorkflowProcess elements are used to define both the main process and all subprocesses. In Figure 12, the originator is responsible for the main process. The nodes 2 and 5 are Subflow activities, which invoke another WorkflowProcess elements. Participants other than the originator are responsible for these subprocesses.

In the MIND architecture, subprocesses can be either predefined by a document designer or added during the execution of workflow by a privileged activity performer (see internal and external subprocess in Section V-B). The latter allows for dynamic modification of the migration path during its execution. In Figure 12, the activities 2 and 5 can be initially defined as tasks to be performed by the workers manually. In the RedefinableHeader element, an author and persons responsible for the current workflow process can be specified. This is optional, but in MIND, the document originator is always responsible for the main process. The activities 2 and 5 has no implementation, i.e., implementation by manual procedures [28]. The extended attribute enables to expand the activities properties with modification rules. The Subflow value of the ModificationRule attribute allows performer to change the selected activity in the subflow and add a new WorkflowProcess element. In this case, the activity implementation alternative is changed from No to SubFlow, which refers to the new WorkflowProcess element. The Performers element is not available for subflow activities. The participant, who modified the activity 2, becomes responsible for the subprocess and can track it using "ground control" service.

The ability to add subprocesses with different responsibles is not yet the choreography policy. It is rather a "set of the orchestrations".

The first step to the choreography is to set different permissions to the participants of the process. As already mentioned, in the MIND architecture, the path component is implemented as XPDL file [28]. The entire migration path (a main process and all subprocesses) definition is bounded together in a model definition, which is contained in one Package element. This element groups together a number of individual process definitions and associated entity data, which is applicable to all the contained process definitions. In particular, the Participant elements can be defined for the Package element and for each WorkflowProcess element separately. Participants defined for the Package can take part in all processes in this Package and, of course, participants defined for WorkflowProcess can take part only in this particular process. Details of the workers participated in the migration path are contained in the worker component (see Figure 3). The Participant element refers to these data and additionally sets the permissions on the migration path.

The document originator is always defined for the Package and, by default, he/she has the permissions: to control the entire migration path using "ground control" service, to cancel the document and to modify the flow. The set of extended attributes allow for indicating permissions and rules on the migration path. The ModificationPermission attribute specifies whether and how the participant can modify workflow during the process execution. The value of that attribute should be one of the: All, Responsible, Performer and No. The All value means the participant can modify activities contained in all processes in this Package, the Responsible value means the participant can modify activities contained in processes for which he/she is assigned as a responsible person, the Performer value means the participant can modify an activity for which he/she is assigned as a performer, and the No value means the participant can not modify any activities in any processes.

The ControlPermission attribute indicates, which process can be tracked and controlled by this participant using the "ground control" service. Possible values of this attribute (All, Responsible, No) have a similar meaning like values of the ModificationPermission attribute. The CancellationPermission attribute is introduced specially for the cancelling pattern (see Section V-B) to separate the permission to cancel the activities or processes from the rest of the permissions that gives the "ground control" service. The privileged participant can cancel the entire document flow ("All"), the subflow for which he/she is responsible ("Responsible") or only particular activities ("Activity").

The permissions delegated to participants are detailed by special rules set to particular activities. The ModificationRule attribute specifies whether and how this activity may be modified. The Subflow value was presented above. It allows for changing the activity in the subflow and add an internal subprocess (see Section V-B). The External rule is wider than the Subflow. It allows for adding an external, internal or mixed subprocess. In this case, the current activity is changed in the subflow, a new WorkflowProcess element is added as well as for the internal subprocess. The external subprocess can be defined as a special activity in this new WorkflowProcess element. Thus, together with this special activities, other activities can be added. The Service value of the ModificationRule attribute allows the performer to use some service to complete this activity. If the activity's ModificationRule attribute has value "No" or it is not specified, even privileged participant is not able to modify this activity. The CancellationRule attribute specifies if, the activity can be canceled. In this case, "Yes" is default, if the attribute is unspecified.

Table II summarizes permission and rule attributes associated with modification and control of the migration path.

The second step to the choreography is defining communication tactics between participants. Each participant, allowed to track process by "ground control" service, can send some signals to performers of activities. Participant, after log in "ground control" service, can track all the processes for which

TABLE II. PERMISSIONS AND RULES ON THE MIGRATION PATH

XPDL ELEMENT	EXTENDED ATTRIBUTE	
	NAME	VALUE
Participant	ModificationPermission	All, Responsible, Performer, No
	ControlPermission	All, Responsible, No
	CancellationPermission	All, Responsible, Activity, No
Activity	ModificationRule	Subflow, External, Service, No
	CancellationRule	Yes, No

he/she is responsible. A tracing application (see Figure 8) marks the currently executing activities and allows for making some top-down decisions by sending appropriate signals to particular LWE. The signals can be either the notification signals required by patterns or some text messages sent to participants via email or other available communicator. Also, LWE is required to have the ability to send and receive messages not directly related to the document but needed to communicate with other workers. Figure 12 shows the communication tactic, that allows the performer to send messages to the immediate responsible and receive messages from all responsibles over this activity. This tactic can be changed, because LWE has access to information about all responsible persons in the process tree.

XPDL is an orchestration language that coordinates multiple tasks and allows for specifying the participants responsible for executing the process. The "ground control" service and LWE enable entering interaction between the participants of the document workflow. Extended attributes enable setting different permissions and rules for defining editing and control strategy. This allows for shifting orchestration idea to more global, multiparty and collaborative choreography policy.

VIII. Case Study and Validation

The MIND architecture was created for facilitate knowledge management in complex knowledge processes, in which the flow of electronic documents and extracting knowledge from them is crucial. Coordination of document workflows may be often enforced by law, especially when the procedures are implemented manually by knowledge workers – as it takes place in court trials, crush investigations or complex medical cases.

The first studied case was the large-scale problem of judicial proceedings. Document in the form of complete files can reach an enormous size. The experiment took place to verify the adequacy of use the proposed document-flow patterns and the required functionality. In court trials, there are many documents (parts of the whole files) that have specified structure. The workflow of the files is precisely defined by the legal proceedings. Therefore, the use of the MIND architecture is justified. It enables to direct the attention of workers to the essence of court trial, through the coordination of complex legal proceedings.

The second case study involved the issue of evaluation of students in a typical university grading process. It allowed to test the validation of implementing the MIND architecture in a real environment. The idea is outlined in Figure 13.

An originator of the grade roster document is the Registrars Office, which recipient is the Course Leader. The Course Leader runs his/her own subprocess of collecting credits from

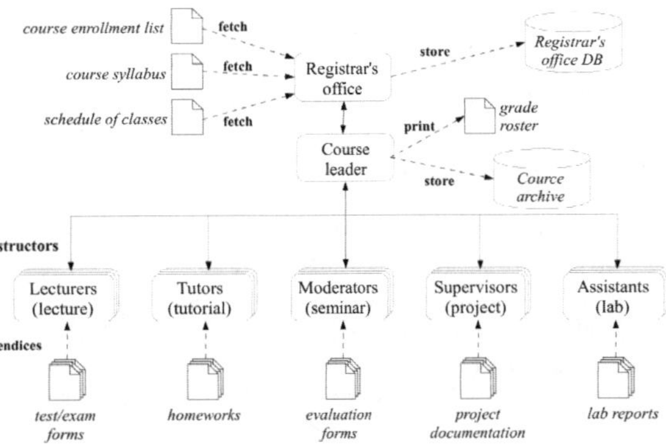

Figure 13. A course grading example [5].

instructors throughout the entire semester; structure and implementation of that subprocess is irrelevant to the Registrars Office. While the Registrars Office may use an online grade system for one-time roster submission and approval, the Course Leader is responsible for all subprocess of collecting credits. He/She has modification, control and cancellation permissions. Instructors receive only a class roster of their students, and it can be filled at any time, taking into account the designated deadline.

The "ground control" service enables the Course Leader tracking the class rosters flow and deadlines, and making decisions in some unforeseen situation. It is not necessary that the Registrars Office has the permission to control the entire process with all subprocesses. In this case, it is sufficient to be able to control the Course Leader work.

The system based on e-mail has been worked satisfactorily and has been accepted by users. The Course Leader is free to implement his/her evaluation process in any way and control the workflow of it. Course instructors can perform their activities using their personal mobile devices in any time, even if they are out of the campus network. The grading process involves both scheduled and unpredictable events, such as project assessment or homework collection for the former, and grade correction or disciplinary actions in a case of academic misconduct. These events may be effectively handled with the document-flow patters outlined in Section V-B, and tracked by "ground control" service presented in Section VI.

IX. Related Work

The presented proposal combines existing technologies and new idea to extract some new functionality in the topics of the distributed electronic document and collaborative environments.

The first significant step in the document-based processing was the Multivalent Document architecture MVD [30] that introduced active functionality to manipulate a document content with dynamically loaded objects called *behaviors*. The concept of behaviors is similar to the MIND embedded services, however MIND expands this concept with local and external services, which can also affect a document behavior, but are not components of the document. This gives documents more flexibility on opening, suiting them better to exploit local resources of visiting devices and to easily add a new functionality.

The Placeless Documents [31] implements document functionality with active properties that cannot only manipulate a document content but also manage of a document structure and workflow. The Placeless Documents are reactive, i.e., they respond to external events, while MIND documents are proactive – they initiate their own behavior.

The concept of a proactive document, capable of traveling between computers under its own control has been introduces with a document-agent platform MobiDoc [32]. This platform was, however, closely related to the particular technology, and thus lacked forward compatibility. On the other hand, solutions proposed by MIND found document-agent mobility on stable email messaging standards. Owing to proactive MIND attachments, any email system could be almost like an agent platform with all the benefits of multi-agent systems, but without a need to implement a full-size agent platform that would have to be updated regularly and require additional skills from administrators to run it.

Workflows have been also implemented by WADE (Workflow and Agents Development Environment) [33] agent platform based on JADE (Java Agent DEvelopment framework) [34]. WADE agents embed a micro-workflow engine, capable of executing workflows and compiled before launching the workflow. Performing of activities may be delegated by one agent to another and in principle is not related to agent mobility. This solution follows the classic central workflow enactment philosophy, and differs from it only in decentralization of a global process state into local process states controlled by micro-workflow engines running inside agents. In the MIND architecture, workflow as a XPDL file is a part of the whole document and it contains its internal state. LWEs run outside of agents as local workflow engines. Workflow, in the form of plain XPDL, may be also modified during the process execution. Moreover, a document-agent is the only communication interface, making MIND based platforms technologically independent and truly loosely coupled distributed systems.

The reliability of distributed workflows processing is associated with the assurance that the object would not be lost and would arrive to the designated location. It requires some tracking service that in distributed loosely-coupled systems may only estimate the real states of migrating objects. The JADE platform provides some control remote agents (Agent Management System – AMS, Remote Monitoring Agent – RMA) that receives messages from JADE agents, while the "ground control" service has a similar task - it receives messages from the MIND documents to tracking their states. Contrary to JADE control agents, the "ground control" is an external, technologically independent service that communicates with the MIND documents through notifications. Document determines whether the notification has to be sent or not. A syntax of the notifications includes also all document-flow patterns.

A process orchestration focuses on the flow of activities performed by participants or services. In contrast, choreography formalizes the way participants coordinate their interactions. Thus, the focus is not on orchestrations of the work performed by these participants, but rather on the exchange of information (messages) between these participants [35]. There are a number of choreography languages, like: Web Services Choreography Description Language (WS-CDL) [36], Business Process Model and Notation (BPMN) [37] or Choreography Extension for Business Process Execution Language (BPEL4Chor) [38]. Many languages try to simultaneously define a meta-model for service choreography and a syntax for orchestration. It creates some limits in the implementation of the choreography with workflow together. For example, BPMN enables put the choreography Message Flow only between the Pools, which means that messages can be sent only between the participants of independent workflows. In the MIND architecture, participants communicate mostly by document - this is the assumption of this architecture. The "ground control" service and LWE enable adding the choreography policy with adjusted communication to workflow enactment.

X. CONCLUSION

Reliable workflow execution of distributed mobile document must be able to handle unforeseen situation when migrating documents fail to reach their destination or get stuck in some worker's device. The "ground control" service, proposed in this paper, is a track and trace service that enables observation of the current document location and stores the history of migration. It allows for checking if the document has reached the recipient LWE or is processed too long on the current device, i.e., if passed the appointed deadline and *sent* notification has not received, it may indicate that the document got stuck in some place. The service does not "tighten" the idea of loosely-coupled distributed system, because it can still execute without this service and the MIND document may decide in which steps the notifications should be sent and in which should not.

The "ground control" service provides new possibilities to MIND, although its introduction was associated primarily with the need of users. Workers report that despite a system based on MIND works, they still does not know what is happening with the document. Without the ability to control the flow, they feel as if they sent an email and been waiting for a response. The limited trust of users was not connected with malfunction of the system. The human naturally wants to have control over the cases, especially those important.

The "ground control" service together with LWE also enables communication between the persons responsible for executing of the process and the activity performers. Additional permissions and rules allow for determining, which participant can control the process execution and make some decision in unforeseen or conflict situations. That allows for introducing the choreography policy into process enactment.

The "ground control" service was created for the purpose of the MIND architecture. However, it may be used to track the workflow of any loosely coupled system. It is only required for the system to send signals via email about its state and to receive and interpret signals from the "ground control" service. It can be also used to track emails in email systems.

Next to reliability and choreography, there is also a security issue, which answers the question: what to do if lost document will get to an unauthorized person? The LWE may require authentication of the worker before unpacking and activating document components. The LWE also verifies if the performer assigned to the current activity is the same person as the recipient of the document. The interesting idea has been proposed in [39] by the MENAID (Methods and Tools for Next Generation Document Engineering) project [40]. It introduces a security by the face recognition algorithm built in the MIND documents.

REFERENCES

[1] M. Godlewska, "Reliable document-centric processing in a loosely coupled email-based system," in ICDS 2015 : The Ninth International Conference on Digital Society. IARIA, 2015, pp. 38–45.

[2] G. D. Bhatt, "Organizing knowledge in the knowledge development cycle," Journal of Knowledge Management, vol. 4, 2000, pp. 15–26.

[3] L. A. Dabbish and R. E. Kraut, "Email overload at work: an analysis of factors associated with email strain," in Proceedings of the 2006 20th Anniversary Conference on Computer Supported Cooperative Work, ser. CSCW'06. New York, USA: ACM, 2006, pp. 431–440.

[4] M. Godlewska, "Agent system for managing distributed mobile interactive documents in knowledge-based organizations," in Transactions on Computational Collective Intelligence VI, ser. LNCS 7190, N. T. Nguyen, Ed. Berlin: Springer-Verlag, 2012, pp. 121–145.

[5] M. Godlewska and B. Wiszniewski, "Smart email - almost an agent platform," in Innovations and Advances in Computing, Informatics, Systems Sciences, Networking and Engineering, ser. LNEE, S. Tarek and E. Khaled, Eds. Berlin: Springer-Verlag, 2015, pp. 581–589.

[6] N. Russell, A. Hofstede, W. Aalst, and N. Mulyar, "Workflow controlflow patterns: A revised view," 2006, BPM Center Report BPM-06-22.

[7] Corporation for National Research Initiatives, "Handle.net (version 7.0): Technical manual," 2010.

[8] C. Peltz, "Web services orchestration and choreography," Computer, vol. 36, no. 10, Oct. 2003, pp. 46–52.

[9] J. Rowley, "The wisdom hierarchy: Representations of the DIKW hierarchy," J. Inf. Sci., vol. 33, no. 2, Apr. 2007, pp. 163–180.

[10] J. Cortada and J. Woods, Eds., The Knowledge Management Yearbook 2000-2001. Boston &c.: Butterworth Heinemann, 2000.

[11] G. Hodge, "Systems of knowledge organization for digital libraries: Beyond traditional authority files," Council on Library and Information Resources, Washington, D.C., Tech. Rep. 91, April 2000.

[12] WfMC. Workflow Management Coalition, "Terminology and glossary," WfMC, Winchester, UK, Tech. Rep. WFMC-TC-1011, Issue 3.0, 1999.

[13] J. Klensin, "Simple Mail Transfer Protocol," RFC 5321, IETF, 2008.

[14] K. Moore, "Simple Mail Transfer Protocol (SMTP) Service Extension for Delivery Status Notifications (DSNs)," RFC 3461, 2003.

[15] C. Lewis, "Overview of Best Email DNS-Based List (DNSBL) Operational Practices," RFC 6471, 2012.

[16] "Java Mail," URL: http://www.oracle.com/ [retrieved: Dec., 2014].

[17] M. Crispin, "Internet message access protocol - version 4rev1," RFC 3501, 2003.

[18] K. Moore, "Recommendations for Automatic Responses to Electronic Mail," RFC 3834, IETF, 2004.

[19] T. Hansen and G. Vaudreuil, "Message Disposition Notification," RFC 3798, IETF, 2004.

[20] "Readnotify," URL: http://www.readnotify.com [retrieved: Dec., 2014].

[21] "Whoreadme," URL: http://www.whoreadme.com [retrieved: Dec., 2014].

[22] G. Coulouris, J. Dollimore, T. Kindberg, and G. Blair, Distributed Systems: Concepts and Design, 5th ed. USA: Addison-Wesley Publishing Company, 2011.

[23] J. Spira and C. Burke, "Intel's war on information overload: A case study," 2009.

[24] International DOI Foundation, "DOI Handbook," 2013.

[25] The PostgreSQL Global Development Group, "PostgreSQL 9.4.0 Documentation," 2014.

[26] G. Decker, O. Kopp, F. Leymann, and M. Weske, "BPEL4Chor: Extending BPEL for modeling choreographies." in ICWS. IEEE Computer Society, 2007, pp. 296–303.

[27] S. Ross-Talbot and N. Bharti, "Dancing with web services: W3C chair talks choreography," 2005, URL: http://searchsoa.techtarget.com/news/1066118/Dancing-with-Web-services-W3C-chair-talks-choreography [retrieved: Aug., 2015].

[28] WfMC. Workflow Management Coalition Workflow Standard, "Process Definition Interface - XML Process Definition Language (Version 2.2)," Workflow Management Coalition, Tech. Rep. WFMC-TC-1025, 2012.

[29] R. Shapiro, A Technical Comparison of XPDL, BPML and BPEL4WS. Cape Visions, 2002.

[30] T. A. Phelps and R. Wilensky, "Multivalent documents: A new model for digital documents," EECS Department, University of California, Berkeley, Tech. Rep. UCB/CSD-98-999, 1998.

[31] P. Dourish, W. K. Edwards, A. LaMarca, J. Lamping, K. Petersen, M. Salisbury, D. B. Terry, and J. Thornton, "Extending document management systems with user-specific active properties," ACM Trans. Inf. Syst., vol. 18, no. 2, 2000, pp. 140–170.

[32] I. Satoh, "Mobile agent-based compound documents," in Proceedings of the 2001 ACM Symposium on Document engineering, ser. DocEng '01. New York, USA: ACM, 2001, pp. 76–84.

[33] Telecom Italia, "Workflows and Agents Development Environment," 2014, URL: http://jade.tilab.com/wade [retrieved: Dec., 2014].

[34] Telecom Italia, "Java Agent Development Framework," 2014, URL: http://jade.tilab.com [retrieved: Dec., 2014].

[35] G. Polani, "Conversation vs collaboration vs choreography," 2014, URL: http://blog.goodelearning.com/bpmn/conversation-vs-collaboration-vs-choreography [retrieved: Mar., 2016].

[36] W3C, "Web Services Choreography Description Language: Primer," 2006.

[37] Object Management Group, "Business Process Model and Notation (BPMN)," Object Management Group, Tech. Rep. formal/2011-01-03, January 2011.

[38] G. Decker, O. Kopp, F. Leymann, and M. Weske, "BPEL4Chor: Extending BPEL for Modeling Choreographies," in Proceedings of the IEEE 2007 International Conference on Web Services (ICWS 2007), I. C. Society, Ed. Salt Lake City: IEEE Computer Society, Juli 2007, pp. 296–303.

[39] J. Siciarek, M. Smiatacz, and B. Wiszniewski, "For your eyes only – biometric protection of pdf documents," in EEE'13 - The 2013 International Conference on e-Learning, e-Business, Enterprise Information Systems, and e-Government, Las Vegas, USA, 2013, pp. 212–217.

[40] MeNaID, "http://menaid.org.pl/," 2012-2014, National Science Center, Poland, grant DEC1-2011/01/B/ST6/06500 [retrieved: Dec., 2014].

A Self-Made Personal Explanation Aid of Learning Materials in a Museum for Naïve Developers

Ayako Ishiyama
Tama Art University, Tokyo Institute of Technology
Tokyo, Japan
ishiyama@tamabi.ac.jp

Satoru Tokuhisa
Yamaguchi University
Yamaguchi, Japan
dangkang@yamaguchi-u.ac.jp

Fusako Kusunoki
Tama Art University
Tokyo, Japan
kusunoki@tamabi.ac.jp

Shigenori Inagaki
Kobe University
Hyogo, Japan
inagakis@kobe-u.ac.jp

Takao Terano
Tokyo Institute of Technology
Kanagawa, Japan
terano@dis.titech.ac.jp

Abstract—**Explanation of museum exhibits must give useful and adequate information to museum visitors. However, good explanation costs a lot and is hard to be maintained by museum curators. To make explanation contents easier, this paper proposes a novel personal support aid: Stamp-On Developers Toolkit (Stamp-On/DT), with which let visitors to easily develop the richer explanation contents by themselves. Stamp-On/DT consists of smart devices with explanation contents and 'stamp' devices attached to corresponding exhibits. The unique features of Stamp-On/DT are summarized as follows: (1) the digital contents of the corresponding explanation can be created by both visitors and curators, (2) the contents are described with conventional web tools such as HTML, CSS, or Java script, and (3) users are only required to save exhibited images in the same exhibited location with the same names. To validate the effectiveness of Stamp-On/DT system, we have conducted a workshop in a museum to let visitors create digital contents and then we have evaluated their performance. Furthermore, we have conducted usability test to evaluate whether naïve users are able to their own explanation aids using Stamp-On/DT system. From both experiments, we conclude that Stamp-On/DT is an effective, easy and interesting aid in understanding museum exhibits.**

Keywords- ***tangible user interface; digital content; museum explanation***

I. INTRODUCTION

The purpose of museums is to collect, store, and educate people with different exhibits. In recent years, lifelong learning has become active and schools have created comprehensive classes. Therefore, demand for education in museums is increasing. With regard to the opportunity for visitors to learn about museum exhibitions, digital exhibition support systems and experiential exhibitions have increased. We have surveyed to identify the expectation of curators from museum visitors. The participants of the survey have indicated that they hope for visitors to have interests in the exhibits, to observe the exhibits more comprehensively, and to feel familiar with the exhibits. Because most visitors often enjoy video games, museum exhibition support systems are required to be both interesting and enjoyable for visitors so that they can engage in observing the exhibits.

Based on such background, in this paper we propose a novel personal support aid: Stamp-On Developers Toolkit (Stamp-On/DT) for visitors, developed by the visitors themselves. This paper is an extended version of our previous work [1] with additional revisions and amendments. The rest of the paper is organized as follows: In Section II, we present a literature survey to highlight the current problems; In Section III, we describe the system configuration and functions of the proposed system; In Section IV, we explain the usage of Stamp-On/DT; In Sections V and VI, in order to validate the effectiveness of Stamp-On/DT, we carry out workshop experiments, then give the findings and discussions; In Section VII, we describe the development of web-based online manual, which we newly designed for provider-visitors to easily use Stamp-On/DT. In Sections VIII and IX, in order to validate the effectiveness of the manual, we carry out the usability test; Finally, Section X concludes the paper.

II. LITERATURE REVIEW

A. Study on Museum Exhibit Explanations

There are many studies on digital explanations for museum exhibits aimed at people accustomed to interactive stimuli, such as video games [2][3][4][5][6][7][8][9].

Such digital explanations have the same structure as video games. If visitors stand in front of a given exhibit, the digital explanation starts. There are interactive elements to push buttons for more details, but in general, visitors watch the exhibit passively. Experts on exhibits system developments (system experts) are responsible for creating such digital content. Therefore, to fix and/or modify these digital contents, hard work from system experts is required.

B. Authoring Tool for Museum Exhibit Explanation

Koleva et al. [10] developed an authoring tool that curators are able to use to connect 3D digital content and sounds for exhibits with a visual programming language. Even with this tool, however, system experts must prepare the 3D parts in advance. Roussou et al. [11] made a website to be used for museum learning, in which they use the pictures drawn by eleven years old children. In Roussou et al.'s study, they report that children made a paper prototype for the web contents. However, finally, a professional web designer created the actual website. Also they reported that the children' s pictures required much time to digitize.

C. Digital Education Tools in Museums

Many museums, including the British Museum and the Louvre, have a digital presence on the Internet. People can watch exhibits remotely [12][13]. On the other hand, Google created a virtual museum for access on the Web in cooperation with different museums, including the National Museum of Western Art [14]. In addition to the Web, museum–display-support applications such as 'Tohaku Navi' [15] and 'e-Museum' [16] are employed. People can confirm the availability of certain exhibitions before visiting a given museum. Okumoto et al. [17] described that watching images and exhibit commentary on the Web before attending a museum was more effective for visitors than using the museum exhibit support system without watching the online commentary prior to visiting the museum. However, it is difficult for all visitors to learn information about exhibits in advance from a museum website. Furthermore, Okumoto et al. indicated that visitors only watched museum exhibits briefly because visitors were preoccupied with awareness of digital content.

D. Summary of the Survey and Research Statements

Currently, experts are required to make digital exhibition support systems. If only experts create the content, there is a limitation in that modifying existing content or adding new content requires considerable time. Although digital exhibition commentary has a level of interactivity because visitors can press a button, visitors mostly watch the exhibition support system passively. There is also a limitation in that visitors observe digital content more closely than the actual exhibits. Therefore, we believe that museum support systems require a mechanism that can help visitors interact more actively with museum exhibits.

From the literature survey, in an exhibition support system, the roles of visitors are considered very low. However, we believe digital contents should be generated by visitors themselves. It can be attained if the contents are easily developed and modified. Furthermore, if visitors are familiar with interactive video games, they are able to enjoy such digital contents interactively. In this paper, we would like to validate such visitor behaviors.

E. Usability Evaluation Experiments with WEB sites

S. E. Ozimek [22] evaluated the effectiveness of a web-game in a museum. They took the online survey from 303 people, then found more than half of the subjects felt that the mobile game will be help in the learning experience. After having visitors play a mobile game, Rubino et al. [23] evaluated the effect of learning through a questionnaire survey about exhibited objects. The results were positive. Yiannoutsou et al. [24] summarized the learning at the museum. They suggested that the involvement of the visitors themselves in the production of content related to the exhibition is important. In this paper, we would like to evaluate these effectiveness with Stamp-On/DT at a real museum environment.

F. Usability Evaluation Experiments of WEB sites

According to Nielsen and Landauer [18] or Albert and Tullis [19], they stated that even the number of the subjects of a usability test is only the five people, it is enough to evaluate the behaviors. We follow the statements in the experiment in Sections V and VI.

III. SYSTEM CONFIGURATION AND FUNCTIONS OF STAMP-ON/DT

Stamp-On/DT system is an extension of Stamp-On exhibition support tool [20] (Figure 1). The system configuration and functions are, thus, almost the same we have already reported. Based on the previous paper, we explain the outline.

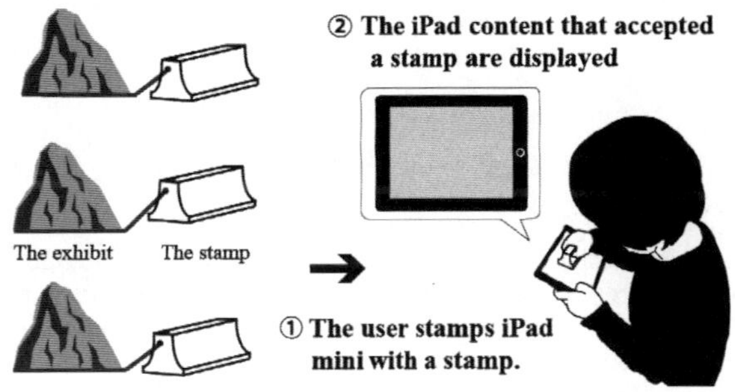

Figure 1. Overview of Stamp-On system[20].

A. Hardware

The Stamp-On/DT system hardware is composed of a Nexus 7 tablet, stamp, scanner, special paper, and stationary (Figure 2).

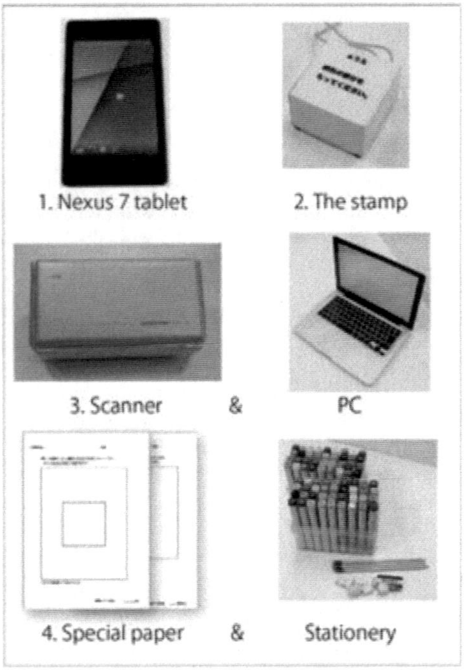

Figure 2. Stamp-On/DT system hardware.

1) Nexus 7 tablet: We need Chrome browser equipped on Nexus 7 tablet: Chrome. However, devices which satisfy the following conditions also run Stamp-On/DT systems:

a) Device with a multi-touch screen, which is used to detect four or more point coordinates.

b) Browser with JavaScript-compatible software.

2) The stamp: Aluminum tape is pasted on a stamp from the bottom of the stamp to the side of the stamp. The stamp has dot patterns on the bottom (Figure 3), on which the stamp has four convex points. When provider-visitors press the Nexus 7 tablet with the stamp, the tablet reads the dot patterns of the bottom. Each of the stamp pattern identifies the corresponding information attached on the pattern. The corresponding digital contents will change through this pattern (Figure 5).

The design of the stamps was improved from the one in Figure 3 to the one in Figure 4. The main difference is that we use simple rivets to specify the dot patterns so that we are able to easily make higher precision patterns and that we easily maintain the work of the stamp. We utilize the new version stamp to evaluate the usability of the online manuals.

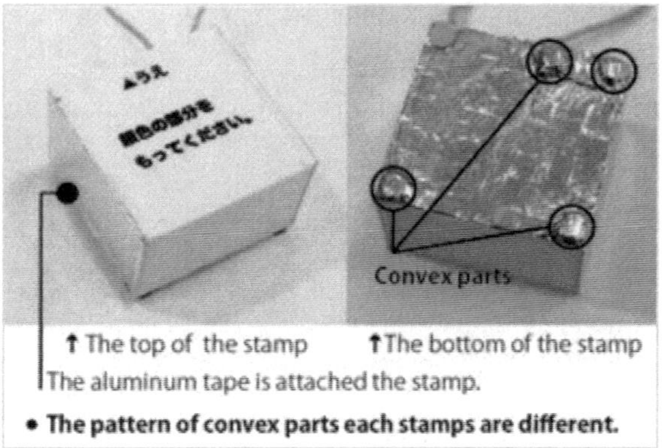

Figure 3. Stamp interface.

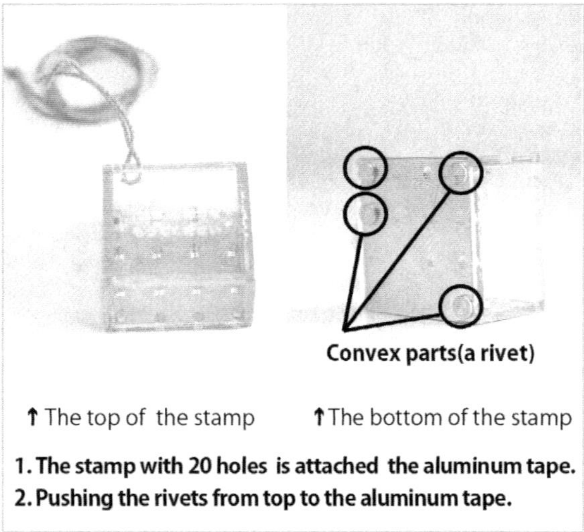

Figure 4. Improvement on Stamps After Experiment

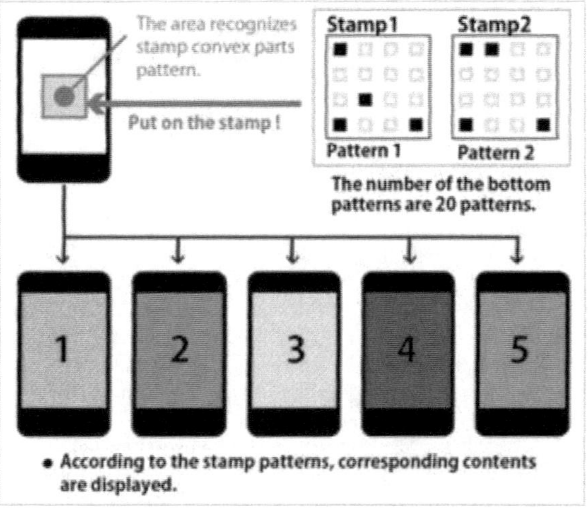

Figure 5. Mechanism to switch digital content.

3) PC and Scanner: A PC and a scanner are required in order to digitize the paper on which provider-visitors write some information on the exhibited items in the form of a single quiz. After the sheet with the quiz is scanned and converted to an image file (jpg format), a support staff will cut unnecessary portions using an image processing software then save the file.

4) Display design sheets and stationeries: To convert digital data, the sheet pre-prints i) a frame in the same screen ratio as the Nexus 7 screen and ii) an area to press the stamp (Figure 6). Stationeries are used by provider-visitors to write the text and / or to draw the picture to be used.

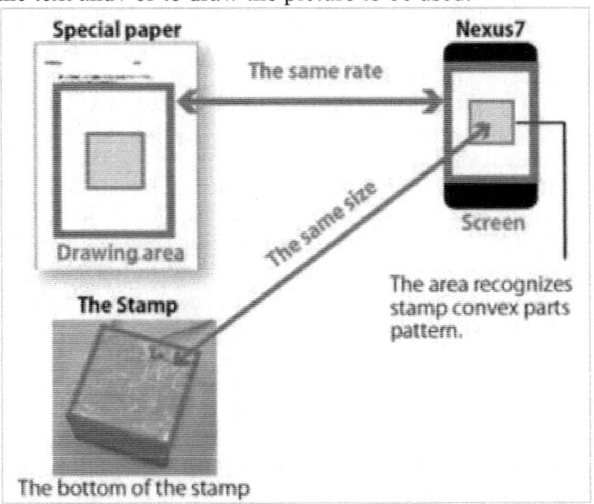

Figure 6. Method for digitizing paper on which provider-visitors draw illustrations for museum exhibits. Method for uploading to Nexus 7 tablet.

B. Software

The software used for the proposed system is written in HTML, CSS, and JavaScript. The image file URLs are written in the HTML source file in advance. A new image file is displayed when the image file in the image folder is overwritten. First, provider-visitors bring their paper with the exhibit quiz and commentary to museum staff. Second, the staff overwrites the image file in the specified folder by scanning with the scanner and PC. Finally, the digital content is completed when the staff copies the folder to the Nexus 7 tablet. (If the PC and the Nexus 7 are connected to a web server, the folder is only required to be uploaded). All these operations are performed on a PC. A general file transfer tool is used between a PC and a Nexus7 terminal. We tune the Stamp sensitivity up, so that a user of Stamp-On/DT smoothly and easily use the system, In the current version, we use Nexus7 as a terminal, however, if we would change the CSS, we would be able to use various conventional portable devices.

IV. USAGE OF STAMP-ON/DT SYSTEM

Provider-visitors who would like to use Stamp-On/DT are required to perform the following two tasks:

1) To create digital contents (Figure 7).
2) To play with the digital contents (Figure 8).

A. Task of the Content Creation Phase

At the first task, provider-visitors are required to follow the steps:

1) Make a quiz regarding a given museum exhibit.
2) Learn about the exhibit while taking notes.
3) Write a quiz related to the exhibition on the sheet with texts and/or illustrations.
4) Scan the sheets then put them into the PC by the staff.
5) Put the generated image files to HTML pages by the staff.
6) Transfer the image files and HTML files to Nexus7 terminal by the staff.

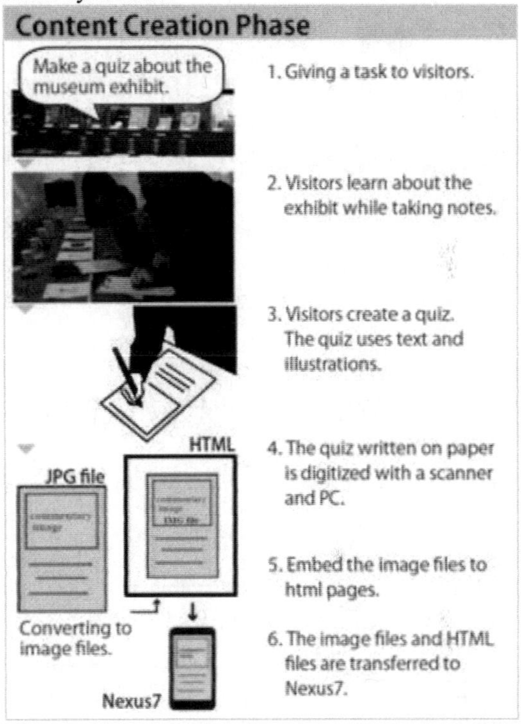

Figure 7. Content Creation Phase.

B. Task of the Playing Phase

At the second task, provider-visitors are required to follow the steps:

1) Place a stamp in front of the museum exhibits.
2) Display the question on the screen of Nexus7.
3) Look for the answer stamp in front of the exhibits.
4) Put the stamp on screen of Nexus7 tablet.
5) Display corresponding contents according to the patterns of the stamp.
6) Display a correct or wrong image. If provider-provider-visitors choose a wrong answer, Nexus 7 displays 'try again'. If provider-visitors choose a correct answer, Nexus7 displays the commentary image which provider-visitors drew.

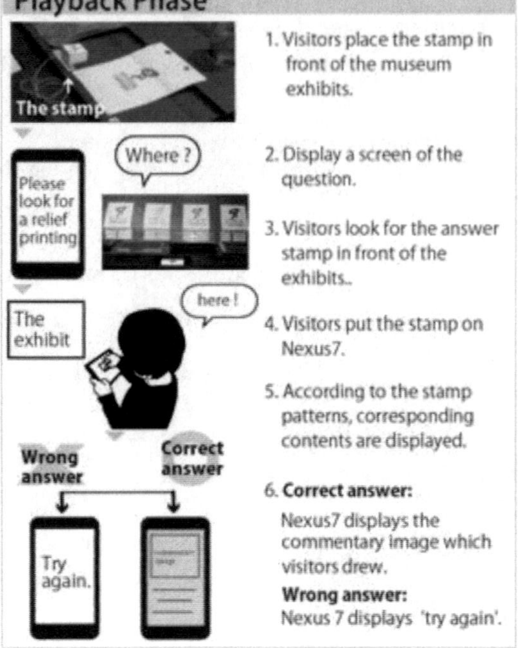

Figure 8. Playback Phase.

V. EXPERIMENT OF STAMP-ON/DT SYSTEM

A. *Design of WorkShop*

To evaluate the effectiveness of Stamp-On/DT, we have organized a workshop in a museum where provider-visitors were able to observe and enjoy the exhibits actively. Provider-visitors to the workshop were instructed to create digital content to explain the museum exhibits.

When provider-visitors create digital contents, we expect them to show the following behavior:

- Provider-visitors will watch the exhibit more carefully than usual.
- Because provider-visitors are required to create a sheet that explains the exhibit, they need to arrange exhibit information in a header and collect it. Therefore, provider-visitors will understand the exhibit more comprehensively than usual.

B. *Experimental Environment*

We conducted an experiment to evaluate our system at the Printing Museum in Tokyo, on Saturday, September 27, 2014. The participants were nine female college students, and none of the participants had seen the exhibits previously. The number of the subjects seems too small to statistically evaluate the experiments, however, the limitation of the cost and the museum capacity, we selected these nine subjects. In order to support the results, instead, we had intensive interviews after questionnaire surveys.

Three days before the experiment, we trained two students for thirty minutes to assist with the activities of the participants to support digitizing, resizing, and saving the information collected during the experiments. Consequently, on the day of the experiment, the participants had no trouble because of the help provided by the student staff members.

Before the experimental workshop, all participants expressed an interest in printing and enjoyed drawing pictures. We divided the students into two groups (four and five people in each group), and the groups were labeled as Group A and Group B.

For both groups, the required task was to create several quizes regarding the exhibition after observing their assigned exhibits (Figure 9, Figure 10). Each person was assigned one of two different exhibits randomly.

After a pre-test, Group A started to create digital contents immediately. On the other hand, after the pre-test, Group B observed the exhibits as usual and required to answer a mid-test. After the mid-test, Group B was required to start to create the corresponding digital contents. As indicated in Table I, we gave the pre- and post-test to Group A as follows:

- T1. pre-test: the participants answered the test without seeing the exhibits in the museum in advance.
- T3. post-test: the participants answer the test after using the Stamp-On/DT system.

As indicated in Table I, to Group B, we gave pre-, mid- and post-tests as follows:

- T1. pre-test: the participants answered the test without seeing the exhibits in the museum in advance.
- T2. mid-test: the participants answered the test just after watching the exhibits as regular visitors.
- T3. post-test: the participants answer the test after using the Stamp-On/DT system.

Figure 9. Experiment participants who observed exhibits.

Figure 10. Subjects drawing picture for exhibit commentary.

TABLE I. FLOW OF THE EXPERIMENTS

Group A

Time	Action	States
10min	Pre questionnaire	T1
1h45min	Digital content creation (Watch Exhibits and production)	
30min	Playing with the digital content they made	
10min	Post questionnaire	T3

Group B

Time	Action	States
10min	Pre questionnaire	T1
20min	Watch as usual	
10min	Intermediate questionnaire	T2
70min	Digital content creation (Watch Exhibits and production)	
30min	Playing with the digital content they made	
10min	Post questionnaire	T3

Figure 11. Staff digitizing exhibition commentary sheet drawn by participants.

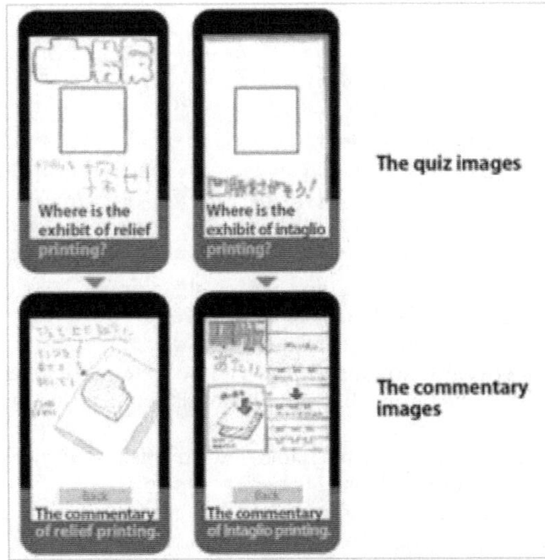

Figure 12. The pictures and texts which subjects painted.

Figure 13. Subjects pressing stamp on Nexus 7 tablet.

C. The Objectives of the Evaluations

We specified the evaluation items of the experiments as follows:

1) How provider-visitors learnt from the observations on exhibited items.

- Evaluate the difference in the observations and the learning effects of pre- and post-tests with Groups A and B between (T1) and (T3).
- Evaluate the difference in the observations and the learning effects of pre-, mid-, and post-tests with Grope B among (T1), (T2), and (T3).

2) How provider-visitors enjoyed the experiences:

- Evaluate how the provider-visitors enjoyed the proposed systems through the questionnaire analyses.
- Let provider-visitors specify the enjoyable points of the proposed system through questionnaire analyses.

D. Evaluation Methods

We use the following methods to carry out the evaluation:

1) Questionnaire Analysis

a) Viewing exhibits and learning effects: Multiple-choice and fill-in-the-blank questions were provided in order to determine how the participants learned from the exhibits. Group A answered two questionnaires, before and after the experiment. Group B answered three questionnaires: before, during, and after the experiment.

For the post-test questionnaire, the participants answered five questions (Q1 to Q5) with five-grade relative estimation.

Q1 and Q2 are related to viewing the exhibits, and Q3, Q4, and Q5 are related to the enjoyability:

Q1. Did you observe the exhibit carefully?

Q2. After the experiment, did you become more careful in observing the general printed information familiar with you and your neighbours?

Q3. Was it interesting for you to make your own descriptions of the exhibited items?

Q4. Was it interesting for you to use the stamp interface?

Q5. Do you like to participate in another similar event, if we would provide the Stamp-On/DT system?

E. Interview

After the questionnaire sessions, we have made oral interview sessions against randomly selected participants.

1) About viewing the exhibits: The interview consisted of the following questions: "Did you carefully observe the exhibits?', 'What were different points between your usual museum visits and this experimental observations on the museum exhibits?', 'What were different points between usual explanations of the exhibits and the digital contents you made?'

2) About enjoyment: The interview questions were as follows: 'Was it interesting for you to play with Stamp-On/DT?', and 'Was it fun to make your own digital contents?'

VI. FINDINGS OF THE MUSEUM EXPERIMENT

A. Discussion of the Experiments

1) Questionnaire Survey Results.

The answers to the questionnaire survey for Groups A and B are summarized in Table II. Table II depicts experimental results about pre- and post-tests. The sign testing method is applied. The results suggest that there are statistical differences with the 95% reliability. To Group B, we apply the Freedman Testing to pre-, mid-, and post-testing. The results also suggest that there are statistical evidences (Table III).

Table IV summarizes the response distributions. Most participants responded positively to all questions. We investigated the response trends after separating the responses obtained from the questionnaire surveys into two groups: positive responses, including 'completely agree' and 'agree', and negative responses, including 'somewhat disagree' and 'completely disagree'. Fisher's exact tests (1×2) showed a statistical significance at 95% level for all items.

TABLE II. THE LEARNING EFFECT ON THE EXHIBIT

The fill-in-the-blank questions from related to the print.

Subjects No.	1	2	3	4	5	6	7	8	9
The pre-test (T1).	6	6	4	8	5	4	1	3	5
The post-test (T3).	15	14	16	18	13	10	8	9	7

p= 0.003906, (p<.05). ↑ The number of correct answers

T1,T3 = states.

Four questions about the type of printing.

Subjects No.	1	2	3	4	5	6	7	8	9
The pre-test (T1).	1	0	1	0	0	0	1	0	2
The post-test (T3).	4	4	4	4	4	4	4	1	2

p=0.007812, (p<.05). ↑ The number of correct answers

T1,T3 = states.

TABLE III. TABOUT THE DIFFERENCES BETWEEN PRE-, MID-, AND POST-TESTING

The fill-in-the-blank questions from related to the print.

	The pre-test (T1).	The intermediate test (T2).	The post-test (T3).
SubjectsB1	6	8	15
SubjectsB2	6	10	14
SubjectsB3	4	6	16
SubjectsB4	8	9	18
SubjectsB5	5	10	13

Friedman chi-squared = 10, p=0.003906 (p<.05).

T1, T2, T3 = states.

Four questions about the type of printing.

	The pre-test (T1).	The intermediate test (T2).	The post-test (T3).
SubjectsB1	1	4	4
SubjectsB2	0	4	4
SubjectsB3	1	1	4
SubjectsB4	0	2	4
SubjectsB5	0	4	4

Friedman chi-squared = 8.375, p=0.01518 (p<.05).

T1, T2, T3 = states.

B. Results of Interview Survey

1) About viewing the exhibits.

- Participant A: I observed the exhibit carefully more than usual with the intention of preparing a quiz about it.
- Participant B: Commentary must be written to be easy to understand because it will immediately become the corresponding digital contents and will be shown to other participants. I observed the exhibit seriously to try to understand it properly in order to clearly make the contents.

TABLE IV. RESULT OF OBSERVATION AND ENJOYABILIT

About Observation.	5	4	3	2	1
Q1. Do you think you carefully viewed the exhibit? **	3	5	1	0	0
Q2. Do you think that you tried to more carefully view a printed item that is more familiar to you? **	3	6	0	0	0

**p<.05, 5=completely agree, 1=completely disagree.

About enjoyability.	5	4	3	2	1
Q3. Do you think that it was fun for you to write a description of the exhibit? **	2	7	0	0	0
Q4. Did you think that it is fun to press a stamp? **	2	7	0	0	0
Q5. If there were another event of this type, do you think that you would want to participate? **	6	3	0	0	0

**p<.05, 5=completely agree, 1=completely disagree.

2) Utterlance of Enjoyable Aspects

- Participant A: I was impressed at the fact that just after making the quiz, it quickly became the corresponding digital content.
- Participant B: When I pressed the stamp, the immediate reactions the system made was quite interesting.
- Participant B: It was interesting to see the digital contents the other participants developed, because the contents gave me different others' perspectives on their focal points and explanations of the exhibits.

C. Summary and Discussion of Experiment Findings

Based on the questionnaire and interview results, the participants viewed exhibits more carefully with the proposed system than usual visits. All participants suggested that (i) it was pleasant to partake of the interview of the experiment, (ii) creating the digital content is much more interesting than making usual paper contents.

The experimental results have revealed that museum provider-visitors would observe exhibits more carefully than usual visits, if the provider-visitors could create quizzes about the exhibits. Furthermore, all participants have interests in the beautiful printing techniques, which curators of the museum usually use to make explanations of the exhibited items. Therefore, the participants have more interests in the various printings among them in the sense of color, styles, and materials.

When the nine participants used the Stamp-On/DT system at the same time, it was possible for them to produce 18 items of digital contents within 2 hours. These results have shown the superiority of the proposed system against prior digital contents research in the literature [11] on the points of the agility and non-professional support to produce the digital contents.

VII. ONLINE MANUAL

We develop web-based online manuals for the Stamp-On/DT system to extend users' community. The manuals describe how to make stamps and the explanation contents, and how to play with Stamp-On/DT. The manuals are available in the Stamp-On/DT website [21]. The web-site contains six movie files. The one is a summary video of the Stamp-On/DT system and the other five contain the instructions about the operation and usage (Figure 14).

A. The Topics of the Online Manuals

The explanation contents of Stamp-On/DT System are different from each other in various museums. As a typical example, in the manual, we deal with wooden materials, which are familiar to both developers and provider-visitors. As a result, a naïve user of the Stamp-On/DT system will make explanation contents to answer the kinds of various wooden materials. They are required to create three quizzes and correct and/or incorrect answers with drawings. Furthermore, they are required to prepare explanation contents referring to various internet and/or book information of the materials.

B. Videos

The video information of the manual contains the following six items:

1) The summary video of the Stamp-On/DT system.

2) How to download Zip files from the WEB site, then to. print out the paper sheets in from the download file.

3) How to draw pictures on the specified paper sheets (Questions 1-3, Answers1-3, and Try again).

4) How to scan the paper sheets and save the resulting scanned image files to the PC (Question1-3, Answer1-3, and Try again).

The scan image files are clipped and saved to the "img" folder (Question1-3).

5) How to clip and save the scanned image files to 'img' folders (Questions 1-3, Answers 1-3, and Try again information).

6) How to install "Android transfer" and "File manager", then how to check both the correctness of image files and playing on Stamp-On/DT system.

That is, VIDEOs 4, 5, and 6 explain the details of how to digitize and edit the image data. In the museum experiment, the trained staffs digitalizes and edited the image data, however, with the web-based manuals the naïve user must digitalize and edit all the information by themselves.

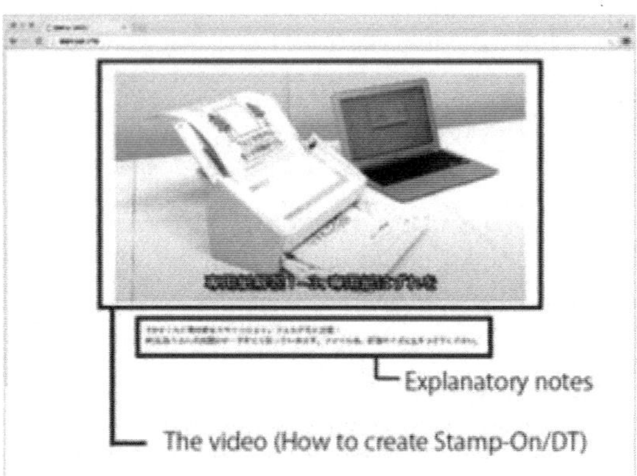

Figure 14. Stamp-On/DT WEB site.

VIII. USABILITY TEST

The purpose of the usability test is to evaluate whether naïve users of Stamp-On/DT are able to develop the explanation information of Stamp-On/DT System by themselves without any experts assistances. For the purpose, we select five female student subjects from Tama Art University in order to let them develop the corresponding explanation materials with the web-based manuals. They are students of the information design course. Thus, they are able to use Photoshop and Illustrator. However, they are less skillful with the computer usage than students at the computer science course. All the subjects have a teacher-training course to be able to be schoolteachers in the future. The reason we choose the subjects are to evaluate whether the system are able to be applied to the development of digital educational contents in a classroom beyond museums explanations settings.

Figure 15. Subjects researches the book of wood.

Figure 16. Subjects drawing picture after checking in the book.

Figure 17. Subjects scaning the paper.

Figure 18. Subjects clipping the image.

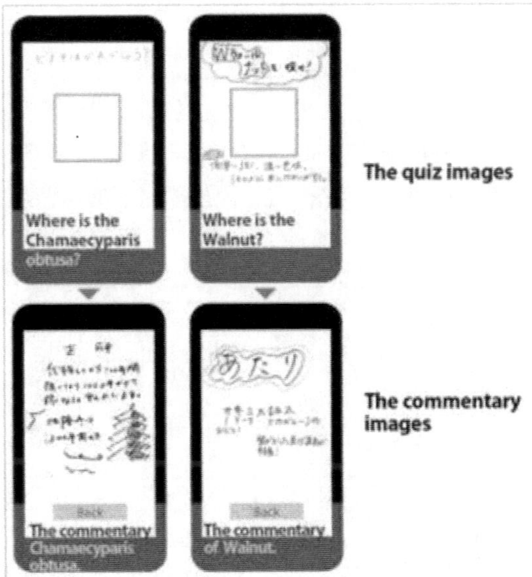

Figure 19. The pictures which subjects painted.

A. Experimental Environment

The experiment continues a three-day period from January 13 to 15, 2016. The subjects are between the ages 20 to 23. The subjects have the teacher-training course. They do not know about the Stamp-On/DT system prior to the test. Of the subjects, the three are fairly familiar with using computers, whereas the rest two are not. The two of the subjects state they often use to image editing software, while the other three are not. The experiment is conducted one person at a time. We set cameras on the side and front of the subjects in order to capture the subject's actions, as well as the computer screen images. Prior to the experiment, the subjects are asked to fill out a survey. We also have interview sessions with them after the experiment.

B. The Criteria of the Evaluations

We evaluate the experiment using the following criteria:

1) Whether the subjects are able to create Stamp-On/DT system contents only referring the web-based information.

2) How long it takes for the subjects to create all of the digital contents. Which processes of the development will takes time. In which part of the development processes, the subjects have troubles.

3) Whether the subjects would like use Stamp-On/DT system to develop digital contents when they will become teachers.

C. Evaluation Methods

We evaluate the subjects whether they complete the assigned task, and if completed, we measure the time needed. After the experiment, we have additional interview sessions.

1) Tasks

We break the flow of usage of Stamp-On/DT system into 52 sub-tasks and we examined whether the sub-tasks are completed.

2) Time

Using video information, the time spent in each sub-task was measured.

3) Interview

After the experiment, we make oral interview sessions against randomly selected participants. The interview involved questions about how they feel when creating the given problem with the web-based manuals.

IX. FINDINGS OF THE USABILITY TEST

A. About the Tasks

Every subject shows successful completion of a given task in Table V. Following the steps shown in the videos in the manuals, the subjects are able to create contents without severe troubles. As a result, all subjects are able to display proper information to the screens. We evaluate the results with the following symbols: AA is very good. A is good, however, less than that of AA. B is not good. Next, we explain why tasks scored A or B occur.

Task 11: Subject 1, who is not familiar with the PC, makes a mistake to save the destination of the scanned data. This is caused by the fact that she does not follow the instruction of the manual, thus, we evaluate the operation is bad (B). But there is no problem in the end.

Task 14: Subjects 1 was lost the way to cutout the image for a while. We evaluate the operation is not good (B).

Tasks 27,31,35: Subjects 2 and 5 are not able to display the commentary screen because of their mistakes. In the image file name, they were not able to notice the difference between character o and number zero. For this reason, although they are able to display the results of tasks 49-51, they fail to display commentary screens. Therefore, the task49, 50 and 51 were evaluated as not good (A).

Such mistake happens because of improper fonts are used in the manuals and videos. Thus, the manual can be modified so that such small mistakes would not happen, again. By telling the subjects the correct file names, they properly manipulate all contents. For tasks 45-47, the stamp's reactions are also important. All subjects are able to load the corresponding digital contents without troubles. Finally, the subjects are able to enjoy interactive contents.

B. Time Measurements

Table VI shows the time required to complete each sub-task. All the subjects create their digital content to for a series stamp work within two hors. The time consuming sub-tasks are (1) to draw the contents information on a designated paper sheet, (2) to transfer the final contents to the terminals, and (3) check the all contents are properly plays. About (1), every subject takes time, while, about (2) some of the subjects must fix the transfer mistakes. Also, subjects without image editing experience encounter difficulty in cropping images.

TABLE V. TASK LIST AND RESULT

No.	Task Details	S1	S2	S3	S4	S5
1	Did she can download the Stamp-On3ver.zip	AA	AA	AA	AA	AA
2	Did she can print out the paper.	AA	AA	AA	AA	AA
3	Did she draw the question1?	AA	AA	AA	AA	AA
4	Did she draw the question2?	AA	AA	AA	AA	AA
5	Did she draw the question3?	AA	AA	AA	AA	AA
6	Was She able to draw the answer1?	AA	AA	AA	AA	AA
7	Was She able to draw the answer2?	AA	AA	AA	AA	AA
8	Was She able to draw the answer3?	AA	AA	AA	AA	AA
9	Did she can draw the screen of "Try again"?	AA	AA	AA	AA	AA
10	Did she can scan the papers?	AA	AA	AA	AA	AA
11	Did she can save the scan data at other than "img" folder?	B	AA	AA	AA	AA
12	Did she can create the "img" folder?	AA	AA	AA	AA	AA
13	To selected the image corresponding to 1.jpg and edited it.	AA	AA	AA	AA	AA
14	Was she able to clipping the 1.jpg?	A	AA	AA	AA	AA
15	Was she able to save as 1.jpg?	AA	AA	AA	AA	AA
16	Was she able to save the 1.jpg at "img" folder?	AA	AA	AA	AA	AA
17	To selected the image corresponding to 2.jpg and edited it.	AA	AA	AA	AA	AA
18	Was she able to clipping the 2.jpg?	AA	AA	AA	AA	AA
19	Was she able to save as 2.jpg?	AA	AA	AA	AA	AA
20	Was she able to save the 2.jpg at "img" folder?	AA	AA	AA	AA	AA
21	To selected the image corresponding to 3.jpg and edited it.	AA	AA	AA	AA	AA
22	Was she able to clipping the 3.jpg?	AA	AA	AA	AA	AA
23	Was she able to save as 3.jpg?	AA	AA	AA	AA	AA
24	Was she able to save the 3.jpg at "img" folder?	AA	AA	AA	AA	AA
25	To selected the image corresponding to 1OK.jpg and edited it.	AA	AA	AA	AA	AA
26	Was she able to clipping the 1OK.jpg?	AA	AA	AA	AA	AA
27	Was she able to save as 1OK.jpg?	AA	B	AA	AA	B
28	Was she able to save the 1OK.jpg at "img" folder?	AA	AA	AA	AA	AA
29	To selected the image corresponding to 2OK.jpg and edited it.	AA	AA	AA	AA	AA
30	Was she able to clipping the 2OK.jpg?	AA	AA	AA	AA	AA
31	Was she able to save as 2OK.jpg?	AA	B	AA	AA	B
32	Was she able to save the 2OK.jpg at "img" folder?	AA	AA	AA	AA	AA
33	To selected the image corresponding to 3OK.jpg and edited it.	AA	AA	AA	AA	AA
34	Was she able to clipping the 3OK.jpg?	AA	AA	AA	AA	AA
35	Was she able to save as 3OK.jpg?	AA	B	AA	AA	B
36	Was she able to save the 3OK.jpg at "img" folder?	AA	AA	AA	AA	AA
37	To selected the image corresponding to NG.jpg and edited it.	AA	AA	AA	AA	AA
38	Was she able to clipping the NG.jpg?	AA	AA	AA	AA	AA
39	Was she able to save as NG.jpg?	AA	AA	AA	AA	AA
40	Was she able to save the NG.jpg at "img" folder?	AA	AA	AA	AA	AA
41	The "img" folder contains the seven images.	AA	AA	AA	AA	AA
42	"img" folder has been overwritten with the same name.	AA	AA	AA	AA	AA
43	Did she can download the "android transfer"	AA	AA	AA	AA	AA
44	Was she able to install the android transfer.	AA	AA	AA	AA	AA
45	To copy the "img" folder by using "android tansfer" to Nexus7.	AA	AA	AA	AA	AA
46	Was she able to install the "File manager app".	AA	AA	AA	AA	AA
47	Display the content using HTML viewer of the file manager.	AA	AA	AA	AA	AA
48	The images was displayed without distortion.	AA	AA	AA	AA	AA
49	Was she able to play Q1.	AA	A	AA	AA	A
50	Was she able to play Q2.	AA	A	AA	AA	A
51	Was she able to play Q3.	AA	A	AA	AA	A
52	Was she able to play NG.	AA	AA	AA	AA	AA

TABLE VI. RESALT OF TIME MEASUREMENT OF EACH VIDEO.

Video No.*	S1	S2	S3	S4	S5
1	**3min36sec.**	**2min42sec**	**2min49sec**	**3min02sec**	**3min10sec**
2	**7min04sec**	**9min10sec**	**8min13sec**	**6min20sec**	**5min02sec**
3	**46min24sec**	**29min26sec**	**14min11sec**	**27min17sec**	**41min17sec**
4	**20min49sec**	**19min23sec**	**21min46sec**	**28min08sec**	**17min43sec**
5	**21min22sec**	**10min37sec**	**12min40sec**	**9min53sec**	**5min57sec**
6	**12min21sec**	**29min43sec**	**19min17sec**	**37min06sec**	**19min05sec**
Total	**1h51min**	**1h41min**	**1h18min**	**1h51min**	**1h32min**

* Video1 : The summary video of the Stamp-On/DT system.
* Video2 : Downloading of the Zip file and Printing out the paper from the download file.
* Video3 : Drawing on the paper (Question1-3, Answer1-3, and Try again).
* Video4 : Scanning the paper and saving to the PC. The scan files are clipped and saved.
* Video5 : The scan image files are clipped and saved to the "img" folder (Answer1-3, Try again).
* Video6 : Installing the two application. Checking the image files and Playing by the Stamp-On/DT.

C. Results of Interview Survey

- Participant A: Though it seems complicated at first, following the video makes it easy. It is actually enjoyable to move the images around.
- Participant B: I feel it important for me to search for information by myself in order to create digital contents. It is a good learning experience.

1) As a teacher candidate.

- Participant C: I think teaching contents by Stamp-On/DT system is immediately effective in an actual science class.
- Participant C: Another way of the usage, I think that it is fun and interesting for both of students and teachers to develop the contents together in the class of Information Study.

D. Discussion

According to the task analysis, to follow the instructions in the web-based manuals, most of the subjects are able to easily create their own contents. All subjects properly display the target information on the screens. However, two of the five subjects cannot open the instruction pages because of mistakes on file names. This was the result of the font used in the video, as well as the lack of adequate explanations in the manuals. Both of these issues are able to be improved in the future. After we suggest to the subjects about the spelling error, they are able to manipulate the contents without a trouble. Also, the stamp interface works well without any troubles.

About the time required to the tasks, the most time-consuming sub-tasks are to draw the information on the problems and explanations on the designated paper sheet. The sub-tasks they tend to get stuck is to crop the images, when they have not used image editing software. The subjects that typed in the wrong file name spend more time to correct the error. At the interview after the test, the subjects claimed it was enjoyable. They mention the searching tasks to create contents are a good learning experience. They also mention that while it seems complicated at first, it is easy to develop the contents following the instructions in the video. Therefore, from the experiment, we conclude that, following the web-based manuals, even naïve users are able to make digital contents for stamp collecting activities.

X. CONCLUSIONS AND FUTURE CHALLENGES

This paper has described the design principles, functions, components, usages, and experiments on Stamp-On/DT system, which is a new extension of our Stamp-On [20]. Stamp-On/DT is a toolkit to let museum provider-visitors develop digital contents. The unique features of Stamp-On/DT are summarized as follows: (1) the digital contents of the corresponding explanation can be created by both provider-visitors and curators, (2) the contents are easily described with conventional web tools such as HTML, CSS or Java script, and (3) users are only required to save exhibited images in the same exhibited location with the same names. To validate the effectiveness of Stamp-On/DT system, we have conducted a workshop in a museum to let provider-visitors create digital contents and to have their performance evaluated. From the workshop experiments, we conclude that Stamp-On/DT is an effective, easy and interesting aid in understanding museum exhibits.

From the experimental workshop, we have suggested that i) Stamp-On/DT system is successful to create digital contents in a short time without professional assistances; ii) the participants observed museum exhibits more carefully than usual, and iii) the learning effects on the exhibits observation was also attained. When the digital contents developed by provider-users will be in real use, the curators will check the correctness, interestingness, and friendliness of the digital contents, again. Thus, the quality of the developed contents will be assured.

The proposed system will be further enhanced so that more kinds of tablet devices other than a Nexus 7 can be used in the proposed system. Also, we will prepare manuals and videos, and improve the stamp shapes so that even naïve users can use the stamps.

The other future work includes 1) the improvement of stamp performance, 2) the introduction of the other kinds of hardware devices to assist the usage, and 3) the improvement of manufacture the stamp development.

ACKNOWLEDGMENT

We would like to express our gratitude to the curator of the Printing Museum in Tokyo, Mr. Nakanishi, and the staff at the Printing Museum. We would also like to thank the Tama Art University students, who participated in the experiment. We would like to thank Miss. Kakuto, who was in charge of the video production. The appropriate comments of anonymous reviewers are very useful to improve the earlier version of the paper. We are also grateful for their help. This research was supported in part by JSPS, the Grants-in-Aid for Scientific Research (A) (No. 24240100) and the Grant-in-Aid for Challenging Exploratory Research (No. 24650521, 26540186, 24650566).

REFERENCES

[1] A. Ishiyama, S. Tokuhisa, F. Kusunoki, S. Inagaki, and T. Terano, " A Self-Made Personal Explanation Aid for Museum Visitors," Proceedings of The Seventh International Conference on Creative Content Technologies (CONTENT 2015), 2015, pp. 49-56.

[2] Y. Ohashi, H. Mashima, F. Kusunoki, and M. Arisawa, "Science Communication from Primary Learning Group to Secondary Learning Group by Adopting Voice Information [in Japanese]," Kagaku Kyoiku kenkyu (Journal of Science Education in Japan) Japan Society for Science Education, 2008, pp. 103-110.

[3] C. Cahill, A. Kuhn, S. Schmoll, W. T. Lo, B. McNallu, and C. Quintana, "Mobile Learning in Museums: How Mobile Supports for Learning Influence Student Behavior," Proceedings of the 10th International Conference on Interaction Design and Children (IDC'11), 2011, pp. 21-28.

[4] F. Kusunoki, T. Yamaguchi, T. Nishimura, and M. Sugimoto, "Interactive and enjoyable interface in museum," Proceedings of the 2nd ACM SIGCHI International Conference on Advances in Computer Entertainment Technology (ACE'05), 2005, pp.1-8.

[5] D. Raptis, N. Tselios, and N. Avouris, "Context-based design of mobile applications for museums: a survey of existing practices," Proceedings of the 7th International Conference on Human Computer Interaction with Mobile Devices and Services (MobileHCI'05), 2005, pp. 153-160.

[6] I. Rose, N. Stash, Y. Wang, and L. Aroyo, "A personalized walk through the museum: The CHIP interactive tour guide," Proceedings of the 27th International Conference Extended Abstracts on Human Factors in Computing Systems (CHI '09), 2009, pp. 3317-3322.

[7] T. Yamaguchi, F. Kusunoki, and M. Manabe, "Design of a System for Supporting Interaction in Museums and Zoos with Mixed Media," Journal of Science Education in Japan, 34(2), 2010, pp. 97-106. (in Japanese).

[8] K. Yatani, M. Onuma, M. Sugimoto, and F. Kusunoki, "Musex: A System for Supporting Children's Collaborative Learning in a Museum with PDAs," Systems and Computers in Japan, 35(14), 2004, pp. 54–63 (in Japanese).

[9] C.M. Medaglia, A. Perrone, M. De Marsico, and G. Di Romano, "A Museum Mobile Game for Children Using

QR-Codes," Proceedings of the 8th International Conference on Interaction Design and Children (IDC '09), 2009, pp. 282-283.

[10] B. Koleva, S. R. Egglestone, H. Schnädelbach, K. Glover, C. Greenhalgh, T. Rodden, and M. Dade-Robertson, "Supporting the Creation of Hybrid Museum Experiences," Proceedings of the SIGCHI Conference on Human Factors in Computing Systems (CHI '09), 2009, pp. 1973-1982.

[11] M. Roussou, E. Kavalieratou, and M. Doulgeridis, "Children Designers in the Museum: Applying Participatory Design for the Development of an Art Education Program," Proceedings of the 6th international conference on Interaction design and children (IDC 2007), 2007, pp. 77-80.

[12] The British Museum Explore. http://www.britishmuseum.org/explore.aspx (accessed 2014-10-20).

[13] Louvre Online Tours. http://www.louvre.fr/jp/visites-en-ligne (accessed 2014-10-20).

[14] Google Cultural Institute. https://www.google.com/culturalinstitute/home?hl=ja (accessed 2014-10-20)

[15] Tohaku Navi. http://www.tnm.jp/modules/r_free_page/index.php?id=1467 (accessed 2014-10-20).

[16] e-Museum. http://www.tnm.jp/modules/r_free_page/index.php?id=168#e-museum (accessed 2014-10-20).

[17] M. Okumoto and H. Kato, "The Learning System Linking Pre-Visit and Museum Learning Materials [in Japanese]," Proceedings of Japan Society for Educational Technology 36 (1), 2012, pp.1-8.

[18] J. Nielsen, and T. K. Landauer, "A mathematical model of the finding of usability problems," Proceedings of ACM INTERCHI '93 Conference (CHI '93), 1993, pp. 206-213.

[19] W. Albert and T. Tullis, "Measuring the User Experience Collecting, Analyzing, and Presenting Usability Metrics," Morgan Kaufmann, July, 2013.

[20] A. Ishiyama, F. Kusunoki, R. Egusa, K. Muratsu, S. Inagaki, and T. Terano, "Stamp-On: A Mobile Game for Museum Visitors," Proceedings of 6th International Conference on Computer Supported Education (CSEDU 2014), 2014, pp. 200-205.

[21] Stamp-On/DT.
http://stampon.info/ (accessed 2016-2-20)

[22] S. E. Ozimek, "Museum Visitors' Perceptions of Mobile Games: A Case Study," Thesis, Rochester Institute of Technology, 2014.

[23] I. Rubino, C. Barberis, J. Xhembulla, and G. Malnati, "Integrating a Location-Based Mobile Game in the Museum Visit: Evaluating Visitors' Behaviour and Learning," Journal on Computing and Cultural Heritage (JOCCH) Volume 8 Issue 3, 2015, Article No. 15.

[24] N. Yiannoutsou and N. Avouris, "Mobile games in Museums : from learning through game play to learning through game design," ICOM Education, vol. 23, 2012, pp. 79-86.

Advanced Knowledge Discovery and Computing based on Knowledge Resources, Concordances, and Classification

Claus-Peter Rückemann
Westfälische Wilhelms-Universität Münster (WWU),
Leibniz Universität Hannover,
North-German Supercomputing Alliance (HLRN), Germany
Email: ruckema@uni-muenster.de

Abstract—**This article presents an extended research of the main results from creating objects equipped with classifications and concordances as base for advanced discovery, processing, and computing based on knowledge resources. Today big data collections and resources sadly combine one or more deficits of being unclassified, unstructured, isolated, and weakly developed on the one hand and in consequence only accessible with insufficient simplistic means on the other hand. New classification features, structures, and components have been developed, which can be flexibly used with multi-disciplinary, multi-lingual long-term knowledge resources. The extended facilities can be used for universal long-term knowledge resources beyond the simple and isolated use of knowledge and data. The goal of this research is to create advanced resources and methods based on classifications and concordances. The focus is to provide facilities for advanced discovery processes based on universal knowledge resources and showing that content, classification, and concordances are valuable long-term assets.**

Keywords–Knowledge Resources; Concordances; Classified Classification; Advanced Computing; Knowledge Discovery.

I. Introduction

This extended research is based on the results from multi-disciplinary project for the creation of objects and concordances, which are intended to be used for long-term knowledge creation knowledge processing, and advanced computing. The basic fundaments of the results were presented at the INFOCOMP 2015 conference in Brussels, Belgium [1].

Advanced knowledge discovery and computing can be based on appropriate knowledge resources, concordances, and classification. The knowledge resources require spanning a reasonable width and depth of knowledge and universal and long-term features.

The fundaments of these required features are the results from the development of advanced object features for long-term knowledge resources, which can be used for universal documentation and consequent purposes. For the consequent purposes like advanced knowledge discovery, further creation and development of knowledge resources, visualisation, and education suitable, data-centred structures have been created being usable for advanced knowledge discovery and processing and for advanced and dynamical computing.

Up to now the world of increasingly big data is limited to data and data collections, which are rapidly growing in quantity, mostly even growing in storage requirements instead of knowledge only. Besides the data being unstructured, isolated, and often inconsistent in content and form it is also missing quality and essential features for conceptional knowledge like classification. One consequence is that in the last decades the means for accessing and handling data have not changed a lot regarding the content, context, and a next generation of features and quality.

The facilities provide advanced features for processing of knowledge as well as for flexible computing. Therefore, the creation and long-term care for suitable knowledge objects is a central issue. The knowledge resources have to be able to document any knowledge and data, e.g., factual and procedural knowledge, which require vertical as well as horizontal scalability for individual and subsequent use. In order to cope with the deficits this architecture can integrate structured and unstructured data, support universal classification and concordances and it can enable advanced knowledge processing, like parallel processing and dynamical visualisation.

The goal of this research is to create advanced resources and methods based on classifications and concordances. The focus of this research is to provide sustainable facilities for advanced discovery processes based on universal knowledge resources and showing that content, classification, and concordances are valuable long-term assets for integrating documentation and applicability. This paper presents the up-to-date research results from the creation of classifications and concordances for long-term knowledge resources' components, structures, and workflows for advanced processing and computing – and in the end most important on the long run, fostering the investments in the development of the data itself. Therefore, the major contributions of this research are the content and context, especially the integration of classification and concordances, on the one hand and on the other hand the new practical insights on improving the state-of-the-art of long-term documentation and application of universal knowledge.

This paper is organised as follows. Section II introduces state-of-the-art and motivation for creating an overall system. Section III discusses the research fundaments. Sections IV and V present the data-centric implementation, the implementation of resources, including concordances and classification with the creation of objects. Section VI shows the definition and organisation of implemented knowledge resources. Section VII provides selected content facets. Section VIII summarises the implemented features for processing and computing. and Sections IX and X provide an evaluation and summarise the main results, lessons learned, conclusions and future work.

II. State-of-the-art and motivation

Conceptual knowledge is an important issue with many aspects of knowledge discovery. Content and context can be provided by structured and unstructured data. Both can be assembled and collected, e.g., in collections and containers. Regarding the value of data it can be seen as a drawback that most public developments are focussing on technical implementations and not on the content [2]. In public presentation and marketing common understanding of containers is reduced to certain aspects, e.g., security features [3], [4]. Other container concepts for handling Big Data, especially scientific data, e.g., the NERSC 'Shifter' at the National Energy Research Scientific Computing Center [5] are focussing on technology-centric and implementation purposes.

These approaches are insufficient from the content and knowledge related point of view of containers. For example, on the one hand, there is nothing general for a container when postulating that it should contain "everything". At the same level, security features have to be considered very special with specific cases of application. In addition, in most cases the advanced application scenarios trigger those secondary conditions. On the other hand, containers must not only provide computational features. The result is that up to now we neither have a commonly discussed container concept nor a set of universal features.

A container is a term for a data or file format bundling the data for certain purpose and application. The features for anything more interesting will include data, documentation, references and so on. Doing so includes how the information is transferred or accessed, which includes to define the modalities for a certain scenario. When discussing containers from the content and knowledge view, many scenarios suggest a target beyond universal application [6], which induces a much more general understanding of containers.

For the required purposes the knowledge resources require a set of features, especially facilities for multi-disciplinary and multi-lingual knowledge and content. Content should be kept consistent and easily accessible, e.g., in collections and containers. One of the most desirable properties are long-term facilities and long-term availability. Especially, the organisational units and objects need to carry conceptual knowledge, e.g., in form of classifications.

III. Fundaments and previous work

Many developments have contributed to the state-of-the-art on knowledge processing and discovery. Also, many developments have provided new technical means to cope with the new developments in computing architectures and services. In the context of knowledge processing, discovery, and search we are often faced with "prominent" examples like Internet search engines, library search engines, specialised expert systems, and maybe social media systems. If at all then there are some interfaces, e.g., for automated requests or web-service creation.

The algorithms applicable to this kind of 'art' are very limited and often not sufficient in delivering a reasonable quality for requested results or for following advanced goals. Therefore, various concepts, developments, and approaches have been created, addressing different aspects and special purposes. Nevertheless, these tools, classifications, and algorithms only try to handle the symptoms of the state of the data.

The approaches cover in-depth classifications and handling, e.g., library classification specialised on geological publications [7], handling historical geographic resources, especially in library context [8], and international patent classification [9]. The algorithms touch processing and automation, e.g., statistical models for online text classification [10] and automation with a classification [11].

The discussions and analyses range from research aspects to reliability and non-disciplinary approaches, e.g., classification as a research tool [12], reliability of diagnostic classification [13], and the Universal Decimal Classification (UDC) [14] as a non-disciplinary [15] universal [16] classification system, and legal and general aspects within Information Science, Security, and Computing [17].

In depth, aspects of mapping, organisation and multi-lingual data have been discussed, e.g., simple mapping between a classification and an "index" [18], simple conceptual methods for using classification in libraries [19], knowledge organisation [20], multi-lingual lexical linked data cloud [21]. In principle, any multi-disciplinary data resources may be used, e.g., projects like Europeana [22], European Cultural Heritage Online (ECHO) [23] or World Digital Library (WDL) [24]. Although these examples are focussed on providing special information they lack in sufficient content, organisation, and structure.

The main motivation for this extended research was the lack of multi-disciplinary data-centric approaches, which can be used for long-term creation of knowledge and scalable implementations. A major reason for the lack of data-centric approaches for these purposes is the missing understanding of value of data, which does not only manifest with data breaches. Considering a possible data breach the analysis has shown an even increased value of data within the last years [25].

With data-centric implementations this is also significant for quality steering [26], evaluation, and acceptance of information systems [27]. In many cases the long-term data value of the results is much higher than the funding value for creating the data [2].

The data used here is based on the content and context from the knowledge resources, provided by the LX Foundation Scientific Resources [28]. The LX knowledge resources' structure and the classification references [29] based on UDC [30] are essential means for the processing workflows and evaluation of the knowledge objects and containers. Both provide strong multi-disciplinary and multi-lingual support.

For this part of the research all small unsorted excerpts of the knowledge resources objects only refer to main UDC-based classes, which for this part of the publication are taken from the Multilingual Universal Decimal Classification Summary (UDCC Publication No. 088) [14] released by the UDC Consortium under the Creative Commons Attribution Share Alike 3.0 license [31] (first release 2009, subsequent update 2012).

The analysis of different classifications, development of concepts for intermediate classifications, and experiences from case studies from the research conducted in the Knowledge in Motion (KiM) long-term project [32] have contributed to the application of UDC and different classifications and concordance schemes in the context of knowledge resources.

The following term definitions for object, container, and matrix can be helpful in this context.

- An object is an entity of knowledge data being part of knowledge resources. An object can contain any documentation, references, and other data. Objects can have an arbitrary number of sub-objects.
- A container is a collection of knowledge objects in a conjoint format.
- A matrix is a subset of the entirety, the "universe", of knowledge. A workflow can consist of many sub-workflows each of which can be based on an arbitrary number of knowledge matrices. The output of any sub-workflow or workflow can be seen as an intermediate or final result matrix.

The flexible creation of objects carrying references, especially classification and concordances is the fundament for advanced. knowledge processing and computing.

IV. DATA-CENTRIC IMPLEMENTATION

In order to concentrate on the challenges of the data itself so-called data-centric, data-defined, document-oriented or document-centric approaches have been developed. This went along with extending features like Structured Query Language (SQL) and "Not only SQL" (NoSQL) [33], e.g., via MySQL [34] and respective SQL [35] and MongoDB [36] and in consequence [37] also in bridging relational and data- or document-centric approaches [38]. Anyhow, implementations like MongoDB, Docker, and CoreOS are technology-centric components, e.g., they are mostly used for Web and application development [39], [40], [41]. The very minimalistic "map" and "reduce" functions approach of MapReduce [42], which attracted many quick and simple solutions is a nice example for building simple workflow elements.

As the knowledge resources' approach [28] is even much more general [29] it allows for arbitrary measures and also for processing implementing map and reduce functions, which can be based on the creation of objects and concordances.

Regarding a distributed computer system theoretical computer science can state the CAP (Consistency, Availability, Partition tolerance) theorem. In condensed form this means: *Consistency*: All nodes see the same data at the same time, *Availability*: A guarantee that every request receives a response about whether it succeeded or failed, *Partition tolerance*: The system continues to operate despite arbitrary message loss or failure of part of the system. Accordingly, learning from decades of case-studies, regarding the long-term knowledge and information sciences we can state a "CLU" theorem:

- *Consistency*: All knowledge in context used is neither in contradiction to other knowledge in context nor disaccording within its content,
- *Long-term sustainability*: Data-centric architectures, the core knowledge resources can be used for an arbitrary number of different implementations,
- *Universal documentation*: Documentation is supported for any knowledge and data, e.g., factual, conceptual, procedural, and metacognitive knowledge.

There is no direct reasonable equivalent for the P and A aspects. Besides the consistency, the items much more important are the long-term sustainability and universal documentation aspects. This includes the requirements for any type of knowledge as well as its multi-lingual documentation and features.

V. IMPLEMENTATION AND RESOURCES

The implementation for dynamical visualisation and computation is based on the framework for the architecture for documentation and development of advanced scientific computing and multi-disciplinary knowledge [43].

The architecture implemented for an economical long-term strategy is based on different development blocks. Figure 1 shows the three main columns: Application resources, knowledge resources, and originary resources.

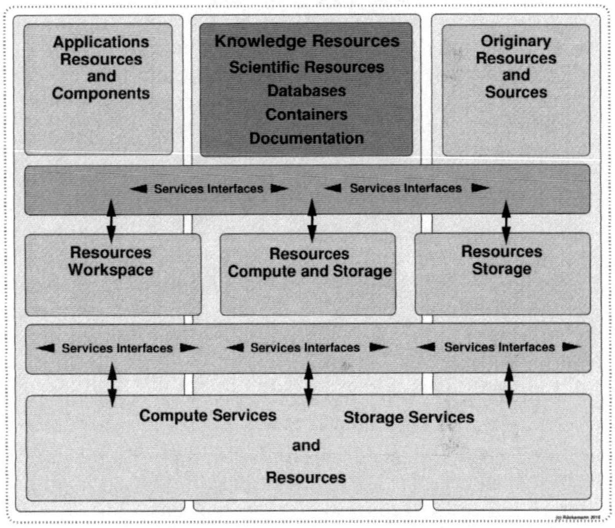

Figure 1. Architecture: Columns of practical dimensions. The knowledge resources are the central component within the long-term architecture.

The central block in the "Collaboration house" framework architecture [29], covers the knowledge resources, scientific resources, databases, containers, and documentation (e.g., LX [28], databases, containers, list resources). These can be based on and refer to the originary resources and sources (photos, scientific data, literature).

The knowledge resources are used as a universal component for compute and storage workflows. Application resources and components (Active Source, Active Map, local applications) are implementations for analysing, utilising, and processing data and making the information and knowledge accessible.

The related information, all data, and algorithm objects presented are copyright the author of this paper, LX Foundation Scientific Resources [28], all rights reserved. The structure and the classification references based on the LX resources and UDC, [44], especially mentioning the well structured editions [14] and the multi-lingual features [45], are essential means for the processing workflows and evaluation of the knowledge objects and containers. Both provide strong multi-disciplinary and multi-lingual support.

The three blocks are supported by services' interfaces. The interfaces interact with the physical resources, in the local workspace, in the compute and storage resources the knowledge resources are situated, and in the storage resources for the originary resources.

All of these components do allow for advanced scientific computing and data processing, as well as the access of compute and storage resources via services interfaces. The resources' needs depend on the application scenarios to be implemented for user groups.

A. Data-centricity

The architecture allows data-centric and computing-centric implementations. In this case, the plan is the integration of long-term creation of knowledge and scalable implementations, which motivates a data-centric approach.

The knowledge resources play the central role. With a data-centric approach the properties of objects may influence workflow decisions and code paths and logics may be defined through references, e.g., relations and constraints, optimising the access of dynamical states of the data and minimising code. Results and object stages can be stored with the data objects and the computing can be done by reading and writing object instances.

Therefore, the focus to provide facilities for advanced discovery processes based on universal knowledge resources is closely linked with data-centric classification and concordances.

B. Context for concordances and classification

Knowledge resources, concordances, and classification are based on an organisation of knowledge. The underlying organisation of knowledge is important for working with knowledge dimensions and for creating computational views, which can be used for advanced knowledge discovery and computing.

The available dimensions depend mostly on features and complexity of the available data. Therefore, a number of essential aspects have been considered when creating content with the knowledge resources. Regarding the views many new arrangements and visualisations are possible. Nevertheless, it can be quite challenging for application developers to create representations, which can be visualised, and to implement suitable components. In many cases so called "Section Views" can be computed, which use n-dimensional sections from 'n+m'-dimensional knowledge context.

Views are supported by knowledge dimensions, meaning the implementation of the types of knowledge, all of which can be integrated in the workflows.

C. Implementation of knowledge dimensions

The implemented knowledge resources integrate factual, conceptual, procedural, and metacognitive knowledge. Table I shows the major types of knowledge as complementary parts of the knowledge resources [46]. The table shows some practical examples, which illustrate the benefits of the integration.

The data itself is represented in knowledge objects containing any kind of information and collections, including content, classifications, and references.

TABLE I. COMPLEMENTARY KNOWLEDGE IN THE KNOWLEDGE RESOURCES, TYPES AND EXAMPLES.

Knowledge	*Examples*
Factual knowledge	Terminologies
	Factual details
Conceptual knowledge	Classifications, categorisations
	Principles, generalisations
	Theories, models, structures
Procedural knowledge	Algorithms, workflows, skills
	Methods, techniques
	Determination on procedures, decision making
Metacognitive knowledge	Strategies
	Self-knowledge
	Cognitive tasks, contexts, conditions

With the content and context documentation the knowledge objects describe the integrated knowledge space, for which any dimensions can be interconnected. Conceptual knowledge can be expressed with classifications.

It is useful to support classifications in general, as there are more than one classification available and in practice. Therefore, also concordances have a strong base in the conceptual knowledge.

D. Section views

The implemented structure and content enable to create section views based on the knowledge dimensions, which can, e.g., be physical or contextual dimensions. Table II shows some section views, which can be based on the combination of contextual and factual knowledge.

Generators can access the knowledge resources and their workflows can apply any appropriate components with their references and algorithms, e.g., classifications, concordances, phonetics [47], associations, references, keywords, and statistics. There will always be different objects, e.g., for different purposes and from different sources.

2016, © Copyright by authors, Published under agreement with IARIA - www.iaria.org

TABLE II. SECTION VIEWS BASED ON THE KNOWLEDGE DIMENSIONS. SECTION VIEWS AND EXAMPLES IN PRACTICE.

Section Views	*Examples*
Attributes	colour, size, ...
	extremes ...
Space and location	spatial distributions
	geo-references
	depth distribution
Time	timelines
	time index
Cultures	context
	history
	time
	location
	society
	inventions
	art
Disciplines	physics
	geophysics
	archaeology
Multi-disciplines	geosciences
	natural sciences – humanities
Multi-lingual	English
	German
	Romanic language
Combinations	depth distribution - timelines
	location-fixed: Objects over time
	time-fixed: Objects over space/locations
	culture-fixed: Objects over space and time

There is no need that such properties are available in all available objects but it can vastly enrich the quality of content and context if they are available. Therefore, the creation and 'development' of knowledge resources and objects is mostly a dynamical process.

E. Creation of objects and conceptual knowledge

Practical creation of objects has shown to be most efficient when three different categories of creation are considered:

- Manually created objects,
- Hybrid (semi-automatically) created objects, and
- Automatically created objects.

In any case creating objects is supported by universal classification, e.g., references to UDC. Therefore, that can also be applied for the creating concordances with objects.

The listing in Figure 2 shows an instance of a simple object excerpt from an object collection. The excerpt shows keywords, content, e.g., including references, documentation, factual knowledge, and conceptual knowledge.

```
Vesuvius [Vulcanology, Geology, Archaeology]:
 (lat.) Mons Vesuvius.
 (ital.) Vesuvio.
 (deutsch.) Vesuv.
 Volcano, Gulf of Naples, Italy.
 Complex volcano (compound volcano).
 Stratovolcano, large cone (Gran Cono).
 Volcano Type: Somma volcano,
 VNUM: 0101-02=,
 Summit Elevation: 1281 m.
 The volcanic activity in the region is observed by the
 Oservatorio Vesuviano. The Vesuvius area has been
 declared a national park on 1995-06-05.
 The most known antique settlements at the Vesuvius are
 Pompeji and Herculaneum.
 Syn.: Vesaevus, Vesevus, Vesbius, Vesvius
 s. volcano, super volcano, compound volcano
 s. also Pompeji, Herculaneum, seismology
 compare La Soufrière, Mt. Scenery, Soufriere
 ...
 UDC:[911.2+55]:[930.85]:[902]"63"(4+37+23+24)=12
 ...
 UCC:UDC2012:551.21
 UCC:UDC2012:551
 UCC:UDC2012:902/908
 UCC:MSC2010:86,86A17,86A60
 UCC:LCC:QE521-545
 UCC:LCC:QE1-996.5
 UCC:LCC:QC801-809
 UCC:LCC:CC1-960,CB3-482
 UCC:PACS2010:91.40.-k
 UCC:PACS2010:91.65.-n,91.
```

Figure 2. Processed instance of a simple object (excerpt) from an object collection.

Both classification and concordances, the Universal Classified Classification (UCC), were collected and created semi-automatically over a period of time. The rest of the object was created manually.

The listing in Figure 3 shows an instance of a simple container entry excerpt from a volcanological features container.

```
CONTAINER_CONCEPTUAL_KNOWLEDGE: UCC:UDC2012:551.21
CONTAINER_CONCEPTUAL_KNOWLEDGE: UCC:UDC2012:551
CONTAINER_CONCEPTUAL_KNOWLEDGE: UCC:UDC2012:551
 .2,551.23,551.24,551.26
CONTAINER_CONCEPTUAL_KNOWLEDGE: UCC:UDC2012:902/908
CONTAINER_CONCEPTUAL_KNOWLEDGE: UCC:MSC2010:86,86A17,86
 A60
CONTAINER_CONCEPTUAL_KNOWLEDGE: UCC:LCC:QE521-545
CONTAINER_CONCEPTUAL_KNOWLEDGE: UCC:LCC:QE1-996.5
CONTAINER_CONCEPTUAL_KNOWLEDGE: UCC:LCC:QC801-809
CONTAINER_CONCEPTUAL_KNOWLEDGE: UCC:LCC:CC1-960,CB3-482
CONTAINER_CONCEPTUAL_KNOWLEDGE: UCC:PACS2010:91.40.-k
CONTAINER_CONCEPTUAL_KNOWLEDGE: UCC:PACS2010:91.65.-n,91.
CONTAINER_CONCEPTUAL_KNOWLEDGE: UCC:PACS2010:91.40.Ge
 ,91.40.St,91.40.Rs,*91.45.C-,*91.45.D-,90
...
CONTAINER_OBJECT_EN_ITEM: Vesuvius
CONTAINER_OBJECT_DE_ITEM: Vesuv
CONTAINER_OBJECT_EN_PRINT: Vesuvius
CONTAINER_OBJECT_DE_PRINT: Vesuv
CONTAINER_OBJECT_EN_COUNTRY: Italy
CONTAINER_OBJECT_DE_COUNTRY: Italien
CONTAINER_OBJECT_EN_CONTINENT: Europe
CONTAINER_OBJECT_DE_CONTINENT: Europa
CONTAINER_OBJECT_XX_LATITUDE: 40.821N
CONTAINER_OBJECT_XX_LONGITUDE: 14.426E
CONTAINER_OBJECT_XX_HEIGHT_M: 1281
CONTAINER_OBJECT_EN_TYPE: Complexvolcano
CONTAINER_OBJECT_DE_TYPE: Komplex-Vulkan
CONTAINER_OBJECT_XX_VNUM: 0101-02=
```

Figure 3. Processed instance of a simple container entry (excerpt).

The excerpt shows a representation of conceptual knowledge for the container and various factual knowledge. The data was collected and created semi-automatically over a period of time. The conceptual knowledge is a matter of more detailed discussion in the next subsections and sections.

The excerpts have been processed with the appropriate `lx_object_volcanology` and `lx_container_volcanology` interfaces, selecting a number of items and for the container also items in English and German including a unique formatting.

The resources' access and processing can be done in any programming language, assuming that the interfaces are implemented. For example, combining scripting, filtering, and parallel programming can provide flexible approaches.

F. Creation of concordances

Many disciplines and large fields of application have developed and used individual adapted frameworks of conceptual knowledge for their purposes. The reasons have been multifold, in that cases either developing a universal approach was too demanding or a distinction for certain reasons might have been considered adequate. In many cases, various classifications required to be "compared" and to be used together.

However, when developing content with conceptual knowledge and classifications sooner or later also the individual classifications get in the focus of development and may require to be "mapped".

In most cases, this can be done with the means of concordances, for example, concordances with classification in medicine and health [48] or the creation concordances between two classifications systems [49], in concordance projects like coli-conc [50] or for benefits in industry classification systems [51], [52]. Therefore, the organisation of the resources and objects is significant for the long-term aspects and the vitality of the data.

Taking advantage of the modular architecture of the overall resources (Figure 1) the main objectives are the knowledge resources, services, and interfaces, which are deployed for creating workflows. Figure 4 illustrates an excerpt of selected knowledge resources' objects. The selected objects are associated to collections and containers and contain references to concordances and classifications. The excerpt in this case shows a distinct handling of manually, hybrid, and automatically created data.

The collection objects carry mostly only their individual conceptual knowledge, as there are concordances and classification, for example. The container objects are commonly similiar types of objects and structures where the container can carry a respective commonly valid conceptual knowledge for the container (symbolised in the figure by brick-structures for the objects). The respective knowledge resource, on the level integrating collections and resources, can also contain a respective commonly valid conceptual knowledge for the resource.

There are different ways of handling the processes for semi-automatically and automatically created concordances. With the main focus on processing and advanced computing we concentrate of the object and references side of the resources. This concept has shown vital benefits, which enables implementations with comparably high flexibility. Disciplines, services, and resources can be integrated in a very scalable way. Practical creation of concordances has shown to be most efficient when three different categories of creation are considered:

- Manually created concordances,
- Hybrid (semi-automatically) created concordances, and
- Automatically created concordances.

Manually-created-concordances is a type of concordances, which has resulted from manually inserting references from objects into a concordance instance. Hybrid-created-concordances is a type of concordances, which has resulted from a combination of manual and automated (semi-automatically) processes.

The processes may work on primary concordances or on any level of secondary data in order to support the creation of concordances. Automatically-created-concordances is a type of concordances, which have been generated, e.g., by an automated workflow process. This is mostly done for big data, which are used as quantity data and not due to their quality. In any way, an integration with the knowledge resources' references and structures is the target.

The workflows can contain several functions comparable to the map and reduce concept. A map function finds the data according to the criteria and creates a map result matrix. A reduce function does the appropriate operation on the map result matrix output.

The listing in Figure 5 shows a simple object instance classification and concordances excerpt (Figure 2) from a volcanological object in a collection.

```
...
UCC:UDC2012:551.21
UCC:UDC2012:551
UCC:UDC2012:902/908
UCC:MSC2010:86,86A17,86A60
UCC:LCC:QE521-545
UCC:LCC:QE1-996.5
UCC:LCC:QC801-809
UCC:LCC:CC1-960,CB3-482
UCC:PACS2010:91.40.-k
UCC:PACS2010:91.65.-n,91.
```

Figure 5. Classification and concordances excerpt of a simple object instance (knowledge resources collection).

The excerpt shows classification concordances in several different classifications as used in different disciplines. Possibly multiple views from different disciplines or author groups on a certain object are not shown in this reduced view but they can also hold the full spectrum of classifications and concordances. The following listing (Figure 6) excerpts classification and concordances of a (volcanological features) container (Figure 3).

The differences in classification and concordances are resulting from the different level of detail in the collections and containers as well as in different potential of the various classification schemes to describe certain knowledge as can be seen from the different depth of classification.

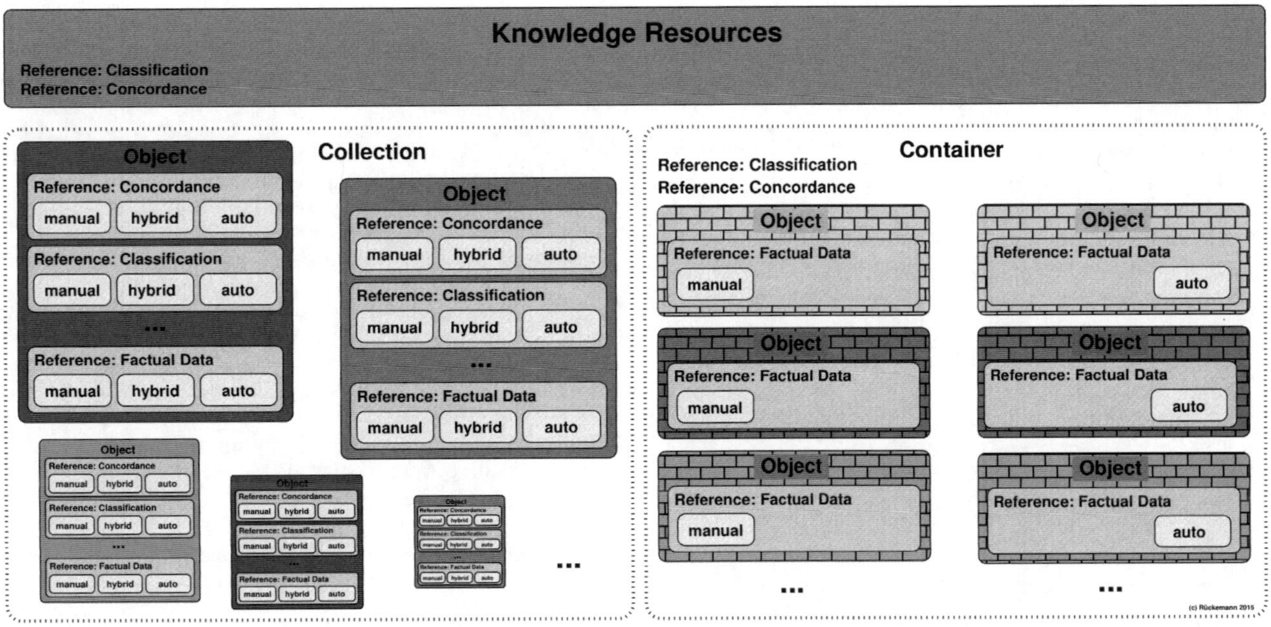

Figure 4. Resources and objects: Selected knowledge resources' objects containing references for concordances and classifications in collections and containers. In this case, the excerpt shows a distinct handling of manually, hybrid, and automatically created data, especially regarding classifications and concordances.

```
UCC:UDC2012:551.21
UCC:UDC2012:551
UCC:UDC2012:551.2,551.23,551.24,551.26
UCC:UDC2012:902/908
UCC:MSC2010:86,86A17,86A60
UCC:LCC:QE521-545
UCC:LCC:QE1-996.5
UCC:LCC:QC801-809
UCC:LCC:CC1-960,CB3-482
UCC:PACS2010:91.40.-k
UCC:PACS2010:91.65.-n,91.
UCC:PACS2010:91.40.Ge,91.40.St,91.40.Rs,*91.45.C-,*91.45.
  D-,90
...
```

Figure 6. Classification and concordances excerpt of a simple container instance (knowledge resources container).

In integration, together the concordances can create valuable references in depth and width to complementary classification schemes and knowledge classified with different classification.

The term concordance is not only used in the simple traditional meaning. Instead, the organisation is that of a meta-concordances concept. That results from the use of universal meta-classification, which in turn is used to classify and integrate classifications [53].

The samples include simple classifications from UDC, Mathematics Subject Classification (MSC) [54], Library of Congress Classification (LCC) [55], and Physics and Astronomy Classification Scheme (PACS) [56]. For PACS the asterisk ($\star$) indicates entries from the "Acoustics Appendix / Geophysics Appendix".

The UCC entries contain several classifications. The UCC blocks provide concordances across the classification schemes. The object classification is associated with the items associated with the object whereas the container classification is associated with the container, which means it refers to all objects in the containers.

VI. Definition and Organisation of Knowledge: Classifications and Concordances

Most content / context documentation and knowledge discovery efforts are based on data and knowledge entities.

Knowledge is created from a subjective combination of different attainments, which are selected, compared and balanced against each other, which are transformed, interpreted, and used in reasoning, also to infer further knowledge. Therefore, not all the knowledge can be explicitly formalised. Knowledge and content are multi- and inter-disciplinary long-term targets and values [57]. In practice, powerful and secure information technology can support knowledge-based works and values.

Computing goes along with methodologies, technological means, and devices applicable for universal automatic manipulation and processing of data and information. Computing is a practical tool and has well defined purposes and goals.

A. Organisation of knowledge

Knowledge requires a universal organisation in order to establish a practical long-term implementation for knowledge objects, which can be flexibly used for varying computing requirements. The sketch of a two-dimensional representation for the organisation of knowledge resources (Figure 7) shows the structure of attributes and references as used for illustration with this research.

The figure illustrates an excerpt of depth and width of resources. These two-dimensional representation is based on n-dimensional resources, which have no general limitations regarding attributes and references.

The knowledge resources contain collections, containers, and other forms of providing information and data.

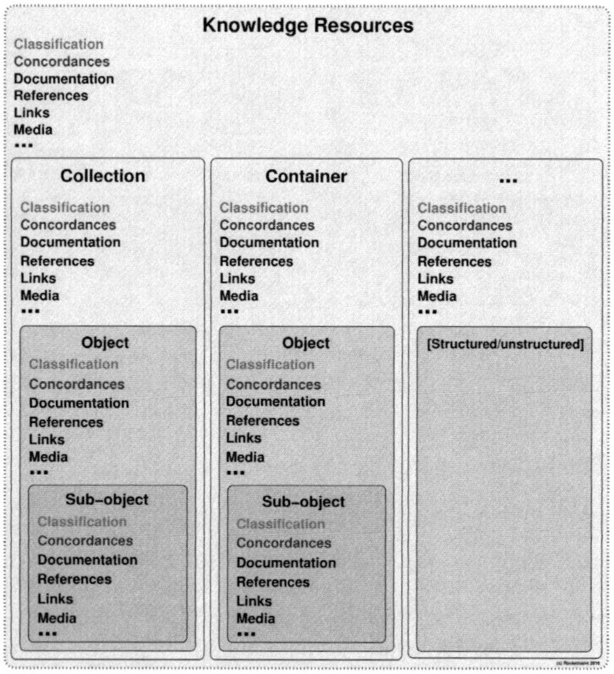

Figure 7. Sketch of a two-dimensional representation for the organisation of knowledge resources, showing an attributes/references structure.

A collection contains objects, which can widely differ, e.g., regarding internal structure, content, and references. For example, different references may be available, classification for objects being available or not. A container contains objects, which can have a common structure and comparable content and data, e.g., a mineral collection container or a volcanic features database. From the conceptual knowledge point of view, classification for the objects in a container will be very much the same.

From this point of view all knowledge objects will have a number classifications, for the resources, for the collection or container, for the object itself, for sub-objects, and probably references to object with classifications in the available dimensions.

Therefore, in this example, in a two-dimensional representation a sub-object in an object, in a container, in knowledge resources can have at least four classifications from the structural hierarchy.

B. Conceptual knowledge: Classification and concordances

The object as described with the creation of concordances is classified by use of one or more classifications. In this case, the UCC concordance holds entries from UDC, MSC, LCC, and PACS.

- UDC is fully integrating the object in a multidisciplinary and multi-lingual context.
- LCC is providing a comparable but much less multilingual integration.
- MSC is a mathematical and natural sciences classification but not providing much depth and details and in this case neither covering volcanology nor archaeology.
- PACS is a traditional classification, which has been used with physics and astronomy and natural sciences context. In this case, it is significant that archaeology is not covered by PACS.

Table III shows the referred conceptual knowledge for an object resulting from more than one classifications.

TABLE III. INSIDE CONCORDANCES: CONCEPTUAL KNOWLEDGE FROM MANY CLASSIFICATIONS (KNOWLEDGE RESOURCES, ENGLISH VERSION).

UDC Code	*Description*
UDC2012:551.21	Vulcanicity. Vulcanism. Volcanoes. Eruptive phenomena. Eruptions
UDC2012:551	General geology. Meteorology.
UDC2012:551.2	Internal geodynamics (endogenous processes)
UDC2012:551.23	Fumaroles. Solfataras. Geysers. Hot springs. Mofettes. Carbon dioxide vents. Soffioni
UDC2012:551.24	Geotectonics
UDC2012:551.26	Structural-formative zones and geological formations
UDC2012:902/908	Archaeology. Prehistory. Cultural remains. Area studies
MSC2010:86	Geophysics
LCC:QE521-545	Volcanoes and earthquakes
LCC:QE1-996.5	Geology
LCC:QC801-809	Geophysics. Cosmic physics
LCC:CC1-960	Archaeology
LCC:CB3-482	History of Civilization
LCC:QC1-999	Physics
LCC:Subclass Q	Science (General)
PACS2010:91.40.-k	Volcanology
PACS2010:91.65.-n	Geology
PACS2010:91.	Solid Earth physics
PACS2010:91.40.Ge	Hydrothermal systems, volcanology of
PACS2010:91.40.St	Mid-ocean ridges, in volcanology
PACS2010:91.40.Rs	Subduction zones, in volcanology
PACS2010:*91.45.C-,91.45.Cg	Continental tectonics
PACS2010:*91.45.D-,91.45.Dh	Plate tectonics
PACS2010:90	Geophysics, Astronomy, and Astrophysics
PACS2010:—	Archaeology

Not only that supporting multiple classifications can be used to integrate resources from multiple sources, which include different classifications. The spectra and focus of many classifications are representing various views and disciplines. Therefore, the use of "complementary" classifications leads to a broader conceptual knowledge with the available content. This is most interesting for multi-disciplinary and multi-lingual knowledge.

VII. Content Facets of Knowledge

A. References and features

For most cases, practically usable knowledge is available at the object level and deeper, e.g., in object elements. That means, within any process available conceptual knowledge can be considered appropriately, according to the respective depths and views. Practically available collection and container reference types from the above examples are, for example:

- Categorisation,
- Multi-lingual elements,
  - Including multi-lingual objects,
  - Including multi-lingual elements in elements of other languages,
- Sorting support,
- Keywords,
- Classification,
- Concordances,
- Content Factor,
- Check sums,
- Signatures,
- Comments,
- Sources, ...
- Formatting elements,
- Links,
- Media,
- Documentation,
  - Including equations and other items,
- Algorithms,
- See,
- Comparison, ...
- Special entries,
- Indexing, general, n-level,
- Indexing, special,
- Glossar, ...

Collections are mostly used for gathering individual objects of any size and content. Containers can be used for keeping objects of comparable thematical content and context. Examples are containers implemented for volcanic features, volcanic eruptions, earthquakes, tsunamis, and minerals.

B. Spanning multi-lingual content

Knowledge resources provide features to document any part of knowledge, e.g., a knowledge resources collection, container, object, or element of an object in any kind and language.

This sounds much simpler than it is for complex knowledge resources. A Latin entry can, e.g., contain documentation for multiple audiences, e.g., English and German. The English references can direct to German objects and vice versa. The German documentation and the German objects can again contain English terms or references. Any of these snippets of language can, e.g., require to provide different views, classification, and formatting. With classification the conceptual knowledge can also provide classification descriptions.

As can be seen from the descriptions, which are available in many languages: It can be reasonable to have support tables, e.g., synonym, variation, and transliteration lists for multilingual descriptions.

C. Spanning classifications

Complementary to the fact that the objects are spanning multi-lingual content is the feature that their conceptual knowledge is also spanning different classification and concordance spaces.

Therefore, they are spanning different conceptual knowledge views, which refer to their trees of knowledge. The complementary views also help improving the quality and robustness of discovery processes based on data, especially long-term and heterogeneous data [58]. Very flexible and extendable trees are, e.g., provided by the decimal architecture of UDC.

Although classification can be used and created dynamically, for many reasons most classifications are long-term conceptual knowledge applied manually and explicitely, persistent to the respective object. This may be met with applying editions for the respective classifications. The result is the benefit of consistent and trackable classification.

D. Application case: Components and cycles

The following example illustrates the components and workflow cycles, especially related to collections and containers including conceptual knowledge.

Table IV shows the specifications with the selected environment, major workflow steps with types of involved information, and the result matrix. The start point for the discovery was Vesuvius. The target was to discover 10 associated ancient locations

The ranking relates to the respective resources, specifications, and workflow. The first matrix elements are more related than the following. The resources and workflow components also allow context associations. However, less related from a primary discovery process can mean more related from a secondary discovery process.

VIII. Knowledge Processing and Computing

The advanced processing of knowledge resources benefits from a significant number of unique attributes in its elements. These attributes can be references, classification, keywords, textual content, links, and many more. The elements can consist of objects or collections of objects, the containers, integrating factual data with object information and structure.

Workflows for creating arbitrary result matrices (Figure 8) have been based on the organisation and object features (Figure 4) in the knowledge resources.

TABLE IV. COMPONENTS AND WORKFLOWS SUPPORTED BY CONCEPTUAL KNOWLEDGE: VESUVIUS-ASSOCIATED ANCIENT LOCATIONS.

Specification	*Selected Environment*
• Knowledge resources,	
Collection,	geosciences, archaeology, ...
Container,	volcanic features, stones, ...
Media,	[no explicit limit]
References,	[no explicit limit]
Links,	[no explicit limit]
Classification,	[no explicit limit]
Concordances, ...	[no explicit limit]
• Internet associations	[no explicit limit]
Workflow and Information	
• Knowledge resources (concordances-manual + structured data)	
• Associated data (concordances-auto + unstructured data)	
• Intermediate result matrix elements (concordance-manual, concordances-auto + structured + unstructured data)	
• Final result matrix elements (English, 10)	
Result Matrix	*Ranking*
Campi Flegrei	[01]
Naples	[02]
Pompeji	[03]
Oplontis	[04]
Stabiae	[05]
Herculaneum	[06]
Nuceria	[07]
Salernum	[08]
Surrentum	[09]
Misenum	[10]

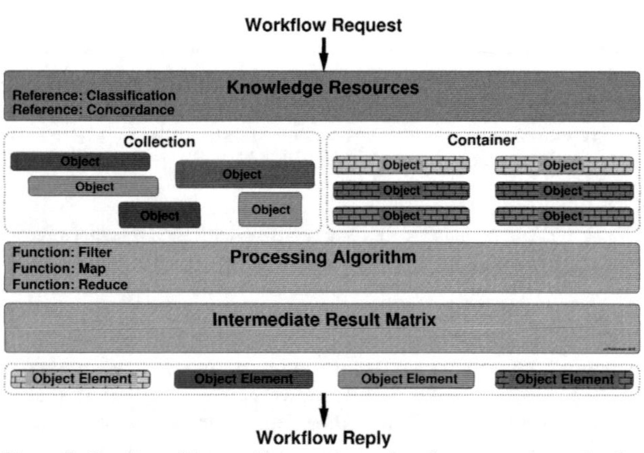

Figure 8. Creation of intermediate result matrices from resources and references (collections and containers) in reply to workflow requests.

The illustration shows that object information is gathered from the objects and references in collections and containers. Configurable algorithms like filters and mapping are then used in order to compute a result matrix. Here, the result matrix is considered "intermediate" because any of such workflows can be used in combination with other workflows, workflow chains or further processing.

For example, there is no "archaeology" in PACS, the concordances refer to resources including "archaeology" via some of the other schemes. MSC also does not contain a classification neither for volcanology or geology nor for associated features. Instead, even the geophysics section classifying geological problems refers to computational methods. The above examples (Figures 5 and 6) also illustrate this. The concordances' blocks allow to bridge between classifications and data resources, which can efficiently increase the available data pool size. Common options are in-depth computation with the container, or in-width with the general object collections. The concordances' blocks allow to follow in-depth or in-width references within data resources, which efficiently supports to improve the quality of result matrices and the quantity of elements, which also impacts on scalability and efficiency of workflows. Table V shows the shares of items regarding processing and computing with the main steps at knowledge resources, processing algorithms, and intermediate result matrices for the Vesuvius / volcanology case (Figures 2–6).

TABLE V. PROCESSING AND COMPUTING WITHOUT (/w) AND WITH (w/) CLASSIFICATION & CONCORDANCES (VESUVIUS/VOLCANOLOGY CASE).

Items of Processing and Computing	*Values*	
	/w	*w/*
Knowledge resources		
Collection	10,000	200
Container	300	5
Processing algorithm		
Mean	750	230
String comparison	90,000	8,000
Associations	344	127
Phonetics	34	22
Weighting	296	84
Intermediate result matrix		
4 result matrix elements	120	20

The number of operations is based on subset of 100,000 collection and container objects from the knowledge resources, which have been accessed for the study. The number of items to be handled by the processing and computing for creating a comparable or higher quality result matrix have been much smaller in the major number of practical workflows when classification and concordances are included in the workflows. Especially, the primary number of requests on the collections and containers can be reduced. Consequently, the number of algorithm calls is reduced. The number of string comparisons and associated algorithms is most prominent here as the majority of objects in the resources contain text.

Figure 9 shows an elementary sample workflow batch implementation of a generated caller script used for the processing parallelisation for the computing tasks, e.g., calling from Integrated System components like actmap [59].

```
#!/bin/bash
#PBS -A ruckema
#PBS -N PARA_Discover
#PBS -j oe
#PBS -l feature=mppl
#PBS -l nodes=16:ppn=6
#PBS -l walltime=00:60:00
cd $PBS_O_WORKDIR
msub para_discover.sh
```

Figure 9. Generated workflow parallelisation with `PARA_Discover`.

Every instance of this sample Portable Batch System (PBS) script uses 16 compute nodes and 6 processors per node in order to execute a `para_discover` call for maximum 60 minutes walltime. A regular run with the above values requires about 5 minutes walltime per instance without and about 25 seconds with classification and concordances. With four times the nodes and cores we can handle about four times the subset data.

However, it is important to choose a right knowledge representation for universal long-term data. The Resource Description Framework (RDF) [60] is a simple example for representing Web data. In many cases, simple directed labeled graphs are not sufficient to represent knowledge. References to directed labeled or other kinds of representations should be possible.

The structure should provide an intuitive and flexible access to the data. There should be features for integrating any kind of external data, e.g., objects, references, links, from structured to unstructured data with the available data. The elementary means of accessing the data should be independent from a certain implementation or certain purpose. The integration, interfaces, and interchange of data should be provided in most sustainable ways. This means any kind of structure and references and conceptual knowledge representation can be integrated. For example, in case of Web data even RDF can be deployed for Uniform Resource Identifiers (URI) naming relationships between data at the "ends" of a link, which in simple context enables to use graph analytics even on powerful High End Computing resources.

IX. Evaluation

The section views were created over longer periods of time while developing the knowledge resources, especially the objects. The implementation of knowledge dimensions is a fundamental means, which is based on complementary knowledge, especially factual, conceptual, procedural, and metacognitive knowledge.

Supporting more than one classification allows to integrate different sources and disciplinary views. This support can be beneficial for the discovery processes and the quality and value of data. Concordances are based on the same classification methods. The integrated use of multiple classifications allows to support a wider and deeper representation of conceptual knowledge.

On the one hand, the wide range of references, which have been implemented and can be extended arbitrarily, enables to support any data and sources. On the other hand, spanning multi-lingual content and spanning classifications allows to document with many languages and even specialised conceptual knowledge and integrate multi-lingual content as well as bridging areas of knowledge, which would be considered 'dark' in a single language or single classification.

As shown, objects and containers can carry complementary information and knowledge. The classifications and concordances feature a fuzzy bridging between resources, which allows modular in-depth as well as in-width workflows. In addition to that, workflows can require strongly adaptive code and algorithms. This may result in significant variations of runtime behaviour and resources' requirements. The workflows can integrate any objects for the processing, e.g., from collections and containers. These objects and their content may result from manual to automated origin. For example, the spectrum of creation includes use of classification, keywords, text analysis, and context analysis for the purpose of integration.

All the elements like classification, concordances, and factual data can result from manual, hybrid, and automatic processes. For example, Big Data [61] resources can be automatically outfitted with classifications and concordances following the container components. The level of details in content, context, and structure is arbitrary and can be scaled defined by the focus of the creator of the respective data. Therefore, associated conditions can be used in workflows for weighting the types of processes and qualities involved.

In practice, during the processing and computing, the numbers of algorithm calls for requests on the collections and containers can be significantly reduced with considering classification and concordances in workflows even when creating result matrices of comparable or higher quality. There will always be non-automated resources, which might be the knowledge intensive ones. The knowledge review can also be supported by distributed authorities as well as by means of automation.

Overall, classifications and concordances can easily be integrated with application components and workflows and allow an improved documentation for object along with additional information for supporting discovery processes, which can, e.g., be used for decision making and relevance considerations within discovery processes.

X. Conclusion and Future Work

With this extended research knowledge resources were created, which integrate flexible facilities for classifications and concordances. The organisation of the knowledge resources allows efficient long-term references structures. Therefore, the resources and objects can include any classification and concordances. Section views and knowledge dimensions have proven to be of long-term benefit for creating and developing knowledge resources.

The support of multiple classifications and concordances is a surplus value in many ways. The support advances the integration of knowledge and the facilities for discovery processes.

The types of objects and concordances shown in this paper have been successfully created and further developed within the knowledge resources. These results have also been integrated into the knowledge resources. The workflows for creating the structures and the features for the advanced processing and computing based on these resources have been successfully implemented with in the last years. From this research, we have learned some major results.

Experiences with the creation and development of objects within the knowledge resources have resulted in the fact that the data-centric approach neither conflicts with the long-term aspects nor with the deployment of advanced processing and computing features. This way, it should be possible to keep knowledge persistent even under changes of technology and paradigms.

The integration of objects, classification, and concordances has provided new means of documenting and accessing knowledge as well as for the efficient application of computational means. The structure of the long-term multi-disciplinary and multi-lingual knowledge resources' components enables to easily integrate objects from collections and containers. In more depth the conceptual knowledge, e.g., the classification can improve the quality of the result matrices. It enables to integrate more objects via strong means of knowledge instead of statistics or pattern matching algorithms only.

The implementation of the concordances and workflows has shown that the integrability of objects regarding multi-disciplinary and multi-lingual aspects has improved. The introduction of a universal classification and concordances is an excellent means of breaking up the isolated state of knowledge resources' content and associated data. In this context, creating concordances mainly contribute in two ways. On the one hand, concordances enable to considers different views of different and even special disciplines with the knowledge processing. On the other hand, concordances can be used to build bridges between isolated data resources.

The flexibility of the knowledge processing benefits from the advanced organisation of the data, which enables various scalable computational means for implementing directed graphs to fuzzy links, for which High End Computing resources can be deployed.

In summary, the wide range of implemented and arbitrarily extendable references and spanning languages and classifications enabled to improve documentation, integrability, and discovery with any data and sources. Creation and development of knowledge resources and knowledge discovery have benefited from classifications and concordances.

Future work will concentrate on advanced methodologies for data description and analysis, which can be applied with structured and unstructured knowledge objects and integrated with classifications, concordances, and references.

ACKNOWLEDGEMENTS

We are grateful to all national and international partners in the GEXI cooperations for the innovative constructive work. We are grateful to the "Knowledge in Motion" (KiM) long-term project, Unabhängiges Deutsches Institut für Multi-disziplinäre Forschung (DIMF), for partially funding this implementation, case study, and publication and to its senior scientific members, especially to Dr. Friedrich Hülsmann, Gottfried Wilhelm Leibniz Bibliothek (GWLB) Hannover, to Dipl.-Biol. Birgit Gersbeck-Schierholz, Leibniz Universität Hannover, and to Dipl.-Ing. Martin Hofmeister, Hannover, for fruitful discussion, inspiration, practical multi-disciplinary case studies, and the analysis of advanced concepts. We are grateful to all national and international partners in the GEXI cooperations for their constructive and trans-disciplinary support.

REFERENCES

[1] C.-P. Rückemann, "Creation of Objects and Concordances for Knowledge Processing and Advanced Computing," in Proceedings of The Fifth International Conference on Advanced Communications and Computation (INFOCOMP 2015), June 21–26, 2015, Brussels, Belgium. XPS Press, 2015, Rückemann, C.-P., Pankowska, M., and Flood, I. (eds.), pages 91–98, ISSN: 2308-3484, ISBN-13: 978-1-61208-416-9, ISBN-13: 978-1-61208-053-6 (CDROM), URL: http://www.thinkmind.org/download.php?articleid=infocomp_2015_4_30_60038 [accessed: 2016-01-24], URL: http://www.thinkmind.org/index.php?view=article&articleid=infocomp_2015_4_30_60038 [accessed: 2016-01-24].

[2] F. Hülsmann and C.-P. Rückemann, "Funding Value and Data Value," KiM Summit, June 15, 2015, Knowledge in Motion, "Unabhängiges Deutsches Institut für Multi-disziplinäre Forschung (DIMF)", Hannover, Germany, 2015.

[3] G. Leopold, "'Can Containers Contain?' Remains Top Security Issue," Enterprisetech, 2015, July 29, 2015, URL: http://www.enterprisetech.com/2015/07/29/can-containers-contain-remains-top-security-issue/ [accessed: 2016-01-24].

[4] G. Leopold, "Goldman Sachs Brokers Container Spec Deal," Enterprisetech, 2015, June 22, 2015, URL: http://www.enterprisetech.com/2015/06/22/goldman-sachs-brokers-container-spec-deal/ [accessed: 2016-01-24].

[5] K. Kincade, "NERSC's 'Shifter' Makes Container-based HPC a Breeze," HPCwire, 2015, August 7, 2015, URL: http://www.hpcwire.com/2015/08/07/nerscs-shifter-makes-container-based-hpc-a-breeze/ [accessed: 2016-01-24].

[6] B. Gersbeck-Schierholz and C.-P. Rückemann, "All-in Folders: Challenges and Benefits," KiMrise, Knowledge in Motion, June 20, 2015, Circle Summit Workgroup Meeting, "Unabhängiges Deutsches Institut für Multi-disziplinäre Forschung (DIMF)", Düsseldorf, Germany, 2015.

[7] R. S. Sasscer, U.S. Geological Survey library classification system. U.S. G.P.O., 1992, USGS Bulletin: 2010.

[8] E. Dodsworth and L. W. Laliberte, Eds., Discovering and using historical geographic resources on the Web: A practical guide for Librarians. Lanham: Rowman and Littlefield, 2014, ISBN: 0-8108-914-1.

[9] "Die Internationale Patentklassifikation (International Patent Classification, IPC)," 2014, Deutsches Patent- und Markenamt (DPMA), Germany, URL: http://dpma.de/service/klassifikationen/ipc/ [accessed: 2016-01-24].

[10] P. Cerchiello and P. Giudici, "Non parametric statistical models for on-line text classification," Advances in Data Analysis and Classification – Theory, Methods, and Applications in Data Science, vol. 6, no. 4, 2012, pp. 277–288, special issue on "Data analysis and classification in marketing" ISSN: 1862-5347.

[11] I. Dahlberg and M. R. Schader, Eds., Automatisierung in der Klassifikation, Proceedings, 7. Jahrestagung der Gesellschaft für Klassifikation e.V. (Teil 1), Königswinter/Rhein, Deutschland, 5.–8. April 1983. Indeks Verlag, Frankfurt a. M., 1983, ISBN: 3-88672-012-X, URL: https://openlibrary.org/books/OL21106918M/Automatisierung_in_der_Klassifikation [accessed: 2016-01-24].

[12] W. Gaul and M. Schader, Eds., Classification As a Tool of Research. North-Holland, Amsterdam, 1986, Proceedings, Annual Meeting of the Classification Society, (Proceedings der Fachtagung der Gesellschaft für Klassifikation), ISBN-13: 978-0444879806, ISBN-10: 0-444-87980-3, Hardcover, XIII, 502 p., May 1, 1986.

[13] J. Templin and L. Bradshaw, "Measuring the Reliability of Diagnostic Classification Model Examinee Estimates," Journal of Classification, vol. 30, no. 2, 2013, pp. 251–275, Heiser, W. J. (ed.), ISSN: 0176-4268 (print), ISSN: 1432-1343 (electronic), URL: http://dx.doi.org/10.1007/s00357-013-9129-4 [accessed: 2016-01-24].

[14] "Multilingual Universal Decimal Classification Summary," 2012, UDC Consortium, 2012, Web resource, v. 1.1. The Hague: UDC Consortium (UDCC Publication No. 088), URL: http://www.udcc.org/udcsummary/php/index.php [accessed: 2016-01-24].

[15] P. Cousson, "UDC as a non-disciplinary classification system for a high-school library," in Proc. UDC Seminar 2009, Classification at a Crossroads: Multiple Directions to Usability, 1992, pp. 243–252, URL: http://www.academia.edu/1022257/UDC_as_a_non-disciplinary_classification_system_for_a_high-school_library [accessed: 2016-01-24].

[16] A. Adewale, "Universal Decimal Classification (UDC): A Most For All Libraries," library 2.0, the future of libraries in the digital age, 2014, URL: http://www.library20.com/forum/topics/universal-decimal-classification-udc-a-most-for-all-libraries [accessed: 2016-01-24].

[17] "EULISP Lecture Notes, European Legal Informatics Study Programme, Institute for Legal Informatics (Institut für Rechtsinformatik, IRI), Leibniz Universität Hannover," 2015, URL: http://www.eulisp.de [accessed: 2016-01-24].

[18] F. Heel, "Abbildungen zwischen der Dewey-Dezimalklassifikation (DDC), der Regensburger Verbundklassifikation (RVK) und der Schlagwortnormdatei (SWD) für die Recherche in heterogen erschlossenen Datenbeständen – Möglichkeiten und Problembereiche," Bachelorarbeit im Studiengang Bibliotheks- und Informationsmanagement, Fak. Information und Kommunikation, Hochschule der Medien Stuttgart, 2007.

[19] T. Riplinger, "Die Bedeutung der Methode Eppelsheimer für Theorie und Praxis der bibliothekarischen und der dokumentarischen Sacherschließung," BIBLIOTHEK Forschung und Praxis, vol. 28, no. 2, 2012, pp. 252–262, 01/2004, DOI: 10.1515/BFUP.2004.252.

[20] S. A. Keller and R. Schneider, Eds., Wissensorganisation und -repräsentation mit digitalen Technologien. Walter de Gruyter GmbH, 2014, Bibliotheks- und Informationspraxis, ISSN: 0179-0986, Band 55, ISBN: 3-11-031270-0.

[21] E. W. De Luca and I. Dahlberg, "Die Multilingual Lexical Linked Data Cloud: Eine mögliche Zugangsoptimierung?" Information Wissenschaft & Praxis, vol. 65, no. 4–5, 2014, pp. 279–287, Deutsche Ges. f. Information und Wissen e.V. (DGI), Ed., De Gruyter Saur, ISSN: 1434-4653, (title in English: The Multilingual Lexical Linked Data Cloud: A possible semantic-based access to the Web?).

[22] "Europeana," 2016, URL: http://www.europeana.eu/ [accessed: 2016-01-24].

[23] Max Planck Institute for the History of Science, Max-Planck Institut für Wissenschaftsgeschichte, "European Cultural Heritage Online (ECHO)," 2016, Berlin, URL: http://echo.mpiwg-berlin.mpg.de/ [accessed: 2016-01-24].

[24] "WDL, World Digital Library," 2016, URL: http://www.wdl.org [accessed: 2016-01-24].

[25] Ponemon Institute, "Ponemon Study Shows the Cost of a Data Breach Continues to Increase," 2014, Ponemon Institute, URL: http://www.ponemon.org/news-2/23 [accessed: 2015-02-01].

[26] G. Isaew and A. Roganow, "Qualitätssteuerung von Informationssystemen: Theoretisch-methodologische Grundlagen," Information Wissenschaft & Praxis, vol. 65, no. 4–5, 2014, pp. 271–278, Deutsche Gesellschaft für Information und Wissen e.V. (DGI), Ed., De Gruyter Saur, ISSN: 1434-4653, e-ISSN: 1619-4292 DOI: 10.1515/iwp-2014-0044, (title in English: Quality Management of Information Systems: Theoretical and methodological basics).

[27] L. Schumann and W. G. Stock, "Ein umfassendes ganzheitliches Modell für Evaluation und Akzeptanzanalysen von Informationsdiensten: Das Information Service Evaluation (ISE) Modell," Information Wissenschaft & Praxis, vol. 65, no. 4–5, 2014, pp. 239–246, Deutsche Gesellschaft für Information und Wissen e.V. (DGI), Ed., De Gruyter Saur, ISSN: 1434-4653, e-ISSN: 1619-4292, DOI: 10.1515/iwp-2014-0043, (title in English: A comprehensive holistic model for evaluation and acceptance analyses of information services: The Information Service Evaluation (ISE) model).

[28] "LX-Project," 2016, URL: http://www.user.uni-hannover.de/cpr/x/rprojs/en/#LX [accessed: 2016-01-24].

[29] C.-P. Rückemann, "Enabling Dynamical Use of Integrated Systems and Scientific Supercomputing Resources for Archaeological Information Systems," in Proc. INFOCOMP 2012, Oct. 21–26, 2012, Venice, Italy, 2012, pp. 36–41, ISBN: 978-1-61208-226-4.

[30] "UDC Online," 2016, URL: http://www.udc-hub.com/ [accessed: 2016-01-24].

[31] "Creative Commons Attribution Share Alike 3.0 license," 2012, URL: http://creativecommons.org/licenses/by-sa/3.0/ [accessed: 2016-01-24].

[32] F. Hülsmann and C.-P. Rückemann, "Summary on Algorithms and Workflows," KiMrise, Knowledge in Motion Winter Meeting, December 12, 2014, Knowledge in Motion, Hannover, Germany, 2014.

[33] S. Tiwari, Professional NoSQL. Wrox, John Wiley & Sons, Inc., 2011, ISBN: 978-0-470-94224-6.

[34] "MySQL," 2016, URL: http://www.mysql.com/ [accessed: 2016-01-24].

[35] D. Wyllie, "MySQL vs. MongoDB: Datenbanksysteme für Web-Anwendungen im Vergleich," Computerwoche, 2014, 2014-05-29, URL: http://www.computerwoche.de/a/datenbanksysteme-fuer-web-anwendungen-im-vergleich,2496589 [accessed: 2015-02-01].

[36] "MongoDB," 2016, URL: http://www.mongodb.org/ [accessed: 2016-01-24].

[37] K. Chodorow, MongoDB: The Definitive Guide. O'Reilly Media, 2013, ISBN: 9781449344689.

[38] J. Roijackers and G. H. L. Fletcher, "On Bridging Relational and Document-Centric Data Stores," in Proc. 29th British National Conf. on Databases (BNCOD 2013), Oxford, UK, July 8–10, 2013, Big Data, LNCS, vol. 7968, 2013, pp. 135–148, ISBN: 978-3-642-39466-9.

[39] G. Rege, Ruby and MongoDB Web Development Beginner's Guide. Packt Publishing, 2012, ISBN: 1849515026.

[40] "CoreOS," 2015, URL: https://coreos.com/ [accessed: 2015-02-01].

[41] "Docker," 2015, URL: https://www.docker.com/ [accessed: 2015-02-01].

[42] J. Dean and S. Ghemawat, "MapReduce: Simplified data processing on large clusters," in Proceedings of the 6th Conference on Operating Systems Design and Implementation (OSDI 2004), 2004, DOI: 10.1.1.163.5292.

[43] C.-P. Rückemann, "High End Computing Using Advanced Archaeology and Geoscience Objects," International Journal On Advances in Intelligent Systems, vol. 6, no. 3&4, 2013, ISSN: 1942-2679, LCCN: 2008212456, URL: http://www.iariajournals.org/intelligent_systems/intsys_v6_n34_2013_paged.pdf [accessed: 2016-01-24].

[44] UDC, Universal Decimal Classification. British Standards Institute (BSI), 2005, Complete Edition, ISBN: 0-580-45482-7, Vol. 1 and 2.

[45] "UDC Online," 2015, URL: http://www.udc-hub.com/ [accessed: 2015-02-01].

[46] C.-P. Rückemann, "From Multi-disciplinary Knowledge Objects to Universal Knowledge Dimensions: Creating Computational Views," International Journal On Advances in Intelligent Systems, vol. 7, no. 3&4, 2014, pp. 385–401, international Academy, Research, and Industry Association (IARIA), Bodendorf, F., (ed.), URL: http://www.thinkmind.

org/download.php?articleid=intsys_v7_n34_2014_4 [accessed: 2016-01-24].

[47] "LX SNDX, a Soundex Module Concept for Knowledge Resources," LX-Project Consortium Technical Report, 2014, URL: http://www.user.uni-hannover.de/cpr/x/rprojs/en/#{}{} [accessed: 2015-02-01].

[48] U. Balakrishnan, "Eine DDC-RVK-Konkordanz - Erste Erkenntnisse aus dem Gebiet Medizin & Gesundheit," 2012, Projekt Colibri / DDC Teilprojekt coli-conc, URL: http://nbn-resolving.de/urn:nbn:de:bsz:ch1-qucosa-82838 [accessed: 2016-01-24].

[49] I. Rauner, "Erstellung einer Konkordanz zwischen BK (Basisklassifikation) und RVK (Regensburger Verbundklassifikation) für das Fachgebiet Germanistik," Master's thesis, University of Vienna, Universitätslehrgang Library and Information Studies, 2010.

[50] U. Balakrishnan, "Das Konkordanzprojekt coli-conc," 2012, Verbundzentrale des GBV, 13. November 2013, Göttingen, Germany, URL: https://www.gbv.de/cls-download/fag-erschliessung-und-informationsvermittlung/arbeitsdokumente-fag-ei/praesentation-zu-konkordanzen/at_download/file [accessed: 2016-01-24].

[51] "North American Industry Classification System (NAICS)," 2014, URL: https://www.census.gov/eos/www/naics/index.html [accessed: 2016-01-24].

[52] "North American Industry Classification System (NAICS), Concordances," 2014, URL: https://www.census.gov/eos/www/naics/concordances/concordances.html [accessed: 2016-01-24].

[53] F. Hülsmann and C.-P. Rückemann, "Intermediate Classification and Concordances in Practice," KiMrise, Knowledge in Motion Meeting, January 9, 2015, Knowledge in Motion, Hannover, Germany, 2015.

[54] "Mathematics Subject Classification (MSC2010)," 2010, URL: http://msc2010.org [accessed: 2016-01-24].

[55] Fundamentals of Library of Congress Classification, Developed by the ALCTS/CCS-PCC Task Force on Library of Congress Classification Training, 2007, Robare, L., Arakawa, S., Frank, P., and Trumble, B. (eds.), ISBN: 0-8444-1186-8 (Instructor Manual), ISBN: 0-8444-1191-4 (Trainee Manual), URL: http://www.loc.gov/catworkshop/courses/fundamentalslcc/pdf/classify-trnee-manual.pdf [accessed: 2016-01-24].

[56] "Physics and Astronomy Classification Scheme, PACS 2010 Regular Edition," 2010, American Institute of Physics (AIP), URL: http://www.aip.org/pacs [accessed: 2016-01-24].

[57] C.-P. Rückemann, F. Hülsmann, B. Gersbeck-Schierholz, P. Skurowski, and M. Staniszewski, Knowledge and Computing. Post-Summit Results, Delegates' Summit: Best Practice and Definitions of Knowledge and Computing, September 23, 2015, The Fifth Symposium on Advanced Computation and Information in Natural and Applied Sciences, The 13th International Conference of Numerical Analysis and Applied Mathematics (ICNAAM), September 23–29, 2015, Rhodes, Greece, 2015.

[58] B. Gersbeck-Schierholz and C.-P. Rückemann, "Coping with Failures in Information and Applied Knowledge," KiMrise, Knowledge in Motion, June 20, 2015, Circle Summit Workgroup Meeting, "Unabhängiges Deutsches Institut für Multi-disziplinäre Forschung (DIMF)", Brussels-Welckenrath, Belgium, 2015.

[59] C.-P. Rückemann, "Active Map Software," 2001, 2005, 2012, URL: http://wwwmath.uni-muenster.de/cs/u/ruckema (information, data, abstract) [accessed: 2012-01-01], URL: http://www.unics.uni-hannover.de/cpr/x/rprojs/en/index.html#actmap [accessed: 2016-01-24].

[60] W3 Consortium (W3C), "Resource Description Framework (RDF)," 2016, W3C Semantic Web, URL: http://www.w3.org/RDF/ [accessed: 2016-01-24].

[61] C.-P. Rückemann, F. Hülsmann, and M. Hofmeister, "Cognostics and Applications for Knowledge Resources and Big Data Computing," KiM Summit, November 9, 2015, Knowledge in Motion, "Unabhängiges Deutsches Institut für Multi-disziplinäre Forschung (DIMF)", Hannover, Germany, 2015.

Smart and Individual Travel Assistance - Barrierfree Mobility for all

Smartphone application for barrierfree cross-modal transportation information in real-time

Nadine Schlueter, Jan-Peter Nicklas, Petra Winzer
Research Group of Product Safety and Quality Engineering
University of Wuppertal
Wuppertal, Germany
schlueter@uni-wuppertal.de; nicklas@uni-wuppertal.de;
winzer@uni-wuppertal.de

Lars Schnieder
Institute of Transportation Systems
German Aerospace Center
Braunschweig, Germany
lars.schnieder@dlr.de

Abstract—**Public transport operators focus on a public transport system, which is inclusive and fair to all groups of society as required in the United Nations´s Convention on the Rights of Persons with Disabilities. This requires an innovative approach reflecting both the users' and the service providers' perspective. From the passengers' point of view it becomes obvious that not only the accessibility of a single mode of transportation is relevant. Furthermore, a systemic view is required as a trip from door to door most likely includes different means of transportation. The interchanges within one transportation system as well as the change-over to other means of transportation must be improved regarding the special requirements of people with reduced mobility and/or sensory restrictions. So, in order to create a public transportation system for all, all public transport service providers and their processes have to be linked with each other. This article describes how this objective can be achieved by a holistic approach that helps developing individual and smart solution available and useable for each passenger.**

Keywords - cross-modal public transportation; barrierfree; smart solutions; customer-orientation; feedback; service application.

I. Introduction

Every mobility chain - not only in public transportation - is accompanied by an information chain. This has to be seen both from the passengers' perspective as well as from the public transport service providers' point of view. Especially passengers with reduced mobility and/or sensory restrictions have to be informed in due time. Not only when operations are affected as planned, but especially in case of unexpected events and service disruptions. In this case, existing travel itineraries have to be updated or new travel itineraries have to be generated and distributed to the relevant passengers. Updates of travel itineraries need to reflect changeover times and have to consider special needs of passengers with reduced mobility. In particular, this means that information needs to be presented in time and in an understandable way, e.g., in sign language [1]. By carrying out the demo research project aim4it (Researchproject aim4it - accessible and inclusive mobility for all with individual travel assistance. EU Funding programme Future Travelling (ENT III, Flagship Call 2013), Projectnumber: 4304059) , barrierfree mobility for all should be achieved as demanded by UN´s Convention on the Rights of Persons with Disabilities [2] as well as corresponding legislation on European [3] and national level [4].

Innovative intermodal transport information systems (ITIS) manage the challenge to provide such relevant pre-trip, on-trip and post-trip information to passengers. Precise and up to date information is the basis for travel assistance applications.

Within the travel assistance application information representation is tailored to the specific requirements of passengers with sensory restrictions, e.g., information display in sign language using an avatar on smartphones. Blind passengers benefit from audible output provided by screen readers.

The offer of travel assistance applications significantly increases service quality perceived by the passenger and can thus increase the use of public transportation. By doing this public transport can make a significant contribution towards a sustainable modal split, which helps to reduce pollution in urban areas. Furthermore, with suitable evaluation algorithms customer feedback can be systematically solicited, evaluated and interpreted by the public transport operators. Better handling of passenger feedback is a solid basis for a continuous improvement of public transport operations. For example, timetables can be adjusted or available digital maps further enhanced furthermore, service personal can be used more appropriate. Overall, this will result in a better service quality for passengers – not only the ones with reduced mobility and/or sensory restrictions. All groups of our society benefit from improved passenger information and value-added services.

In the following sections, it will be described how an innovative approach can support the development of a barrierfree public transportation system. The technical components have to fulfill the passenger´s needs as well as the public transport service provider´s needs and will be further described below. Furthermore, the chosen use case example "UC6: Passenger feedback function" will be explained in more detail to point out the innovative methodological approach, which helps to continuously improve value-added services for passengers with reduced mobility. Finally, a conclusion will sum up the most important facts and show the next steps on the way to a barrierfree public transportation system for all.

II. Innovative Approach for Barrierfree Public Transportation

The project aim4it (accessible and inclusive mobility for all with individual travel assistance) incorporates and integrates both the user's and service provider's point of view. In order to bring together both views service blueprints of the passenger processes and use cases from the public transport service provider´s point of view are linked to each other. Demands and requirements from passengers and public transport service providers are linked to the processes and sub-processes of service maps and use cases (see Figure 1) in order to gain known-ledge about all relevant requirements (for more information refer to [5]) that need to be fulfilled.

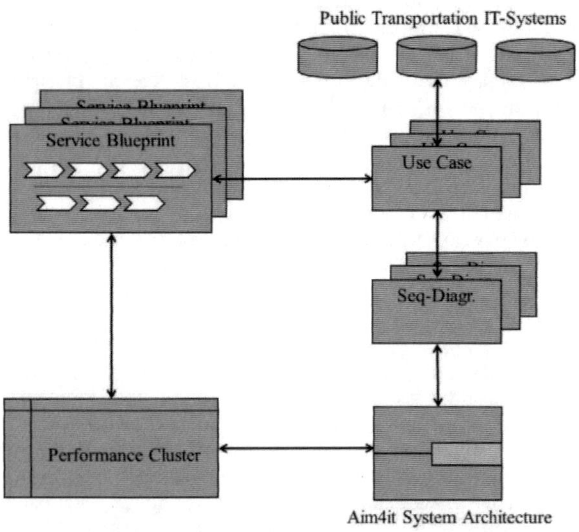

Figure 1. Innovative approach for developing barrierfree public transportation systems in accordance to [6]

Furthermore, a requirements management approach for networks is implemented to evaluate, structure, assess and monitor the process of requirement fulfillment [7] and to assure the quality of the project outcome. In order to show the way how the system is developed, based on elicited requirements and processes, a short use case example is given in the following.

When a journey is viewed from the perspective of the customer/user, it becomes clear that it is not enough to design individual transport modes and facilities for just one transport system. In order to be passenger-friendly and suitable for use by passengers with special mobility needs (in this use case visually impaired passengers as well as the deaf and hard of hearing) all transport modes and, therefore, all service providers have to be considered [8]. For a given destination to be reachable by everyone, barrierfree mobility chains for all transport modes should be set up. As every mobility chain is accompanied by an information chain passengers with reduced mobility and/or sensory restrictions have to get all relevant information about departure and arrival times as well as necessary transfer procedures at interchange stations. This information must be up-to-date, precise and understandable at important nodes before, along as well as after the journey. Significant information needs to be conveyed in optical, acoustical and/or tactile form [9].

These demands and requirements lead to several use cases (UC), which will be addressed in the aim4it project:

- UC1: Request for connection protection especially for passengers with reduced mobility who have a need for prolonged changeover times at interchange stations.
- UC2: Information about current incidents in the public transport network in sign language.
- UC3: Request for staff assistance to get on and off the vehicle to facilitate use of public transport services for passengers with reduced mobility.
- UC4: Re-Routing especially in case of incidents, but also in case of delays in public transport operations.
- UC5: In-Vehicle passenger information based on the integrated on-board information system (IBIS).
- UC6: Passenger feedback function to trigger continuous improvement activities of public transport operators.

Afterwards those use cases are transferred, based on their storyline, into Unified Modelling Language (UML) sequence diagrams in order to support the development of technical interfaces between the different information systems of the service providers. For the use case 5 "in-vehicle passenger information" such a sequence-diagram is shown as an example in Figure 2. It shows how the background system (the journey planner, which is part of the intermodal transport information system, ITIS), the travel assistance application on the passengers' smartphones, the Bluetooth-Gateway on board of the vehicle as well as the on-board unit of the intermodal transport control system (ITCS) interact with each other.

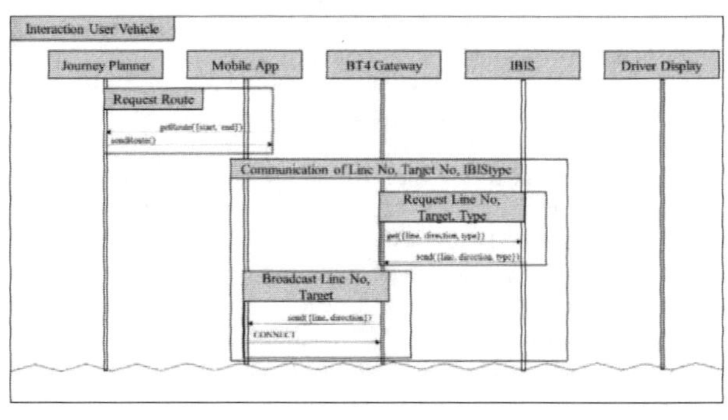

Figure 2. Detail of sequence diagram about "In-Vehicle Passenger Information" use case

Based on the defined use cases and the sequence diagrams that show, which information sources are available and how they should interact with each other, the whole system architecture with its components was set up. The following section describes those components, based on the use cases in more detail.

III. Components of the aim4it System Architecture

The intended overall aim4it system provides a benefit from the user's as well as the public transport service provider's point of view. The key idea of the aim4it system architecture is to use industry standards. This facilitates implementation of the aim4it travel assistance application as well as field integration in the test field in Vienna. Furthermore, it allows easy transfer of project results to other regions after the project.

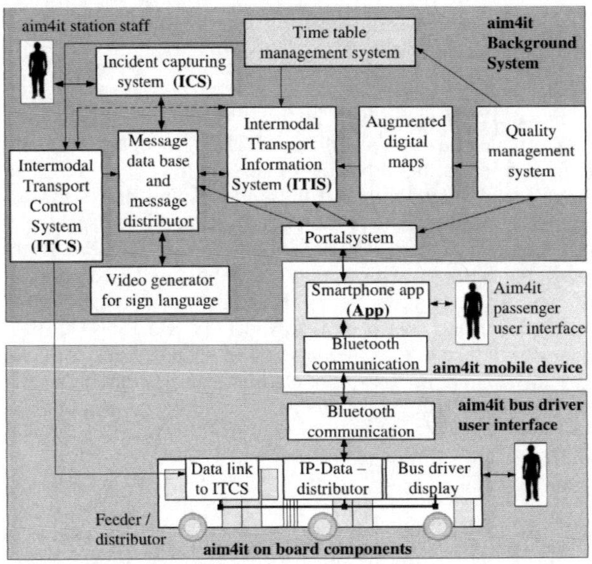

Figure 3. Aim4it system architecture [10]

Thereby the aim4it smartphone app is the key element as shown in Figure 3. The following sections will explain the aim4it sub-systems and their interactions in more detail.

A. *aim4it smartphone app*

With the aim4it smartphone app passengers with reduced mobility and/or sensory restrictions get assistance in both trip planning and execution. At home the passenger can start the planning of the trip by entering information about the start and the destination into the app. Data entry and display on the aim4it user interface are designed in a user-centered way. All information provided will be displayed as multi-sensual output to secure information for the different groups of passengers. For example, blind and visually impaired passengers receive audible output. Once all data is entered, the aim4it smartphone app sends a request for a barrierfree trip to the Intermodal Transport Information System (ITIS) [11]. This way a bi-directional communication between passengers and service providers can be established [12]. This bi-directional link will be maintained once the passenger started his journey. This means once a triggering condition for a route-update has been identified by the ITIS the passenger will receive a new itinerary on his smart phone (see Figure 4). With the app the passenger can also "book" other value-added services. If required prolonged change-over times at interchange stations can be requested as well as boarding assistance to enter or leave the public transport vehicle.

Figure 4. Push-updates for passenger´s smartphones

The passenger receives updates about current public transport operations with push-updates. Figure 4 shows a sample screen shot of the aim4it smartphone app. The example shows a trip with the subway line U2 in Vienna to the convention center. The trip from start to destination requires an interchange from subway line U2 to the bus line 82A. The connection from subway to bus is successfully booked and the bus driver is informed. The passenger receives a positive acknowledgement about this.

B. *Intermodal Transport Information (ITIS)*

Based on the start and end point of the requested trip the ITIS performs barrierfree routing from start to destination. In order to do this, the system is supplied with all relevant time table information from time table planning systems. Furthermore, the available infrastructure at stations (e.g., lifts and escalators) is part of the system. The combination of time table data and infrastructure modelling allows the execution of barrierfree routings. In addition to "just" reflecting time table data, the ITIS also reflects real-time data [13] of current public transport operations. Real-time data is provided by the Intermodal Transport Control System (ITCS). Furthermore, available information from augmented digital maps (e.g., based on crowdsourcing projects such as wheelmap) and incident from the incident capturing system (ICS, see section III, D) are considered in the routing function. For example, incident messages can be entered by local service staff at stations (e.g., defect of an escalator). The barrierfree route compiled by the ITIS is sent to the smartphone app. There it is displayed for barrierfree navigation along the planned trip chain. Besides this routing function, the ITIS also serves as a "message broker" between the passenger and the public transport operators. For the use cases "connection protection" and "staff assistance" the ITIS receives the requests, maps the requests to specific vehicle movements and forwards these requests to the intermodal transport control system (ITCS). If required by the usecase feedback from the ITCS will be forwarded to the passenger by the ITIS (e.g., acknowledgement of staff assistance request). The passenger will receive corresponding information on his/her smart phone.

C. *Intermodal Transport Control Systems (ITCS)*

The intermodal transport control system (ITCS) continuously monitors the current status of public transport operations (see Figure 5). Each day the current time table is loaded into the system.

Figure 5. Operations control center

Each vehicle receives information, that is relevant. Time table information is displayed to the driver who adheres to the schedule in the best possible way. Based on GPS-tracking the vehicles send updates about schedule adherence and their current position to the ITCS. Based on the available information, existing conflicts in public transport operations can be detected (or future conflicts predicted) and appropriate corrective action is triggered by the staff in the operations control center. In the operations control center previously booked connection requests are monitored. The same applies for previously booked requests for staff assistance. In case planned connections cannot be kept or planned staff assistance at a station cannot be guaranteed any more, appropriate action is taken. Connection monitoring is visualized in the screenshot in Figure 6 below. This list provides information, which connections are subject to monitoring and if these are critical due to delays especially of the feeding bus.

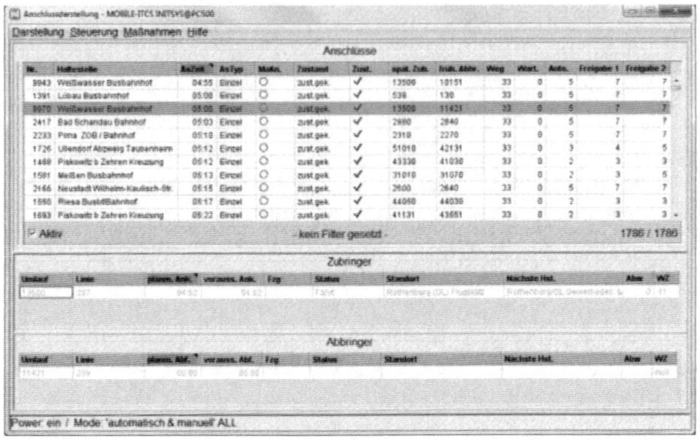

Figure 6. Display of secured connections at the operator's terminal in the operations control center

Besides this equipment in the operations control center each vehicle (bus and tram) has an ITCS on-board unit. By implementing a new bi-directional interface between the aim4it smart phone app and the onboard unit new services become available to the passengers. An example of a possible new feature is the request for bus driver assistance e.g., to board the vehicle. This request can be processed in two different ways. In a first option, the request is entered into the smart phone app and is sent to the ITIS. By the ITIS this request is passed to the ITCS where the corresponding vehicle is identified. Via the existing data link between the ITCS and the vehicle the request for bus driver assistance is sent to the bus (see Figure 7) [11]. In a second option, a direct communication link between app and vehicle (e.g., WiFi or Bluetooth) can be used.

Figure 7. Bus driver display shows requested assistance

On board of the vehicle the boarding request is displayed to the bus driver within the aim4it bus driver user interface when the vehicle approaches the proposed station. Figure 7 shows how a boarding request of a wheel chair user is displayed to the bus driver.

D. *Incident Capturing System (ICS)*

During operations the initial route of the passenger will be updated based on available information about timetable deviations or changes in the status of the network infrastructure (real-time data). Real-time data also includes incidents and disruption information due to their mostly short-term nature. For this reason public transport service providers have to capture incidents in their route network [14]. For example, this can be line closures (e.g., due to an accident) or a defect of facilities at stations. With the incident capturing system the operator can enter currently existing problems. This information is made available to the ITIS. ITIS determines which line/station is affected by the entered incident message. Furthermore, ITIS has an overview, which passengers need to be informed about currently existing restrictions within the public transport network. The existing incident is reflected in the routing of passengers (see section IV.D). With the push service all passengers receive information that is relevant to them in their specific usage context. For example, a wheel chair use will get an adequate route information in case a lift is broken. In this case, he/she might be asked to use a different route or to leave the subway at another station. In case an incident has been solved the incident message is revoked. In this case, the ITIS can determine a new route.

IV. Value-Added Services and their Continuous Improvement

With the aim4it smartphone app passengers with reduced mobility and/or sensory restrictions get on-trip assistance. This includes several services, which are based on pre-defined use cases. The implemented use cases are further described in the following sections.

A. *UC 1: Request for connection protection*

Most often trips in a public transportation network can only be realized with at least one transfer [10]. To provide a dependable transportation chain time tables have to be matched and transport operators have to monitor connections in order to synchronize transportation chains in case of incidents. If needed, the connecting vehicle can wait for passengers of the feeding vehicle. The request for connection protection in the aim4it system takes into account that passengers with mobility or sensual restrictions need a longer transfer time to the vehicle. Based on this service the connection is guaranteed and the passenger is informed in due time. The driver of the receiving vehicle is informed about the prolonged waiting time at the requested station. In addition, connections can also be cancelled if no longer required (e.g., due to re-routing, see Section IV.B – Incident information in sign language) to avoid delay [1, 10]. If a connection cannot be kept because of delays or incidents within the public transport network the passenger will get an automatic route update.

B. *UC 2: Incident information in sign language*

All passengers need to get access to detailed and reliable information regarding their trip. To provide such comprehensive information by the travel assistance application for sensory restricted passengers, this information have to be made available in an appropriate way. Whenever service irregularities (e.g., delays, cancellations, missed connections) are detected in the ITCS error information is forwarded to the passenger. In order to provide barrierfree information, this process includes several media types, which supply information for the passenger in a way suitable for his special needs.

The aim4it project pays special attention to deaf and hearing-impaired passengers. As this passenger group has difficulties in deciphering complex linguistic structures relevant information will be provided by sign language-based avatar videos. The aim4it message generator automatically transforms the text message to a video stream, *displaying error information in sign language* for deaf and hard of hearing passengers on their smartphones [1, 10]. Figure 8 shows the video avatar for displaying information in sign language.

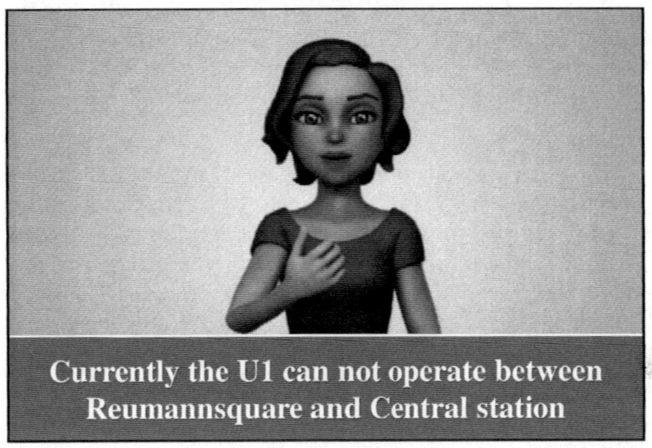

Figure 8. Video avatar for displaying information in sign language [10]

C. *UC 3: Request for staff assistance*

On trip the passenger can make stop requests along with requests for bus driver assistance. For instance, a blind or sensory restricted passenger can call for help to get on the vehicle (see Figure 9). It is also possible to call for help to get off the vehicle. Therefore, the bus driver can assist, e.g., a wheelchair user by a bus integrated ramp (see Figure 10).

Figure 9. Sensory restricted passenger requests via aim4it application

. Figure 10. Assistance for wheelchair user

This service provides an easier usage of public transportation services for passengers with reduced mobility or with sensual restrictions. Information about a staff assistance request is sent by the passenger prior to the trip. The staff member awaits the passenger at the previously defined station and helps to board the vehicle. At the designated station the staff member helps again by alighting from the vehicle [1, 10].

D. UC 4: Re-routing

During the trip of a passenger, a previously defined trip may become impractical. This may be due to

a) the passenger changing his or her mind about basic parameters of the initial trip,
b) the passenger showing up to late at the start station or missing a connection or
c) irregularities of public transport operations, for example, in case of delays, cancellation or detours.

Therefore, dynamic *re-routing* is an integral part of the system. Once one of these triggering conditions is identified by the smartphone app a new trip request is initiated. Using available information in the ITIS as well as the information about the passenger´s disability profile a new route is generated considering current position of the passenger and real time data of public transport operations (including delays and incident information). If re-routing involves another use case, e.g., "Request for staff assistance" information is updated or the request is cancelled [1, 10].

E. UC 5: In-vehicle passenger information based on IBIS IP

In order to establish internet protocol (IP) based communication, wireless communication between the aim4it application and the public transportation vehicle will be implemented by means of Bluetooth 4.0-interface. This way waiting passengers can recognize, which line the approaching vehicle is assigned to (Figure 11).

Figure 11. Recognition of approaching line via aim4it application

Additional information is sent from the vehicle to the application on board. This contains information about the travel directions, route and stop sequences, real-time information to catch connected services, etc. Deviations from the scheduled timetable can be sent as well [1, 10].

F. UC 6: Feedback for continuous improvement

To realize a continuous improvement of the public transportation system, as well as the aim4it services, the passengers have to be surveyed. With the aim4it feedback function passengers with sensory restrictions or restricted mobility will be directly involved in this improvement process during their travel [15]. Based on these assessed performances and opinions of the passengers, the public service providers can improve performances of service quality in a precise way. The public transport operators can set up the right priorities for the adaptation of existing facilities and services or add new, gathered requirements for further design, planning and – after implementation - assessment of public transportation systems. To realize this actual state of the art customer satisfaction measurement concepts have to be enhanced and combined with the potentials of up-do date information and communication technology [16, 17].

In detail, this means that passengers, their processes and their contact points are used to implement a concept for customer- and process-oriented satisfaction measurement, which is based on real time data.

The service blueprint showing the passenger processes, their contact points and links to service providers [8] offer input for the performance cluster that is a knowledge base for survey questions and their results. Furthermore, it is used as basis for the use cases of each function that is supplemented with available information systems and standards in public transportation [15]. The execution of every journey generates data that is sent to and from the smartphone device of the passenger. This data can serve as a kind of direct performance measurement in the sense of the European standard specifying service quality for the public transport domain [15]. With this data the actual quality delivered by the public transport operator can be measured by using statistical matrices.

One possible measurement concept is the so called direct performance measures (DPM) [18]. DPM have proven to be an adequate method of monitoring the actual performance of services based on operational data records. Examples of data collected in public transportation are information indications of passengers arriving on time, indications of passengers departing early/late from the (re)routing service. This data can be used as a DPM for the service criterion "adherence to schedule" [15]. Another example is the indication of connections met, which is a result of the connection protection service in connection with the (re)routing service. This can also be used to quantify actual service performance regarding the service criterion "process data" (e.g., successful execution of service) or the request for bus driver assistance (e.g., successful execution of staff assistance) [6].

Furthermore, the aim4it smartphone app allows to conduct customer satisfaction surveys (see Figure 12).

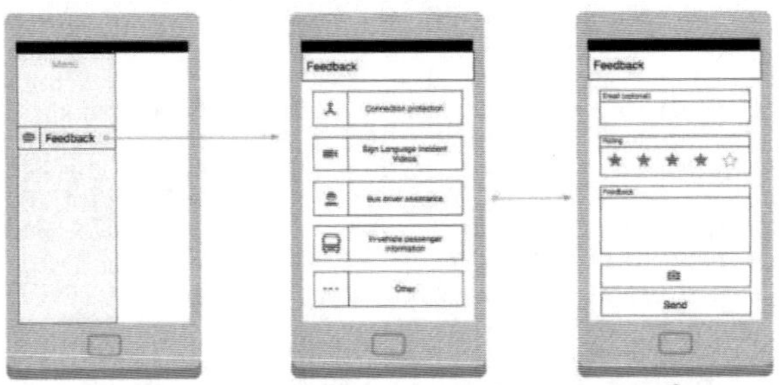

Figure 12. Mock-up of graphical user interface for customer feedback [6]

Customer satisfaction surveys shall assess the degree to, which a customer believes his or her demands with respect to public transport services have been met [15]. These levels of satisfaction with a provided service can be compared against defined scales of quality expected by the customer. With the integration of customer satisfaction surveys into the travel assistance application surveys can be conducted and reported just in time of delivering the service. By using a star-rating for different categories of service quality the customer can evaluate the service he just consumed and the assessment can be linked to the system data. This way, the actually achieved service performance is linked to the customer satisfaction, not to the planned service performance [6].

The gathered data will be analyzed with respect to different kind of criteria that are based on the passengers' service requirements. In this case, two different kind of analysis are possible. A simple one offers KPIs to get an overview about the actual performance while the complex analysis offers widespread facts to gain knowledge about correlations of service attributes [6].

Both analyses support the implementation of a continuous improvement process of service quality in different ways:

(1) existing quality levels are identified,
(2) areas for potential improvement are identified and
(3) corrective action can be taken. Corrective actions include actual improvement of performance, appropriate communication to the customers as well as corrective action in the case of unacceptable performance [6].

While KPIs are a simple analysis to achieve an overview on the actual performance, the customer satisfaction index is a more complex analysis. For this product, attributes will be defined, which have an effect on customer satisfaction. In the smartphone application questions regarding the product attributes (in this case e.g., kindness of staff during staff assistance) are presented to the passenger, when the product criteria are used.

The customer is asked to evaluate each attribute he or she just consumed [7]. The evaluation includes their perception and expectation of *performance* and *importance*. The smartphone application provides a five-point scale (but you can use x-point scale also). Where for example, for performance: 1-means very dissatisfied, 2-somewhat dissatisfied, 3-neither dissatisfied and satisfied, 4-somewhat satisfied, 5-very satisfied. For the measurement of importance a different scale applies, where 1-means is not important, 2-little importance, 3-neutral, 4-important, 5-very important [6]. As a result, a customer quality map can be set up (see Figure 13).

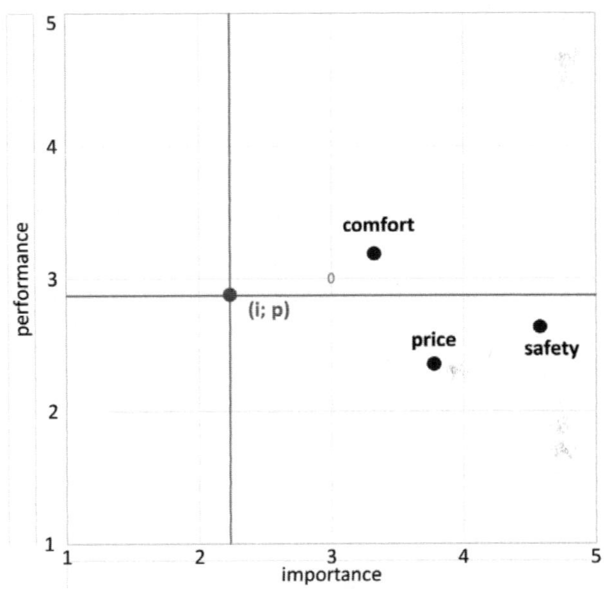

Figure 13. Importance/Performance portfolio of the CSI [6]

The customer quality map is split into four areas. The areas of this map indicate, which attributes should be kept at the current level, and, which should be improved. Section I shows quality attributes whose values should be kept. Section II shows service characteristics whose attributes should be improved first (in the short time). Section III contains insignificant attributes. Public transport operators should transfer their resources they spend on those criteria to other areas. Section IV includes characteristics for improvement, but they are rated as insignificant by the passenger [19]. For this reason, these service characteristics should be considered as last for service improvement [6].

By implementing such a feedback function into the aim4it system and carrying out the KPI and CSI analysis continuously the service providers are able to improve their services constantly while avoiding mismanagement of resources.

V. CONCLUSION

Currently, the demonstrator of the aim4it app is tested and implemented by the consortium members. First results of the integration in the city of Vienna (Austria) show the enhanced possibilities of such an application. A first prototype of the smart phone application has been tested with a focus group of passenger with reduced mobility in Vienna (two blind persons, three deaf persons, two persons in a wheel chair). Based on the project results and future real scenario tests the local public transport operator in Vienna evaluates if project results can be incorporated into the productive version of the travel assistance application after the end of the project. Based on the project results, further value added services for travel assistance can be developed in the future, which is facilitated by using industry standards in the project. The results of the aim4it project will be the basis for further standardization projects (further enhancement of the outcomes of the previous national standardization project IP-based communication in public transportation, IP-KOM-ÖV). In close cooperation with the VDV (German Transport Companies) aim4it project results will be integrated into the existing set of standards. Aim4it project results will be formulated as change requests and fed into the standardization process carried out by VDV. Only this way it will be possible to enable a nationwide implementation of smart applications as they need some kind of common standards so that needed data can be exchanged. Thus, domain experts will review the project's deliverables and will reflect project outcomes in an updated revision of the TRIAS standard (Travellers‘ Real-time Information and Advisory Standard).

ACKNOWLEDGMENT

The promotion plan 64.004/2014 of the European research program era-net transport has been funded by the German Federal Ministry of Transport and Digital Infrastructure based on an enactment of the German Parliament.

REFERENCES

[1] J.-P. Nicklas, N. Schlüter, L. Schnieder, and P. Winzer, "Barrierfree Mobility for All by a Smart and Individual Travel Assistance," Proceedings of SMART 2015: The Fourth International Conference on Smart Systems, Devices and Technologies, IARIA, ISBN 976-1-61208-414-5, Brüssel, pp. 22–23, 2015.

[2] United Nations, "Convention on the Rights of Persons with Disabilities," [A/RES/61/106], January, 24th, 2007.

[3] European Commission, "European Disability Strategy 2010-2020: A Renewed Commitment to a Barrier-Free Europe", COM(2010)636, Brussels, 15.11.2010.

[4] Federal Ministry of Justice and Consumer Protection, Bundesministerium der Justiz und Verbraucherschutz „Personenbeförderungsgesetz (PBefG)", [Online] Available from: http://www.gesetze-im-internet.de/pbefg/, Berlin, 2013.08.07

[5] J.-P. Nicklas and P. Winzer, "Approach for Using Requirements Engineering in Collaborative Networks," in Entering the Experience Economy from product quality to experience quality, S.M. Dahlgaard-Park and J.J. Dahlgaard, Eds. Proceedings of the 17th QMOD-ICQSS International Conference on Quality and Service Sciences, 2014.

[6] L. Schnieder, A.-M. Ademeit, M. Barrilero, N. Schlüter, J.-P. Nicklas, P. Winzer, B. Starzyńska, A. Kujawińska, and J. Diakun, "Systematic improvement of customer satisfaction for passengers with special mobility needs," in: Urban Transport 2015, J.L. Brebbia and G. Miralles, Eds. XXI International Conference on Urban Transport and the Environment. Spanien: Valenica. WitPress, pp. 375–390, 2015, DOI: 10.2495/UT150301.

[7] B Starzyńska, A. Kujawińska, M. Grabowska, J. Diakun, E. Więcek-Janka, L. Schnieder, N. Schlüter, J.-P. Nicklas, „Requirements Elicitation of Passengers with Reduced Mobility for the Design of High Quality, Accessible and Inclusive Public Transport Services," in: Management and Production Engineering Review (MPER), Vol. 6, No.3, Sept. 2015, S. 70–76. DOI: 10.1515/mper-2015-0028.

[8] J.-P. Nicklas, N. Schlüter, and P. Winzer, "Integrating customers‘ voice inside network environments," in: Special Issue: QMOD 2011-2012 Conferences: Selected Best Papers. Total Quality Management & Business Excellence Journal. Volume 24, numbers 7-8, J. Dahlgaard, Ed. July-August 2013. Taylor & Francis, 2013. ISSN: 1478-3363, pp. 980–990. DOI 10.1080/14783363.2013.791104.

[9] H. Bandelin, T. Franke, R. Kruppa, A. Wehrmann, and D. Weißert "Einheitliche Plattform für ÖPNV-Kommunikation auf gutem Weg," in: Der Nahverkehr 30, issue 7-8, 2012, p. 44.

[10] J.-P. Nicklas, N. Schlüter, P. Winzer, and L. Schnieder "Accessible and inclusive mobility for all with individual travel assistance – aim4it," in: 2015 IEEE 18th International Conference on Intelligent Transportation Systems (ITSC), Las Palmas de Gran Canaria, Spanien, 14.-18. September 2015, S.1569-1574, DOI 10.1109/ITSC.2015.256.

[11] L. Schnieder, D. Wermser, and M. Barrilero, "Integrated Modelling of Business Processes and Communication Events for Public Transport," in: Proceedings of Symposium FORMS/FORMAT - Formal Methods for Automation and Safety in Railway and Automotive Systems. Braunschweig (Germany), pp. 233–242, 2014.

[12] A. Stelzer, F. Englert, H. Stephan, and C. Mayas, "Using Customer Feedback in Public Transprotation Systems", in: Proceedings of 3rd International Conference on Advanced Logistics and Transport, A. M. Alimi, M., Abed, M. Benaina, M. Benttalima, M., Negi, H.M. Kammoun, and M., Wali, Eds. ICACT, S.42-47, 2014.

[13] CEN TS 15531 "Service Interface for Real time Information" (SIRI)

[14] VDV-Schrift 720 [Print-Version] "Kundeninformationen über Abweichungen vom Regelfahrplan," Ausgabe 07, 2011.

[15] EN 13816:2002: "Transportation - Logistics and services - Public passenger transport- Service quality definition, targeting and measurement".

[16] J.-P. Nicklas, N. Schlüter, and P. Winzer, "Measurement Concept for Security in Mass Transportation," in: Future Security. N. Aschenbruck, P. Martini, M. Meier, and J. Tölle, Eds. 7th Security Research Conference, Future Security 2012, Bonn, Germany, September 4-6, 2012. Proceedings: Springer-Verlag New York Inc, ISBN 978-3-642-33160-2, pp. 1–4.

[17] N. Schlüter, J.-P. Nicklas, and P. Winzer, "Measurement of Customer Satisfaction in Business Networks," in: Proceedings 14. QMOD Conference on Quality and Service Science 2011.

C. Jaca, R. Mateo, E. Viles, and J. Santos, Eds. Pamplona, Spain: Servicios de Publicaciones Universidad de Navarra (14). ISBN: 84-8081-211-7, pp. 1321–1336

[18] C. Lovelock and J. Witz, "Service Marketing - People, Technology, Strategy," New Jersey: Peasron, Vol.5, 2006.

[19] A. Töpfer, "Konzeptionelle Grundlagen und Messkonzepte für den Kundenzufriedenheitsindex (KZI/CSI) und den Kundenbindungsindex (KBI/CRI)," in: Handbuch Kundenmanagement. Anforderungen, Prozesse, Zufriedenheit, Bindung und Wert von Kunden. 3. Vollst. Überarbeitete und erw. Auflage. A. Töpfer, Ed. Springer, Berlin/Heidelberg, 2008.

International Journal on Advances in Intelligent Systems, vol 9 no 1 & 2, year 2016, http://www.iariajournals.org/intelligent_systems/

Appliance Scheduling Optimization for Demand Response

Armin Ghasem Azar and Rune Hylsberg Jacobsen
Department of Engineering, Aarhus University, Denmark
Email: {aga, rhj}@eng.au.dk

***Abstract*—The paper studies the challenge of the electricity consumption management in smart grids. It focuses on different impacts of demand response running in the smart grid engaging consumers to participate. The main responsibility of the demand response system is scheduling the operation of appliances of consumers in order to achieve a network-wide optimized performance. Each participating electricity consumer, who owns a set of home appliances, provides the desired expectation of his/her power consumption scenario to the demand response system. It is accompanied with time limits on the flexibility of controllable appliances for shifting their operational time from peak to off-peak periods. The appliance scheduling optimization for demand response is modeled as an optimization problem. It concentrates on reducing the total electricity bills and CO_2 emissions as well as flattening the aggregated peak demand at the same time. This paper categorizes the appliances based on shiftability and interruptibility characteristics. It uses information of dwellings to determine an effective appliance scheduling strategy. This strategy gets influenced by grid constraints imposed by distribution system operators. The simulations confirm that scheduling appliances of 100 consumers yields a significant achievement in the peak demand reduction while averagely satisfying the comfort level of consumers.**

Keywords–Smart grid, demand response, appliance scheduling, knapsack problem, dynamic programming, multi-objective optimization.

NOMENCLATURE

Constants

PDT	Peak Demand Threshold
PPD	Peak Power Demand
A_i	Number of appliances in D_i
$a_{i,j}$	Appliance j in dwelling i
D_i	Dwelling i
G	Number of generations
N	Number of dwellings
p_c	Crossover propability
p_m	Mutation propability
$p_{i,j}$	Priority of appliance $a_{i,j}$
Q	Population size
T	Number of time intervals
$DF_{i,j}$	Deadline flexibility of appliance $a_{i,j}$
$TPD_{i,j}$	Total power demand of appliance $a_{i,j}$

Indices

i	Index of dwellings
j	Index of appliances
t	Index of time intervals

Variables

$x^t_{i,j}$	Decision variable of selecting $PD^t_{i,j}$
CO_2E^t	Amount of CO_2 emission at time interval t
EP^t	Electricity price at time interval t
$PD^t_{i,j}$	Power demand request of appliance $a_{i,j}$ at time interval t
$RP^t_{i,j}$	Number of remaining power requests of appliance $a_{i,j}$ at time interval t

I. INTRODUCTION

The smart grid has emerged as a novel infrastructure aiming to transform the existing power system into a reliable and consumer-centric one. It forms a distributed energy delivery network using the electricity and information streams simultaneously. This network possesses a self-healing characteristic toward facing unforeseen electricity outage circumstances. Its reliability and stability are based on intelligent controllers, in which they try to establish bilateral communication channels between consumers and Distribution System Operators (DSOs). The demand side management service provides an opportunity to energy actors for an active participation in counterbalancing the *demand response*. It helps to find the most reliable and effective energy solutions in real-time. This paper extends the work presented in [1]. Here, the key contributions include the extended mathematical formulation and description of the demand response system along with a presentation of an extensive simulation performance analysis.

Demand response is one of the most challenging issues in demand side management, which is responsible for providing effective and comprehensive energy solutions [2]. From the consumers' point of view, demand response attempts to motivate them to modify their electricity usage patterns, in response to potential grid incentives. In contrast to this point of view, DSOs intend to equilibrate demands with responses to reduce peak power demands as much as possible [3]. These purposes can be achieved through both *curtailing the power demand* and *controlling the activation time of electricity usages*. However, a mutual challenge behind these procedures is how to motivate consumers to modify their power demand profiles [4][5].

One of the most pragmatic incentives for consumers to modify their consumption behavior is electricity prices. Although demand response includes efforts to change the electricity usage of consumers with respect to the alterations in the electricity prices, however, reducing the peak demand and CO_2 emission also help to decrease the greenhouse gas emissions [6]. This reduction results in a co-optimization approach of power demand cost and CO_2 emission. In some peak hours, the demand response system has to shift some *power demand requests* from diverse dwellings to another time interval. This shifting can occur several consecutive/separate times over a day. Obviously, this leads to some changes in the daily power consumption of consumers. This causes a problem named *dissatisfaction of consumers*. As a result, maximizing the satisfaction of consumers is an essential objective as well.

Consumers are also interested to reduce their electricity cost while contributing to CO_2 emission reduction program. From the DSOs' point of view, they aim to shave the peak period, which results in flattening the aggregated power demands over time.

Figure 1 shows a conceptual view of various communications in the grid. Each dwelling has a specific scenario for its own appliances. This scenario includes the desired timetable of using appliances in a day. First, appliances are classified based on the *shiftability* feature [7]. Second, shiftable appliances are categorized by the *interruptibility* feature. These classifications permit consumers to give a priority to appliances, which is important for their starting time. Once the consumer chooses to operate an appliance in demand response ready mode, the consumer offers flexibility to the grid and provides an opportunity to the demand response system for reducing the peak demand.

This paper proposes a local power scheduling algorithm attempting to schedule power demand requests of appliances. Here, local means receiving the power demand requests with a specific time resolution and scheduling them accordingly. As its principal novelty, the algorithm runs concurrently and need not know the whole operating period of appliances. The scheduler intends to schedule power demand requests optimally once they arrive. At each time interval, its main responsibility is to allow some appliances to operate and shift the operating cycle of the remaining appliances to the future. This shifting is enabled by utilizing Peak Demand Thresholds (PDTs) imposed by DSOs. The scheduling algorithm attempts to keep the aggregated power consumptions below PDTs continuously.

This rest is organized as follows: Section II overviews the related work. Section III presents the system model. Section IV proposes the power scheduling algorithm. Section V discusses the simulation setup and analysis. Finally, Section VI concludes the paper and provides the possible future extensions.

II. Related Work

A considerable amount of literature is published on smart grids due to concerns on the inefficient structure of the current electrical grid in responding to the growing demand for electricity [8][9]. Farhangi [8] investigated the differential impacts of transforming the current electrical grid to a complex system of systems, named the smart grid while Fang *et al.* [9] surveyed the enabling technologies for data communications in the smart grid. With the advent of smart grids, new solutions are becoming available. To support these, demand response programs endeavor to change the electricity usage patterns of consumers in response to electricity prices or other signals. These programs are considered as reliable solutions to improve the energy efficiency and reduce the peak demand [10]. To reach these goals necessitates demand response service providers investing on proposing functional and potential power scheduling services to the smart grid.

Most of the current research on the power scheduling problem focuses on scheduling power demand requests of appliances of consumers wrapping as a single-objective framework while relying on historical data and forecasting services [11][12]. Agnetis *et al.* [11] defined the problem of optimally scheduling a limited number of manageable appliances of only one dwelling solving with a high computational algorithm based on the mixed integer linear programming. O'Brien [12] proposed a greedy algorithm for automatically scheduling the shiftable appliances with completely predetermined power profiles while missing to take any grid stability constraint into account.

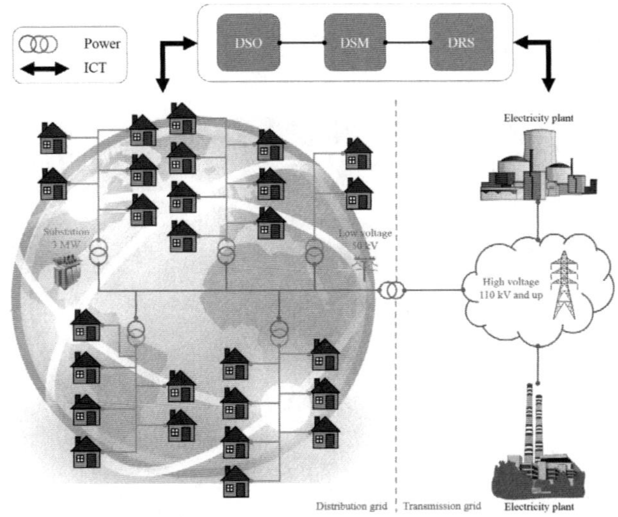

Figure 1. Conceptual view of various communications in the grid

Nevertheless, far too little attention has been paid by smart grid researchers to design a system model where power scheduling is done near real-time. Jacobsen *et al.* [1] found this gap and developed a simple but efficient smart appliance power scheduling mechanism based on the peak demand reduction strategy. Consecutively, Azar *et al.* [13] followed a design methodology that efficiently utilized a time-independent PDT policy for decreasing the aggregated peak demand considering the appliance reception minimization method. It successfully flattened the aggregated power consumption based on a centralized demand response system.

This paper advances the state of the art in formulating a demand response service where appliances send their power demand requests with a specific time resolution accompanying the consumer's time-limit flexibilities. The DSO schedules the incoming power demand requests according to the customers' and its objectives. It attempts to keep the aggregated power demands below PDTs over time.

III. System Model

This section clarifies the proposed system model, as Figure 2 illustrates its conceptual view. Consumers play a major role in this system model since they provide their desired electricity consumption scenarios and corresponding flexibilities to the demand response system. In addition, DSOs impose some grid stability constraints to maintain the electrical grid, such as PDT. Electricity prices of a typical day with the corresponding CO_2 emission data are another system input. The demand response system will receive these input data and then, executes the scheduling algorithm attempting to schedule appliances of dwellings with respect to the objectives and constraints settled in the demand response system.

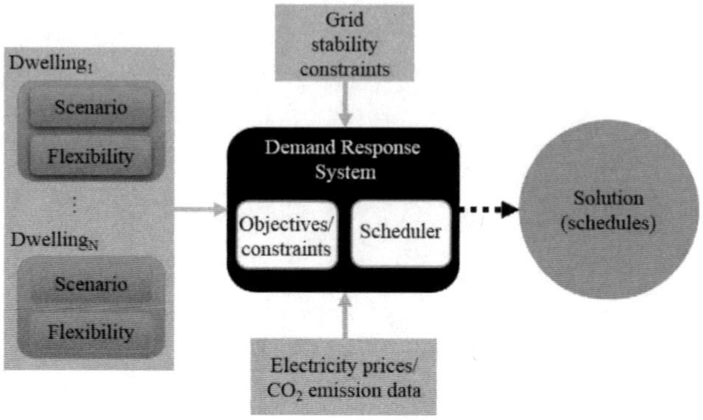

Figure 2. System model of the appliance power scheduling

A. Consumers: Appliance Point of View

This paper assumes there are $N \in \mathbb{N}$ dwellings connected to a feeder in the electrical grid. Each dwelling D_i, where $i \in \{1, 2, \ldots, N\}$, possesses $A_i \in \mathbb{N}$ appliances. Each appliance $a_{i,j}$, where $j \in \{1, 2, \ldots, A_i\}$, is a driver of residential power demands. To guarantee the full operation of appliances, the demand response system should check whether appliances have completed their responsibilities during the day or not. Therefore, Equation (1) shows this hard constraint.

$$\sum_{t=1}^{T} \left(PD^t_{i,j} \times x^t_{i,j}\right) = TPD_{i,j}, \tag{1}$$

where $PD^t_{i,j} \in \mathbb{R}^*$ (watts) is the power demand of appliance $a_{i,j}$ at time interval t. Notation $x^t_{i,j} \in \{0,1\}$ is the decision variable of the optimization problem. $x^t_{i,j} = 1$ allows appliance $a_{i,j}$ to operate at time interval t while $x^t_{i,j} = 0$ shifts its operation to the future. Furthermore, $TPD_{i,j} \in \mathbb{R}^+$ (watts) is the total power demands of the appliance.

Appliances are classified according to some smart features named shiftability and interruptibility [7][13]. Shiftability means giving permission to the demand response system to shift the power demand requests of shiftable appliances to later time intervals. However, some appliances cannot be shifted, for instance the refrigerator. These appliances are members of non-shiftable appliances. Afterwards, shiftable appliances are divided into two groups based on the interruptibility feature. The electric vehicle is a typical example of an appliance exhibiting this feature. The demand response system can both shift and interrupt the duty cycle of charging the electric vehicle. Nevertheless, those appliances, which can be shifted, but are infeasible to be interrupted are called uninterruptible appliances (e.g., dishwasher). Their whole operating duty cycle can be shifted to another time interval. However, they should not be interrupted because of the continuity in their cycle. Equation (2) formulates this hard constraint, which is valid at each time interval:

$$\begin{aligned} &\text{Non-shiftable appliances} \rightarrow x^t_{i,j} = 1, \\ &\text{Uninterruptible appliances} \rightarrow \begin{cases} x^t_{i,j} = 1 & \text{if } x^{t-1}_{i,j} = 1, \\ x^t_{i,j} \in \{0,1\} & \text{otherwise}, \end{cases} \\ &\text{Interruptible appliances} \rightarrow x^t_{i,j} \in \{0,1\}. \end{aligned} \tag{2}$$

At each time interval t, the demand response system is signaled with power demand requests of appliances. Once it receives a power demand request from a non-shiftable appliance, it is allowed to operate. If the request belongs to an uninterruptible appliance first it should check whether the relevant appliance has been allowed to start its work at the previous time interval. If so, the system cannot interrupt and shift it to another time interval. Otherwise, it is possible to shift it, if needed. Finally, if an interruptible appliance sends a power demand request at any interval, it is possible to either allow or shift it.

In real world, consumers sometimes give priorities to use their appliances based on their preferences. For instance, the stove has higher priority compared to the laundry machine. There are two kinds of priority preference named *static* and *dynamic*. The former denotes time-independent priorities of appliances, where the pairwise comparison between each two appliances is constant with respect to some criteria such as emergent usage, welfare, or electricity cost. Each consumer can set $0 < p_{i,j} \leq 1$ as the priority of using appliance $a_{i,j}$ over the day. As a result, if the demand response system confronts a circumstance, when it should decide to select one appliance among two or more, then, the appliance, which has the highest priority will be selected [14]. Finally, as a brief description of the dynamic priority, sometimes consumers change the priorities of their appliances as time moves on. For instance, one consumer gives a priority to his/her dishwasher in the morning. In the afternoon, he/she changes its priority since the washing machine is needed to operate at the same time. Therefore, dishwasher's priority is decreased. Nevertheless, for simplifying the model, the dynamic priority constraint is not considered in this paper.

Consumers participating in demand response programs provide some flexibilities to the demand response system for operating their appliances. Let us assume one consumer is interested to plug in his/her Nissan Altra electric vehicle at 18:00. The charging cycle will typically take five hours [15]. Nonetheless, he/she is flexible to receive the electric vehicle in the finished state at most at 08:00 the next day. Therefore, the flexibility that the consumer offers to operate his/her electric vehicle is 14 hours. We name this concept as a *deadline* flexibility, which is a time-oriented constraint. This kind of flexibility helps the demand response system to shift some appliances, which relatively consume more than others, to the future. The demand response system should consider the remaining power demand flexibility (with given time limits) before shifting them. Equation (3) describes this constraint:

$$RP^t_{i,j} \leq \left(DF_{i,j} - t\right), \tag{3}$$

where $RP^t_{i,j} \in \mathbb{Z}^*$ relates to the number of remaining power demand requests of appliance $a_{i,j}$ from time interval t until the end of its duty cycle. Moreover, $DF_{i,j}$ (e.g., UTC) denotes the deadline flexibility of this appliance. The demand response system satisfies this constraint while it receives the power demand requests continuously. If the remaining power demand of an appliance is still less than its provided time limit flexibility, the demand response system can decide to allow it to start/continue in this time interval or to shift it to another time interval. To shift a power demand request, it is essential to ensure the satisfaction of all constraints.

Considering the aforementioned descriptions, each dwelling D_i has a specific scenario showing how the consumer intends to operate the appliances. Table I lists a sample scenario of operating the appliances in a typical dwelling. As described previously, deadline flexibility in using appliances means a firm deadline for finishing the related activity. For example, the consumer provides two hours of flexibility to the demand response system for charging the electric vehicle. More in details, it receives the first power demand request for charging the electric vehicle at the defined time. The demand response system has an opportunity to deliver the charged electric vehicle later in time by utilizing the provided deadline flexibility. It is possible to both shift and interrupt the charging process during the defined time period since the electric vehicle is a member of the interruptible appliances. Here, the priorities are time-independent (static). It is worthwhile emphasizing that the priority is applied to only shiftable appliances. Hence, the refrigerator and lighting will not undergo any scheduling procedure. They will receive an infinite priority since they are members of non-shiftable appliances.

B. Distribution System Operator: Grid Constraint Point of View

Currently, electricity producers generate more electricity since they are experiencing an insufficiency of electricity generation capacity because of the power demands by consumers. However, it can be avoided using demand shaping schemes. DSOs currently apply a threshold policy, in order to shave the peak, which results in shaping the demand profiles over time [1]. From an electricity grid point of view, the upper limit of the PDT may be enforced by the DSO by the installation of fuses and other safety-related measures such as protective relays. These devices may be dimensioned differently and the subscription fee for a dwelling often depends on the installed capacity. As a complement, adaptive schemes can be deployed as a control loop between a DSO-controlled generator side and individual dwellings [16]. Let

$$\sum_{i=1}^{N}\sum_{j=1}^{A_i}\left(PD_{i,j}^{t} \times x_{i,j}^{t}\right) \leq PDT, \tag{4}$$

where $PDT \in \mathbb{R}^{+}$ (watts) is a constant and time-independent power demand threshold, in which the demand response system attempts to keep the amount of allowed power demand requests below it. Nevertheless, Equation (4) sometimes cannot be satisfied owing to the provided deadline flexibilities and uninterruptibility feature of some appliances. Therefore, the demand response system will consider this constraint for power demand requests, in which the corresponding appliances: 1) still have time to start operating or 2) have not started yet. For the former the demand response system can still use the provided flexibility while for the latter it can shift the starting time of the appliance to the later time intervals. It is worth noting that priorities of appliances could be also considered in Equation (4).

C. Demand Response System: Objective Point of View

While the demand response system receives power demand requests of appliances, it cannot globally optimize the objectives since they are received at specific time intervals continuously. As a result, all objectives are based on a local controlling strategy, as follows.

TABLE I. A SIMPLIFIED EXAMPLE OF A DWELLING' SCENARIO

Start	End	Activity description	Deadline flexibility	Priority
00:00	24:00	Using the refrigerator	24:00	Infinite
08:00	24:00	Turning the lights on	00:30	Infinite
08:05	09:50	Putting the dishes into the dishwasher	10:30	0.2158
13:00	14:15	Putting the laundry into the washing machine	17:00	0.1063
17:25	18:15	Putting the washed laundry into the laundry dryer	22:00	0.1499
11:30	22:40	Using the computer	23:30	0.2649
19:50	22:00	Watching the TV	24:00	0.1293
20:00	22:00	Charging the electric vehicle	24:00	0.1338

1) Minimizing the Electricity Cost: Equation (5) formulates the willingness of the demand response system to minimize the electricity cost of consumers at each time interval. Here, $EP^t \in \mathbb{Z}^*$ (DKK per watts per hour) is the electricity price at each time interval.

$$f(x) = \min\sum_{i=1}^{N}\sum_{j=1}^{A_i}\left(PD_{i,j}^{t} \times x_{i,j}^{t} \times EP^{t}\right). \tag{5}$$

2) Minimizing the CO_2 Emission: Equation (6) shows the interest for reducing the CO_2 emission of dwellings at each time interval by applying the decision variable $x_{i,j}^t$ for all power demand requests. Here, $CO_2E^t \in \mathbb{R}^*$ (grams per watts per hour) is the amount of CO_2 emission at each time interval.

$$g(x) = \min\sum_{i=1}^{N}\sum_{j=1}^{A_i}\left(PD_{i,j}^{t} \times x_{i,j}^{t} \times CO_2E^{t}\right). \tag{6}$$

3) Maximizing the Comfort Level of Consumers: Equation (7) formulates how the demand response system is interested to maximize the comfort level of consumers over time. Comfort level indicates the consumers' desire to have their activities being done as they exactly expect from their scenarios. In fact, appliances aim to get permission to run their operations at each time interval as much as possible.

$$h(x) = \max\sum_{i=1}^{N}\sum_{j=1}^{A_i}\left(x_{i,j}^{t} \times p_{i,j}\right). \tag{7}$$

In conclusion, the demand response system considers the appliance power scheduling optimization as a mixed-integer linear programming problem including Equations (5) to (7) as its objective functions subject to Equations (1) to (4) as the relevant constraints. Next section will describe how the proposed scheduling algorithm attempts to solve this optimization problem applying diverse approaches.

IV. Scheduling Algorithm

Algorithm 1 presents the pseudo-code of the power scheduling algorithm. Considering the system model shown in Figure 2, the demand response system executes the scheduling algorithm to produce a specific schedule for appliances of dwellings based on the objectives and constraints, described in Section III. It receives power demand requests at specific time intervals. Apart from the PDT, the scheduler allows the non-shiftable power demand requests to start or to continue their

Algorithm 1: Power scheduling

```
Input  : The scenarios, power profiles, classification of appliances, PDT.
Output: Schedule of appliances of all dwellings.
Preprocessing the input data;
while receiving the power demand requests over time do
    Allow the non-shiftable appliances to start or to continue;
    Update PDT;
    if there are uninterruptible appliances, which have started previously then
        Allow them to continue;
        Update PDT;
    end
    if there are appliances, which cannot be shifted due to their deadline flexibility constraint then
        Allow them to start or to continue;
        Update PDT;
    end
    if there are some remaining power demand request then
        if their total consumption is less than the remaining PDT then
            Allow them to start or to continue;
            Update PDT;
        else
            Refer to the single/multi-objective Knapsack procedure;
            Allow the output power demand requests of the Knapsack procedure to start or to continue;
            Shift the remaining power demand requests to the next time interval;
        end
    end
end
```

duties. Furthermore, if there is an uninterruptible appliance, which has started at the previous time interval, it should be allowed to continue. Finally, if there is a power demand request, where shifting it to the next time interval violates its provided deadline flexibility, then, the same action of allowing it to start takes place. After finishing these procedures, the algorithm will check whether the total power demand of the remaining requests is below the remaining PDT (capacity) or not. If so, all will be permitted to start or to continue their procedure. Otherwise, the algorithm refers to the Knapsack procedure to select some requests from the remaining power demand requests to enable them to start or to continue, and shift the unselected requests to the next time interval.

Two challenging circumstances can occur during the scheduling, and handling them confirms the robustness of the scheduling algorithm. If there is a sudden drop in the electric power, indeed no appliance can send any power demand request. Therefore, the scheduling algorithm waits until the appliance sends its new power demand request. Furthermore, if all appliances in all dwellings are configured as non-shiftable with high priorities, the scheduling algorithm will allow all of them to operate, when they send their power demand requests. This is based on respecting the consumers who do not provide any flexibility to non-shiftable appliances. However, this is considered to be an infeasible and greedy setup.

A. The Knapsack Problem

The Knapsack problem is one of the traditional problems of computer science in combinatorial optimization literature [17]. Given F items, the Knapsack tries to pack the items to obtain the maximum total value. Each item gets a weight and value. The maximum weight that the Knapsack can tolerate is limited by a fixed capacity W. This problem has two versions: "0-1" and "fractional". In the former, items are indivisible meaning it is possible to either take an item or not. In contrast, in the fractional version, items are divisible and, therefore, the Knapsack can take any fraction of an item.

This paper gets the benefit from the first version since the remaining power demand requests are similar to the indivisible items in "0-1" Knapsack problem. The "0-1" Knapsack problem is NP-Complete since the time complexity of solving it in a brute-force approach is $O(2^F)$. Time complexity measures the time that an algorithm takes as a function of the size of its input. Applying brute-force approach means calculating the fitness of 2^M solutions to locate the optimal one. The power scheduling problem is reducible to this version since the demand response system should decide to allow those indivisible power demand requests, which optimize the objective(s) and satisfy the constraints simultaneously. Therefore, the discussing problem is also NP-Complete. Hereinafter, we the scheduler needs to refer to the Knapsack problem, we name it the Knapsack procedure.

Indeed, the Knapsack procedure requires not only to decide, which power demand requests have to be processed now and delay the others afterwards, but should also consider the starting (ending) times of the latter. The latter is reflected in the flexibility that consumers provide.

Table II defines the equivalent parameters of the Knapsack and power scheduling optimization problems according to various objectives. As described previously, the Knapsack procedure receives the remaining power demand requests, which their total power demand is indeed more than the remaining capacity. It calculates the fitness of produced feasible solutions, in which each solution includes some power demand requests.

TABLE II. EQUIVALENT PARAMETERS OF THE KNAPSACK PROCEDURE AND POWER SCHEDULING OPTIMIZATION PROBLEM

	Values (items)	Objective(s)	Weights	Capacity
Single-objective	Electricity cost of power demand requests	Minimizing the total electricity costs	Power demand requests	PDT
	CO_2 emission of power demand requests	Minimizing the total CO_2 emissions	Power demand requests	PDT
	Priority of power demand requests	Maximizing the total allowed power demand requests	Power demand requests	PDT
Multi-objective	Electricity cost and priority of power demand requests	Minimizing the total electricity costs and maximizing the total number of allowed power demand requests	Power demand requests	PDT
	CO_2 emission and priority of power demand requests	Minimizing the total CO_2 emission and maximizing the total number of allowed power demand requests	Power demand requests	PDT

As a result, the solution to this problem is a subset of received power demand requests, which should be allowed to start or to continue in this time interval. Then, there will most likely be some remaining power demand requests, which cannot successfully start or continue. These power demand requests should be shifted to the future.

Depending on the number of objectives chosen by the demand response system, different approaches can be used to run the Knapsack procedure. On the one hand, if the demand response system decides to run the scheduling with one objective, the scheduling problem turns into a single-objective optimization problem. This is equal to run the single-objective "0-1" Knapsack procedure with dynamic programming at each time interval (if needed) [14]. On the contrary, if at least two objectives are chosen, the scheduling algorithm corresponds to a multi-objective optimization problem, which has to be solved with relevant techniques [18]. It is worth noting that these approaches are used at each time interval, if needed. The following describes them.

1) Dynamic Programming: We utilize a dynamic programming approach to solve single-objective power scheduling problem. As Figure 3 demonstrates its principles, this approach first characterizes the structure of an optimal solution. Then, it decomposes the problem into smaller problems. Meanwhile, it finds a relationship between the structure of the optimal solution of the original problem and solutions of the smaller problems. It recursively expresses the solution of the original problem in terms of optimal solutions to smaller problems, which supports the optimality.

To this end, it follows a bottom-up computation approach. The value of an optimal solution is computed in a bottom-up manner using a table structure. This table is repeatedly filled to use in each iteration [19]. The structure of an optimal solution to the power scheduling problem is a subset of the remaining power demand requests, which optimizes the relevant objective. Algorithm 2 declares the dynamic programming method for running the single-objective Knapsack procedure. The time complexity of approaching the Knapsack procedure using dynamic programming is $O(M \times PDT)$.

2) Multi-Objective Optimization: Multi-Objective Optimization (MOO) is an area of multiple criteria decision-making, where mathematical optimization problems involving more than one objective function should be optimized simultaneously [20]. Optimal decisions are taken in the presence of trade-offs between two or more conflicting objectives. Solving a MOO problem necessitates computing all or a representative set of Pareto-optimal solutions. In this paper, a Pareto solution comprises a subset of remaining power demand requests. When decision-making is emphasized, the objective of solving a MOO problem is to support a decision-maker in finding the most preferred Pareto-optimal solution. Here, the decision-maker is the demand response system, which should decide to allow only a subset of the remaining power demand requests to optimize the objectives and satisfy the constraints at each time interval accordingly. The objective functions are in

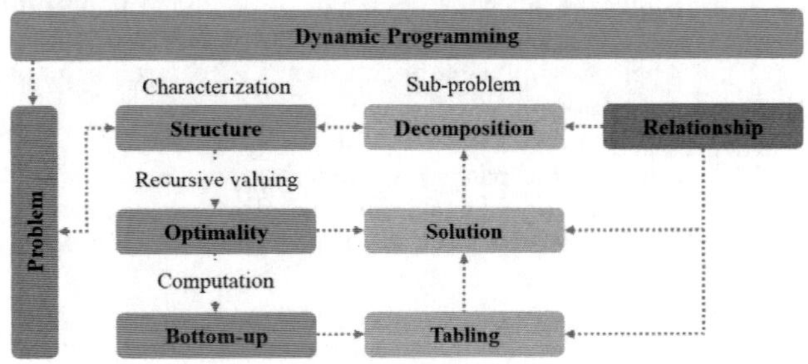

Figure 3. Principles of the dynamic programming approach

Algorithm 2: Approaching the Knapsack procedure: Dynamic programming

Input : power demand requests, PDT.
Output: The optimal solution at the current time interval.

Set F as the number of input power demand requests;
Create a $(F+1) \times (PDT+1)$ table named V;
if *the objective is minimization* **then**
  Set $V[0, 0 : PDT+1]$=Inf;
else
  Set $V[0, 0 : PDT+1]$=0;
end
for $i = 1$ *to* F **do**
  for $j = 1$ *to* PDT **do**
    if $PD[i] \leq j$ **then**
      if *the objective is minimization* **then**
        $V[i, j] = \min(V[i-1, j], PD[i] + V[i-1, j-PD[i]])$;
      else
        $V[i, j] = \max(V[i-1, j], PD[i] + V[i-1, j-PD[i]])$;
      end
    else
      $V[i, j] = V[i-1, j]$;
    end
  end
end
Return the $V[F, PDT]$ as the final solution;

Algorithm 3: Approaching the Knapsack procedure; Multi-objective evolutionary algorithm

Input : Remaining power demand requests, PDT, population size (Q), number of generations (G), crossover (p_c) and mutation (p_m) probabilities.
Output: A near-optimal solution at the current time interval.
Randomly produce initial solutions and combine them as the parent population;
Evaluate the parent population based on the objective functions;
Calculate the Pareto-fronts and the crowding distance of solutions inside the parent population;
$c = 1$;
while $c \leq G$ **do**
    Apply the selection operator on the parent population and forward to the crossover operator;
    Apply the crossover operator on the received solutions with a probability of p_c and forward to the mutation operator;
    Apply the mutation operator on the received solutions with a probability of p_m and put them into the offspring population;
    Evaluate the offspring population based on the objectives;
    Combine the parent and offspring populations into a temporary population;
    Calculate the Pareto-fronts and crowding distances of solutions inside the temporary population;
    Select solutions from the Pareto-fronts orderly while replacing them with solutions in the parent population until reaching Q;
end
Return a Pareto-solution from the first Pareto-front as a near-optimal solution;

conflict, when there exist an infinite number of Pareto-optimal solutions. A Pareto-optimal solution does not improve for one objective unless it satisfies others. The main goal in MOO problems is to find a finite Pareto-front in the objective space including a finite number of diverse Pareto-solutions.

Evolutionary Algorithms (EAs) are one of the most well-known meta-heuristic search mechanisms utilized for the MOO problems since their structure is free of search space and objective capacities [21]. EAs form a subset of evolutionary computation, in which they generally involve techniques and implementing mechanisms inspired by biological evolutions such as reproduction, mutation, recombination, natural selection, and survival of the fittest. The main advantage of EAs, when applied to solve MOO problems, is the fact that they typically generate sets of solutions, allowing computation of the entire Pareto-front. Currently, most Multi-Objective Evolutionary Algorithms (MOEAs) apply Pareto-based ranking schemes such as the Non-Dominated Sorting Genetic Algorithm-II (NSGA-II) [22]. Algorithm 3 describes the procedure of running the multi-objective Knapsack procedure using the NSGA-II. The time complexity of approaching the Knapsack procedure using the NSGA-II is $O(G{\times}M{\times}Q^2)$, where G is the number of generations, M is the number of objectives, and Q is the population size.

The NSGA-II randomly generates an initial Pareto-population, and then, applies some evolutionary procedures such as tournament selection with crossover and mutation operators. Next, it generates an offspring population from parents in each generation. It classifies the temporary population, as the combination of parent and offspring populations, based on the dominance principle to some fronts f_1, f_2, f_3 and so on. A solution Sol_1 dominates a solution Sol_2, if Sol_1 is better than Sol_2 in some objectives and perhaps equal to others. All the solutions, which lie in one specific front are non-dominant. In addition, for each solution Sol_a in f_k, there exists a solution Sol_b in $f_{k'}$ such that Sol_b dominates Sol_a, where $k' < k$. In the last step, the NSGA-II fills the next generation's population starting from the first front and continuing with solutions in the next fronts. Since the size of the combined population is twice the new one, all fronts, which could be unable to accommodate are removed. However, it needs to handle the last allowed fronts, in which some of its solutions are possibly considered in the new population. In this situation, the NSGA-II uses a niching strategy to choose solutions of the last allowed fronts, which lie in the least crowded regions of the solution space. To this end, it finds the distance between each solution and its nearest left and right neighbors in the last allowed fronts for each dimension in the objective hyperspace. Finally, it sums up such distances for each solution as the largest hypercube around it, which is empty from other solutions. The largest hypercube shows a solution with the least crowd. Figure 4 elaborates a conceptual view of Pareto-fronts and Pareto-solutions with corresponding crowding distances.

V. Simulation Setup and Analysis

This section first describes the simulation setup and subsequently, analyzes the results.

A. Simulation Setup

This work has been implemented with Matlab R2014b on a personal computer with an Intel Core i7-2.0 GHz CPU and 6 GB memory. Power profiles of all appliances are captured from the TraceBase open repository, which comprises a collection of real power traces of electrical appliances [23]. The electricity prices in the Danish day-ahead market, known as Elspot market, are provided by Nord Pool Spot with an hourly resolution on the day before the power delivery [24]. CO_2 emission intensity prognosis data are also provided in an hourly resolution by the Danish transmission system operator [25]. It is significant to note that the demand response system is set to receive the power demand requests at five-minute time intervals until finishing all activities. At each hour, it receives the power demand requests 12 times. As a result, T has been set to 24×12. $N = 100$ dwellings are assumed to provide their power demand requests over time.

A precise scenario for each dwelling is created randomly based on power profiles of appliances. Corresponding power

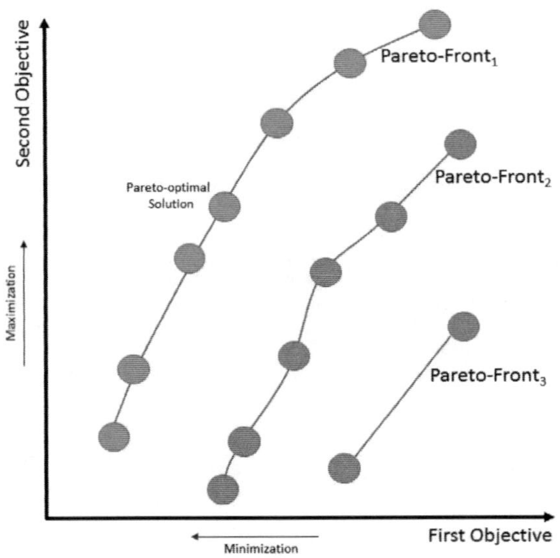

(a). Pareto-fronts and solutions

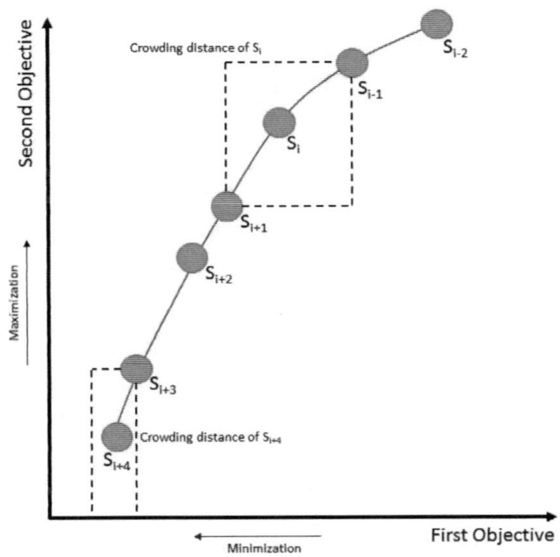

(b). Crowding distance of the Pareto-solutions

Figure 4. Conceptual view of Pareto-fronts and Pareto-solutions with corresponding crowding distances

demand requests are established in each scenario. To streamline the model, each appliance is operated only one time. Regarding flexibilities, we generate a random flexibility value for each appliance. A lower bound for each flexibility value is the following time interval from the moment, at which the operating cycles should finish without scheduling. An upper bound for each flexibility value is the end of the day.

It is considered that priorities are generated randomly. Figure 5 shows the aggregated power demand of the appliances of one dwelling in a typical day. Figure 6 shows the aggregated power demands of 100 dwellings. Peak power demand occurs at 20:30, which is 293 kW. Therefore, in order to allow all requested power demands at each time interval without shifting

TABLE III. SIMULATION CASE STUDIES INSPIRED FROM TABLE II

	Objective(s)
Case study 1	1) Minimizing the electricity cost
Case study 2	1) Maximizing the comfort level of consumers
Case study 3	1) Minimizing the electricity cost 2) Maximizing the comfort level of consumers

or interrupting any of them, the PDT should be at least 293 kW since it has been indicated that the PDT is constant and time-independent. However, the demand response system desires to flatten the aggregated demand by shifting power demand requests from on-peak periods to off-peak times. Therefore, it modifies the PDT to enable the shifting and interruption.

As described earlier, the MOEA includes some evolutionary parameters. As a selection operator, this paper utilizes the tournament selection. Linear crossover and exchange mutation are also utilized as the exploitation parameters. Their probabilities are set to p_c=80% and p_m=20%, respectively. Finally, the population size (Q) and the number of generations (G) are both adjusted to 100.

B. Simulation Analysis

This section analyzes the results obtained based on three simulation case studies, as Table III lists. The first case study is single-objective and aims to minimize the electricity cost as its objective function (see Equation (5)). The second case study is also single-objective and attempts to only maximize the comfort level of consumers (see Equation (7)). Finally, the third case study is multi-objective and intends to both minimize the total electricity cost and maximize the comfort level of consumers. We omit to show a case study including minimization of the CO_2 emission as an objective function since it would be similar to minimizing the electricity cost. The results will be analyzed based on variations of the PDT as follows:

$$PDT = \{(10\% \sim 100\%) \times PPD\}, \tag{8}$$

where $PPD \in \mathbb{R}^+$ (watts) denotes the peak power demand. It is equal to 293 kW (see Figure 6). We change the PDT from 10% to 100% to analyze the obtained results. Hereinafter, when PDT is equal to R%, where $10\% \leq R \leq 100\%$, it means PDT=R×PPD. We examine the effects of these variations on:

- Computation time of running the algorithm over time;
- Number of referrals to the Knapsack procedure;
- Computation time of the total number of referrals to the Knapsack procedure;
- Total electricity costs of the dwellings in a day;
- Deviation between the reception and delivery times of appliances;
- Aggregated power demands of the scheduled scenarios in a day.

Figure 7 analyzes the computation of running the scheduling algorithms based on different case studies. In Figure 7(a), according to Algorithm 1, non-shiftable power demand requests will be allowed to start or to continue apart from the assigned PDT. Considering computation time, when PDT is equal to 10%, the remaining capacity for allowing the remaining power demand requests is very low or even below zero.

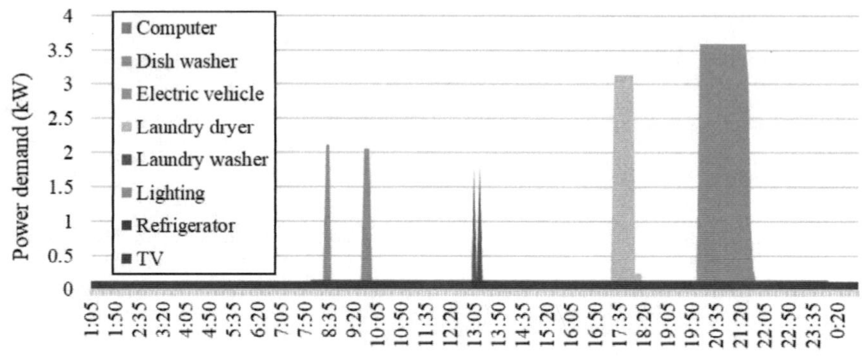

Figure 5. Aggregated power demand of appliances used in Table I

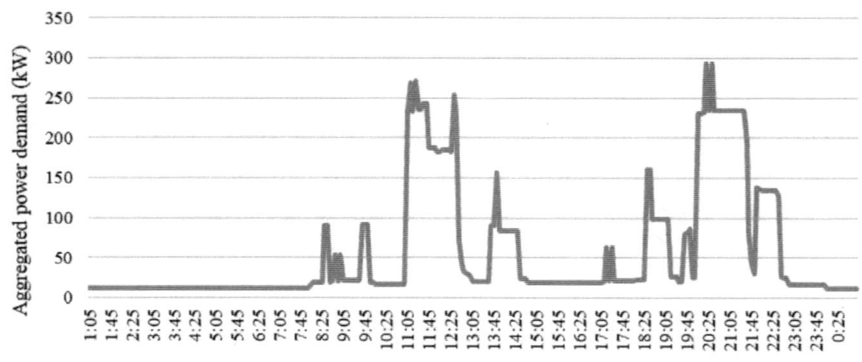

Figure 6. Aggregated power demands of 100 dwellings based on randomly generated scenarios in a typical day

The reason is that the algorithm should satisfy Equations (1) to (4). Therefore, it is not possible to run the Knapsack procedure since the minimum consumption of the remaining power demand requests is greater than the remaining capacity. In the next intervals, the system, apart from the remaining capacity, should allow some power demand requests to start or to continue, for which shifting or interrupting them is not possible due to their deadline flexibility constraints. As a result, the number of remaining power demand requests as inputs to the Knapsack procedure will be few and, therefore, computation time will be lowered accordingly. Nevertheless, when PDT increases, the Knapsack procedure will allow more power demand requests to start or to continue at each interval. Some of these allowed power demand requests are members of the uninterruptible set. Therefore, at the next intervals, the system has to allow the corresponding appliances to continue their operation apart from the PDT. The demand response system will confront more remaining power demand requests compared to lower assigned PDT in later time intervals. This will increase the complexity and computation time of running the Knapsack procedure.

We experience more complexity and higher computation time, when assigned PDT increases. Nevertheless, the number of intervals, in which the Knapsack procedure should run decreases. Having some uninterruptible appliances and time limit flexibility constraints make this decreasing. If the system allows an uninterruptible power demand request to start at a certain time interval, it will be unable to interrupt it in the following intervals. Therefore, it will have to shift more power demand requests since the remaining capacity has decreased. These shifted power demand requests will be accumulated and, finally, the Knapsack procedure will face several remaining requests. When PDT is 90%, we observe a noticeable decrease in computation time compared to previous figures. The reason is the reduced amount of the Knapsack procedure's inputs. Since the aggregated power demands of the remaining power demand requests are less than the remaining capacity at most of the time intervals, it is not necessary to run the Knapsack procedure. Obviously, there is no need to run the Knapsack procedure at any of the time intervals, when the threshold is equal to 100%.

Figure 7(b) demonstrates the same analysis based on the second case study. The description of this figure is almost the same as Figure 7(a). However, there are some minor differences, which are linked to the differences in the nature of the objectives. The main reason is underlining the intention of consumers to pay for the highest comfort as little as possible. The computation time of running the third case study is illustrated in Figure 7(c). In contrast to Figures 7(a) and 7(b), here, the computation time is completely different. The main reason is the repetitive manner of the MOEA in finding the non-dominated near-optimal solution at each time interval. As described previously, there is no exact solution for multi-objective problems. Therefore, the near-optimal solutions ob-

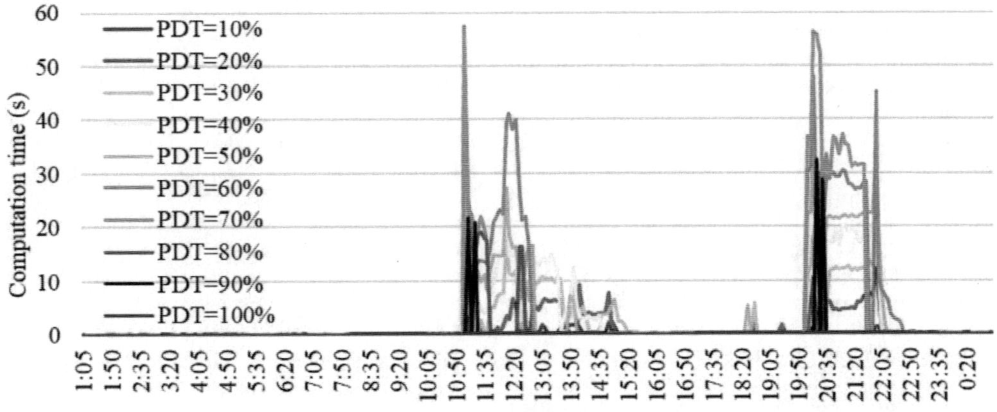

(a). Computation time of running the scheduling algorithm based on the first case study

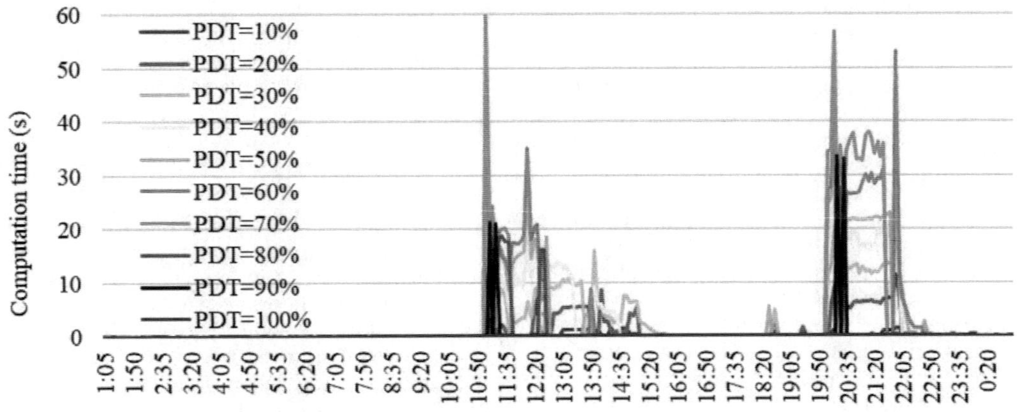

(b). Computation time of running the scheduling algorithm based on the second case study

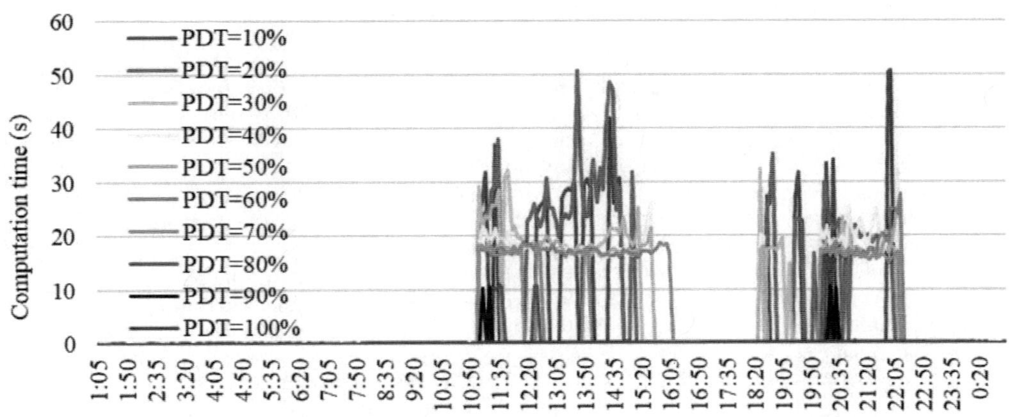

(c). Computation time of running the scheduling algorithm based on the third case study

Figure 7. Computation time of running the scheduling algorithms based on different case studies

tained from running the algorithm at each time interval, affect the computation time of subsequent intervals. Computation times for the next intervals may change due to the randomized nature of finding near-optimal solutions. If all scenarios and relevant information are known before scheduling, it will be possible to limit the computation time. However, in this situation, when the system receives the power demand requests with a specific time resolution, it is not possible to do it since there is no future prediction or even forecasted data to learn before scheduling.

According to Figure 7(c), the computation time decreases, when PDT is 50% or more. The total power demand of remaining requests at 22:00 is a bit more than the remaining capacity. Also, most of the corresponding appliances are members of the uninterruptible appliances. Therefore, the Knapsack procedure's output comprises most of them. The demand response system should allow them to continue their duties at the next time intervals apart from the remaining capacity. This decreases the computation time at the next time intervals since the number of inputs to the Knapsack procedure decreases. As the final note, in this analysis, only 35% of the CPU speed and 400 MB of memory have been employed by the local power algorithm in all three case studies in the worst case.

Figure 8 analyzes the number of referrals to the Knapsack procedure in Algorithm 1. Figure 9 studies the corresponding computation time, when PDT changes. According to Figure 8, the number of referrals to the Knapsack procedure in the first two case studies is different, when PDT is equal to 10%. The reasons are first the reductive nature of Equation (5) and second the remarkable difference between the assigned PDT and the power demand of the remaining requests. When the threshold changes to at least 20%, uninterruptible power demand requests will roughly be allowed to start or to continue their work at the time they desire. Therefore, the number of inputs to the Knapsack procedure will decrease and the total number of referrals to the Knapsack procedure in the first two case studies will be almost the same. Now, due to the multi-objective nature of the third case study, the total number of referrals will also be more than previous case studies since the outcome solutions of the Knapsack procedure at each time interval are near-optimal.

According to Figure 9, the computation time of the total referrals to the Knapsack procedure increases when the number of referrals rises. However, this fact is applicable to only the first two case studies. The computation time of running the multi-objective algorithm is decreased when the number of referrals to the Knapsack procedure increases. Similar to the provided descriptions to Figure 7(c), this algorithm does not seek to obtain the optimal solution of the problem. As a result, the near-optimal solutions contain a mix of interruptible and uninterruptible power demand requests. Intuitively, the uninterruptible power demand requests will not be shifted to the next intervals and, therefore, the number of Knapsack procedure's inputs will decrease.

As the next analysis, Figure 10 displays the differences between the total electricity costs in the three case studies based on the variations in PDT. With respect to Figure 7, computation time increases nearly linearly when PDT changes. The total electricity cost is the same since the total number of interruptions decrease when the threshold increases. Thus, appliances start operating roughly at their desired time. This causes the peak times to remain over the time (see Figure 6). Nevertheless, with decreasing the PDT, some of the power demand requests should be shifted to the low price intervals, which result in decreasing the total electricity costs. As can be easily seen, the electricity cost is reduced for 1%, when PDTs are equivalent to 10% and 100%. Having almost low fluctuating Danish electricity prices make this very low reduction.

The third case study performs better in terms of electricity cost reduction. This is due to having a multi-objective problem. For instance, in the second case study, the algorithms tries to find an optimal solution at each time interval. An optimal solution should include the maximum number of possible power demand requests. However, this is different in the third case study since objectives are conflicting. Therefore, the solution's size is smaller, which causes the requests being shifted to lower electricity price periods.

Table IV analyzes the actual required PDT and the differences at peak time intervals when the assigned PDT changes based on Equation (8). The variation rates of PDT required for scheduling the power demand requests in first two case studies are almost the same. If we compare the maximum needed PDT in the first case study with the second one when assigned PDT rises, we observe that the gradients of maximum needed PDTs are almost similar to one another. Nevertheless, the decreasing gradient of PDT, when the system applies the third case study, is lower than the other case studies. The time interval, at which the peak demand happens, is equivalent in the first two case studies. This time interval is different in the third case study due to its multi-objective nature.

According to Equation (7), consumers desire to receive their appliances in the completed status at the time they expect. This expected time for each appliance is the sum of the time periods provided in the scenarios and the corresponding additional deadline flexibility period. However, it is not possible to satisfy all consumers due to some restrictions such as PDT. The average deviation between reception and delivery times of each appliance of each dwelling for all case studies is pictured in Figure 11. These waiting times do not result in a violation of the deadline flexibility constraint. Assigning 60% is beneficial to minimize the deviation between delivery and reception times of each appliance in the first two case studies. Consumers have to wait to receive their charged electric vehicle almost 30 minutes when PDT is 60%. For the multi-objective case study, if PDT is 80%, consumers should wait averagely almost 20 minutes for receiving their charged electric vehicle. It is worth emphasizing that these waiting times are in addition to the time it takes to actually charge the EV.

As the final analysis, Figures 12 demonstrates the aggregated consumption of the scenarios after applying the scheduling algorithm. The demand response system endeavors to flatten the aggregated power consumption over the day. According to Figure 12(a), it shows the best condition of aggregated power demand when PDT is equal to 60% (17 kW). If the system does not apply any scheduling algorithm on the received power demand requests, i.e., PDT is 100%, the total maximum consumption will be approximately 293 kW. It proves that the demand response system can reduce the peak demand by 40%. This fact is also applicable to the second case study shown in Figure 12(b). Finally, it is worthy to note that since the complexity of the multi-objective case study is high, it needs a high PDT. Figure 12(c) pictures the

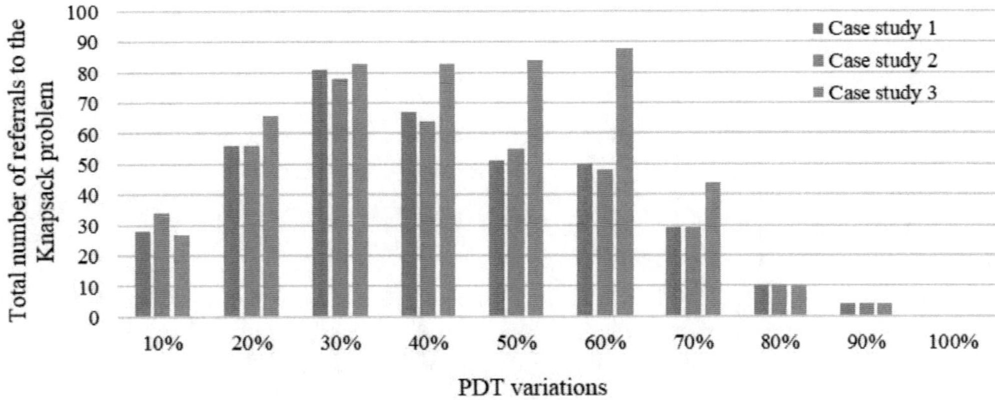

Figure 8. Total number of referrals to the Knapsack procedure in Algorithm 1

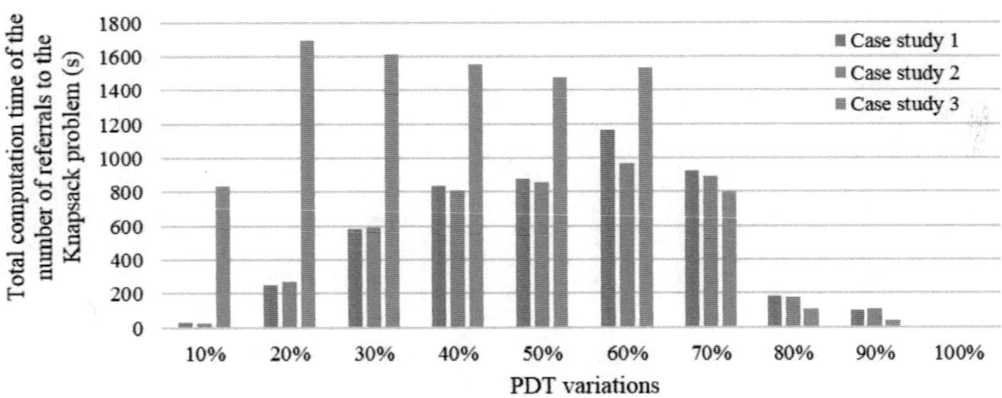

Figure 9. The computation time of referrals to the Knapsack procedure in Algorithm 1

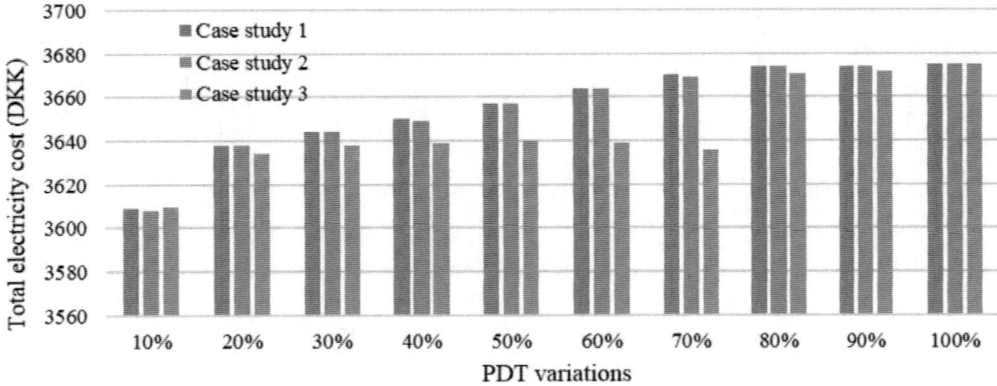

Figure 10. Total electricity costs of dwellings in a day based on three case studies

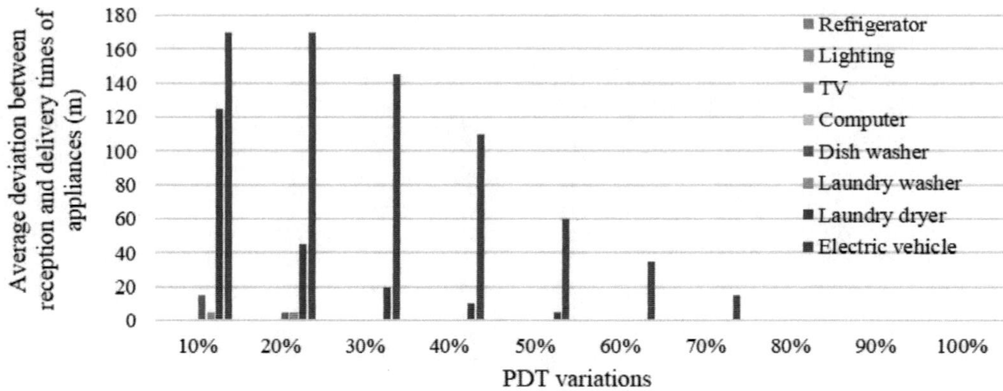

(a). Deviation time between appliance delivery and reception times based on the first case study

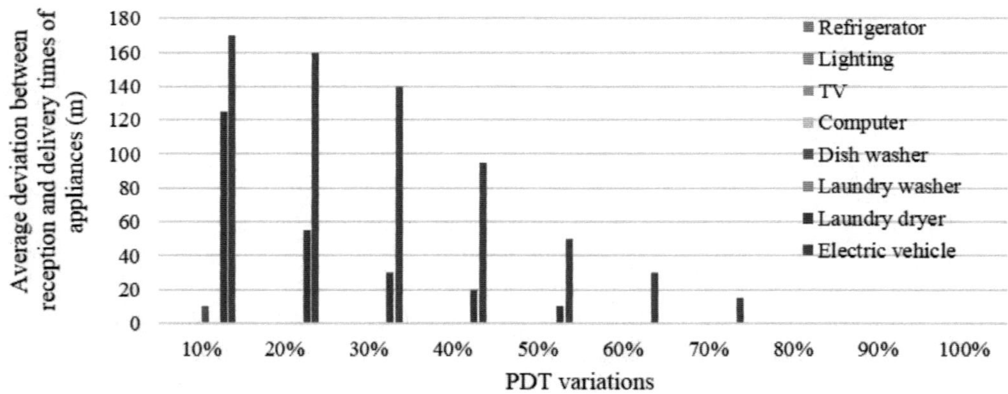

(b). Deviation time between appliance delivery and reception times based on the second case study

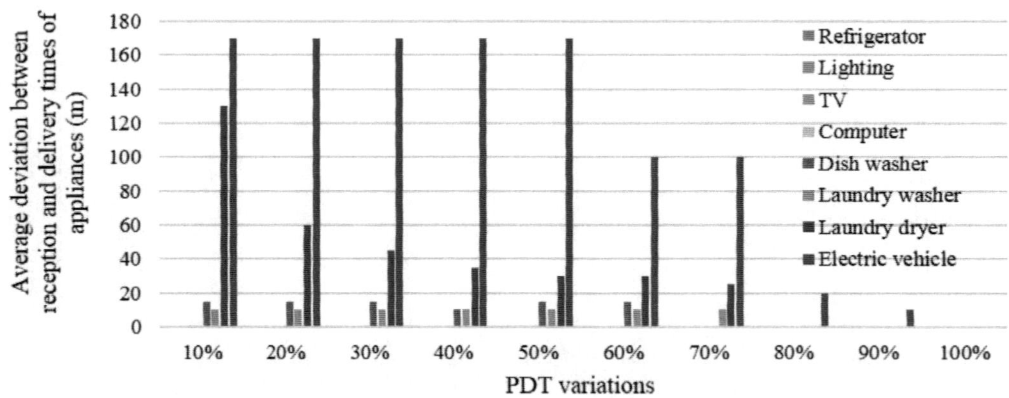

(c). Deviation time between appliance delivery and reception times based on the third case study

Figure 11. Deviation time between appliance delivery and reception times based on different case studies

TABLE IV. MAXIMUM NEEDED PDT AND CORRESPONDING PEAK TIME INTERVAL WHEN THE ASSIGNED PDT CHANGES

		Assigned PDT									
		10% 293 kW	20% 586 kW	30% 879 kW	40% 117 kW	50% 146 kW	60% 175 kW	70% 205 kW	80% 234 kW	90% 263 kW	100% 293 kW
Maximum needed PDT	Case study 1	360 kW	282 kW	222 kW	218 kW	200 kW	175 kW	205 kW	234 kW	263 kW	293 kW
	Case study 2	363 kW	287 kW	242 kW	192 kW	155 kW	175 kW	205 kW	234 kW	263 kW	293210
	Case study 3	360 kW	322 kW	213 kW	300 kW	298 kW	291 kW	291 kW	234 kW	254 kW	293 kW
Peak time interval	Case study 1	23:35	23:05	22:30	22:30	22:30	11:05	20:20	20:35	11:20	20:30
	Case study 2	23:35	23:05	23:05	23:05	22:35	11:20	11:05	20:35	11:20	20:30
	Case study 3	23:35	23:05	23:05	23:05	23:05	23"05	23:05	20:35	12:30	20:30

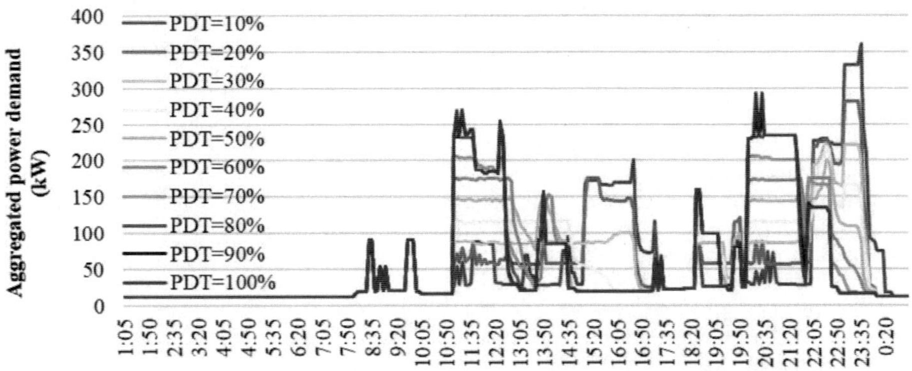

(a). Aggregated power demand of 100 dwellings based on the first case study

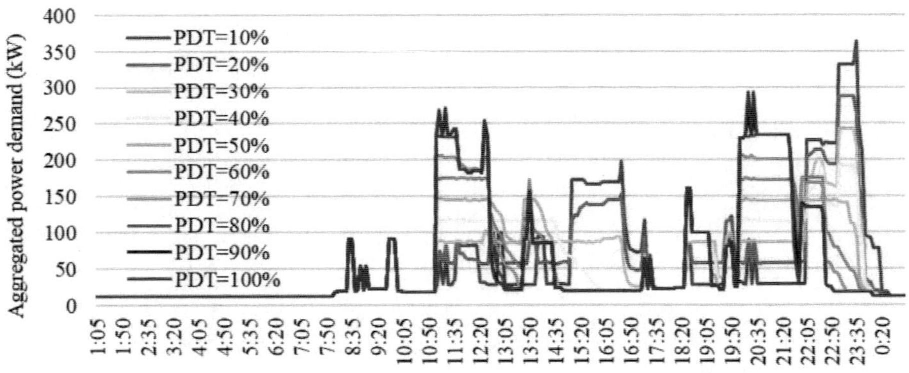

(b). Aggregated power demand of 100 dwellings based on the second case study

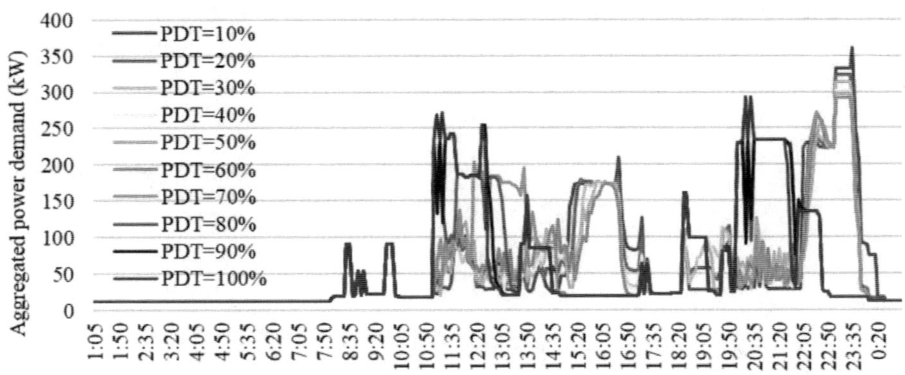

(c). Aggregated power demand of 100 dwellings based on the third case study

Figure 12. Aggregated power demand of 100 dwellings based on different case studies

aggregated consumption of 100 dwellings when the system applies the third case study. In this figure, the demand response system will receive the minimum aggregated power demand, when PDT is equal to 80%. In this status, the maximum power demand is 234 kW and the achievement is 20%.

VI. Conclusion and Future Work

This paper developed a demand response system. It received power demand requests of appliances continuously and scheduled them accordingly. Appliances are classified based on the shiftability and interruptibility features. The well-known "0-1" Knapsack procedure has been applied to the scheduling problem, when it is necessary to choose some requests to allow them to start or to continue their duties at the current time interval and shift the remaining to the future time intervals. The objectives of the proposed scheduling algorithm are minimizing the total electricity costs and CO_2 emission intensities coupling with maximizing the satisfaction of consumers. In addition, as constraints, the system attempts to keep the total power demands under a constant and time-independent power demand threshold provided by distribution system operators at each time interval. Consumers may provide time limits of flexibilities of electricity powers to the demand response system. These time limit flexibilities of power demand requests vary among appliances. It helps the system to find an optimal or near-optimal solution (based on the approach used) to decide when to shift or to interrupt power demand requests. The results were analyzed based on changing the thresholds. It was confirmed that applying this kind of threshold led to a reduction in the total electricity costs, a change in the daily behavior of consumers in a beneficial way, and additionally, a flattened aggregated power demand.

An investigation of reformulating the current power scheduling algorithm to a hierarchical scheduling algorithm to run in each dwelling is a promising future work. It would be also interesting to investigate the sensitivity of the scheduling algorithm to the stochasticity of power profiles. In practice, the adaptation of power demand thresholds can be accomplished by implementing a control loop between the demand response system and a gateway deployed in each dwelling.

Acknowledgment

The work in this document has been funded by European Union Seventh Framework program (FP7/2007-2013) under grant agreement n° 619560 (SEMIAH).

References

[1] R. H. Jacobsen, A. G. Azar, Q. Zhang, and E. S. M. Ebeid, "Home Appliance Load Scheduling with SEMIAH," in the Fourth International IARIA Conference on Smart Systems, Devices, and Technologies (SMART), 2015, pp. 1–2.

[2] J. Gao, Y. Xiao, J. Liu, W. Liang, and C. P. Chen, "A Survey of Communication/networking in Smart Grids," Future Generation Computer Systems, vol. 28, no. 2, 2012, pp. 391–404.

[3] A. Soares, Á. Gomes, and C. H. Antunes, "Categorization of Residential Electricity Consumption as a Basis for the Assessment of the Impacts of Demand Response Actions," Renewable and Sustainable Energy Reviews, vol. 30, 2014, pp. 490–503.

[4] M. Rastegar, M. Fotuhi-Firuzabad, and F. Aminifar, "Load Commitment in a Smart Home," Applied Energy, vol. 96, 2012, pp. 45–54.

[5] J. S. Vardakas, N. Zorba, and C. V. Verikoukis, "Scheduling Policies for Two-State Smart-Home Appliances in Dynamic Electricity Pricing Environments," Energy, vol. 69, 2014, pp. 455–469.

[6] P. Stoll, N. Brandt, and L. Nordström, "Including Dynamic CO_2 Intensity With Demand Response," Energy Policy, vol. 65, 2014, pp. 490–500.

[7] X. He, L. Hancher, I. Azevedo, N. Keyaerts, L. Meeus, and J.-M. GLACHANT, "Shift, Not Drift: Towards Active Demand Response and Beyond," 2013.

[8] H. Farhangi, "The Path of the Smart Grid," IEEE Power and Energy Magazine, vol. 8, no. 1, 2010, pp. 18–28.

[9] X. Fang, S. Misra, G. Xue, and D. Yang, "Smart grid-The New and Improved Power Grid: A Survey," IEEE Communications Surveys & Tutorials, vol. 14, no. 4, 2012, pp. 944–980.

[10] P. Palensky and D. Dietrich, "Demand Side Management: Demand Response, Intelligent Energy Systems, and Smart Loads," IEEE Transactions on Industrial Informatics, vol. 7, no. 3, 2011, pp. 381–388.

[11] A. Agnetis, G. Dellino, P. Detti, G. Innocenti, G. de Pascale, and A. Vicino, "Appliance Operation Scheduling for Electricity Consumption Optimization," in Proceedings of 50th IEEE Conference on Decision and Control and European Control Conference (CDC-ECC), 2011, pp. 5899–5904.

[12] G. O'Brien and R. Rajagopal, "A Method for Automatically Scheduling Notified Deferrable Loads," in Proceedings of IEEE American Control Conference (ACC), 2013, pp. 5080–5085.

[13] A. G. Azar, R. H. Jacobsen, and Q. Zhang, "Aggregated Load Scheduling for Residential Multi-Class Appliances: Peak Demand Reduction," in Proceedings of the 12th International IEEE Conference on the European Energy Market-EEM, 2015.

[14] O. A. Sianaki, O. Hussain, and A. R. Tabesh, "A Knapsack Problem Approach for Achieving Efficient Energy Consumption in Smart Grid for End Users' Life Style," in IEEE Conference on Innovative Technologies for an Efficient and Reliable Electricity Supply (CITRES), 2010, pp. 159–164.

[15] F. Rassaei, W.-S. Soh, and K.-C. Chua, "Demand Response for Residential Electric Vehicles With Random Usage Patterns in Smart Grids," IEEE Transactions on Sustainable Energy, vol. 6, no. 4, 2015, pp. 1367–1376.

[16] M. T. Beyerle, J. A. Broniak, J. M. Brian, and D. C. Bingham, "Manage Whole Home Appliances/loads to a Peak Energy Consumption," 2011, US Patent App. 13/042,550.

[17] H. Kellerer, U. Pferschy, and D. Pisinger, Knapsack Problems. Berlin, Heidelberg: Springer Berlin Heidelberg, 2004, ch. Introduction to NP-Completeness of Knapsack Problems, pp. 483–493. [Online]. Available: http://dx.doi.org/10.1007/978-3-540-24777-7_16

[18] K. Florios, G. Mavrotas, and D. Diakoulaki, "Solving Multi-objective, Multi-constraint Knapsack Problems Using Mathematical Programming and Evolutionary Algorithms," European Journal of Operational Research, vol. 203, no. 1, 2010, pp. 14–21.

[19] R. E. Bellman and S. E. Dreyfus, Applied Dynamic Programming. Princeton university press, 2015.

[20] K. Deb, Search Methodologies: Introductory Tutorials in Optimization and Decision Support Techniques. Boston, MA: Springer US, 2014, ch. Multi-objective Optimization, pp. 403–449. [Online]. Available: http://dx.doi.org/10.1007/978-1-4614-6940-7_15

[21] H. Ishibuchi, N. Akedo, and Y. Nojima, "Behavior of Multi-objective Evolutionary Algorithms on Many-Objective Knapsack Problems," IEEE Transactions on Evolutionary Computation, vol. 19, no. 2, 2015, pp. 264–283.

[22] K. Deb, A. Pratap, S. Agarwal, and T. Meyarivan, "A Fast and Elitist Multi-objective Genetic Algorithm: NSGA-II," IEEE Transactions on Evolutionary Computation, vol. 6, no. 2, 2002, pp. 182–197.

[23] A. Reinhardt, P. Baumann, D. Burgstahler, M. Hollick, H. Chonov, M. Werner, and R. Steinmetz, "On the Accuracy of Appliance Identification Based on Distributed Load Metering Data," in Proceedings of the 2nd IFIP Conference on Sustainable Internet and ICT for Sustainability (SustainIT), 2012, pp. 1–9.

[24] Nord Pool Spot. Last access on May 4, 2016. [Online]. Available: http://www.nordpoolspot.com

[25] Energinet. Last access on May 4, 2016. [Online]. Available: http://www.energinet.dk/

Decentralized Energy in the Smart Energy Grid and Smart Market – How to master reliable and secure control

Steffen Fries, Rainer Falk
Corporate Technology
Siemens AG
Munich, Germany
e-mail: {steffen.fries|rainer.falk}@siemens.com

Henry Dawidczak, Thierry Dufaure
Energy Management
Siemens AG
Berlin, Germany
e-mail: {henry.dawidczak|thierry.dufaure}@siemens.com

Abstract—**The reliable integration of decentralized energy resources and loads into the smart energy grid and into a smart energy market is gaining more importance to cope with the increasing energy demand and the installation of renewable energy sources. Ideally, the load on the energy transmission network shall not be affected by direct energy exchange between local generation and consumption within a distribution network. Characteristic for the involved control systems is the data exchange between intelligent electronic devices (IEDs) that are used to monitor and control the operation. For the integration of Decentralized Energy Resources (DER), these IEDs provide the data for obtaining a system view of connected (decentralized) energy resources. This system view builds the base to manage a Virtual Power Plant (VPP) by combining a number of DER, reliably. In substation automation, the standard IEC 61850 is used to enable communication between IEDs to control the central energy generation and distribution. This standard is being enhanced with web services, features and mappings to support its application also for DER. One difference to the classical application in substations is the integration of IEDs residing on a customer network, most likely to be operated behind Firewalls and Network Address Translation (NAT). Nevertheless, end-to-end secured communication between DER and control center also over public networks must be ensured to maintain a consistent security level. Here, adequate IT security measures are a necessary prerequisite to prevent intentional manipulations, affecting the reliable operation of the energy grid. This paper investigates into the currently proposed security measures for the communication architecture for DER integration. In addition to the original paper, the contributions to the International Electrotechnical Commission (IEC) for enhancements of the security for the standard IEC 61850 are elaborated more deeply with the focus not only on pairwise connections but also for multicast communication. Besides that, this paper also investigates into open issues related to the secure integration of DER.**

Keywords–security; device authentication; pairwise security; multicast security; firewall; decentralized energy resource, substation automation; smart grid; smart Market, IEC 61850, IEC 60870-5, IEC 62351, XMPP

I. INTRODUCTION

As described in [1], renewable energy sources like the sun or wind power are becoming increasingly important to generate environmentally sustainable energy and thus to reduce greenhouse gases leading to global warming. Integrating these decentralized energy resources (DER) into the current energy distribution network poses great challenges for energy automation: DER need to be monitored and controlled to a similar level as centralized energy generation in power plants to keep the stability of the power network frequency. As DER are typically geographically dispersed, widely distributed communication networks are required for exchanging control communication not only between the DER and the control center but also between DER. Multiple DER may also be aggregated on a higher architecture level to form a so-called virtual power plant. Such a virtual power plant can be controlled from the overall energy automation system in a similar way as a common centralized power plant with respect to energy generation capacity. But due to its decentralized nature, the demands on automation and communication, necessary to control the virtual power plant are much more challenging.

Furthermore, the introduction of controllable loads on residential level requires enhancements to the energy automation communication infrastructure as used today. It allows network operators to control more fine grained the amount and time of energy consumption. This is typically supported by mechanisms provided by a smart energy market allowing the exchange of information about energy prices and demand. Clearly, secure communication between a control station and DER equipment or energy loads of users as well as with decentralized field equipment must be achieved to avoid unauthorized access or manipulation of the data exchanged. Standard communication technologies based on IEC 61850 [2], which are used today for substation automation, cannot directly be applied and need enhancements.

Figure 1 below depicts the integration of DER into the Smart Grid and Smart Market from an abstract view. The lower part of the figure shows the distributed generators and loads, which shall be managed by the control function shown in the upper part. All peers are connected via a communication network and shielded by firewalls to avoid unauthorized inbound or outbound connections. The control function may be located at a Distribution Network Operator (DNO), a VPP operator, or a smart energy market operator.

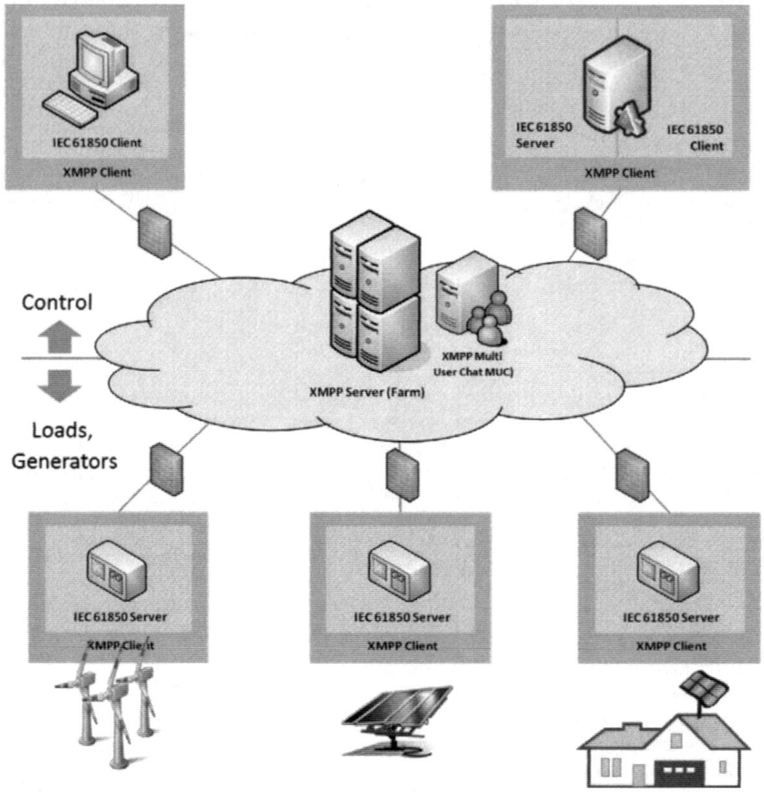

Figure 1. DER Integration based on IEC 61850 over XMPP

For the description of use cases in a smart grid environment the so called traffic light concept has been introduced by the regulation. This concept subdivides use cases into three different scenarios. The green phase allows using all market mechanisms, while yellow and red traffic light scenarios are defined by electrical network constrains due to problems like critical power unbalancing or power flow congestion in the electrical network.

The requirements of communication between DNO and DER Systems regarding for instance transfer times may differ compared to a pure market-driven use cases. It may be necessary to request a larger number of DER systems to change their generating or consuming power in a short time with a high priority. Group communication can be a required option for such use cases.

Grouping (sometimes called clustering) is a function of the DER management that consists in defining and using lists of DER systems by special characteristics (e.g., size of power, location in the topology of the network, type of connected DER units). Groups are created by each DER management entity for a special purpose. Using groups for a fast communication can require special means of the communication protocol.

Also shown are typical security infrastructure elements – Firewalls – which shield the different sub-networks. Communication is realized by applying IEC 61850 transmitted over the eXtensible Message and Presence Protocol (XMPP) [1][3]. XMPP is a well-known protocol standardized in the Internet Engineering Task Force (IETF) as RFC 6120 and is used for instance in chat applications. It supports Firewall and NAT traversal and also device registration and discovery. As XMPP, IEC 61850 itself is a client-server protocol. In the scenario shown in Figure 1, the IEC 61850 server part resides at the DER sides. Thus, a direct connection to control the DER may not be possible due to blocked inbound connections at the Firewall of the network the DER is connected to. This is the part where XMPP is utilized, as the XMPP client resides on the DER and starts establishing a connection with the XMPP server, that can be used to facilitate the IEC 61850 communication.

Note that this paper is an extended version of [1] that describes the environment in more detail, and also takes recent advancements in the definition of the IEC standard as well as the underlying scenarios and technology into account. The remaining part of this paper is organized as following: Section II provides an introduction to IEC 61850 and also investigates into missing parts for the integration of DER into Smart Grids. Section III analysis the security requirements and also potential security measures, by applying existing technology as far as possible. Section I discusses the resulting security approach, which is also proposed for standardization. Compared to [1], this section is enhanced with the discussion of multicast communication security. This functionality has been identified in the original paper as being required to better control a larger number of IEDs individually, but provides a combined view at the control center level. Section V concludes the paper and provides an outlook for further work.

This paper targets the identification of existing security means as well as existing gaps for the concept of secure DER integration. Implementations as proof of concept have not been finished, yet.

II. IEC 61850 OVERVIEW

A. The IEC 61850 principles

While the first edition of the IEC 61850 series[2], published in 2003 focused on standardizing communication between applications within a Substation Automation Domain, the second edition published in 2010 extends its domain of application up to the Power Utility Automation System (see also [3]).

The IEC 61850 series specifies:

- An Abstract Communication Service Interface (ACSI),
- A semantic model based on an object oriented architecture,
- Specific Communication Service Mappings (SCSM),
- A project engineering workflow including a configuration description language (SCL) based on the XML language.

Using the IEC 61850 philosophy, i.e., decoupling the IEC 61850 object model and associated services from the communication technologies, allows the standard to be technology independent, that is, specifying new technologies when a set of new requirements is being processed by the standardization body without modifying the system architecture.

Services in IEC 61850 include:

- Client and Server communication within the scope of a Two Party Application Association (or session), for discovering, controlling and monitoring objects implemented in the device model,
- Peer to peer communication within the scope of a Multicast Application Association, for providing a unidirectional information exchange from one source to one or many destinations.

The IEC 61850-8-1 SCSM part has specified the mapping of IEC 61850 object model and associated services to the Manufacturing Message Specification (MMS, ISO 9506 series [4]). While IEC 61850-8-1 SCSM has proven to be a very efficient communication technology within the substation, i.e., within a private network, new challenges appear with the integration of the DER. A current effort in the standardization has gathered the requirements for an IEC 61850 SCSM to Web technologies.

Public network/infrastructure are neither administered by the DER owners nor by the control function operator; the use of public network represents therefore a major change in comparison to the way IEC 61850 Systems and communication have been deployed within the substation.

The gathered requirements [5] show also that the response times are less critical than they are in the substation environment. Both the number of devices connected to the Smart Grid as well as the dynamic changes of the system (continuous integration of new resources) encourage the use of a technology that supports the volatility of the system.

The decision criteria used in the standardization committee lead to the election of XMPP [6] technology as a network layer in the SCSM.

B. The XMPP principles

XMPP is a communication protocol enabling two entities (XMPP clients) to exchange pieces of XML data called stanzas. As shown in Fig.1, both the DER (IEC 61850 servers) and the VPP or DNO control center (IEC 61850 client) are then exposed as XMPP clients. They are not directly connected together but can exchange XML messages over the XMPP server(s) they are connected to. Each XMPP client is responsible for initiating a TCP/IP connection to the XMPP server of the domain the XMPP client belongs to. The XMPP servers are located in the WAN and their location can either be statically configured in the DER or can be discovered by the DER via DNS-SRV records [7].

Since DER will be located behind (most of the time unmanaged) firewalls, the XMPP servers cannot reach/connect to them (requirement – blocked inbound connection); nevertheless, DER can reach/connect to the XMPP server of their domain over the stateful firewall of their infrastructure.

As soon as the TCP/IP connection to its XMPP server is established, each XMPP client starts a bi-directional XML stream with its XMPP server.

Each XMPP client has a unique system identifier, a so-called JIDs (Jabber Identification), whose format is quite similar to the well-known mail addresses format: entity@domain.tld.

Communication between XMPP clients occurs over the XML streams, each client has negotiated with their XMPP server, the server acting then as router forwarding the message exchange.

The XMPP series define three different XML message formats called stanza. Similar to the mail message, each stanza contains an attribute "from" (from="JID of the source of the message") and an attribute "to" (to="JID of the destination of the message"). The message formats are:

- of type <iq> (dedicated for request/response exchange - solicited service),
- of type <message> (dedicated for push-exchange - unsolicited communication),
- or of type <presence> (dedicated for presence announcement).

C. Mapping of IEC 61850 to XMPP

IEC/CDV 61850-8-2 foresees XER encoding of MMS using following mapping of the services to the XMPP stanza:

- request/response services will be mapped to the <iq> stanza (e.g., initiate-RequestPDU, initiate-ResponsePDU, writeRequestPDU, ...)
- reporting services will be mapped to the unsolicited <message> stanza (e.g., informationReportPDU, ...)
- monitoring of association connectivity will use the <presence> stanza

The monitoring of the IEC 61850 association connectivity is a crucial part in an XMPP environment as the two ends of the IEC 61850 two party associations are not directly connected with means of a TCP socket. The XMPP Server monitors the connectivity to each of the two XMPP Clients, and informs the remaining one with mean of a presence (unavailable) stanza when the other end has disconnected (e.g., due to communication outage).

Through the mapping of MMS to XMPP, the MMS defined security measures are directly applicable as outlined in the next section.

D. Additional XMPP feautures for solving system management use cases

The XMPP standard provides protocol extensions (so called XEPs [8]), i.e., optional technical specifications to solve additional communication requirements (e.g., group communication). The developments of the specifications are hosted and coordinated by the XMPP foundation [9]. For example, the XEP-0045 specifies the Multi-User Chat (MUC) environment, with which XMPP clients can exchange messages in the context of an administrated room. The IEC 61850 multicast application association defined the abstract model could easily be mapped to a moderated room, where the moderator is the publisher of the unidirectional information, and the subscribers are dynamically invited to join the room in which the information is being published.

XEP-0030 specifies an XMPP protocol extension for a generic Service Discovery, with which XMPP clients can discover services associated to a domain (support of MUC, time synchronization scheme, security actors, ...) or to a given XMPP Client (support of MUC, support of service discovery, support of additional XEPs). To fulfill the plug and play requirements of a secured Smart Grid environment, XMPP Service Discovery offers an alternative to DNS-SRV records within a domain, having trusted entities (XMPP Server of the domain, or XMPP Clients) responding to service discovery requests. XEP-0060 specifies an XMPP protocol extension for a generic Publish-Subscribe functionality: an XMPP client can be configured to create a node onto the XMPP server, in which it will publish information for subscribers. With means of the Service Discovery protocol extension, XMPP Clients can discover the publish nodes and can request a subscription to them. Publish-subscribe model can be useful for publishing tariff data.

III. Security Considerations

This section describes IT security requirements that are connected with the reliable operation of a smart energy grid. The security requirements are mapped to standardized IT security measures.

A. Security Requirements

Security requirements targeting the integration of DER into power system architectures are typically derived from a given system architecture like the one shown in Figure 1, and from use cases describing the interactions of the components. Also, further security requirements may be posed through national regulations, depending on the country the DER integration is done. These regulations specifically target the privacy protection of end user related information.

The main focus in the context of this document is placed on the investigation of the communication relations and data assets exchanged between the components. Table I below provides the most relevant data assets.

TABLE I. Data Assets

Asset	Description, example content	Security relation
Customer related information	Name, identification number, location data, schedule information, electrical network topology data	Effects on customer privacy
Meter Data	Meter readings that allow calculation of the quantity of electricity consumed or supplied over a time period.	Effects on system control, billing, and customer privacy
Control Commands	Actions requested by one component. These may include Inquiries, Alarms, Events, and Notifications.	Effects on system stability and reliability and also safety
Tariff Data	Utilities or other energy providers may inform consumers of new or temporary tariffs as a basis for purchase decisions.	Effects on competition and customer privacy as tariff depends on consumption.

Data exchange of this information typically depends on the underlying system architecture and may comprise hop-to-hop, end-to-end, or multicast communication, depending on the context and the involved entities. To determine the connected security requirements, the trust relations between the different entities are essential. Based on Figure 1 the following trust relations are assumed:

- DER resource (XMPP client on IEC 61850 server) belongs to DER owner
- DER control (XMPP client on IEC 61850 client/server) belongs to DNO or 3rd party grid service
- XMPP server may belong to DNO or 3rd party grid service provider
- Trust relation between DER resource owner and DNO (e.g., based on contract)
- XMPP server operator trusted regarding resource discovery and message transfer service (not processing!)

These trust assumptions for the data exchange lead to base security requirements enumerated in Table II below.

TABLE II. SECURITY REQUIREMENTS

	Security requirements
R1	End-to-middle source authentication ensures peers are properly identified and authenticated. It is required between XMPP client and XMPP server or between XMPP servers. Note that here it may target mainly component authentication.
R2	End-to-end source authentication ensures peers are properly identified and authenticated. It is required between IEC 61850 client and server instances. This authentication goes across the XMPP server ("application layer") and may be bound to a dedicated instance running on the IEC 61850 host.
R3	End-to-middle integrity protection to ensure that data in transit has not been tampered with (unauthorized modification) between the XMPP client and XMPP server.
R4	End-to-end integrity protection to ensure that data in transit has not been tampered with (unauthorized modification) between the IEC 61850 client and server instances. Based on the different communication relations, the protection needs to support a) unicast: peer-to-peer related communication b) multicast: group based communication (via the MUC)
R5	End-to-middle confidentiality protection to ensure that data in transit has not been accessed (read) in an unauthorized way between the XMPP client and XMPP server.
R6	End-to-end confidentiality protection to ensure that data in transit has not been accessed (read) in an unauthorized way between the IEC 61850 client and server instances. Based on the different communication relations, the protection needs to support a) unicast: peer-to-peer related communication b) multicast: group based communication (via the MUC)

Mapping the enumerated requirements to the base architecture shown in Figure 1 is depicted in Figure 2 below. Note that the figure shows the unicast communication as well as potential multicast communication relations.

Based on the trust assumptions and the enumerated security requirements in Table II, the consequent next step is the investigation into existing security measures to evaluate their effectiveness to cope with the base requirements. These security measures are used to identify a first target system security architecture and also potential missing pieces. For the missing pieces, target architecture specific security measures have to be defined. The following subsections map the existing measures based on standardized solutions and also investigating into enhancements of the considered standards.

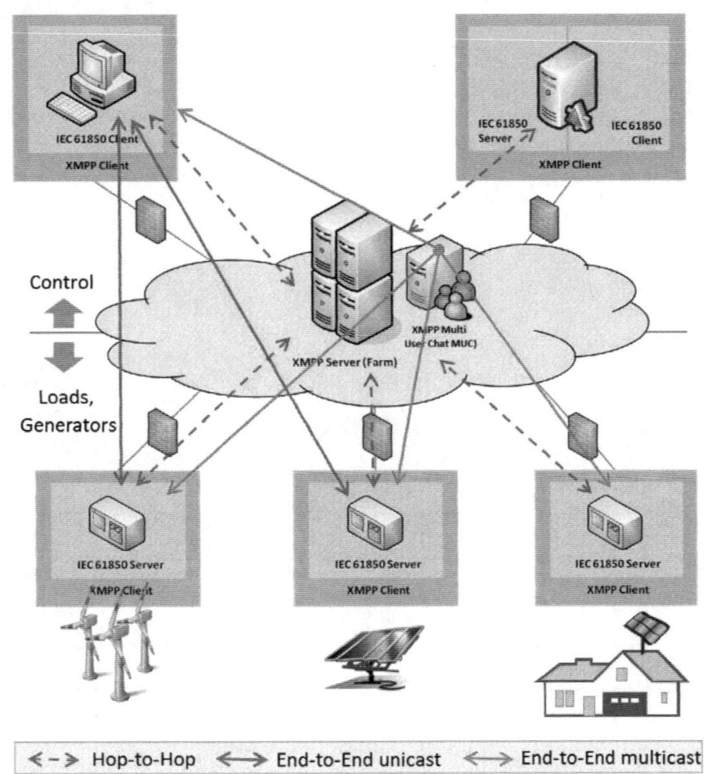

Figure 2. Security Relations for DER Integration

B. Mapping of exisiting Security Measures

The following subsections map standardized security measures to the security requirements, to discuss their applicability.

1) Security Options in XMPP

XMPP as defined in RFC 6120 [6] and shown in Figure 3 already considers the following integrated security measures:

- Transport layer protection using the Transport Layer Security protocol (TLS, specified in RFC 5246 [10]), allows for
  - mutual authentication of involved peers,
  - integrity protection of data transfer, and
  - confidentiality protection of data transfer.

  Depending on the chosen cipher suite, the application of this security mean addresses the security requirements R1, R3, and R5.
- XMPP peer authentication with two options
  - Rely on TLS authentication (addresses R1), or
  - Using the separate Simple Authentication and Security Layer (SASL) authentication (in XMPP [11], addresses R1) to authenticate users.

Note that the XMPP security features target the communication between a XMPP client and XMPP server in the first place. Additional means to address end-to-end security support (between XMPP clients) on higher protocol layers are available or are currently discussed within standardization groups. Examples are:

- IETF RFC 3923 [12] describes end-to-end signing and object encryption utilizing S/MIME, like a secure email. This approach addresses the security requirements R2, R4a, and R6a by applying asymmetric cryptography on a per-message base. Two important points to note here are the following ones: Asymmetric cryptography in this context relates to the application of X.509 certificates and corresponding private keys in a similar way as in email applications. Note that the asymmetric encryption is typically much more costly in terms of required computational power compared to symmetric encryption, in particular for frequently exchanged messages. Hence, applying this approach may influence the performance in a negative way. Secondly, RFC 3923 is restricted to the application of RSA (Rivest, Shamir, Adleman) as asymmetric cryptographic algorithm for digital signature and encryption. More recent standards also support elliptic curve cryptography, which provides an adequate security level utilizing a much shorter key. Moreover, the operation is much more performant.
- The IETF draft draft-miller-xmpp-e2e [13] describes end-to-end object encryption and signatures between two entities with multiple devices. This addresses the situation, where some end points for a given recipient may share keys, some may use different keys, some may have no keys and some may not support encryption or signature verification at all. The draft defines a symmetric key table that is managed via three mechanisms that enable a key to be pushed to an end point, to be pulled from an originator or negotiated. If applicable it addresses R4a and R6a. Note that this draft Internet standard document has expired. It is mentioned here, as the general approach may provide a solution.
- The IETF draft draft-meyer-xmpp-e2e-encryption [14] describes XTLS as end-to-end TLS (like) channel. It would have been applicable to address R 2, R 4a, and R 6a, but the work has stopped and the draft has expired. The draft is stated here for completeness, as the mechanism intended to evolve the security provided in IEC 62351-4 uses a similar approach (see the next subsection).

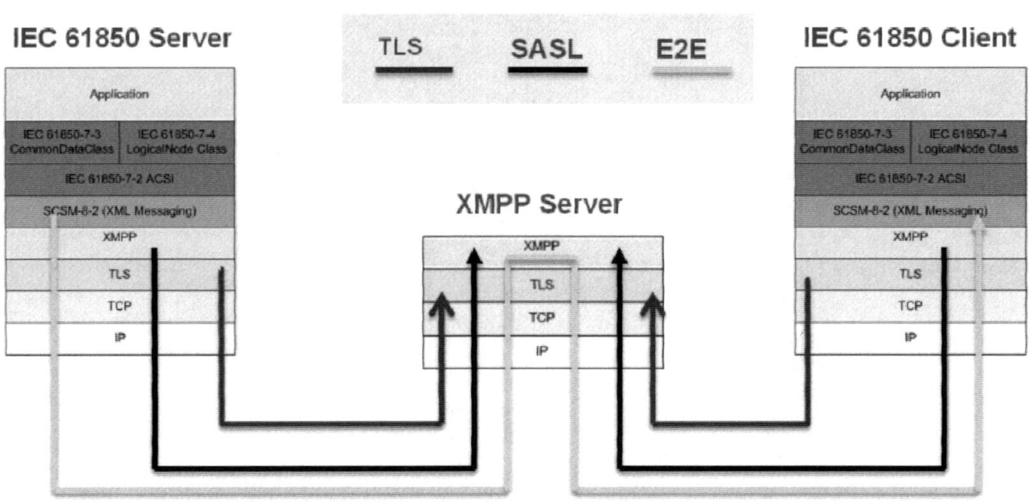

Figure 3. XMPP Security Options

2) IEC 62351 – Security for IEC 61850 and beyond

The working group IEC TC 57 WG15 is responsible for maintaining and evolving different security mechanisms applicable to the power systems domain. Here, IEC 62351 [15] has been defined, which is meanwhile split into 14 different parts with different level of completeness. Figure 5 shows the existing parts and their relation to the target energy automation standards.

Out of this set of specific security parts, mainly four parts are within the scope for the further discussion of security mechanisms that help to protect XMPP communication. Note that three parts are already available as technical standard (TS), but are currently being revised and updated, while the fourth one is defined in edition 1. The parts referred to are:

- IEC/IS 62351-3: Profiles including TCP/IP: This part basically profiles the use of TLS and is referenced from part 4, 5, 6, and 9. Profiling here relates to narrowing available options in TLS like the requirement to utilize mutual authentication reducing the number of allowed algorithms or the disallowance of utilizing certain cipher suites, not providing sufficient protection. Moreover, this part also provides guidelines for utilizing options, which depend on the embedding environment. An example is the relation of using session renegotiation and session resumption in conjunction with the update interval of the certificate revocation information.
- IEC/TS 62351-4: Profiles including MMS: This part is currently in revision. The current document defines protection of MMS messages on transport and application layer. The application layer provides only limited protection as it does only allow for an authentication during the initial MMS session handshake without a cryptographic binding to the remaining part of session. As new scenarios arise, involving intermediate devices, this protection is no longer sufficient. Hence, IEC/TS 62351-4 is being revised to enhance the protection of MMS traffic with additional application layer security profiles. Now, MMS session integrity and confidentiality protection is targeted as depicted in Figure 4 below.

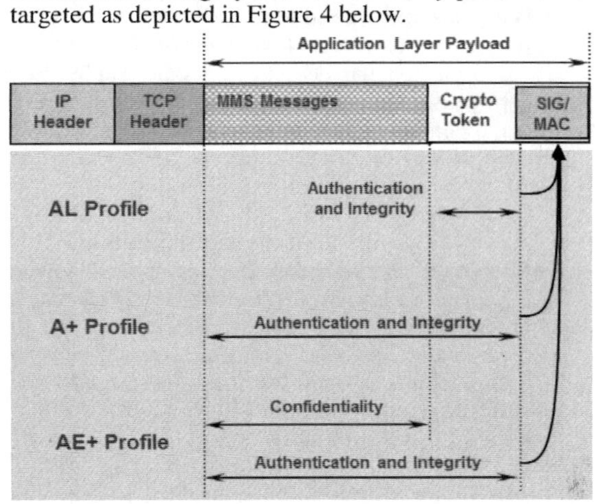

Figure 4. IEC 62351-4 A-Profile enhancements

This approach can be leveraged for the transport over XMPP to address R2, R4a and R6a.

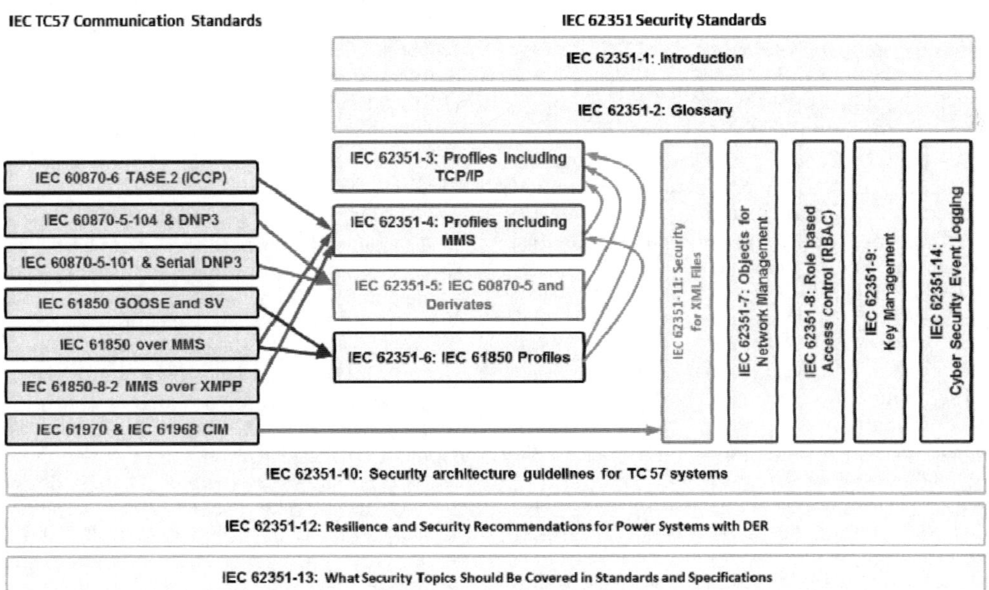

Figure 5. IEC62351 addressing energy automation communication

- IEC/TS 62351-6: Security for IEC 61850: This part targets the integrity protection of Ethernet multicast communication exchanges in substations utilizing GOOSE (Generic Object Oriented Substation Event), but can also be applied to the exchange of synchrophaser communication over wide area networks, also utilizing the GOOSE protocol. The originally standardized security measure employs on digital signatures on a per message base is currently being reworked to address performance shortcomings. It will be enhanced to allow for a group security approach utilizing symmetric cryptography to better cope with the performance requirements of GOOSE communication. This approach can also be leveraged to support the secure integration of DER addressing R4b and R6b in multicast environments.
- Draft IEC/TS 62351-9: Cyber security key management for power system equipment: This part focuses on the base key management of asymmetric key material like X.509 certificates and corresponding private keys, including the enrollment and revocation of certificates, but also symmetric keys applicable for group communication. For the latter, the IETF defined Group Domain of Interpretation (GDOI), RFC 6407 [16], is used to provide the key material for IEC/TS 62351-6. To achieve the transport of the IEC 61850 related key material and the connected security policy, GDOI had to be enhanced with the appropriate key data payloads. This enhancement is described in [18].

As there are some fundamental differences between automated pairwise (unicast) and group based (multicast) key management and the application of the key, the following two subsections provide some background on both issues.

a) Pairwise or unicast security

A typical protocol example for pairwise key establishment and application is TLS, which is already used by IEC 62351 to secure TCP based traffic. Here, both peers possess a X.509 certificate and a corresponding private key that are used to authenticate and to protect the negotiation of a session secret and an associated security policy between these peers. As TLS is required to be used with mutual authentication, the session key negotiation is best done by applying the Diffie-Hellman key agreement scheme that is already part of several TLS cipher suites. As a result, both peers possess a pairwise shared secret as session key that is the base for the further symmetric protection of the message exchanges. The combination of the key with dedicated security services (integrity, encryption or both) is negotiated during the handshake based on proposed cipher suites. Just the same approach is being used to setup the session keys in the realization of the A-profiles shown in Figure 4. Here, there are much less security options provided compared to TLS. Figure 6 provides an overview on this handshake.

The base for the session key establishment is the signed handshake in the initiation phase. This handshake carries the Diffie Hellman parameter of both peers in a signed message. After the exchange both sides can derive the Diffie Hellman secret and utilize it to secure the concurrent session. The cleartokens shown in Figure 6 carry the necessary information for the Diffie Hellman key agreement.

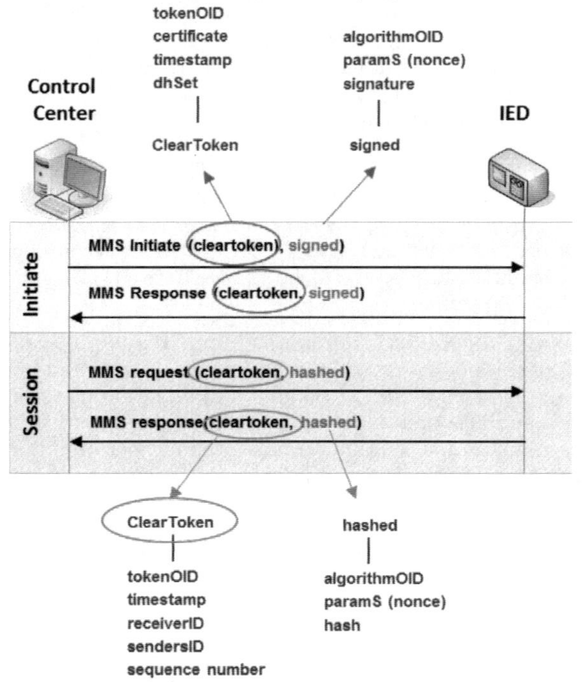

Figure 6. IEC 62351-4 Session Key establishment for A-Profiles

The trust in the certificates on both peers is provided through a trusted third party that has issued these certificates. This is a typical task of a certification authority (CA), which is part of a Public Key Infrastructure (PKI). It is assumed that both peers trust the same CA. This CA can issue the certificates offline. The certificates are verified during the TLS handshake that does not involve the trusted third party directly. Note that the revocation state may also be provided offline through the use of certificate revocation lists (CRLs), which are typically refreshed once a day.

b) Group based or multicast security

The general approach of group based security clearly differs from the more common unilateral security approach. As stated before, the chosen approach for IEC 62351 is GDOI [16]. An overview of multicast security options for power systems can be found in [17].

In case of GDOI a trusted third party, the key distribution center (KDC), needs to be online as part of the session key establishment. Here, the session key is a key shared between a group of participants.

Figure 7 shows the setup of a group of three IEDs, which form a group. The authentication towards the KDC is performed based on X.509 certificates and corresponding private keys. According to the security policy, the KDC distributes the key information (Key-ID) for the associated message flow (Stream-ID) to the authenticated IEDs. Each IED can then apply the group key to secure the message exchange between the three IEDs.

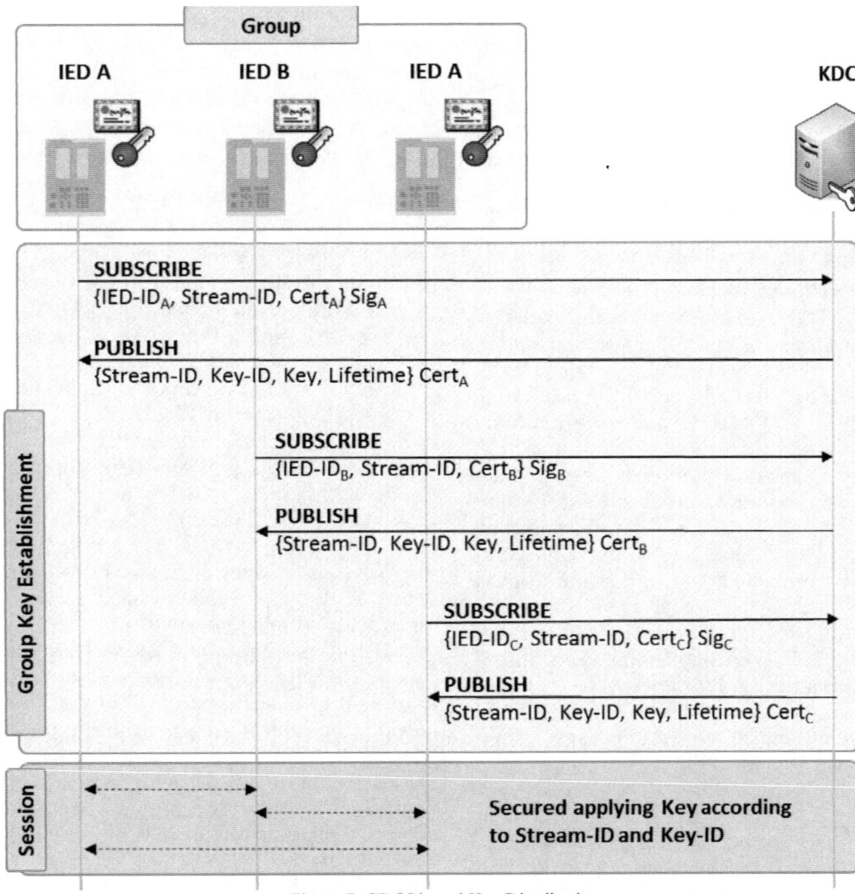

Figure 7. GDOI based Key Distribution

IV. Proposed Communication Security Approach

Based on the discussed trust assumptions, the security requirements and the security means in Section III, the following measures are proposed as base for a secure communication architecture to enable the secure integration of DER systems into the Smart Grid. The measures are distinguished into unicast and multicast communication. Also identified are open issues, which have to be addressed.

A. *Unicast security means*

For unicast communication, the security requirements can be fulfilled by the security means described in the sequel. Both hop-to-hop and end-to-end security are required to fulfill the security requirements.

Mutual authentication, session integrity and confidentiality of an XMPP-based client, -server, or server-server communication are protected (hop-to-hop security from IEC 61850 point of view). This fulfills the requirements R1, R3, and R5. The TLS security protocol as specified in RFC 6120 (XMPP Core) is applied, using the cipher suites and settings defined in IEC/IS 62351-3 defining a TLS profile for protecting TCP based IEC 61850 traffic. The credentials used for authentication are X.509 certificates and corresponding private keys of the involved peers. The verification of XMPP client or XMPP server certificates requires that the root certificate of the issuing certificate authority (CA) is available at the other peer. Most likely the CA has a relation to the DNO or another 3rd party grid service provider.

End-to-end authentication, i.e., between two XMPP client instances, integrity, and confidentiality can be achieved by applying the draft IEC/IS 62351-4 MMS secure session concept as stated in section 2) utilizing the AE+ profile to address R2, R4a, and R6a.

Open at this point in time is if there is a distinction between the transport layer authentication and the application layer authentication in terms of utilized credentials. Using the same credentials for both may require a provisioning of access lists of allowed XMPP clients (DER resources) for the XMPP server upfront provided by the DNO (as blacklist or white list) to the XMPP server operator. This is especially necessary, if the DNO uses an own PKI infrastructure. Also, it may be in the interest of the XMPP server operator to utilize an own PKI for issuing certificates used to access the provided service to better divide potential liability issues. This is especially interesting if the DNO and the XMPP service provider are two distinct legal entities.

B. *Multicast security means*

For multicast communication, the multicast distribution point is the MUC, residing at the XMPP server side. Using XMPP out of the box, the multicast communication is protected only hop-to-hop between MUC and XMPP clients. Access to the MUC is controlled by user authentication. Here two basic approaches are possible:

- If TLS is used with mutual authentication, the client certificate needs to carry the JID to provide the information about the authorization to use a dedicated JID to the MUC and/or presence service.
- Alternatively, if TLS is used with either unilateral authentication or in case of mutual authentication, with a certificate not carrying the JID and thus bound to the device and not the user, user authentication is performed using SASL to control access to the MUC and/or the presence service.

To achieve cryptographic end-to-end integrity and confidentiality protection, additional means are necessary. As the aforementioned group based key management protocol GDOI is already considered in the overall security architecture, it is also recommended for utilization to reuse existing features and components as far as possible. This establishes a group key shared between the authenticated members of the group. The security solution defined in IEC 61351-6, i.e., the application of a group key for multicast communication, in conjunction with IEC 62351-9 defining the group key distribution, can be re-used directly to address security requirements R2, R4b and R6b.

The realization of the group key management functionality is open, i.e., which entity generates the group key, and distributes it to the clients. Based on the given requirements, and the trust assumptions, the group key generation would be performed at the DNO or VPP side, while the group key distribution would be performed using the MUC of the XMPP architecture. This distributed key management certainly requires a protected end-to-end transport of the group key to avoid that the XMPP server operator has access to this sensitive information. The final mapping of the group based security scheme heavily depends on the underlying trust model. This trust model and the connected scenarios are currently under discussion in the IEC working group. The proposed solution builds one option to realize the group based communication technically. Note that there is currently work ongoing to also invest on one hand into the feasibility of using other group based key management schemes and also regarding the placement of the KDC in the overall architecture.

V. IDENTIFIED OPEN ISSUES

As stated in the previous section, open issues have been identified regarding the credentials used for the peer authentication (hop-to-hop, and end-to-end) in unicast communication, and also regarding the mapping of certain multicast security related functions to the various involved entities. Another issue besides the selection of the authentication credential relates to the performance of peer authentication of XMPP clients towards the XMPP server. It has to be determined, which entity performs the authentication and access control. Different options have been identified:

- Option 1: The XMPP server performs the client authentication locally, using a locally available access control list. The access control list can be provided by the DNO, or by another 3rd party grid service provider over a secure configuration protocol.
- Option 2: The DNO, or another 3rd party grid service provider, performs the authentication, and access control check remotely, based on a redirection from the XMPP server. Frameworks like OAuth [19] could be involved here. This would allow also the utilization of already established solutions.
- Option 3: While the user authentication is performed locally by the XMPP server, e.g., using SASL, or a user certificate with included JID, the access control check is performed remotely. This approach would lead to a token based approach, which may utilize functionalities like SAML (Security Assertion Markup Language) tokens [20] or JSON web tokens [21].

These topics require further research, and the results will have to be part of future standardization work to ensure interoperable solutions.

Based on a threat and risk analysis, the options for using single credential or different credentials for hop-to-hop, and end-to-end security, have to be compared in the specific application context. This is the basis to make a well-founded design decision. It has to be defined whether the choice can be left to the energy operator to provide flexibility for both options. If all peers authenticate using X.509 certificates, and corresponding private keys, the creation, and distribution of these operational certificates needs to be defined from a process, and also a technical point of view. The standard IEC 62351-9 (targeting key management) provides guidance here, but the involved peers need to be identified, and their responsibility needs to be described for all use cases at a fine granularity to assure interoperability.

Further issues requiring research are the management of multicast membership: Which entity serves as the room creator that is aware of the group communication need for the current use case and determines, which XMPP client is allowed to participate in which MUC multicast room. How is the multicast key distribution being performed? It could be performed independently from the MUC, or alternatively using the MUC for distribution of the (encrypted) multicast key. The final solution will heavily depend on the underlying trust model, especially, if the XMPP server, including the MUC is operated by the DNO itself or a third party. This underlying trust model also builds the main point designing a solution to protect the information collected on the XMPP server itself. The information of published resources collected (and provided) at the XMPP server can be considered as essential asset, as it allows the potential control and information exchange with the connected energy resources, and can therefore be used to influence the connected energy grid in a sensitive way.

VI. Conclusions and Outlook

This paper proposes security measures for the integration of DER systems into Smart Energy Grid and Smart Market, utilizing and combining mostly existing, or security means currently defined by different standardization organizations. The focus in this paper was placed on securing the information exchange between a DER system and a DNO controlling the energy grid. This approach considered the utilization of a potentially untrusted or less trusted environment for the communication exchange. The process for the definition of a standardized security solution is currently ongoing within the IEC taking the proposed solution as base.

Open issues relating to authentication options of peers to the different service points (DNO, XMPP server operator) and also for leveraging multicast communication requiring further research have been identified, and possible directions for defining a suitable solution have been outlined. While open issues lie in the technical domain, they have dependencies also in the operational domain as security management operations have to be aligned with general operational use cases. The means to address have not been decided yet and need further research. A proof of concept implementation of the proposed technical security approach to protect unicast communication is currently ongoing.

As outlined, but not address in this paper, the protection of collected information at the XMPP server is a necessary prerequisite to ensure a reliable management of DER. This is especially important as the number of connected DER is increasing and thus, the amount of energy, which can be controlled over publish subscribe mechanisms will increase.

References

[1] S. Fries, R. Falk, H. Dawidczak, and T. Dufaure, "Secure Integration of DER into Smart Energy Grid and Smart Market," Proceedings IARIA SMART 2015, June 2015, ISBN: 978-1-61208-414-5, page 56-61, https://www.thinkmind.org/download.php?articleid=smart_2015_4_20_40020, [retrieved: January 2016]

[2] ISO 61850-x: Communication networks and systems for power utility automation, http://www.iec.ch/smartgrid/standards/ [retrieved: Jan. 2015]

[3] "Efficient Energy Automation with the IEC 61850 Standard Application Examples," Siemens AG, December 2010, http://www.energy.siemens.com/mx/pool/hq/energy-topics/standards/iec-61850/Application_examples_en.pdf [retrieved: Dec. 2014].

[4] ISO 9506: Industrial Automation Systems – Manufacturing Message Specification.

[5] IEC TR 61850-80-3: Mapping to Web Protocols – Requirement Analysis and Technology Assessment

[6] P. Saint-Andre, "Extensible Messaging and Presence Protocol (XMPP): Core," RFC 6120, https://tools.ietf.org/html/rfc6120 [retrieved: Jan. 2014].

[7] A. Gulbrandsen, P. Vixie, and L. Esibov, "A DNS RR for specifying the location of services (DNS SRV)," RFC 2782, http://tools.ietf.org/rfc/rfc2782.txt [retrieved: Jan. 2015].

[8] XMPP Protocol extensions: http://xmpp.org/xmpp-protocols/xmpp-extensions/ [retrieved: Jan. 2015].

[9] XMPP foundation: http://www.xmpp.org [retrieved: April. 2015]

[10] T. Dierks and E. Rescorla, "The Transport Layer Security (TLS) Protocol Version 1.2," RFC 5246, Aug. 2008, http://tools.ietf.org/html/rfc5246 [retrieved: Jan. 2015].

[11] A. Melenikov and K. Zeilenga, "Simple Authentication and Security Layer (SASL)," RFC 4422, http://tools.ietf.org/html/rfc4422 [retrieved: Jan. 2015].

[12] P. Saint-Andre, "End-to-End Signing and Object Encryption for the Extensible Messaging and Presence Protocol (XMPP)," RFC 3923, https://tools.ietf.org/html/rfc3923 [retrieved: Jan. 2015].

[13] M. Miller and C. Wallace, "End-to-End Object Encryption and Signatures for XMPP," expired IETF draft, https://datatracker.ietf.org/doc/draft-miller-xmpp-e2e/ [retrieved: Jan. 2016].

[14] D. Meyer and P. Saint-Andre, "XTLS: End-to-End Encryption for the Extensible Messaging and Presence Protocol (XMPP) Using Transport Layer Security (TLS)," expired IETF draft, https://www.ietf.org/archive/id/draft-meyer-xmpp-e2e-encryption-02.txt, [retrieved: Jan. 2016]

[15] IEC 62351-x Power systems management and associated information exchange – Data and communication security, http://www.iec.ch/smartgrid/standards/ [retrieved: Jan. 2015].

[16] B. Weiss, S. Rowles, and T. Hardjono, "The Group Domain of Interpretation," RFC 6407, Oct. 2011, http://tools.ietf.org/html/rfc6407 [retrieved: Jan. 2015].

[17] R.Falk and S. Fries, "Security Considerations for Multicast Communication in Power Systems," International Journal on advances in Security, 2013 vol 6 nr. 3&4, ISSN: 1942-2636, [retrieved: Jan. 2016]

[18] B. Weiss, M. Seewald, and H. Falk, "GDOI Protocol Support for IEC 62351 Security Services," IETF draft, June 2015, https://tools.ietf.org/id/draft-weis-gdoi-iec62351-9-06.txt, [retrieved Dec. 2015]

[19] OAuth - OAuth 2.0 authorization framework, http://oauth.net/ [retrieved Jan. 2015].

[20] Web Services Security SAML Token Profile Version 1.1.1, OASIS Standard, March 2012, http://docs.oasis-open.org/wss-m/wss/v1.1.1/os/wss-SAMLTokenProfile-v1.1.1-os.html, [retrieved Jan. 2016].

[21] M. Jones, J. Bradley, and N. Sakimura, " JSON Web Token (JWT)." IETF RFC 7519, May 2015, https://tools.ietf.org/html/rfc7519, [retrieved Jan. 2016].

Architecture Overview and Data Analysis Approach of the eTelematik ICT-System

Outline of System Requirements, Implementation Design, Field Test Results and Analysis approach

Steffen Späthe
Department of Computer Science
Friedrich Schiller University Jena
Jena, Germany
steffen.spaethe@uni-jena.de

Robert Büttner
Navimatix GmbH
Software Department
Jena, Germany
robert.buettner@navimatix.de

Wilhelm Rossak
Department of Computer Science
Friedrich Schiller University Jena
Jena, Germany
wilhelm.rossak@uni-jena.de

***Abstract*—Electrical vehicles are not only passenger cars but also commercial vehicles and, in particular, municipal vehicles. Their acceptance and usage depends primarily on everyday usability, aiming for a smart vehicle with intelligent energy and range supervision as well as driver support. In our funded research project eTelematik, we conceptualized, implemented and proved an Information and Communication Technology (ICT) System with directly connected vehicle components, driver interface and back end applications as well as an analytical evaluation process for our prediction model. In order to expand the usage of electric vehicles, we predict energy consumption of complex work task sets and guide vehicle drivers while driving.**

Keywords - Municipal vehicles; ICT-support for fully electric vehicles; range prediction; mobile client; in-car module; trajectory; Dynamic Time Warping.

I. INTRODUCTION

This paper is an extended version of a paper that was presented at the Forth International Conference on Smart Systems, Devices and Technology, SMART 2015 [1].

Worldwide electrical vehicles are seen as the future of mobility. The primary focus in this vision is mainly on private cars [2]. However, commercially used vehicles have a much better starting point for electrification. Based on prescheduled tasks and daily high usage work, the capability of commercial vehicles can be predicted. At the current state of development commercially used, fully electrical vehicles are not able to fulfill a full day's work without recharging. Therefore, hybrid vehicle concepts are developed and currently in advanced prototype state. A special class of commercial vehicles are municipal vehicles. These universal vehicles can be used with different setups and add-on structural parts in various scenarios.

In our research project eTelematik, we developed a system based on Information and Communication Technologies (ICT), which supports daily commercial usage of electrical municipal vehicles and allows for new usage scenarios with hybrid vehicles.

The project eTelematik was a federal funded research project during 2012 and 2014. The consortium included four main partners [3]:

1. EPSa GmbH: industry, electronics and communication devices
2. Navimatix GmbH: mobile and server applications
3. Friedrich Schiller University Jena: research, distributed software systems, range estimation
4. HAKO GmbH Werk Walterhausen: electrical municipal vehicles

The paper presented here, focuses on summarizing the project and its general accomplished results as well as giving a detailed overview of the analysis approach used for the evaluation of the produced data within the project.

The remainder of the paper is organized as follows: In Section II we will provide an overview of the project's overall ICT architecture including the main challenges of our distributed system. From there we will highlight the usage of collected data inside the vehicle and on back end systems. In Section III the analysis process for the evaluation of work task sets will be described and in Section IV some information and findings of the project's long-term field test will be presented. We close with a short review of goal reaching in Section V.

II. THE ETELEMATIK PROJECT

The main focus of the project was the creation of a complete ICT infrastructure to enable an improved usage of electrical municipal vehicles.

Our main requirements for this system were

a) to gather data from mobile electrical vehicles and store them in a central universal database,
b) to interpret gathered data in order to evaluate the influence of various parameters on energy consumption during the fulfillment of certain work tasks with required work equipment,
c) to adjust the internal energy consumption and range prediction model with computed factors of influence and
d) to support the driver with information about estimated and real energy consumption of current and scheduled work tasks, irrespective of the status of the connection to the central server.

Excluded from the project focus was the development of a new work force management or fleet management/ optimization system. Thus, all required business data had to be provided from an external fleet management system via designated service interfaces.

Based on these requirements, we developed our system as schematically shown in Figure 1.

Fig. 1. eTelematik system architecture overview (adapted figure, based on original by Johannes Kretzschmar, University Jena)

The eTelematik solution consists of a communication hardware ("in-car module"), a mobile application ("mobile client") and a central server ("central instance") with a prediction model ("flexProgno").

Externally computed work task sets are evaluated in regard to their practicability in our central instance *eTelematik Server*. We use our energy consumption and range prediction model *flexProgno* to estimate the power consumption for every single part of the given work task set. While power consumption depends on various parameters like vehicle model, payload, environmental temperature (as already shown in [4]), we need to know more about the work task, required add-on structural parts and settings of them. Moreover, we require knowledge about the concrete routing and their elevation profile between different work task places. We use the commercial available route calculation service and map height services of project partner Navimatix GmbH to gather this data.

If a working set is estimated as achievable, the assigned driver gets this set shown on his mobile client.

Inside the vehicle the communication hardware, developed by EPSa GmbH, collects vehicle specific data in real-time, aggregates and sends them to the mobile client. Communication between the communication hardware and the vehicle is realized by Controller Area Network (CAN) connections. The mobile client, developed by Navimatix GmbH, is an Android application running on established consumer devices. The mobile client informs the driver about the actual operating status of the vehicle, the current status prediction based on the assigned working task set and the probability of fulfillment of this set. All collected vehicle data combined with sensor data from the mobile phone are transferred to and stored at the central instance.

Figure 2 shows the internal conceptual system design of the mobile client application. The mobile client is subdivided into a user interface related part and some background services. While the data storing modules are responsible for realizing business logic, which is used by the UI module, the ICM Communicator Service takes care of establishing a connection to the in-car module and keeping it alive. We use plain TCP socket connections at this communication channel to minimize transport size and delay overhead. The eTele App Communicator Service realizes the reliable communication to the central instance. All other services, background as well as UI-related, use this service to communicate to and receive data from the central instance. At this channel, we use HTTP as transport layer. Since our JBoss Application Server based central instance is realized by using Java Servlets and Enterprise Java Beans, HTTP is a natural choice. As payload, we used data objects with an own implemented key-value based object serialization which represents our business data.

In summary, our system has to handle the following data from central instance to vehicle:

- master data of vehicles and drivers
- general and vehicle specific configuration setting for communication between in-car module and mobile client
- current work task sets depending on logged in driver

From vehicles to central instance we send:

- updates of work task status
- vehicle's positions and velocity
- electrical vehicle specific measurements

The electrical vehicle specific measurements and especially their representation on in-car communication buses vary between vehicle manufacturers and even between vehicle types of one manufacturer. Within our project consortium, we are able to gather and transfer the following electrical vehicle specific measurements:

- state of charge
- primary battery voltage
- current in high voltage circuit
- connection state, settings and power of battery recharger
- state and settings of range extender (if applicable)

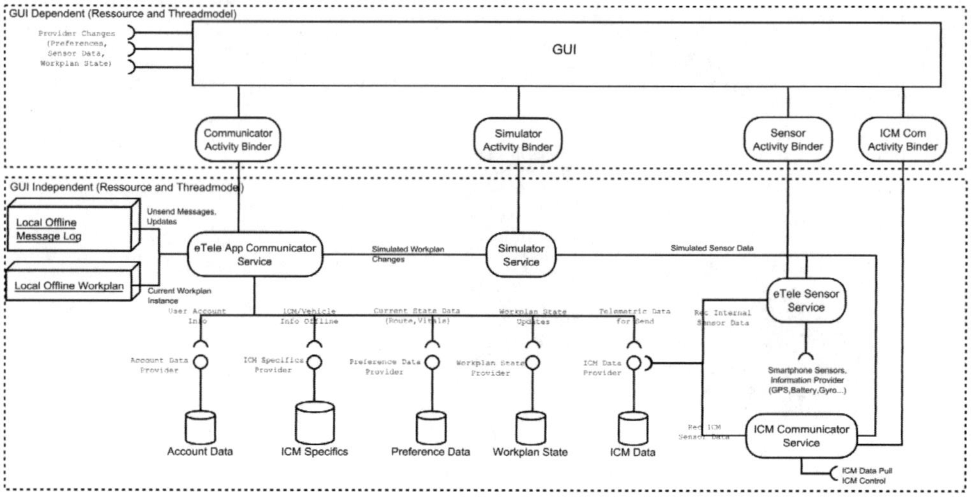

Fig. 2. eTelematik mobile clients internal module overview

This data is used in different situations. The data supports the driver inside the vehicle in driving between work task places of action and while task fulfillment. On server side, we use recorded data in different analyses. Some are shown in Section III of this paper.

Inside the vehicle, we are able to realize "enhanced foresighted driving". Since we know, based on the scheduled work task sets, which route has to be driven and what kind of working task has to be accomplished, we are able to predict if this planning is still valid. Usually, only average statistics about energy consumption per kilometer are available to the vehicle and the driver. We know the exact route to drive as well as the required settings of add-on components. Thus, we are able to predict the required energy consumption on a much more detailed basis. This advanced, detailed knowledge allows us to warn the driver that he will not reach his destination, even if the average statistics would tell him so. Alternatively, we can relax him in situations where average statistics would show a much too low range, for example, when the planned route has many downhill sections. Furthermore, we can delay the usage of the range extender in hybrid cars when it would be triggered by the vehicle's management system, because we know when the user's preferred charging stations are in reach.

By doing so, we are able to optimize the battery usage and extend the usability of electrical vehicles.

In vehicles with range extender, we can optimize the point in time for recharging. In certain situations, work tasks have to be fulfilled without any avoidable emission, e.g., noise or exhaust. If recharging is only controlled by battery state of charge, it could happen that the driving to the workplace is realized fully out of battery and that the recharging has to be started at the workplace. With our knowledge about the complete work task set and desired or required restrictions in work task fulfillment, we can foresee and avoid such situations.

On server side, we use recorded data of the vehicle in different scenarios.

A long-term use case, which is very important to vehicle manufactures as well as to the vehicle owner, is predictive maintenance. With data mining techniques, we are able to detect deviations in characteristic gradients long before the vehicle breaks down. This is of particular interest to our project partners due to the lack of long-term experience with the completely new designed power train and the used battery system.

In addition, for the first time, this process enables insight into exhaustive detailed real world usage records of these vehicles. This information is very helpful to vehicle manufactures for further improvements and new developments.

A short-term use case is monitoring the overall resource consumption for certain work tasks. It is not possible to date the direct assignment of fuel consumption to single work tasks. Since we record work task state changes as well as energy consumption parameters continuously, we are able to match them.

Inside our project's system, we also process recorded data for intrasystem usage. The main task is to adjust and improve our energy consumption and range prediction model flexProgno. Our model is based on assumptions, e.g., required energy stays equal if all influencing parameters do not change or stay very close to situations before. Initially, we did not have many vehicle specific data. By processing recorded data, the vehicle specific parameter set gets more accurate over time. The basic approach of our model is shown in [5].

Energy consumption does not only depend on vehicle or work task parameters, but also on driver characteristics. Hence, it is important to include the driver's start and stop behavior in energy consumption prediction. Since these parameters cannot be measured beforehand, they need to be determined from the recorded data.

III. Location-based analysis for work task sets

A working task set is defined as a round trip with several work task places.

Figure 3 shows an abstract work task set. A driver starts the trip at a central point ("start"), driving over to his work task places, e.g., A, B and C, where the driver will then fulfill the work tasks. After finishing all tasks in the given order, the driver will then drive back to the central point ("end"), which is not necessarily the same as the starting point.

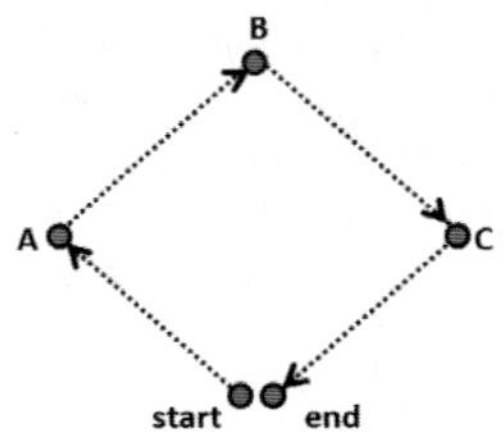

Fig. 3. Work task set definition as round trip with work task places A, B and C

To verify our assumptions about a certain work task set with its predicted routes between task places, it is worth to compare recorded data with the predicted data or even with other recorded data of the same task set. Furthermore, the comparison of different trip records of the same route at specific spatial scenarios, e.g., uphill, downhill, highway or city traffic, can help us to understand the behavior of drivers and vehicles. Hence, enables us to evaluate and adjust our prediction model.

While doing so, the data can be examined from different perspectives and all of them may raise different questions. For example:

A) *Geographically*, i.e., "Is the driven route equal to the predicted route?"
B) *Energy consumption*, i.e., "Is the predicted consumption close to the real consumption?" or "Which driver was saving most energy on the same route as others and why?"
C) *Trip time*, i.e., "Is the predicted estimated trip time close to real trip times?"

For the analysis, we use the recorded trajectory data of each municipal electric vehicles using our system architecture. As above mentioned, we want to analyze them at specific location-based scenarios. Thus, we always need to specify a spatial reference track which defines the road segment that is going to be analyzed. Both, trajectory and reference track, are defined as follows in definitions 1 and 2:

Definition 1. *A trajectory* $T = \{p_1, p_2, \ldots, p_N\}$ *is a finite sequence of points. Each point* $p_i = \{ts, pos, o\}$ *consists of a timestamp (ts) and a geo-position* $pos = \{lon, lat, alt\}$ *with longitude (lon), latitude (lat) and altitude (alt). An optional set of attributes (o) with additional measurements for each spatio-temporal point can be defined. All points are in temporal order* $p_1.ts < p_2.ts < \ldots < p_N.ts$.

Definition 2. *A reference track* $rT = \{p_1, p_2, \ldots, p_N\}$ *is a finite ordered sequence of points. Each point* $p_i = \{pos\}$ *consists of a geo-position* $pos = \{lon, lat, alt\}$ *with longitude (lon), latitude (lat) and altitude (alt).*

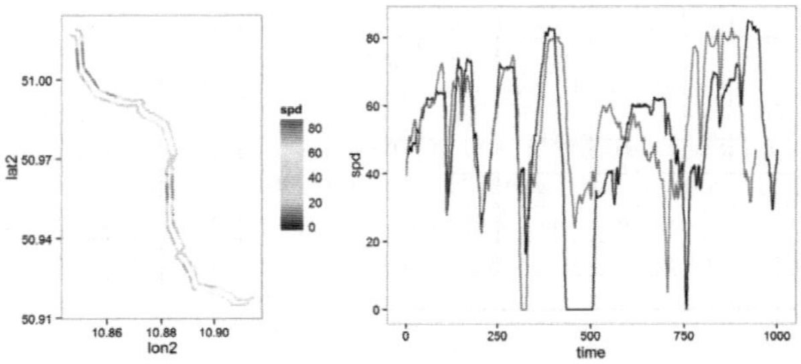

Fig. 4. Two similar recorded tracks, side by side, with colored speed (left); speed vs. time graph of the same two tracks (right)

However, the representation form of a temporal trajectory is very unsuitable for a comparison on a local basis. In fact, looking at the left graph of Figure 4, the human brain might be able to perform such a comparison given the appropriate visual representation. Unfortunately, a computer using algorithms cannot do that, due to temporal shifts or distortion and the consequential difference in length, as shown in the right graph of Figure 4. Thus, it is necessary to synchronize the data at a geographical-spatial basis to be also able to analyze it automatically through algorithms.

The synchronization is realized using the *Dynamic Time Warping* (DTW) Algorithm. The DTW Algorithm is well known in the area of time series alignment and clustering. One of its first applications was speech recognition back in the 70s and since then it is also used in handwriting and gestures recognition, to only name a few [6], [7]. To overcome the limitations of shifts in time series, it generates a warping path which represents an optimal alignment between the two, not necessarily equally long, time series, as shown in Figure 5.

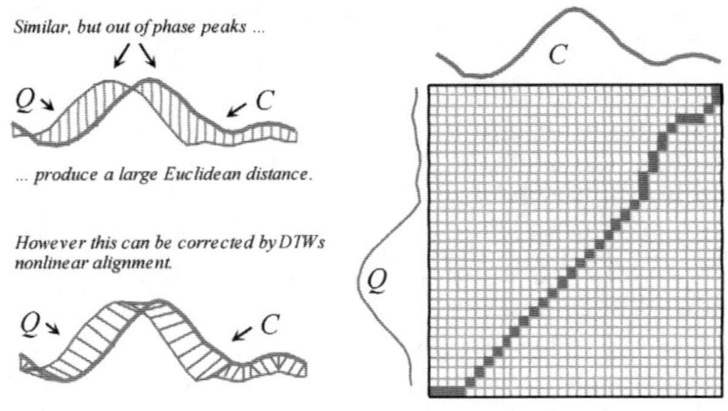

Fig. 5. Point correspondence when two similar time series contain local time shifting using Euclidean distance (upper left); using DTW (lower left); Search for an optimal alignment or warping path (red squares) within the distance matrix between the same two time series (right) Image source: [8]

A. Methodology

Our analysis process can be divided into the three subprocesses *(i)* Data preparation, *(ii)* Identification of analyzable segments and *(iii)* Spatial synchronization:

(i) Data preparation: Before it is possible to perform a data analysis, the data needs to be structured in a way that consistent processing can be guaranteed.

As already mentioned in Section II, the electrical vehicle specific measurements and their representation can vary between vehicle types, but also the time intervals in which the various measurements are collected within the vehicle can differ. Taken all that into account, it is necessary to convert the data into an homogeneous data scheme. To overcome the measure interval differences, the data will be embedded into a fixed time interval, e.g., every n seconds. Emerging temporal gaps will eventually be filled using a linear interpolation.

Due to the possible occurrence of errors during data collection, it is also necessary to perform a data cleansing. Especially when using GPS, it is not uncommon to receive erroneous or inaccurate GPS positions. In order to correct these position data, we use a map-matching algorithm which brings off-track positions back to their corresponding road element using the map service of project partner Navimatix GmbH.

After homogenization and data cleansing, we also perform a data enrichment to combine our vehicle specific measurements with more general information, e.g., traffic, temperature and weather or even more accurate altitude information, to improve our data even more.

The result of this subprocess is an homogenized, revised trajectory dataset $QT = \{T_1, T_2, \ldots, T_N\}$, which now can be used as a basis for the analyzing process.

(ii) Identification of analyzable segments: Given a preselected reference track rT, which could contain interesting sections for an analysis task, we need to determine all common sub-trajectories between rT and the dataset QT in order to find all track segments $RT' = rT \cap QT$ that can possibly be covered by the dataset. Those segments need to be clustered into distinct groups and will be afterwards presented to an expert who will finally choose one segment, which will serve as the selected reference track $rT' \in RT'$ for the further detailed analysis process.

(iii) Spatial synchronization: Since a reference track rT' has been selected by the expert, the spatial synchronization to enable the location-based analysis can be performed.

To do that, we need to find all common sub-trajectories $CS = rT' \cap QT$ that cover the selected reference track entirely. Afterwards, the spatial synchronization takes place between rT' and every common sub-trajectory $cs \in CS$ and results in synchronized common sub-trajectories cs_{sync} with the same length as the selected reference track. This implies that, with the definition of the preselected reference track rT, it is possible to control the level of detail of the synchronization outcome, i.e., sample points and distance between them.

The trajectories cs_{sync} are now equally long and it is guaranteed that the i-th element of each trajectory refers to the same spatial position. Hence, can be compared with each other using algorithms.

B. Algorithms

To reflect the spatial synchronization process two key-algorithms have to be implemented: *(i)* Determining common sub-trajectories and *(ii)* Spatial synchronization of common sub-trajectories.

(i) Determining common sub-trajectories: This algorithm determines common subsegments between two location-based data series, in our case reference track and trajectory, where local distances of corresponding points are within a tolerated distance r. The DTW algorithm is used to determine the corresponding points. For this, a pair-wise local distance matrix $D(rT, T) \in \mathbb{R}^{M \times N}$ is built between all positions of the reference track rT with M elements and the trajectory T with N elements. The distance between two positions will be calculated using great-circle distance calculation, i.e., a low-costed matrix, with a minimum of zero, will represent more geographic similarity than a high-costed matrix.

Based on matrix D the DTW algorithm calculates an alignment path, i.e., warping path, which runs through the low cost areas of the local distance matrix. It represents a complete assignment of all indices between both data series, starting with the first and ending with the last indices of both, to guarantee that every index is used at least once. The indices-pairs of the warping path are by default in a monotonically increasing order with a maximum step-size of 1.

Afterwards, the local distances of the warping path will be analyzed. Here, all index-pairs with a lesser local distance than the predefined tolerance radius r will be determined. These pairs are describing geographical common points CP between rT and T. Multiple consecutive common points can form a common sub-trajectory. To avoid large gaps between consecutive points, it is necessary to define a tolerance distance. The gap distance g represents the maximum distance two subsequent common points can be apart from each other to be recognized as "real consecutive" and, hence, forming a common sub-trajectory cs.

Figure 6 shows the local distances of the warping path's index-pairs. The straight colored line at the bottom side represents the tolerance radius for determining common points. Furthermore, aside from a common sub-trajectory, a gap between common points as well as a case of a possible crossing between the two trajectories is highlighted.

(ii) Spatial synchronization of common sub-trajectories: To make the local points of a common sub-trajectories $CS = \{cs_1, cs_2, \ldots, cs_N\}$ locally comparable with each other, the length of both data series needs to be equalized. Therefore, the points of the reference track will serve as spatial reference points. Each data series needs to be realigned to match the length of the reference track in order to return data for each

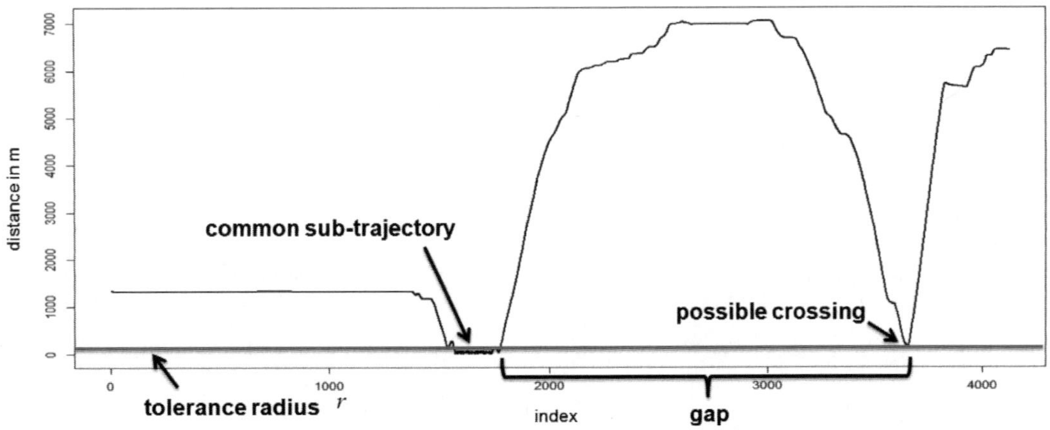

Fig. 6. Interpretation of the warping path's local distances in order to determine common sub-trajectories

spatial reference point. The alignment to realize this is already given by the warping path. However, before it can be used, multiple assignments of indices within the warping path need to be handled. They occur to compensate differences in length between the time series. The following cases of assignments are possible and need the given action:

- **normal case:** Exactly one index of cs is assigned to exactly one index of rT. Nothing needs to be done.
- **reduction case:** Multiple indices of cs are assigned to exactly one index of rT. Here, the multiple assigned points of cs need to be aggregated into one point, as shown in Figure 7.
- **extension case:** Exactly one index of cs is assigned to multiple indices of rT. This case needs to be handled very carefully to preserve the reference point count. Hence, an aggregation cannot be done. Instead the point of cs needs to be duplicated until every point of rT finds exactly one match, as also shown in Figure 7.

The result of the synchronization is a trajectory cs_{sync} which is exactly as long as the reference track rT' and can now be locally compared, i.e., by location, to other trajectories cs_{sync} synchronized on the same reference track.

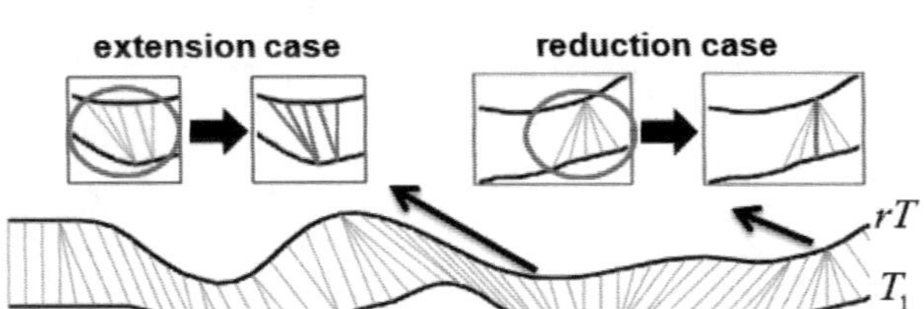

Fig. 7. Approaches of solving different multiple assignments problems within the warping path using duplication and aggregation (in this case mean calculation).

IV. The Project's Field Test

As we developed our system from scratch, we designed a long running field test. In this section, the test will be reviewed from two different perspectives. The technical perspective reviews the overall functionality of the system and whether all components are working well together. The analytical perspective is concerned with the resulting data produced by the system and the analytical potential of them.

A. Technical perspective

We built up a complete system installation to validate the system's long term stability, data transfer reliability especially in areas with unreliable mobile network connection and to validate and harden our prediction model.

In our build up test, we installed our system components in five electrical vehicles. These vehicles were used on a regular daily basis. In terms of the test, the following findings are worth mentioning:

A) Our system setup is running very stable over all components. During the development, there were some doubts about wireless local area network (WLAN) communication between in-car module and mobile client. However, we did not register any significant disturbance in this communication channel. All relevant data provided by the electrical vehicles in the field test were recorded by the in-car module and were transferred properly to the mobile client.

B) We succeeded in establishing a robust communication between mobile client and central instance. Even in our test region where mobile network coverage is very patchy, we had no data loss.

C) Synchronization of master data as well as measurement data between mobile client and central instance is working very solid, even if network connection gets lost while transfer. Thus, the required offline capability of the mobile client is achieved.

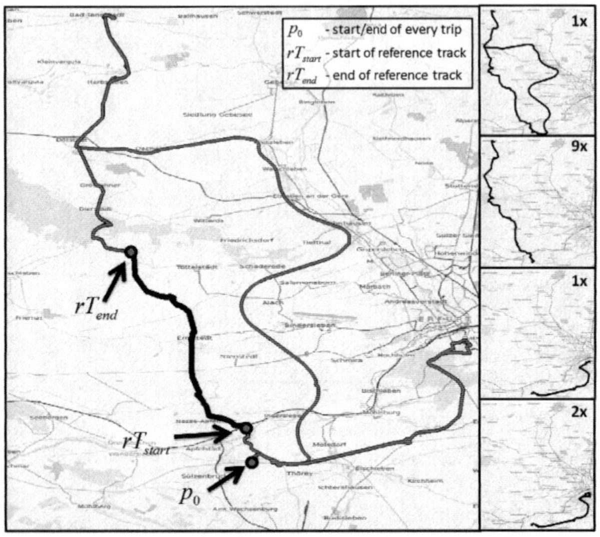

Fig. 8. Recorded subset of the road network with highlighted reference track and start/end point of every trip (left); trip types and their occurrences (right)

TABLE I. A part of the synchronized speed data of Figure 9

rT index	rT lon	rT lat	track1.spd	track2.spd
1000	10.88224	50.94711	37.0	17.3
1001	10.88224	50.94716	28.3	14.8
1002	10.88224	50.94720	28.3	14.8
1003	10.88224	50.94724	28.3	13.3
1004	10.88223	50.94729	20.5	8.9
1005	10.88223	50.94733	20.5	6.3

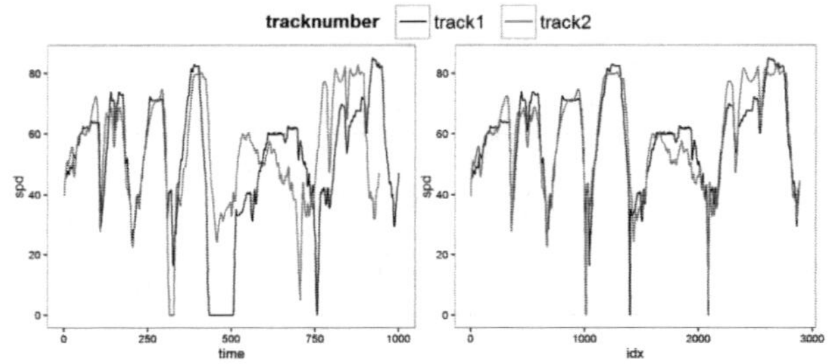

Fig. 9. Speed profile of two different trips on the same road segment in asynchronous representation (left); synchronized (right)

B. Analytical perspective

During the field test, the electrical vehicle specific measurements, mentioned in Section II, as well as GPS positions are collected and stored for each trip together with their corresponding timestamps per measurement, and hence forming trajectories. We are using the programming language R for our location-based analysis process to evaluate the consistence of the recorded data and our assumption about working task sets and the behavior of electrical vehicles in general.

For demonstration purposes, we examine an isolated and complete subset of the whole road network produced during the field test. Figure 8 shows the subset which was recorded in the area of Erfurt, Germany. It consists of 13 single trips which were all driven by the same car at different days. Each trip starts and ends at the same position p_0. The distinct tracks with the number of times they were used for the trips within the recorded data are listed at the right side of the figure. For the analysis, we choose the reference track highlighted in black and defined by the starting point rT_{start} and ending point rT_{end}.

During data preparation the recorded trip data is converted into a common data scheme and our map matching algorithm corrects positions that are off the road, which is crucial for the detection of common sub-trajectories. Additionally, the data is enriched with altitude data in order to complete the 3D position tuple and is now prepared for further analysis.

During the determining of common sub-trajectories between the reference track rT and the recorded trip data QT, ten common segments were found. All ten segments are fully covering the reference track. As Figure 8 indicates, this is expected, since this is equal to the number of trips sharing visually the same route as the reference track.

On these ten common segments, the spatial synchronization process is performed. To visualize the results of the process, Figure 9 is showing the speed profile of two of the ten common segments in an asynchronous state before and in a spatial synchronized state after the process. It is worth pointing out that the x-axis, which was representing time beforehand, has changed into the spatial dimension (namely "idx" for index) after the synchronization. The index scale is directly linked to the numbered elements of the reference track and their positions. A part of the data of Figure 9 together with the corresponding position data from the reference track is shown in Table I and proofs that the data can now be compared in a local dimension.

The representation in the local dimension opens up for new analysis perspectives. In order to see how different attributes depend on each other, we can now for example, analyze them not only over the course of one trip but across multiple trips with an identical route.

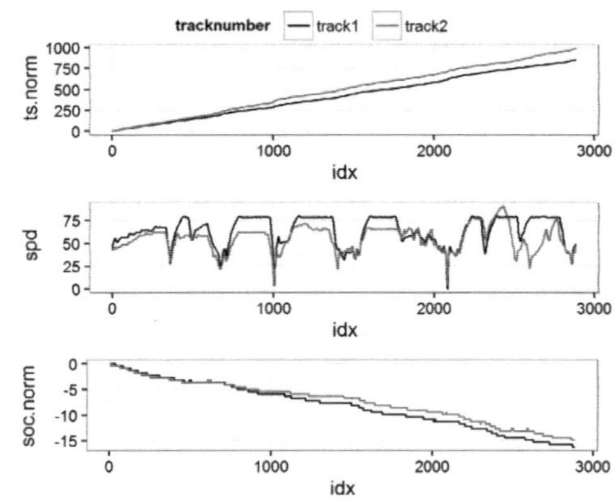

Fig. 10. Analysis of multiple attributes over two or more common segments

Figure 10 shows a possible visualization of such an analysis. Here, the three attributes *ts.norm* (trip duration), *spd* (speed) and *soc.norm* (state of charge loss) are presented. Note that, even though we left the time dimension due to the spatial synchronization, time data can still be restored as an analyzable attribute by storing the difference in time between two local positions as an attribute. The trip duration graph shows the duration of each trip in seconds. The state of charge graph allows us to identify the energy consumption on each trip. The speed graph shows the speed used at each position. It is noticeable that the difference in speed used during the different trip is responsible for the different trip durations that emerged. However, it could also be responsible for the difference in energy consumption, given our assumption that the speed, or better, the acceleration process has a significant impact on the energy consumption. Other attributes such as weather or altitude data could also show dependencies and could easily be added to the set of analyzable attributes for even more insight.

The synchronized data can also be aggregated on a local level. This can be used to create an energy consumption profile for a route with a mean energy consumption difference between positions of all trips. This could then be used to evaluate our predicted energy consumption model for a given route. Figure 11 shows the energy consumption profile for the reference track produced during the field test visualized by putting it on a map with a color indication for the mean energy consumption.

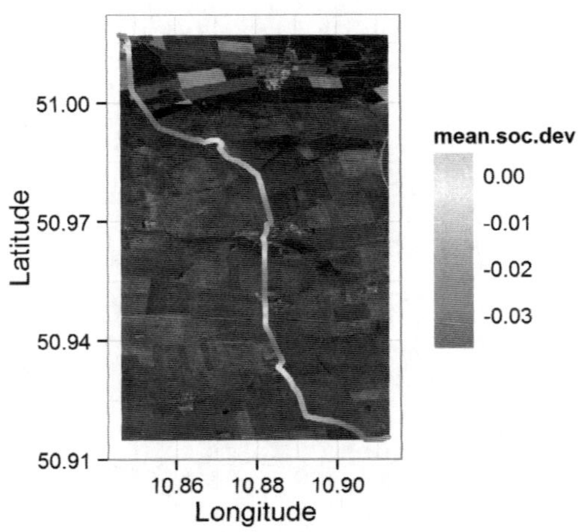

Fig. 11. Map of the reference track with mean energy consumption difference of all trip data of the route as color indication

During the analysis of the field test data, we noticed that the attribute *state of charge* is not satisfying our needs for range prediction evaluation purposes. The state of charge represents a percentage of the energy capacity in a battery. However, this maximum capacity can decrease due to extreme temperature or bad health state. The state of charge is calculated in relation to the current capacity. Without the current capacity measured in our system, it is needless to say that the state of charge cannot give us any information about the actual energy that is drained from the battery. This information is crucial for the comparison with our prediction model. Hence, in the future, instead of measuring the energy consumption as a relative value, we need to measure real energy values in kilowatt.

V. Summary and Future Work

Based on the evaluation of our long-term field test, we can state that we achieved our primary goals.

From a technical point of view, the overall data recording is satisfying, data transfer reliability is sufficient and offline capability for mobile client is achieved.

Therefore, we can determine that our selected system design and implementation are adequate to meet our overall requirements. However, we have to reassess our selection of mobile phone as primary communication channel. We deployed mass market mobile phones in the field test. So far we did not have substantial failures. Nevertheless, based on other tests we expect thermal problems in very cold and warm to hot situations. These problems will become more serious when running more applications and parallel tasks on the mobile phone's hardware.

Accordingly, the partitioning between in-car module and mobile client has to be reviewed very carefully. An alternative approach could be to transfer all permanent running processes of data collection and aggregation to the fixed-powered in-car module. This could as well include data transfer from and to the central instance. This process should be realized in a proxy-like way to keep this functionality transparent to the mobile client. The main function of the mobile phone still has to be the communication to the driver of the vehicle. This includes the exchange of information about working sets, as well as electrical vehicle state of charge, and driving instructions, to reach optimal range and energy usage.

A disadvantage within this alternative approach is the limited updatability and extensibility of the in-car module. The software for the in-car module has to be written system-specific and very closely fitted to the underlying hardware. Due to the rapid development of embedded Linux systems and their possibilities, we see now the option to overcome the above mentioned drawback by implementing our software on a Linux-based embedded system together with a scripting language to build a generic base system that is easily adaptable for the use on a specific underlying hardware.

From the analytical point of view, a process was introduced to synchronize spatial time series on a spatial-geographical basis. Although this process has to be tested thoroughly in the future, the evaluation of the field test shows that the overall functionality is working. Its provided functionality is helpful, as it allows us to evaluate our whole prediction model and the recorded data produced by our system, which would otherwise not be possible.

Thanks to the field test data evaluation, it is revealed that there is a lack of significance in some of our data attributes (namely state of charge), which provoked us to reconsider the electrical vehicle specific measurements that we are recording in general. However, at the time the field test took place, no other data was available for our system to measure. This has changed as the project proceeded and to date a lot more measurements can and will be recorded with our system. Hence, we can easily measure the required data, e.g., real energy consumption in kilowatt.

Until now, the analysis process has to be initiated manually on a specified reference track. In the future, the process could also be automatized to directly adjust our prediction model if multiple trips are showing a pattern of high deviations.

Still many questions and tasks are left open. Our work will be continued, partly in cooperation with the federal funded project called "Smart City Logistik Erfurt" (SCL) [9].

In SCL, we address aspects of inner city freight logistic processes with full electric vehicles. The logistic partners of SCL intend to deploy available medium sized electrical vehicles into their business as freight transporters for the last mile, from the city's perimeter to the final destination. The project's focus is on ICT support to optimize vehicle's utilization and integration in existing fleets and processes.

Therefore, we have to adapt our in-car module to the selected vehicle models. The driver assistance mobile application needs adjustments to meet the specific needs in delivery logistic applications. Our range prediction has to be adjusted to the new domain as we have differing influence factors like weight or specific vehicles accessories. In SCL, we will not only validate existing working sets. Implementation of route calculation and tour optimization with electrical vehicle's additional restrictions will be an important task. Overall, we have to improve usability and user experience in our driver assistance application as well as in the back-end system's user interface, which was not the focus of eTelematik, but is undoubtedly important to bring our research and development into real world applications.

VI. Acknowledgment

We would like to thank all members and partners of eTelematik research project, especially S. Gebhardt from HAKO GmbH for long lessons on battery chemistry and vehicle driving dynamics.

VII. Funding sources

This project was funded by the Federal Ministry for Economic Affairs and Energy (KF3012602).

References

[1] S. Späthe and W. Rossak, "etelematik: Ict-system for optimial usage of municipal electric vehicles," in *SMART 2015, The Fourth International Conference on Smart Systems, Devices and Technologies*, pp. 80–83.

[2] S. Lukic and Z. Pantic, "Cutting the cord: Static and dynamic inductive wireless charging of electric vehicles," *Electrification Magazine, IEEE*, vol. 1, no. 1, pp. 57–64, Sept 2013.

[3] etelematik project website. [Online]. Available: http://www.etelematik.de/ [Accessed Jun. 6, 2016].

[4] V. Schau *et al.*, "Smartcitylogistik (scl) erfurt: Deriving the main factors that influence vehicle range during short-distance freight transport when using fully electric vehicles," in *LBAS Conference on Location Based Applications and Services*, pp. 101–108.

[5] J. Kretzschmar, F. Geyer, S. Späthe, and W. Rossak, "etelematik: Prognose und ausfhrungsberwachung elektrifizierter kommunaler nutzfahrzeuge," in *LBAS Conference on Location Based Applications and Services*, pp. 119–125.

[6] P. Senin, "Dynamic time warping algorithm review," [Online]. Available: http://seninp.github.io/assets/pubs/senin_dtw_litreview_2008.pdf [Accessed Jun. 6, 2016].

[7] E. J. Keogh and M. J. Pazzani, "Derivative dynamic time warping," in *First SIAM International Conference on Data Mining (SDM)*, 2001.

[8] T. Rakthanmanon, B. Campana, A. Mueen, G. Batista, B. Westover, Q. Zhu, J. Zakaria, and E. Keogh, "Searching and mining trillions of time series subsequences under dynamic time warping," in *Proceedings of the 18th ACM SIGKDD International Conference on Knowledge Discovery and Data Mining*, ser. KDD '12. New York, NY, USA: ACM, 2012, pp. 262–270, [Online]. Available: http://doi.acm.org/10.1145/2339530.2339576 [Accessed Jun. 6, 2016].

[9] Smart city logistik project website. [Online]. Available: http://www.smartcitylogistik.de/ [Accessed Jun. 6, 2016].

International Journal on Advances in Intelligent Systems, vol 9 no 1 & 2, year 2016, http://www.iariajournals.org/intelligent_systems/

Smart Spaces Based Construction and Personalization of Recommendation Services for Historical e-Tourism

Oksana B. Petrina

Faculty of Mathematics and Information Technology
Petrozavodsk State University
Petrozavodsk, Russia
Email: petrina@cs.karelia.ru

Aleksey G. Varfolomeyev

Faculty of Mathematics and Information Technology
Petrozavodsk State University
Petrozavodsk, Russia
Email: avarf@petrsu.ru

Dmitry G. Korzun

Department of Computer Science
Petrozavodsk State University
Petrozavodsk, Russia
Email: dkorzun@cs.karelia.ru

Aleksandrs Ivanovs

Department of History
Daugavpils University
Daugavpils, Latvia
Research Institute for Regional Studies (REGI)
Rezekne University
Rezekne, Latvia
Email: aleksandrs.ivanovs@du.lv

Abstract—**The smart spaces approach enables development of advanced digital services referred now as "smart services". In this paper, we discuss the development problem of smart services for the domain of historical e-Tourism. We show the applicability of recommender systems for constructing and personalizing such services within a smart space. The latter is created to accompany a tourist or a group of them. A corpus of historical data distributed among multiple sources in the Internet is collected the tourist's smart space, forming a kind of custom and dynamic historical knowledge. In particular, context-aware semantic relations between historical objects are established and manipulated. This semantics-rich information is an input for recommendation-making. Personalized recommendations with quantitative and qualitative estimates can be constructed. The result then is visualized to assist a historian tourist in historical analysis of points of interests. The contribution consists of the concept definition and system design for creating a smart space with assistance services of personalized recommendations.**

Keywords–Historical e-Tourism; Cultural Heritage; Point of Interest; Recommender Systems; Semantic Network; Smart Spaces; Personalized Services.

I. Introduction

This work extends the results presented in our UBICOMM 2015 paper [1] on the role and smart spaces based design of e-Tourism recommender systems. A lot of research has been already done, especially in the direction of making the services of e-Tourism systems mobile and intelligent [2], [3]. A topical subdomain is historical tourism [4], which we distinguish from more general cultural heritage tourism. In particular, the historical tourism focuses on visiting historical Points of Interest (POI) and on studying their history-aware relation with other historical objects (POIs, events, persons, etc.).

For a historian tourist, a POI is recommended not only if it is nearby and within user's interests. Such a tourist would like to see a spectrum of historically related POIs; some are closely located and some can be faraway. Clustering important POIs for recommendation needs semantic analysis of their relation with historical objects and can be performed by means of ontologies [5]. The content for reasoning about, however, must be extracted from some historical databases or digital archives. Moreover, some historical relations are subjective, e.g., depend on context or personal vision of historical facts.

The study presented in this paper is motivated by the lack of "smart" assistants for historian tourists, although there is a lot of them for mobile e-Tourism in general [2]. Based on our previous work [1], [6]–[9], we expect that development of recommendation services with built-in semantic analysis of historical data can be implemented using ontology-based technologies of the Semantic Web. Furthermore, traditional web-based architectures and mobile standalone applications seem insufficient for this development. We focus on the emerging approach of smart spaces [10], [11]. A ubiquitous computing environment is created where mobile users, multisource data, and various services constructed over these data are intelligently connected based on ontology-driven information sharing and self-generation. Services can be personalized by means of augmentation of personal data to the shared content and customization of required reasoning about the content.

In this paper, we analyze the historical POIs recommendation problem. Our research scope is limited to such important phases of service development as concept definition and system design. To define the concept we provide a reference scenario of recommendation services for historical e-Tourism. Additionally, we explain the concept by a detailed example. The proposed system design consists of a smart space based architecture and operation description for participating software agents. The proposed design supports multiple data sources and adopts various ranking methods. This contribution enables creation of a personalized smart space with services assisting its historian tourists by means of recommendations. We also perform experimental performance evaluation for iterative acquisition of historical knowledge from available data sources in the Internet.

The rest of the paper is organized as follows. Section II discusses the related work motivating our study of POI recommendation services in historical tourism. Section III introduces our reference service scenario for historical e-Tourism. Section IV illustrates by a detailed example the semantic network construction and its use for POI ranking. Section V describes the smart space based system design. Section VI provides details of the software agents that cooperatively construct the recommendation service in the smart space. Section VII analyses the proposed concept definition and system design using experiments and contrasting with the existing solutions. Section VIII concludes the paper.

II. Motivation and Related Work

Historical tourism has distinctive features [4] compared with the general application domain of cultural heritage tourism. The latter embraces both historical and present-day cultural phenomena. According to Nora [12], historical tourism addresses the so-called "sites of memory". They present any material traces of historical events, which sometimes coincide with cultural heritage artifacts. For instance, an architectural monument is directly "involved" in historical developments related to its construction. Another example is any place or a spot associated with a historical event. Traces of historical facts are presented in the multitude of historical sources, including open sources in the Internet.

In general, a point of interest (or attraction) is an actual spot with precise localization on the geographical map (e.g., geo-position coordinates or postal address). Nowadays, POI recommender systems form an important services class in e-Tourism [2]. In addition to POIs, historical tourism takes into consideration a lot of other historical-valued objects such as persons, events, and data sources (written records and narratives, artifacts, alternative information sources, data and knowledge bases available on the Web, etc.). Relations between historical objects define important semantics [13]. Moreover, any historical event might be conditionally defined as a semantic relation between several historical objects [14]. Ontologies become of high application interest for knowledge representation and reasoning in historical research [5] and e-Tourism [3].

In historical tourism, we expect that semantic relations can be effectively represented and manipulated using the technologies of the Semantic Web. To the best of our knowledge, no specialized knowledge base that comprise semantically enriched information about historical objects has been created yet, e.g., see [15]. To a certain extent, a corpus of historical information is represented in the ontological form in such knowledge bases for cultural heritage as DBpedia, Freebase, or YAGO. Additional information can be extracted from web publications of historical sources [6], [16]. In these settings, the methods of web-based systems, mobile programming, and multi-agent systems provide effective means for implementation of data search, access, and reasoning [2], [3].

Semantic Web methods and technologies help to solve the problems of creation, design, enrichment, editing, retrieval, analysis and presentation of historical information [15]. There are mobile services for cultural heritage e-Tourism developed using semantic technologies, e.g., see the review in [17]. For instance, an intelligent tourist guide [18] utilizes cultural heritage information. Nevertheless, the present-day application developments do not take into account the principal peculiarity of historical tourism—semantic relations among historical data. The problem of the semantic-aware retrieval information from multiple data sources can be settled by using semantic technologies, e.g., by parsing the query and ranking the relevance of content [19]. However, effective POI ranking requires the combination of different algorithms. One of the ranking parameters can be the recalls of the users with similar interests that have been posted on a Smart Tourism Website [20]. In addition to users recalls, other parameters should be taken into account, e.g., such context attributes of visited places as time and weather.

Methods of ubiquitous computing and, in particular, the recent progress in communication technologies of the Internet of Things make possible creating environments where diverse devices and computer systems cooperatively construct services surrounding the user [10], [11], [21]. New programming paradigms emerge, such as smart spaces. A smart space supports cooperation by establishing a shared view of resources in the environment. The shared view is ontology-based, applying the technologies of the Semantic Web. For e-Tourism services, a smart space is mobile and personalized, i.e., created around a traveling tourist, attracting appropriate web services and other data sources from the Internet [6], [22], [23]. In particular, smart service attributes and their smart space based implementation were proposed in [9]. As a result, these attributes introduce a new level of adaptation and personalization for e-Tourism services.

The discussion above motivates our research focus on POI recommendation services for historical tourism. First, semantic relations between historical objects cannot be bypassed in recommendation making. Second, there is no single source of needed information. The latter is distributed within multiple sources, each represents the information either in ontological form or requires an extraction procedure. Third, a historian tourist needs personalized services, i.e., source information and the result are subject to her/his preferences and context. Last but not least, a recommendation service is "ubiquitous", i.e., the service accompanies a mobile tourist in the anywhere and anytime style. In this paper, we propose the concept model and system design for the smart space based implementation of recommendation services for historical tourism. The key advantage of the proposed solutions is their support for various smart services attributes.

III. Recommendation Scenario

Consider a historical POI recommendation service that provides personal assistance for a tourist during her/his journey. This way, we introduce a reference scenario that defines our concept model of a historical e-Tourism service. Table I summarizes the formal symbol notation.

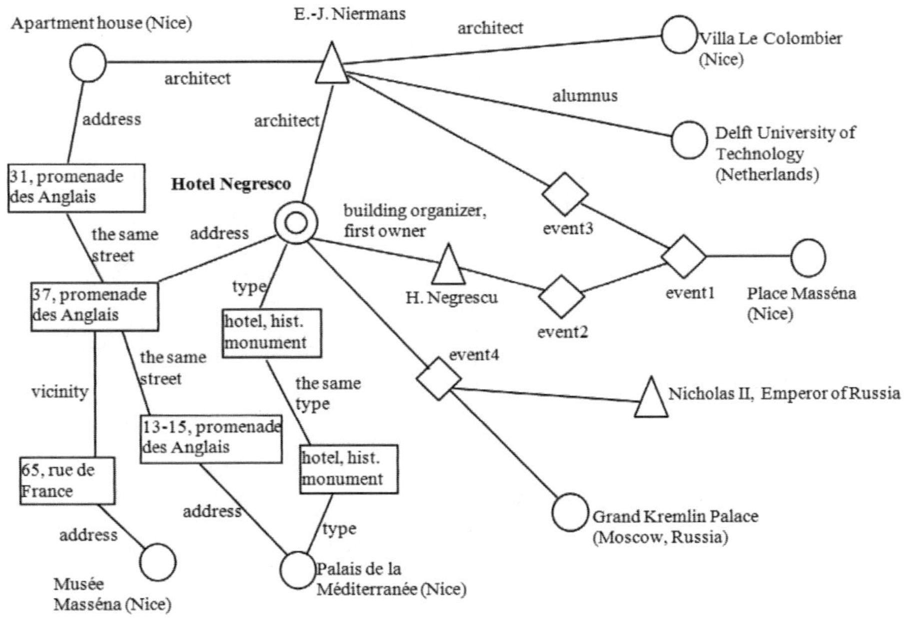

Figure 1. Sample semantic network: historical relations built around Hotel Negresco.

Let P consist of POIs that are accessed from multiple sources. Typical examples of historical POIs are buildings, monuments, fountains, bridges, squares, etc. Spacious objects, such as streets or rivers, are not POIs. As a rule, a historical POI has a particular name. There can be several names associated with a given $p \in P$, e.g., due to historical developments or due to the use of different languages. Each POI has distinctive properties: coordinates and/or address, date, architect, etc. In the service, POIs and other historical objects form the set H.

A historical POI recommendation is essentially based on relations between the elements of H. First, "direct" links exist between historical objects. For instance, a person x is the architect of a building y. Second, links can appear between objects due to similarity. For instance, two buildings have been constructed by the same architect or they are located on the same street. Third, links are a result of involving diverse objects and POIs in a common historical event. Therefore, a semantic network G with nodes H can be constructed.

TABLE I. SYMBOL NOTATION.

Symbol	*Description*
H	The set of all historical objects $H = H_1 \cup \ldots \cup H_n$ acquired from n data sources. Overlapping $H_i \cap H_j \neq \varnothing$ is possible.
$P \subset H$	The set of all POIs $P = P_1 \cup \ldots \cup P_n$, where $P_i \subset H_i$ for any data source i.
G, G_p	Semantic network G where nodes are from H and links are historical relations. In G_p, an initial POI $p \in P$ is fixed.
O	Ontology O describes the historical domain: possible classes and properties of historical objects as well as relations and restrictions for them.
R_p	Star graph R_p is a POI recommendation, where the internal node is the initial POI $p \in P$ and leaves are recommended POIs $q \in P$.
$r_q > 0$	Real-valued rank r_q shows the recommendation degree of $q \in P$ in respect to the initial POI p.
t_q	Annotation t_q summarizes (in a human-readable form) the reason of recommending q if the initial POI is p.

The historical relation semantics have a personalized character: some relations are treated differently by different historians or dependently on a context. For instance, there can be several visions of the role of a person for a certain POI. An important context corresponds to an initial POI; a tourist selects $p \in P$ and considers a semantic graph G_p. The all three types of links mentioned above can be a subject to context consideration and personalization.

Figure 1 shows a sample semantic network that is built manually around Hotel Negresco, one of the most famous buildings of Nice. Small circles are POIs, triangles denote historical persons, text rectangles describe POI properties, and rhombuses represent historical events. The initial POI ($p =$ "Hotel Negresco") is linked with seven other POIs (five of them are located in Nice). The links are based on different properties: one and the same architect, close location, involvement in common historical events, etc. Hotel information is extracted mainly from Wikipedia (see the next section for detailed description).

Based on G_p, a tourist would like to understand which POIs are interesting for her/his personal consideration from historical perspective. An important context for this understanding is that she/he starts from p (e.g., being actually or virtually in this POI). The recommendation result can be represented as a star graph R_p. Its internal node is p and the leaves represent all recommended POIs $q \in P$. Ranks $r_q > 0$ can be associated with the POIs to describe the recommendation degree of q (the higher rank the more recommendable). In a visual representation of G_p the length of edge (p, q) is proportional to the rank. Additional annotations t_q, which describe the reason of recommendation (in an aggregative form), can be also associated. Visual layout of R_p can also take into account the geographical position of q in respect to p (e.g., when q is on the North-East of p).

An example of recommendation is shown in Figure 2 in the form of a star graph derived from the semantic network (it was shown in Figure 1). The example star graph has been built by hand. With this example, we considered the possibility of processing unstructured data sources [8]. If text information is automatically processed, then the star graph will be identical. Geographical positions of the POIs are not reflected.

Now we can formulate our reference scenario of recommendation services for historical e-Tourism as consisting of the following steps.

Step 1: Initial POI selection. It can be made either manually (e.g., pointing out coordinates, a spot on the map, or POI's name) or automatically (e.g., within a definite area pointing out the nearest POI). The area can be either set by the tourist (for instance, on a map), or determined automatically taking into consideration the location of the tourist.

Step 2: Semantic network around the initial POI. The sets H and $P \subset H$ as well as semantic relations among them are searched for and retrieved from available knowledge bases and other data sources. Since the network G_p is potentially infinite, the process is limited. For instance, if the construction reaches another POI q from p, then the search for additional historical objects interconnected with q is terminated. Note that the path from p to q is subject to analysis in order to derive the reason of recommending q (construction of an annotation t_q). This example of limiting the construction process straightforwardly leads to a star graph R_p.

Step 3: POI ranking. Differentiation of recommended POIs can be based on ranks r_q. They are computed based on tourist's preferences. For instance, she/he needs to find a building constructed by the same architect, an edifice that built in the same architectural style, or another historical building located on the same street. Such preferences can be defined in the user's profile. They can be manually defined for the initial POI (before the implementation of the second scenario step). A significant component of the user's profile is the history of the choices of previous initial POIs (e.g., history of visits). For instance, the previously chosen POIs acquire lower ranks, since these POIs should not be repeatedly recommended.

Step 4: Visualization. The recommendation results achieved on Steps 2 and 3 are visually presented in a user friendly way, i.e., by means of a star graph possibly augmented with a map

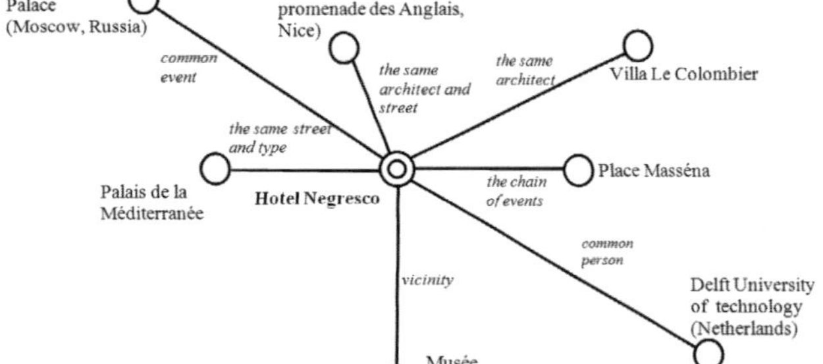

Figure 2. Star graph example: Hotel Negresco and recommendations on its historical surrounding.

and textual/visual descriptions. For instance, annotations t_q show the reasons of the provided POI recommendations.

Step 5: Feedback. The recommendation process is iterative. Based on the presented results (the star graph with ranks and annotations), the tourist supplements this information by expanding the semantic network G (additional data retrieved from historical sources). The process—supplementing and expanding network—is represented in G: new historical events appear in which both the user and the objects are involved. The user becomes a historical person—a network node in G.

In summary, this reference scenario defines our concept model of a recommendation service for the considered class of recommender systems in historical e-Tourism.

IV. Example of Semantic Network Construction and POI Ranking

The previous section showed the construction of a semantic network around POIs. Let us now illustrate some important details of the construction. We continue the handmade example on Hotel Negresco from Section III. The example reflects the operations to be implemented in the proposed smart space based system design.

The initial POI of the semantic network in Figure 1 is Hotel Negresco. It attracted our attention by its position in the center of Nice and its role of an architectural symbol, the most popular siteseeng in that city. Hotel information is widely represented on several pages in Wikipedia. Not surprisingly, the French version is the most complete one, but it is quite interesting that the same information from different pages is slightly different: for example, there are few differences in the histories how the unique chandelier under the hotel canopy is linked to the Russian Emperor Nicholas II. The Russian version simply states that two chandeliers were made. The first one is for Nicholas II, who placed it in the Grand Kremlin Palace. The second one is for the hotel. The French version says that the chandelier in the hotel was also originally intended to the Russian Tsar. The English version sais that Nicholas II was not able to take the chandelier because of the October Revolution.

By this example, we can see the deficiencies of Wikipedia as a source of historical information. There are no precise references to the sources. The connection between Hotel Negresco, Nicholas II, and the Grand Kremlin Palace is expressed using "event4" event, as it is shown in Figure 1.

From the text of Wikipedia pages, it should be noted that the hotel is connected with two bright personalities: 1) the author of the idea, the customer of the construction, the first owner of the hotel, the Romanian adventurer and businessman Henri Negresco, and 2) Dutch architect Edouard-Jean Niermans. There are other persons as well, for example, Jeanne Augier, the owner of the hotel in the last decades, who has breathed new life into the hotel, aligning it with the art museum. There are also many links away with directors and actors through the movies that were filmed there, or with great people who lived in the hotel. That is, the semantic network around the hotel could be much more extended. We decided to stay at Negresco and Niermans because additional links were discovered between them, and quite an interesting network with no other persons is constructed. In practice, limiting the expansion of the semantic network can be implemented by input of specific parameters, e.g., the network depth or the number of POIs.

Shortly before the start of construction of the hotel Henry Negresco had become the director of the restaurant in Municipal Casino in Nice. In this period, Niermans performed work on the reconstruction of the premises in that building. Apparently, they met there; as a result Niermans was embodied in the idea to build the hotel. Unfortunately, the Municipal Casino of Nice has not survived to the present time; it was demolished in 1979. It was located on Place Massena, now this place is just a square. The existing connection between the Place Massena, Negresco and Niermans is expressed in Figure 1 by three events: "event2" and "event3" link Niermans and Negresco with the Municipal Casino (the historical object that do not exist now), and "event1" connects the Municipal Casino with Massena Square (the event is that there was casino that had been constructed and then disassembled). The last case can also be described as two events.

In addition to Hotel Negresco, Niermans was the architect of many other buildings, but there are few of them in Nice. For example, the apartment house, which is not far from the hotel (on the same street Promenade des Anglais), and Villa Le Colombier, which is quite far from the center (it was built by the architect for his daughter). These objects do not have their own pages on Wikipedia, but the Niermans' page has references to them. In addition, Niermans' page describes that Niermans was graduated from Delft University of Technology.

In addition to these connections of Hotel Negresco, the semantic network also embraces other historical monuments, which are located in the nearest neighbourhood like Villa (museum) Massena, or located on the same street as the historic hotel-casino Mediterranean Palace.

Thus, the initial POI is associated with seven related POIs, five of which are in Nice, the sixth one is the Grand Kremlin Palace in Moscow, and the seventh one is Delft University of Technology. Of course, the location (proximity to the initial POI) should influence the rank of an object: the closer the POI, the higher the rank. In addition, it is necessary to take into account the convenience of the route - it is the best when objects are located on the same street. By proximity and convenience the POIs could be ranked as follows:

1) Musée Masséna;
2) Apartment house (31, promenade des Anglais, Nice);
3) Palais de la Méditerranée;
4) Place Masséna;
5) Villa Le Colombier;
6) Delft University of Technology;
7) Grand Kremlin Palace.

It is also necessary to take into account the degree of interest for a historian tourist. This degree can be estimated by the number of connections and the level of facts saturation. For example, the story of Nicholas II and the chandelier is much fuller of facts relevant to the initial POI, than the mention of the fact that the architect Niermans studied in Delft. The same can be said about the Place Massena in comparison with any other POI. If Casino Municipal was preserved, it certainly would have to take the top spot in the ranking. However, as a look at the square, where once there was this casino, still is not as interesting as a building, in the final ranking, it would be put on the 3rd place:

1) Apartment house (31, promenade des Anglais, Nice) – the same street and the same architect;
2) Palais de la Méditerranée – the same street and the same type of building (historical hotel-casino);
3) Place Masséna – rich history closely related with the initial POI, but now it is not so interesting;
4) Musée Masséna – very close to the initial POI, but the relation is rather weak (it is also a historical monument);
5) Villa Le Colombier – it is interesting to see it because it was built by the same architect, but it is very far from the initial POI.

V. SMART SPACE BASED DESIGN

The smart spaces paradigm considers computing networked environments equipped with a variety of devices and with access to the Internet [10], [11], [24]. Software agents act as knowledge processors (KPs) running on the devices and interacting via information sharing. A semantic information broker (SIB) is a mediator for information collection and exchange. Each KP produces its share of information and makes it available to others via the SIB. Similarly via the SIB, a KP consumes information of its own interest. The information storage employs RDF (Resource Description Framework) [25]. Agents can apply such advanced Semantic Web technologies as SPARQL Protocol and RDF Query Language or Web Ontology Language (OWL) for shared information maintenance, search, and reasoning [26].

This programming paradigm suits well for the development of e-Tourism services, as recent work [6], [22], [23] indicated. Figure 3 shows the multi-agent system architecture that we adopted from [6] for the case of historical recommendation services. Data source KPs for historical sources provide the smart space with extracted historical data. Client KPs allow the user to participate in the smart space receiving and consuming its services. Semantic network combiner constructs personalized

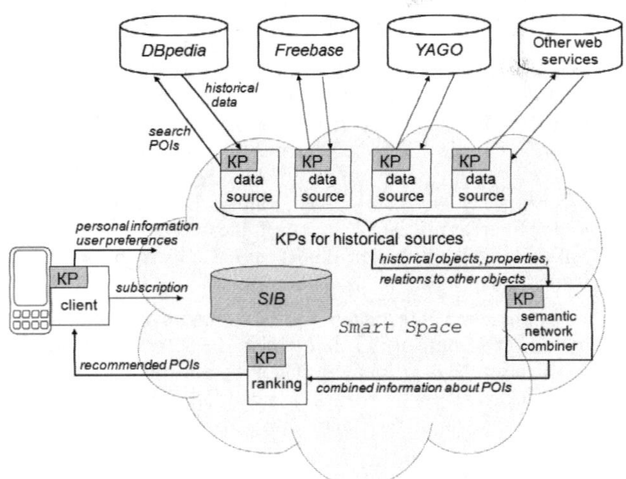

Figure 3. Multi-agent system architecture: historical information from multiple sources and other relevant information are semantically related and collectively processed in the smart space.

structures of POIs and builds the semantic network. Ranking KP makes ranking POIs using different ranking algorithms.

The recommendation service is constructed by cooperative work of multiple KPs on historical data and other information. Consider the properties of the proposed architecture to analyze the advantages that the smart spaces approach provides to the development of recommendation services for historical tourism. Some advantages are valid even for the more general case of e-Tourism.

Popular architectural styles for e-Tourism recommender systems are web-based, agent-based, and mobile [2], [3]. Smart spaces support them to be applied in a composition. SIB is deployed on a host machine in the Internet, similarly as it happens with web services now. Each user (tourist) is mobile, acts using her/his client KP (e.g., on smartphone or tablet), and consumes the service anywhere and anytime. Other KPs produce the information collecting it in the smart space for the use by the service. They can be hosted on the same machine with SIB (web-like solution) or on other computers (agent-based solution). The latter property leads to higher flexibility for system deployment. For instance, some KPs are provided by a travel agency and some KPs are attached from the user side in order to augment the system for personalized operation.

The recommendation service becomes not attached to a fixed source of historical information. A wide pool of available sources is used, where a data source KP is assigned per source (DBpedia, Freebase, YAGO, etc.). Configuration of the pool is flexible and a subject to dynamic inclusion/exclusion. Some data source KPs are set up by system administrators. Some KPs can be attached by the users if the appropriate rights are delegated. Each data source KP has to implement its source-specific interface to access and search for information. Note that a client KP can also provide historical information to the smart space, in addition to her/his preferences, context, and control. The information is further used for personalization.

The function of the data source KPs is to extract historical information from two key types of data sources. The first type is tourism-oriented or universal knowledge bases (e.g., DBpedia). They store many POIs and related information. The POI search is primarily based on coordinates, similar to popular location-based systems. The other type is historical publications (as a rule, in HTML—HyperText Markup Language or in PDF—Portable Document Format) or archival databases records (e.g., in XML—eXtensible Markup Language). XML-files can be mapped into OWL [6]. HTML sources can be processed by means of NLP (Natural Language Processing) tools. In treating data sources of the second type, the main difficulty is that historical objects are usually identified by their names only.

As a result, the smart space contains a representation of the semantic network G, integrating the information extracted from multiple data sources. Their parallel activity is coordinated by combining KPs. The common ontology O is used to represent G in the smart space. The ontology provides a system of classes, relations, and restrictions that collected historical information must confirm. As a result, they constitute a historical semantic network for the reference recommendation scenario. A combining KP reasons over the extracted historical information and establishes semantic relations between historical objects. There can be several combining KPs, and the consistency of G is ensured by O. A combining KP can represent interests of a given tourist, act on behalf of a group of tourists, or perform generic context-aware construction.

Based on the whole semantic network G in the smart space, a ranking KP constructs recommendations. Each recommendation is represented as star graph R_p for a given tourist, initial POI p, and context. Visualization on the client KP can utilize additional information such as ranks r_q and annotations t_q for all recommended POIs from R_p. Importantly that there can be many ranking KPs, each employs own computational method of POI selection for the recommendation. For instance, in POI selection method [6], values of r_q reflect the closeness of q's categories to the categories the initial POI p has. Then an annotation t_q can describe the common categories of p and q.

The proposed architecture reduces the service construction to the interactions of KPs. It follows the principle that a smart space service is knowledge reasoning over the shared content and delivering the result to the users [27]. In our case of historical recommendation services for e-Tourism, the proposed model of KPs interaction is presented in Figure 4.

Smart space content is shared, forming a subject to self-generation. That is, the steps in Figure 4 are performed simultaneously, with event-driven synchronization. An important event to activate data extraction is specifying the initial POI of a tourist (step 1). Content self-generation also supports the service personalization. New historical objects can be found and new semantic relations can be associated with this given POI (the iteration in steps 2a and 2b). Request for additional information about historical objects (step 2b) occur until semantic network around a tourist is being formed. The POI recommendation and ranking are further personalized (the iteration in steps 4a and 4b) when personal information is directly integrated into the rank computation, e.g., the POIs that a tourist has already visited. Updating the user's personal information or preferences (step 4a) requires the rank conversion. This conversion can occur until the user likes the recommended POIs (step 4b).

Table II illustrates this content self-generation model by showing the construction of the semantic network from Figure 1 and, consequently, the star graph from Figure 2. Note

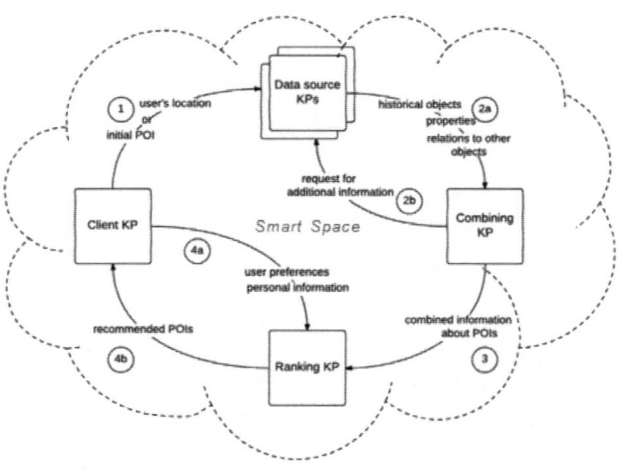

Figure 4. Many KPs interact in a smart space to construct a service.

TABLE II. EXAMPLE OF CONTENT GENERATION.

Step	Interaction	Generated content
1	Initial POI	Hotel Negresco
2	Data source KPs retrieve facts about the initial POI from different data sources.	Hotel Negresco is located at Promenade des Anglais, 37. The architect of Hotel Negresco is E.-J. Niermans. The first owner of Hotel Negresco is H. Negresco.
3	Combining KP collects an information about other POIs which relate with initial POI to create a semantic network.	POIs on the same street: Apartment house, Palais de la Méditerranée. POIs by the same architect: Villa le Colombier, Apartment house. POIs related with H. Negresco: Place Masséna.
4	Ranking KPs differentiate the POIs in the semantic network, selecting the most attracting for the user.	Rank-sorted list: Apartment house, Place Masséna, Palais de la Méditerranée, Villa le Colombier.

that in this paper we do not focus on a particular ranking criterion. Intuitively, the closer the POI and the richer and more appropriate the established relations then the rank becomes higher. For instance, Apartment house receives the highest rank since the POI is a) located on the same street and b) designed by the same architect.

VI. KNOWLEDGE PROCESSORS

The proposed system architecture defines the service-oriented application as a system of KPs interacting in the smart space. We classify these KPs as follows: A) Historical data source KP, B) Semantic network combiner, and C) POI Ranking KP. This section provides our design details of such KPs with an overview of possible algorithms that such KPs can implement.

A. Historical data source processors

Each data source KP provides the smart space with cultural heritage data. As shown in the previous section, different sources — universal knowledge bases (e.g., DBpedia), HTML-pages, databases records etc. can contain historical information about POIs. Consider design of a data source KP for the case of DBpedia knowledge base.

Dbpedia is created by means of automatic transmission of structured information from the Wikipedia pages to a semantic network [28]. Structured information in DBpedia consists of categories related with a Wikipedia page, references to other pages as well as to external resources, and facts presented in the so-called "infoboxes". They are the fragments of the pages, which provide data structured according to a certain pattern. DBpedia is a source that is conceptualized with a fixed ontology. DBpedia uses RDF for representation of the information, which is automatically extracted from Wikipedia. The scheme of data source KP operation with the DBpedia knowledge base is shown in Figure 5.

TABLE III. DBPEDIA INFORMATION ABOUT HOTEL NEGRESCO.

Property	Value
geo:lat	43.694443
geo:long	7.257500
foaf:homepage	http://www.hotel-negresco-nice.com/
is dbo:knownFor of	dbr:EdouardNiermans(architect)
rdfs:comment	The Hotel Negresco is a famous hotel and site of the equally famous restaurant Le Chantecler, located on the Promenade des Anglais on the Baie des Anges in Nice, France. It was named after Henri Negresco

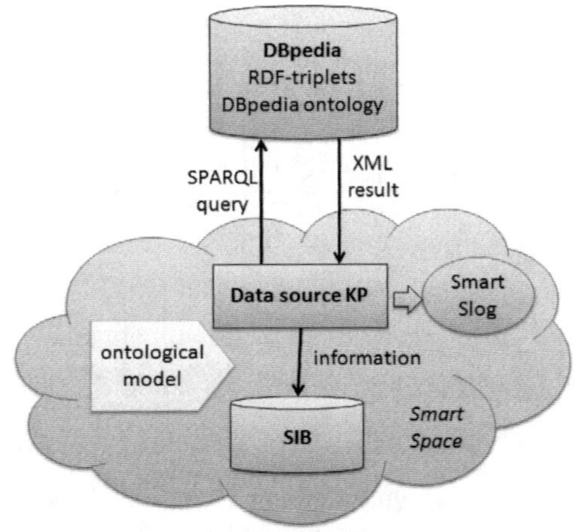

Figure 5. Data source KP operation with DBpedia.

Information representation in the format of RDF triples supports effective searching through the knowledge base using SPARQL queries. The data source KP is oriented to the Dbpedia ontology. The KP implements SPARQL queries to DBpedia, which also provides a certain set of query templates. Application development tool SmartSlog [26] is used to convert the SPARQL query XML result into a local data structure. The KP publishes the information in the smart space using the application ontological model [29]. This ontological model encompasses several important aspects of the tourism problem domain, including tourist places (cities, towns), tourist attractions, tourist events (concerts, shows, etc.), and transport issues. As a result, the KP provides POIs and other objects to construct the semantic network in the form of an RDF graph.

An example of information acquisition about Hotel Negresco from DBpedia is shown in Table III. Experimental performance evaluation of the data source KP operation is presented further in Section VII.

B. Semantic network combiner

Each combining KP is responsible for processing the information extracted from different sources. It aggregates the information received from the data source KPs. A combining KP constructs a personalized structure of POIs according to a given ontological model. The fragment of the ontological model is shown in Figure 6.

The ontology describes the three main entities: POI, Person, Event, and relations between them. Class Location represents POI location in the form of geographical coordinates. Geographical coordinates correspond WC3 Geo with data properties *lat* and *long* to designate geographical latitude and longitude, respectively. Class User is linked to class POI with two object properties *hasVisitPoint* and *hasFavoritePoint*. Thus, the user can mark a POI that she/he has visited and that she/he wants to visit.

If the received information is insufficient for semantic network extension, then the combining KP can send specifying queries to fill information structure of a POI. It is provided with a certain set of query templates that can be put to information sources. Thus, the combining KP establishes semantic relations for the semantic network between POIs and other historical objects. The constructed semantic network is ensured by ontological model; it also takes into account users' preferences and generic context.

In summary, each combining KP publishes information about POIs and the relations between POIs and other historical objects in the smart space. Then the published information is used to determine rank of each POI.

C. POI ranking methods

Ranking KP can use various algorithms to calculate the rank of a POI. In this section some methods are listed that can be used for future research. The proposed system design potentially adopts various ranking methods. Let us consider three classes of ranking algorithms. They show the spectrum of possible solutions, while the implementation and its analysis is the subject of our further research.

The simplest case is when basic information about POI is used, e.g., categories (a particular case of keywords or tags). Computational method in [6] solves the problem of ranking the available POIs by the level of proximity to the tourist's context based on the information about the set of the categories relating to a POI. Different knowledge bases (e.g., DBpedia, Freebase, and YAGO) are found on rich systems of categories. In different knowledge bases, there will be systematic differences in the values of distances between the sets of categories, thus the method used probabilistic approach determining distances between the subsets of a finite set.

Besides the possibility to compare the distances between the sets of categories, the probabilistic distance provides one more advantage: it provides an opportunity to evaluate the value of distance in the terms "long"/"short" before the whole set of the distances has been obtained. In the mobile environments, this extra opportunity is very useful, since it reduces the amount of computation by means of ranking POIs in accordance with the preferences and interests of a user.

The second class of algorithms comes from the recommender systems. Such systems are typically divided into the following three types [22]:

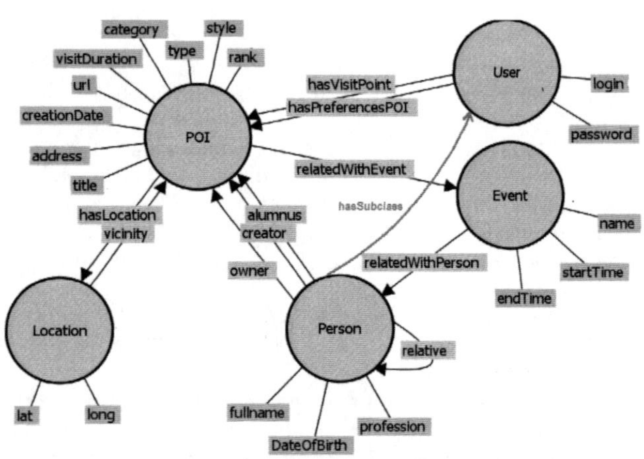

Figure 6. Example fragment of the ontological model.

1) content-based, which are based on similarity of POI's characteristics;
2) collaborative filtering, which are based on similarity of user preferences;
3) hybrid, which are combining 1 and 2.

In particular, a context-aware recommender system from [22] ranks a POI in terms depending on similarity to user preferences. It considers the following context attributes: time, company in which a tourist has visited an attraction, and weather.

The tourist can evaluate the attractiveness of POIs from one to five. Attraction rating estimation for a given tourist is performed in two steps: a group of tourists with ratings similar to the given tourist is determined; rating of attraction is estimated based on ratings of this attraction assigned by the tourists of the group. A recommendation is based on assessment of the similarity between the two tourists depending on the tourist evaluations. Then it calculates the group which the tourist can be classified to. A tourist group is determined by k-Nearest Neighbors method. It composes the resulting list of POIs.

Estimation of rank r_{uq} for POI $q \in P$ and tourist u is based on ratings (scores) of that POI. They are assigned by other tourists of the group with respect to their similarity to the tourist u. The resultant list of attractions L presented to the tourist u is sorted in descending order of:

$$s_q = kr^*_{uq} + (1-k)(1 - \frac{d^w_q}{\max_{i \in L} d^w_q})$$

where $k \in [0, 1]$ is a model parameter reflecting the importance of the POI rating estimation in favor of its reachability; d^w_q is the estimation of time for u to reach q.

Since the semantic network provides rich structural information, we can use the methods of structural ranking. For instance, a variant of the well-known PageRank algorithm can be applied. The basic idea behind PageRank for any directed graph is that a link from a node to another states an endorsement of the latter node, indicating the quality. PageRank takes advantage of the global link structure to order nodes according to their perceived quality. Various algorithms for computing PageRank in general graphs are presented in [30]. Consider the basic idea.

Given a semantic network G_p for $p \in P$. Ranks r_q for all $q \in P$ can be computed iteratively starting from some initial values $r^{(0)}_q$:

$$r^{(i+1)}_q = \alpha \sum_{\forall s: q \to s} p_{sq} r^{(i)}_s + (1-\alpha)\pi_q,$$

where $q \to s$ is a link in G_p, p_{qs} is the weight of the link, α is the damping factor denoting the probability of following the link structure, and π is a personalization vector of damping factors for all POIs.

VII. Comparison and Applicability Analysis

One of the key performance bottlenecks of the proposed smart space based architecture is the need to search and retrieve information from multiple data sources, which are available in the Internet. We experimentally analyze the performance of information acquisition from DBpedia. We assume

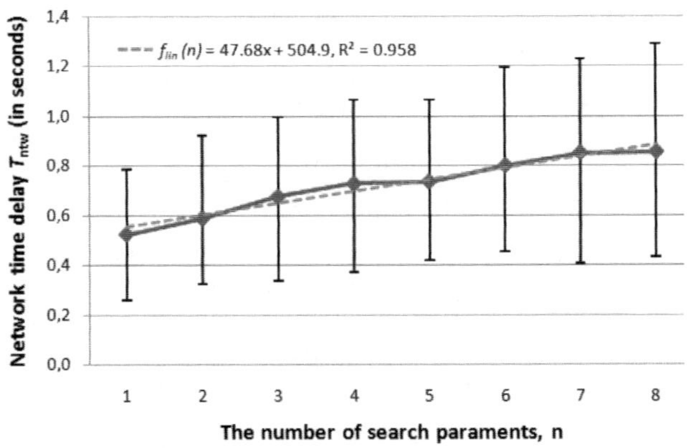

Figure 7. Estimated average time $T_{ntw}(n)$ of sending a query in DBpedia and getting a result.

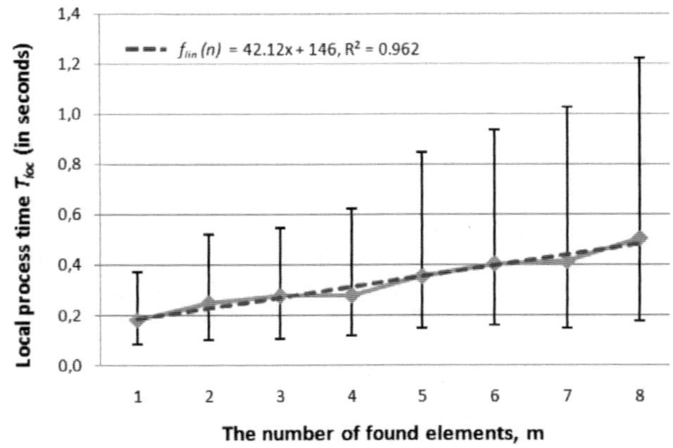

Figure 8. Estimated average time $T_{loc}(m)$ of processing the XML-result and publishing the information in smart space.

that the source has enough information on the studied history-aware problem. The information completeness in open data sources is a subject of our further research.

For this experiment we cannot use Hotel Negresco and its surroundings since it has a modest representation in DBpedia. Let us consider the case of Eiffel Tower to evaluate the performance of the data source KP. DBpedia information about Eiffel Tower is shown in Table IV. The information is much richer than about the Hotel Negresco (see Table III above). There are at least 8 parameters to search with the known coordinates of Eiffel Tower. As a result of the search, relations with 3 persons can be found (Stephen Sauvestre, Emile Nouguier, and Maurice Koechlin) and one historical event (Exposition Universelle in 1989). They define the first relations in the semantic network. Consider data source processing performance under specified conditions.

To retrieve information from DBpedia the data source KP sends a SPARQL query, processes the XML-result, and publishes the found information in the smart space in accordance with the application ontological model. In the experiments, we varied from one to eight query parameters ($n = 8$). The resource-expensive operations for our service are sending a query in DBpedia and receiving its result by network communication (time delay T_{ntw}). Then the XML result is processed and the information is published in the smart space (time T_{loc}).

The experimental behavior of $T_{\text{ntw}}(n)$ and $T_{\text{loc}}(m)$ is shown in Figure 7 and Figure 8, respectively. The number of parameters is varied for $1 \leq n \leq 8$. The number of found elements is varied for $1 \leq m \leq 8$. Although the higher number of published RDF triples can be, we consider only ones which are necessary for the semantic network construction. For each n and m we made 50 runs, and the plot shows the average with the standard deviation bars. The presented plots also include the linear regression to show the trend.

TABLE IV. DBPEDIA INFORMATION ABOUT EIFFEL TOWER.

Property	*Value*
geo:lat	48.858223
geo:long	2.294500
dbo:architect	dbr:StephenSauvestre
foaf:homepage	http://www.tour-eiffel.fr
dbo:openingDate	1889-03-31
dbo:thumbnail	wikipedia-en:Special:FilePath/TourEiffelWikimediaCommons.jpg
dbp:height	300
dbp:structuralEngineer	dbr:EmileNouguier dbr:MauriceKoechlin
rdfs:comment	The Eiffel Tower is an iron lattice tower located on the Champ de Mars in Paris, France. It was named after the engineer Alexandre Gustave Eiffel, whose company designed and built the tower.
is dbp:building of	dbr:ExpositionUniverselle (1889)

We can see that DBpedia lets to get some important information about POI, including, in particular, the coordinates and some relations with other historical objects. Nevertheless, this information is not sufficient to build a rich semantic network around the POI. It is necessary to develop other Data source KPs, which would be able to analyze the information from different types of sources (e.g., HTML pages).

The case of HTML-page analysis is considered in [8]. It describes the extraction of historical facts as RDF-triples from the regional history database "Latgales Dati" (http://latgalesdati.du.lv) by means of PHP Simple HTML DOM Parser. An example of this activity is shown in Table V.

Now let us consider distinctive properties of our system design based on results published in previous works.

The proposed service scenario differs from other proposals. The most close to our work is [18]. The authors explore the use of location aware mobile devices for searching for and browsing a large number of general and cultural heritage information repositories. The application—Mobile Cultural Heritage Guide— searches for POIs in the current tourist's physical location and constructs a "mental map" of nearby POIs within a circular shape. Next semantic crawling is applied

TABLE V. HTML TO RDF TRANSFORMATION.

HTML	*RDF triples in Smart-M3 format*
<div class='page-header'> <h1>Edids Udems</h1> </div>	123, fullName, "Edids Udems"
<div class='person'>	
<div class="birth">Dzimis 1877. gada 15. maijā </div>	123, Birthday, "1877. gada 15 maijā" (15 May 1877)
<div class="info"> Uzņēmējs (tirgotājs). ...</div>	123, profession, "Uzņēmējs (tirgotājs)" (Businessman (trader))

to resemble the process of a human using the Web to find other information relevant to these POIs. Finally, augmented reality is used in combination with facet selection to present this POI-related information to an active tourist on her/his mobile device. Similarly to our scenario, this application aims at dynamic provision of semantically-enriched information in favor of a classical travel guide. In contrast, our scenario introduces both nearby and faraway POIs, which are semantically related within a variety of historical objects, including common historical persons and events. Our scenario supports automation of semantic crawling with POI ranking; the ranks are then used for visual representation of POI recommendations to the user.

Paper [31] considers a prototype application with POI ranking. It supports content-based recommendations for generating personalized routes along cultural heritage assets in outdoor environments (e.g., city tours). The case of indoor environments, such as museums, is studied in recent work [32]. The mobile application helps the visitors to access information concerning exhibits that are of primary interest to them during pre-visit planning, to provide the visitors with relevant information during the visit, and to follow up with post visit memories and reflections. In contrast, our scenario resembles the process of a historian studying historical facts.

Based on recent studies of the Smart-M3 performance, we expect the proposed system design is applicable in real-life setting and has advantages over the other approaches to recommender system development. The applicability of the smart space based architecture, similar to the one shown in Figure 3, is discussed in [10]. A realistic case is a smart space [22] where the number of large data sources, such as web-based databases and repositories, is of the 10-order magnitude and the number of mobile users is of the 10^3-order magnitude.

In contrast to mobile standalone applications, the workload is delegated from a personal mobile device to smart space infrastructure deployed on powerful hosts. Experiments in [33] confirm that this design solution additionally improves reliability and fault tolerance, essentially in wireless network settings. In our scenario, the delegated workload includes the construction of semantic networks for many users and POI ranking over these networks. A personal mobile device visualizes aggregated fragments (e.g., a star graph) of the whole semantic network enriched with derived ranks.

In comparison with web-based recommender system, the proposed smart space based system design provides flexibility in selection of 1) data sources, 2) semantic network construction, 3) POI ranking, and 4) personalization. Although the cost is performance, Semantic Web technologies are now capable to create and maintain relatively large RDF triple stores [25], where the number of RDF triples is of the 10^5-order magnitude and more. In particular, Smart-M3 SIB employs the Redland library for RDF triple store and SPARQL support [11], [24].

VIII. Conclusion

This paper addressed recommendation services development for historical e-Tourism. We studied the problem of historical POI recommendation, the necessity of using semantic relations between historical objects, and the personalized (subjective, contextual) aspect of services. We proposed the smart space based system design for implementing such a recommender system. The proposal provides a concept definition and design solutions for creating a smart space to accompany a historian tourist. Multiple external sources of historical data can be attached to the smart space and used for provision of information relevant to the situation and user's interests. The information is integrated using Semantic Web technologies and analyzed to produce personalized recommendations. The result is visually presented with quantitative (POI ranks) and qualitative (reason annotations) estimates.

Our study makes a step towards concept development for historical e-Tourism. Feasibility study of the proposed concept model, including ontology engineering for integrated representation of historical objects, analysis of POI ranking methods over a semantic network of historical objects, and comprehensive experimental evaluation, is a subject to our further research.

Acknowledgment

This work is financially supported by the Ministry of Education and Science of the Russian Federation within project # 2.2336.2014/K from the project part of state research assignment and project # 14.574.21.0060 (RFMEFI57414X0060) of Federal Target Program "Research and development on priority directions of scientific-technological complex of Russia for 2014–2020". The reported study was partially funded by RFBR according to the research project # 14-07-00252.

References

[1] A. G. Varfolomeyev, A. Ivanovs, D. G. Korzun, and O. B. Petrina, "Smart spaces approach to development of recommendation services for historical e-tourism," in Proc. 9th Int'l Conf. on Mobile Ubiquitous Computing, Systems, Services and Technologies (UBICOMM). IARIA XPS Press, Jul. 2015, pp. 56–61.

[2] D. Gavalas, C. Konstantopoulos, K. Mastakas, and G. Pantziou, "Mobile recommender systems in tourism," J. Netw. Comput. Appl., vol. 39, Mar. 2014, pp. 319–333.

[3] J. Borràs, A. Moreno, and A. Valls, "Intelligent tourism recommender systems: A survey," Expert Syst. Appl., vol. 41, no. 16, Nov. 2014, pp. 7370–7389.

[4] V. L. Smith, Hosts and Guests: The Anthropology of Tourism. University of Pennsylvania Press, 1989.

[5] N. Ide and D. Woolner, "Historical ontologies," in Words and Intelligence II: Essays in Honor of Yorick Wilks, ser. Text, Speech and Language Technology, K. Ahmad, C. Brewster, and M. Stevenson, Eds. Springer, 2007, vol. 36, pp. 137–152.

[6] A. Varfolomeyev, D. Korzun, A. Ivanovs, and O. Petrina, "Smart personal assistant for historical tourism," in Recent Advances in Environmental Sciences and Financial Development. Proc. 2nd Int'l Conf. on Environment, Energy, Ecosystems and Development (EEEAD 2014), C. Arapatsakos, M. Razeghi, and V. Gekas, Eds., Nov. 2014, pp. 9–15.

[7] A. Varfolomeyev, D. Korzun, A. Ivanovs, H. Soms, and A. Pashkov, "Smart space services as a teaching aid in history and cultural heritage studies," in ICERI2015 Proceedings. 8th International Conference of Education, Research and Innovation. IATED, Nov. 2015, pp. 1373–1380.

[8] A. Varfolomeyev, D. Korzun, A. Ivanovs, H. Soms, and O. Petrina, "Smart space based recommendation service for historical tourism," in ICTE in Regional Development 2015 Valmiera, Latvia, ser. Procedia Computer Science, E. Ginters and M. Schumann, Eds. Elsevier, 2015, vol. 77, pp. 85–91.

[9] K. Kulakov, O. Petrina, D. Korzun, and A. Varfolomeev, "Towards an understanding of smart service: The case study for cultural heritage e-tourism," in Proc. 18th Conf. Open Innovations Framework Program FRUCT. ITMO Univeristy, Apr. 2016, pp. 145–152.

[10] D. Korzun, S. Balandin, and A. Gurtov, "Deployment of Smart Spaces in Internet of Things: Overview of the design challenges," in Proc. 13th Int'l Conf. Next Generation Wired/Wireless Networking and 6th Conf. on Internet of Things and Smart Spaces (NEW2AN/ruSMART 2013), LNCS 8121, S. Balandin, S. Andreev, and Y. Koucheryavy, Eds. Springer, Aug. 2013, pp. 48–59.

[11] J. Kiljander, A. D'Elia, F. Morandi, P. Hyttinen, J. Takalo-Mattila, A. Ylisaukko-oja, J.-P. Soininen, and T. S. Cinotti, "Semantic interoperability architecture for pervasive computing and Internet of Things," IEEE Access, vol. 2, Aug. 2014, pp. 856–874.

[12] P. Nora, "Between memory and history: Les lieux de mémoire," Representations, no. 26, 1989, pp. 7–24, Special Issue: Memory and Counter-Memory.

[13] M. Kalus, "Semantic networks and historical knowledge management: Introducing new methods of computer-based research," The Journal of the Association for History and Computing, vol. 10, Dec. 2007.

[14] A. Ivanovs and A. Varfolomeyev, "Computer technologies in local history studies: Towards a new model of region research," Acta Humanitarica Universitatis Saulensis, vol. 19, 2014, pp. 97–107.

[15] A. Meroño-Peñuela, A. Ashkpour, M. van Erp, K. Mandemakers, L. Breure, A. Scharnhorst, S. Schlobach, and F. van Harmelen, "Semantic technologies for historical research: A survey," Semantic Web journal, vol. 6, no. 6, 2015, pp. 539–564.

[16] E. Ahonen and E. Hyvonen, "Publishing historical texts on the semantic web - a case study," in Proc. 2009 IEEE Int'l Conf. on Semantic Computing (ICSC '09). IEEE Computer Society, 2009, pp. 167–173.

[17] L. Ardissono, T. Kuflik, and D. Petrelli, "Personalization in cultural heritage: The road travelled and the one ahead," User Modeling and User-Adapted Interaction, vol. 22, no. 1-2, Apr. 2012, pp. 73–99.

[18] C. van Aart, B. Wielinga, and W. R. van Hage, "Mobile cultural heritage guide: Location-aware semantic search," in Proc. 17th Int'l Conf. on Knowledge Engineering and Management by the Masses (EKAW'10), LNCS 6317, P. Cimiano and H. S. Pinto, Eds. Berlin, Heidelberg: Springer, 2010, pp. 257–271.

[19] F. Zhao, Z. Sun, and H. Jin, "Topic-centric and semantic-aware retrieval system for internet of things," Information Fusion, vol. 23, 2015, pp. 33–42.

[20] A. Becheru, C. Badica, and M. Antonie, "Towards social data analytics for smart tourism: A network science perspective," in Linguistic Linked Open Data. Springer International Publishing, 2016, pp. 35–48.

[21] J. Augusto, V. Callaghan, D. Cook, A. Kameas, and I. Satoh, "Intelligent environments: a manifesto," Human-centric Computing and Information Sciences, vol. 3, no. 1, 2013.

[22] A. Smirnov, A. Kashevnik, A. Ponomarev, N. Teslya, M. Shchekotov, and S. Balandin, "Smart space-based tourist recommendation system," in Proc. 14th Int'l Conf. Next Generation Wired/Wireless Networking and 7th Conf. on Internet of Things and Smart Spaces (NEW2AN/ruSMART 2014), LNCS 8638, S. Balandin, S. Andreev, and Y. Koucheryavy, Eds. Springer, Aug. 2014, pp. 40–51.

[23] K. Kulakov and A. Shabaev, "An approach to creation of smart space-based trip planning service," in Proc. 16th Conf. of Open Innovations Association FRUCT. ITMO Univeristy, Oct. 2014, pp. 38–44.

[24] I. Galov, A. Lomov, and D. Korzun, "Design of semantic information broker for localized computing environments in the Internet of Things," in Proc. 17th Conf. of Open Innovations Association FRUCT. ITMO Univeristy, IEEE, Apr. 2015, pp. 36–43.

[25] C. Gutierrez, C. A. Hurtado, A. O. Mendelzon, and J. Pérez, "Foundations of semantic web databases," J. Comput. Syst. Sci., vol. 77, no. 3, May 2011, pp. 520–541.

[26] D. G. Korzun, A. A. Lomov, P. I. Vanag, J. Honkola, and S. I. Balandin, "Multilingual ontology library generator for Smart-M3 information sharing platform," International Journal on Advances in Intelligent Systems, vol. 4, no. 3&4, 2011, pp. 68–81.

[27] D. Korzun and S. Balandin, "A peer-to-peer model for virtualization and knowledge sharing in smart spaces," in Proc. 8th Int'l Conf. on Mobile Ubiquitous Computing, Systems, Services and Technologies (UBICOMM 2014). IARIA XPS Press, Aug. 2014, pp. 87–92.

[28] C. Bizer, J. Lehmann, G. Kobilarov, S. Auer, C. Becker, R. Cyganiak, and S. Hellmann, "DBpedia – a crystallization point for the Web of Data," Web Semantics: Science, Services and Agents on the World Wide Web, vol. 7, 2009, pp. 154–165.

[29] K. Kulakov and O. Petrina, "Ontological model for storage historical and trip planning information in smart space," in Proc. 17th Conf. Open Innovations Framework Program FRUCT. ITMO Univeristy, Apr. 2015, pp. 96–103.

[30] A. D. Sarma, A. R. Molla, G. Pandurangan, and E. Upfal, Fast Distributed PageRank Computation, ser. Lecture Notes in Computer Science. Springer Berlin Heidelberg, 2013.

[31] N. Stash, L. Veldpaus, P. D. Bra, and A. P. Rodeirs, "Creating personalized city tours using the CHIP prototype," in Late-Breaking Results, Project Papers and Workshop Proceedings of the 21st Conf. on User Modeling, Adaptation, and Personalization (UMAP 2013): Proc. Workshop on Personal Access to Cultural Heritage (PATCH 2013), ser. CEUR Workshop Proceedings, S. Berkovsky, E. Herder, P. Lops, and O. C. Santos, Eds., vol. 997, Jun. 2013, pp. 68–79.

[32] T. Kuflik, A. Wecker, J. Lanir, and O. Stock, "An integrative framework for extending the boundaries of the museum visit experience: linking the pre, during and post visit phases," Information Technology & Tourism, vol. 15, no. 1, 2015, pp. 17–47.

[33] I. Galov and D. Korzun, "Fault tolerance support of Smart-M3 application on the software infrastructure level," in Proc. 16th Conf. of Open Innovations Association FRUCT. ITMO Univeristy, Oct. 2014, pp. 16–23.

International Journal on Advances in Intelligent Systems, vol 9 no 1 & 2, year 2016, http://www.iariajournals.org/intelligent_systems/

RBF-metamodel driven multi-objective optimization and its applications

Tanja Clees, Nils Hornung, Igor Nikitin, Lialia Nikitina, Daniela Steffes-lai
Department of High Performance Analytics
Fraunhofer Institute for Algorithms and Scientific Computing
Sankt Augustin, Germany
Tanja.Clees|Nils.Hornung|Igor.Nikitin|Lialia.Nikitina|Daniela.Steffes-lai@scai.fraunhofer.de

***Abstract*—Metamodeling of simulation results with radial basis functions (RBF) is an efficient method for the continuous representation of objectives in parametric optimization. In the multi-objective case a detection of non-convex Pareto fronts is especially difficult, which is a point where many simple algorithms fail. In this paper we consider different formulations of the multi-objective optimization problem: as a sequential linear program (SLP), as a sequential quadratic program (SQP) and as a generic nonlinear program (NLP). We compare their efficiency and apply them in three realistic test cases. In the first application we consider a bi-objective optimization problem from non-invasive tumor therapy planning, where the typical goal is to maximize the level of tumor destruction and to minimize the influence to healthy organs. The second application case is safety assessment in automotive design. Here the crash intrusion in the driver and passenger compartment is minimized together with the total mass of the vehicle. The third application comes from the simulation of gas transport networks, where the goal is to fulfil the contract values, such as incoming pressure and outgoing flow delivery, providing the best energetic efficiency of the transport.**

Keywords-complex computing in application domains; advanced computing in simulation systems; advanced computing for statistics and optimization.

I. INTRODUCTION

This paper is a continuation of our previous work [1], significantly extended by new material. Particularly, in the paper [1] we have proposed three algorithms for the detection of non-convex Pareto fronts in multi-objective optimization problems, where the objectives are represented by RBF metamodels. The algorithms have been applied to a bi-objective optimization problem in focused ultrasonic therapy planning. In the current paper we give more details on the implementation of the algorithms and present two more applications. The first application is a bi-objective optimization problem in the field of automotive design. The statement of the problem has been given in [2], while the special methods for finding non-convex Pareto fronts described in this paper have never been applied to this problem and we do it here for the first time. The next application is a four-objective problem in optimization of gas transport networks, which has not been considered before. Here we give the detailed statement of the problem and find an optimal solution, providing 27% energy savings for the realistic network.

Related work on metamodeling techniques, multi-objective optimization and their industrial applications is presented in [2-8]. Our contribution with regard to the state-of-the-art is the development of efficient algorithms for detection of non-convex Pareto fronts in combination with RBF metamodeling of objectives.

RBF metamodeling is often used in applied problems for the continuous representation of optimization objectives from a discrete set of simulation results. It represents the interpolated function f(x) as a linear combination of special functions Φ() depending only on the distance to the sample points x_k:

$$f(x) = \sum_{k=1..Nexp} c_k\, \Phi(|x-x_k|). \qquad (1)$$

The coefficients c_k in (1) can be found from known function values in sample points $f(x_k)$ by solving a moderately sized linear system with a matrix $\Phi_{kn} = \Phi(|x_k-x_n|)$. A suitable choice for the RBF is the multi-quadric function $\Phi(r)=(b^2+r^2)^{1/2}$, b=Const, which provides non-degeneracy of the interpolation matrix for all finite datasets of distinct points and all dimensions [3]. RBF interpolation can be extended by adding polynomial terms, allowing the exact reconstruction of polynomial (including linear) dependencies and generally an improved precision of interpolation. The number of points should be greater than the number of available monomials to avoid overfitting. An adaptive sampling and a hierarchy of metamodels with appropriate transition rules are used for further precision improvement. RBF metamodels are directly applicable to the interpolation of high dimensional bulky data, e.g., complete simulation results can be interpolated at a rate linear in the size of the data, and even faster in combination with PCA-based dimensional reduction techniques. The precision can be controlled via a cross-validation procedure. RBF metamodels, enhanced in this way, are a part of our software tool for design parameter optimization DesParO [2,4,5].

Single objective optimization selects a point in parameter space, providing an optimum (e.g., maximum) of the objective function. In multi-objective optimization the optimum is not an isolated point but a hypersurface (Pareto front, [6]) composed of points satisfying a tradeoff property, i.e., none of the objectives can be improved without simultaneous degradation of at least one other objective. E.g., for a bi-objective problem, the Pareto front is a curve on the 2D plane of the objectives bounding the region of possible solutions. Efficient methods have been previously developed for determining the Pareto front.

The simplest way is to convert multi-objective optimization to single objective one, by linearly combining all objectives into a single target function

$$t(x)= \sum w_i f_i(x) \quad (2)$$

with user-defined constant weights w_i. Maximization of the target function (2) gives one point on the Pareto front, while varying the weights allows to cover the whole Pareto front. In this way only convex Pareto fronts can be detected, because non-convex Pareto fronts do not produce maxima but saddle points of the target function. For non-convex Pareto fronts this method just skips non-convex segments and jumps to the nearest convex part.

There are methods also applicable to problems with non-convex Pareto fronts. The non-dominated set algorithm (NDSA) finds a discrete analogue of the Pareto front in a finite set of points. For two points f and g in optimization criteria space the first one is said to be dominated by the second one if $f_i \leq g_i$ holds for all i=1..Ncrit , where Ncrit is a number of objectives (optimization criteria). A point f belongs to the non-dominated set if there does not exist another point g dominating f. There is a recursive procedure [7] finding all non-dominated points in a given finite set. The drawback of the algorithm is an extremely large number of samples necessary to populate multidimensional regions for a good approximation of the Pareto front.

The normal boundary intersection method (NBI) [8] provides a good heuristic for sampling the Pareto front. The idea is to find individual minima of objectives, to construct their convex hull, to sample it, e.g., with Delaunay tessellation, to build normals in tesselation points and finally to intersect them with the boundary of the par $\rightarrow$ crit mapping. The approach has problems, e.g., at Ncrit>2, when non-Pareto points or not all Pareto points are covered, or if the number of minima is >Ncrit, when several local Pareto fronts can be mixed together.

Meanwhile, practical applications just require an elementary algorithm that performs a local improvement of a current design towards the optimum. Being iterated such an algorithm proceeds towards the Pareto front. For definiteness, an improvement direction in the space of objectives can be fixed, e.g., if at every step all objectives are improved by a given increment. The algorithm stops when no further improvement in the given direction is possible. Normally it happens when the solver reaches the Pareto front. Convex or non-convex Pareto fronts can be encountered and the algorithm should work equally efficient for both. The improvement can also stop at a non-Pareto boundary point. In this case the algorithm is allowed to return another point on Pareto front, which does not necessarily belong to the original improvement direction.

In Sections II-V we consider different approaches for this algorithm: sequential linear programming (SLP), sequential quadratic programming (SQP) and generic 1- or 2-phase nonlinear programming (NLP). We also consider the question of scalarization, i.e., the possibility to reformulate the multi-objective optimization problem as constrained optimization with a single objective, which allows to employ available NLP solvers for its solution. In Section VI we discuss the implementation details of the algorithms. In Sections VII-IX we describe the applications of the algorithms to the optimization problems in focused ultrasonic therapy planning, safety assessment in automotive design and simulation of gas transport networks, respectively. The relative benefits of the algorithms are summarized in Section X.

II. Using Sequential Linear Programming

Considering RBF metamodels (1) and linearizing the mapping y=f(x) using the Jacobi matrix $J_{ij}=\partial y_i/\partial x_j$, let us define a polyhedron of possible variations

$$\Pi_\varepsilon: \Delta y=J\Delta x\ ,\ \Delta y \geq \varepsilon > 0\ ,\ -\delta \leq \Delta x \leq \delta, \quad (3)$$
$$x_{min} \leq x+\Delta x \leq x_{max}\ ,\ y_{min} \leq y+\Delta y \leq y_{max}.$$

Here we require that all criteria Δy are improved, parameter variations Δx are bounded in a trust region $[-\delta,\delta]$ for linear approximation, while parameters and criteria satisfy bounding box or other polyhedral restrictions in xy-space. By requiring in (3) that a maximally possible improvement of the criteria in Π_ε is achieved, we formulate a linear program that can be solved, e.g., by the simplex method [9] and repeated sequentially:

Algorithm SLP:

Solve LP: max ε, s.t. $(\Delta x,\Delta y)\in\Pi_\varepsilon$.

Repeat steps $x+\Delta x \rightarrow x$ until convergence.

The algorithm terminates at the Pareto front, where no further improvements are possible.

Property [9]: In general position the LP-optimum is achieved in the corners of the polyhedron Π_ε.

E.g., $\Delta y=\varepsilon$ corresponds to linear trajectories in y-space, $|\Delta x|=\delta$ corresponds to linear trajectories in x-space. Therefore, the method tends to generate linear trajectories in certain projections.

SLP is formulated above for the case dim(x)=dim(y). At dim(x)<dim(y) the multi-objective problem is ill defined, i.e., full dimensional regions in parameter space become Pareto equivalent. At dim(x)>dim(y) there are unstable directions from the kernel of Jacobi matrix Ker(J): $J\Delta x=0$, i.e., there are Δx not influencing Δy. These directions can be suppressed by the additional condition $J_\perp\Delta x=0$, where $J_\perp$ is the orthogonal complement to J, constructed, e.g., with the Gram-Schmidt algorithm.

Example: Let us consider a fold transform: $|y|=2|x|/(1+|x|^2)$, shown in Fig. 1 for the 2D case. An upper right arc corresponds to a global Pareto front (PF) max y_1,y_2. There is also a degenerate local PF at $y_{1,2}=-0$, corresponding to an image of $x_{1,2}=-\infty$.

The SLP algorithm generates trajectories shown by red lines in Fig. 1, in x-space in the left column and in y-space in the right column. The algorithm reconstructs correctly both global and local PFs, shown by blue points in the images. The bottom closeups demonstrate piecewise linear trajectories described above. Particularly, there is a dashed linear trajectory in y-space tending to the non-Pareto part of the boundary (nPF), which at a certain moment switches from the $\Delta y=\varepsilon$ corner to the $|\Delta x|=\delta$ corner, becomes curved and finally stops at the PF.

III. USING SEQUENTIAL QUADRATIC PROGRAMMING

The polyhedron Π_0 is defined as above (with $\varepsilon=0$). Let v be a fixed search direction in y-space, ε a constant. The following quadratic program [10] tries to perform $\Delta y=\varepsilon v$ steps if possible in Π_0:

Algorithm SQP:

Solve QP: min $\|\Delta y-\varepsilon v\|^2$, s.t. $(\Delta x,\Delta y)\in\Pi_0$

Repeat steps $x+\Delta x \rightarrow x$ until convergence.

Property [10]: In general position the QP-optimum can be achieved inside Π_0, in the corners of Π_0 or on the edges/faces of Π_0.

In the first case $\Delta y=\varepsilon v$ linear trajectories will be generated in y-space, in the second case $|\Delta x|=\delta$ linear trajectories will be generated in x-space, in the third case the trajectories become nonlinear.

Example: Fig. 1 also shows 5 trajectories from SQP method (green lines). Performance of SQP is analogous to SLP and we prefer to use SLP due to simplicity of its implementation.

IV. USING 1-PHASE NONLINEAR PROGRAMMING

Nonlinear target functions of the form $t(x)=\sum w_i \, crit_i^p$ can, under certain conditions, detect non-convex Pareto fronts. Here the target function is represented by a scaled L_p-norm with weights $w_i\geq0$, $\sum w_i=1$. Fig. 2 left shows the level curves for a 2D target function for different p. One has a straight line at p=1, a quadric at p=2, a superquadric at p>2 and a corner at $p=\infty$.

Property (see Fig. 2 left): Nonlinear target functions can be used to detect non-convex PFs, if the curvature of the level curve exceeds the curvature of the PF.

Also at higher dimensions, considering the level set (LS) tangent to the PF, performing Taylor expansions of the LS and the PF: $z=u^TMu+o(u^2)$, where u,z are, respectively, the parallel and normal components to a common tangent hyperplane to the LS and the PF, and requiring $z_{LS}\geq z_{PF}$, one can reformulate the property above as positive definiteness for the difference of the curvature matrices M_{LS}-M_{PF}.

Note that L_∞ =max is applicable in any case (minmax method [11]), but the corresponding NLP will be non-smooth. Practically, one can use large finite p. It is also convenient to normalize y_i in [0,1] and take the logarithm of the target function for numerical stability. In this way one achieves a so called scalarization of the multi-objective optimization, i.e., the conversion of a multi-objective problem to a single objective one. As a result, the problem becomes solvable with standard NLP-solvers, e.g., Ipopt [12]. Here one can impose any additional constraints, e.g., require that $y(x) \leq c$. By putting $c=y_0$ one ensures that the result is better in all criteria than a starting point and finds only a corresponding segment of the PF. One can also leave $c=\infty$ and vary w_i to cover the whole PF.

Algorithm NLP1(c):

minimize $t(x)=\log \sum (w_i y_i)^p$, s.t. $y(x) \leq c$.

V. USING 2-PHASE NONLINEAR PROGRAMMING

The following algorithm combines the concepts of linear search from NBI and the optimization of a nonlinear target function. The first phase performs the linear search in a given direction v in y-space towards the PF and the second phase tries to perform further improvements (if possible). The problem is solvable with two calls to ipopt.

Algorithm NLP2:

NLP2.1: maximize t, s.t. $y(x)=y_0+tv$; result y_1;

NLP2.2: call NLP1(y_1); result y_2.

Properties (see Fig. 2 right):

if $y_1 \in$ PF, phase 2 quits immediately;

if $y_1 \in$ non PF boundary, trajectory is bounced to PF.

In NLP2.2 not the whole PF is targeted, but a smaller part ΔPF possessing better criteria values than y_1. Here one can use a smaller p, while even for too curved PFs the result y_2 will be still better than y_0 and y_1.

VI. IMPLEMENTATION DETAILS

The SLP and SQP algorithms with their specific definition of a polyhedron of variation and with their internal iteration loop are better to implement as separate program modules. The NLP algorithms can use existing NLP solvers, such as Ipopt, Snopt, Minos etc. An implementation can use one of the following interfaces:

AMPL environment (A Mathematical Programming Language, [13]) can be used to specify the optimization problem in a human-readable format. Fig. 3 top shows a snippet of code defining a constraint.

NL stub [14] is a standard format for optimization problems, containing the objective and constraints recorded in Polish prefix notation (PPN). The code forms an expression tree, whose branches are formed from a predefined set of operators (o…) extendable by user defined functions (f…), the leaves are numerical constants (n…) and variables (v…). Such a representation is suitable for the automatic differentiation of expressions using the chain rule. Fig. 3 middle shows the definition of a constraint in NL format.

Ipopt's C++ API [12] allows to inherit a new program from a base class TNLP (The Non-Linear Program or Template Non-Linear Program). The class possesses an evaluator of constraints and objectives, as well as their first and second derivatives, expressed in analytical or numerical form. Fig. 3 bottom represents the corresponding function prototypes.

Although AMPL and NL interfaces have a small overhead in comparison with the direct C++ API, in practice all these possibilities provide comparable performance.

VII. APPLICATION IN FOCUSED ULTRASONIC THERAPY PLANNING

Focused ultrasonic therapy is a non-invasive therapy using magnetic resonance tomography for the identification of tumor volume and focused ultrasound for the destruction of tumor cells. Numerical simulation becomes an important step for the therapy planning. Efficient methods for focused ultrasonic simulation have been presented in paper [15]. It uses a combination of the Rayleigh-Sommerfeld integral for near field and of the angular spectrum method for far field computations, which allows determining the pressure field in heterogeneous tissues. The bioheat transfer equation is used to determine the temperature increase in the therapy region. Thermal dose is defined according to the cumulative equivalent minutes metric (CEM, [16]) or the Arrhenius model [17] as a functional of temperature-time dependence in every spatial point in the therapy region. These methods have been accelerated by a GPU based parallelization and put in the basis of software FUSimlib (www.simfus.de), developed by our colleagues at the Fraunhofer Institute for Medical Image Computing.

3D visualization is used for the interpretation of the simulation results, in particular, for the detailed inspection of MRT images (magnetic resonance tomography), corresponding material model and spatial distribution of the resulting thermal dose, see Fig. 4. Stereoscopic 3D visualization in virtual environments based on modern 3D-capable beamers with DLP-Link technology (Digital Light Processing), described in more details in [18], is especially suitable for this purpose. Such commonly available beamers do not require special projection screens and can turn every regular office to a virtual laboratory providing full immersion into the model space. We use 3D visualization software Avango (www.avango.org), an object-oriented programming framework for building applications of virtual environments. Our interactive application overlays three voxel models: The original MRT sequence, the material segmentation and the resulting thermal dose. The user can mix the voxel models together, interactively changing their levels of transparency, set the breathing phase, cut the model with a clipping plane, etc.

TABLE I. BI-OBJECTIVE OPTIMIZATION IN FOCUSED ULTRASONIC THERAPY PLANNING, PROBLEM CHARACTERISTICS

Parameter bounds: frequency 0.25…0.75 MHz ini.speed 0.23...0.282 m/s	**Timing per solution** @ 3GHz Intel i7:
Criteria bounds: ∑TDin 0…3000 eq.min ∑ TDout 0…6000 eq.min	SLP 7ms NLP1 16ms NLP2 13ms+12ms

A generic workflow for ultrasonic therapy simulation has been described in our paper [19]. Numerical simulation with FUSimlib software uses a 512 x 512 x 256 voxel grid. Ultrasound has been focused in the center of the target zone for the neutral breath state. The result after 10 seconds of exposure time (200 steps x 0.05sec) has the form of spatial distributions of the pressure amplitude, the temperature and the thermal dose. Fig. 4 top-right shows a typical result for thermal dose on slice 97/256 near the focal point. The frequency of the transducer is taken as an optimization parameter controlling the focused ultrasonic therapy simulation. The other one, initial particle speed, is proportional to an acoustic intensity emitted by the transducer [15]. The objective of therapy planning is a maximization of the thermal dose inside the target zone (TDin) and a minimization of the thermal dose outside (TDout). The thermal doses are defined as sums of the thermal dose over corresponding voxels, ∑TDin / ∑TDout. The variation range of the optimization parameters was regularly sampled with 25 simulations, from which 16 fall in the region of interest, shown in Fig. 5 by red points. Our RBF metamodel constructed on simulation results is used to oversample the region by green points, from which the discrete method NDSA selects the Pareto front, shown by blue points. We see that the Pareto front is of non-convex type. Magenta lines show the application of the three continuous methods described above. The trajectories generated by SLP and NLP2 coincide in every detail. Even bouncing from the non-PF boundary works similarly, although the mechanisms of this bouncing are different. NLP1 with p=8 and w_1=0.01, 0.15, 0.27, 0.5, 0.99 produces the other set of trajectories. Table I shows a summary of the problem characteristics. SLP provides the best performance for the given application case. On the other hand, NLP provides an easier integration with existing scalar solvers. In the NLP class, NLP1 is faster than NLP2 for bounced trajectories, otherwise NLP2 is faster. Numerically NLP2 (with small p) is less singular than NLP1 (with large p) and, therefore, it is more robust for the detection of strongly curved Pareto fronts.

VIII. Application in Audi B-pillar Crash Test

We apply the algorithm NLP2 for the detection of Pareto fronts in automotive crash test simulation, described in [2]. The PamCrash software (www.esi.com.au/Software/PAM-CRASH.html) is used for simulation. The model of a B-pillar shown in Fig. 7 contains 10 thousand nodes. 45 timesteps of crash process are simulated. 101 simulations were made by varying two design parameters, i.e., the thicknesses of two layers composing the B-pillar. The optimization objective is the simultaneous minimization of the total mass of the B-pillar and of the crash intrusion in the contact area. Crash intrusions in the driver and passenger compartment are commonly considered as critical safety characteristics of car design, while the total mass influences other important characteristics, i.e., fuel consumption, CO2 emissions and production costs. Two extreme designs corresponding to lower and upper bounds of both thicknesses are shown in Fig. 7.

Further, we apply RBF metamodeling to represent the relation between design parameters and optimization criteria and study this problem in our interactive optimization tool DesParO, see Fig. 6. At first, we impose constraints on the optimization criteria, as indicated by red ovals in Fig. 6 top. As a result, islands of available solutions become visible along the axes of design parameters. The islands are combined cross-like, as shown in Fig. 6 bottom. For these combinations both constraints on mass and intrusion are satisfied, while all alternative combinations violate the constraints. In this way a complex structure of the Pareto front in the considered problem is revealed.

Fig. 8 shows the results of the NDSA and NLP2 methods on two different projections. On the left the Pareto front on the criteria plane is presented. Blue points indicate the first piece of the Pareto front found by NDSA and corresponding to the first island of solutions. Meanwhile NLP2 trajectories sometimes stop earlier and indicate the second piece of the Pareto front shown by a dashed line. Fig. 8 right part shows a different projection, where both pieces become visible. There is a hill separating solutions like a watershed, so NLP2 trajectories go to the one or to the other side dependently on a starting point. This projection produces also a fold, a small overlap near the second piece of the Pareto front. It does not disturb the convergence of the NLP2 algorithm, the trajectory jumps directly from the starting point to the second piece of the Pareto front, displayed by the dashed line in the figure.

We note that NDSA considers a dataset as a cloud of discrete points in the space of criteria, without any notion of continuity in parameter and criteria space, and detects only one piece of the Pareto front (global optimum). NLP2 is a continuous method and detects also the second piece (local optimum). In the considered problem both optima are close to each other and represent the underlying symmetry of the problem. Indeed, the Pareto optimal solution for this problem belongs to a boundary of the parameter space. It corresponds to a minimal thickness of one layer and varied thickness of the other layer, representing a compromise between stiffness and mass. Two possibilities in a choice of the minimal layer become two pieces of the Pareto front.

TABLE II. Bi-objective optimization in Audi B-Pillar crash test simulation, problem characteristics

Parameter bounds:	
thickness1,2	0.5…3 mm
Criteria bounds:	
intrusion	0…174 mm
mass	7.8…26.9 kg

IX. Application in gas transport networks

The simulation of gas transport networks is performed by a software package Mynts (Multi-phYsics NeTwork Simulator, www.scai.fraunhofer.de/en/business-research-areas/high-performance-analytics-en/products/mynts.html) developed in our group. A small training network used here for experiments is shown in Fig. 9. It contains 100 nodes, 111 pipes and other connecting elements. We note that real life problems are much larger. In cooperation with our partners we solve stationary and transient problems for gas networks with ten thousands of elements.

The network of Fig. 9 has two supply nodes with specified pressure values (PSETs) and three consumer nodes with specified flow values (QSETs). There are two compressor stations, providing the necessary throughput in the network, see Fig. 10. Every station consists of two separate compressors, each can be configured to provide a fixed output pressure (SPO) or a fixed flow value (SM). In the considered scenario one compressor is set to SPO mode and three others to SM mode and these four values are used as optimization parameters. The purpose of the optimization is to run the compressors at minimal possible power (POW) sufficient to satisfy all contract values, such as PSETs and QSETs. The result is a particular solution of a network feasibility problem, possessing the best energetic efficiency.

For this study we have prepared 1000 simulations in the bounds given in Table III. Fig. 11 shows a solution of the optimization problem in our DesParO Metamodel Explorer. It is achieved at a minimal SPO value for the first compressor and a particular distribution of SM values, corresponding to individual properties of the three other compressors. The result of the NLP2 optimization is given in Table IV. We see that the optimization provides 27% energy savings relative to the starting point.

TABLE III. FOUR-OBJECTIVE OPTIMIZATION IN GAS TRANSPORT NETWORK SIMULATION, PROBLEM CHARACTERISTICS

Parameter bounds: SPO1 71…91 bar SM2-4 400...600 x1000m^3/h
Criteria bounds: POW1-4 2…16 MW

TABLE IV. FOUR-OBJECTIVE OPTIMIZATION IN GAS TRANSPORT NETWORK SIMULATION, STARTING POINT AND OPTIMAL SOLUTION

	STARTING POINT	OPTIMAL SOLUTION
SPO1	81	71
SM2	500	510
SM3	500	508
SM4	500	502
POW1	8.5	6.3
POW2	8.6	6.4
POW3	8.4	6.2
POW4	7.8	5.6

X. CONCLUSION

Several algorithms of continuous multi-objective optimization applicable to the detection of non-convex Pareto fronts have been discussed: sequential linear programming (SLP), sequential quadratic programming (SQP) and generic 1- or 2-phase nonlinear programming (NLP1,2). Performance of SQP is analogous to SLP and we prefer to use SLP due to simplicity of its implementation. Scalarization, i.e., the reformulation of the multi-objective optimization problem as constrained optimization with a single objective, allows to employ available NLP solvers for its solution. The algorithms have been applied to a realistic test case in focused ultrasonic therapy planning. In the given problem SLP possesses the best performance, while NLP provides an easier integration with existing scalar solvers. NLP1 is faster than NLP2 for bounced trajectories, otherwise NLP2 is faster. Numerically NLP2 is less singular than NLP1 and is therefore more robust for the detection of strongly curved Pareto fronts. All these optimization methods provide real-time performance necessary for the interactive planning of focused ultrasonic therapy. Further, NLP2 has been applied to a multi-objective optimization problem in the safety assessment of automotive design. Here the Pareto front is also non-convex and consists of two separate pieces, global and local parts of the Pareto front. NDSA detects only the global part, while NLP2 finds both. Finally, we have applied NLP2 to improve the energetic efficiency of a gas transport network, where the optimization allows to achieve 27% energy savings.

REFERENCES

[1] T. Clees et al., "RBF-metamodel Driven Multi-objective Optimization and its Application in Focused Ultrasonic Therapy Planning", in C.-P. Rückemann et al. (Eds.), ADVCOMP 2015, The Ninth International Conference on Advanced Engineering Computing and Applications in Sciences, July 19-24, 2015, Nice, France, pp. 71-76.

[2] T. Clees et al., "Analysis of bulky crash simulation results: deterministic and stochastic aspects", in N.Pina et al. (Eds.): Simulation and Modeling Methodologies, Technologies and Applications, AISC 197, Springer 2012, pp. 225-237.

[3] M. D. Buhmann, "Radial Basis Functions: theory and implementations", Cambridge University Press, 2003.

[4] G. van Bühren et al., "Aspects of adaptive hierarchical RBF metamodels for optimization", Journal of computational methods in sciences and engineering JCMSE 12 (2012), Nr.1-2, pp. 5-23.

[5] T. Clees et al., "Nonlinear metamodeling of bulky data and applications in automotive design", in M. Günther et al. (eds), Progress in industrial mathematics at ECMI 2010, Mathematics in Industry (17), Springer, 2012, pp. 295-301.

[6] M. Ehrgott and X. Gandibleux (Eds.), "Multiple criteria optimization: state of the art annotated bibliographic surveys", Kluwer 2002.

[7] H. T. Kung et al., "On finding the maxima of a set of vectors", Journal of the ACM, 22(4), 1975, pp. 469-476.

[8] G. Eichfelder, "Parametergesteuerte Lösung nichtlinearer multikriterieller Optimierungsprobleme", Friedrich–Alexander-Universität Erlangen–Nürnberg, Dissertation 2006.

[9] G. Dantzig, "Linear programming and extensions", Princeton University Press and the RAND Corporation, 1963.

[10] R. Fletcher, "Practical Methods of Optimization", Wiley 2000.

[11] D. Müller-Gritschneder, "Deterministic Performance Space Exploration of Analog Integrated Circuits considering Process Variations and Operating Conditions", Technische Universität München, Dissertation 2009.

[12] A. Wächter, "Short Tutorial: Getting Started With Ipopt in 90 Minutes", IBM Research Report, 2009.

[13] R. Fourer, D. M. Gay, and B. W. Kernighan, "AMPL: A Modeling Language for Mathematical Programming", Cengage Learning, 2002.

[14] D. M. Gay, "Writing .nl Files", Albuquerque, Sandia National Laboratories, Technical report, 2005.

[15] J. Georgii et al., "Focused Ultrasound - Efficient GPU Simulation Methods for Therapy Planning", in Proc. Workshop on Virtual Reality Interaction and Physical Simulation VRIPHYS, Lyon, France, 2011, J. Bender, K. Erleben, and E. Galin (Editors), Eurographics Association 2011, pp. 119-128.

[16] S. Nandlall et al., "On the Applicability of the Thermal Dose Cumulative Equivalent Minutes Metric to the Denaturation of Bovine Serum Albumin in a Polyacrylamide Tissue Phantom", in Proc. 8th Int. Symp. Therapeutic Ultrasound (AIP), 1113, 2009, pp. 205-209.

[17] J. A. Pearce, "Relationships between Arrhenius models of thermal dose damage and the CEM 43 thermal dose", in T. P. Ryan (ed.), Proc. of Energy-based Treatment of Tissue and Assessment V, SPIE, 2009, p. 7181.

[18] T. Clees et al., "Focused ultrasonic therapy planning: Metamodeling, optimization, visualization", J. Comp. Sci. 5 (6), Elsevier 2014, pp. 891-897.

[19] T. Clees et al., "Multi-objective Optimization and Stochastic Analysis in Focused Ultrasonic Therapy Simulation", in Proc. of SIMULTECH 2013, SCITEPRESS, 2013, pp. 43-48.

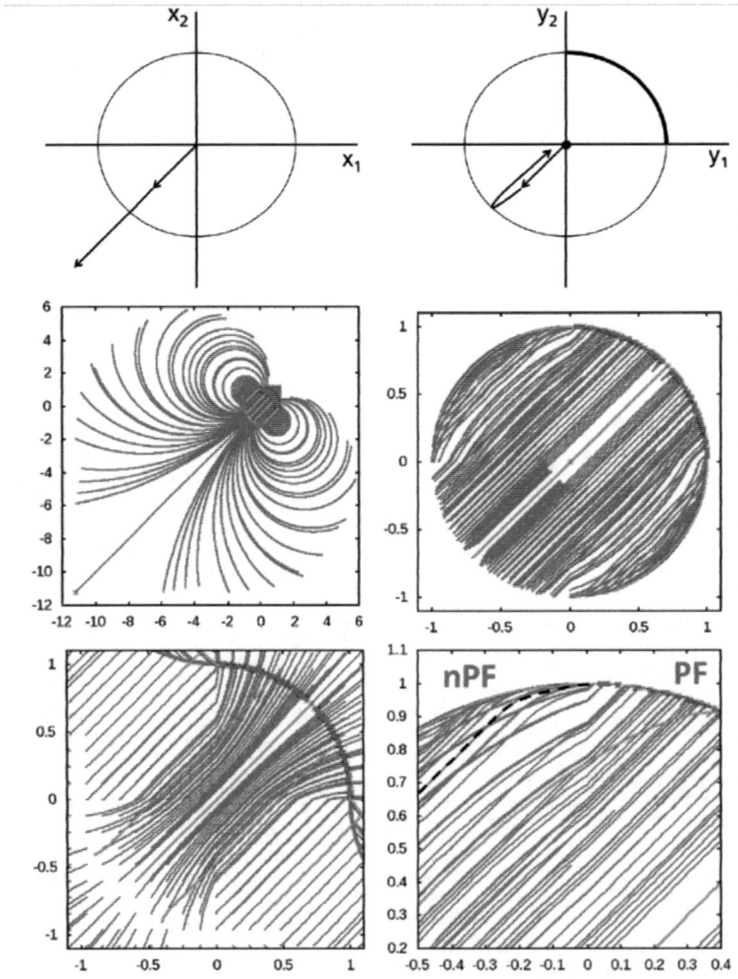

Figure 1. Pareto front detection for 2D fold transform (see Sections II-III for details).

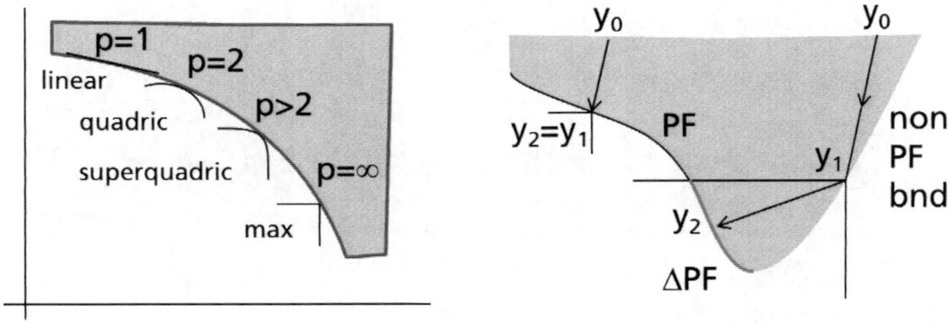

Figure 2. Scalarization of multi-objective optimization problem. On the left: algorithm NLP1; on the right: algorithm NLP2.

```
maximize obj: t*1e6;
subject to y0constr:
y0=sqrt(0.01+((x0-250000)/500000-0)**2+((x1-0.23)/0.052-0)**2)*(4208.98)+sqrt(0.01+((x0-250000)/500000-
0)**2+((x1-0.23)/0.052-0.25)**2)*(-938.255)+sqrt(0.01+((x0-250000)/500000-0)**2+((x1-0.23)/0.052-
0.5)**2)*(-310.969)+sqrt(0.01+((x0-250000)/500000-0)**2+((x1-0.23)/0.052-0.75)**2)*(-
1405.99)+sqrt(0.01+((x0-250000)/500000-0)**2+((x1-0.23)/0.052-1)**2)*(-527.836)+sqrt(0.01+((x0-
250000)/500000-0.25)**2+...
```

```
C0 o54 28 o2 n-4208.98 o39 o54 3 n0.01 o5 o3 o0 n-250000 v0 n5e+05 n2 o5 o3 o0 n-0.23 v1 n0.052 n2 o2
n938.255 o39 o54 3 n0.01 o5 o3 o0 n-250000 v0 n5e+05 n2 o5 o0 n-0.25 o3 o0 n-0.23 v1 n0.052 n2 o2
n310.969 o39 o54 3 n0.01 o5 o3 o0 n-250000 v0 n5e+05 n2 o5 o0 n-0.5 o3 o0 n-0.23 v1 n0.052 n2 o2
n1405.99 o39 o54 3 n0.01 o5 o3 o0 n-250000 v0 n5e+05 n2 o5 o0 n-0.75 o3 o0 n-0.23 v1 n0.052 n2 o2
n527.836 o39 o54 3 n0.01 o5 o3 o0 n-250000 v0 n5e+05 n2 o5 o0 n-1 o3 o0 n-0.23 v1 n0.052 n2 o2 ...
```

```
bool eval_f(Index n, const Number* x, bool, Number& f); // objective function
bool eval_grad_f(Index n, const Number* x, bool, Number* gf); // gradient of objective function
bool eval_g(Index n, const Number* x, bool, Index m, Number* g); // constraints
bool eval_jac_g(Index n, const Number* x, bool, Index m, // Jacobian of constraints
                      Index njac, Index* iRow, Index *jCol, Number* values);
bool eval_h(Index n, const Number* x, bool, Number obj_factor, Index m, const Number* lambda, bool,
                      Index nhess, Index* iRow, Index* jCol, Number* values); // Hessian of Lagrangian
```

Figure 3. Example of NLP code in different interfaces. Top: AMPL model file. Center: NL stub file. Bottom: Ipopt C++ API.

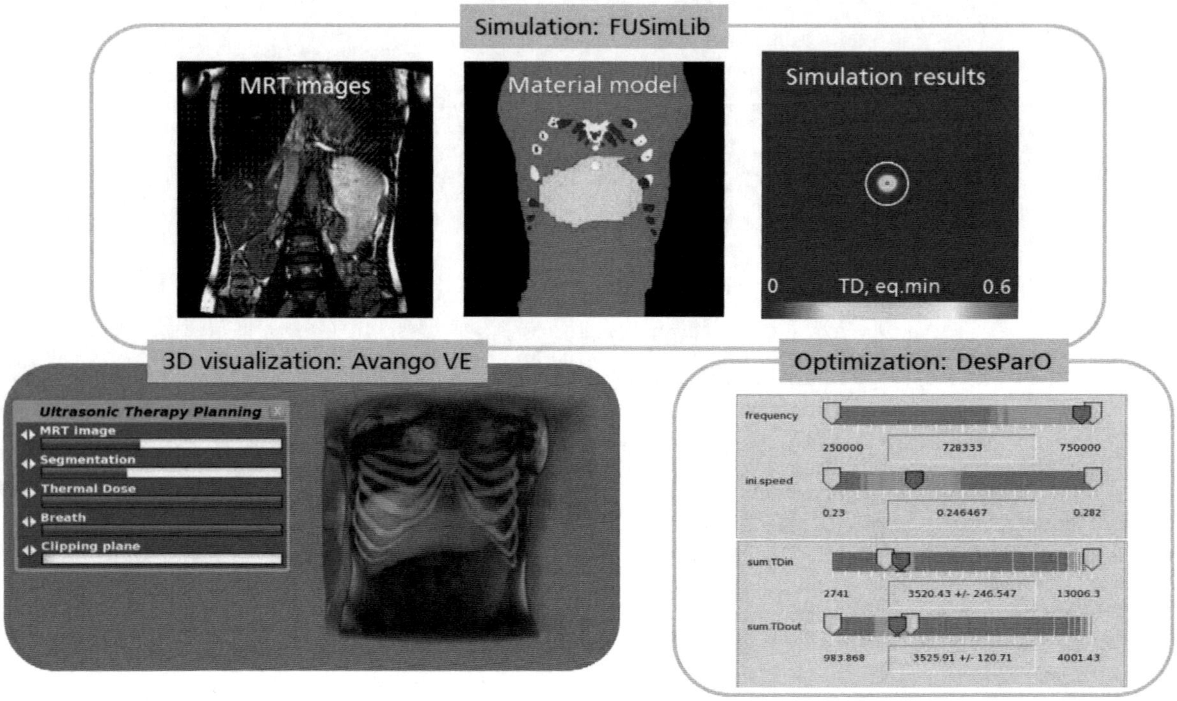

Figure 4. Focused ultrasonic therapy planning and its software components.

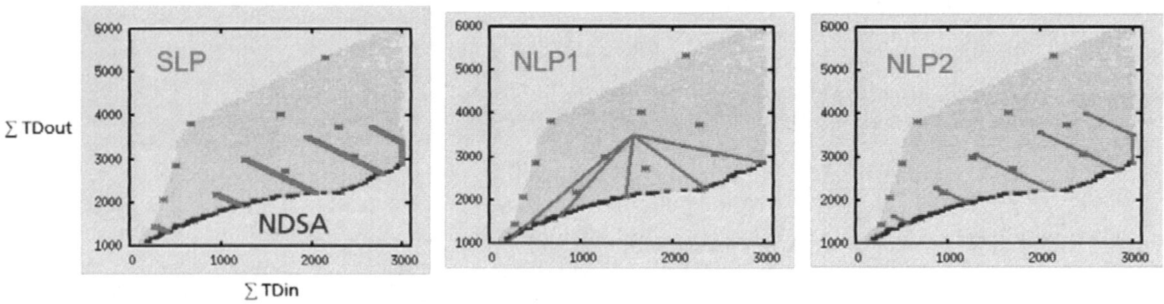

Figure 5. Non-convex Pareto front in focused ultrasonic therapy planning, comparison of different methods.

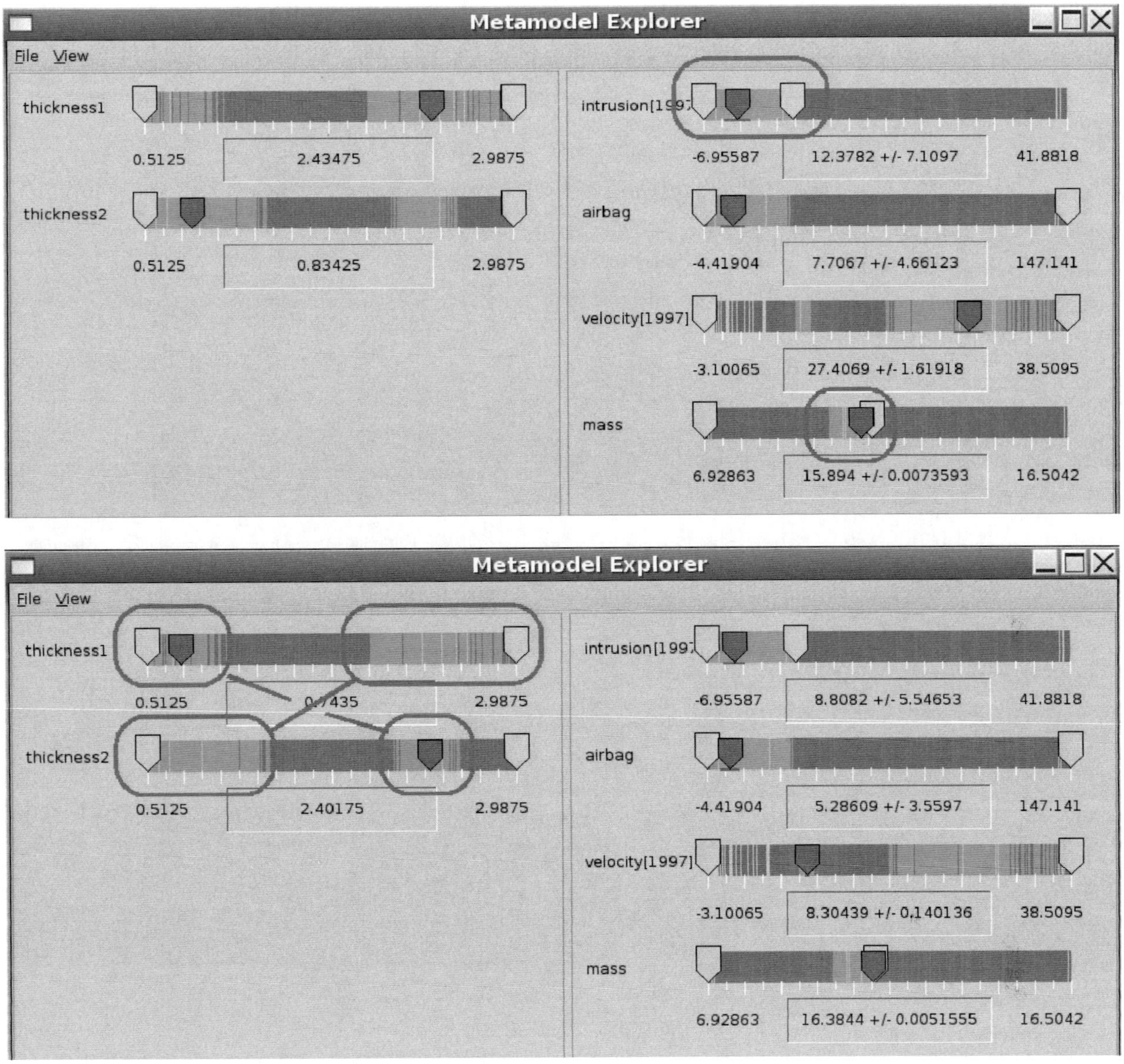

Figure 6. Studying Audi B-Pillar crash test in DesParO Metamodel Explorer. Top: an attempt to minimize simultaneously intrusion and mass by setting upper constraints on these criteria. Bottom: two islands of available solutions become visible.

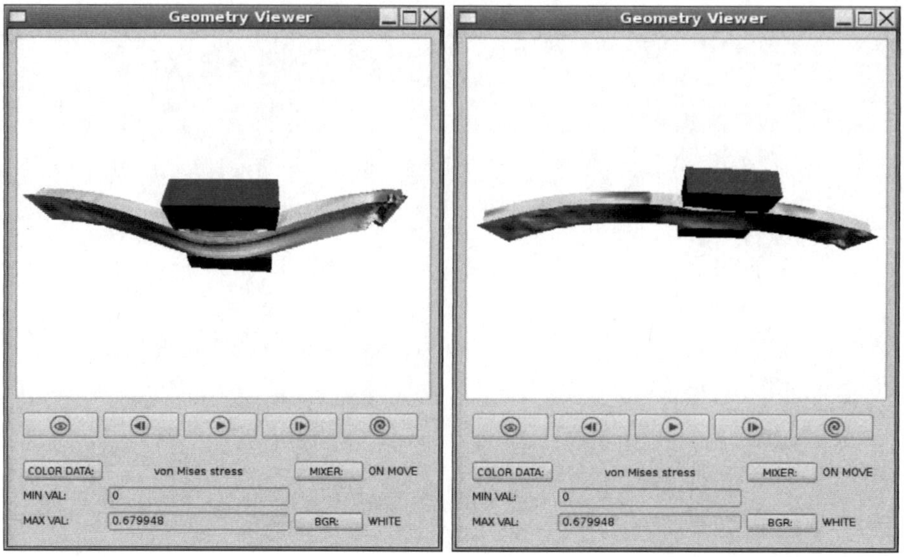

Figure 7. Audi B-Pillar crash test in DesParO Geometry Viewer. Two extreme designs are shown. On the left: small stiffness, small mass. On the right: large stiffness, large mass.

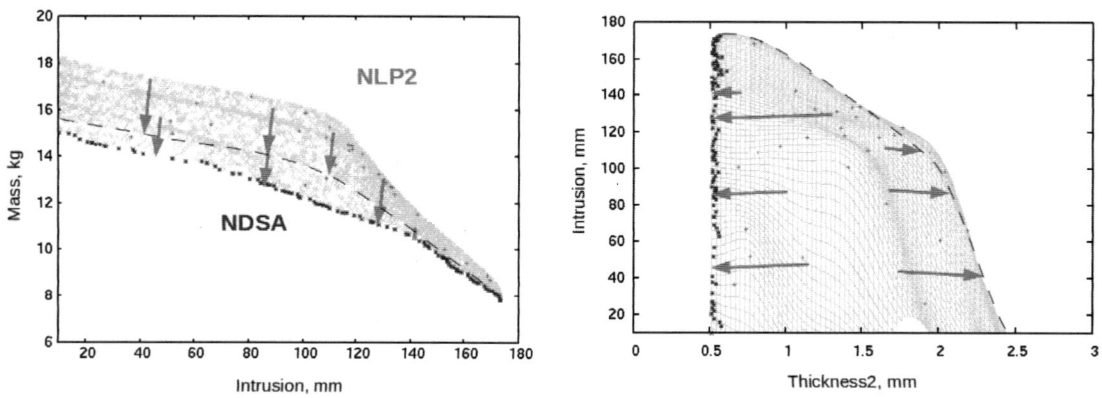

Figure 8. Pareto front of Audi B-Pillar crash test. On the left: intrusion vs mass projection. On the right: intrusion vs thickness2 projection. Red points show simulation results, green area - RBF interpolation, blue points - global Pareto front found with NDSA. Magenta arrows are trajectories of NLP2 algorithm. Dashed line shows a local Pareto front, corresponding to the second island of solutions.

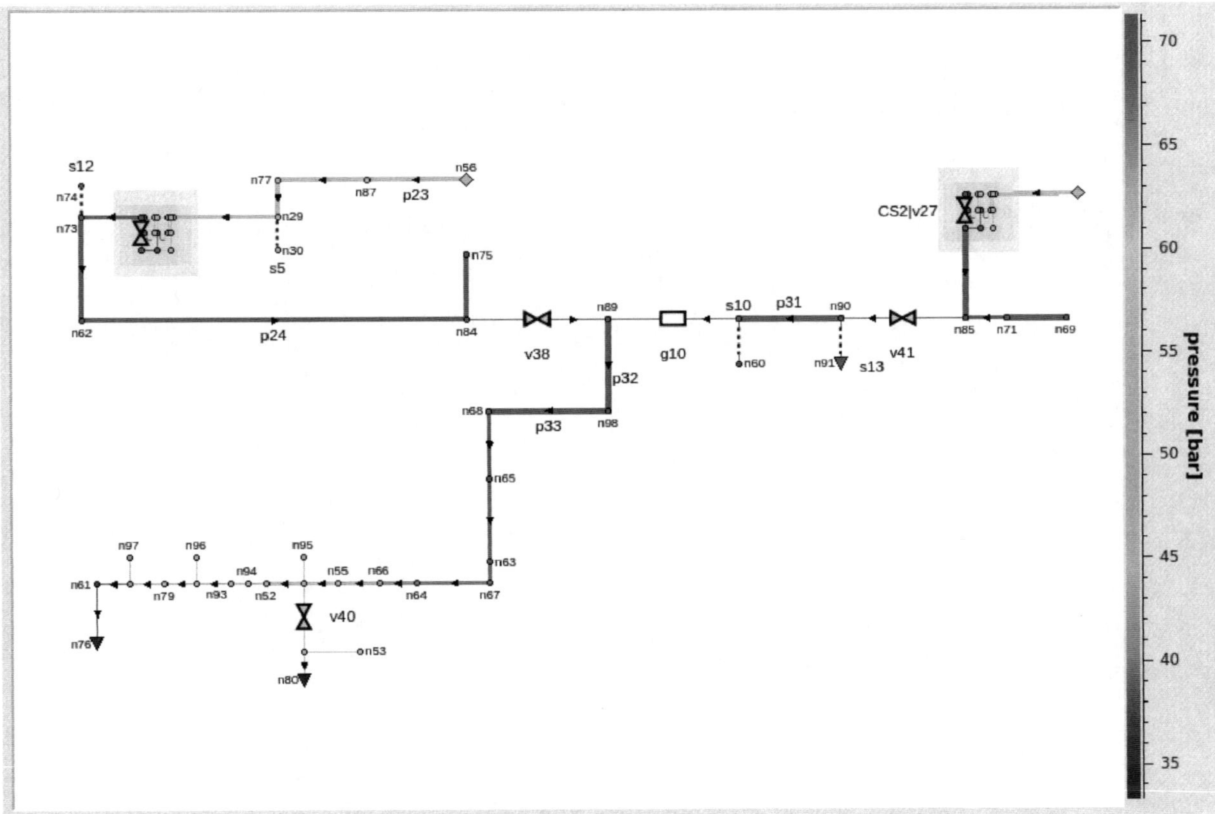

Figure 9. Gas transport network simulation in Mynts, the network topology with the resulting pressure distribution, shown by color.

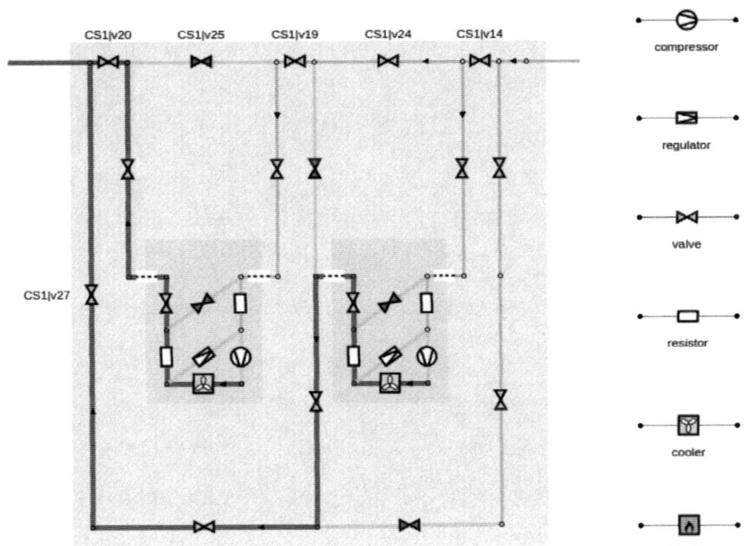

Figure 10. Gas transport network simulation in Mynts, closeup to a compressor station.

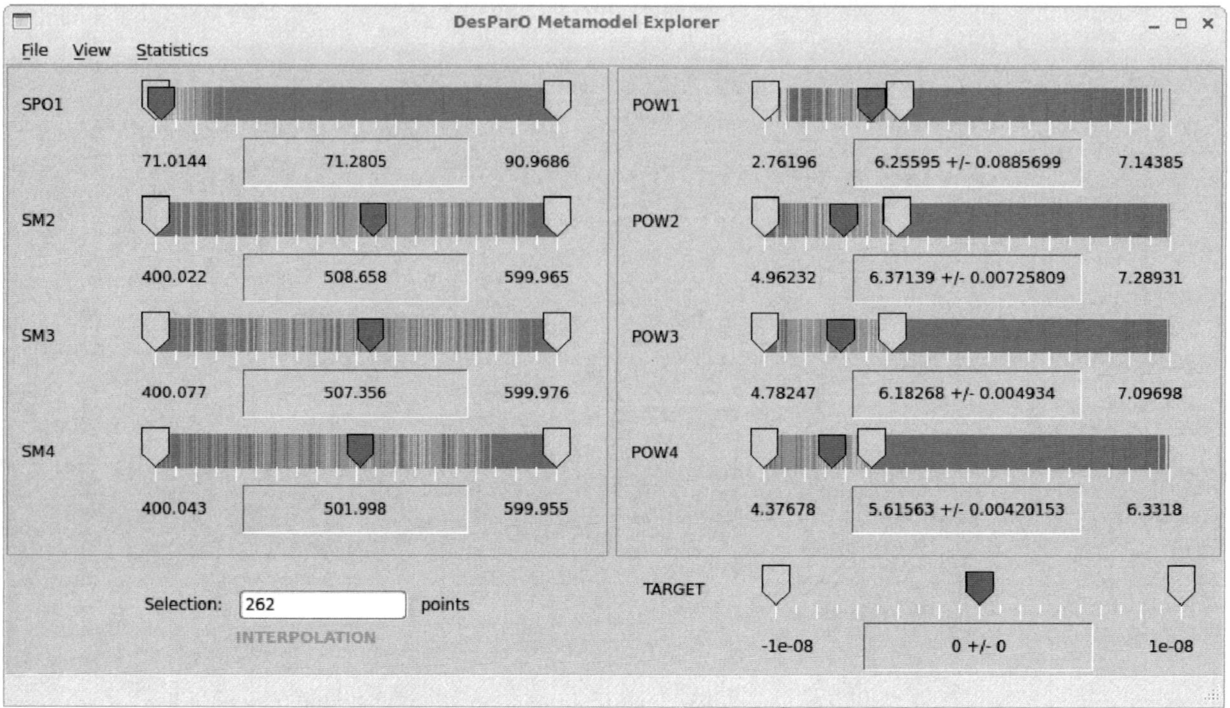

Figure 11. Four-objective optimization problem for gas transport network simulation in DesParO Metamodel Explorer.

Toward an Adaptive Application Builder: Two Communication Systems for an Ontology-Based Adaptive Information System Framework

Louis Bhérer
Luc Vouligny, Mohamed Gaha

Institut de recherche d'Hydro-Québec, IREQ
Varennes, Québec, Canada
Email: bhererlouis@gmail.com
Vouligny.Luc@ireq.ca, Gaha.Mohamed@ireq.ca

Christian Desrosiers

École de technologie supérieure
Montréal, Québec, Canada
Email: christian.desrosiers@etsmtl.ca

***Abstract*—Software development does not usually end with the final release of the application. The software application must be maintained throughout its lifetime to keep in step with the user's needs. Most software applications are built around a rigid data model, which whenever modified will have an impact on the application, resulting in additional maintenance costs. A way to mitigate this problem would be to have an ontology-based software framework for building information systems that can auto-adapt to an evolving data model. Such a framework has been built and used in the development of a client-server application as a proof of concept. This application can adapt dynamically to numerous changes that can be made in the data model without recompiling the client side or server side of the application. Two communication systems between the client and server have been tested to compare their performance, code length and capabilities. In order for this framework to be efficiently used for the development of applications, it must be combined with other components to form an adaptive application builder, whose design is discussed with regard to the ontology-driven architecture paradigm.**

Keywords–Adaptive Information System; Ontology; RDF; RDFS; OWL; Ontology-Driven Architecture; Model-Driven Engineering, Autonomic Computing.

I. Introduction

This article is an extended version of an earlier paper that described an ontology-based framework for building applications capable of adapting to changes in the data model. Here, it will be explained how this framework can be part of a more complex entity: an adaptive application builder (AAB). In addition, two communication systems between client and server are compared [1].

Many of today's software applications are developed around a rigid data model drawn from relational database (RDB) technologies. Though RDB technologies are mature and perform well when storing and accessing data, their data models are hard to change when modifications must be made. Modification of the software itself is rather time-consuming as most of the changes to the data model also require adjustments to the corresponding objects' model. Migration usually requires a transitional program to transfer stored information to the new data model, recompile and republish the application. Usually, when the application is on a client-server system in a large organization, all this work must be synchronized between departments, adding to the overall refactoring effort.

When ontologies are used to model information, they can be established and refined as new knowledge is acquired and as needs evolve. However, the ease with which models are modified within the ontology can be constrained by the applications' rigid development framework and resulting programs. Staab *et al.* recommend gathering all the modifications made to an ontology in order to test all possible consequences to the applications before deploying a new version [2]. We conclude that developing applications able to self-adapt to data models would reduce both development and maintenance costs. This paper shows how ontology repository technologies such as triplestores, i.e., database management systems (DBMS) for data modeled using the resource description framework (RDF) [3], can be used in applications built to take into account how the data model evolves. Moreover, such applications do not require a compilation process in order to adapt to an evolving data model, contrary to most current applications.

The main focus of this work is the design and implementation of a framework that allows for a fast and easy building of information systems that can auto-adapt to evolving data models. This framework has been used in the development of a client-server application as a proof of concept. The application adapts dynamically to numerous changes that can be made in the model without recompile of the client side or server side of the application. The goal of this framework is to reduce the costs associated with application development, deployment and maintenance at Hydro-Québec, the utility that generates, transmits and distributes electricity in the province of Québec. At IREQ, Hydro-Québec's research institute, studies on the application of semantic technologies are currently underway as a means to solve problems related to the increasing number of databases within the organization [4][5]. In addition, self-adapting technologies have already been applied successfully [6]. Since the adaptive properties of applications hinges on the communication system between the server side and the client side, two communication approaches have been tested and compared within the framework developed. The main contribution of this paper is the development of this framework as a new approach to generating an information system that auto-adapts to its data model.

In order to give the framework more complex adaptive capabilities and facilitate its implementation into future company applications, an adaptive application builder (AAB) is being developed. Since this AAB influences the development of the framework, its main principles will be discussed. As semantic technologies enable domain-independent meta-modeling of information systems, model-driven engineering (MDE) seems a natural approach to guide the development of an AAB.

Section II of this paper reviews earlier work in two areas: MDE and ontology-driven architecture (ODA), and then systems, frameworks and user interfaces (UI) with self-adaptive capabilities. Section III presents the framework, its design and main functions, an application built with it and an alternative communication system for the framework. Section IV presents the results, including the comparison between the two communication systems. Section V discusses the benefits of the proposed framework and future developments.

II. Related work

This section first examines how MDE and semantic technologies relate to one other and what has been done to bridge the two worlds, and second, reviews works on auto-adaptiveness, or more generally on the self-* properties of applications and information systems.

A. *Model-driven engineering and ontology-driven architecture*

Since the 1990s, MDE methodologies have focused on enabling software development from models. In order to maximize productivity, the model of the software application would be sufficient for programs to automatically generate the software itself. Though there are some success stories in MDE, it has not become a universal approach since adopting it remains complex and time consuming. Even so, researchers and companies are still devoting much attention to MDE because of its great promises [7]. In [8], Douglas C. Schmidt described MDE as a promising approach to shield developers from platform complexity, just as early programming languages protected programmers from the complexity of machine code. Schmidt stated that third-generation languages failed to alleviate this complexity due to their own complexity and to the rapid evolution and proliferation of platforms.

Ontologies have also been a popular research subject in the recent years, due primarily to their interoperability capabilities, which could facilitate the advent of the semantic web. Since an ontology is the "description of the concepts and the relationships that can formally exist for an agent or community of agent" [9], it is understandable why researchers have tried to use them with MDE.

The object management group (OMG), proponents of the model-driven architecture (MDA) [10], states that the goals of their approach include application re-use, complexity reduction, cross-platform interoperability, domain specificity and platform independence. Since these are also objectives of semantic technologies, synergy may presumably be achievable by combining the two paradigms. The World Wide Web Consortium (W3C), providers of the foundation of the semantic web, suggests that even if MDA is a good framework for software development, it could be improved by the use of semantic web technologies to disambiguate domain vocabularies, validate model consistency and increase the expressivity of the constraints representation. By thus augmenting the OMG methodology stack, ontologies could lead to the rise of ODA [11].

Pan *et al.* propose using ontologies and MDA together to reap the best of both worlds [12]. Their approach is to build bridges between the ModelWare and OntologyWare technical spaces. Both technical spaces are constructed on different layers, from metalanguages (M3), languages (M2) and models (M1) to running instances (M0). By bridging each of these layers, the ontologies' capabilities would be enabled in an MDA approach during software development. Ontologies should be integrated with model-driven software development in order to validate the consistency of models, guide software developers and causally connect specifications during the development process [12].

In what seems like a much simpler and straightforward way to bring those two worlds together, Martins Zviedris *et al.* describe how they automatically build ontology-based information systems [13]. Following the Sowa's principle that every software system has an ontology, implicit or explicit [14], the authors believe it possible to develop a universal platform-independent meta-model using an MDA approach.

They do so by first developing an ontology of web applications and then instantiating this ontology each time they wish to build a new information system. An engine they built is then used to "understand" the instance of a particular application and automatically generate its code. The result is a hard-coded non-adaptive application with a one-to-one mapping of the domain ontology classes and properties into JAVA classes. The resulting application can be easily rebuilt if any change is made in the data model but must be recompiled to use.

The main difference between the work of Pan *et al.* and of Zviedris *et al.* is that the former are trying to bring the capabilities of ontologies into the MDA world, while the latter are focusing on bringing MDA learning into semantic standards. Although the approach of Pan *et al.* to bridging all the standards enables the use of many tools already developed with both technologies, it is far more complex to implement. By ignoring OMG standards, Zviedris *et al.* more easily bring MDA learning into the semantic realm, but at the cost of coding their own MDA tools, i.e., their web application builder and their web application runtime engine. In our view, both teams are working to achieve ODA in opposite ways. Our ODA approach is similar to Zviedris, enhancing upon it by incorporating auto-adaptive capabilities.

B. *Self-* properties*

In 2001, IBM proposed the Autonomic Computing Initiative [15] with the objective to develop mechanisms that would allow systems and subsystems to self-adapt to unpredictable changes. Conferences such as Software Engineering for Adaptive and Self-Managing Systems (SEAMS) [16] or Engineering of Autonomic and Autonomous Systems (EASe) [17] show that system and software self-adaptability is still an important research area, now divided into a variety of subfields. Amongst them, one could include information system self-adaptability to an evolving data model.

As Dobson *et al.* pointed out [18], the Autonomic Computing Initiative did not fulfill the promises announced [19]. Though many individual advancements have yielded some of the expected benefits, there is still no integrated solution resulting in an autonomous system. This is a task being undertaken by some researchers, such as Bermejo-Alonso who is attempting to develop an ontology for the engineering of autonomous systems [20]. All those individual advancements fall into the category of "self-* properties", i.e., ways for systems to automatically maintain themselves throughout different scenarios [21].

The self-adaptability mechanisms of the framework we proposed could help develop self-aware or self-adjusting properties [22] leading to the development of autonomic components. Within the hierarchies of self-* properties of both Salehie and Tahvildari [23] and Berns and Ghosh [21], our framework would be classified as a set of self-configuring properties. Once the framework is integrated into an AAB, some self-optimizing properties are likely to emerge.

As the framework's ultimate goal is semi-automatic development of completely adaptive applications, it is important to look at current adaptive user interfaces (UIs), and systems to study their strengths and weaknesses. Recently, Akiki *et al.* [24] presented an overview of the most important adaptive UIs, evaluating and classifying them. They divided the design of adaptive UIs into two approaches: (1) MDE and (2) window managers and widget toolkits. They then proposed seven criteria to evaluate the two approaches and concluded that the first has more advantages than the second. They next established 21 criteria to evaluate adaptive model-driven development systems, specifying whether each criterion applies to architectures, techniques or development tools. Lastly, they evaluated many UIs adapting to their context of use. This set of criteria provides a valuable starting point and checklist for devising a new adaptive UI.

At Hydro-Québec, progress has been made in self-adapting applications with the dynamic information modelling (DIM) development environment [6]. Some client-server applications built using this system have been put into production and are still in use today. Self-adaptation, even though it is only to the data model, has proven to be beneficial, especially when evolutionary prototyping is used as a development methodology [25]. In DIM, the proposed development library was not a client-server framework and was used as a private, closed semantic modeling system. Those benefits were an incentive to continue following the evolutionary prototyping approach, as does the framework and even more so the AAB. The use of standards like RDF makes it possible to continue developing this research field in concert with other researchers world-wide.

McGinnes and Kapros circumscribe the problem of non-adaptive applications as a conceptual dependence upon the data model [26]. They describe this dependence between the data model and the resulting application as undesirable software coupling. The authors use the term “adaptive information system” (AIS) for an information system that adapts to changes made to the underlying data model. They conclude that most applications based on information systems in use today are dependent on their domain model. Such systems must thus be maintained every time the data model is changed, even the slightest change potentially resulting in costly, time-consuming adaptation.

McGinnes and Kapros propose six principles to achieve conceptual independence over any data source (see Table I). Using those principles, they show that it is possible to build an AIS based on an Extensible Markup Language (XML) mapping of an RDB data source [26]. Applying those principles to ontologies based on RDF brings useful insights (see Table I) on the use of those technologies in an AIS. Achieving conceptual independence using RDF-based technologies such as Resource Description Framework Schema (RDFS) and Web Ontology Language (OWL) is arguably more intuitive than using RDB data sources. RDF-based technologies actually have many of the required properties inherently built into their design, thus reducing the complexity of achieving conceptual independence. In Table I, principles 3, 5 and 6 may be considered inherent to this technology. Use of the other principles is discussed in Section III.

The proposed ontology-based adaptive information system framework (OBAISF) is presented in the next section. The applications built with OBAISF are conceptually independent from their data model, like McGinnes and Kapros but with independence achieved using semantic technologies.

III. Proposed Ontology-Based Adaptive Information System Framework

As stated previously, our current goal is to develop an AAB that will use an ontology-based adaptive information system framework (OBAISF) to construct auto-adaptive applications. The AAB is the combination of an ontology browser (OB), a SPARQL query builder (SQB) and an OBAISF. SPARQL stands for "SPARQL Protocol and RDF Query Language" [27]. The OB and SQB designs will be the subject of a future paper. In the coming months, the OB will be enhanced with an editing module supporting the instantiation of a web application ontology (WAO), in line with the work of Zviedris *et al.* [13] presented in Section II. With this editing module, web application components can be added to a particular instantiation of the WAO and customized through OB and SQB functionalities.

A. Proposed adaptive application builder

The OB has been developed to navigate any OWL ontology. It first presents all the classes of an OWL graph in a tree. Then, upon selection, a box shows all the properties of the selected object and those of its superclasses. From then on, the user can navigate the ontology using object-type properties, which open new boxes (Figure 1). In the AAB, the OB will be used to choose classes and properties of an ontology and link them to application components. For example, two classes linked by an object-type property could be selected so their instances become the branches and leaves of a data tree component.

The SQB is built on top of the OB and uses a recursive JAVA engine to translate a user-originated visual query into a proper SPARQL query. The SQB supports querying data-type properties and applying filters to them (Figure 1). In the AAB, the SQB will be used to build views on the semantic data. This way, the end user of an application can be presented with any view that could be made from the ontology.

All this is made possible by the semantic properties in Table I, which enable the creation of the OBAISF. The framework is basically a set of generic functions that dynamically query the ontology before querying a set of its instances. Those generic functions were first developed to be compatible with RDFS ontologies but are now being updated to also suit OWL ontologies. The remainder of this section will present an AIS built with an OBAISF for a decision support application.

TABLE I. CONCEPTUAL INDEPENDENCE PRINCIPLES AND APPLICATIONS.

CONCEPTUAL INDEPENDENCE PRINCIPLES [26]	**APPLICATIONS OF THE PRINCIPLES WITH RDF-BASED TECHNOLOGIES**
1. Reusable functionality (structurally- appropriate behavior): The AIS can support any conceptual model. Domain-dependent code and structures are avoided. Useful generic functionality is invoked at run time for each entity type.	This principle applies similarly using a triplestore data source. Generic SPARQL requests will be obtained by exclusively hard-coding resources from the RDF, RDFS or OWL semantics, leaving other resources soft-coded. The data model can be inspected at run time using generic SPARQL requests.
2. Known categories of data (semantically- appropriate behavior): Each entity type is associated with one or more predefined generic categories. Category-specific functionality is invoked at run time for each entity type.	All ontologies using RDFS or OWL languages contain *ipso facto* the same conceptual basis. The definition of those meta-entities is the semantics of RDF, RDFS and OWL. By employing those meta-entities as the most generic entities of the AIS, any RDF-based ontology can be used. McGinnes and Kapros use archetypal categories taken from the field of psychology to classify entities according to the behaviours the AIS should adopt in their presence. This interesting idea will be considered later on in the development of this AIS, but is not yet essential.
3. Adaptive data management (schema evolution): The AIS can store and reconcile data with multiple definitions for each entity type (i.e., multiple conceptual models), allowing the end user to make sense of the data.	Firstly, RDF technology uses what McGinnes and Kapros call "soft schemas": data models stored as data. Secondly, RDF technology allows individuals with different valued properties to coexist in the same class. Moreover, individuals can belong to more than one class. Axioms like *OWL:sameAs* or *OWL:equivalentClass* make it possible to reconcile data from distinctly described entities. Two previously distinct classes declared as equivalent will have, by inference, the same set of properties and then two individuals of this new class may have only different valued properties. This mechanism thus supports reconciliation of data from different conceptual models. As the model evolves, data using different conceptual models remains available and is instantly accessible without any refactoring of the AIS.
4. Schema enforcement (domain and referential integrity): Each item of stored data conforms to a particular entity type definition, which was enforced at the time of data entry (or last edit).	In technologies such as OWL, domain integrity and referential integrity can be validated with reasoners. As for data types, literal data is usually associated with basic types upon entry in a semantic store.
5. Entity identification (entity integrity): The stored data relating to each entity is uniquely identified in a way that is invariant with respect to schema change.	In RDF technology, entity identification is provided by the URI mechanism, and is already invariant with respect to schema change.
6. Labelling (data management): The stored data relating to each entity is labelled such that the applicable conceptual models can be determined.	Using RDF technology, this principle means that every individual must belong to a class. It then does not matter how much the class has changed over time since all individuals in it can have any number of valued or non-valued properties. However, human-readable labels are necessary to present the information to the users and it is mandatory to assign such labels to each entity.

B. Proposed adaptive information system

This AIS was developed as a three-tier client-server system: a triplestore, a generic server and a web interface.

The triplestore is used to store the knowledge bases constituted by a conceptual model and its individuals. In the proposed AIS, two knowledge bases are used: one for the domain of expertise and one for the presentation of information. The triplestore used in this framework is an Oracle 12c RDF Semantic Graph.

The server-tier is coded using a standard JAVA Enterprise Edition technology. It is built as a web service offering different generic functions with a REST client-server interface. These services are implemented using the Jena library [28] to process requests written in the SPARQL query language.

The user interface is implemented in JavaScript with the Ext.js 4.2.2 library [29]. It uses the REST interface to communicate with the server. It is thus independent from the server and could be coded using another technology.

We used our framework to implement a decision support application to be used at IREQ. The purpose of the application is to gather power transformer oil sampling data, such as methanol and ethanol concentrations, to monitor power transformer health and provide suitable maintenance advice to specialists. The application acts as a dashboard, within which the users can add, update or delete entries, and do simple searches. It also perform automated calculations, e.g., adjusting concentrations of specific molecules depending on the oil temperature. Engineers use the application to record maintenance operations and measurements, track and compare the health of transformers, and test and refine parameters used in concentration adjustment equations.

The conceptual model of this application has six classes that will be used in the subsequent examples:

1) PowerStation,
2) PowerTransformer,
3) Measurement,
4) MaintenanceIntervention,
5) ConversionParameter, and
6) PowerStationAndTransformerAssociation.

Each of these classes has between two and twelve properties and comprises up to 7,000 individuals. This application has been chosen to validate the framework since it requires a variety of functionalities that would be suitable for a wide range of applications in addition to having a small and simple ontology, easy to build and test at this stage of the project.

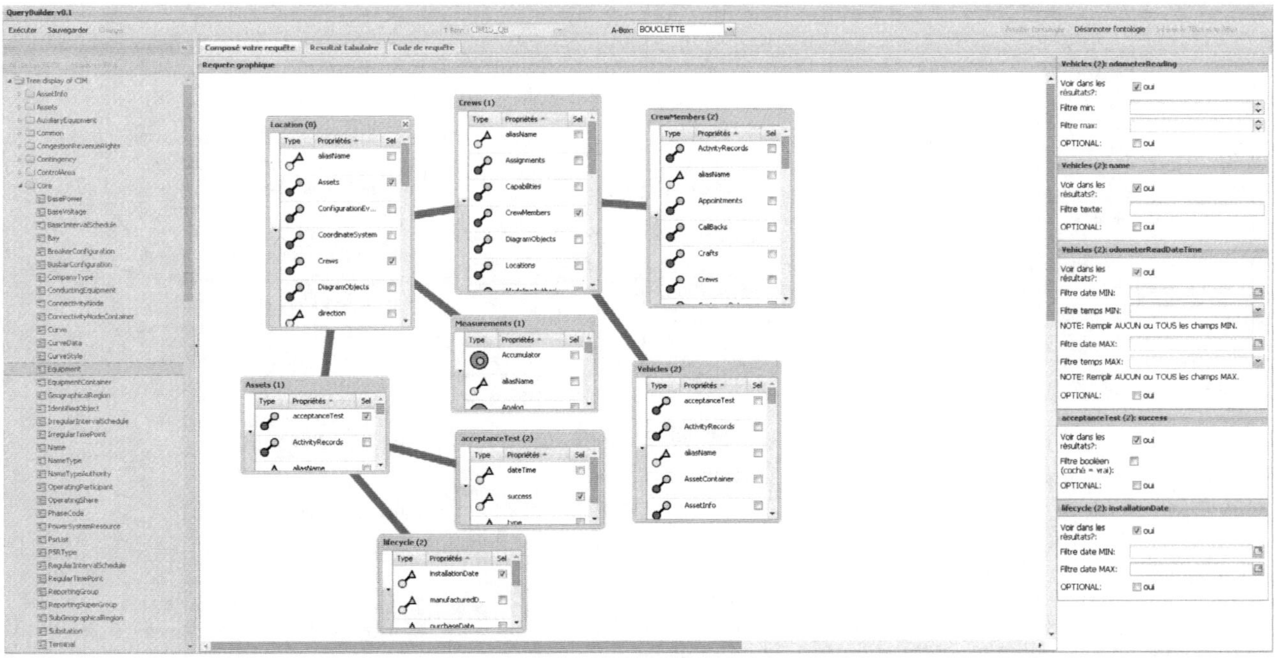

Figure 1. Ontology Browser and Sparql Query Builder overview: Center - Ontology Browser for navigating classes. Right - Filters on datatype properties to be used in the Sparql Query Builder.

1) Application triplestore setting: Most of this transformer monitoring application's data is stored in a RDB. A semantic meta-model (T-Box) has been designed to model the required classes (PowerTransformer, PowerStation, etc.). Then, by using the D2RQ library [30], the data from the RDB has been converted into an RDF graph of individuals (A-Box). The T-Box has been designed using RDFS semantics. It contains solely association relationships and essentially describes the classes and the properties with their domain and range. Each class, property and individual has been labeled in order to be displayed on the visual interface.

In order to better understand this application, Figure 2 presents a high-level view of its architecture. At the initialization phase, the application requests the triplestore via a web service to show a tree view of the data model. The user can view an individual of a class (e.g., a power transformer) by selecting a leaf in the tree. When the user clicks on this leaf, the interface sends a request to the server through its web service. Upon receipt of the request, the server dynamically gathers a number of classes determined by the model, all of which have an association relationship with the class of the selected individual. For each of these classes, the server will then gather the list of its properties and the list of its individuals related to the user's selection. This information can be transferred to the client using two systems: (1) a generic JAVA object and its corresponding JSON representation or (2) a generic triple model and its corresponding JSON-LD representation. A triple is "the fundamental RDF structure" [31] consisting of a subject, a predicate and an object. The W3C describes JSON-LD as "a JSON-based format to serialize Linked Data [whose] syntax is designed to easily integrate into deployed systems that already use JSON" [32]. As both JSON and JSON-LD

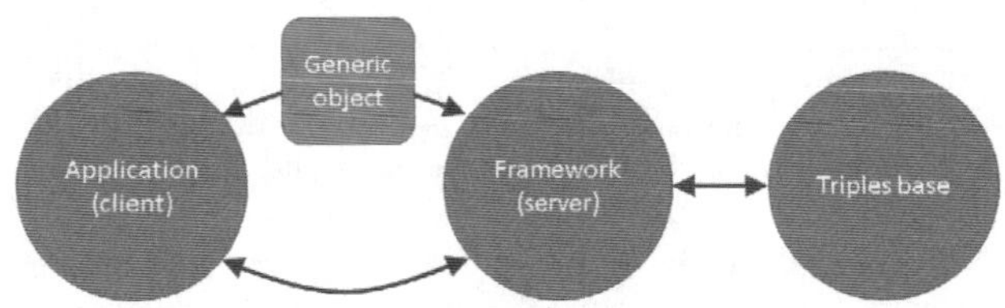

Figure 2. Adaptive information system framework.

share a similar data structure, they can both be processed by most web APIs or frameworks, with the difference that JSON-LD must be processed by a library beforehand. Those generic objects or models contain all the information to display on the UI and to request for further operations to the server, as Create, Read, Update, and Delete (CRUD) operations.

The next section will describe both data communication systems (using a generic JAVA object or using a generic triple model).

2) Two systems for dynamic visualization of the semantic data: Here are the main design elements for both systems for dynamic visualization of the information.

a) System 1 - Generic object system: In this system, a generic JAVA class (meta-class) was designed to support dynamic gathering of information from the semantic store. The resulting object is used to transfer information from the semantic store to the UI. A given object's instance is built from generic SPARQL requests using RDF and RDFS semantics. The object has fixed attributes used to hold information about the RDFS class, its properties and individuals. It also holds the path and filters used to select the individuals or the class

- Class
  - URI
  - Label
- List of properties, each element containing:
  - URI
  - Label
  - Range
  - Presentation information
- List of individuals, each element containing:
  - Property-value mapping of each element in the list of properties for every listed individual
- Access
  - Filter (Specified individual of the range class)
  - Path (Bridge predicate)

Figure 3. Definition of the JAVA generic object.

itself. See Figure 3 for the definition of the object.

Note here that each individual contains a property-value mapping for each property in the list of properties and its corresponding value, if any. The access elements contain the path in the graph to go to the class (i.e., the property linking the individuals of the two classes) and the filter (i.e., an individual in the range class) used to select the individuals in the domain class. The term "Bridge predicate" will be used to refer to the property linking the domain class and range class, i.e., the path (see Figure 5).

In the application developed, selecting a power transformer in the tree will result in a request to find individuals linked to it from all classes having a property whose range is the Transformer class, i.e., individuals from the domain classes of the Transformer class. For each class found, a generic object is created.

The example in Figure 4 helps to better understand how generic objects are created. In this example, the user has selected the power transformer numbered 123. The framework then queries the model and finds three classes having an associative relationship with the PowerTransformer class: Measurement, MaintenanceIntervention and PowerStationAndTransformerAssociation. Those three classes will be fetched but, for the sake of simplicity, this example only presents the Measurement class case. Its uniform resource identifier (URI) [33] and label have first been retrieved, followed by the list of its properties and the list of its individuals. This second list contains a mapping for each individual, between every property in the list of properties and its value for this individual, if any.

In the example in Figure 4, the filter is the specified individual of the range class, i.e., the power transformer numbered 123. It is considered a filter because it reduces the number of individuals to retrieve. Here, the path is simply the Bridge predicate between the range and the domain classes. Further development should lead to the creation of more filter and path options, as well as sequences and aggregations of these options.

In our AIS, every time a power transformer is selected in the tree, the model is inspected dynamically to find all the domain classes of the PowerTransformer class and all individuals linked to the selected power transformer. Hence, if a new domain class is added, the application will automatically present it to the user.

- Class
  - URI: <hydroquebec:Measurement>
  - Label: "Measurement"
- List of properties
  - Prop 1
    - URI: <hydroquebec:Measurement#ETH
    - Label: "Ethanol_Concentration"
    - Range: <xsd:decimal>
    - Presentation information: "numberField"
  - Prop 2
    - URI: <hydroquebec:Measurement#METH
    - Label: "Methanol_Concentration"
    - Range: <xsd:decimal>
    - Presentation information: "numberField"
  - ...
- List of individuals
  - Ind 1
    - Ethanol_Concentration: 127.6
    - Methanol_Concentration: 156.7
    - ...
  - Ind 2
    - Ethanol_Concentration: 126.7
    - Methanol_Concentration: 157.6
    - ...
- Access
  - Filter: <hydroquebec:PowerTransformer#123>
  - Path: <hydroquebec:Measurement#PowerTransformerURI>

Figure 4. Example of a JAVA generic object.

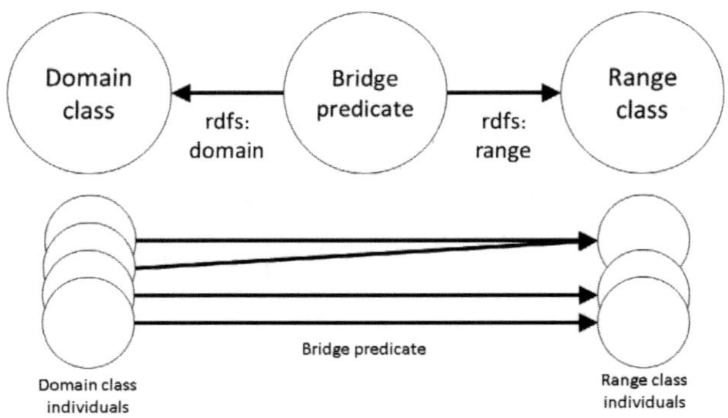

Figure 5. Graph representation of the range and domain classes in an associative relationship.

The application uses a tree to show the user a specific portion of the semantic graph (see Figure 7). In our case, the tree first shows all the power stations as folders that can be expanded to see the power transformers in each.

When the user selects a node (e.g., power transformer 123), the client UI sends a request to the AIS server using a generic process to dynamically gather the domain classes (e.g., the Measurement class) in relationship with the range class (e.g., the PowerTransformer class). For each of these classes, the properties will first be found, and then all the individuals of the domain classes linked with the user-selected individual will be retrieved. As a result, a list of generic JAVA objects will be generated, where each object corresponds to a domain class.

These JAVA objects are then automatically converted to JSON, using the Jackson library [34] and sent to the UI.

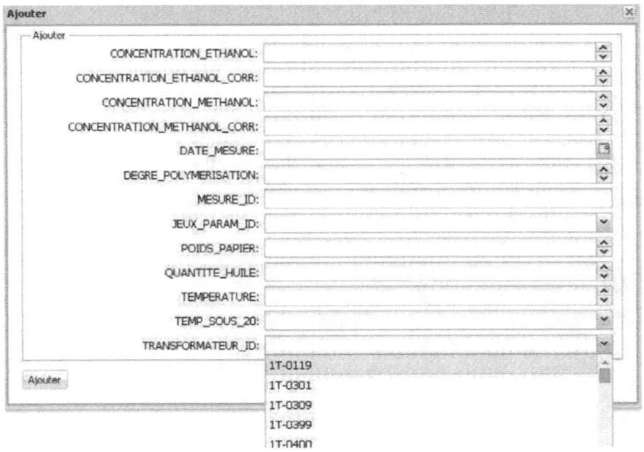

Figure 6. Example of individual CRUD form.

b) System 2 - Generic triples system: Using JAVA generic objects and transmitting them in the JSON format seems natural in an object-oriented paradigm. However, since the database is part of the semantic world, keeping the data in RDF format should also be appropriate.

An important difference between the first and the second system is that generic SELECT queries in the former are replaced by a generic CONSTRUCT query in the latter. The use of SELECT queries leads to the parsing of result sets in the object-oriented paradigm, i.e., the generic JAVA object. The CONSTRUCT query, on the other hand, leads to the creation of a new set of RDF statements. Using the Jena library, this set can be directly mapped into JSON-LD format.

By building the generic CONSTRUCT query, it was possible to extract the same data from the triplestore as when using System 1. This query was designed to produce an RDF graph with the same data structure as that of the JAVA generic object of System 1, so the client interface could use both transmission methods without any major change.

In order to transform the JSON-LD RDF graphs into a tree-like structure, the JSON-LD library for JavaScript was used [35]. This library enables the system to frame the RDF graph in a non-redundant data tree and to compact its URIs into keywords, thus presenting the information just as a normal JSON would do.

3) After data transmission: No matter which method is used, once transmission is complete and the data is sent to the client side, the UI will produce a 2D matrix for every class in the list (see Figure 7). These matrices show the information to the user using human readable labels. The user can then request CRUD operations on individuals represented in the matrices (see Figure 7).

Due to the genericity of the functions, changes made to the data model are immediately available to all AIS users. This genericity was obtained as discussed in the first and second principles of Table I. From then on, every request will retrieve individuals and classes from the new model with no need to recompile the client or server. This is because both the data model and its instances are queried. In addition to adapting to any model, a request used in runtime will inspect the actual version of the model.

In the current state of the framework implementation, if changes are made in the T-Box, either by modifying the properties of some domain classes or by adding a new domain class related to the class of the tree leaves, the users will instantly begin to navigate in the new model. Without code refactoring, no other changes are possible in this implementation.

The main presentation tree does not grant access to every class in the semantic graph. Therefore, the UI has been given other access points, from which the user can request directly previously inaccessible classes. The system uses a similar generic function to request this information, except that it retrieves the class itself and all its individuals instead of using the previously presented domain class mechanism. Either the same generic JAVA object or generic triples model can be used, but they do not contain any access information. The same CRUD operations can still be performed on individuals.

4) The CRUD services: Our framework allows CRUD services only on individuals, not on classes or properties. Other means are used to edit the conceptual model. Further work will be done to allow modeling of the T-Box from the UI, either by adding capabilities to the OB or by developing ontology edition components usable in any AIS made with the AAB. The CRUD services on the A-Box are done on the client side using forms showing the properties of the class and their value for the selected individuals, if any (see Figure 6). These forms are created from the properties listed in the generic JAVA object or the generic triples model.

In order to help the user and validate the input, a presentation knowledge base comprising the various presentation options has been established. This information is associated with every property of the domain knowledge base and is passed on by the JAVA generic object or the generic triples model. It indicates how to establish every entry field of the forms. Those forms are constructed dynamically, adapting the user's interaction options based on the values of properties according to the presentation knowledge base information. This dynamic type retrieval is in line with conceptual independence principle 4 in Table I.

In further developments, mechanisms will be designed to automatically link domain ontology properties to presentation ontology individuals. Some ontologies contain semantics, such as Enumeration or Bag, that can be used to predict the correct entry field's type for a given property. Enumeration, for instance, can be represented as a list of individuals that may be selected by the user. In general, the range of a property is a good indicator of the required type of a given entry field. Finally, functions will be implemented to allow the user to change the type of the entry field at runtime.

In the current state of the framework, four types of entry fields are implemented: numerical field, text field, list field and date field. Upon expansion, the list field requests a service that finds all the existing values associated to this property. For the fields used to update literals, the range type of the property is used for validation. Cardinalities exist in the presentation knowledge base so the forms can specify to the user the required fields, if any.

5) Graphics: Graphic classes and related properties have been added to the presentation knowledge base to represent graphic views, such as histograms or clouds of points. Graphic

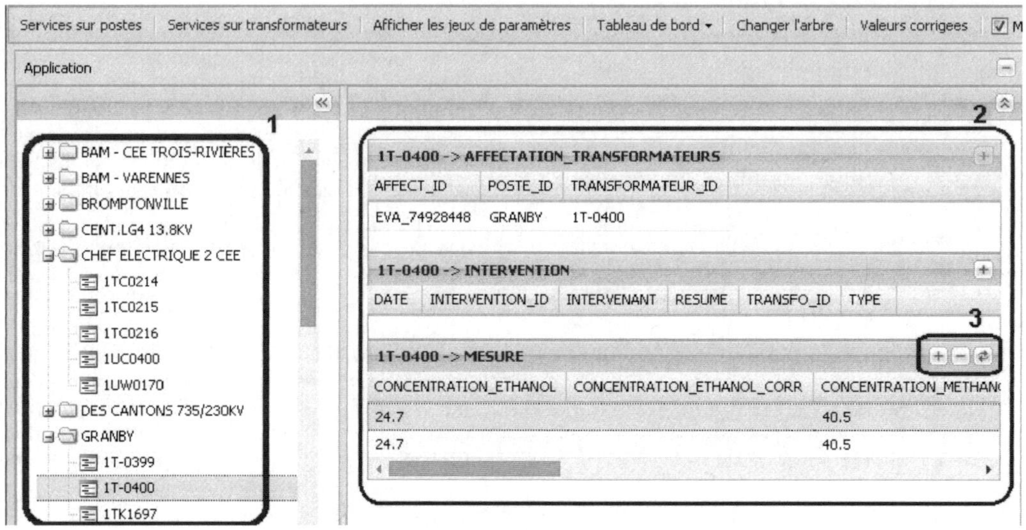

Figure 7. Application -(1) tree view, (2) matrices and (3) buttons for CRUD operations.

properties are used to specify the association between the graphic elements such as X-axis data, Y-axis data, labels, etc. The axes are linked to domain ontology properties.

C. *Organization of knowledge bases*

This use-case application required the use of multiple stores to distinguish between domain information, presentation information, conceptual-model knowledge, individuals, editable and non-editable information. The application requires that all this information integrate seamlessly on the UI. When information is requested, a virtual aggregation is done, depending on which data sources the user wants to visualize.

The semantic graphs are organized as follows: the T-Box semantic models, one for the presentation knowledge and one for the domain knowledge, are separated from their respective A-Box semantic models (see Figure 8).

The presentation T-Box graph represents knowledge that will be common to all applications using the framework. Its A-Box contains form entry field types and application-specific graphics.

The domain T-Box graph represents knowledge specific to the application domain of expertise. Its A-Box is divided into four semantic graphs. It is first split into two graphs since data may come from two sources: the organization RDB or users themselves. For security reasons, it is impossible to apply changes to the organization RDB from the application. The A-Box is hence split into two graphs depending on the origin of the data: a non-editable one with data from the organization RDB and an editable one with user-created data. It is then easy to synchronize the non-editable graph to keep it updated, while not losing any user-created information. Moreover, this division enables the two data sets to be displayed independently, but only if another separation is created.

Independent data can be presented on their own to the user but other data depend upon these independent data to be shown. Therefore, a division relative to the dependence of the information is needed. Dependent A-Box individuals are

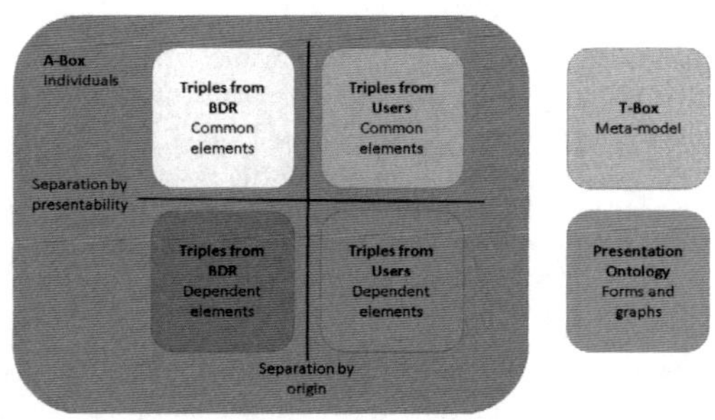

Figure 8. Organization of semantic graphs.

located in one graph and independent individuals are located in another. For example, if the user only wants to see the user-entered power transformer measurements imported from the organization database, information from both sources will be needed. Holding the power transformers in the independent graphs and the measurements in the dependent one will allow the display of user-entered measurements exclusively, even the ones describing power transformers held in the RDB. When CRUD services are used, a service is called upon to indicate on the form whether data can be modified or suppressed, depending on its source.

This organization of the A-Box in four semantic graphs was established for convenience, but it would be beneficial for this mechanism to be generic to the many applications used in an organization where information comes from various sources with different security constraints. Further testing must be done to establish a completely generic methodology.

IV. RESULTS

The OBAISF has been used to create a client-server decision support application. Using the generic services of the framework, the classes and properties in the conceptual model can be modified directly in the triplestore without affecting the application. The UI presentation will adjust automatically according to the latest update of the conceptual model, since the request queries the semantic graph dynamically. The proposed framework supports all CRUD operations to be performed on individuals. Moreover, the framework will query the conceptual model in the semantic graph for each request. This differs from a standard application where the conceptual model is taken into consideration only at compile time. The resulting application is ready to be put into production. Once in production, since it will be able to automatically adapt to conceptual model changes, it should easily evolve as the framework is extended.

As stated, the OBAISF will enable the AAB. The AAB will help to create many information systems to be used throughout Hydro-Québec and its research institute. This should shorten the time needed to create applications. In research institute context where new knowledge in the domain of electric utilities is constantly emerging, auto-adaptive applications should require minimal time to maintain, thus reducing the time between discoveries and their practical implementation. As seen in Table I, RDF technologies have inherent properties facilitating the design of adaptive applications.

The adaptiveness of those applications is in large part due to the way the database is queried. Of the various ways that could have been used to obtain the data in a generic manner, the two below have been tested and compared.

A. Results - Comparison of two communication systems

Two client-server communication systems were tested on the same virtual machine using 16 gigabytes of RAM and four cores. The first involves a generic JAVA object populated by generic SPARQL queries and automatically transformed to the JSON data format. The second uses another generic SPARQL query but to construct triple models sent to the client in the JSON-LD data format. Both communication systems manage to transmit the same data, formatted in the same structure, in a generic manner, thus bringing the same flexibility to the applications. Except for the communication systems, all the other methods of the AIS were shared between the two configurations. The two communication systems were compared for speed, code length and possibilities.

In our implementation, the generic JAVA object system retrieved small data sets faster, but became slower than the JSON-LD system as the data sets increased in size. This is primarily because the generic JAVA object is populated by several SPARQL SELECT queries; whereas the JSON-LD system is populated by only one CONSTRUCT query, less efficient for processing small data sets but gaining efficiency with larger ones.

To be completely fair in comparing the speed of the two systems, an effort should be made to minimize the number of queries in the first, and to optimize all the queries in both. Even doing so, the first technique will always require more queries than the second to obtain the same results. This is because SPARQL SELECT query outputs are result sets organized as 2D matrices. In order to have meaningful result sets, it is useful to split the queries; failing to do so creates numerous near identical lines in 2D matrices due to data replication. The number of queries needed for the first system is $1 + 2c$, where c is the number of classes describing the selected individual retrieved. CONSTRUCT query output being a set of triples, the results are in the form of an oriented graph. In the second system, a single CONSTRUCT query can thus yield all the required results in a meaningful manner.

Code length was compared between the two systems. Though not a really meaningful metric, it is a first attempt at characterizing the two systems. Further work is needed to calculate better metrics to account for code maintainability, readability and complexity when comparing systems. For code length, the JSON-LD system is more advantageous, requiring three times fewer lines on the server side to yield the same result. On the client side, the code is almost exactly the same in both cases with the exception of the use of the JSON-LD.JS library [35] for the second system. This library is used to transform the triples in the received JSON-LD into JSON format by first rearranging them into a tree shape by framing them according to a pre-defined frame and then compacting the properties' URI into pre-set keywords. These two operations result in a JSON object usable by any JSON-friendly library.

A major advantage of the second system is only visible when picturing the AAB. With this system, SPARQL queries used for application customization can be stored as a set of triples. As the visual queries made from the SQB are stored in the form of triples, they can be easily linked to the domain ontology by simply joining the query repository with the ontology. This enables automatic validation of applications upon modification of the ontology. Thus, the changes in the ontology that will not be tackled by the auto-adaptive properties of the OBAISF will still be automatically spotted, marked and sent to a power user or an administrator. The same mechanism is conceivable with the first system but would be more difficult to implement.

Another advantage of the second system is potential use of inference capabilities on the client side of the applications. While it has not yet been tested, bringing triples from the triplestore to the client side would make it possible to use RDF-friendly algorithms, like inferencing, without any communication with the database server. This could be useful in some use cases, like for portable applications.

B. Limitations

The main limitation of the entire framework is how it explores the model at each request. It can now only retrieve individuals from classes that are one associative relationship away from a desired individual. Further work is required to find ways to expand this exploration, a crucial factor for the framework to be effective in large-scale ontologies. The OB should help to develop this mechanism rapidly. Associating classes and properties with annotations seems like an easy way to solve this problem but more sophisticated solutions may yield better results.

Tests must still be run to determine performance differences between a dynamic application such as the one we developed and a static one, and to observe the scaling potential. The resulting application from the proposed framework is not expected to perform as well as a similar application developed from a more conventional framework but the difference in performance has yet to be established. It will then be possible to evaluate over the long run how much the lower costs incurred during the AIS development and maintenance processes offset any reduced performance.

C. Lessons learned

While implementing this proof of concept, we learned that many of the properties needed to achieve conceptual independence are inherent to RDF technology. Exclusively hard-coding resources from RDF, RDFS and OWL semantics in all SPARQL requests and leaving all other resources soft-coded are necessary conditions to obtain conceptual independence. Because the semantics of these three languages (RDF, RDFS, and OWL) are shared across RDF-based ontologies, they form a common conceptual basis to all the domains they can represent. Limiting conceptual dependencies to their semantics, the applications developed can use any such ontology, regardless of its knowledge domain.

AISs built using the AAB will fall into the MDE paradigm, in the sense that a meta-model language is used to describe all AISs independently of their domain and that by designing their model using WAO components will suffice to generate their code. The AIS will be considered M0; WAO, M1; OWL, M2; and RDFS, M3. This architecture mainly uses RDF for the platform-independent model (PIM) and JavaScript for the platform-specific language (PSL). By encapsulating the PSL into the PIM, i.e., by inserting application components inside the classes of an ontology, the transformation model can become generic. This transformation model will work independently from the PSL. Indeed, as long as the engine reading the WAO instances and transforming them into web applications uses generic functions, it can build them in any web-friendly language. This should also make it possible to easily change PSL components, thus making application maintenance processes even more flexible. This technique should also increase code reuse across the entire application-building process since all applications built with it can share the same components and processes. Lastly, this should reduce refactoring efforts.

V. Conclusion and Future Work

As hypothesized, an AIS based on a triplestore is easier to implement than an AIS using XML to dynamize functions on an RDB. Many artifices must be considered to build an AIS from a RDB, something not required with semantic technologies, as seen from Table I. The use of a library to map the RDB into a triplestore appears a judicious way to quickly and easily achieve the conceptual independence needed in an AIS.

With the use of an RDF representation to store the information, generic SPARQL queries that can search any semantic graph for both conceptual knowledge and individual information are easily devised. This makes the AIS able to adapt to changes in the conceptual model and to be used for different application domains. The framework could also be used with evolutionary prototyping application development as the future AAB. At Hydro-Québec, other large-scale client-server applications have already been successfully developed using evolutionary prototyping, highlighting the benefits of such technologies compared to standard development processes [25].

A deeper analysis is needed to determine which of the two communication systems to choose. So far, the second system seems more promising, mainly due to greater speed in processing large data sets and its capability to automatically spot the impact a modification to the ontology will have on the applications. More exhaustive tests are underway and should improve results.

Based on this proof of concept, the proposed AAB will be designed to use this OBAISF in order to build numerous AISs. Our goal is to produce interpreted applications with their code and processes maintained inside the domain ontology. Any instantiation of the WAO will be a custom aggregation of different generic components using the generic functions of the OBAISF. The last part of the AAB is building an engine capable of reading a WAO instantiation and generating the application on the fly. A technique to encode treatment of the data inside the ontology should also be developed.

Using the OBAISF through the AAB to build new applications will further test the approach. In doing so, new functions will be developed eventually leading to more complete AISs. Ideally, the AISs should be able to take advantage of all RDF, RDFS, and OWL semantics. The current OBAISF uses only RDFS semantics; adding OWL capabilities will make the use of inference reasoners possible. This will be a major benefit to the AAB, the reasoner supporting validation during the creation of applications.

In the current release, only individuals can be edited by the user through forms. Editing features on the meta-model should be enabled by adding an ontology editor on top of the OB and by incorporating these capabilities into the framework. The OB should eventually also be enhanced to enable the insertion of treatments of data inside the domain model. This will help reduce refactoring time and improve code reuse throughout the company.

The framework and the application demonstrate that an AIS can work easily and efficiently by capitalizing on RDF technology and its inherent properties. The future AAB should leverage the framework by giving power users an easy means to implement it in a wide variety of adaptive applications. Such systems can be useful in fast-evolving knowledge domains. They are fully in line with the AGILE development philosophy, allowing the data model to evolve freely at each iteration. Those considerations suggest that OBAISF and self-adapting applications could bring substantial cost reductions in application development and maintenance in the coming years.

Acknowledgment

The authors would like to thank Jérôme Côté, Arnaud Zinflou and Billel Redouane.

References

[1] L. Bhérer, L. Vouligny, M. Gaha, B. Redouane, and C. Desrosiers, "Ontology-based adaptive information system framework," in IARIA SEMAPRO 2015, The Ninth International Conference on Advances in Semantic Processing, Nice, France, July 2015, pp. 110–115.

[2] S. Staab, R. Studer, H.-P. Schnurr, and Y. Sure, "Knowledge processes and ontologies," IEEE Intelligent Systems, vol. 16, no. 1, Jan. 2001, pp. 26–34.

[3] J. Sequeda. Introduction to: Triplestores. [retrieved: 02, 2016]. [Online]. Available: http://www.dataversity.net/introduction-to-triplestores/ (2013)

[4] A. Zinflou, M. Gaha, A. Bouffard, L. Vouligny, C. Langheit, and M. Viau, "Application of an ontology-based and rule-based model in electric power utilities," in 2013 IEEE Seventh International Conference on Semantic Computing, Irvine, CA, USA, September 16-18, 2013, 2013, pp. 405–411.

[5] M. Gaha, A. Zinflou, C. Langheit, A. Bouffard, M. Viau, and L. Vouligny, "An ontology-based reasoning approach for electric power utilities," in Web Reasoning and Rule Systems - 7th International Conference, RR 2013, Mannheim, Germany, July 27-29, 2013. Proceedings, 2013, pp. 95–108.

[6] L. Vouligny and J.-M. Robert, "Online help system design based on the situated action theory," in Proceedings of the 2005 Latin American Conference on Human-computer Interaction, ser. CLIHC '05. New York, NY, USA: ACM, 2005, pp. 64–75.

[7] T. Gherbi, D. Meslati, and I. Borne, "MDE between promises and challenges." in UKSim, D. Al-Dabass, Ed. IEEE Computer Society, 2009, pp. 152–155. [Online]. Available: http://dblp.uni-trier.de/db/conf/uksim/uksim2009.html#GherbiMB09

[8] D. C. Schmidt, "Model-driven engineering," IEEE Computer, vol. 39, no. 2, February 2006. [Online]. Available: http://www.truststc.org/pubs/30.html

[9] T. R. Gruber, "Toward principles for the design of ontologies used for knowledge sharing?" International Journal of Human-Computer Studies, vol. 43, no. 5–6, 1995, pp. 907 – 928. [Online]. Available: http://www.sciencedirect.com/science/article/pii/S1071581985710816

[10] O. M. Group. Executive overview model driven architecture. [retrieved: 02, 2016]. [Online]. Available: http://www.omg.org/mda/executive_overview.html/ (2014)

[11] W3C. Ontology driven architectures and potential uses of the semantic web in systems and software engineering. [retrieved: 02, 2016]. [Online]. Available: https://www.w3.org/2001/sw/BestPractices/SE/ODA/ (2006)

[12] J. Z. Pan, S. Staab, U. Aßmann, J. Ebert, and Y. Zhao, Eds., Ontology-Driven Software Development. Berlin: Springer, 2013.

[13] M. Zviedris, A. Romane, G. Barzdins, and K. Cerans, Semantic Technology: Third Joint International Conference, JIST 2013, Seoul, South Korea, November 28–30, 2013, Revised Selected Papers. Cham: Springer International Publishing, 2014, ch. Ontology-Based Information System, pp. 33–47. [Online]. Available: http://dx.doi.org/10.1007/978-3-319-06826-8_3/

[14] J. Sowa, "Serious semantics, serious ontologies, panel," in Presented at Semantic Technology Conference (SEMTEC 2011), San Francisco, 2011.

[15] P. Horn, "Autonomic Computing: IBM's Perspective on the State of Information Technology," Tech. Rep., 2001.

[16] T. Vogel. Software engineering for self-adaptive systems. [retrieved: 06, 2015]. [Online]. Available: https://www.hpi.uni-potsdam.de/giese/public/selfadapt/ (2015)

[17] I. T. C. on Software Engineering. IEEE EASe 2014. [retrieved: 06, 2015]. [Online]. Available: http://tab.computer.org/aas/ease/2014/index.html (2014)

[18] S. Dobson, R. Sterritt, P. Nixon, and M. Hinchey, "Fulfilling the vision of autonomic computing," Computer, vol. 43, no. 1, 2010, pp. 35–41.

[19] J. O. Kephart and D. M. Chess, "The vision of autonomic computing," Computer, vol. 36, no. 1, Jan. 2003, pp. 41–50.

[20] J. Bermejo-Alonso, R. Sanz, M. Rodríguez, and C. Hernández, "Ontology-based engineering of autonomous systems," in Proceedings of the 2010 Sixth International Conference on Autonomic and Autonomous Systems, ser. ICAS '10. Washington, DC, USA: IEEE Computer Society, 2010, pp. 47–51.

[21] A. Berns and S. Ghosh, "Dissecting self-* properties," 2013 IEEE 7th International Conference on Self-Adaptive and Self-Organizing Systems, 2009, pp. 10–19.

[22] R. Sterritt and M. Hinchey, "SPAACE IV: Self-Properties for an Autonomous Computing Environment; Part IV A Newish Hope," in Engineering of Autonomic and Autonomous Systems (EASe), 2010 Seventh IEEE International Conference and Workshops on, March 2010, pp. 119–125.

[23] M. Salehie and L. Tahvildari, "Self-adaptive software: Landscape and research challenges," ACM Trans. Auton. Adapt. Syst., vol. 4, no. 2, May 2009, pp. 14:1–14:42. [Online]. Available: http://doi.acm.org/10.1145/1516533.1516538

[24] P. A. Akiki, A. K. Bandara, and Y. Yu, "Adaptive model-driven user interface development systems," ACM Comput. Surv., vol. 47, no. 1, May 2014, pp. 9:1–9:33. [Online]. Available: http://doi.acm.org/10.1145/2597999

[25] L. Vouligny, C. Hudon, and D. N. Nguyen, "Design of MIDA, a web-based diagnostic application for hydroelectric generators." in COMPSAC (2), S. I. Ahamed, E. Bertino, C. K. Chang, V. Getov, L. L. 0001, H. Ming, and R. Subramanyan, Eds. IEEE Computer Society, 2009, pp. 166–171.

[26] S. McGinnes and E. Kapros, "Conceptual independence: A design principle for the construction of adaptive information systems," Inf. Syst., vol. 47, 2015, pp. 33–50.

[27] D. Beckett. What does SPARQL stand for? [retrieved: 02, 2016]. [Online]. Available: https://lists.w3.org/Archives/Public/semantic-web/2011Oct/0041.html (2011)

[28] T. A. S. Foundation. Apache jena. [retrieved: 02, 2016]. [Online]. Available: https://jena.apache.org/ (2015)

[29] Sencha. Ext js 4.2. [retrieved: 02, 2016]. [Online]. Available: http://docs.sencha.com/extjs/4.2.2/ (2014)

[30] C. Bizer. D2RQ. [retrieved: 02, 2016]. [Online]. Available: http://http://d2rq.org/

[31] T. C. L. C. Inc. Definition of: RDF. [retrieved: 02, 2016]. [Online]. Available: http://www.pcmag.com/encyclopedia/term/50223/rdf (2016)

[32] W3C. Json-ld 1.0. [retrieved: 02, 2016]. [Online]. Available: https://www.w3.org/TR/json-ld/ (2014)

[33] T. Berners-Lee. Naming and addressing: Uris, urls, ... [retrieved: 02, 2016]. [Online]. Available: https://www.w3.org/Addressing/ (1993)

[34] Cowtowncoder. Jackson. [retrieved: 06, 2015]. [Online]. Available: http://jackson.codehaus.org/ (2015)

[35] W. J.-L. C. Group. JSON for linking data. [retrieved: 02, 2016]. [Online]. Available: http://json-ld.org/ (2014)

Gamification of Tour Experiences with Motivational Intelligent Technologies

Mei Yii Lim, Nicholas K Taylor
School of Mathematical and Computer Sciences
Heriot-Watt University
Edinburgh, UK
e-mail: {M.Lim, N.K.Taylor}@hw.ac.uk

Sarah M Gallacher
Intel Corporation, London, UK
e-mail: sarah.m.gallacher@intel.com

Abstract— **SUMMIT is a mobile app that aims to gamify the experience of walkers and hikers and benefit the local communities through which they perambulate. It encourages physical activity through gamification of the user experience by adding additional elements of social fun and motivation to walking and hiking activities. It rewards users for their physical effort by offering access to local resources, hence increasing awareness and appreciation of the local assets and heritage and contributing to the local economy. The evaluation results show that both businesses and walkers were very receptive to the idea. A modified version of SUMMIT, the Science Safari App was implemented in a zoo setting and its potential implications are discussed.**

Keywords-Location based; gamification; personalisation; rewards; tourism; mobile application.

I. INTRODUCTION

SUMMIT [1] is a location-based mobile app that encourages the walking and hiking community to avail themselves of local resources including hospitality businesses, product vendors, tourist attractions and local information.

Romanticism era in the 18th century brought forth a shift in attitudes to the landscape and nature leading to the manifestation of the idea of walking through the countryside for pleasure [2]. An explosion of long distance walking routes occurred in the late 20th century with the Appalachian Trail in the USA [3] and the Pennine Way in Britain [4] as early examples. In Scotland, tourism figures from 2012 show that walking and hiking was the second most popular tourist activity among domestic visitors [5]. However, for many of these visitors, the walk can be the sole purpose of their trip and they may not access any other local attractions or local businesses.

The key goal of SUMMIT is to "gamify" the user experience by adding additional elements of social fun, motivation and rewards to walking activities whilst increasing cultural appreciation through promotion of the local amenities and services to the benefit of the local economy.

The idea behind it is to challenge walkers and hikers to reach checkpoints (geo-fenced areas) that are located along popular walking and hiking routes. When walkers reach a checkpoint they are presented with a list of rewards on their mobile app from which they can choose their favourite as illustrated in Fig. 1. The rewards are provided by local businesses in the area and may include things like a free muffin or a 20% discount on a product. For example, if the walker decides to choose a free muffin as his reward at some checkpoint, he selects this in his app and a virtual muffin is added to his "reward knapsack". He then takes this virtual muffin to the local shop that offered this reward to exchange his virtual muffin for a real one. While he is there he may also buy a coffee or take friends with him who may also make some purchases.

Figure 1. SUMMIT reward scheme.

In this way, SUMMIT benefits both walkers and local businesses. It encourages physical activity by making such activities more fun and rewarding but also introduces walkers and hikers to new local resources in the area that they might not have visited otherwise.

Additionally, a great advantage of SUMMIT is its flexibility and extensibility. With some adaptations SUMMIT is deployable at different tourist sites with many points of interests where a stimulating route can be generated to improve visitors' tour experiences. One such place is the zoo. During Explorathon'15 [6] at RZSS Edinburgh Zoo [7], the Science Safari App, a modified version of SUMMIT was released to visitors. The Explorathon'15 at RZSS Edinburgh Zoo held on the European Researcher's Night, which takes place simultaneously every year in hundreds of cities across Europe and beyond is a mini science festival where scientists from Edinburgh's universities showcased their ground breaking research to the public. The Science Safari App was used to guide visitors around the different science exhibits on display.

The rest of this paper is organised as follows. Section II presents the related work. Section III presents the findings from a focus workshop carried out prior to development while Section IV presents the design of SUMMIT, both the mobile and web apps. An evaluation of the first prototype that was carried out in the wild on Arthur's Seat in Edinburgh, Scotland is detailed in Section V along with the results and discussions. Section VI presents the Science Safari App and some potential implication of its application in the zoo setting. Section VII concludes the paper.

II. Related Work

Pervasive gaming takes the gaming experience into the real world, focusing on introducing game elements into the everyday life of players. It exploits interaction devices such as handhelds to display virtual elements [8], generates location-sensitive responses to interaction [9], employs technology through which human game-masters can exercise control of the game experience [10] and involves interactive actors to perform non-player characters [11].

Pirates! [12] was one of the first successful attempts to port the computer game into the real world and the IPerG project [13] has successfully executed a number of pervasive games in real spaces such as Epidemic Menace [14] and Day of the Figurines [15]. Other groups have produced educational pervasive games such as Virus [16] and Paranoia Syndrome [17]. Artistically oriented pervasive games such as Can You See Me Now? [8] used whole cities as the game environment. Ludocity [18], a collection of pervasive games inspired by theatre, painting, dance and other art forms also exploits public places such as city streets and parks for social play. All Ludocity games are released under creative commons licences, which allow everyone to run the games for free. Ingress by Google [19] is a near real-time augmented reality massively multiplayer online pervasive game with a complex science fiction back story and continuous open narrative.

On the other hand, SUMMIT is a real-world outdoor treasure hunt game using Global Positioning System (GPS)-enabled devices inspired by geocaching [20]. Analogous to geocaching, SUMMIT "hides" rewards of different categories at different places along a popular route for users to find and collect. These rewards reflect the distinctive resources offered by the local area and community encouraging users to appreciate and take advantage of the local amenities on offer. SUMMIT also logs users' achievements and allows them to perform social comparison of their performance against others, thus introducing a competitive element to the overall walking/hiking experience.

To date, quite a few treasure hunt based pervasive applications aiming at increasing cultural heritage appreciation have emerged including the Stealit App [21], Regensburg REXplorer game [22], the Global Treasure Apps [23], the Museum Explorer [24] and Huntzz [25].

The Stealit App was developed for the National Museum of Scotland in Culture Hack Scotland 2011 by Alex Waterson and Jen Davies. It maps over 1000 items from the museum collections onto Festival venues throughout Edinburgh and encourages players to "steal" them. The Global Treasure App entice users to follow clues at different tourist attractions to collect gold, silver or bronze treasure tokens and real-world rewards such as a badge or money off in gift-shops and cafes. In the Museum Explorer App, users have a mission to track down nine mystery objects within the museum to unlock special explorer badge. The Huntzz App allows anyone to create and share treasure hunts.

The main difference between these applications and SUMMIT is that these applications do not reward users based on physical achievements but on solving puzzles and clues. Only the Global Treasure Apps include real-world rewards but the focus is on promoting artifacts and attractions rather than local businesses and communities.

Although other stamping schemes for tourist checkpoints exist [26], these schemes usually require all checkpoints to be reached to validate the completion of a tour with the aim of collecting badges or similar rewards. On the other hand, SUMMIT users do not need to reach all checkpoints to collect rewards and have the flexibility of choosing their desired rewards. Instead of automated checkpoint verification, the stamping schemes involve manually dating and stamping of a personal completion brochure or manually entering codes collected from checkpoints on the respective websites for electronic validation.

Many zoos have created their own mobile apps such as the ZSL London Zoo App [27], Chester Zoo App [28], the Smithsonian National Zoo App [29] and the Dinosaurs Return App [30]. Most of these applications focus on helping visitors find their way around and discover the different animals and attractions available.

The ZSL London Zoo App, the Chester Zoo App and the Smithsonian National Zoo App all present animal facts, photos and videos, incorporate a GPS-enabled interactive zoo map and a planner showing all daily events around the zoo. Additionally, the ZSL London Zoo App features a Walkabout Game where visitors have to find and photograph animals to win prizes. Users of the Chester Zoo App can collect special animal badges as they walk around the zoo. The Smithsonian National Zoo App on the other hand lets anyone with Android or iOS mobile devices enjoy the zoo wherever they are with its virtual component.

The Dinosaurs Return App was developed in conjunction to the Dinosaurs exhibition [31] at RZSS Edinburgh Zoo. The exhibition took place from April to November 2015 aiming to raise awareness about the real threat of extinction faced by many endangered species today. Visitors can watch dinosaurs come alive in the palm of their hand by scanning augmented reality tags scattered around the site. There is also a dinosaur quiz and an exhibition map to aid visitors.

The Science Safari App was developed from the SUMMIT project and targeted a range of scientific research exhibits at RZSS Edinburgh Zoo as part of the Explorathon'15 event [10]. SUMMIT is easily extensible to any locations in the world by adding new routes information and checkpoint coordinates, hence providing a quick way to generate interesting routes and create awareness in visitors about what is on offer at one-off events such as Explorathon'15 as well as longer term local resources.

III. Design Workshop

SUMMIT was proposed for the Fort William area [32]. To inform the design of SUMMIT, we met with our contact from Visit Fort William [33] to discuss requirements both from hikers and businesses point of view. Through this collaboration, we identified three interesting routes around the area including Ben Nevis, Glen Nevis and Kinlochleven.

A site analysis of the Ben Nevis area confirmed our expectations that the 3G signal is intermittent and cannot be relied upon. GPS and mobile network connectivity loss can have a negative impact on the user experience if not handled appropriately. Hence, a mechanism that allows users to have an undisrupted interaction is vital to the system.

Additionally, we ran a focus workshop with hikers and walkers to understand more about their use of technology when out in the wild. The group provided some interesting suggestions for before, during and after the hike.

Before the hike, it was proposed that weather forecast, route information on a map, predicted completion time and a checking in feature to say that they are going for a hike would be useful. During the hike, the ability to connect to social network for sharing, performance measure, alert to possible interesting diversion and emergency button to call for help are desirable. After the hike, there need to be a feature for checking out to say that they have completed the journey as well as the ability to view collected rewards.

Some interesting issues were also raised such as concerns about draining battery power, suggestion for group specific rewards and some views that information about the local town might be more important than real-world rewards. They also mentioned that during a walk/hike, they usually keep their phones in the pocket.

Moreover, there seemed to be a consensus that the target group for the app is the younger generation. Personalisation of rewards to age groups or user types can be beneficial.

These feedbacks informed the design of the SUMMIT service including seamless connectivity, availability of a route map, information about estimated distance and completion time, a check-in check-out feature, ability to share on social network sites such as Facebook, ability to view an assortment of rewards and select them as well as the need for minimum interaction with the service while en route.

Unfortunately, due to limited time and resources, we were not able to implement suggestions such as weather forecast, real-time performance measure, interesting diversion alert, emergency help button or personalisation of rewards but focused on those deemed important for the purpose of the SUMMIT service.

IV. The Summit System

The SUMMIT system consists of two main components: a web app, which allows business users to manage the rewards that they provide, and a mobile app, which is used by the walkers and hikers. Fig. 2 illustrates the SUMMIT system deployment including the server where information about business users and app users are stored.

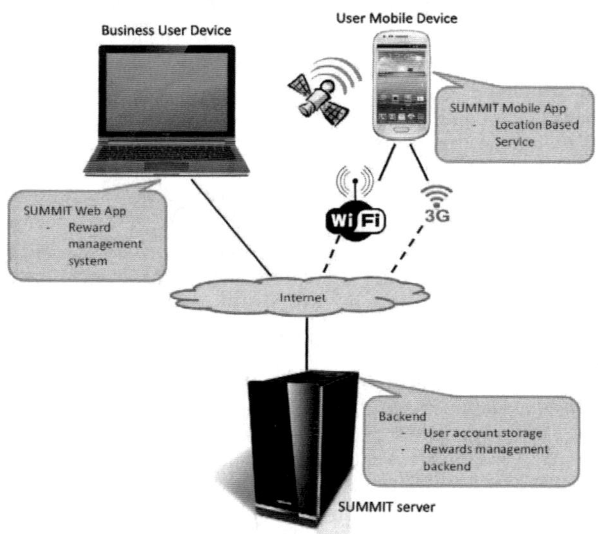

Figure 2. SUMMIT system deployment.

A. SUMMIT Mobile Application

The mobile app was developed for the Android platform. It aims to enhance the walking activities by supporting the users' personal achievement element through a reward scheme and the social competition element through comparisons of their progress against others via the social network site, Facebook.

The mobile app monitors the users' outdoor locations while they are en route using GPS. Each route has several pre-defined checkpoints, usually selected based on their touristic values to the respective region that are geo-fenced areas. The app does not provide real-time navigation but as users reach checkpoints, the phone will start vibrating and notifications will appear on the system bar. When this happens, users will unlock new virtual reward items provided by local businesses, which they can exchange into real rewards.

Prior to the hike, users can check out different routes and rewards associated with each of the routes. They can then select a route that provides the rewards they desire and suits their constraints in terms of time and distance. This flexibility enables users to personalise their tour experience based on their needs at any particular time.

Fig. 3 shows the workflow of the mobile app. Before users can use the mobile app, they have to register. After they have registered and logged in, they will see 5 tabs including "Route", "K-sack", "Reward", "Claim" and "Facebook". Fig. 4 shows the Login Screen of the app while Fig. 5 shows the "Route" tab, which lists the available routes, estimated distance and time as well as the checkpoints and rewards associated with each route.

When users select a route, the route information will be downloaded onto their phone assuming Internet connection is available. By pre-loading the routes, the issue of unreliable 3G signal is avoided as the route information is now locally stored, hence will always be available to users when en route.

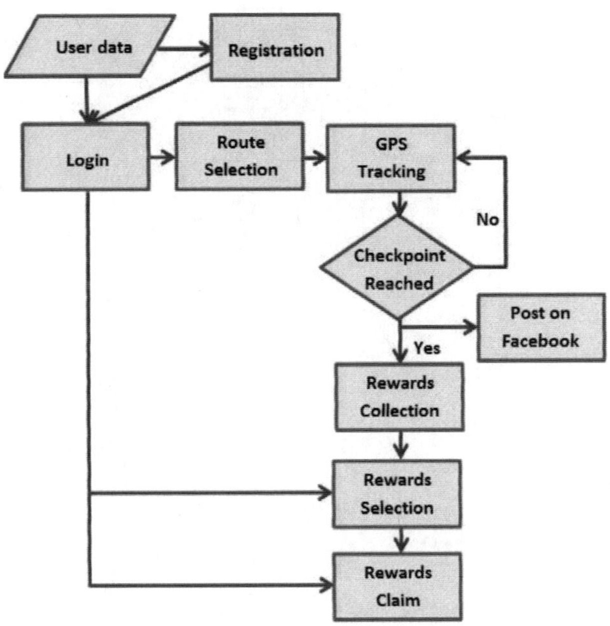

Figure 3. SUMMIT mobile app workflow.

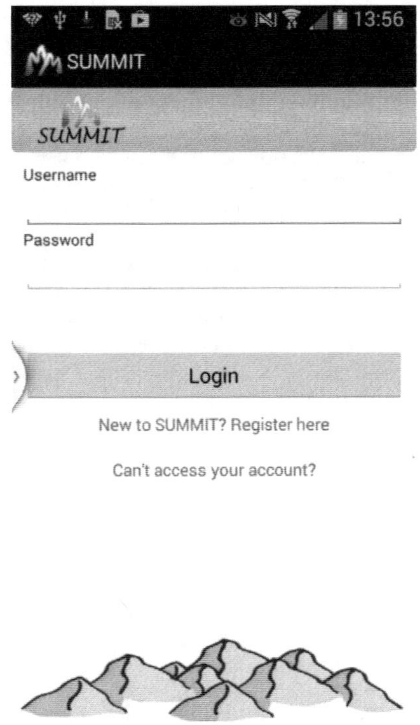

Figure 4. "Login" screen.

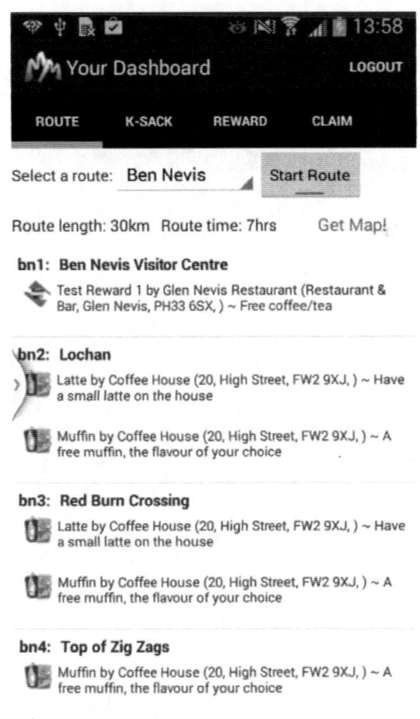

Figure 5. "Route" tab.

When the user is ready for the hike, they check-in by pressing the "Start Route" button, which activates checkpoints tracking. During the hike, only GPS signal is required to track users' position. Since each checkpoint covers an area of 50 metre radius, a short loss of GPS signal does not affect the performance of the app. These approaches give users a virtual "Always-On" connectivity impression allowing them to have an undisrupted interaction experience. The problem of draining the battery power is also minimised as the phone is not constantly connected to the network. Synchronisation with the server occurs the next time network connectivity is available and activated by the user when all logged data on the mobile device is uploaded.

To help users locate the rewards, a map that shows the locations of the different checkpoints is provided as illustrated in Fig. 6. The associated rewards will automatically be added to the user's knapsack ("K-sack" tab) at each checkpoint. When network connection is available, users can select one reward for each checkpoint through a selection dialog as shown in Fig. 7.

After they have made their selection, the rewards will appear under the "Reward" tab. To claim a particular reward on this list, the user needs to tap on the reward and a claim dialog as shown in Fig. 8 will appear. By clicking claim, the reward will appear under the "Claim" tab and on the supplier system (for the web app description, please refer to Section B) where the claim can be authorised.

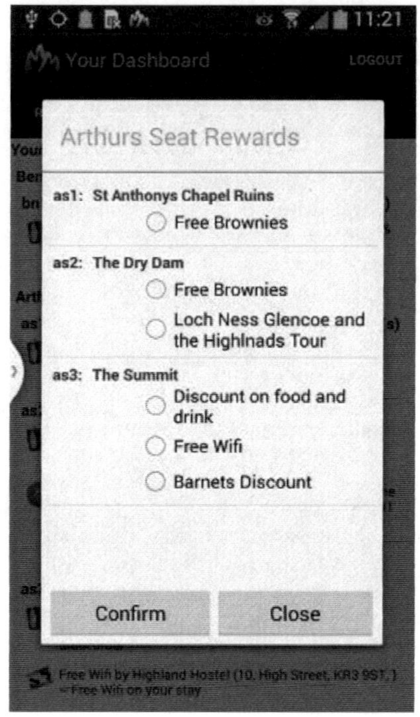

Figure 7. Rewards selection dialog box.

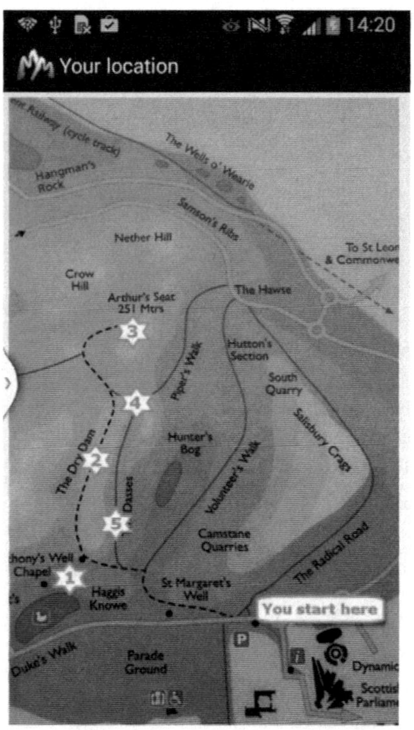

Figure 6. Map with checkpoints.

Figure 8. Claim dialog box.

Users can also post their achievements onto Facebook if they wish as illustrated in Fig. 9 allowing them to compare their progress against others en route. When they have completed the hike, they check-out by pressing the "End Route" button, which will subsequently stop checkpoints tracking and upload all the users' progress onto the server when Internet connection is available.

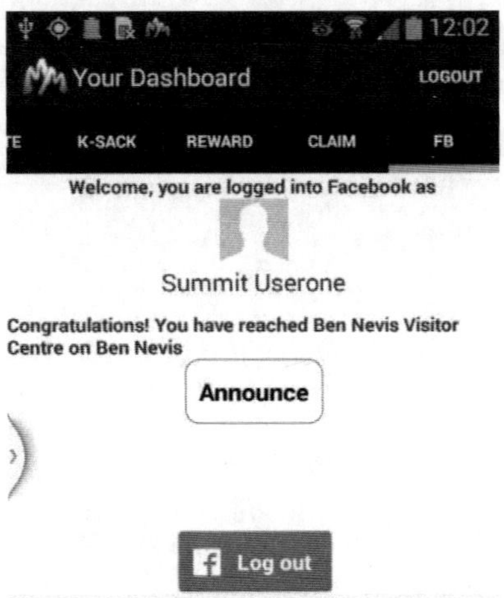

Figure 9. Facebook announcement feature.

B. SUMMIT Web Application

The web app was developed to enable easy sign-up of local businesses as reward providers. Once registered as business users, they can perform the actions depicted in the workflow diagram in Fig. 10.

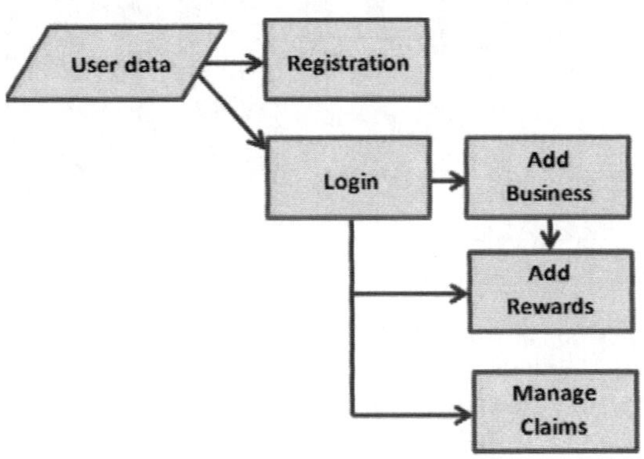

Figure 10. SUMMIT web app workflow.

The supplier can add, edit or delete a business. They can add, deactivate, re-activate, delete and edit a specific reward item. They can also approve claims from the mobile app users.

Fig. 11 shows the web app dashboard with four tabs: Your Information, Add Business, Add Rewards and Manage Claims. The "Your Information" tab displays the list of businesses and rewards owned by a provider as well as the available actions. Alert icons will appear beside reward items that reach zero count so that the provider can decide to add more of the reward or delete it.

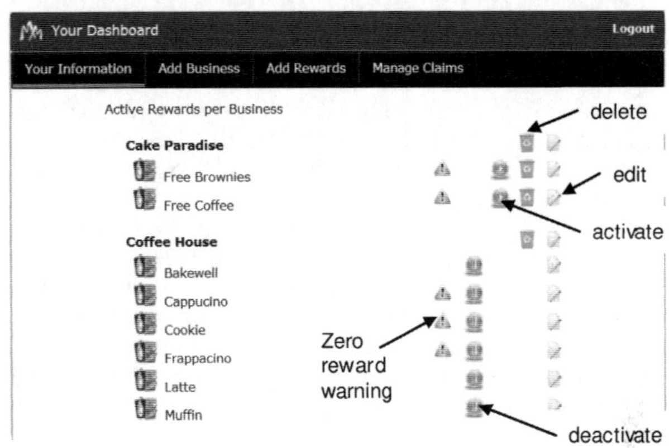

Figure 11. Web app dashboard.

The "Add Business" tab allows the suppliers to add business(es) while the "Add Reward" tab allows them to add reward(s). The "Manage Claims" tab in Fig. 12 lists all pending claims from the mobile app users. To authorise a claim from a specific user, the supplier has to click on the approve icon to the right of the claim with the respective user name.

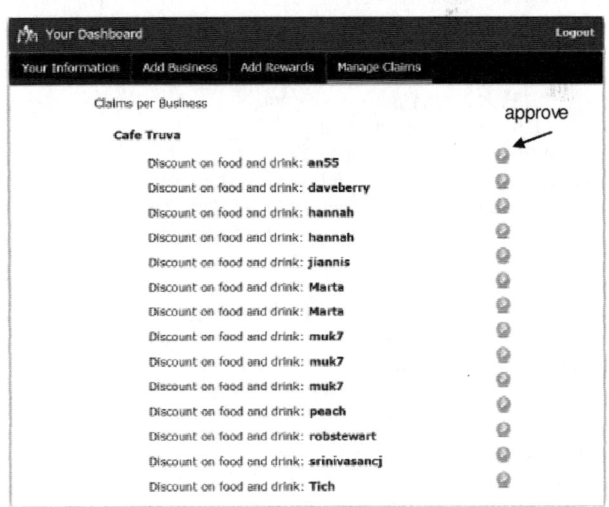

Figure 12. "Manage Claims" tab.

V. EVALUATION

This section details the evaluation we carried out on the SUMMIT Mobile App and Web App.

A. *Experimental Setup*

The experimental setups for both platforms are presented below.

1) *The Mobile App*

A trial of the SUMMIT mobile app has been carried out with 24 participants; 18 males and 6 females. Participants were volunteers who are either interested in mobile applications or hikers and walkers. They were issued with Samsung Galaxy SIII phones with the mobile app pre-installed and were asked to hike up Arthur's Seat (Fig. 13), a popular rural area within the City of Edinburgh with many local businesses in proximity.

One of the main reasons we chose Arthur's Seat for the trial was because it is much more accessible from Heriot-Watt University making recruitment of participants easier as compared to routes around the Fort William areas such as Ben Nevis, Glen Nevis and Kinlochleven. Logistically, it is almost impossible to organise a group up north for a hike and back within a day. The unpredictable weather made the task even more difficult. On the other hand, participants can go up Arthur's Seat at their own convenience when the weather permitted anytime during the 3 weeks period of the trial.

After participants had completed the hike, they were asked to complete a questionnaire. They were asked to rate different features of the app on a 5-point Likert scale. These features included:

S1: route information
S2: map
S3: rewards motivation
S4: advance knowledge of rewards
S5: rewards selection
S6: claim system
S7: rewards choices
S8: claim intention
S9: Facebook functionality and
S10: ease of use of the app.

Additionally, they were given the freedom to provide further comments about any part of the mobile app or their experience of using it. Please refer to Appendix I for the full list of questions.

2) *The Web App*

A total of 7 businesses signed up to the rewards scheme. In order to participate, the suppliers were asked to create a business account and add their own reward(s). The rewards were to remain active during the period of the trial and the following couple of months.

A week after the trial ended, they were contacted to gather their feedback on the web app. Some personal information and previous experience in using apps for advertising purposes were gathered. Other questions included the number of customers the mobile app brought into the shops, other desired features for the web app and free comments on the web app and their experience in using it. Please refer to Appendix II for the full list of questions.

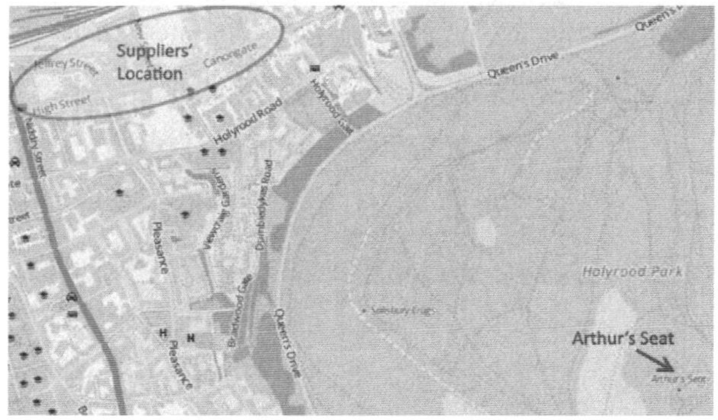

Figure 13. Arthur's Seat and part of Edinburgh's World Heritage Old Town (©OpenStreetMap contributors)

B. *Results and Discussion*

In the following subsections, we present the results of our evaluation of both platforms and relevant implications are discussed.

1) *The Mobile App*

The chart in Fig. 14 shows the overall average rating of all 24 participants. On average participants were neutral on the usefulness of the route information (S1). Taking the level of significance, α = 0.05, a Mann-Whitney test on this variable between the younger (less than 40 years old, n=17, M=3.418, SD=0.425) and the older (more than 40 years old, n=7, M=2.286, SD=0.694) users showed a significant difference with U(24)=13, Z=-3.050, p=0.002 (see Fig. 15).

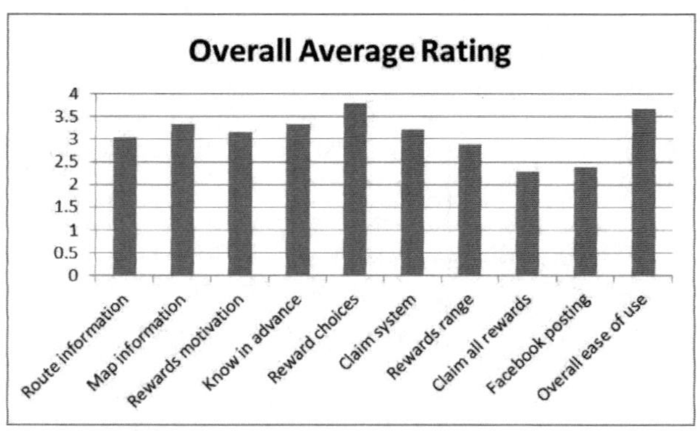

Figure 14. Overall average rating of all 24 participants.

The older generation found the route information not useful while the younger generation found it useful. This might be because the older users were used to using guidebooks when walking and were expecting directional information such as descriptions of terrain and photographs of each checkpoint, which was not provided via the app and might have led to some of them getting lost along the way.

On average the participants found the map informative (S2). However, they would have preferred an interactive map, which tells them their position in relation to the checkpoints at any particular time instance, "a real-time blue dot" as they called it.

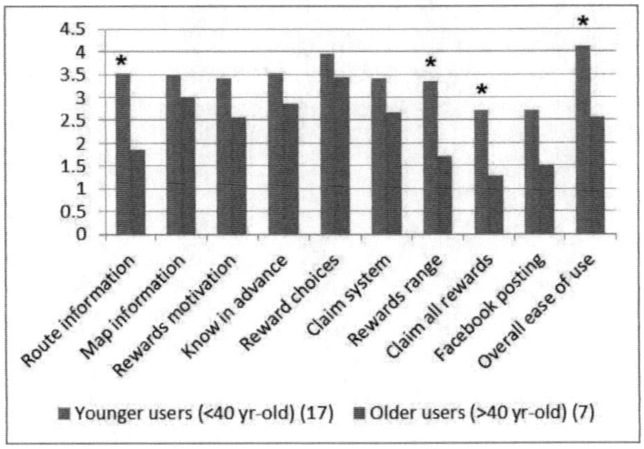

Figure 15. Average rating comparison between younger and older users. (* denotes variables with significant differences, $\alpha = 0.05$)

The participants found the rewards motivated them to go on the hike (S3). Although not statistically significant, a closer look at the comparison between novice (n=8), intermediate (n=11) and experienced hikers (n=5) in Fig. 16 revealed that novice and intermediate hikers found the rewards more motivating than experienced hikers. This could be due to the fact that experienced hikers have the passion to hike and thus will do it irrespective of whether they are being rewarded or not.

Some participants mentioned in their questionnaire that the rewards served as an initial motivation. As they moved from one checkpoint to another, the fact that there were rewards attached to each of the checkpoints became less important to them and, instead, their ultimate goal was to reach all the checkpoints and complete the route as reflected in the participants' comments.

"The motivation was the challenge to reach all the checkpoints."

"The biggest motivation to keep walking weren't the rewards but the challenge to reach the next checkpoint."

This interesting finding suggests that the gamification aspect of numbering the checkpoints itself provided enough motivation for the user to carry on once they had started. This implies that it might not be necessary to assign rewards to all checkpoints but only to a few important ones to give them the initial push.

Overall, participants thought that it was important to know the rewards in advance (S4) and to be given the option to choose from a selection of rewards (S5). They also found the claim system easy to use (S6).

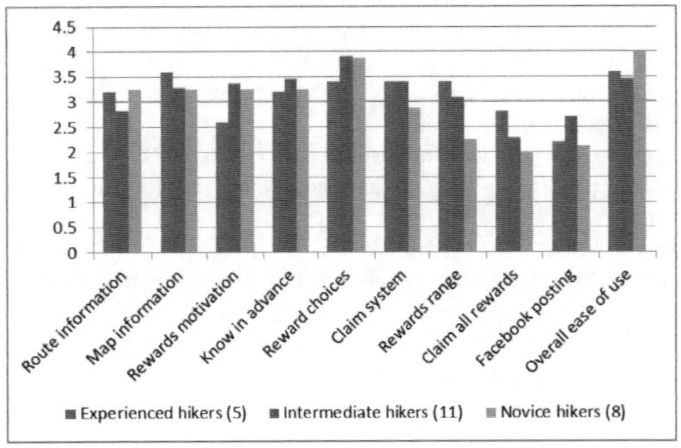

Figure 16. Average rating comparison between Experienced, Intermediate and Novice hikers.

In terms of the range of rewards provided (S7), there was again a significant difference between younger (n=17) and older (n=7) users. This was revealed by applying the Mann-Whitney test, with $U(24)=17$, $Z=-2.842$, $p=0.005$, to the results in Fig. 15. The younger users seemed to be satisfied with the type of rewards provided, which included discounts on food, drinks, shoes, sweets, clothes, souvenirs and tours, while the older users were not.

The older users would have liked some rewards that they could redeem immediately after the hike, for example, refreshments, discount at a local hotel or B&B and rewards targeted at kids. The younger users also mentioned that free rewards, money-off vouchers for tourist attractions such as National Trust locations, the storytelling centre, museums, zoos and castles as well as offers related to sport or physical activities would be beneficial.

The intention to claim all rewards (S8) also revealed a significant difference between the two age groups. Many of the participants were exhausted after the hike and selected their rewards only after they were home and once they were not in the vicinity of the shops. They were therefore less keen to make the effort to return to the area to collect their rewards at a later date. Their need during the short period before and after the trial may also determine whether the participants will claim their rewards, for example, discount on shoes will be useful if the participant is in need of a new pair of shoes but might be worthless otherwise. Again, the Mann-Whitney test showed a significant difference between the older and younger users, $U(24)=21.5$, $Z=-2.529$, $p=0.013$. Since the older users were less interested in the rewards, they were also less inclined to claim them.

The participants rated the ability to post their achievement onto Facebook (S9) fairly low. One reason for this might be because, as the app was only a prototype, the users had to use test user accounts instead of their own accounts. As a result the achievement posts did not appear on their own Facebook wall or timeline. Observing the chart in Fig. 15, younger users seem to have a more positive outlook on this feature than older users although the Mann-Whitney test did not show a significant difference.

Finally, the average rating for ease of use of the app (S10) was good. However, there was again a significant difference between the older and younger users, as confirmed by the Mann-Whitney test, U(24)=17.5, Z=-2.801, p=0.005. This could be due to the fact that the younger users were more accustomed with mobile apps and thus had a better idea about the flow of control and operations of the app and phone in general. For example, a couple of the older participants were having some technical problems such as locating the back button on the phone and getting Facebook login to work as reflected in their comments:

> *"Hardest bit was finding the 'Back' button."*

> *"Couldn't get the Facebook login to work"*

Moreover, only 2 out of the 7 older participants are experienced mobile apps users while 10 out of 17 younger participants are experienced users.

The feedback on subjective questions revealed that some participants would have liked the mobile app to provide more interesting information about the route and checkpoints. One of the experienced hikers suggested that it would be useful if the app could show real-time progress such as the time he took to go from one checkpoint to another and the overall time he took to complete the route. This would allow users to compare their real-time progress with each other, hence increasing the competitive element of the app.

The mobile app has also been found to provide motivation for a second time visitor to hike a hill/mountain that they have conquered before, as one of the participants stated:

> *"Thanks for giving me a reason to walk up Arthur's Seat. I am feeling revitalised and refreshed now I'm home! This serves as an excellent reason to walk up hills/mountains that you have already conquered (I've been up Arthur's Seat twice)."*

2) The Web App

From the perspective of the suppliers, overall they were very satisfied with the usability of the web app. The participating suppliers' age ranges from 30 to 70 and only one of them has previous experience of using an app for advertising purposes. Moreover, many of the shops have staffs working on shifts. As a result, they were not very meticulous in recording or updating the actual rewards that were redeemed in their system so we are unable to report actual numbers but we were assured that rewards were indeed claimed.

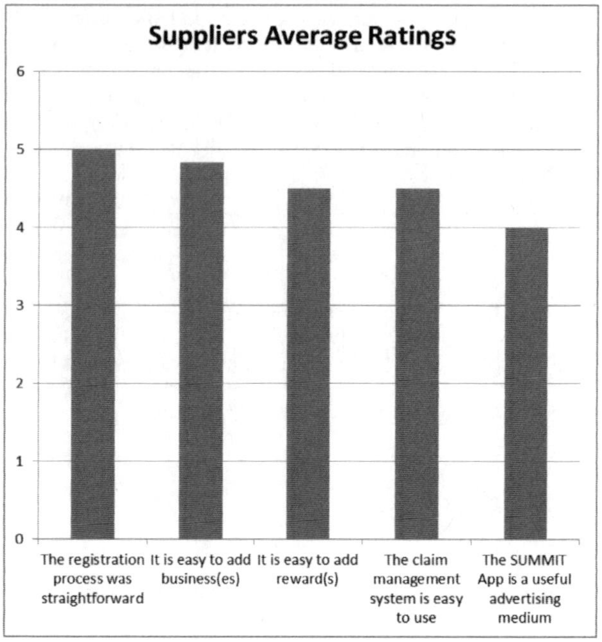

Figure 17. The average suppliers rating of different Web app features.

Observing Fig. 17, they found the registration process straightforward (S1), an average rating of 4.857 out of 5. It is also easy to add business(es) (S2) and reward(s) (S3). They found the claim management system easy to use (S4). All the suppliers who took part in the trial think that the app can potentially be a useful advertising medium (S5), hence the rating of 4 out of 5.

In order to encourage claims after the trial, one of the suppliers offered an additional deal on top of those provided on the mobile app if participants claimed within a particular period of time.

The suppliers remained very enthusiastic about the SUMMIT system following the trial. One of the suppliers suggested that it might be useful to include an online claim facility, which might encourage more claims as the participants would be able to redeem their rewards anywhere at their own convenience.

VI. THE SCIENCE SAFARI APP

As previously stated, SUMMIT is easily extensible to new routes and attractions. Consequently, the Science Safari App [34] was created for the Explorathon'15 event [6] at RZSS Edinburgh Zoo [7] to guide visitors around the science exhibits.

A. *Explorathon '15 Event*

At the Explorathon'15 event [6], visitors were invited to download the Science Safari App [34] onto their Android device when they arrived at the zoo. All available exhibits were listed on the "Route" tab and as the visitors attended each of them, the app registered the entry with notional reward. Depending on the number of exhibits clocked, a final reward was delivered as the visitor was leaving the zoo. Various rewards were offered including sweets, pens, keyrings and badges. The "Explorer" badges personalised with name was the most popular among children.

B. Future Potential

Successively, the Science Safari App enabled the visitor movement around the site to be captured as illustrated in Fig. 18. This information is invaluable to RZSS Edinburgh Zoo for future planning such as identifying where new services should be located and how to minimize congestion.

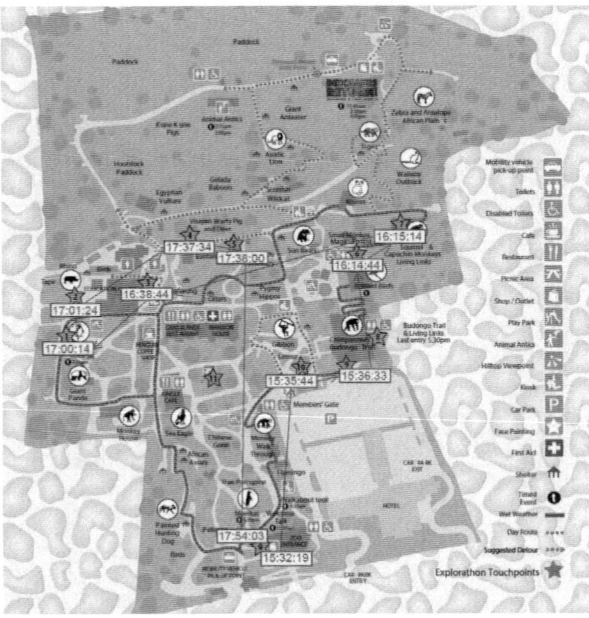

Figure 18. Example visitor route around the exhibits with time stamps.

RZSS Edinburgh Zoo recognises the potential of this type of technology to enhance visitors' experience and how it could be used to support its mission to engage the public in conservation issues. It already employs technology such as the Dinosaur Return App discussed earlier, online webcams (for pandas, penguins and squirrel monkeys) and the online learning system Moodle [35] through which the public can take courses in relevant subjects.

As a result, RZSS Edinburgh Zoo is exploring further with us how the reward-based gamification aspects of SUMMIT can be used to encourage and create awareness in visitors about conservation, hence fulfilling its aims of providing recreational and educational value to visitors.

In order to realise this potential, the first step would be to capture the visitor flow with a much larger monitoring programme using portable device such as suitably located RFID reader while issuing each visitors with RFID labels, which permit both indoor and outdoor tracking. The data gathered will then be mined to identify pattern for daily and seasonal variations. The rewards may then be assigned to less "popular" locations or where important messages on conservation are being delivered.

Additionally, to maximize the visitors learning experience, delivery of meaningful and coherent content is crucial. Visitors usually determine their own routes around different points of interests and this variability can make it difficult to deliver understandable content to them. A way to overcome this is by recording movement history as visitors traverse the zoo and alert them to other related exhibits based on this information. We have developed such solutions in a number of previous projects [36, 37, 38, 39].

A further novel information delivery approach in which content is personalised and adapted to a visitor's prior knowledge based on what they have already received would avoid the annoying repetition common to current information delivery systems. This will provide visitors with unique narratives and experiences evolving around their own interests and knowledge.

The opportunity to deploy and test these ideas in a public setting such as RZSS Edinburgh Zoo will enable us to further our research in this field.

VII. FUTURE WORK

In its current state, the SUMMIT Mobile app is easily extensible to other locations by adding new routes information and checkpoints coordinates. However, there are still room for improvement which could further the potential of the app.

- It would be beneficial to include an interactive map that dynamically updates the user's position on the map during the hike, for example a real-time 'blue dot' that tracks the user on the map.
- To increase cultural appreciation, the app can take advantage of attractions along a certain route and uses these as checkpoints. This will encourage visitors to make diversions and visit places that they might not be visiting when they do the usual hike. The user experience and engagement can also be improved if the app can provide the users with interesting and meaningful information about these locations.
- To target users of all ages, the app may benefit from a wider range of rewards with greater intrinsic values for example useful information about the local area, discounts on tickets for local events or entrance to local attractions and offers related to sports or physical activities available in the local area.
- It might also be useful to personalise the rewards according to age group or type of users so that their needs are better met as suggested by the focus group.

- It would be worthwhile to grade the route with different level of difficulty so that the user can choose routes that are suited to their capability reducing the possibility of struggles or lose of interests.
- Information regarding personal progress can be valuable for some users who are interested in how they are performing such as the overall completion time and the time taken to go from one checkpoint to another.
- Presentation of personalised and coherent information based on users' prior knowledge will increase engagement and improve recreational and educational experiences.

An improvement to the SUMMIT Web app would be the inclusion of an online claim facility which allows the user to make the claim online without the need to physically visit the shops. This might benefit hikers who travel through regions that take hours or days. However, this will work only for intangible rewards or rewards that can be sent through post. This will also encourage the participation of more businesses as the constraint of location is eliminated. Care has to be taken to ensure that priorities are still given to local businesses in the target area.

A larger scale evaluation at the Fort William area will provide us with more insights about users' perception and experiences of the apps.

VIII. Conclusion

SUMMIT has successfully added the elements of social fun and motivation to walking and hiking activities. It helps to promote local resources around a route by making users aware of their existence through its rewards scheme and checkpoints assignment. Business users were satisfied with its ease of use and appreciated its potential as a useful medium for advertising and delivering their wares and services. Its application in a public "in-the-wild" setting at RZSS Edinburgh Zoo has also proved successful and demonstrated the potential of such technology in improving visitor experiences and education.

Acknowledgments

The SUMMIT work was supported by the dot.rural Research Councils UK Digital Economy Hub, through the Scottish Funding Council's SICSA Smart Tourism Programme.. The Science Safari work was additionally supported by HW Engage, whose mission is to embed public engagement activities into academic life at Heriot-Watt University. The authors are solely responsible for the content of this publication.

References

[1] M. Y. Lim, S. M. Gallacher, and N. K. Taylor, "SUMMIT: Supporting Rural Tourism with Motivational Intelligent Technologies," Proceedings of the 9th International Conference on Mobile Ubiquitous Computing, Systems, Services and Technologies : UBICOMM 2015, Nice FRANCE, pp. 50-55, 2015.

[2] *The Norton Anthology of English Literature*, ed. M. H, Abrams, 7th ed., vol. 2, pp. 9-1, 2000.

[3] Appalachian Trail FAQ, http://www.outdoors.org/conservation/trails/appalachian-trail/at-faq.cfm, available online, accessed May 18, 2016.

[4] National Trails: Pennine Way, http://www.nationaltrail.co.uk/pennine-way, available online, accessed May 18, 2016.

[5] Visit Scotland – Key Facts on Tourism 2012, http://www.visitscotland.org/pdf/VS%20Insights%20Key%20Facts%202012%20%282%29.pdf, available online, accessed May 18, 2016.

[6] European Researchers' Night, Explorathon'15, http://www.explorathon.co.uk/edinburgh/zoo, accessed May 18, 2016.

[7] RZSS Edinburgh Zoo, http://www.edinburghzoo.org.uk, accessed May 18, 2016.

[8] S. Benford, A. Crabtree, M. Flintham, A. Drozd, R. Anastasi, and M. Paxton, "Can you see me now?," ACM Transactions on Computer-Human Interaction, vol. 13, no. 1, pp. 100–133, 2006.

[9] G. Chen and D. Kotz, "Solar : A pervasive computing infrastructure for context-aware mobile applications," Technical Report TR2002-421, Department of Computer Science, Dartmouth College, 2002.

[10] J. Soderberg, A. Waern, K. P. Akesson, S. Bojrk, and J. Falk, "Enhanced reality live role playing," Workshop on Gaming Applications in Pervasive Computing Environments, Second International Conference on Pervasive Computing, Vienna, Austria, 2004.

[11] J. Stenros, "Between Game Facilitation and Performance," International Journal of Role-Playing, Special Issue: Role Playing in Games, Issue 4, pp. 78-95, 2013.

[12] S. Bjork, J. Falk, R. Hansson, and P. Ljungstrand, "Pirates! Using the physical world as a game board," Proceedings of Interact '01, pp. 9-13, 2001.

[13] IPerG: Integrated Project on Pervasive Gaming. http://iperg.sics.se, available online, accessed March 17, 2015.

[14] I. Lindt, J. Ohlenburg, U. Pankoke-Babatz, and S. Ghellal, "A report on the crossmedia game Epidemic Menace," Computers in Entertainment, vol. 5, no. 1, 2007.

[15] M. Flintham, G. Giannachi, S. Benford, and M. Adams, "Day of the Figurines: Supporting Episodic Storytelling on Mobile Phones," Virtual Storytelling, Using Virtual Reality Technologies for Storytelling, Lecture Notes in Computer Science, Vol. 4871, pp. 167-175, 2007.

[16] V. Collella, R. Bororvoy, and M. Resnick, "Participatory simulations: Using computational objects to learn about dynamic systems," SIGCHI conference on Human factors in computing systems (CHI'98), Los Angeles, USA, pp. 9-10, 1998.

[17] G. Heumer et al., "Paranoia Syndrome - A pervasive multiplayer game using PDAs, RFID, and tangible objects," Third International Workshop on Pervasive Gaming Applications on Pervasive Computing 2006, Dublin, Ireland, 2006.

[18] Ludocity, http://ludocity.org/wiki/Main_Page, available online, accessed May 18, 2016.

[19] Ingress: Niantic Labs, https://www.ingress.com/, available online, accessed May 18, 2016.

[20] Geocaching: http://www.geocaching.com, available online, accessed May 18, 2016.

[21] Cultural Hack: Stealit, http://culturehack.org.uk/prototypes/stealit/, available online, accessed May 18, 2016.

[22] R. Ballagas, A. Kuntze, and S. P. Walz, "Gaming tourism: Lessons from evaluating REXplorer, a pervasive game for tourists," Pervasive Computing, Lecture Notes in Computer Science, Vol 5013, pp.244-261, 2008.

[23] Global Treasure Apps: http://globaltreasureapps.com/, available online, accessed May 18, 2016.

[24] National Museum of Scotland: Museum Apps. http://www.nms.ac.uk/our_museums/national_museum/museum_explorer_app.aspx, available online, accessed May 18, 2016.

[25] Huntzz Treasure Everywhere, 2011, http://www.huntzz.com/about-us.html#.VU4sjZNWIhQ, available online, accessed May 18, 2016.

[26] Proposed features/Checkpoint for Tourism, http://wiki.openstreetmap.org/wiki/Proposed_features/Checkpoint_for_Tourism, available online, accessed May 18, 2016.

[27] ZSL London Zoo App, http://www.zsl.org/zsl-london-zoo/visitor-information/zsl-london-zoo-smart-phone-app, available online, accessed May 18, 2016.

[28] Chester Zoo App, http://www.chesterzoo.org/campaigns/download-our-app, available online, accessed May 18, 2016.

[29] SmithsonianNationalZooApp, https://nationalzoo.si.edu/smithsoniannationalzooapp/, available online, accessed May 18, 2016.

[30] The Dinosaurs Return App, http://www.edinburghzoo.org.uk/app/, available online, accessed May 18, 2016.

[31] The Dinosaurs Return Exhibition, http://www.edinburghzoo.org.uk/animals-attractions/dinosaurs-return/, available online, accessed May 18, 2016.

[32] Fort William, https://www.visitscotland.com/info/towns-villages/fort-william-p236531, accessed May 18, 2016.

[33] Visit Fort William, http://www.visitfortwilliam.co.uk, accessed May 18, 2016.

[34] N. K. Taylor, M. Y. Lim, and L. Morris, "Beyond the Pandas : Enhancing the Visitor Experience at Edinburgh Zoo," ACM CHI 2016 Workshop: HCI Goes to the Zoo, 2016.

[35] Moodle, https://moodle.org, available online, accessed May 18, 2016.

[36] D. S. Bental, E. Papadopoulou, N. K. Taylor, M. H. Williams, F. R. Blackmun, I. S. Ibrahim, M. Y. Lim, I. Mimtsoudis, S. W. Whyte, and E. Jennings, "Smartening up the Student Learning Experience with Ubiquitous Media," ACM Transactions on Multimedia Computing, Communications and Applications, 12 (1s), pp. 1-23, 2015.

[37] S. M. Gallacher, E. Papadopoulou, Y. Abu-Shaaban, N. K. Taylor, and M. H. Williams, "Dynamic Context-Aware Personalisation in a Pervasive Environment," Journal of Pervasive and Mobile Computing, 10 Part B, pp. 120-137, 2014.

[38] S. M. Gallacher, E. Papadopoulou, N. K. Taylor, and M. H. Williams, "Learning User Preferences for Adaptive Pervasive Environments," ACM Transactions on Autonomous and Adaptive Systems, 8 (1), pp. 1-5, 2013.

[39] E. Papadopoulou, S. M. Gallacher, N. K. Taylor, and M. H. Williams, "A Personal Smart Space Approach to Realising Ambient Ecologies," Journal of Pervasive and Mobile Computing, 8 (4), pp. 485-499, 2012.

Appendix I: SUMMIT Android App User Trial Questionnaire

About You

Username : __________

Age : __________

Gender : male female

Prior experience with mobile apps:
novice intermediate experienced

Hiking experience :
novice intermediate experienced

How often do you go on hiking trips? __________

About SUMMIT Android App

Please rate your degree of agreement with the following statements: From Disagree (1) to Agree (5)

1) The route information was useful

2) The map was informative

3) The rewards motivate me to continue hiking

4) It is important to know what rewards are available in advance

5) It is important to be given some choices of rewards to select from

6) The reward claim system was easy to use

7) I found the rewards useful

8) I intend to claim all the rewards I have chosen

9) I found the ability to post my achievements onto Facebook useful

10) Overall, the SUMMIT Android App was easy to use

____

What other type of reward would you like to be included?

____

Other comments

____

Appendix II: SUMMIT Web App User Trial Questionnaire

About You

Age : ____________

Type of business : ____________

Have you used any app for advertising purposes before? :
Yes No

About SUMMIT Web App

Please rate your degree of agreement with the following statements: From Disagree (1) to Agree (5)

The registration process was straightforward

It is easy to add business(es)

It is easy to add reward(s)

The claim management system is easy to use

The SUMMIT App is a useful advertising medium

____

Did the SUMMIT app bring you customers? If yes, how many?

____

What other features would you like the app to provide?

____

Other comments

____

Bamboo in a Sandpile

Methodological Considerations for Leveraging Data to Enhance Infrastructural Resilience

Robert Spousta III, Steve Chan
Sensemaking Fellowship
San Diego, California, The United States of America
spousta@mit.edu, stevechan@post.harvard.edu

Stef van den Elzen, Jan-Kees Buenen
SynerScope BV
Helvoirt, The Netherlands
s.j.v.d.elzen@tue.nl, jan-kees.buenen@synerscope.com

Abstract—**The onset of the Big Data phenomenon presents significant technological challenges in managing massive amounts of information, yet it also presents tremendous opportunities for enhancing societal resilience and directly serving the public good. The Internet of Everything, which is driving such massive connectivity and growth in data generation is a highly complex system, continuously giving rise to new communication capabilities, yet also becoming increasingly vulnerable to destabilizing forces and malicious threats. Creating systems that are truly intelligent and capable of balancing these interrelated dynamics in the management of data demands a deliberate approach that is scalable, adaptive, and extensible. In this paper, we discuss three primary considerations for conducting Collaborative Big Data Analytics, including data acquisition, layered analytics, and visualization in order to grow resilient cyber-physical infrastructures that are capable of withstanding significant destabilization. With regard to data acquisition, we present the basic characteristics of so-called Big Data, namely the Six Vs of data variety, volume, velocity, veracity, volatility, and value. In addition, we outline the development of analytical tools and techniques for processing data, as well as methods for effectively visualizing the products of a layered analytic approach. In order to illustrate the utility of such an approach, we summarize findings from our participation in Orange Telecom's Data for Development Challenges in the Republic of Côte d'Ivoire and Senegal, as well as introduce initial findings from our ongoing study of infrastructural resilience in archipelagos. We conclude that while Collaborative Big Data Analytics hold great promise, forums for the open development and validation of methodologies for its conduct are needed to generate more and better uses of the Big Data that have come to dominate our world.**

Keywords—Collaborative Big Data Analytics; Decision Engineering; Infrastructural Resilience; Sensemaking Methodology

I. Introduction

This paper is an extension of work presented at the 2015 IARIA Data Analytics Conference [1]. Whereas the dot-com boom of the late 1990s and early 2000s ushered in a wholly novel industry, replete with information-based products and virtual services marketed via the Internet, collaborative approaches for conducting civil-centric and public service-oriented data analytics have taken longer to develop [2]. This fact notwithstanding, the rise of the Internet of Everything (IoE) has introduced unprecedented levels of artificial complexity within many cyber-physical systems, which demand constant attention, lest areas of brittleness and blind spots compromise the delivery of essential services through infrastructures that are the backbone of modern civilization. In bridging this gap, we present three basic layers that comprise a framework for gaining insight from data. In previous work [3], we posed the question of whether the protection architectures of critical infrastructure are improving or deteriorating with age; in other words, are they more like milk or like wine? Our investigation suggests that in the case of electric grid systems, infrastructures become more vulnerable with age, particularly as new threats evolve more quickly than existing protective measures are able to adapt. To ameliorate such a circumstance and improve the security and stability of critical infrastructural systems like the grid, we advocate for increased data collection, and more robust analytic capability employed in a Big Data Paradigm. This is illustrated by our juxtaposition of bamboo and the sandpile. Whereas the Abelian Sandpile or Bak-Tang-Wiesenfeld model serves as an effective metaphor for self-organized criticality and cascading effects in complex systems [4], the structural flexibility and dynamic responsiveness of bamboo [5] characterizes a system in which adaptation facilitates resilience. In turn, adaptation is facilitated by a timely and precise leveraging of data. The **Sensemaking Methodology** addresses three primary concerns, namely, the capturing of data, the processing and refinement of data into insight, and the visualization of insight to guide Decision Engineering endeavors. In this manuscript, we briefly outline the system of methods that comprise our three-layer framework, as illustrated by ongoing research focused on the resilience of critical infrastructures such as electric power systems.

The remainder of the paper is organized as follows. Section II discusses some of the primary considerations for data identification and capture, including the variety of sensor platforms that are responsible for producing data. Section III describes the basic categories of analytic tools and techniques that have been developed for data processing, and argues the importance of counterpoising heuristic and algorithmic analytics, which is a core component of our methodology. Section IV addresses primary considerations for effective data visualization. Section V summarizes major findings and lessons learned from our participation in the first two Data for Development (D4D) Challenges as an exemplar of the Sensemaking Methodology for **Collaborative Big Data Analytics**. In Section VI, we articulate how such an approach stands to enhance resilience in complex systems, in particular the employment of data-driven isomorphic and biomimetic applications to critical infrastructures such as the electric grid. Specifically, we explore the context of power grid resilience, and discuss our investigation of a synchrophasor analytics system for archipelagos. We conclude in Section VII with general thoughts on the state of the art with regard to Collaborative Big Data Analytics, and identify areas for future advancement of our Sensemaking Methodology.

II. Data Acquisition: Prospecting for Diamonds of the Information Age

Just as various phases of the Industrial Revolution were fueled by human ability to derive value from the planet's natural resources though technology, the ongoing Information Revolution is being fueled by our ability to derive value from data through technology [6]. However, this derivation results in more than the generation of wealth. Data management impacts nearly every facet of society, from economic development and education, to international security and environmental stewardship. In formulating a data-centric approach to complex problem-solving of any sort, it is prudent to first observe basic characteristics of data that impact its selection and acquisition. Whereas multivariate criteria exist for evaluating the quality of natural mineral resources such as diamonds (e.g., the "Four Cs" of color, clarity, cut, and carat weight) [7], so too must data be evaluated from various perspectives. At the most basic level, the phenomenon of Big Data is being propelled by the so-called "Three Vs" of volume, variety, and velocity, which concern objectively quantifiable aspects of how much and how quickly different kinds of information are being communicated. However, in order to make any sense out of this torrent of data, we argue that an additional three qualitative aspects of veracity, value, and volatility are of equal importance, as depicted in Table I below.

TABLE I. CHARACTERISTICS OF DATA

V	The 6 Vs of Big Data	
	Description	*Units of measure / Dimensions*
Volume	Massive amounts of data	Bytes => Petabytes
Variety	Multiple forms / formats	video, sms, .pdf, .doc, .jpg, .xls, .rtf, .tif, PMU, etc
Velocity	Speed of data feeds	Event-driven / Streaming
Veracity	Trustworthiness of data	Provenance / Pedigree
Volatility	Shelf-life of data	Time-Sensitive / Static
Value	Usefulness of data	Ambiguity / Uncertainty; Correlation / Causation

a. An alternate V of Viability has also been proposed in [2], which we believe is subsumed above

Size does matter. The Big Data phenomenon is perhaps most commonly linked with the sheer volume of data being generated by a host of remote sensors, household appliances, mobile communication devices, and human content generators worldwide that totals over 2.5 quintillion bytes of data per day [8]. Although difficult to comprehend quantitatively, these reams of data come in many forms, from the millions of photos and videos shared daily from smart phones through applications like Facebook, Sine Weibo, and Snapchat, to telemetric data and raw system measurements recorded by a multitude of sensor types and fed into industrial control systems (ICS), transportation management networks, meteorological forecasting services, and other information management systems [9]. Whereas human beings have historically been the primary generators and collectors of data contributing to knowledge development, with the number of devices connected to the Internet surpassing the global human population in 2008 [10], machines are now responsible for an increasing preponderance of the world's data. Indeed, the growing linkage of people, data, things, and processes is central to the so-called IoE [11], and the driving force behind change in myriad interdependent complex systems. This massive increase in IOE-generated data is both a significant challenge and a promising opportunity. On the one hand, conventional mechanisms for capturing and analyzing data cannot scale up effectively to accommodate the explosive growth in data generation. On the other hand, such abundance can enable us to use data to guide our decision-making and problem-solving in ways that have not been possible until now. A key to unlocking this potential is the ability to rapidly assimilate huge volumes of data and accurately identify useful pieces of information.

Integrating a large variety of data stands to yield the most robust insights. In order to achieve quantitative exactitude in identifying insightful information, a maximally inclusive variety of data types and sources is essential. To generate a complete picture of a system, we must be able to view it from multiple perspectives. In this regard, a critical determinant for perspicacity is the incorporation of diverse data that each relate to a given system or problem set through unique angles that allow for cross-referencing and comparison. This includes the acquisition of both structured and unstructured forms of data. By way of example, when someone is interested in a particular topic or event, they may initially hear a broadcast about it on the radio, then read an article about it, download images, or watch a video on the Internet. As with the parable of the blind men and the elephant; each source of information takes a different form, yet contributes to a more complete understanding when taken together. Similarly, in researching issues of infrastructural resilience, we are striving to utilize a host of data gathering mechanisms, including the collection of electric power signals from monitoring equipment such as Phasor Measurement Units (PMU) and Digital Fault Recorders (DFR), to visual and geospatial data from Unmanned Aircraft Systems (UAS), Ocean Data Acquisition Systems (ODAS), Synthetic Aperture Radar (SAR) and other weather observation tools, to human sensor networks in the form of crowdsourced event observation and reporting.

Data velocity is a determining factor for agile systems. In addition to harvesting a large variety of data, the speed with which data are gathered and communicated is another significant variable, as time-critical operations from financial management and news reporting, to emergency response, law enforcement, and national defense all must be able to quickly sense the occurrence of anomalous events in order to operate effectively [12]. Several factors influence the velocity of data, including the capacity of communication channels, as well as the granularity of observations. The continuous expansion of fiber optic and wireless communication networks enable many individuals and sensors to rapidly exchange data. In addition, sensors are capable of recording measurements at increasingly precise spatial and temporal scales, resulting in more frequently observed change and data generation. At the same time, the increase in data velocity challenges our ability to keep pace. As information is communicated at greater speed, decision cycles are compressed, and we have less time to assimilate more information. To illustrate this point, consider that over 100 hundred hours of video are uploaded every minute to the video sharing site YouTube [13], which accounts for over 400 million years' worth of viewing time in the 11 years since the site's creation in 2005 [14].

Whereas adapting to these quantitative aspects of data are sufficiently challenging, simply capturing a large amount of fast-moving information from different places is not enough to generate improved insight. We must also consider the more qualitative aspects of data, which ultimately determine how useful it can be. In managing both emergency responses and routine system operations, all data consumers rely on the authenticity or veracity of data in order to gain actionable insight. The consistency of data taxonomy is an important aspect of veracity, and, in this regard, discovery standards for electronic resources such as the Dublin Core standards for Metadata are essential for datasets held by diverse curators to remain compatible with one another [15].

A more persistent challenge regarding veracity is the ability to establish the provenance and pedigree of data, particularly in the context of data manipulation and spoofing, or counterfeiting in the information supply chain. While gathering redundant data from multiple sources, and cross-referencing particularly specious data are prudent strategies for mitigating the negative impact of false or corrupted data, ensuring data veracity is a challenge that requires vigilance and adaptation. By way of example, the April 2013 issuance of a false tweet from the Associated Press's hacked Twitter account alleging injury to President Obama during an explosion at the White House caused the Dow Jones Industrial Average to plummet 142 points in just two minutes [16]. Such a resourceful, yet malicious use of technology illustrates that data need not be characterized by great volume or variety in order to generate massive impact. In turn, methods to ascertain and safeguard the authenticity of data must be equally resourceful.

Data veracity is particularly significant for operating and safeguarding critical infrastructures. With regard to electric power systems, the lack of a shared standard for grid performance metrics can compromise the value of system-wide measurements, as U.S. grid ownership is fractured between a diverse mix of privately-owned corporations, rural cooperatives, municipalities, the federal government, and a host of independent power providers, with over three thousand organizations distributing power to consumers, each with varying standards of performance monitoring [17]. Internationally, in addition to a lack of shared performance metrics, grid operations are also challenged by the lack of a shared grid event lexicon, which in extreme cases can actually prevent system interoperability [18].

In addition to its veracity, the shelf life of data also has a large impact on its utility. Volatility or duration of relevance depends largely on the nature of the decision which data are serving to inform. Whereas certain digitally preserved historical records maintain their relevance or value in perpetuity, other datasets that pertain to rapidly evolving circumstances may remain relevant for only a matter of days, if not seconds, or less. By way of example, international standards for the operation of power grids dictate that the onset of electrical islanding events amongst distributed power generating sites be detected and addressed in no more than two seconds [19]. Although the granularity of time series data is a vital consideration for decision making on compressed time scales, the continuity of data collection similarly impacts the longitudinal analysis of slower developing patterns. By way of example, a maintenance gap in 2012 of the Tropical Ocean Atmosphere array led to a 70% drop in data collection, thus compromising the consistency of measurements, and potentially skewing the analysis of long-term anthropogenic climate change and global warming studies [20].

Whereas an evaluation of each of the Four Cs are combined to determine a diamond's overall quality, the aforementioned Vs can be similarly combined to determine the utility of data. Data value loosely correlates to how much of any given decision can be engineered from it. In other words, can we decide a course of action based on a single dataset? If so, then that dataset is of high value. If many disparate datasets are required in order to engineer a single decision, then each of those datasets is of comparatively lower value, taken in isolation. Determinants of value include such factors as the level of ambiguity with regard to data meaning, as well as discernibility between correlation and causation (i.e., whether multiple variables simply change together, or whether a particular variable directly catalyzes change in others). Amongst the sea of data corresponding to myriad variables, a principal challenge is determining which pieces of data are the most significant indicators of change or phenomena of interest. Although no formalized schema yet exists for evaluating these Six Vs of data, recognizing the significance and employing methods for addressing each is a fundamental aspect of operating in a Big Data Paradigm.

The actual task of data acquisition is no less complex. For all organizations - public, private, and any permutation in between – how best to gather and disseminate data remain open questions [21]. With the United Nations (UN) having asserted that information in itself is a life-saving need for people in crisis, just as important as water, food, and shelter, the necessity of publicly-accessible data is clearly a global one that now transcends the realm of scholarly open access [22]. Yet, there is no comprehensive, authoritative single source for information, and so we must get data from as many places as we can, in as many ways as we can. By extension, an intelligent system is ideally capable of continuously ingesting data from multiple sources, through diverse media. However, there are a variety of practical limitations on such a capability, including human controls over data accessibility (e.g., personal privacy, political sensitivity, national security, commercial ownership, etc.), as well as technological challenges with data capture and curation [23]. Moore's Law for semiannually doubling transistor capacity, Gilder's Law for annually doubling communication bandwidth capacity, and Koomey's Law for annually doubling computational energy efficiency have each held steady for years to yield the current explosion of Big Data. Yet, at the same time, system input/output (I/O), memory, and storage capacities have each increased at a much slower rate [24], creating a dynamic whereby data is generated faster than it can be consumed, as pictured below in Figure 1.

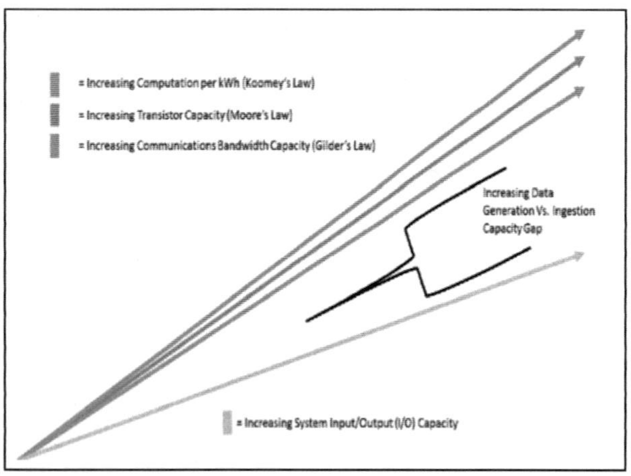

Figure 1. Technology Trends Impacting Big Data

Such limitations notwithstanding, an important component of our Sensemaking Methodology involves prioritizing the most critical data requirements, and where these cannot be met directly, identifying suitable proxies. Just as the UN employs rates of electrification as a proxy to gauge a nation's level of development, we can employ statistics such as the penetration of renewable energy sources to infer probability of electrical islanding and other disturbance events. As a commodity, data in and of itself is not particularly valuable. However, the more of it that we can gather, then the greater the chances are to yield valuable insights through intelligent refinement. Generally speaking, the onset of the Big Data phenomenon is not an automatic boon to the generation of deep insight into complex problem sets. On the contrary, Big Data itself presents unique challenges that necessitate new ways of working with information, through robust analytic techniques.

III. Stacking the Deck: Tools and Techniques for Layered Data Analytics

The analytic phase of the Sensemaking process is designed to extract actionable insights from the raw material of massive datasets. It is constituted by layers of algorithmic and heuristic techniques, high performance, distributed, and cloud computing, machine learning, signal resolution, video analytics, and natural language processing, nested under the Unstructured Information Management Architecture (UIMA) [25]. Whereas the significance of structured information such as that contained in relational databases is by nature unambiguous, the various components comprising UIMA are geared towards discerning meaning and significance from a variety of unstructured information sources, such as sensors, video, and natural language. Many of these components are rooted in mathematical concepts that have developed over centuries, and therefore some brief accounting of their evolutionary pathway is instructive.

Mathematicians and logicians of the 17th century realized that the painstaking work of numerical calculation could be conducted automatically in order to free up the mind to focus on higher level analytical work. First the Pascaline, then the Leibniz Computer represent some of the earliest automated calculating machines, later advanced in the 19th century by Charles Babbage in the form of the Analytical Engine, which was the first programmable computer designed to solve a variety of mathematical and logical problems [26]. Although Babbage's inventions are certainly significant achievements, the detailed instructions that his protégé and peer, Augusta Ada Byron Lovelace wrote for using the Engine are arguably even more lasting for being the first computer programming code [27]. Indeed, a case can be made that modern computer programming evolved from Lovelace's early conceptual programming work, as indicated by the fact that one of the U.S. military's first high level programming languages was eponymously called "Ada" [28]. In addition, George Boole's work on representing the process of logical thought in binary mathematical form paved the way for digital computer logic and the electromechanical switching processes that remain foundational to the operation of computers today [29].

While providing early functional models for computational intelligence, the work of early mathematicians and philosophers also served to inform the ontological basis on which many modern platforms have been constructed. Specifically, the theories of knowledge and logic proposed by the American Triumvirate of Pragmatism in the late 19th century have played a significant role in influencing the trajectory of the Information Revolution in the 20th and 21st centuries. The Triumvirate, comprised of William James, Charles Pierce, and John Dewey, established three postulates that would later serve as the philosophical underpinning for modern information retrieval and search engine systems, namely applications of the semblance of indeterminacy, order in chaos, and long-run convergence [30]. When combined with such an ontological orientation and the invention of semi-conductive transistors, the Shannon-Weaver model of communication opened the door to modern information and communication technology, by establishing a theory of information that conceptually integrated disparate elements of data source, message, transmitter, signal, channel, noise, and receiver into a coherent system [31]. Finally, the works of mathematician and cryptanalyst Alan Turing and others at Bletchley Park to unlock the signals intelligence encrypted by Nazi Germany's Enigma Machine, as well as John Mauchly and Presper Eckert's Electronic Numerical Integrator and Computer (ENIAC) [32] not only helped to turn the tide of World War II, but also gave birth to the field of computer science [33].

From this shared lineage, the modern analytical toolkit of computation has evolved into far too many instruments to concisely summarize here. However, there are fundamental components of the analytic process, which we will strive to articulate. Upon acquiring data, the initial step in the analytic layer of our framework is data ingestion and cleansing, which can actually account for up to 80% of work in data science [34]. By way of example, satellite imagery is unfortunately not as simple as an "eye in the sky" beaming down neat pictures to a computer console for analysis and distribution. The many 0's and 1's that make up the digital representation of a physical object must first be processed and translated into an intelligible picture. Once raw data are refined into a malleable commodity, that commodity can then be annealed into meaningful insight through a systematic layering of Analytics on Analytics (A2O). The most critical aspect of A20 is the contrasting or counterpoising of diverse datasets. This process begins with a foundational geospatial and or temporal matrix of data points, and proceeds through a set of systematic organizational steps that include data clamping, normalization, and hierarchical clustering, in order to reveal patterns and detect aberrations.

Given the importance of data veracity, a significant aspect of analytics in a Big Data Paradigm is the ability to recognize latent relationships in seemingly unrelated phenomenon. The case of the Boston Marathon Bombing well illustrates this point, as minor human error inputting one of the perpetrator's names into a federal database prevented law enforcement and intelligence officials from recognizing a critically predictive event in the month's leading up to the attack [35]. In a Big Data Paradigm, the mistaken addition of an extra "y" included in the Treasury Enforcement Communication System (TECS) record for Tamerlan Tsarnaev would not have prevented the issuance of an alert to detain him during re-entry to the United States from Chechnya, upon the recommendation of the Russian State Security Service (FSB). The application of fuzzy logic [36] and similar techniques in an A20 approach accommodates uncertainty in information granulation, which recognizes approximate relations in data instead of relying solely on exact similarity and total certainty. In general, morphological analysis and aberration detection serve to evaluate the role of myriad variables in the dynamics of complex systems and networks over time. This is depicted below in Figure 2, which is a snapshot from the SynerScope visualization suite showing change in international communication network connectivity.

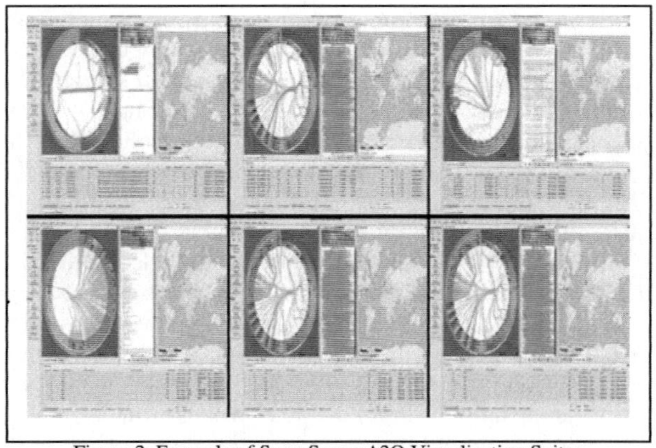

Figure 2. Example of SynerScope A2O Visualization Suite

Whereas many high performance computing applications rely on synthesized data (i.e., Monte Carlo Simulations, etc.), our approach is predicated on the acquisition and analysis of empirical data. However, a fundamental prerequisite for effective A2O is the storage and management of massive datasets. In this regard, distributed computing architectures and parallel processing are critical capabilities [37].

Impressive though they may be, machine capabilities comprise but one half of the analytic layer of our methodological framework. The remaining half relies on the inherently human capabilities of contextual orientation and intuitive leaping [38]. Whereas machines are capable of generating, processing, and storing massive quantities of data, the human mind remains unique in its ability to superimpose context over data in order to discern relevance and meaning. Hence, the Sensemaking Methodology is characterized by its fusion of technological and sociological perspectives. On the one hand, we leverage the technical advantages of machine capability in an algorithmically inductive pathway accumulating specific observations to build generalizable insights. On the other hand, we also leverage intuitive capacity in a heuristically deductive pathway applying general knowledge in particular circumstances to yield precision insights.

This socio-techno unification is at the heart of our methodology for pattern recognition and Decision Engineering. Going back to the example of satellite imagery, let us consider the case of the Global Earth Observing System of Systems (GEOSS) and the view of Somali villages at night as an illustration of counterpoising algorithmic versus heuristic insight. With the rise of both maritime piracy off the Horn of Africa, and the violent extremist organization Al-Shabaab in Somalia, international security organizations were keen to establish a link between the two groups [39]. As assets in the GEOSS satellite constellation observed significant variances in the night-time illumination of various towns along the Somali Coast and provincial capitals, analysts sought to employ the algorithmic insight of seeing more lights at night as evidence for a correlation between the dispensation of pirate ransoms and the buildup of jihadi strongholds [40]. However, heuristic insight suggested that the ideological and religiously-motivated nature of Al-Shabaab was incompatible with the financially-driven motives of the criminal piracy network, and therefore a link was unlikely. The truth of this insight would later be established through data gathered by the International Criminal Police Organization (INTERPOL) and the United Nations Office on Drugs and Crime (UNODC) [41], which verified that although pirates invest in infrastructure improvements (e.g., electrification and lights), Al-Shabaab degrades local infrastructure to fund arms purchases and maintain secrecy. Such an example shows us that while technology and algorithms are more than capable of identifying patterns of interest, we still need heuristic insight to decipher what those patterns actually mean.

IV. A PICTURE TELLS A THOUSAND WORDS: IMPARTING INSIGHT THROUGH DATA VISUALIZATION

Upon recognizing patterns of interest through an analytic process, relevant insight must be visualized in a way that directly informs the engineering of decisions. The primary aim of the data visualization phase is to establish the relevance of insight gained through the A20 process, and help to guide the actions of decision makers by parsing out critical points of useful information from massive amounts of data. Figure 2, above, displays output from one of our visualization platforms, the SynerScope. SynerScope and other similar tools use a coordinated multi-view approach with a scalable and flexible visual matrix in order to visualize key morphological insights into how complex systems and networks change over time. However, before we progress into any further detail with regard to contemporary visualization techniques, let us briefly consider data visualization in its broader context.

Efforts to visualize and impart insight are as old as human knowledge and communication; from cave paintings, to pictographs, hieroglyphs, numerology, symbolic logic, and language. In order to understand what methods have been developed over time for effectively conveying knowledge, it is instructive to visit certain historical examples. One case in point is the work of the Mixtec civilization of Oaxaca, Mexico [42], depicted above in Figure 3. Although the figure above depicts the Mixtec's primordial cosmology and creation mythology, it is an early example of how human insights gained through observation of natural phenomenon (i.e., data analysis) were preserved for distribution and posterity. This and other similar precedents from early civilization remain germane to many data-related fields, including Education, the Arts, Public Information, Manufacturing, Product Advertisement, Device Instruction Manuals, Traffic Signage, Emergency Management, and Information Technology (IT) [43]. With the advent of the Internet, and eventually the World Wide Web, the tradition of data visualization has continued to evolve. Today, such professional disciplines as Cognitive Science, Behavioral Psychology, Computer-Assisted Design (CAD), and Strategic Communication all build on the work of early visualization specialists by combining machine capability with human insight to generate socio-techno innovations in how the brain senses and interprets information. In turn, our interpretation and assimilation of information drives our ability to engineer decisions and determine appropriate courses of action, as individuals in daily life, as agents in organizations, and as members of the global citizenry.

Nevertheless, this does not mean that modern data visualization is a perfected science. Rather, visualization is a principled art that requires both intelligence and intuition in its composition. In turn, efforts to visualize pseudo-insights that are not informed by robust analytics run the risk of proliferating misinformation, bias, conflict, and spoilage of resources [44]. In addition to these pitfalls, data-informed visualizations also can be subject to information overload, if insights are not concisely crystallized in a digestible form, as depicted below in Figure 4 [45].

Figure 3. Image from the *Codex Vindobonensis Mexicanus*

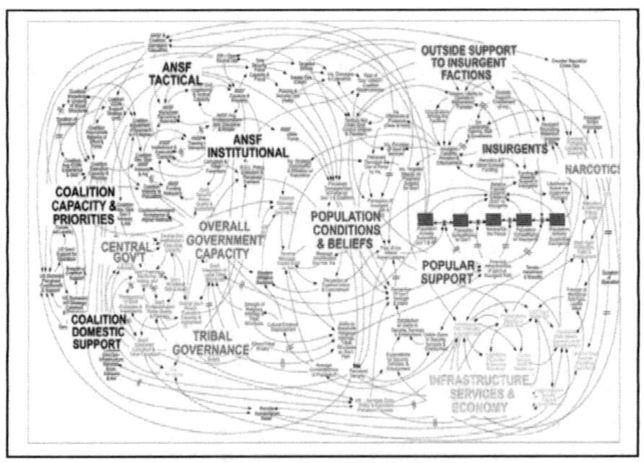

Figure 4. Example of Counterinsurgency Diagram

The design of any given data visualization is driven by two primary factors; the nature of the decision it serves to engineer, and the demographic characteristics of the audience or decision maker. Firstly, is the aim of the visualization simply to impart generally useful information, or is it intended to inform a specific choice? If the aim is the former, then visualizations such as that in Figure 4 may be suitable. However, decision-quality visualizations must clearly depict actionable insight, and inform implementable courses of action in a timely manner. Secondly, how much does the target audience for a given data visualization already know? An audience of laymen will require a significant amount of context in order to make sense out of visualizations depicting complex phenomena. Conversely, too much context will be superfluous (and potentially distracting) to an audience of experts. Therefore, constructing an effective data visualization means striking a delicate balance between sufficient context and specific insight.

With this in mind, we turn to a key consideration regarding the value of data visualization; the depiction of changing dynamics and identification of brittleness in complex systems. In light of the many layers of interdependence that characterize our most critical infrastructural systems (e.g., electric grids, the Internet, etc.), there is significant potential for percolation effects or cascading failure [46]. Therefore, to ensure the resilience of such systems, it is essential to closely track changes in system states over time, to identify areas of brittleness or weak links in the chain, and actuate corrective measures before these weak links fail. With regard to the resilience of the Internet in particular, tools such as the SeeSoft System, pictured below in Figure 5, enable analysts to visualize statistics of interest in software code [47]. In the case of Figure 5, a color-coding scheme displays how recently lines of code have been changed, with red lines having been most recently changed, and green lines having remained unchanged the longest.

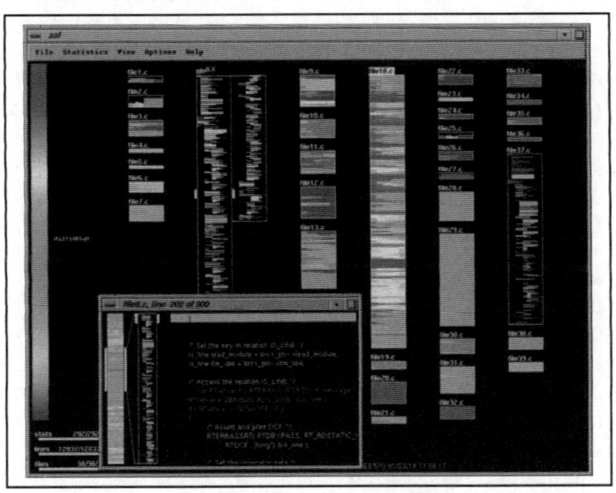

Figure 5. SeeSoft software code visualization system, Lucent Technologies

Visualization tools are invaluable assets that enable us to quickly and clearly see areas of potential brittleness in complex systems. In the case of Figure 5, above, we have a mechanism to visualize answers to questions such as whether software security improves with age, as lines of code not recently updated to address proliferating cyber threat vectors are likely brittle [48]. Therefore, visualization is not only a product of the analytic phase of the Sensemaking Methodology, but can actually be a feedback loop that helps to inform the A2O process. In general, visualization is a fluid endeavor, whereby patterns that reside in large amounts of data can be quickly and easily recognized by a human user, and help to guide their decision making amidst dynamic environments and changing circumstances.

V. PROOFS OF CONCEPT: SYNERSCOPE AND THE DATA FOR DEVELOPMENT CHALLENGE

To demonstrate the utility of our approach, we come to the shores of West Africa and the Data for Development Challenge (D4D) [49]. Since its inauguration in 2012, the annual D4D Challenge has represented a unique opportunity for Big Data analysts to experiment with diverse tools and techniques for harvesting insight from mobile phone data. For each challenge, international competitors from academia and private industry are given the chance to analyze a multitude of datasets pertaining to mobile phone use in a designated country during a circumscribed portion of the year [50]. We have had the privilege to participate in the first two such challenges, in the Republic of Côte d'Ivoire and Senegal, with a sampling of our results displayed below in Figure 6 [51].

Figure 6. 2013 D4D Best Visualization: *"Exploration and Analysis of Massive Mobile Phone Data: A Layered Visual Analytics Approach"*

In conducting our analysis of the D4D datasets and generating the illustrations sampled above, two lessons became clear to us. First, we needed a large variety of data sources, through which to contrast and correlate mobile phone activity with other significant trends and events. For the first D4D in Côte d'Ivoire, we contrasted the given mobile phone data with UN reports of violent conflict and significant social disturbance, as well as meteorological data for the given timeframe. This helped to reveal regional political affiliations and ethnic enclaves, as violent events targeting certain political and ethnic groups in the capital city, Abidjan, catalyzed notable increases in call activity to specific communities elsewhere in the country. In addition, we observed that abundant rainfall in areas of significant cocoa and yam cultivation correlated with heightened call activity, likely indicating increased agro-business developments at specific points in the growth and harvest cycles in response to favorable weather conditions. Our second key learning was the need to adopt multiple perspectives from which to interrogate the datasets. Our normalization and clustering algorithms produced dendograms, with which we were able to sort items (e.g., cell towers) of similar calling behavior into groups for further investigation. By grouping cell towers of similar call behavior, we were then able to further explore what other commonalities linked these disparate regions.

Although such techniques are still relatively nascent, we believe that the work of our team and fellow D4D participants is a clear demonstration that Collaborative Big Data Analytics can help to increase insight into complex interrelated phenomenon, and thus improve Decision Engineering in a variety of social, political, and economic arenas. However, the implementation of our **Sensemaking Methodology** remains in the early stages, and inevitably there is room for improvement in such an approach. Specifically, increasing the volume and variety of data included in the A2O phase will yield greater insight in future D4D Challenges, and other applications of our methodological framework. In addition, the deliberate articulation of alternate frameworks for Collaborative Big Data Analytics will help to progress the state of the art, by revealing common best practices as well as shortfalls and gaps.

VI. KEEPING THE LIGHTS ON: THE ROLE OF SENSEMAKING IN SMART ELECTRIC GRIDS

In addition to work on the D4D Challenges, our exploration of infrastructural resilience also helps to illustrate the utility of a systematic approach for data acquisition, analytics, and visualization. As society has evolved, technology has advanced, and the complexity of systems has increased. In turn, this rise in complexity and interdependence leads to increased vulnerability in the social and physical systems upon which we rely for essential services [52]. In response, a resilience-oriented approach assumes that unpredictable and destabilizing events will inevitably occur, and accordingly focuses on how flexibility and adaptation can be instilled across systems. Making good use of data is central to such an effort. Therefore, we present initial findings from the application of our Sensemaking Methodology to an investigation of electric grid systems, and the development of a synchrophasor analytics system for archipelagos.

The concept of resilience is a core area of study in a wide variety of disciplines, from human psychology [53] and childhood development [54], to ecosystems [55], economics [56] and disaster preparedness [57]. Generally speaking, resilience refers to the capacity of a system to absorb shocks while maintaining functionality. However, resilience is a highly conditional state and the determinants of system resilience vary depending on the nature of the system and the context of specific shocks or destabilizing forces [58]. Factors that promote resilience in one system do not always translate neatly into other system contexts. By way of example, while a diverse social network can enhance individual resilience, the interdependence of diverse infrastructural components may itself be a source of vulnerability for the collective infrastructural system. In addition, a particular system cannot be broadly characterized as either vulnerable or resilient in perpetuity, because each threat affects a system differently, and threats continually evolve.

Nonetheless, we maintain that insights generated from the study of resilience in social-ecological systems [59] do bear relevance for the promotion of resilience in cyber-physical systems, such as the electric grid. In particular, the so-called "R4" framework is a helpful tool for conceptualizing the key harbingers of resilience, namely robustness, redundancy, resourcefulness, and rapidity [60]. With regard to lifeline critical infrastructure systems like the electric grid, robustness; or the ability to withstand shocks is of particular importance [61]. Although rapidity (i.e., the ability to return to a state of normal functioning in a timely manner) is also a chief concern, it is an outcome of how effectively the redundancy and resourcefulness of contingency measures can augment a system's robustness.

Resilience can take many forms. In particular, research in ecological systems has evolved through two fundamental categories of systemic resiliency that differ over the balance between resilience and stability, or the flexibility to operate in multiple states of equilibrium or basins of attraction, as depicted below in Figure 7. Systems of inherent or engineering resilience are characterized by relatively low resilience and high stability, whereby systems operate within a comparatively narrow envelope of equilibrium that are designed for efficiency and productivity and thus do not tolerate instability. Systems of engineering resilience typically operate within a rigid set of parameters, or a single basin of attraction, and therefore have been able to operate effectively on a comparatively sparse data paradigm. In contrast, systems of adaptive or ecological resilience are characterized by relatively high resilience and low stability, whereby systems can function in multiple states of equilibrium or instability in order to persist or remain functional [62]. These multiple states of equilibrium or basins of attraction enable systems of adaptive resilience to remain viable in a more fluid set of parameters.

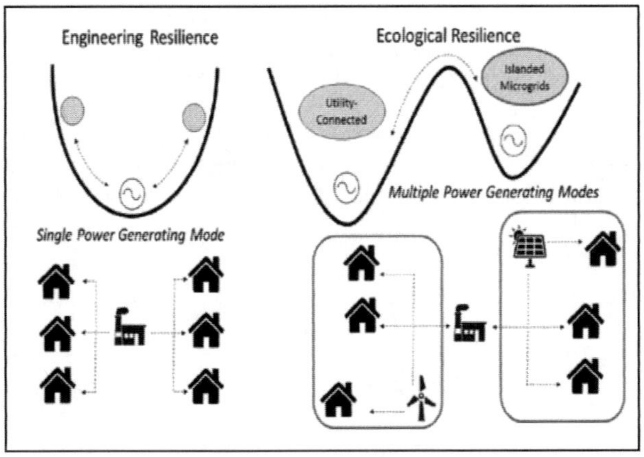

Figure 7. Engineering & Ecological Resilience, adapted from Scheffer et al, 1993

The ecological resilience concept pictured on the right of Figure 7 more closely approximates the aspirational "Smart Grid" of future power delivery. In this conception, resilience is a dynamic process that unfolds within a stability landscape, determined by a system's latitude, resistance, precariousness, and panarchy [63], which necessitates the adoption of a Big Data Paradigm in light of the many variables that must be managed within a given system. A resilience-oriented approach differs from a stability-oriented approach in that it does not require complete knowledge of all possible future events, but rather assumes that the unexpected will occur, and accordingly, it focuses upon devising systems that can respond adaptively to new and changing circumstances through the timely acquisition and analysis of granular data. These divergent conceptions of resilience raise interesting questions as to the nature of increasingly complex cyber-physical systems, such as the electric grid, particularly in light of the electric grid's shift toward a heterogeneous blend of power providers and distributed energy resources.

While engineering resilience characterizes the grid of the past and present, in which stability and efficiency are prioritized, the grid of the future has the potential to operate in an ecological resilience paradigm, whereby continuity is prioritized and power is provided in increasingly varied ways. In light of many technological advancements, perhaps the characterization need not be one of mutual exclusivity, but rather, how systems like the electric grid can be a hybrid enjoying the benefits of both stability and resilience. In this vein, a complementary focus in resilience research explores the effects of long-term change on the functionality of systems. In contrast to quick-onset shocks, the effects of gradual transformation can be equally disruptive and challenging to the resilience of systems, thereby demanding an adaptive capacity on the part of human operators [64]. The move towards a smarter grid represents just such a transformation, with multiple competing priorities that must be balanced in order to maintain infrastructural systems that are both sustainable and secure. This includes the deployment of newly developed hardware and software tools, as well as human capital investment for training operators to work in a more adaptive and data-centric paradigm.

Indeed, as societies become more reliant on an increasingly complex web of infrastructural systems, the need for both resilience and stability cannot be mutually exclusive. The imperative for many infrastructural providers to operate their systems at a profit adequately incentivizes stability in routine operations. However, a comparably salient incentive to invest in measures that enhance resilience to rare — yet devastating — black swan events [65] is lacking. The interdependence of modern critical infrastructure systems is itself a chief vulnerability or blind spot, in that the disruption of one critical service or system can potentially catalyze the catastrophic failure of all systems [66]. As evidence of this potential, we need only consider how many devices in our homes and communities rely upon electricity to function, from refrigerators and cash machines, to life-saving medical devices and water treatment facilities. In the event of a power outage, any such device not supported by its own independent power source would cease to function. When disaster events compromise the operation of critical infrastructure systems, the potential arises for situations to quickly transform from emergencies into crises. In such scenarios, societal or community resilience and the ability of citizens to cope effectively with crisis becomes a crucial consideration, albeit with its own set of unique challenges [67].

To hedge against such catastrophe, enhancing the resilience of even a single infrastructural component increases the collective resilience of the entire mosaic of critical infrastructure. Therefore, the focus of our study is on enhancing resilience in the electric grid as a vital component in the broader infrastructural system. In doing so, we aim to provide a blueprint for Decision Engineering that can be translated to other infrastructural sectors, public services, and missions that are challenged with the management of large and complex systems.

The first step in this effort is understanding data related to an electric power system, and the means for acquiring it. An electric grid is an integration of four distinct networks of electricity generation, transmission, distribution, and consumption, each of which produce distinct metrics. While each of these networks present their own idiosyncratic challenges to be overcome, the overarching problem for the grid is that electricity supply must constantly satisfy ever expanding consumer demand in a reliable, efficient, and increasingly sophisticated manner [68]. In order to do so, electricity is transported through many buses or nodes and, in many cases, over long distances; the overload or failure of any single node or edge between nodes forces the redistribution of load to other nodes, which can compromise the operation of the entire network through a cascading or percolating effect [69]. Percolation is not unique to electric grids, and other networks that have demonstrated potential resilience to the phenomenon appear to share common topological features, such as modularity and long path length across the network, which serve to isolate disturbances, provide alternate flow routes, and delay total network exposure [70]. However, robustness to percolation is not a viable solution, as grid operators must also deliver electricity efficiently, which excessively circuitous or entangled transmission and distribution lines would preclude. In contrast, optimally efficient networks are characterized by short path lengths formed around highly linked central nodes or hubs [71]. Ideal grid architectures strike a balance between resilience and efficiency by featuring a core of interlinked hubs and a periphery of leaf nodes, which facilitate connectivity throughout the network while maintaining resilience to percolation [72]. However, the North American bulk power grid was not designed with resilience in mind, and it contains a very limited corpus of hubs, which are so highly connected that it has been characterized as a scale-free network [73]. While these hubs are the main source of the grid's connectivity, they are also a critical vulnerability if they are compromised.

The development of smart grid technologies is precipitating several significant changes in data generation, network topology, and system dynamics that impact resilience. First, automated metering infrastructure and other communications enhancements are increasing the volume, variety, and velocity of power system data. In addition, power generation resources are becoming increasingly diverse and decentralized, with the flow of electricity transitioning from unidirectional to bidirectional as energy consumers also become part-time energy providers [74]. These changes add layers of complexity to electric grid operations, which in turn drives an increase in the amount of information required to maintain operability that exceeds human capabilities to process in terms of speed and volume [75]. In naturally occurring complex adaptive systems, biodiversity is an asset that enables various components to self-organize effectively in response to disturbances [76]. As the electric grid becomes an increasingly complex system of diverse components, it is prudent to consider what measures can be taken to catalyze resilience as an emergent property among these components.

In this regard, key principles from corporate enterprise governance provide an informative isomorphic contrast to those of ecosystem resilience. For service-oriented enterprises that must cope with discontinuity and uncertainty, the ability to sense and respond to change is paramount; context and coordination replace command and control as procedural operating paradigms, with the addition of an adaptive loop that facilitates systemic learning and the ability to improve responses to successive perturbations [77]. The Sense and Respond concept was originally articulated in the context of managing large corporations with diverse teams working on a variety of missions; however, it also bears relevance to a large physical system with diverse components that must fulfill a variety of functions. In this regard, the need to acquire maximally granular data regarding the operational status of the grid's various components becomes a principal requirement, and the advent of phasor measurement units (PMU) or synchrophasors represent a significant increase in granularity over conventional supervisory control and data acquisition (SCADA) capabilities [78].

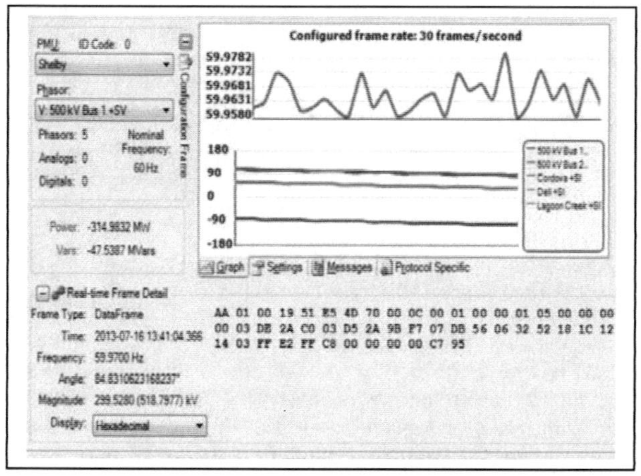

Figure 8. Sample phasor measurement unit output, Open PMU

Leveraging the PMU as a primary data acquisition platform enables the operation of power systems in a Big Data Paradigm. Measurements, such as the example pictured above in Figure 8, translate electric power signals into sinusoidal waveform and are capable of recording as many as 120 geo-referenced time-synchronized measurements per second in a streaming fashion, whereas conventional SCADA monitoring systems are event-driven, and typically record a single measurement every 2-4 seconds. In addition to acquiring a larger volume of data, PMUs are capable of measuring a variety of variables, such as voltage and frequency fluctuations, rate of change of frequency, harmonics, and phase angle difference. The veracity of these measurements is ensured with time synchronization via GPS arbiter clocks in each unit. By employing such an increased observational capacity, grid operators can sense the onset of disturbance or fault events with much greater precision. However, this requires both the ability to ingest large continuously streaming datasets [79], as well as the analytic capability to perform complex computations on the incoming data in order to discern between typical system fluctuations and dangerous anomalies. In this regard, standards for PMU performance, such as IEEE C.37.118 continue to evolve as thresholds for harmonic and interharmonic filtering are calibrated to preserve valuable signal components [80].

With regard to data ingestion and the velocity of PMU record generation, communications latency is a nontrivial issue worthy of note. In order to maximize the utility of PMUs, they must be able to communicate through a robust protocol such as TCP/IP, with significant bandwidth (i.e., at least 5 Megabytes per second). In light of the synchronized nature of PMU data, a network of geographically dispersed devices can facilitate a wide-area measurement system (WAMS), provided that each device enjoys uniform connection speed. Whereas conventional fault recording devices are generally triggered only in event-driven circumstances, the need for persistent Internet connectivity between substations and central monitoring facilities is a novel requirement for many utility operators. Similarly, the streaming nature of synchrophasor data requires utility operators to develop data retention strategies or policies in order to effectively manage such a large increase in data generation. Although the dynamic nature of power systems means that PMU data are highly volatile for functions that demand a fast response, the preservation of data over time is critical to yielding deep insights through an A2O process.

As an electric power signal contains numerous variables of interest, the analytic phase of our approach involves numerous procedural layers. A variety of competing algorithmic techniques exist for detecting anomalies, such as analyzing rates of change of voltage, frequency, and phase angle difference, detecting fluctuations in harmonic distortion, and measuring voltage unbalance, many of which have historically been executed independently of one another. As computational capability has advanced, the ability to leverage support vector machines, artificial neural networks, decision trees, and other intelligent classifiers presents the opportunity to more quickly and accurately detect events of interest. In particular, we are exploring how cognitive computing in a layered analytic process has the potential to enable the rapid detection of the onset of electrical islanding scenarios. By developing an integrated islanding detection method that is both sensitive to target events and stable against false tripping, we aim to improve the integration of renewable energy sources such as photovoltaics and wind turbines. In turn, we intend that such an advanced analytic process will also help to identify and visualize patterns related to other destabilizing events in electric power systems. We have chosen to focus our research on archipelagos due to the unique set of circumstances which these environments represent. Given their physical isolation, islands are inherently bounded problem sets. In addition, the power systems that serve islands are characterized by lower inertia and lower blackstart/quickstart ratios than larger systems such as the North American bulk power grid.

In exploring these problem sets, we employ a combination of algorithmic and heuristic analytics. Although the PMU's increase in observational granularity coupled with advanced computational analytic capabilities represent the value of algorithmic insight for enhancing power system resilience, the generation of heuristic insight will also be a significant pathway towards a more resilient and adaptive operating paradigm. In addition to its internal system dynamics, many external natural and anthropogenic environmental factors each exert influence on the operation of the grid. Therefore, including data on seismic events, weather patterns, and other natural phenomena as layers in the analytic stack will help to enrich the observational space in which we analyze power system dynamics. In addition, human-generated content is a valuable source of situational awareness regarding service disruptions, power outages, and latent vulnerabilities. By way of example, power companies in the U.S. have historically become aware of the majority of outages only after their customers called in to report that they were without power [81]. However, vigilant customers can serve as sensors not only to detect instances of power outage, but also to identify conditions that may be pre-cursors to fault or disturbance events, such as vegetation overgrowth affecting power lines, abnormal spark emission from transformers, and suspicious activity around substations. Similar to the U.S. Department of Homeland Security's "See Something, Say Something" public ad campaign, the encouragement of customer vigilance and crowdsourced infrastructure protection can be a useful tool for augmenting the limited capacity of system operators and public safety officials charged with safeguarding the grid. As depicted below in Figure 9, our approach aims to integrate these various data sources and analytic capabilities in order to achieve power systems that operate with greater resilience.

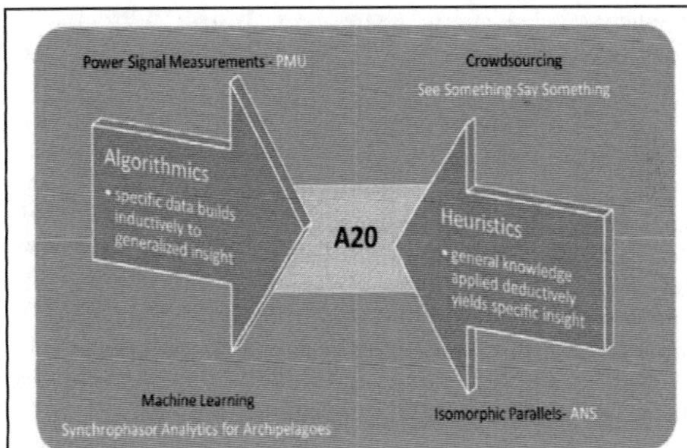

Figure 9. Analytics on Analytics (A2O) Concept

As technology and connectivity advance us closer to the realization of a smart grid, a coherent and logical integration of data acquisition, analytics, and visualization will be critical. The ability to assimilate system state data from PMUs and other devices deployed across the grid with a variety of environmental data and geo-referenced content from human observers and remote sensors will be vital for operating power systems that are both reliable and sustainable. In addition, gaining a better understanding of how complex dynamics impact the grid's operation will directly inform how automated protocols can be established to develop computer-assisted dynamic fine tuning measures.

In this regard, nature-inspired engineering and insight from the life sciences may be instructive. In particular, the autonomic nervous system (ANS) is one potentially useful source of biomimetic and isomorphic insight for how a self-healing smart grid could operate. Also known as the involuntary nervous system, the ANS maintains conditions for a steady state or homeostasis within the body and plays a role in many of its critical processes, including the defense reaction or "fight or flight" response, thermoregulation, coping with metabolic challenges [82], and regulation of organ functions related to the biological clock [83]. The ANS is composed of two primary subsystems that influence bodily functions; the sympathetic nervous system, which activates function, and the parasympathetic nervous system, which limits function [84].

An important aspect of the ANS that translates well to the electric grid is its feedback-regulated nature; as conditions within the body change, the ANS acts to mitigate potentially harmful effects. For example, when we stand up after sitting for an extended period, the potentially dangerous drop in blood pressure that could result from blood pooling in the legs is counteracted as the ANS initiates a series of baroreceptor reflexes that increase heart rate and blood flow while mediating constriction of the blood vessels to restore steady blood pressure throughout the body. However, the ANS is also capable of anticipatory responses that serve to manage the danger presented by system perturbations or destabilizing events before they occur. The anticipatory release of insulin prior to a meal is one simple example. And yet, maintaining a homeostatic steady state may not always be the best strategy for ensuring the long-term survival of a system. In response to stress imposed by extreme circumstances, ANS processes within the body may need to shift to an altered state or allostasis[1] characterized by adaptive levels of system output like increased heart rate and blood flow through the muscles in order to facilitate escape from or confrontation with a physical threat [85]. Similarly, cyber-physical infrastructures such as the grid must also operate during periods of unusually high demand, or acute instability such as in the midst or aftermath of natural disaster.

[1] Allostasis refers to a system's ability to maintain functionality through change. In contrast to a homeostatic state in which a system maintains a relatively stable balance, an allostatic state is characterized by temporarily unbalanced ratios in system input vs. output, or other adaptations to internal processes that enable the system to remain in operation during external perturbations, after which the system returns to homeostasis.

In light of its role in both feedback-regulated and anticipatory responses that facilitate homeostatic and allostatic system states, the ANS offers conceptual parallels for enhancing the resilience of critical infrastructure systems like the electric grid. Just as the ANS acts within the body to mitigate against potentially harmful conditions without an individual's conscious awareness, machine automation or computer assisted dynamic fine tuning can act within the grid to mitigate against potentially harmful conditions before they are even recognized by human system operators. Yet, just as the ANS relies on input from the five senses to drive its operation, human-engineered systems like the grid require robust, precise, and diverse data in order to operate effectively. Technological advances such as synchronized phasor measurements, cognitive computing, and machine learning capabilities are particularly beneficial for operating large infrastructural systems such as the electric grid, and are therefore the primary components of our synchrophasor analytics system for archipelagos.

VII. Conclusion

As machine capability continues to accelerate giving rise to big and bigger data, the power and promise of robust analytics will grow along with potential areas of vulnerability introduced by increased system connectivity and interdependence. At the same time, our ability to make sense out of evolving circumstances quickly, and adapt social and physical structures accordingly will be important determinants in the shape of things to come. Such competing dynamics call for a suitably balanced approach to data management and systems operation. While complex cyber-physical infrastructures such as the electric grid are akin to the Abelian Sandpile in its susceptibility to cascading effects, tools such as PMU-enabled response mechanisms are the bamboo that can enable such systems to remain resilient amidst destabilizing events. In the context of electric grids in particular, the increasing penetration of distributed sources of renewable energy necessitates an improvement in the ability to detect and counteract the destabilizing effects of unintentional electrical islanding and similar phenomenon. In response, our synchrophasor analytics system for archipelagos aims to achieve a precise islanding detection capability by integrating the granularity of PMU data acquisition with the robust analytic capabilities of cognitive computing and machine learning.

Our participation in the D4D Challenges as well as our investigation of infrastructural resilience demonstrate that much opportunity exists to improve our understanding of how systems operate through the application of analytics in a Big Data Paradigm. We believe that open and inclusive approaches such as the **Sensemaking Methodology** have the potential to enhance numerous dimensions of resilience, including those of cyber-physical systems, societies, and individuals. Systematic Decision Engineering requires a robust and iterative process of data collection, layered analytics, and insight visualization that in turn has the ability to identify critical blind spots and mitigate harmful vulnerabilities. We hope that such a methodology can facilitate positive developments, such as the smart integration of green technologies into sustainable Blue Economies [86], and improvement in our roles as both environmental stewards and engines of social progress. Each of these areas represent exciting and relatively unexplored realms of research that we have designated as targets for future work. Specifically, we plan to further investigate how technological capabilities such as remote sensing and cognitive computing can be effectively integrated with human Sensemaking techniques to achieve increasingly useful insights and practical Decision Engineering solutions.

ACKNOWLEDGMENT

The authors would like to thank our mentors and collaborating partners, as well as the advisory board of the Sensemaking Fellowship.

REFERENCES

[1] R. Spousta, S. van den Elzen, S. Chan, and J. K. Buenen, "From Cheese to Fondue: A Sensemaking Methodology for Data Acquisition, Analytics, and Visualization," in *IARIA 2015 Data Analytics* Nice, France, 2015, pp. 38-43.

[2] N. R. Council, *Frontiers in Massive Data Analysis*. Washington, DC: The National Academies Press, 2013.

[3] R. Spousta and S. Chan, "Milk or Wine: Are Critical Infrastructure Protection Architectures Improving with Age? ," *Journal of Challenges,* vol. 2, pp. 43-57, 2015.

[4] P. Bak, C. Tang, and K. Wiesenfeld, "Self-organized criticality: An explanation of the 1/f noise," *Physical Review Letters,* vol. 59, p. 381, 1987.

[5] W. Bryant, "Cyberspace Resiliency: Springing Back with the Bamboo," in *Evolution of Cyber Technologies and Operations to 2035*, M. Blowers, Ed., ed Cham: Springer International Publishing, 2015, pp. 1-17.

[6] M. E. Porter and V. E. Millar, "How information gives you competitive advantage," *Harvard Business Review,* vol. 63, July-August 1985.

[7] E. Fritsch and B. Rondeau, "Gemology: The Developing Science of Gems," *Elements,* vol. 5, pp. 147-152, 2009.

[8] N. Biehn. (2013, May) The Missing V's in Big Data: Viability and Value. *Wired*. Available: http://www.wired.com/2013/05/the-missing-vs-in-big-data-viability-and-value/. Accessed May 27, 2016

[9] C. Alcaraz and J. Lopez, "Wide-Area Situational Awareness for Critical Infrastructure Protection," *Computer,* vol. 46, pp. 30-37, 2013.

[10] L. Atzori, A. Iera, and G. Morabito, "The internet of things: A survey," *Computer Networks,* vol. 54, pp. 2787-2805, 2010.

[11] D. Evans, "The internet of everything: How more relevant and valuable connections will change the world," *Cisco IBSG,* pp. 1-9, 2012.

[12] K. M. Chandy, "Sense and respond systems," in *Int. CMG Conference*, 2005, pp. 59-66.

[13] T. Yu, L. Bai, J. Guo, and Z. Yang, "Construct a Bipartite Signed Network in YouTube," *International Journal of Multimedia Data Engineering and Management (IJMDEM),* vol. 6, pp. 56-77, 2015.

[14] T. Ray, "YouTube's 2 Billion Videos, 197M Hours Make it an 'Immense' Force, Says Bernstein," in *Barron's*, ed, 2016.

[15] S. Weibel, J. Kunze, C. Lagoze, and M. Wolf, "Dublin core metadata for resource discovery," *Internet Engineering Task Force RFC,* vol. 2413, p. 132, 1998.

[16] D. ElBoghdady, "Market quavers after fake AP tweet says Obama was hurt in White House explosions," in *Washington Post*, ed, 2013.

[17] T. D. Heidel, J. G. Kassakian, and R. Schmalensee, "Forward Pass: Policy Challenges and Technical Opportunities on the U.S. Electric Grid," *Power and Energy Magazine, IEEE,* vol. 10, pp. 30-37, 2012.

[18] Y. Pradeep, S. A. Khaparde, and R. K. Joshi, "High Level Event Ontology for Multiarea Power System," *Smart Grid, IEEE Transactions on,* vol. 3, pp. 193-202, 2012.

[19] "IEEE Standard for Interconnecting Distributed Resources with Electric Power Systems," *IEEE Std 1547-2003,* pp. 1-28, 2003.

[20] D. M. Legler, H. J. Freeland, R. Lumpkin, G. Ball, M. J. McPhaden, S. North, *et al.*, "The current status of the real-time in situ Global Ocean Observing System for operational oceanography," *Journal of Operational Oceanography,* vol. 8, pp. s189-s200, 2015.

[21] M. Alavi and D. E. Leidner, "Review: Knowledge Management and Knowledge Management Systems: Conceptual Foundations and Research Issues," *MIS Quarterly,* vol. 25, pp. 107-136, 2001.

[22] C. Hajjem, S. Harnad, and Y. Gingras, "Ten-year cross-disciplinary comparison of the growth of open access and how it increases research citation impact," *arXiv preprint cs/0606079,* 2006.

[23] C. L. Philip Chen and C.-Y. Zhang, "Data-intensive applications, challenges, techniques and technologies: A survey on Big Data," *Information Sciences,* vol. 275, pp. 314-347, 2014.

[24] S. F. Oliveira, K. Furlinger, and D. Kranzlmuller, "Trends in Computation, Communication and Storage and the Consequences for Data-intensive Science," in *High Performance Computing and Communication & 2012 IEEE 9th International Conference on Embedded Software and Systems (HPCC-ICESS), 2012 IEEE 14th International Conference on*, 2012, pp. 572-579.

[25] D. Ferrucci and A. Lally, "UIMA: an architectural approach to unstructured information processing in the corporate research environment," *Natural Language Engineering,* vol. 10, pp. 327-348, 2004.

[26] R. Kurzweil and M. L. Schneider, *The age of intelligent machines* vol. 579: MIT press Cambridge, 1990.

[27] L. van Zoonen, "Gendering the Internet: Claims, Controversies and Cultures," *European Journal of Communication,* vol. 17, pp. 5-23, March 1, 2002.

[28] D. Gurer, "Pioneering women in computer science," *Communications of the ACM,* vol. 38, pp. 45-54, 2002.

[29] H. H. Goldstine, *The computer from Pascal to von Neumann*: Princeton University Press, 1980.

[30] M. Glassman and M. J. Kang, "Pragmatism, connectionism and the internet: A mind's perfect storm," *Computers in Human Behavior,* vol. 26, pp. 1412-1418, 2010.

[31] C. E. Shannon and W. Weaver, *The mathematical theory of communication*: University of Illinois press, reprinted 2015.

[32] S. McCartney, *ENIAC: The Triumphs and Tragedies of the World's First Computer*: Walker \& Company, 1999.
[33] A. M. Turing, "Turing's treatise on Enigma," *Unpublished Manuscript,* 1939.
[34] S. Lohr, "For big-data scientists, janitor work is key hurdle to insights," *New York Times,* vol. 17, 2014.
[35] M. Viser, "House panel details failures in run-up to Marathon attack," in *Boston Globe*, ed, 2014.
[36] L. A. Zadeh, "Toward a theory of fuzzy information granulation and its centrality in human reasoning and fuzzy logic," *Fuzzy Sets and Systems,* vol. 90, pp. 111-127, 1997.
[37] G. S. Sureshrao and H. P. Ambulgekar, "MapReduce-based warehouse systems: A survey," in *Advances in Engineering and Technology Research (ICAETR), 2014 International Conference on*, 2014, pp. 1-8.
[38] N. Ford, "Information retrieval and creativity: towards support for the original thinker," *Journal of Documentation,* vol. 55, pp. 528-542, 1999.
[39] J. Stevenson, "Jihad and Piracy in Somalia," *Survival,* vol. 52, pp. 27-38, 2010.
[40] A. Shortland, "Treasure mapped: using satellite imagery to track the developmental effects of Somali Piracy," *London: Chatham House,* 2012.
[41] S. Yikona, *Pirate Trails: Tracking the Illicit Financial Flows from Pirate Activities Off the Horn of Africa*: World Bank Publications, 2013.
[42] B. E. Byland and J. M. Pohl, *In the realm of 8 Deer: The archaeology of the Mixtec codices*: University of Oklahoma Press, 1994.
[43] J. Z. Gao, L. Prakash, and R. Jagatesan, "Understanding 2D-BarCode Technology and Applications in M-Commerce - Design and Implementation of A 2D Barcode Processing Solution," in *Computer Software and Applications Conference, 2007*, pp. 49-56.
[44] W. Neil Adger, N. W. Arnell, and E. L. Tompkins, "Successful adaptation to climate change across scales," *Global Environmental Change,* vol. 15, pp. 77-86, 2005.
[45] E. Bumiller. (2010, April 26) We Have Met the Enemy and He is Powerpoint. *New York Times.* Available: http://www.nytimes.com/2010/04/27/world/27powerpoint.html?_r=2. Accessed May 27, 2016.
[46] S. H. Strogatz, "Exploring complex networks," *Nature,* vol. 410, pp. 268-276, 2001.
[47] S. G. Eick, J. L. Steffen, and E. E. Sumner, Jr., "Seesoft-a tool for visualizing line oriented software statistics," *Software Engineering, IEEE Transactions on,* vol. 18, pp. 957-968, 1992.
[48] A. Ozment and S. E. Schechter, "Milk or wine: does software security improve with age?," in *Proceedings of the 15th conference on USENIX Security Symposium-Volume 15*, 2006, p. 7.
[49] J. K. Laurila, D. Gatica-Perez, I. Aad, J. Blom, O. Bornet, T. M. T. Do, *et al.*, "From big smartphone data to worldwide research: The Mobile Data Challenge," *Pervasive and Mobile Computing,* vol. 9, pp. 752-771, 2013.
[50] V. D. Blondel, M. Esch, C. Chan, F. Clérot, P. Deville, E. Huens, *et al.*, "Data for development: the d4d challenge on mobile phone data," *arXiv preprint arXiv:1210.0137,* 2012.
[51] J. Poole. (2013, May 6) Winning Research from the Data 4 Development Challenge. *United Nations Global Pulse.* Available: http://www.unglobalpulse.org/D4D-Winning-Research. Accessed May 27, 2016.
[52] N. Elhefnawy, "Societal Complexity and Diminishing Returns in Security," *International Security,* vol. 29, pp. 152-174, 2004.
[53] V. Hughes, "Stress: The roots of resilience," *Nature,* vol. 490, pp. 165-167, October 10, 2012 2012.
[54] S. S. Luthar and L. B. Zelazo, "Research on resilience: An integrative review," in *Resilience and vulnerability: Adaptation in the context of childhood adversities*, ed New York, NY, US: Cambridge University Press, 2003, pp. 510-549.
[55] C. S. Holling, "Resilience and Stability of Ecological Systems," *Annual Review of Ecology and Systematics,* vol. 4, pp. 1-23, 1973.
[56] L. Briguglio, G. Cordina, N. Farrugia, and S. Vella, "Economic Vulnerability and Resilience: Concepts and Measurements," *Oxford Development Studies,* vol. 37, pp. 229-247, 2009.
[57] S. E. Chang and M. Shinozuka, "Measuring Improvements in the Disaster Resilience of Communities," *Earthquake Spectra,* vol. 20, pp. 739-755, 2004.
[58] Y. Y. Haimes, "On the Definition of Resilience in Systems," *Risk Analysis,* vol. 29, pp. 498-501, 2009.
[59] B. Walker, "Resilience, Adaptability and Transformability in Social--ecological Systems," *Ecology & Society (formerly Conservation Ecology),* vol. 9, p. 5, 2004.
[60] K. Tierney and M. Bruneau, "Conceptualizing and measuring resilience: A key to disaster loss reduction," *TR news,* 2007.
[61] T. McDaniels, S. Chang, D. Cole, J. Mikawoz, and H. Longstaff, "Fostering resilience to extreme events within infrastructure systems: Characterizing decision contexts for mitigation and adaptation," *Global Environmental Change,* vol. 18, pp. 310-318, 2008.
[62] C. S. Holling, *Engineering Resilience versus Ecological Resilience*: The National Academies Press, 1996.
[63] B. E. Beisner, D. T. Haydon, and K. Cuddington, "Alternative stable states in ecology," *Frontiers in Ecology and the Environment,* vol. 1, pp. 376-382, 2003/09/01 2003.
[64] C. Folke, "Resilience: The emergence of a perspective for social–ecological systems analyses," *Global Environmental Change,* vol. 16, pp. 253-267, 2006.
[65] N. N. Taleb, *The black swan: The impact of the highly improbable fragility*: Random House, 2010.
[66] T. D. O'Rourke, "Critical infrastructure, interdependencies, and resilience," *Bridge - Washington National Academy of Engineering,* vol. 37, p. 22, 2007.
[67] A. Boin and A. McConnell, "Preparing for Critical Infrastructure Breakdowns: The Limits of Crisis Management and the Need for Resilience," *Journal of Contingencies and Crisis Management,* vol. 15, pp. 50-59, 2007.
[68] J. O. Petinrin and M. Shaaban, "Smart power grid: Technologies and applications," in *Power and Energy (PECon), 2012 IEEE International Conference on*, 2012, pp. 892-897.
[69] M. E. J. Newman, "The Structure and Function of Complex Networks," *SIAM Review,* vol. 45, pp. 167-256, 2003.
[70] J. Ash, "Optimizing complex networks for resilience against cascading failure," *Physica A,* vol. 380, p. 673, 2007.
[71] V. Colizza, J. R. Banavar, A. Maritan, and A. Rinaldo, "Network Structures from Selection Principles," *Physical Review Letters,* vol. 92, p. 198701, 2004.

[72] M. Brede, "Networks that optimize a trade-off between efficiency and dynamical resilience," *Physics letters. A*, vol. 373, p. 3910, 2009.

[73] D. P. Chassin and C. Posse, "Evaluating North American electric grid reliability using the Barabási–Albert network model," *Physica A: Statistical Mechanics and its Applications*, vol. 355, pp. 667-677, 2005.

[74] E. Zio and G. Sansavini, "Vulnerability of Smart Grids With Variable Generation and Consumption: A System of Systems Perspective," *Systems, Man, and Cybernetics: Systems, IEEE Transactions on*, vol. 43, pp. 477-487, 2013.

[75] H. Yih-Fang, S. Werner, H. Jing, N. Kashyap, and V. Gupta, "State Estimation in Electric Power Grids: Meeting New Challenges Presented by the Requirements of the Future Grid," *Signal Processing Magazine, IEEE*, vol. 29, pp. 33-43, 2012.

[76] J.-M. Lehn, "Toward Self-Organization and Complex Matter," *Science*, vol. 295, pp. 2400-2403, March 29, 2002 2002.

[77] S. H. Haeckel, "Adaptive enterprise design: The sense - and - respond model," *Planning review*, vol. 23, p. 6, 1995.

[78] A. G. Phadke, "Synchronized phasor measurements-a historical overview," in *Transmission and Distribution Conference and Exhibition 2002: Asia Pacific. IEEE/PES*, 2002, pp. 476-479 vol.1.

[79] "IEEE Standard for Synchrophasor Measurements for Power Systems," *IEEE Std C37.118.1-2011 (Revision of IEEE Std C37.118-2005)*, pp. 1-61, 2011.

[80] K. E. Martin, "Synchrophasor Measurements Under the IEEE Standard C37.118.1-2011 With Amendment C37.118.1a," *Power Delivery, IEEE Transactions on*, vol. 30, pp. 1514-1522, 2015.

[81] D. W. Caves, J. A. Herriges, and R. J. Windle, "Customer Demand for Service Reliability in the Electric Power Industry: A Synthesis of the Outage Cost Literature," *Bulletin of Economic Research*, vol. 42, pp. 79-121, 1990.

[82] C. B. Saper, "The Central Autonomic Nervous System: Conscious Visceral Perception and Autonomic Pattern Generation," *Annual Review of Neuroscience*, vol. 25, pp. 433-469, 2002.

[83] R. Buijs, C. van Eden, V. Goncharuk, and A. Kalsbeek, "The biological clock tunes the organs of the body: timing by hormones and the autonomic nervous system," *Journal of Endocrinology*, vol. 177, pp. 17-26, April 1, 2003.

[84] G. G. Berntson, M. Sarter, and J. T. Cacioppo, "Autonomic nervous system," *Encyclopedia of cognitive science*, 2003.

[85] B. S. McEwen and J. C. Wingfield, "The concept of allostasis in biology and biomedicine," *Hormones and Behavior*, vol. 43, pp. 2-15, 2003.

[86] G. Pauli, "The blue economy," *Our planet*, pp. 24-27, 2010.

Interactive Mirror for Smart Home

Chidambaram Sethukkarasi, Vijayadharan SuseelaKumari HariKrishnan, Karuppiah PalAmutha
National Ubiquitous Computing Research Centre
Centre for Development of Advanced Computing
Chennai, India
{ctsethu, harikrishnans, palamuthak}@cdac.in

Raja Pitchiah
Department of Electronics and Information Technology
Government of India
Delhi, India
pitchiah@mit.gov.in

Abstract—**This paper describes the design and development of a smart artifact called "Interactive Mirror" for smart home users. The idea is to transform a normal mirror into an intelligent artifact by embedding various technologies to support users in their daily activities. This paper explains the state of the art technologies for building the intelligent mirror. It identifies the user using facial recognition technique and provides services such as recognizing emotions, progress representation of measured health parameters, height identification, identify garments, suggest garments with suitable color, and reminds important events. The prototype is developed, and demonstrated in ubiquitous computing laboratory. The algorithms are being tested in the deployed environment and the results are discussed in detail in this paper. Initial user studies indicated a high appeal of the Interactive Mirror features.**

Keywords - Ubiquitous Computing; Interactive mirror; Face Recognition; Emotion Recognition; Human Height Identification; Smart Artifact; RFID (Radio Frequency IDentification); Garment Identification; Garment Suggestion.

I. INTRODUCTION

A home environment consists of variety of devices and there exists huge information due to technology advancements. An effort towards ubiquitous computing is to intelligently collect or sense the information from the environment and make it smarter. Nowadays, not only the computers but also any devices like mobile phone, PDAs, tablets have network connectivity and offer various intelligent services to us. The devices used in our daily life can be made smart enough to assist the smart home users. In general, people normally spend considerable time in front of mirror and it has been considered as an ideal artifact for embedding intelligence for demonstrating proposed interactive mirror concept. The general approach is to extract information about the scene using computer vision, and use this information to update a scene model to be rendered using computer graphics.

An effort towards this results in the development of an interactive mirror [1], which augments a normal mirror with intelligence and provides value added services. To identify the user, we propose to utilize facial recognition technology since it is a non contact based recognition method. The mirror assists the individuals in aiding a healthier life style by providing feedback on the measurement of basic health parameters. The user's garments are identified using RFID technology and its details/descriptions are displayed in the mirror. The mirror also guides user in selecting a suitable garment color according to their skin color. The system has been designed, developed, and deployed in ubiquitous research lab.

The contributions of this paper are: 1) conceptualization, design and development of interactive mirror prototype. 2) Emotion Recognition. 3) Human height identification using image processing technique. 4) Garment Identification using RFID technology. 5) Guidance in selecting suitable garment based on skin color. 6) Accuracy improvements of image processing modules.

The reminder of this paper is organized as follows. Section II briefly comments on some related work. The system and functional overview are described in Section III and IV respectively. Section V presents implementation details of the prototype. The experimental results are discussed in Section VI. Conclusion and future work are given in Section VII.

II. RELATED WORK

In several investigations, smart homes have been developed by combining monitor and mirror systems. The AwareMirror [2] is an augmented display that is placed in the bathroom for presenting personalized information to the user. It detects the person's position using proximity sensor and identify using RFID tag embedded in toothbrush. It provides useful information such as closest schedule, transportation information, and the weather forecast. The mirror is constructed by attaching an acrylic board in front of a monitor. Using tooth brush as a tool for identification might not produce accurate results since it needs to be replaced more frequently and tagged properly. This paper uses face recognition technique, a biometric identification system for person identification.

The Memory Mirror [3], developed at the Everyday Computing Lab, aims at helping people remember tasks that have to be repeated. It uses a camera and face-recognition software to identify different users in a home. The drugs are tagged with RFID tags and readers to locate and keep track of drug usage. It alerts consumers if they have taken the wrong bottle or if it is the right bottle at the wrong time. Besides, the cabinet enables patients to monitor blood pressure, heart rate and cholesterol levels, and share this information with their doctor via the Internet. The cabinet also provides a trend chart, and if this one shows a problem tendency, the system will suggest the user to make an appointment with their doctor. The drug usage factor heavily depends on RFID technology and all items need to be tagged properly. The proposed system facilitates users to set remainders. When user comes in front of the mirror, he/she will be reminded. In our system, user needs to set reminders, which will be reminded by the mirror when they use the system.

A mirror that detects and analyzes a human behavior, is demonstrated under persuasive mirror [4]. It makes use of behavioral data in order to provide its user with continuous visual feedback on their behavior. A mirror that provides a natural means of interaction through which the residents can control the household smart appliances and access personalized services is described in [5]. It uses face recognition to authenticate the user and provides widget based interface to access data feeds and other services. Tomoki Hayashi, Hideaki Uchiyama, Julien Pilet and Hideo Saito proposed an Interactive Digital Mirror [6], which captures the ambient light with a camera, extract information about the scene, and display appropriate information to the user, combining real-time computer vision systems with realistic computer graphic. The computer vision routine includes human face detection, tracking and 3D head pose estimation.

Philips research lab demonstrated an Intelligent Bathroom Mirror [7], which supports people need and enable people with new possibilities in the daily use of the bathroom space. It comprises two display mirrors connected to the PC having Internet access, a TV tuner, a wirelessly connected electric toothbrush, a weight and height sensors and two video cameras. It provides personalized services according to the user's preferences such as children can watch their favorite cartoon while brushing their teeth, provide live TV feeds, monitor the latest weather, check the traffic information, provides health information and so on. Personnel recognition has been proposed by using weight, height, etc. Two methods of interaction without physically touching the mirror have been demonstrated. The bathroom lighting comprise of 50 light sources of different kind. Various light sources have been used, which generates light of different color and temperature. Similar to this intelligent mirror, [8] presents i-mirror, which attempts to create an interactive information environment within a mirror interface in a natural way. A special optical system is designed using ac camera, a projector, mirror and a screen to bring a mirror like interface. The three main characteristic of i-mirror are: it shows images in dark, younger/older views of a person and memory to playback the older scenes. The mirror records the scene, which may lead to privacy issues.

A Magic mirror [9] can function like a good friend who listens to the user's questions and automatically responds to their request. It is an interactive multimedia mirror system, which includes speech recognition, speech synthesis, face detection/modified/recognition, 3D virtual genius, hidden LCD (Liquid Crystal Display) mirror, and camera, performs simple syndication to capture information about peripherals and network connections. It can detect an user's feeling based on speech and image recognition features to select the appropriate music and speech to alter the user's mood. Our interactive mirror is also an intelligent mirror, which recognizes the user's mood and attempts to assist the user in leading a healthier lifestyle by providing feedback on measured health parameters.

One of the main usages of mirror is to see how we look like in particular attire? Ching-I Cheng and Damon Shing-Min Liu developed an Intelligent Dressing Advice System [10] to help women choose correct attire for attending a specific occasion. Fuzzy logic rules were used to search good matches in the garment database and showing the matched results. Our application analyzes the skin color of the user and suggests a suitable list of garments based on both the color parameter and occasions to wear.

In comparison with the other works described above, our work is different in that we aim to develop a system for assisting smart home users in their daily activities such as selecting suitable garment, recognizing emotions, and represents the progress in health parameters. The normal mirror is transformed into a smart device by preserving its metaphor in addition to embedding technologies.

III. SYSTEM OVERVIEW

The Interactive Mirror [1] shown in Figure 1 comprises of a LCD display placed behind a dielectric coated mirror, a camera, a weight measurement platform, and a RFID reader.

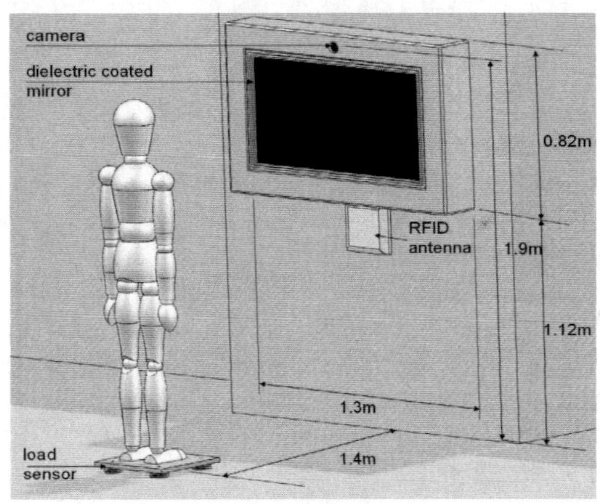

Figure 1. Engineering of Interactive Mirror

The Interactive mirror display can be used in two different modes by placing a dielectric coated mirror over the LCD display. The modes of operation are 1) Normal Mirror: When the display is OFF, it will act as a normal reflective mirror; 2) Interactive Mirror: When the display is ON, it will act as a see through glass and the display can be viewed. A web camera of resolution 640 x 480 is used for capturing the images in front of the mirror. A weighing platform, designed using four load sensors is placed in front of the mirror to measure the person's weight. A RFID reader and an antenna are connected to the system for identifying the tags attached with the garments.

IV. Functional Overview

The system has the following functionalities, as shown in Figure 2.

A. Person Identification

Recognizing the user is the first step towards providing personalized services. The system recognizes the user using face recognition technique.

B. Health Information Services

The users can measure their health parameters such as weight, height, BMI (Body Mass Index) and BMR (Basal Metabolic Rate) daily with the help of mirror. The system maintains a health database and analyzes the progress of health parameters over the recent days and displayed to the user in the form of 3D graph.

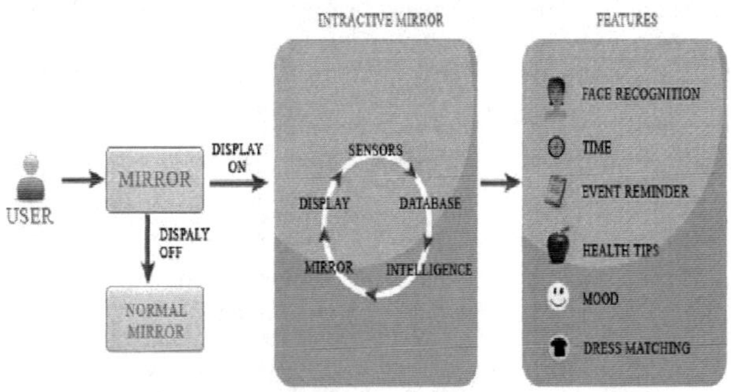

Figure 2. Functional Overview of Interactive Mirror

C. Clothing advisor

The mirror assists the user in selecting a suitable garment for a particular occasion out of users garment. It also suggests suitable dress colors based on their skin color.

D. Recognize emotion

The emotion of the person is recognized using image processing technique. The emotions like Happy, Sad, Surprise and Normal are identified.

E. Reminder assistance

The important messages and reminders are displayed to the recognized users like bill payments, tour plans, meeting schedule, etc. The user needs to set reminders with the help of a GUI (Graphical User Interface).

V. Prototype Development

The prototype is developed using various technologies and tools such as: face recognition, emotion recognition, RFID, PostgreSQL and java programming language. The mirror uses a display with a camera and a weighing platform for user identification and providing personalized services in smart home environment. The system comprises of the following modules: Face recognition, Emotion Recognition, Health Progress Representation, Garment Identification and Suggestion and other features.

A. Face Recognition

The mirror identifies the person using face recognition technique. When the user starts using the system, the camera triggers ON and captures the image in front of it. The image contrast is improved by histogram equalization technique before processing by face recognition module.

Naturally, human identifies and recognizes the face based on the characteristics of facial features such as eyes, nose, mouth, and lips. Same process is followed in image processing routines for person identification. The steps involved in face recognition module are shown in Figure 3. The first step is to find faces in an image called as face detection. There exist many techniques such as viola-jones face detection, skin color based detection, LBP (Local Binary Patterns), Adaboost, facial geometry [11], etc. We adopted viola-jones face detection algorithm [12] for our system since it is the most adopted algorithm for face detection in real time. The algorithm has high detection speed with relatively high detection accuracy. It is an especially successful method [13] with very less false positive rate.

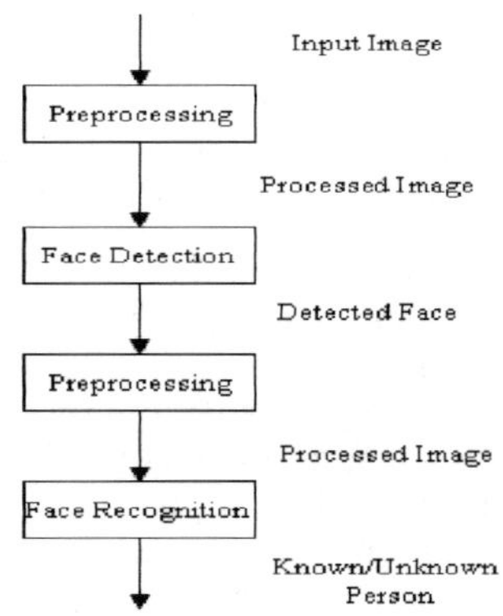

Figure 3. Steps involved in Face Recognition Module

This method makes use of HAAR features, which describes the properties common to human face. The basic principle of the Viola-Jones algorithm [14] is to scan an input image using a sub-window capable of detecting faces. The sub window looks for Haar like features in the image. The standard image processing approach would be to rescale the input image to different sizes and then run the fixed size detector through these images. This approach is a time consuming due to the calculation of the different size images. Here, the detector is rescaled instead of the input image and run the detector many times through the image (each time with a different size). There exists an enormous amount of such features in a sub image. Among all these features few are expected to give almost consistently high values when on top of a face. In order to find these features Viola-Jones uses a modified version of the AdaBoost algorithm [14] developed by Freund and Schapire in 1996. AdaBoost is a machine learning boosting algorithm capable of constructing a strong each containing a strong classifier. The job of each stage is to determine whether a given sub-window is definitely not a face or maybe face. When a sub-window is classified to be a non-face by a given stage it is immediately discarded. Conversely, a sub-window classified as maybe-face is passed on to the next stage in the cascade. It follows that the more stages a given sub-window passes, the higher the chance of sub-window contains a face. A window that passes through all classifiers is classified as face image.

Prior to face recognition, the detected face image has to be pre-processed to remove the background pixels other than the facial features. The detected face image will have few background pixels such as hair pixels other than the facial features. This may affect the recognition accuracy. In order to remove these pixels from consideration, we used ellipse fitting procedure for segmenting facial features region alone from others pixels. We created an elliptical mask (shown in Figure 4a) that has a pixel value of 0 in the region we are interested in and 1 elsewhere. The mask is bitwise ORed with the detected face image (shown in Figure 4b) to segment the interested region of the face image from other pixels. The segmented image (shown in Figure 4c) having facial features is an input for the face recognition module.

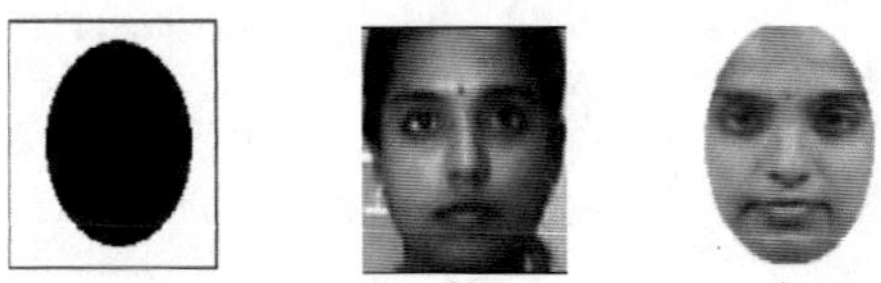

a) b) c)

Figure 4. a) Elliptical Mask b) Detected face c) Segmented face image

The next step is face recognition, which is the process of telling whose face is this? There exist a lot of algorithms and methods for recognizing human faces [15]. We were using eigen face recognition [16][17][18] technique, which is one of the global feature based approach. The Eigen face approach has the following advantages and limitations [19] over other methods:

Advantages:

- Recognition is simple, efficient and easy to implement
- No knowledge of geometry or special feature of the face is required
- Little preprocessing work

Limitations:

- Sensitive to scale, pose and illumination variation
- Suitable only for frontal face images
- Good performance under controlled background.

The system is designed for smart home environment where the background and lighting may not change frequently. Based on this consideration, we adopted eigen face approach for our system. The steps involved in eigen face recognition algorithm are described below. The face objects such as eyes, nose and mouth and its relative distances between these object forms the characteristic features of a face image. These characteristics features are called eigenfaces or principal components. These principal components are identified using a mathematical tool called PCA (Principal Component Analysis). By means of PCA, each original image of the training set is transformed into a corresponding eigenface. An important feature of PCA is that one can reconstruct any original image from the training set by combining the eigenfaces. The original image can be reconstructed with the weighted sum of all eigen faces. This weight specifies to what degree the specific feature (eigenface) is present in the original image. Based on the weights, the face images are grouped into classes. The weight vectors for the training and test images are calculated in training and testing phase respectively. For classification, compute the average distance measure between the training and test image weight vectors using distance measure techniques. The least distance measure is compared against the threshold values t_1 and t_2 to classify the test image as known or unknown person. The details about choosing the threshold values and criteria for classification are described in detail under results section.

B. *Emotion Recognition*

Facial Expression is an inevitable factor in analyzing the emotion of a person. K-nearest neighbor algorithm is used for classifying the input images into four facial expression happy, sad, normal, and surprise. Human Emotions are the most valuable aspects of human life. By the analysis of facial expression and emotional aspect of person, the interactive mirror detects the emotion of a person. The emotional analysis data is recorded for a period of time (say 1 year or 1 month) can be used to identify the mental state of the person such us conditions like depression, fear and enthusiastic factors of user. If required, the details are provided to a doctor. This will be helpful also for depression monitoring of patients.

The camera mounted on the top of the mirror captures the user's image. The captured image is passed through the face detection process to detect and segment the face image. The detected face image will be given as an input to the preprocessor module of facial expression recognition algorithm. The mouth and eyes play an important role in determining or extracting user's emotion. We have extracted mouth features for classifying the expression.

There exist various methods for extracting the facial features [20][21][22][23][24]. The emotion recognition framework based on video sequences and the challenges involved in it are discussed in [25]. The experiments show that the proposed facial expression recognition framework yields relatively little degradation in recognition rate, when faces are partially occluded, or under a variety of levels of noise introduced at the feature tracker level.

Different training and classification methods are being analyzed, which includes Support Vector Machines, Hidden Markov Models, Bayes Classifiers. [26] tells about six classification methods used for facial expression recognition using the above algorithms. The image processing techniques like PCA, LFA (Local Feature Analysis), ICA

(Independent Component Analysis), or FLD (Fisher's Linear Discriminant) are some of the methods used for feature extraction. Lucas-Kanade tracking algorithm for tracking eyebrows and cheeks, canny edge detector for detection of wrinkles are used in preprocessing steps. Approach in [27] describes about using topological mask and similarity measurement for classification of facial expression. Approach in [28] calculates difference image sequence by subtracting the pixel value at the same position (x,y) from video image sequences of adjacent frames and makes use of hidden markov model for classification of facial expression. Approach in [29] creates active appearance model in the form of 2D or 3D mesh of the training sample images and uses the algorithms nearest neighbor and support vector machine for classification of expression. Approach in [30] also extracts 2D images from 3D image sequences and uses the algorithms combined k Nearest Neighbor/rule-based classifier and SNoW (Sparse Network of Winnows) classifier for training and expression classification. Approach in [31] uses SVM (Support Vector Machine) for classification of facial expression for images from video sequences. Approach in [32] uses Tree Augmented Naïve Bayes Classifier.

The popular databases used in the above experiments include Yale database [33], Cohn-Kanade database (video image sequences) [34], MMI –Facial Expression Database [35], The JAFEE (JApanese Female Facial Expression JAFFE) Database [36].

Facial Action Coding System [37] is a widely used method for encoding facial expression based on contraction of facial muscles. It was developed by Paul Ekman and W.V. Friesen in 1970s.

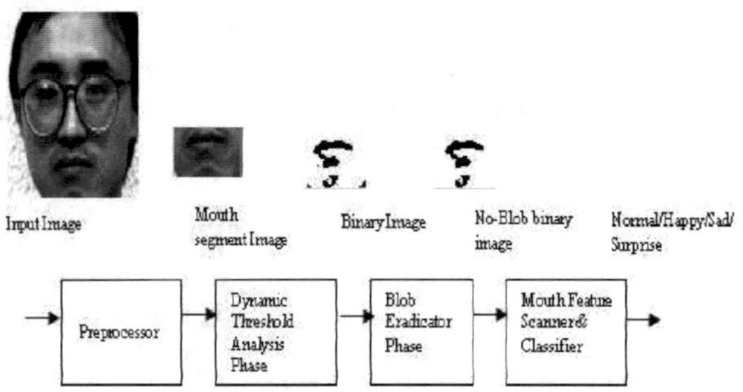

Figure 5. Mouth Feature Extraction.

The steps involved in extracting the mouth features are shown in Figure 5.

1) Preprocessor

The preprocessor takes the input image from the face detection module. From the face image, the mouth region is segmented in order to extract the mouth features. Based on facial geometry property, the mouth region is segmented.

2) Dynamic Threshold Analysis Phase

In the dynamic threshold analysis phase, the segmented mouth image is converted into binary image. Determining the proper threshold value for thresholding an image is too complex. The threshold value for accurate and legible extraction for binary facial images may vary depending on various environmental factors like illumination, the deviation from camera where the person is standing, the facial color of person etc. of the input facial image. To resolve this issue, the dynamic threshold analysis module calculates the mouth segment pixel density factor. Mouth segment pixel density factor is the number of black pixels in the segmented binary mouth image. From our observation, the value of 100 and 230 for mouth segment pixel density factor is the apt for accurate extraction.

Dynamic binary image selection is the method used by the dynamic threshold analysis module. The input image should be threshold with a random threshold value (T) to obtain a binary facial image. Dynamic threshold analysis module calculates the mouth segment density factor of the binary image. If the mouth segment pixel density factor is less than 100, the thresholding process should be repeated with a new threshold value of $T_1=T+10$, else if the mouth segment pixel density factor is greater than 230, the thresholding process is repeated for the new threshold value of $T_1=T-10$. The above thresholding process is repeated with new value of $T=T_1$, until the MSPDF (Mouth Segment Pixel Density Factor) reaches a saturation, i.e., until the condition $100<MSPDF<230$ is achieved.

Let t_c be a threshold increment/decrement factor, the numerical value by which T should be incremented or decremented. In the above occasion, we took the value of t_c as 10. The equation can be written as

$$T_1 = T \pm t_c \quad (1)$$

If we choose t_c as a fixed value like 10, it may lead to infinite repetition of dynamic binary image selection as the Mouth Segment P. This is because MSPDF does not converge to $100<MSPDF<230$ for higher values of t_c. To resolve this issue dynamic threshold analysis phase changes the value of t_c as $t_c = t_c/2$ (t_c is always a natural number). The threshold increment/decrement factor t_c is updated only after every 10 iteration of the dynamic binary image selection described above. The decrease in value of t_c helps the threshold value to converge to a better option of T for which $100<MSPDF<230$. The binary image obtained with MSPDF value between 100 and 230 is used as output of dynamic threshold analysis module, which is further sent for blob detection. We choose MSPDF boundaries lower bound as 100 and upper bound as 230 based on visual observations experienced in clarity of mouth image segment.

3) Blob Eradicator Phase

The obtained binary image may have small unwanted black blobs surrounding the lip. This may be because of non uniform lighting in face image or mustache or beard. To extract the mouth features more accurately, the unwanted blobs needs to be removed. Blob Eradicator use OpenCV blob detection functions to filter all the blobs having blob length less than a count of 12 pixels. After the blobs are removed, the mouth segment image is sent to mouth scanner module.

4) Mouth Feature Scanner and Classifier

The mouth feature scanner module scans the mouth image pixel by pixel along the row pixels. The starting point of scanning is always the middle topmost pixel of mouth segment. Mouth feature scanner divides the mouth segment image into two parts cutting it along the middle pixel column (vertically). Left scanning involves scanning the left portion of the mouth segment to determine left lip tip point A co-ordinates. Right scanning involves scanning right portion of the mouth segment to determine right lip tip point C co-ordinates. The top most first detected black pixel becomes the lip top point B. The points A, B, C in the extracted binary lip image forms a lip triangle ABC shown in Figure 6. The altitude of the triangle ABC gives lip height and the length of side AC gives lip length.

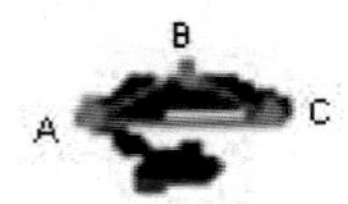

Figure 6. Mouth Triangle.

5) Facial Expression Classification using K-Nearest Neighbour Algorithm

The knn (k-nearest neighbor) algorithm is a method for classifying objects based on closest training examples in the feature space. In k-NN, an object is classified by a majority vote of its neighbors, with the object being assigned to the class most common amongst its k nearest neighbors. The feature space used in this classification is a two dimensional feature space.

The following assumptions have been made: 1) Constant lighting and illumination; 2) Front Face image; 3) No scaling variations for testing of facial expression recognition.

C. Health Progress Representation

The mirror assists the user in leading a healthier life by advising on health parameters such as weight, height, BMI and BMR. The weighing platform measures the weight of the user when he/she starts using it.

There exist several methods to measure the human height, which includes using IR (Infrared) sensor, Ultrasonic sensor and camera. The human height is used as a biometric identity for identifying home residents [38]. Height is typically a weak biometric, but it is well suited for identifying among a few residents in the home, and can potentially be improved by using the history of height measurements. The system has been tested with 20 subjects in 3 homes and that height sensors could potentially achieve at least 95% identification accuracy. A similar work is described by Hsin-Chun Tsai [39], which combines both height measurement and face recognition to identify the person in long distances. The human height identification is used in surveillance application [40] to spot persons coming from the dark area.

We used camera captured image and image processing technique to measure the human height. The steps involved in height detection module (shown in Figure 7) are described as follows.

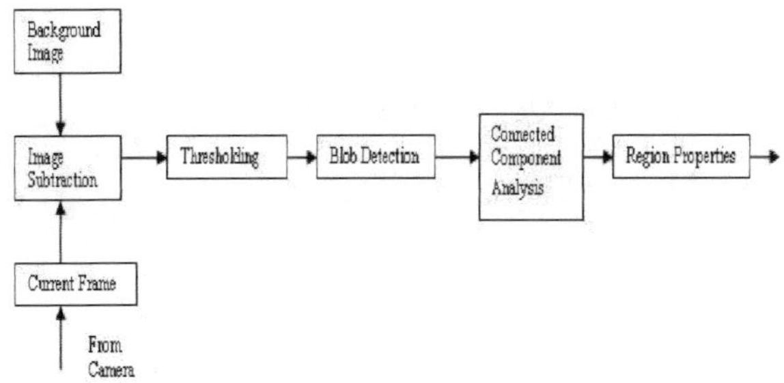

Figure 7. Height Identification

1) Background frame initialization: The image is preprocessed to improve the contrast and remove noise pixels. After preprocessing, a background frame needs to be initialized. There are many ways to obtain the initial background image. For example, take the first frame as the background directly, or the average pixel brightness of the first few frames as the background or using a background image sequences without the prospect of moving objects to estimate the background model parameters.

2) Background Segmentation and thresholding: The current frame denoted as F (shown in Figure 9b) is subtracted from the background image denoted as B (shown in Figure 9a) and if the difference is greater than the threshold value th, then the pixel belongs to foreground otherwise it belongs to background. Mathematically, it can be written in equation as follows:

$$P(x,y) = 255 \quad \text{if } F(x,y) - B(x,y) > th \tag{2}$$

$$P(x,y) = 0 \quad \text{otherwise} \tag{3}$$

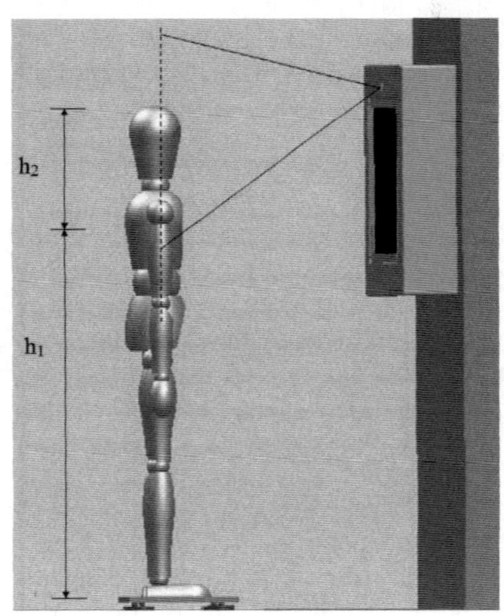

Figure 8. Height Measurement

Figure 9. a) Background Image b) Foreground Image c) Output Image after connected component analysis

3) Blob Detection and Analysis: The Morphological operations such as filtering the holes, filling up of holes, dilation, erosion and removal of smaller blobs are carried out to detect the foreground object. Obtain the height of the blob using connected component labeling and region properties. It gives the height of the human in terms of pixel. The obtained height is converted to actual units. The distance between the camera and human is too short to cover the entire human in an image. The height between the weighing platform and the camera coverage area (h1) is added upon with the obtained height output (h2) to determine the user's height h (h= h1 + h2 as shown in Figure 8).

From the measured weight and height values, parameters such as BMI and BMR were calculated. These parameters were measured and recorded regularly in a health database. BMI is a factor that determines a person's weight according to his height and BMR is the measure of number of calories burned by the body when the user is at rest. This helps in determining how much calories he/she needs to intake in order to maintain an energy balance and balanced diet condition. The measured BMI value is analyzed for the conditions such as normal, overweight, underweight and obesity. Drastic weight change over a short time is the main symptom of identifying certain major diseases in human body. Therefore, the measured values are saved in a health database and its progress over a period of time is reported and displayed to the user in the form of 3D graph.

D. Garment Identification and Suggestion

The textile industries and fashion garments started adopting RFID technology for tagging the garments and other clothes for rapid identification of items throughout its life cycle. Each tag has a unique ID number associated with the garments model name and description, including size, color and fabric, price, material, etc. As the user comes near the mirror wearing a tagged garment/cloth, the system identified it and captures the ID number. The application updates the garment database and the description of that particular garment is retrieved from the database and displayed in the mirror. The user is given feedback on how often he/she is using the particular garment.

The mirror detects the user skin color and attempts to suggest suitable colors for garments. It also tries to suggest according to the occasions such as party, outing, traditional program, competitions, etc.

To suggest a suitable garment color, the skin color of the user needs to be detected and categorized. Skin pixel detection and segmentation is employed in many tasks related to the detection and tracking of humans and human-body parts. The goal of skin pixel detection is to locate the pixels belongs to the skin and discard other pixels in an image.

Figure 10. Skin Pixel Segmentation

The simplest way to decide whether a pixel belongs to skin color [41] or not is to explicitly define a boundary based on color channels. Brand and Mason [42] constructed a simple one dimensional skin classifier: a pixel is labeled as a skin if the ratio between its R and G channels is between a lower and an upper bound. The color spaces that are frequently used in studies are RGB, HIS, HSV, TSL and YUV.

The Kovac model [43] contains four sub-rules as follows. Pixel is skin color pixel if:

$$R > 95 \text{ and } G > 40 \text{ and } B > 20$$
$$Max(R, G, B) - Min(R, G, B) > 15$$
$$|R - G| > 15$$
$$R > G \text{ and } R > B$$

This rule can be interpreted as the range of R value is from 96 to 255, the range of G value is from 41 to 239, and the range of B value is 21 to 254. Since R value is always greater than G and B, the second rule and third rule are always positive values. Tomaz et al. [44] described that if R-value is too high, and the G and B values are too low, it will result in a pixel more close to red, and should not be considered as skin pixel. In other cases when R < 100 and G < 100 and B < 100, it will result to dark color that may be non-skin pixel, and when

G > 150 and B < 90 or R + G > 400, it will result in yellow like color. Swift's rule [45] is simpler as compared to Kovac's rule and can be described as follows. Pixel is not skin color pixel if:

$$B > R, G < B, G > R, B < 1/4R \text{ or } B > 200$$

The range of R-value is from 4 to 255, the range of B-value is from 1 to 200, and the range of G-value is from 1 to 255. This rule is unable to detect some dark skin color and yellow like color, which is detected as skin color. Finally, a very simple rule was introduced by Saleh [46], which considers only the value of R and G. This rule defines that a pixel is skin pixel when R – G is greater than 20 and less than 80. This rule does not consider a present of B-value that contributed to the whitish color. This rule is also unable to detect dark skin color or skin cover under shadow, and yellow like color and redder color problems, which is detected as skin pixel. We used HSV color space for detecting skin pixels. The steps involved in skin detection module are shown in Figure 10. The face image from the face detection module was converted to HSV color space and the following rule was applied for identifying skin color pixels.

$$P(x, y) = 0 \quad \text{if } H < 20, S > 48, V > 80 \qquad (4)$$

$$P(X, y) = 255 \quad \text{otherwise} \qquad (5)$$

The image was then converted to binary image with skin color pixels as black and other pixels as white according to the above rule. Based on segmentation, the average pixel value of the skin color is calculated and classified into three categories dark, medium, and bright. Based on the category, a suitable garment color is suggested for the user. For example, light color garments can be suggested for dark skin complexion, dark color garments for light skin complexion and both light and dark colors for medium complexion. It can also suggest a suitable garment according to the events like marriage function, birthday party, family outing, pilgrim functions, etc. based on the parameters such as price, usage factor, material, and type. The information about the events and occasions are acquired from the event reminder database.

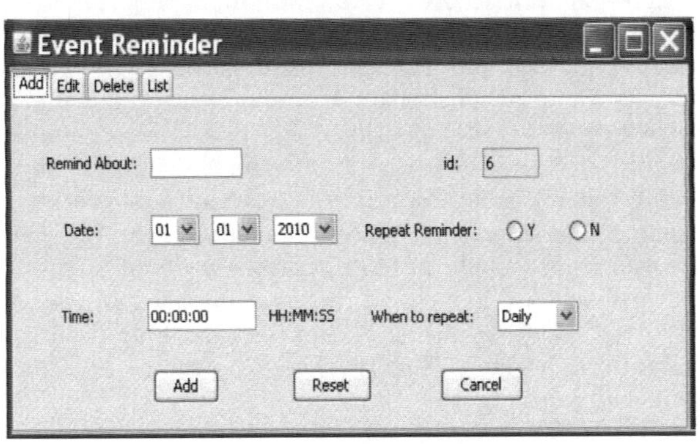

Figure 11. Event Reminder GUI

E. Other Features

The mirror observes how long a user is using it. The weighing platform senses the user presence and absence and calculates the mirror usage time. It can intimate the user if they are getting late for an office, school, or meetings, etc. It also acts as a reminder device, which reminds the user on important things such as Bill payments, prioritized works, birthdays, etc. The user needs to set details such as what to remind, when to remind, repeat reminder, etc. with the help of a GUI shown in Figure 11.

VI. EXPERIMENTAL RESULTS

The prototype has been deployed in our ubiquitous computing laboratory (shown in Figure 12).

A. Face Recognition Algorithm Test Results:

We created our face database with 42 images of 9 different subjects. The images were collected in a semi-controlled environment. To maintain a degree of consistency throughout the database, the same physical setup was used in capturing the images. We maintained constant lighting and the distance between the mirror and weighing platform were kept constant to avoid major scaling variations. The images were collected on different days and at different time. In order to collect front face images, the user were asked to look straight at the mirror and there were no other instructions or restrictions given to the user. Therefore, the images were not exactly frontal face but little variation exists. This created a real practical testing environment.

The face recognition module was trained with 45 images of 9 different subjects. We created a test set of 24 face images with both known and unknown subjects. For distance measure, we explored both euclidean and mahalanobis distance method. The Euclidean Distance is the most widely used distance metric.

Figure 12. Deployment of Interactive Mirror in Ubicomp Laboratory.

The euclidean distance between two points is given as:

$$d(x, y) = \sqrt{(x_2 - x_1)^2 + (y_2 - y_1)^2} \quad (6)$$

The Mahalanobis Distance is a better distance measure when it comes to pattern recognition problems. It takes into account the covariance between the variables and hence removes the problems related to scale and correlation that are inherent with the Euclidean Distance. It is given as:

$$d(x, y) = \sqrt{(x - y)^T S^{-1}(x, y)} \quad (7)$$

Therefore, we adopted Mahalanobis distance method for recognition. The distance measure will give the least distance match or score of the test image out of the training images. When an unknown face image comes up for recognition task, it will still say the test image is recognized as the training image with the lowest score. It is for this purpose that we decided the threshold t_1. Also, to classify non face images with face images, another threshold t_2 for the distance measure was evolved. These threshold values t_1 and t_2 were evolved experimentally and heuristically.

To choose the threshold we chose a set of random images (both face and non-face); we then calculated the distance measure for images of subjects in the database and also for this random set and set the threshold t_2 accordingly. Threshold t_2 decides whether the test image is a face or non face image. If the test image is a face image, then it should fall near some face class in the face space. Again, threshold t_1 decides whether it is a known or unknown face image. When the training set changes, then these threshold values need to be calculated again.

There are four possible combinations on where an input image can lie:

$$(d < t_1) \,\&\&(d < t_2) \quad (8)$$

$$(d > t_1) \,\&\&(d < t_2) \quad (9)$$

$$(d > t_1) \,\&\&(d > t_2) \quad (10)$$

$$(d < t_1) \,\&\&(d > t_2) \quad (11)$$

1. Near a face class and near the face space: The test image is a facial image of a known subject.
2. Near face space but away from face class: The test image is a facial image of an unknown subject.
3. Distant from face space and near face class: The test image is a non face image but still resembles like the one in dataset (False Positive).
4. Distant from both the face space and face class: The test image is not a face image.

The algorithm was tested with 24 images of known and unknown faces and the above said criteria were used for recognition. The results obtained are tabulated in Table I.

TABLE I. FACE RECOGNITION ALGORITHM TEST RESULTS

No of Test Images	Successfully Recognized	Success Percentage
24	20	83%

The images that produced false results were not frontal face images. Those images were pose varied, tilted and with expressions. Overall, the performance of the face recognition module has found to be reasonable to work with front face images.

Not all the eigenfaces play important role in recognition task. Few eigenfaces may increase the error rate in recognition. The associated eigenvalues allow us to rank the eigenvectors according to their usefulness in characterizing the variation among the images. Therefore, eigenfaces having low eigenvalues can be discarded.

For the Eigenface method (PCA), it has been suggested that by discarding the three most significant principal components, variations due to lighting can be reduced [47]. In [48], experimental results show that the Eigenface method performs better under variable lighting conditions after removing the first three principal components. However, the first several components not only correspond to illumination variations, but also some useful information for discrimination. Besides, since the Eigenface method is highly dependent on the training samples, there is no guarantee that the first three principal components are mainly related to illumination variations and it is evident that discarding first several principal components cannot improve the performance significantly.

The face recognition can be integrated with height measurement to improve the recognition accuracy.

B. Emotion Recognition Algorithm Test Results:

We used 2 face databases for testing our application. The databases used are 1) Yale database and 2) CDAC (Centre for Development of Advanced Computing) Face Database. We used Yale facial expression database images of 15 subjects for training and testing our facial expression recognition algorithm. Yale database images of 10 subjects (Lip length and half of 'mouth opening height' values) are used for training the K-NN classifier. Figure 13 is the knn-classifier feature space plotted after completion of training for Yale Database. We used openCV library functions for training the classifier. To visualize the two dimensional estimated feature space points for KNN (k=6) with Lip length and Lip Height at X-axis and Y-axis, respectively, we used four colors to denote four expressions in the feature space. The red, green, blue and black color represents normal, happy, surprise and sad expression respectively in feature space. The test results of the algorithm with the Yale database images are listed in Table II. The best accuracy level was obtained for the k value of 6.

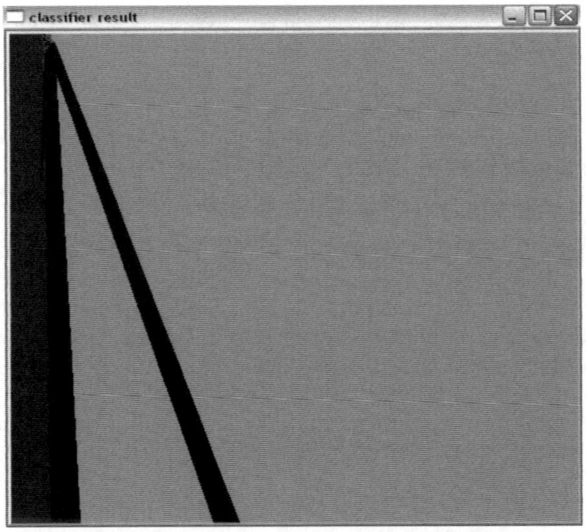

Figure 13. Classification Output (Yale Database Images)

TABLE II. EMOTION RECOGNITION ALGORITHM ACCURACY(YALE DATABASE)

K	Happy	Surprise	Normal	Sad
3	93.33	53.33	66.66	33.33
6	100	60	46.6	26.66

The Emotion recognition algorithm had been tested with CDAC database images in the deployment environment. The algorithm was trained with the mouth features like mouth width and mouth height. The results are presented in Table III. The algorithm was capable enough to recognize the happy expression when compared to other expressions.

Figure 14 describes knn-classifier feature space plotted after completion of training CDAC Database. On K-NN training phase completion, the estimated feature space points are plotted with Lip length and Lip Height at X-axis and Y-axis, respectively. The feature space used is a two dimensional feature space. The k value was selected as 6 for k-NN classifier as it is found to be more accurate when tested with CDAC database images. The training was performed to classify four expressions happy, sad, normal and surprise. Our database consists of 400 images of 5 different subjects. For each expression, there are 20 images per subject. For each expression, 5 images per subject were used for training and 15 images per subject were used for testing. The restricted lab environment with fixed illumination and fixed distance from camera was used for testing.

TABLE III. EMOTION RECOGNITION ALGORITHM ACCURACY (C-DAC DATABASE)

K	Happy	Surprise	Normal	Sad
6	90.67%	52.00%	42.67%	50.66%

Figure 14. Feature Space Plot (C-DAC database Images)

The following are some of the issues faced in mouth feature extraction:

1) Segmentation Problem:

When segmenting the mouth region, in certain images a small portion of the nose is also included. The nose part is identified as the mouth top point B by the mouth feature scanner algorithm as shown in Figure 15. This reduces the algorithm accuracy.

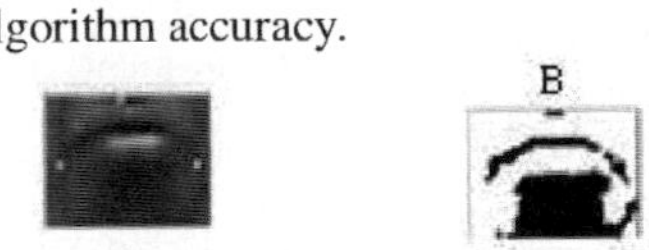

Figure 15. Mouth Feature Extraction – Segmentation Problem

Our facial expression database images for the expressions happy, surprise and sad are shown in Figures 16, 17, and 18, respectively. Our approach uses extraction of lip length and lip height features and using K-Nearest Neighbor algorithm for classification as described in the above sections. We are planning to enhance the classification accuracy using facial action coding units.

Figure 16. Happy Expression Database Images.

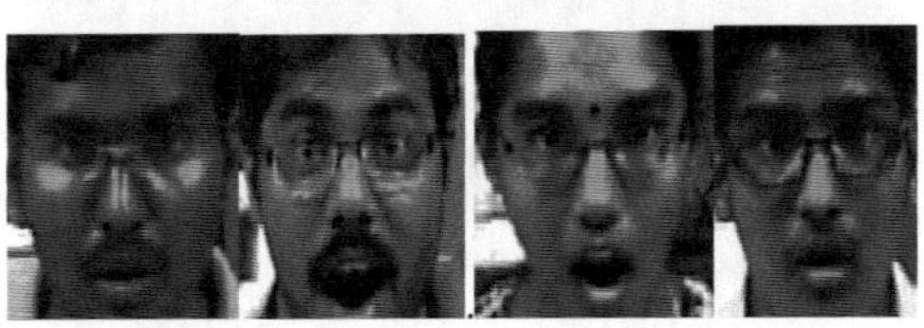

Figure 17. Surprise Expression Database Images.

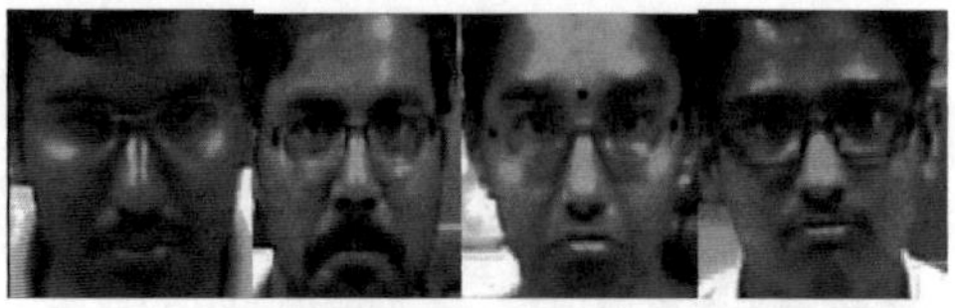

Figure 18. Sad Expression Database Images.

2) Non-uniform lighting problem:

The mouth portion is not segmented properly during thresholding process, because of non uniform lighting in the face region. Only ¾ length of the original mouth is visible in binary image and the corners are not visible shown in Figure 19. This results in inaccurate feature point extraction.

Figure 19. Mouth Feature Extraction – NonUniform Lighting Problem

C. Weight Measurement Accuracy

The four digital load sensors each capable of measuring maximum 50 lb are used to build a weighing platform. The weight measurement accuracy depends on the load sensor accuracy.

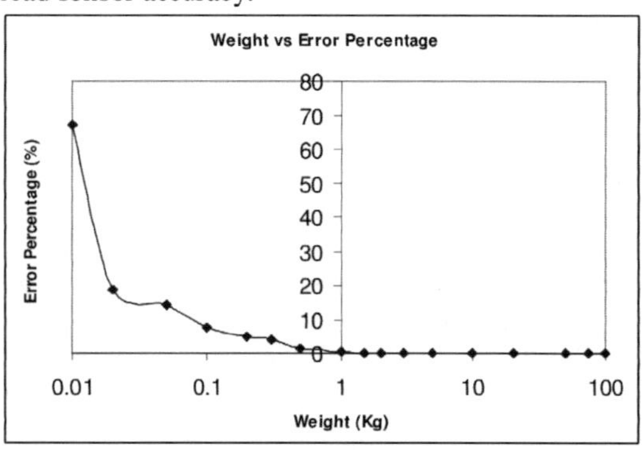

Figure 20. Weight versus error percentage.

We tested the load sensor accuracy with standard weights. The percentage error for various loads on a 50 lb load sensor is shown in Figure 20. It is concluded that the error rate is less when it is loaded with maximum capacity. Also, it was found that the error rate is found to be high for the weights equal to or less than 1 kg. That is not considered as the major problem, since the weight of the user who will use the system might be of more than 1 kg.

D. Others

The RFID tag performance on different dress materials and human body needs to be analyzed. The proper placement of tags and antenna has to be tested for better read performance. The performance of garment integrated RFID antennas are studied and detailed in [49]. The results show that embroidery technique can be used to fabricate RFID tag and wireless sensor antennas, which are intended to be used in clothing very near the human body.

The rest of the features like mirror usage time and event reminder were found to be useful. The proper placement of RFID antenna and tags in garments need to be evolved to achieve better read performance.

E. User Evaluation

The use case scenario is as follows: When a person enters the dressing room, he/she stands in front of the mirror. The weighing platform detects the user's presence and triggers camera ON to capture the image. The initial step is to recognize the user using face recognition technique with the help of the captured image. The health parameters are measured and saved in the database. The progress of health parameters are analyzed and displayed in the form of 3D graph. The weight is displayed using java speedometer component with a needle moves over a weight scale. The garment details are then identified and its descriptions are shown on the screen and followed by suggestion on suitable garments. This information is also provided in audio output using MBROLA TTS (Text To Speech) engine.

The system is deployed in our UBICOMP (UBIquitous COMPuting) laboratory for testing. The users of age group 24 to 32 used the mirror for a period of say 10 or 12 days and gave feedback. The feedback rating is plotted in Figure 21. The rating is done considering the comfort/convenience level achieved in each service. The rating 5 represents that the user is more comfortable and 1 represents that the user is not at all comfortable.

Few suggestions from the user are as follows:

1) In addition to recognizing the emotions, they want the mirror to entertain them in case they are not in good mood.

2) Want more interactions like voice output other than displaying information.

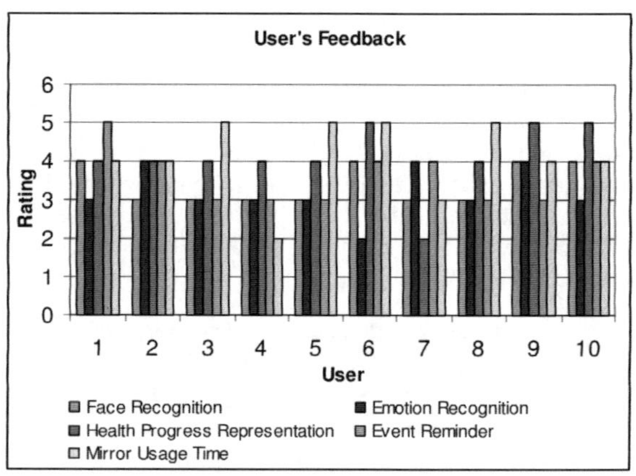

Figure 21. User's Feedback

3) Feeling little incomfort in asking them to particularly stand on the weighing platform.

4) Can this system be adoptable for more than one users using the mirror at same time?

5) Color lighting environment can be created as per the user's preference.

The user's feedback and suggestions were collected and improvements are being done.

VII. Conclusion and Future Work

This paper demonstrated a smart artifact for assisting smart home users in their daily activities. It incorporates intelligence into a normal mirror by embedding image processing and RFID technologies. The mirror recognizes the user using face recognition technique and offers personalized services. These services include recognizing emotions, identifying garments, suggesting suitable garment colors, remind important events, and monitor the progress of health parameters. It functions in two different modes of operation: In normal mode, it acts like a traditional mirror and in interactive mode it acts as an intelligent device that recognizes information and provides personalized services. The prototype has been developed and deployed in ubiquitous computing laboratory and kept for user evaluation. The image processing algorithms were tested in the deployed environment and the results were discussed in detail. The primary user feedbacks were mostly positive and the system is found to be highly satisfied and useful. Our future work includes improvement of image processing algorithms in terms of accuracy, automate the training process of face recognition algorithm, enrich the features using machine learning techniques, introduce additional technologies such as speech recognition, and enable touch screen facility for user interaction. Empirical evaluation of users feedback in the laboratory environment is given in this paper. More exhaustive evaluation of users experience in real-life environments could be carried out as further scope of work. The features of the mirror can be enhanced for deploying in other environments such as Beauty Parlors, Textile shops, and Hotels. However, security and privacy requirements need to be adequately addressed.

Acknowledgment

The work is developed under National Ubiquitous Computing Research Centre, funded by Department of Electronics and Information Technology, Government of India. We would like to thank Department of Electronics and Information Technology for providing us an opportunity to develop this smart artifact.

References

[1] C. Sethukkarasi, V. S. Harikrishnan, and R. Pitchiah, "Design and Development of Interactive Mirror for Aware Home," The First International Conference on Smart Systems, Devices and Technologies, pp. 1-8, 2012.

[2] K. Fujinami, F. Kawsar, and T. Nakajima, "Aware Mirror: A Personalized Display Using a Mirror," Third International Conference, User Interaction, Pervasive Computing, vol. 3468, pp. 315 332, May 2005.

[3] Everyday Computing Lab, Memory Mirror, Available from: http://we-make-money-not-art.com/memory_mirror_a/ 2016.05.18

[4] A. C. Andres del Valle and A. Opalach, "The Persuasive Mirror: computerized persuasion for healthy living," Accenture Technology Labs, France. Available from: http://www.consultoras.org/frontend/movil/descargar.php?idf=6700 2016.05.18

[5] M. A. Hossain, P. K. Atrey, and A. E. Saddik, "Smart Mirror for Ambient Home Environment," 3rd IET International Conference on Intelligent Environments, pp. 589-596, 24-25 Sep 2007.

[6] C. H. Morimoto, "Interactive Digital Mirror," IEEE Proceedings on Computer Graphics and Image Processing, pp. 232-236, 2001.

[7] T. Lashina, "Intelligent Bathroom," Philips Research, Netherlands. Available from: https://www.researchgate.net/publication/228881021_Intelligent_bathroom 2016.05.10

[8] K. Ushida, Y. Tanaka, T. Naemura, and H. Harashima, "i-mirror: An interaction/information environment based on a mirror metaphor aiming to install into our life space," Proceedings of the 12th International Conference on Artificial Reality and Telexistence (ICAT2002), pp. 113-118, 2002.

[9] J. Ding, C. Huang, J. Lin, J. Yang, and C. Wu, "Magic Mirror," IEEE International Symposium on Multimedia, pp. 176-185, December 2007.

[10] C. Cheng and D. S. Liu, "Discovering Dressing Knowledge for an Intelligent Dressing Advising System," Fourth IEEE International Conference on Fuzzy Systems and Knowledge Discovery, pp. 339-343, 2007.

[11] H. H. J. Kim, Survey Paper : Face Detection and Face Recognition. Available from http://citeseerx.ist.psu.edu/viewdoc/download?doi=10.1.1.93.4859&rep=rep1&type=pdf 2016.05.10

[12] P. Viola and M. J. Jones, "Rapid Object Detection using a Boosted Cascade of Simple Features," IEEE Conference on Computer Vision and Pattern Recognition, pp. 511-518, 2001.

[13] V. Gupta and D. Sharma, "A Study of Various Face Detection Methods," International Journal of Advanced Research in Computer and Communication Engineering, vol. 3, Issue 5, pp. 6694-6697, May 2014.

[14] O. H. Jensen, "Implementing the Viola-Jones Face Detection Algorithm," IMM-M.Sc.: ISBN 87-643-0008-0, ISSN 1601-233X, 2008.

[15] W. Zhao, R. Chellappa, A. Rosenfeld, and P. Phillips, "Face Recognition : A Literature Survey," ACM Computing Survey, pp. 399-459, 2003.

[16] M. Turk and A. Pentland, "Eigenfaces for Recognition," J. Cognitive Neuroscience, Vol. 3, pp. 71-86, 1991.

[17] M. A. Turk and A. P. Pentland, "Face Recognition using Eigen Faces," IEEE Computer Society Conference on Computer Vision and Pattern Recognition, pp. 586-591, 1991.

[18] Face Recognition using Eigenfaces and Distance Classifiers: A Tutorial. Available from: http://onionesquereality.wordpress.com/2009/02/11/face-recognition-using-eigenfaces-and-distance-classifiers-a-tutorial/ 2016.05.31

[19] R. K. Gupta and U. K. Sahu, "Real Time Face Recognition under Different Conditions," International Journal of Advanced Research in Computer Science and Software Engineering, Vol. 3, Issue 1, pp. 86-93, January 2013.

[20] W.K. Teo, L. C. D. Silva, and P. Vadakkepat, "Facial Expression Detection and Recognition System," Journal of the Institution Engineers, pp. 14-26, 2004.

[21] H. Gu, G. Su, and C. Du, "Feature points extraction from Faces," Image Vision and Computing, pp. 154-158, 2003.

[22] R. S. Feris, T. E. D. Campos, and R. M. C. Junior, "Detection and tracking of Face features in video Sequences," Lecture Notes in Artificial Intelligence, vol. 1793, pp. 129-137, Apr. 2000.

[23] M. Deriche, "A Simple Face Recognition Algorithm using Eigeneyes and a Class-Dependent PCA Implementation," International Journal of Soft Computing 3(6), pp. 438-442, 2008.

[24] M. Gargesha and S. Panchanathan, "A Hybrid Technique for Facial Feature Point Detection," Fifth IEEE Southwest Symposium on Image Analysis and Interpretation, pp. 134-138, 2002.

[25] F. Bourel, C. C. Chibelushi, and A. A. Low, "Robust Facial Expression Recognition Using a State-Based Model of Spatially – Localised Facial Dynamics," Proceedings of the Fifth IEEE international Conference on Automatic Face and Gesture Recognition, pp. 106-111, 2002.

[26] C. C. Chibelushi and F. Bourel, "Facial Expression Recognition: A Brief Tutorial Overview". Available from: http://homepages.inf.ed.ac.uk/rbf/CVonline/LOCAL_COPIES/CHIBELUSHI1/CCC_FB_FacExprRecCVonline.pdf 2016.05.31

[27] X. Wei, J. Loi, and L. Yin, "Classifying Facial Expressions Based on Topo-Feature Representation," Affective Computing, pp. 69-82, 2008. Available from: http://www.intechopen.com/books/affective_computing/classifying_facial_expressions_based_on_topo-feature_representation 2016.05.31

[28] F. Hulsken, F. Wallhoff, and G. Rigoll, "Facial Expression with Pseudo-3D Hidden Markov Models," 23rd DAGM-Symposium on Pattern Recognition, pp. 291-297, 2001.

[29] S. Lucey, I. Matthews, C. Hu, Z. Ambadar, F. D. L. Torre, and J. Cohn, "AAM Derived Face Representations for Robust Facial Action Recognition," 7th International Conference on Automatic Face and Gesture Recognition, pp. 155-162, 2006.

[30] M. Valstar, M. Pantic, and I. Patras, "Motion History for Facial Action Detection in Video," IEEE International Conference on Systems, Man and Cybernetics, pp. 635-640, 2004.

[31] P. Michel, and R. E. Kaliouby, "Real Time Facial Expression Recognition in Video using Support Vector Machines," The 5th International Conference on Multimodal interfaces, pp. 258-264, 2003.

[32] I. Cohen, N. Sebe, A. Garg, L. Chen, and T. S. Huang, "Facial Expression Recognition From Video Sequences," IEEE International Conference on Multimedia and Expo, pp. 121-124, 2002.

[33] Yale Face Database. Available from: http://cvc.cs.yale.edu/cvc/projects/yalefaces/yalefaces.html 2016.05.24

[34] Cohn-Kanade AU-Coded Expression Database. Available from: http://www.pitt.edu/~jeffcohn/CKandCK+.htm 2016.05.24

[35] MMI Face Database. Available from: http://www.mmifacedb.com/page/About/ 2016.05.24

[36] The Japanese Female Facial Expression (JAFFE) Database. Available from: http://www.kasrl.org/jaffe.html 2016.05.24

[37] Y. Tian, T. Kanade, and J. F. Cohn, "Recognizing Upper Face Action Units for Facial Expression Analysis," IEEE Conference on Computer Vision and Pattern Recognition, pp. 294-301, 2002.

[38] V. Srinivasan, J. Stankovic, and K. Whitehouse, "Using height sensors for bio-metric identification in Multi-resident Homes," Pervasive Computing, pp. 337-354, 2010.

[39] H. Tsai, W. Wang, J. Wang, and J. Wang, "Long Distance Person Identification Using Height Measurement and Face Recognition," IEEE TENCON 2009, pp. 1-4, 23-26 Jan 2009.

[40] E. Jeges, I. Kispal, and Z. Hornak, "Measuring Human Height using Calibrated Cameras," IEEE Conference on Human System Interactions, pp. 755-760, 2008.

[41] R. Sohal and T. Kaur, "Skin Pixel Segmentation Using Learning Based Classification: Analysis and Performance Comparison," International Journal of Engineering Research and Applications, Vol. 4, Issue 5 (Version 3), pp. 49-56, May 2014.

[42] J. Brand and J. S. Mason, "A Comparative Assessment of Three Approaches to Pixel-Level Human Skin Detection," Proc. IEEE International Conference on Pattern Recognition, vol. 1, pp. 1056-1059, Sep. 2000.

[43] J. Kovac, P. Peer, and F. Solina, "Human skin colour clustering for face detection," IEEE EUROCON 2003, pp. 144-148, 2003.

[44] F. Tomaz, T. Candeias, and H. Shahbazkia, "Improved automatic skin detection in color images," VIIth Digital Image Computing: Techniques and Applications, Sydney, pp. 419-427, 2003.

[45] D. B. Swift, "Evaluating graphic image files for objectionable content," US Patent US 6895111 B1, 2006.

[46] S. A. Al-Shehri, "A simple and novel method for skin detection and face locating and tracking," Asia-Pacific Conference on Computer-Human Interaction (APCHI 2004), LNCS 3101, 2004.

[47] W. Chen, M. J. Er, and S. Wu, "Illumination Compensation and Normalization for Robust Face Recognition Using Discrete Cosine Transform in Logarithm Domain," IEEE Transactions on systems, man, and cybernetics, Vol. 36, no. 2, pp. 458-466, Apr. 2006.

[48] P. N. Belhumeur, J. P. Hespanha, and D. J. Kriegman, "Eigenfaces versus Fisherfaces: recognition using class specific linear projection," IEEE Trans. Pattern Anal. Mach. Intell., vol. 19, no. 7, pp. 711–720, Jul. 1997.

[49] K. N. Goh, Y. Y. Chen, and E. S. Lin, "Developing a Smart Wardrobe System," IEEE Consumer Communications and Networking Conference, pp. 303-307, 2011.

International Journal on Advances in Intelligent Systems, vol 9 no 1 & 2, year 2016, http://www.iariajournals.org/intelligent_systems/

Type of Stochastic Dependence and its Impact on the Performance of Regression Type Classifiers

Olgierd Hryniewicz

Systems Research Institute
Polish Academy of Sciences
Warszawa, Poland
Email: hryniewi@ibspan.waw.pl

***Abstract*—Six regression type binary classifiers based on linear and logistic models have been evaluated using a complex simulation experiment. The classifiers were compared with respect to the robustness to unexpected changes of the models that describe data in training and test sets. The data used for this comparison were generated using different models describing their interdependence. This dependence was modeled by different copulas. The experiments revealed that the performance of considered classifiers strongly depends upon the type of copula. However, the simple logistic regression has appeared to be the best one in these circumstances. Thus, this classifier could be recommended for practitioners when the type of dependence may vary in time.**

Keywords–Binary classification; Regression type classifiers; Copulas; Simulation of dependent data; Robustness.

I. INTRODUCTION

This paper is a significant extension of the conference paper "On the Robustness of Regression Type Classifiers" presented in the Proceedings of INTELLI'2015 conference, held in St. Julians, Malta [1], and is focused on rarely discussed aspects of classification problems. Classification algorithms are probably the most frequently used tools of data mining. The methods of their construction in the Artificial Intelligence (AI) community is known under the name of *supervised learning*. There are thousands of books and papers devoted to their theory and applications. Thomson Reuter's scientific database Web of Science displays information (as on 2016 February 24th) on nearly 400 papers with the phrase "classification algorithms" in the title, and nearly 7000 papers with this phrase in the topic. The information about theoretical foundations of classification algorithms can be found, e.g., in books by Duda et al. [2] and Hastie et al. [3]. Comprehensive description of application aspects of classification algorithms can be found in the book by Witten et al. [4].

The main problem with the evaluation of each, from among hundreds of already proposed, classifier is estimation of its quality characteristics. Japkowicz and Shah in their excellent book [5] write about two general approaches to this problem: *de facto* approach based on computing of many different quality characteristics, and *statistical* approach, in which unavoidable randomness of classification results is taken into account. The *de facto* approach can be used for any type of testing procedure, and is predominately used by the AI community. The applicability of the statistical approach is somewhat restricted, as the analyzed data should fulfill some requirements precisely described in terms of the theory of probability. These requirements are easily verified if we use for testing purposes artificially generated data. However, the usage of such data is not appreciated by the AI community, who prefers to use real-life benchmarks for evaluation purposes. When we use benchmark data for evaluation, the data used for the construction of an algorithm and the data used for its evaluation come from the same set of real-life values. In order to assure validity of comparisons different schemes of randomization, e.g., cross-validation techniques, are used. This approach is commonly accepted, and valid for the great majority of potential applications. It is, usually rightly, assumed that a classifier (in fact, the method of its construction) is of good quality if it performs well on many different benchmarks. However, in nearly every case (see, e.g., Hand [6]) it is assumed that the classifier is constructed and further used on *the same population* of classified objects. In some cases, however, this assumption may be questioned.

Robustness is well defined in statistics. According to Wikipedia, robust statistics "is a statistical technique that performs well even if its assumptions are somewhat violated by the true model, from which the data were generated". This definition of robustness can be directly applied to these methods of classification, which are based on well established statistical methodology, such as, e.g., regression. In general, however, many classification methods, such as, e.g., neural networks or decision trees, are not based (at least, directly) on statistical models. Therefore, in the machine learning community robustness is often understood somewhat differently, as the ability to perform well for many different sets of real data. David Hand, one of the most renowned researchers in the area of machine learning, in his overview paper [6] discusses consequences of breaking the assumption that the data in the design (training) set are randomly drawn from the same distribution as the points to be classified in the future. He gives references to some works related to this problem, and presents examples of problems encountered in the area of the credit scoring and banking industries. It has to be noted, however, that the number of papers devoted to the problem of robustness, understood as in [6], is rather small. For example, Japkowicz and Shah [5], while discussing this type of the robustness of classifiers, cite only the paper by Hand [6]. One can consider the concept of robustness in even more general sense, as to perform reasonably well when data are described or generated using different mathematical models. This understanding of robustness is close to the one used by the AI community, but is different to it as takes into account the knowledge about the mathematical models of analyzed data. In this paper we understand the concept of robustness in this, more general, sense.

Hryniewicz [7] [8] considers the case when binary classifiers are used for quality evaluation of items in production processes. In many cases of such processes, quality characteristics cannot be directly evaluated during production time. Sometimes it is impossible, when a testing procedure is destructive or impractical, or when a testing procedure is costly or lasts too long. In such cases, an appropriate classifier, which labels monitored items as "good" or "bad" is constructed using the data coming from specially designed (and usually costly) experiments, and then used in production practice. The situation does not rise any objections if the process, from which items used in the construction phase of a classification algorithm are taken is *the same* as a process, in which obtained classifiers are used. Hryniewicz [7], [8] has demonstrated that deterioration of such process may have detrimental effects on the quality of classification. Similar problems may be also encountered in other fields of applications. Consider, for example, a classifier that is used for the prediction of cancer recurrence who may change its quality characteristics when future patient will undergo a treatment, which was not used at the moment when this classifier was built.

The problems described in the previous paragraph may suggest that in the evaluation of classifiers we should add another dimension, namely the robustness to the change of population understood as the change of probability distributions that describe input variables in the classification process. It was the topic of the paper by Hryniewicz [1] whose work was focused on the analysis of robustness understood in this way. In our analysis we take into account in a more comprehensive way the impact of the type of stochastic dependence on the performance of classifiers. Therefore, we supplement the results already presented in [1] with new results whose aim is to present this impact.

At the moment the analysis of the robustness of classifiers, understood in a general way, can be achieved using artificially generated data, because appropriate, and widely known, benchmarks seem not to exist. Hryniewicz [1] analyzed the problem of robustness using software designed for the generation of complex nonlinear processes with statistically dependent data. This software has also been used for obtaining new results described in this paper. A detailed description of this software can be found in Section II. Similarly as in [1] we have evaluated binary classifiers whose construction is based on generalized linear models and regression techniques. In particular, we have analyzed classifiers based on

- Simple linear regression,
- Linear regression with interactions,
- Simple logistic regression,
- Logistic regression with interactions,
- Linear Discrimination Analysis with a symmetric decision criterion,
- Linear Discrimination Analysis with an asymmetric decision criterion.

We have assumed that the dependence between variables in our simulation model may be described by different copulas, characterized by different strength of dependence. The main goal of the research was twofold. First, as it is presented in [1], we have evaluated the robustness of the considered classifiers to shifts of the expected values of input variables (attributes). Second, we have tried to find if the strength and type of dependence influences performance of the considered classifiers. In contrast to the results published by other authors, we present the results of experiments performed in a strictly controlled environment that simulates conditions, which are significantly different from those usually assumed for the considered classification models.

This paper is organized similarly to its predecessor [1]. In Section II we describe considered models of data dependence, simulation software, and evaluated classifiers. Then, in Section III we describe used methods of evaluation. The most important results of experiments will be illustrated with examples in Section IV. Finally, in Section V we will conclude the experiments, and present the original results of this research.

II. Description of Simulation Experiments

Except for few particular cases the problems described in the previous section cannot be solved analytically. Therefore, statistical simulations are widely accepted by the AI community as a sufficient tool for solving different problems of classification.

A. *Simulation software*

Realization of the task formulated in Section I requires an implementation of a complex mathematical model in a form of simulation software. On the most general level, let us assume that a general mathematical model that describes dependence of input variables (predictors) with an output binary variable is a simple one. Let $Z_1, \ldots, Z_p$ be p output characteristics whose values are not directly observed in an experiment. Assume now that these values should be predicted using observations $X_1, \ldots, X_k$ of k predictors. This problem is easy to solve if we assume that we know the joint probability distribution of input and output variables, i.e., the probability distribution of a combined vector $(Z_1, \ldots, Z_p, X_1, \ldots, X_k)$. According to the famous Sklar's theorem this distribution is unequivocally described by a $(p+k)$-dimensional copula, and marginal probability distributions of $Z_1, \ldots, Z_p$ and $X_1, \ldots, X_k$, respectively. Such a general model is hardly applicable, as only two-dimensional copulas $C(u, v)$ are widely used in practice. Therefore, our simulation software should be based on a model, which is simpler and more easy for practical interpretation. In this research we have used a hierarchical 3-level model, originally proposed in [7]. On the top level of this model there is an auxiliary one-dimensional real-valued variable T. This value is transformed to a binary one (in which we are interested in) by means of the following transformation

$$Z_t = \begin{cases} 0 & , \quad T \geq t \\ 1 & , \quad T < t \end{cases} \tag{1}$$

The instances with the value $Z_t = 1$ we will call "positive cases" or "Positives", and the instances with the value $Z_t = 0$ we will call "negative cases" or "Negatives". This model has a direct interpretation in the case considered by Hryniewicz [7] who modeled a monitoring of a production process with indirectly observable quality characteristic. The first level of our model describes the predictors $X_1, \ldots, X_k$. In order to simplify simulations we assume that consecutive $k-1$ pairs of predictors $(X_i, X_{i+1}), i = 1, \ldots, k-1$ are described by $k-1$ copulas $C_{i,i+1}(F_i(X_i), F_{i+1}(X_{i+1})), i = 1, \ldots, k-1$, where $F_1(X_1), \ldots, F_k(X_k)$ are the cumulative probability functions of the marginal distribution of the predictors. In order to simulate the input variables we have to assume the type of the proposed copulas, and the strength of dependence between the pairs of random variables whose joint two-dimensional probability distributions are described by these copulas. In the AI community Pearson's coefficient of correlation r is often used as the measure of dependence. Unfortunately, its applicability is limited to the case of the classical multivariate normal distribution, or - in certain circumstances - to the case of the multivariate elliptic distributions (for more information see [9]). When dependent random variables cannot be described by such a model, and it is not an unusual case in practice, we propose to use Kendall's coefficient of association τ defined, in its population version in terms of copulas, as (see [10])

$$\tau(X,Y) = 4 \int\int_{[0,1]^2} C(u,v)dC(u,v) - 1. \quad (2)$$

Numerical comparisons of the values of Pearson's r, Kendall's τ, and - another popular nonparametric measure of dependence - Spearman's ρ are presented in [11], and show that the usage of Pearson's r in the analysis of data that cannot be described by the normal distribution may lead to wrong conclusions, especially in the case of negative dependence. Therefore, Kendall's τ is, in such cases, a much better measure of dependence.

In order to have a more realistic model for simulation purposes, it was proposed in [7] to use an in-between second level of latent (hidden) variables $H_1, \ldots, H_k$ described by cumulative probability functions $F_{H1}(h_1), \ldots, F_{Hk}(h_k)$. Each hidden variable H_i is associated with the predictor variable X_i, and its fictitious realizations are measured on the same scale as the predicted continuous random variable T. The dependence between H_i and X_i is described by a copula $C_{i,i}(F_{Hi}(H_i), F_i(X_i))$. Moreover, in our model we assume that there exists a certain linear relationship between the expected value of H_i and the expected value of X_i. This assumption is needed if we want to model the effects of the shifts in the expected values of the predictors on the expected value of the predicted auxiliary variable T, which is related to the hidden variables by a certain, possibly nonlinear, function

$$T = f(H_1, \ldots, H_k). \quad (3)$$

In real circumstances, such as those described in [7], the probability distribution of T, and hence the probability distribution of Z_t, can be observed only in specially designed experiments. The results of such experiments can be viewed upon as data sets coming from supervised learning experiments. In our research we simulate similar experiments, and we use actual (i.e., generated by our software) and predicted (i.e., the results generated by classifiers) binary outputs for constructing and testing, several, say s, classifiers, $K_1, \ldots, K_s$, each of the form

$$Z'_t = K(X_1, \ldots, X_k). \quad (4)$$

The mathematical model described above was implemented in a software system written in FORTRAN. The reason for using this old programming language was twofold. First, because of a great amount of needed computations the usage of popular among statisticians interpreted languages like R is completely inefficient. Second, because of the long history of the usage of this programming language in statistics many numerically effective procedures are widely available.

B. Description of the experiment

In this paper, we describe the results for only four input variables. This limited number of input variables may be justified by findings of Hand [6] who noticed that in many real-life problems of classification only few predictors (attributes) have real impact on the results of classification. Another reason for making this restriction is limited time of computations. One has to note that even in this restricted model one run of Monte Carlo simulations may last several days of continuous work of a fast PC computer. The simulation process described in this paper consists of three parts. First, a stream of data points, i.e., the values of predictors, the values of hidden variables, the value of the unobserved auxiliary output variable, and the observed output binary variable are generated. Next, these simulated data serve as training data sets for building several classifiers. Finally, test data sets are generated, and used for the evaluation of considered classification (prediction) algorithms.

In our simulation experiment the probability distributions of predictors defined by a user on the first level of the model can be chosen from a set of five distributions: uniform, normal, exponential, Weibull, and log-normal. For the second level of the model a user can choose the probability distributions of the hidden variables from a set of distributions, that are defined on the positive part of the real line: exponential, Weibull, and log-normal. The information about these probability distributions can be found in any textbook on probability and statistics.

The dependence between the pairs of predictors, and between predictors and associated hidden variables, can be described by the following copulas:

- independent

$$C(u,v) = uv, \quad (5)$$

- Normal (Gaussian)

$$C(u,v;\rho) = \Phi_N(\Phi^{-1}(u), \Phi^{-1}(v); \rho) \quad (6)$$

where $\Phi_N(u,v)$ is the cumulative probability distribution function of the bivariate normal distribution, and $\Phi^{-1}(u)$ is the inverse of the cumulative probability function of the univariate normal distribution (the quantile function). Parameter ρ is equal to the well known Pearson's coefficient of linear correlation r only in the case of normal marginal probability distributions,

- Clayton

$$C(u,v) = \max\left(\left[u^{-\alpha} + v^{-\alpha} - 1\right]^{-1/\alpha}, 0\right), \alpha \in [-1,\infty) \setminus 0, \quad (7)$$

- Frank

$$C(u,v) = -\frac{1}{\alpha}\ln\left(1 + \frac{(e^{-\alpha u}-1)(e^{-\alpha v}-1)}{e^{-\alpha}-1}\right), \quad (8)$$
$$\alpha \in (-\infty,\infty) \setminus 0,$$

- Gumbel

$$C(u,v) = \exp\left(-\left[(-\ln u)^{1+\alpha} + (-\ln v)^{1+\alpha}\right]^{\frac{1}{1+\alpha}}\right), \quad \alpha \in (0,\infty), \tag{9}$$

used only for positive dependencies, and

- Fairlie-Gumbel-Morgenstern (FGM)

$$C(u_1,u_2;\theta) = u_1u_2 + \theta u_1u_2(1-u_1)(1-u_2), |\theta| \leq 1, \tag{10}$$

used for modeling only weak dependencies. The detailed description of these copulas can be found, e.g., in [10]. The strength of this dependence is defined by the value of Kendall's coefficient of association τ, calculated for each of the considered copulas using (2). The expected values of the distributions of the hidden variables in this simulation model depend in a linear way on the values of its related predictors. At the next stage of simulation, hidden random variables are transformed to the auxiliary output random variable T. The relation between the hidden variables and T is strongly non-linear, and is described by operators of a "min-max" type. Finally, the auxiliary output random variable T is transformed to the binary output variable, which is used for classification purposes. The proposed model allows to generate data with great variety of properties (non-linear dependence of a different strength, different probability distributions, etc.) that are significantly different from those usually assummed for linear regression models.

The scheme of the simulation of a data point, for an exemplary set of input parameters (probability distributions, copulas, and values of Kendall's τ), is presented in Figure 1. The values of four input attributes are generated, respectively, from the normal, exponential, logarithmic normal, and Weibull distributions. The generated values are statistically dependent, and the dependencies are described, respectively, by the following copulas: Clayton (with $\tau = 0.8$), Normal (with $\tau = -0.8$), and Frank (with $\tau = 0.8$). Then, for each input attribute the system generates an unobserved (hidden) value. These hidden values are generated, respectively, from the logarithmic normal, exponential, exponential, and Weibull distributions. The parameters of these distributions depend in a linear way upon the values of the respective input attributes (this dependence is not depicted in Figure 1). Moreover, they are also statistically dependent upon the values of the generated input attributes, and these dependencies are described, respectively, by the following copulas: Normal (with $\tau = -0.8$), Frank (with $\tau = 0.9$), Gumbel (with $\tau = -0.9$), and Normal (with $\tau = -0.8$), and Clayton (with $\tau = -0.8$). Finally, the real-valued output is calculated using the formula depicted in Figure 1, and this value is transformed, by using (1), to the binary output variable. The generated 5-tuple (4 input attributes, and a binary output value) describes one point in the training data set. The points of the test set are generated similarly, with the same or different (when robustness is evaluated) parameters of the model. The number of input variables (four) has been chosen in accordance with the opinion presented in [6] that in real situations the number of attributes, which really influence quality characteristics of a classifier is usually small.

Several types of classifiers have been implemented in our simulation program. The classifiers are built using samples

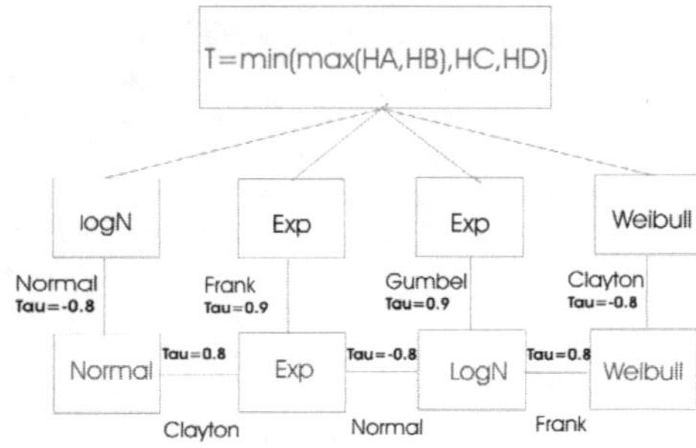

Figure 1. An exemplary scheme of the simulation of a data point

of size n_t of training data consisted of the vectors of the values of predictors (x_1, x_2, x_3, x_4), and the actual value of the assigned class. In this paper, we consider only six of them, which represent three different general approaches to the classification problem.

Binary linear regression. The first considered classifier is a simple (of the first order) binary linear regression (LINREG4). We label the considered classes by 0 and 1, respectively, and consider these labels as real numbers, treating them as observations of a real dependent variable in the linear regression model of the following form:

$$R_4 = w_0 + w_1 * X_1 + w_2 * X_2 + w_3 * X_3 + w_4 * X_4, \tag{11}$$

where R is the predicted class of an item described by explanatory variables X_1, X_2, X_3, X_4, and w_1, w_2, w_3, w_4, w_0 are respective coefficients of the regression equation estimated from a training set of n_t elements. The value of R estimated from (11) is a real number, so an additional requirement is needed for the final classification (e.g., if $R < 0,5$ an item is classified as belonging to the class 0, and to the class 1 otherwise). The second considered classifier is also a linear one, but with additional variables describing interactions of the second order between the input variables (LINREG14). The regression function (of the second order) in this case is the following

$$\begin{aligned} R_{14} = \; & w_0 + w_1 * X_1 + \cdots + w_5 * X_1^2 + \cdots + \\ & w_9 * X_1 * X_2 + \cdots + w_{14} * X_3 * X_4. \end{aligned} \tag{12}$$

The main advantage of these two classifiers is their simplicity. Moreover, the classical linear regression is implemented in all spreadsheets, such as, e.g., MS Excel. For this reason we have chosen these classifiers as the easiest to implement in practice without any specialized software.

Logistic regression. The next two classifiers are built using a generalized linear regression model, namely the logistic regression. The logistic regression is recommended by many authors (see, e.g., [3]) as the best regression tool for the analysis of discrete data. In this model the dependence of the output R_L upon the input variables is modeled by the logistic function

$$R_L = \frac{1}{1 + exp(-f(X_1, \ldots, X_4))}, \tag{13}$$

where the function $f(X_1, \ldots, X_4)$ is described either by the right side of (11) of the LOGREG4 model, or by the right side of (12) of the LOGREG14 model. Unfortunately, the implementation of the logistic regression is not as simple as in the case of the linear regression. The estimation of its parameters requires the usage of numerical procedures that are implemented in specialized software (available, e.g., in the WEKA package).

Linear Discriminant Analysis (LDA). The last two classifiers implement the LDA introduced by Fisher, and described in many textbooks on multivariate statistical analysis and data mining (see, e.g., [3]). This method is historically the first classification method used in practice, and according to [6] its efficiency has been proved empirically by many authors. In the LDA statistical data are projected on a certain hyperplane estimated from the training data. New data points, projected on this hyperplane, which are closer to the mean value of the projected on this hyperplane training data representing the class 0 than to the mean value of training data representing the remaining class 1 are classified to the class 0. Otherwise, they are classified to the class 1. The equation of the hyperplane is given by the following formula:

$$L = y_1 * X_1 + y_2 * X_2 + y_3 * X_3 + y_4 * X_4 + y_0, \quad (14)$$

where L is the value of the transformed data point calculated using the values of the explanatory variables X_1, X_2, X_3, X_4, and y_1, y_2, y_3, y_4, y_0 are respective coefficients of the LDA equation estimated from a training set. If Z_L denote the decision point, a new item is classified to the class 0 if $L \leq Z_L$, and to the class 1 otherwise. The LDA may not perform well in the case of imbalanced data. Therefore, in our simulation we implemented two methods of the calculation of Z_L. First, the classical one (LDA-SYM), when this point is just the average of the mean values of the transformed data points from the training set that belonged to the class 0 and the class 1, respectively. Second, an asymmetric one (LDA-ASYM), recommended for the analysis of imbalanced data sets, where Z_L is located asymmetrically between the two mean values mentioned above, depending upon the number of items belonging to each class in the test set. The calculation of the LDA equation (14) is not so simple. However, it can be done using basic versions of many statistical packages such as SPSS, STATISTICA, etc. Moreover, the LDA problem can be reformulated in terms of a simple linear regression, so the statistical tools available in spreadsheets may also be used for computations.

III. Evaluation of binary classifiers

Proper evaluation of binary classifiers is not as simple as it looks like. If we do not consider any costs of misclassification the whole information about the quality of classifiers is contained in the so called confusion matrix, presented in Table I [5].

TABLE I. Confusion matrix

	Pred_Negative	Pred_Positive	
Act_Negative	True negative (TN)	False positive (FP)	N=TN+FP
Act_Positive	False negative (FN)	True positive (TP)	P=FN+TP

All measures of the quality of classifiers are built using the information contained in this matrix. A comprehensive overview of these measures can be found in many sources such as, e.g., Chapter 3 of the book by Japkowicz and Shakh [5]. The most frequently used measure is *Accuracy*

$$Acc = \frac{TN + TP}{N + P} \quad (15)$$

It estimates the probability of correct classification. However, in certain circumstances (e.g., when classes are imbalanced) this measure does not let to discriminate the quality of different classifiers. This happens to be the case in experiments described in this paper.

Other popular and important measures, such as

- *Precision*

$$Prec = \frac{TP}{TP + FP}, \quad (16)$$

- *Sensitivity* or *Recall*

$$Sens = \frac{TP}{TP + FN}, \quad (17)$$

- *Specificity*

$$Spec = \frac{TN}{FP + TN}, \quad (18)$$

describe only certain features of binary classifiers. For example, high values of *Precision* in statistical terms are equivalent to low values of type I classification error when "Positives" are considered as the relevant class. Similarly, high values *Sensitivity* in statistical terms are equivalent to low values of type II classification error. When quality of the classification of "Negatives" is also worth of consideration, one has to take into account the value of *Specificity*.

In the performed experiment we used all these measures for the evaluation purposes. However, in this paper we present the analysis of two aggregate measures recommended for the evaluation of performance especially in presence of imbalanced data. First of these measures is *F1 score* (or *F1 measure*), defined as the harmonic average of *Precision* and *Sensitivity*, and calculated using the following formula

$$F1 = \frac{2TP}{2TP + FP + FN}. \quad (19)$$

Low values of this measure indicate that a classifier has a large value of at least one of type I or type II errors. Second aggregate measure is known as *G-mean*, defined as the geometric mean of *Sensitivity* and *Specificity*, and calculated as

$$G = \sqrt{\frac{TP * TN}{((TP + FN)(FP + TN)}}. \quad (20)$$

This measure is recommended for the evaluation of classifiers for highly imbalanced data when percentages of "Positives" and "Negatives" are significantly different, as it was the case in our experiments. It has to be noted that a popular among AI specialists measures such as ROC or AUC cannot be applied in our comparisons, as all considered classifiers are based on the same linear model, and are characterized by the same (or nearly the same) ROC characteristics.

IV. RESULTS OF EXPERIMENTS

The simulation system described in Section II was used in many experiments with the aim to evaluate different binary classifiers. In this paper, we describe only one of them. In each instance of this particular experiment we simulated 50 runs, each consisted of one training set of 100 elements and 100 test sets of 1000 elements each. This small size of a training set was chosen in order to compare the results of simulations with those described in [7], [8], where it had a particular practical meaning. In each instance of the experiment, we used the same type of a copula for the description of all dependent random variables (in other experiments, not described in this paper, we used different copulas in one considered model). The strength of dependence was categorized into 6 categories: strong positive (Sp), medium positive (Mp), weak positive (Wp), weak negative (Wn), medium negative (Mn), and strong negative (Sn). For the Sp category the value of Kendall's τ was randomly chosen for each training set from the interval $[0.7, 0.9]$. The respective intervals for the remaining categories were the following: $[0.4, 0.6]$ for Mp, $[0., 0.2]$ for Wp, $[-0.2, 0.]$ for Wn, $[-0.6, -0.4]$ for Mn, and $[-0.9, -0.7]$ for Sn. For each of the simulated 50 training sets the expected values of input variables (predictors) varied randomly in certain intervals. The simulated training sets were used for the construction of six classifiers described in Section II. For all test sets in one simulation run the description of the dependence between considered random variables (i.e., the copula, and the set of the values of Kendall's τ) was the same as in the respective training set. However, in choosing the expected values of the input variables (predictors) we considered two cases. In the first case, these expected values were the same as in the training set. Thus, the test sets were simulated using the same model as the respective training set. In other words, the considered classifiers were evaluated, in this case, on data generated by the same model as it had been used for their construction. In the second case, the expected values of the input variables used in the generation of test sets were *different* than the values used in the generation of the respective training sets. Those different values were chosen randomly around the values used for the generation of the training sets (by maximum $\pm 30\%$).

The presentation of the obtained results let us start with the analysis of the influence of the type of a copula describing the type of dependence on the *Accuracy* (i.e., fraction of correctly classified objects) of considered classifiers, which is the most frequently used quality characteristics of classification. In Table II we present the obtained average values of *Accuracy* for 4 different copulas, and the strength of dependence belonging to the category Mp. We can see that the quality of the considered classifiers for a given copula is similar. Only the asymmetric LDA classifier is visibly worse. However, this quality is different for different types of copulas. This seems to be a very important finding, as the type of dependence is rarely (if ever) considered in the evaluation of classifiers. In the case described in Table II the observed (marginal) probability distributions are the same, and the estimates of the strength of dependence are also the same. Nevertheless, the accuracy of classification is visibly different, depending upon the type of dependence defined by the respective copula.

From Table II we can see that the highest fraction of correctly classified objects appears when data are generated

TABLE II. AVERAGE *Accuracy*. THE SAME MODEL FOR TRAINING AND TEST SETS. MEDIUM POSITIVE DEPENDENCE

Classifier	*Normal*	*Clayton*	*Gumbel*	*Frank*
LINREG4	0.769	0.835	0.741	0.752
LINREG14	0.769	0.833	0.735	0.751
LOGREG4	0.789	0.849	0.757	0.773
LOGREG14	0.769	0.832	0.736	0.751
LDA-SYM	0.741	0.765	0.729	0.729
LDA-ASYM	0.697	0.732	0.683	0.685

by the Clayton copula, and the LOGREG4 classifier is the best one for all considered types of dependency, described by four considered copulas.

Now, let us consider the case of the similar (of medium strength) dependence, but a negative one. In Table III we compare the values of Accuracy for three copulas: Normal, Clayton, and Frank (the Gumbel copula does not allow negative dependence).

TABLE III. AVERAGE *Accuracy*. THE SAME MODEL FOR TRAINING AND TEST SETS. MEDIUM NEGATIVE DEPENDENCE

Classifier	*Normal*	*Clayton*	*Frank*
LINREG4	0.356	0.279	0.321
LINREG14	0.432	0.411	0.404
LOGREG4	0.424	0.333	0.379
LOGREG14	0.436	0.422	0.408
LDA-SYM	0.428	0.438	0.460
LDA-ASYM	0.483	0.472	0.486

From Table III we see that in the case of negative dependence the situation is totally different in comparison to the case of positive dependence of the same (in absolute values) strength. For classifiers based on linear and logistic regression models the best results of classification are observed when data are described by the Normal copula. Moreover, classifiers that use the linear model with interactions perform much better than the simple ones. However, when data are analysed using classifiers based on linear discriminant analysis the best results are observed when they are described by the Frank copula. It is worth to note that in the considered case of negative dependence the LDA-ASYM classifier is visibly the best one.

It is a well known fact that for imbalanced classes (i.e., when objects belonging to one of the two considered classes, usually the "Positives", appear much less frequently than the objects belonging to the second class) *Accuracy* may not be a good quality characteristic. In such a case, an aggregate characteristics, such as, e.g., *F1 score*, are used for evaluation purposes. The results of such evaluation (averaged for the same data!) are presented in Table IV.

TABLE IV. AVERAGE *F1 score*. THE SAME MODEL FOR TRAINING AND TEST SETS. MEDIUM POSITIVE DEPENDENCE

Classifier	*Normal*	*Clayton*	*Gumbel*	*Frank*
LINREG4	0.358	0.561	0.266	0.324
LINREG14	0.490	0.623	0.419	0.472
LOGREG4	0.537	0.662	0.464	0.509
LOGREG14	0.500	0.630	0.430	0.487
LDA-SYM	0.101	0.061	0.072	0.089
LDA-ASYM	0.549	0.598	0.484	0.562

It is evident that the situation in this case becomes quite different. First of all, we can see unacceptably low values of the *F1 score* for the symmetric LDA classifier. Despite its quite good accuracy (see Table II) classification errors of this classifier are completely imbalanced. As the matter of fact, the precision of this classifier was good, but its sensitivity was really very low. The variability of the *F1* score observed in Table IV is much greater than the variability of the *Accuracy*. It means that for different copulas the quality of considered classifiers measured by the *F1 score* may be significantly different. Moreover, if we look simultaneously on Tables II and IV, we can see that the simple logistic regression classifier seems to be quite visibly the best when it classifies data generated by the same model as it had been used for the generation of the training set.

The situation completely changes when consider the case of negative dependence, presented in Table V.

TABLE V. AVERAGE *F1 score*. THE SAME MODEL FOR TRAINING AND TEST SETS. MEDIUM NEGATIVE DEPENDENCE

Classifier	*Normal*	*Clayton*	*Frank*
LINREG4	0.356	0.279	0.321
LINREG14	0.432	0.411	0.404
LOGREG4	0.424	0.333	0.379
LOGREG14	0.436	0.422	0.408
LDA-SYM	0.428	0.438	0.460
LDA-ASYM	0.483	0.472	0.486

The observed values of the *F1 score* behave similarly to the case observed for *Accuracy*. Both classifiers built using the discriminant analysis (LDA-SYM and LDA-ASYM) perform much better than classifiers built on linear and logistic regression. What is interesting, however, that the values of the *F1 score* of the LDA-ASYM classifier (the best one!) observed for different copulas are similar. It means that in case of negative dependence this classifier is robust against possible variations of the type of dependence.

A close look at the definition of the *F1 score* reveals that this quality characteristic is related to the classification of "Positives", and does not take into account the quality of classification of "Negatives", which usually form a much more numerous class. So, in the next step of our analysis let us examine the impact of the strength of dependence on the performance of considered classifiers evaluated using the *G-mean*. From the definition of this characteristic one can see that quality of classification of both "Positives" and "Negatives" is taken into account in this case. In Tables VI– IX we present a similar, as above, comparison for four cases: two levels of the strength of dependence of both positive and negative sign.

TABLE VI. AVERAGE *G-mean*. THE SAME MODEL FOR TRAINING AND TEST SETS. STRONG POSITIVE DEPENDENCE

Classifier	*Normal*	*Clayton*	*Gumbel*	*Frank*
LINREG4	0.806	0.860	0.796	0.820
LINREG14	0.834	0.893	0.831	0.847
LOGREG4	0.868	0.918	0.858	0.877
LOGREG14	0.835	0.896	0.831	0.847
LDA-SYM	0.055	0.037	0.058	0.063
LDA-ASYM	0.848	0.874	0.796	0.844

The results presented in Tables VI– IX show a rather complex picture. In the case of strong positive dependence ($\tau \in [0.7, 0.9]$) between all variables the quality of classification, measured using the *G-mean*, is consistently the highest when dependencies are described by the Clayton copula. However, the differences between considered copulas are not very strong. The best results are observed for the LOGREG4 classifier based on the simple (i.e., without interactions) logistic regression. When the strength of positive dependence is weaker ($\tau \in [0.4, 0.6]$) the data generated by the Clayton copula are still classified in the best way, but in this case the best classifier is the LDA-ASYM, based on Fisher's linear discrimination model with asymmetric decision criterion. The situation changes dramatically when the dependence is negative. In both considered cases of strong negative ($\tau \in [-0.9, -0.7]$) and medium negative ($\tau \in [-0.6, -0.4]$) dependencies the best results of classification are observed for the Normal (Gaussian) copula. For the Clayton copula (the best in case of positive dependencies) the observed quality is the worst. What is also very important that in the case of negative dependencies none of the considered classifiers is the best one. However, the classifiers based on logistic regression seem to be more stable, as their performance does not depend so visibly on the strength of dependence between observed (predictors) and hidden variables.

TABLE VII. AVERAGE *G-mean*. THE SAME MODEL FOR TRAINING AND TEST SETS. MEDIUM POSITIVE DEPENDENCE

Classifier	*Normal*	*Clayton*	*Gumbel*	*Frank*
LINREG4	0.513	0.665	0.434	0.496
LINREG14	0.625	0.725	0.567	0.617
LOGREG4	0.665	0.758	0.602	0.642
LOGREG14	0.634	0.736	0.576	0.629
LDA-SYM	0.281	0.195	0.261	0.287
LDA-ASYM	0.699	0.756	0.651	0.704

TABLE VIII. AVERAGE *G-mean*. THE SAME MODEL FOR TRAINING AND TEST SETS. STRONG NEGATIVE DEPENDENCE

Classifier	*Normal*	*Clayton*	*Frank*
LINREG4	0.708	0.637	0.712
LINREG14	0.809	0.774	0.785
LOGREG4	0.815	0.731	0.790
LOGREG14	0.809	0.775	0.785
LDA-SYM	0.309	0.180	0.234
LDA-ASYM	0.370	0.305	0.300

Let us now consider an interesting case when the model of data in test sets is *different* from that of training data. In reality, it means that a classifier is used on data described by a different probability distribution than the data used during its construction. In Tables X– XI we present average values of the *Accuracy*, and in Tables XII– XIII we present average values of the *F1 score*, when the expected values of the input variables in the test sets have been randomly shifted around the values used for the generation of the training sets (by maximum $\pm 30\%$).

Similar results for the case of the *G-mean* are presented in Tables XIV– XV.

As we can expect, the values of quality indices in this case

TABLE IX. AVERAGE *G-mean*. THE SAME MODEL FOR TRAINING AND TEST SETS. MEDIUM NEGATIVE DEPENDENCE

Classifier	*Normal*	*Clayton*	*Frank*
LINREG4	0.488	0.431	0.464
LINREG14	0.566	0.557	0.545
LOGREG4	0.553	0.482	0.519
LOGREG14	0.572	0.568	0.550
LDA-SYM	0.566	0.458	0.575
LDA-ASYM	0.605	0.527	0.592

TABLE X. AVERAGE *Accuracy*. DIFFERENT MODELS FOR TRAINING AND TEST SETS. MEDIUM POSITIVE DEPENDENCE

Classifier	*Normal*	*Clayton*	*Gumbel*	*Frank*
LINREG4	0.730	0.773	0.705	0.728
LINREG14	0.678	0.741	0.670	0.687
LOGREG4	0.759	0.809	0.725	0.749
LOGREG14	0.680	0.728	0.669	0.683
LDA-SYM	0.745	0.775	0.730	0.731
LDA-ASYM	0.643	0.672	0.631	0.646

TABLE XI. AVERAGE *Accuracy*. DIFFERENT MODELS FOR TRAINING AND TEST SETS. MEDIUM NEGATIVE DEPENDENCE

Classifier	*Normal*	*Clayton*	*Frank*
LINREG4	0.765	0.738	0.757
LINREG14	0.718	0.669	0.701
LOGREG4	0.759	0.736	0.755
LOGREG14	0.717	0.666	0.693
LDA-SYM	0.527	0.423	0.529
LDA-ASYM	0.537	0.501	0.544

TABLE XII. AVERAGE *F1 score*. DIFFERENT MODELS FOR TRAINING AND TEST SETS. MEDIUM POSITIVE DEPENDENCE

Classifier	*Normal*	*Clayton*	*Gumbel*	*Frank*
LINREG4	0.317	0.440	0.259	0.300
LINREG14	0.443	0.519	0.356	0.420
LOGREG4	0.482	0.577	0.406	0.451
LOGREG14	0.452	0.528	0.367	0.430
LDA-SYM	0.138	0.126	0.101	0.124
LDA-ASYM	0.470	0.524	0.411	0.484

TABLE XIII. AVERAGE *F1 score*. DIFFERENT MODELS FOR TRAINING AND TEST SETS. MEDIUM NEGATIVE DEPENDENCE

Classifier	*Normal*	*Clayton*	*Frank*
LINREG4	0.340	0.274	0.308
LINREG14	0.367	0.394	0.372
LOGREG4	0.399	0.320	0.358
LOGREG14	0.365	0.399	0.373
LDA-SYM	0.427	0.434	0.457
LDA-ASYM	0.470	0.473	0.486

TABLE XIV. AVERAGE *G-mean*. DIFFERENT MODELS FOR TRAINING AND TEST SETS. MEDIUM POSITIVE DEPENDENCE

Classifier	*Normal*	*Clayton*	*Gumbel*	*Frank*
LINREG4	0.540	0.632	0.494	0.525
LINREG14	0.626	0.685	0.561	0.610
LOGREG4	0.652	0.723	0.599	0.629
LOGREG14	0.631	0.692	0.567	0.615
LDA-SYM	0.326	0.287	0.294	0.325
LDA-ASYM	0.653	0.692	0.618	0.661

TABLE XV. AVERAGE *G-mean*. DIFFERENT MODELS FOR TRAINING AND TEST SETS. MEDIUM NEGATIVE DEPENDENCE

Classifier	*Normal*	*Clayton*	*Frank*
LINREG4	0.499	0.461	0.473
LINREG14	0.551	0.583	0.554
LOGREG4	0.557	0.506	0.522
LOGREG14	0.549	0.587	0.558
LDA-SYM	0.572	0.479	0.581
LDA-ASYM	0.591	0.564	0.602

are lower in comparison to the case when training and test data are described by the same probability distributions. The relative changes of their values are presented in Tables XVI–XVII for *Accuracy* and *F1 score*, respectively.

TABLE XVI. RELATIVE CHANGE OF *Accuracy* DUE TO DIFFERENT MODELS FOR TRAINING AND TEST SETS

Classifier	*Normal*	*Clayton*	*Gumbel*	*Frank*
LINREG4	0.950	0.925	0.950	0.968
LINREG14	0.883	0.889	0.911	0.914
LOGREG4	0.962	0.953	0.957	0.969
LOGREG14	0.884	0.875	0.909	0.910
LDA-ASYM	0.923	0.918	0.924	0.943

TABLE XVII. RELATIVE CHANGE OF *F1 score* DUE TO DIFFERENT MODELS FOR TRAINING AND TEST SETS

Classifier	*Normal*	*Clayton*	*Gumbel*	*Frank*
LINREG4	0.887	0.785	0.974	0.925
LINREG14	0.904	0.834	0.850	0.890
LOGREG4	0.897	0.872	0.875	0.886
LOGREG14	0.904	0.837	0.853	0.884
LDA-ASYM	0.855	0.876	0.848	0.862

In the case of the *G-mean* the results are presented in Table XVIII. In this table we have deleted the LDA-SYM classifier, as its behaviour looks quite random, and thus cannot be compared with the other considered cases.

TABLE XVIII. RELATIVE CHANGE OF *G-mean* DUE TO DIFFERENT MODELS FOR TRAINING AND TEST SETS. STRONG POSITIVE DEPENDENCE

Classifier	*Normal*	*Clayton*	*Gumbel*	*Frank*
LINREG4	0.829	0.777	0.833	0.803
LINREG14	0.827	0.820	0.852	0.850
LOGREG4	0.906	0.845	0.906	0.884
LOGREG14	0.828	0.818	0.851	0.848
LDA-ASYM	0.791	0.773	0.842	0.790

The analysis of the robustness of the considered classifiers to an unexpected change of the underlying model of observed data is not simple and unequivocal. For example, in the case of data described by the Clayton copula the loss of efficiency seems to be the biggest one, so the type of data that yields the best results of classification when training and test data are generated by the same model becomes the worst one when test data are generated from a different model. When we want to compare the quality of considered classifiers, the simple logistic regression classifier (LOGREG4) still seems to be the best. However, its loss of efficiency is the best one only in the case of G-mean. There is also another interesting observation: the robustness of classifiers built on extended models (i.e., that take into account interactions) is generally worse than the robustness of simple models.

Finally, let us consider the problem how the strength of dependence influences the robustness of classifiers to an unexpected change of the underlying model of observed data. We will illustrate this problem on the example of the LOGREG4 classifier, which seems to be the best from among all classifiers considered in this paper. It seems to be quite obvious that there exists a general rule that "the stronger dependence (positive or negative) the better classification". However, the relationship between the strength and type of dependence and the quality of classification may be not so simple. In Table XIX, we show

how the values of the *F1 score* are changing for different copulas and different strengths of dependence.

TABLE XIX. AVERAGE *F1 score* FOR THE LOGREG4 CLASSIFIER. THE SAME MODEL FOR TRAINING AND TEST SETS. DIFFERENT LEVELS OF THE STRENGTH OF DEPENDENCE

Dependence	*Normal*	*Clayton*	*Gumbel*	*Frank*	*FGM*
Sp	0.799	0.866	0.813	0.813	X
Mp	0.537	0.662	0.463	0.509	X
Wp	0.041	0.062	0.044	0.052	0.052
Wn	0.088	0.060	X	0.056	0.056
Mn	0.424	0.333	X	0.379	X
Sn	0.763	0.647	X	0.730	X

The results displayed in Table XIX reflect the complexity of the stated problem. First of all, the quality of classification strongly depends upon the type of dependence described by a respective copula. Only in the case of the normal (Gaussian) copula (the classical multivariate normal distribution is a particular case of a distribution described by this copula) the relationship between the strength of dependence and the quality of classification (measured by the *F1 score*) is symmetric. For the remaining copulas this relationship is visibly asymmetric (negative dependence leads to worse classification), and the values of the *F1 score* may be quite different despite the same strength of dependence.

When the data in the test sets are generated by different models than in the training sets the values of the *F1 score* are changing. This is illustrated in Table XX for the case of the LOGREG4 classifier.

TABLE XX. AVERAGE *F1 score* FOR THE LOGREG4 CLASSIFIER. DIFFERENT MODELS FOR TRAINING AND TEST SETS. DIFFERENT LEVELS OF THE STRENGTH OF DEPENDENCE

Dependence	*Normal*	*Clayton*	*Gumbel*	*Frank*	*FGM*
Sp	0.642	0.618	0.633	0.625	X
Mp	0.482	0.577	0.406	0.451	X
Wp	0.069	0.089	0.064	0.077	0.076
Wn	0.110	0.082	X	0.074	0.075
Mn	0.399	0.320	X	0.358	X
Sn	0.648	0.558	X	0.633	X

For strong and medium positive dependencies the strongest worsening of quality of classification has been observed when data are described by the Clayton copula. However, when dependencies are negative, the case of the Normal copula seems to be the worse. It is also surprising that for weak dependencies the values of the *F1 score* have even improved. It shows that in such cases this quality index is rather inappropriate as the results of classification to great extent seem to be random.

V. CONCLUSIONS

In the paper we have evaluated six binary regression type classifiers. For the comparison we used three measures of quality: the *Accuracy* (i.e., the probability of correct classification), the *F1 score*, which is the harmonic average of *Precision* (equal to one minus the probability of type I error) and *Sensitivity* (equal to one minus the probability of type II error), and the *G-mean*, which is the geometric average of *Sensitivity* and *Specificity*. The evaluation was performed using a complex simulation software that allowed to model strongly nonlinear dependencies of different types (described by different copulas) and different strength (measured by Kendall's τ). The distinctive feature of this research is taking into consideration the impact of the type and the strength of dependence between all variables in the considered model. Moreover, we have considered a practical problem when objects classified by a certain classifier are described by a different probability distribution than the objects used for building (training) this classifier.

The performed experiments revealed that the quality of classification is strongly related to the type of dependence (type of the respective copula). This relationship may have different impact on the performance of different classifiers. For example, a simple linear regression classifier is quite robust to the change of the data model when the data are described by the Gumbel copula, but not robust when the data are described by the Clayton copula, even if the strength of dependence is in both cases the same. What is more important, and from a practical point of view quite undesirable, that the impact of the type of a specific copula strongly depends upon the sign of dependence. For example, when the data are generated by the Clayton copula the performance of considered classifiers is the best in the case of (strong) positive dependence, but the worse for the negative one.

The performed experiments do not reveal unquestionable superiority of anyone of the considered classifiers. It is hardly unexpected, as according to the famous Wolperts "no free lunch theorem" such the best classifier cannot exist. However, classifiers based on linear and logistic regressions are generally (with some exceptions) better than those based on Fisher's linear discrimination. If we take into account both the quality of classification and the robustness to the change of the underlying model, *the classifier based on a simple (without interactions) logistic regression is the best one*. This could serve as the general recommendation for practitioners. However, when some additional information is available, other classifiers could be preferred. For example, if we know that input attributes are dependent, and their dependence is described by the Frank copula, then the LDA classifier with an asymmetric decision criterion would be preferred. In practice, however, obtaining such specific information seems to be rather unlikely, so our general recommendation seems to be valid for the great majority of practical cases.

In the research described in this paper we have analysed the case with when considered classes are imbalanced. We have assumed that the class of main interest contains the minority of observations. This is a situation frequently met in practice, e.g., in medicine or in quality control. Moreover, we have analysed only the case of binary classification. The consideration of more realistic, in some applications, cases of multiple classes requires further research. Moreover, the behaviour of more complex classifiers (e.g., based on decision trees) also requires further investigation. Preliminary investigations (see, e.g., [8]) show, however, that these more complex non-linear classifiers may perform much better in the case of the same data model for training and test data (it is a usual case considered in the data mining community), but loose its superiority when the data models for training and test data sets are different, as in the case considered in this paper.

REFERENCES

[1] O. Hryniewicz, "On the robustness of regression type classifiers," in *Proceedings of INTELLI'2015*, October 11–16, St. Julians, Malta. IARIA, 2015, pp. 16–22.

[2] R. Duda, P. Hall, and D. Stork, *Pattern Classification, 2nd Edition*. Wiley, 2000.

[3] T. Hastie, R. Tibshirani, and J. Friedman, *The Elements of Statistical Learning. Data Mining, Inference and Prediction, 2nd Edition*. Springer, 2009.

[4] I. Witten, E. Frank, and F. Hall, *Data Mining. Practical Machine LearningTools and Techniques, 3rd Edition*. Morgan Kaufman, 2011.

[5] N. Japkowicz and M. Shah, *Evaluating Learning Algorithms. A Classification Perspective*. New York: Cambridge University Press, 2015.

[6] D. Hand, "Classifier technology and the illusion of progress," *Statistical Science*, vol. 21, pp. 1–14, 2006.

[7] O. Hryniewicz, "Spc of processes with predicted data: Application of the data mining methodology," in *Frontiers in Statistical Quality Control 11*, S. Knoth and W. Schmid, Eds., 2015, pp. 219–235.

[8] ——, "Process inspection by attributes using predicted data," in *Challenges in Computational Statistics*, ser. Studies in Computational Intelligence 605, S. Matwin and J. Mielniczuk, Eds. Springer Int. Publ. Switzerland, 2016, pp. 113–134.

[9] P. Embrechts, F. Lindskog, and A. McNeil, *Modelling Dependence with Copulas and Applications to Risk Management*. Amsterdam: Elsevier, 2015, ch. 8, pp. 329–384.

[10] R. Nelsen, *An Introduction To Copulas*. New York: Springer, 2006.

[11] O. Hryniewicz and J. Karpiński, "Prediction of reliability - pitfalls of using pearsons correlation," *Eksploatacja i Niezawodnosc - Maintenance and Reliability*, vol. 16, pp. 472–483, 2014.

A Context-Aware Collaborative Mobile Application for Silencing the Smartphone during Meetings or Important Events

Remus A. Dobrican, Gilles I. F. Neyens and Denis Zampunieris

University of Luxembourg
Luxembourg, Grand-Duchy of Luxembourg
Email: remus.dobrican@uni.lu, gilles.neyens@uni.lu, denis.zampunieris@uni.lu

Abstract—**This study describes a mobile application, i.e., SilentMeet, that uses group-driven collaboration and location-based collaboration for automatically switching smartphones into silent mode during meetings or important events. More precisely, for the first step of the collaboration, a partial agreement algorithm will be used for establishing if a meeting is confirmed by its participants and, for the second round, confirming if the meeting will take place, based on the location of the participants. The application tries to avoid those cases when a meeting is accepted but the participants are not coming to the meeting or when participants do not reply to the meeting invitations but they are still attending the meeting. SilentMeet uses a new technique for exchanging information, for coordinating and for taking distributed decisions, called Global Proactive Scenarios (GPaSs). For executing GPaSs, a rule-based middleware architecture for mobile devices is utilised. GPaSs and the middleware architecture allow developers of collaborative applications to define the actions of their applications in a structured way without having to take care of the communication and coordination of the mobile devices. Also, there is no need for developing a server-side application; all the logic is integrated into GPaSs. Apart the main goal of the application, which is to silence mobile phones during meetings, there are three secondary objectives: a) to provide an collaborative application capable of acquiring contextual information from various devices, b) to check if it is possible to achieve collective reasoning using a rule-based middleware architecture for mobile devices, and c) to validate GPaSs in a real-case example.**

Keywords–Mobile application; Context-Awareness; Location-based collaboration; Collective Reasoning; Proactive Computing; Middleware architecture.

I. Introduction

This work extends the previous application [1], which was checking if a meeting was potentially validated between the invited users of that meeting. The new application includes an extra checking step, based on location sharing between the mobile devices of the participants, involving multiple rounds of collaboration. Moreover, the application is taking into account contextual information such as the time and the location of the users involved in the collaboration.

Latest studies show a significant increase of mobile devices all over the world [2]. This offers great advantages for developing collaborative mobile applications. However, this brings new challenges like how to handle the high complexity of efficient collaborative mechanisms, how to detect various contexts of users that are continuously on the move or how to automate part of the user's interaction with the applications, as too many actions are required from the users in order to perform even the most basic operations.

Communication and collaboration, more precisely interactive collaboration, are two key aspects in today's mobile world. Basic mobile applications that are able to perform only local tasks do not address the increasing needs of the users any more. The demand for services and applications that support communication and collaboration of mobile devices has raised significantly in the past years [3]. The latest interest in mobile collaboration can be explained by the large number of mobile devices around the world, which is continuing to grow from one year to another [4]. However, this mobile environment capable of performing distributed operations brings new challenges, such as intermittent connectivity, data heterogeneity, limited computational capabilities and users' mobility. Also important, is the fact that mobile networks, due to the high mobility of their users [5], differ a lot from static systems, where the users are always connected. This leads to the issues like determining the context information needed to trigger the collaboration process or like users being temporarily unavailable while they are still engaged in the collaborative operations.

Another important aspect to be addressed, when designing collaborative applications, is to establish up to which level will the users interact with the system. Because users may have basic skills or only limited experience when interacting with complex applications or because they do not want to spend a lot of their time giving instructions to the system, the applications can automate a lot of their processes. One of the solutions for doing this is Proactive Systems, which are able to act on their own initiative and to take decisions on behalf of their users [6]. Recently, the possibility of implementing a Proactive Engine for mobile devices was investigated [7]. The added value is that, with the help of a mobile Proactive System, which is essentially an advanced rule-based system, developers can directly add the functionality they want to their applications by using Proactive Rules. From the developer's point of view, a Proactive Rule represents a tool for writing a set of instructions, while from the system's point of view, a Proactive Rule is a piece of code that has to be executed. More about Proactive Rules and examples with the rules used for this study will be shown in Section V-C.

In order to have a rule-based system capable of executing Proactive Rules on mobile devices, a middleware model was created for Android-based mobile devices [8]. This represents an important achievement as until now only lightweight basic rule-based engines like [9] and [10] were developed for mobile platforms. These engines would allow applications to use simple conditional rules. The middleware model is also providing an information sharing method between the devices called Global Proactive Scenario (GPaS) [11]. This method was implemented to give the possibility to the applications to perform collaborative tasks.

In this study, we investigate how a context-aware mobile application, i.e., SilentMeet, which uses a proactive rule-based middleware system, is automatically turning the devices into silent mode if a meeting is detected and confirmed between a predefined group of users and if the location of the users is the same as the location of the meeting, on the same date, at approximatively the same hour.

The rest of the paper is structured as follows. Section II discusses related work relevant to this study. Section III introduces the problem statement and a situation that points out the need for automatizing certain tasks and processes inside applications in order to reduce the user's involvement in unnecessary situations. Section IV contains explanations about SilentMeet's architecture, design and about its way of reaching a global decision based on multiple rounds of collaboration. The Proactive Scenarios that were used for this application and the Proactive Rules that compose them are explained in Section V. Tests on real devices are discussed in Section VI and their results in Section VI-B. And finally, Section VII contains the main conclusions and future work.

II. RELATED WORK

Related work was divided into several categories considered relevant for this study. The first one examines context-aware mobile collaborative systems, where the focus is on the context of groups of users, the second one discusses relevant collaborative middleware architectures, the third one has examples of collaborative mobile applications developed for other fields than the ones that turn the mobile phone into silent mode and the last one contains several examples of mobile applications developed for silencing smartphones in various situations.

A. Context-aware mobile collaborative systems

A key characteristic of mobile collaborative systems, where groups of users perform common activities and have the same interests, is the ability to acquire different contextual information from multiple sources, not only from local, individual sources. The idea is that multiple devices can observe and reason about the same event from different angles. Multiple frameworks were developed to ease the creation of context-aware mobile applications [12] [13] [14], but the aspect of reasoning about the shared contextual information, coming from multiple applications, was not explored. Wang et.al [15] propose a context-aware strategy for collaborative mobile applications based on location. However, the collaboration process is limited as the context information depends only on the near proximity of the participants. Despite a collaborative strategy for sharing context between devices, the authors only provide in [16] a simple integration of the context, which is just added to the knowledge base.

B. Collaborative Middleware Architectures

Numerous studies [5][17][18] have been conducted that provide middleware architectures as tools for developing collaborative applications. One important difference is that these studies look at collaboration from a different angle. More precisely, they concentrate on user-centred collaboration, where the focus is to get the users to interact more and more with their applications on the mobile devices. The issue is that these applications would depend too much on the actions of their users and, if the users do not engage properly in each step of their interaction with their devices, the applications may remain at the same step. Opposite to this, Proactive Computing, which was defined by Tennenhouse as a new way of computing, for and on behalf of the user [19], tries to reduce the users' involvement by automatizing some processes. By doing so, the users can concentrate more on the most important parts of the collaboration. MobiSoC [20], a middleware enabling mobile social applications, showed on initial tests indicated that this framework provided good response times for 1000 users for location-based matching and place-based matching.

C. Collaborative Mobile Applications

Using the WMP (WatchMyPhone) toolkit, a shared text editing collaborative application was developed in [21] with the help of Mobilis Framework [22]. The proposed toolkit is compressed into a library and can be used by other collaborative applications by including this library into their project. Another domain where collaboration is crucial is represented by mobile-based games. In [23], the authors created a mobile game based on collaborative game play. The game was developed on top of a middleware architecture. However, the whole framework consisted not only from a client side middleware but also from a server side middleware.

D. Applications for silencing the Smartphone

Many mobile applications exist on the market, like Silence[24], Go Silent [25] or Advanced Silent Mode [26], which automatically switch off the sounds of mobile devices based on the user's preferences. These simple applications are focused on one user and perform only local tasks like checking the user's predefined preferences or detecting calendar events. They do not use any kind of collaboration with other devices to make the application smarter.

For example, SilentTime [27] searches for weekly events in the local schedule and automatically silences the user's phone if a future event is detected. It offers the user the possibility to add exceptions, in case he/she is waiting for an important phone call. However, the application has a couple of downsides. First, it is exclusively based on the user's input, i.e., a calendar event or exceptions of a special situations will only be detected if the user creates them before, and second, it does not use any kind of communication with other devices to check if the events will take place or not. Another example is AutoSilent [28], which is slightly different from SilentTime because it adds an extra step of verification before muting the user's phone, i.e., it will verify if the user's location corresponds with the event's location at a certain time. This extra feature is again just a simple check because it does not use any kind of collaboration, like, for example, checking also the location of the other participants.

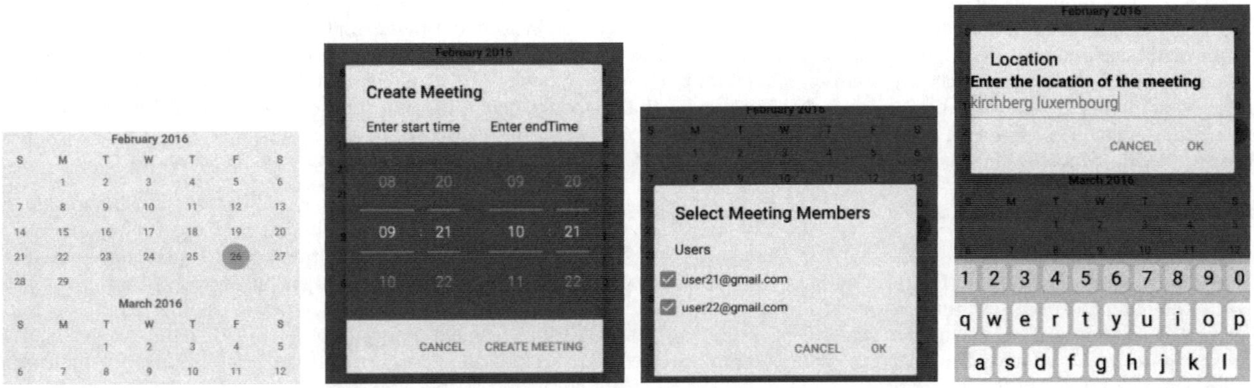

(a) The main screen of the SilentMeet (b) Selecting the start and end time of a meeting (c) Selecting users from the same group for sending meeting invitations (d) Entering the location of the Meeting

Figure 1. Creating a meeting

Figure 2. Receiving a meeting invitation

III. Problem Statement

There are quite a few mobile users who went through embarrassing situations when their phones rang during important meetings, lectures, exams, presentations, concerts, interviews or key talks offered at international conferences. Imagine, for example, that during a viola recital of a famous musician, the mobile phone of a person start ringing, like it did during a recital in Slovakia [29]. The musician is not only interrupted but he/she could also loose focus and find it difficult to continue. There are many more other examples when muting the phone is a mandatory requirement. The main problem is that each user has to manually configure his/her phone to be silent during important events. And often, they forget. A general common strategy or approach which performs collaborative actions is missing.

Let us imagine the following real-world situation: an important event is about to begin. The mobile devices of the participants, located in their pockets, go automatically into silent mode. The participants do not have to worry they forgot to silence their mobile phones, they can focus more on their important tasks. The meeting can continue without any interruptions or embarrassing situations.

IV. A Rule-Based Solution - SilentMeet

SilentMeet is a mobile collaborative application that is developed in order to minimize the risk of interruptions and their distracting effects during an important event such as a meeting, interview or public event. Moreover, in order to have an efficient collaboration algorithm, part of the user's actions are automated by using Proactive Computing. The main difference between SilentMeet and other applications is that SilentMeet does additional checks, based on collaboration with the other mobile devices, to establish if a meeting is taking place or not. More precisely, it checks, among the possible participants of the meeting, if there are at least 2 users that have accepted to attend the meeting and have the meeting in their calendar, and, finally, on the date of the meeting, it will check the location of the users 15 minutes before the start of the meeting. The additional checks are necessary for trying to avoid cases such as silencing a smartphone even if the meeting is not taking place.

A. The graphical user interface (GUI)

SilentMeet is an application developed for the Android Operating System and consists of a main Activity with a calendar view working as a date picker, laid out in Figure 1a. The basic idea is to provide the user with a simple interface for creating the meeting, i.e., selecting the participants for this meeting, the place where the meeting will take place and the starting and ending hour of the meeting. In Figure 1, an example of creating a meeting using SilentMeet is provided. At the start, the user selects a date from the calendar when the meeting should take place. The date of the meeting should be higher or equal to the current date otherwise the meeting will not be created. Afterwards, a new dialog opens asking the user for the start time and end time of the meeting, as shown in Figure 1b. Again, the start time has to be bigger than the current time if the meeting is on the same day or, if the meeting is on a further day, the start time has to be smaller than the end time.

Then, the user has to select the participants for the meeting. He/she will have to choose from a list of predefined users, as presented in Figure 1c, i.e., the users that have agreed to be part of the same group for creating future meetings. Additional information about how these groups are created are given in Section IV-B. And finally, before sending the invitation to the other members, the user has to input the location of the meeting, depicted in Figure 1d. The location is given by the user as text, which is then converted into GPS coordinates. These coordinates are stored locally on the phone, and, just before the meeting takes place, they are compared with the current GPS coordinates.

The members selected for the meeting receive an invitation with the date, location, start time and end time of the meeting, depicted in Figure 2. Then, a user can accept, reject or not respond to the invitation by selecting another area on the application's screen. If the invitation is accepted, the response is sent back to the initiator of the meeting. For a meeting to be confirmed there needs to be at least 2 participants that accepted to participate. The initiator of the meeting can cancel anytime the meeting if he/she decides that the meeting should take place only if all the invited members accept the invitation or for other reasons.

B. Grouping the participants for a meeting

We assume that groups of people are predefined when an event is created by each user. More precisely, when a calendar event is created, the user also adds the participants. Users can perform collaborative actions only if they are part of the same group of the same event. So, users first have to build their own groups or agree to be part of already created groups. For example, in a company, the secretary of a department creates a group for the employees of that department that have meetings regularly. By joining this group, the members agree that their mobile phones can be silenced by the application of the other members, after multiple rounds of negotiation. More about the negotiation process is presented in Section V-I. Also, more conditions and checks are taken into account like the location of the event and the participants, the date and the hour of the event and the local preferences of each user. In Figure 1c, a user is about to start a new meeting and decides to invite both members of his/her group, i.e., *user21@gmail.com* and *user22@gmail.com*, to this meeting. In this example, these members are part of the same group as the user that creates the new meeting, i.e., *user20@gmail.com*. More about how the users are recognized by the application and how their IDs are handled and the possibility of having multiple groups is explained in Section VI.

C. Middleware model - Proactive Engine for Mobile Devices

The Proactive Engine (PE) for mobile devices is a framework created to support the development of collaborative applications. It contains a middleware architecture capable of executing tasks in the background, of automatically exchanging information with other PEs and of performing actions specific for each application in a structured way. From a technical point of view, the only thing the framework needs from the application developers is a set of Proactive Rules, which is then analyzed, processed and executed. The Proactive Rules represent the structured method of an application of passing instructions to the PE.

1) The Rules Engine: The Rules Engine is the core of the Proactive Engine and is used to process rules provided by different applications [8]. It it composed of two Queues, i.e., two FIFO(first in first out) lists, which contain rules to be executed at each iteration. It is continuously checking for rules to be executed each n seconds, where n is a parameter for establishing the frequency of the checking.

2) Communication between PEs: PEs communicate with each other by sending JavaScript Object Notation (JSON) messages. The messages can contain questions, answers or commands, depending on their purpose. For example, a Proactive Engine can send a question to another engine to ask for various context information. Based on the received answer, if some conditions are fulfilled, the engine can then send a command to the other engine to perform an action. Messages are forwarded to a local server and to Google's Cloud Messaging(GCM) server on the cloud. The GCM server is in charge of assigning each device with a device ID and with forwarding the JSON messages to the targeted devices. They also handle special cases such as lost JSON messages or devices that are not temporarily available on the network. Message forwarding is done either via WiFi or via 3G/4G, if available. The users of SilentMeet have to have unique identifiers, e.g., in this case unique email addresses, because the PE needs to know where to forward the message or the request for additional information.

V. Proactive Scenarios

A Proactive Scenario is the high-level representation of a set of Proactive Rules that is meant to be executed on the Proactive Engine. It describes a situation and a set of actions to be taken in case some conditions are met. For example, creating a meeting with SilentMeet is achieved with the help of a Proactive Scenario. The set of actions includes defining the date, time, location and the members of the meeting, asking for the members' confirmation, altering the GUI of the application, etc. For each of these actions a Proactive Rule is defined. The Proactive Scenario also consists of defining the order of how the Proactive Rules should be generated and executed by the Proactive Engine. More precisely, a Proactive Rule that asks members for confirming the meeting will only be triggered after a meeting is defined, by another Proactive Rule, on the smartphone of the person that initiated the meeting. Proactive Scenarios are divided into two main categories: Local Proactive Scenarios and Global Proactive Scenarios. An application can have a combination of both types of scenarios depending on its goals.

A. Local Proactive Scenarios (LPaSs)

This type of scenarios is used when defining a situation where only local actions are performed and no collaboration with other devices is needed. They range from simple scenarios that perform simple actions like creating other scenarios when some conditions are fulfilled to complex scenarios, e.g., when the system needs to acquire relevant context information for changing different parameters in order to increase the performance of a PE. Previous examples of LPaSs include supporting students in their learning process through the creation of coaching messages inside their Learning Management System

(LMS) [30] and the creation, maintenance and termination of social groups inside a LMS [31].

B. Global Proactive Scenarios (GPaSs)

On the other hand, a GPaS is a data exchange mechanism, which involves the collaboration of one or more devices. It is based on the data acquisition from multiple sources and it works between all mobile devices with an integrated Proactive Engine. The new generation of interactive applications need collaborative methods that will allow them to find more advanced solutions for addressing existing challenges.

The idea of SilentMeet is that the devices participating in a collaboration process can take decisions based on global information, coming from other PEs, which enhances the local information. Each device is able to make use of the global knowledge that is created by all the devices involved in the collaboration. For example, a basic application would only be able to detect an event based on the local information provided by the calendar of a device. SilentMeet is able to query all the relevant devices to obtain more precise information about that event by using a particular GPaS.

SilentMeet uses two GPaSs: one for creating and establishing if a meeting will take place and the other one to check, just before the meeting, the location of the users and to decide if they are close to the meeting's location in order to put the mobile phones into silent mode. A meeting is confirmed in two steps: the first step checks if the participants of the meeting have accepted the invitation to the meeting and have that particular meeting in their calendars, and the second step checks the location of the participants to see if it corresponds with the meeting's location, on the exact date, 15 minutes before the meeting is about to start. This algorithm with all the extra checking steps is useful because we want to avoid false positives, i.e., those cases where the meeting is not taking place but the phones are still put into silent mode.

1) Global Proactive Scenario 1.: The purpose of the first GPaS is to create a meeting and establish if a meeting is confirmed by checking with the mobile devices of the other participants. This is only the first step of verifying if the meeting is going to take place. It is necessary for starting the second verification step, i.e., the second GPaS. Each device needs additional information from the other devices before taking a decision. The idea is that if multiple devices, part of a collaboration group, have an event in their local calendar, with the same date, time and location, it is very probable that the event will take place. We presume that the same information about an event coming from 2 different devices part of the same group is enough for the application to decide what to do next, e.g., in this case, it will activate the second GPaS. The minimum number of 2 devices is motivated by the fact that a device should not be able to mute, by itself, other devices without any kind of agreement. This GPaS allows a decision to be taken without the confirmation of the meeting coming from all the participants, as this is very difficult to achieve in real-life situations, where each user is expected to manually add the event into the calendar.

2) Global Proactive Scenario 2.: The second GPaS is in charge of the second verification step by exchanging the location of participants, if they are close to the meeting's location. So, it is not enough for accepting the invitation when the meeting is created by a user, for example, 1 week before the actual meeting takes place, but there are 2 extra steps to be completed. The first one is that the users that accepted the invitation have to be near the location of the meeting 15 minutes before the meeting will begin and the second one is that they have to exchange their location with at least one other participant that is also near the meeting's location. Only when these steps are fulfilled, the silent mode will be activated. These extra steps of verification are useful for cases when even if persons confirm their attendance at a meeting, they are stuck in traffic, or they had an emergency and cannot attend the meeting, and so, activating the silent mode on their smartphones is not necessary.

```java
public abstract class AbstractRule implements
    Serializable{

 @DatabaseField(generatedId = true)
 private long id;

 private boolean activated;
 protected QueueManager engine;

 public AbstractRule(){} // default constructor

 // methods to be implemented
 protected abstract void dataAcquisition();
 protected abstract boolean activationGuards();
 protected abstract boolean conditions();
 protected abstract boolean actions();
 protected abstract boolean rulesGeneration();

 @Override
 public abstract String toString();

 // method used for creating other Rules
 // or for cloning the same rule
 public final void createRule(final
     AbstractRule rule){...}

 // the order of the execution of the methods
 public final boolean execute(){
   dataAcquisition();
   if(activationGuards()){
     this.activated=true;
     if(conditions()){
       actions();
     }
   }
   boolean ret=rulesGeneration();
   return ret;
 }

 // setters and getters
 ...
}
```

Figure 3. The code of the AbstractRule in Java

C. Proactive Rules

GPaSs are composed of sets of Proactive Rules, which are written by the developer and which, among others, contain a series of instructions. These rules are to be executed by the Proactive Engine when their activation conditions are met, such as, when different events are detected or when they are missing. The initial structure of a Proactive Rule [32] was used for creating the rules necessary for SilentMeet. It contains 5 main parts such as *data acquisition*, *activation guards*, *conditions*, *actions* and *rules generation*, as depicted in Figure 3, where the code of the **AbstractRule** is provided in the Java programming language used for the Android Operating System. All the other Proactive Rules extend the **AbstractRule**, meaning they have to implement its methods. These methods are important as they decide when a rule is executed, if the rule performs its actions, if the rule will generate other rules or will just simply clone itself. Proactive Rules can have different execution times because their activation depends on the local settings of each device and on the user's actions. For example, 2 users creating a new calendar event at different hours on their phones, trigger, at different time intervals, the rule that starts the negotiation process of SilentMeet.

The SilentMeet application is composed of 2 GPaSs, each being implemented through a small set of proactive rules. These rules are installed together with SilentMeet's user interfaces on each mobile device equipped with a Proactive Engine. Initially, only the Proactive Rules that will continue to clone themselves and be in the Queue at each iteration will be executed by the Proactive Engine. Then, all the rules can be activated, if their execution conditions are met. One of the rules that is executed at the beginning by the PE is called **RegisterToServerRule** that registers the user on the GCM server, if not already registered. This will give the user a unique ID, which is then used in the communication with the other PEs.

D. Proactive Rules that compose the first GPaS

GPaS1 is composed of 4 Proactive Rules, i.e., **R011**, **R021**, **R012** and **R022**. **R011** is one of the rules that is running from the beginning, when the application is installed, and is checking for new meetings in the local database. The code of rule **R011** is shown in Figure 4. The PE executes an Iteration each 5 seconds, so, **R011** will be checking each 5 seconds for a new meeting. When creating a meeting, as seen in Figure 1, SilentMeet registers the meeting's location, date, start time, end time and the persons invited to that meeting. The status of the meeting, after it was created locally, is *pending* and *unsent*. **R011** checks for all the pending unsent meetings, this step being part of the **data acquisition** method of this rule, and, only if such meetings are detected, the **actions** method will be activated. Inside this method, an invitation will be sent to the users selected to attend the meeting. The invitation will contain all the meeting's details like its location, start time, end time, date and members. The name of rule to be activated on the receiving PEs is included among the parameters when the message is sent to the receiving PEs. And so, rule **R021** will be activated on the devices of the receivers. For example, if user1 decides to create a meeting and invite user2 and user3 to that meeting, on the devices of user2 and user3 the PE will activate rule **R021**.

When rule **R021** gets activated, it means that the receiver of the message is invited to a new meeting. In its **data acquisition** phase it looks in its own calendar if there is no other meeting

```
@DatabaseTable(tableName="R011")
public class R011 extends AbstractRule{

   // local parameters
   private long startTime, date;
   private boolean newMeeting = false;
   private List<Meeting> meetings;

   @Override
   protected void dataAcquisition() {
      // if a new meeting is detected
      newMeeting = engine.getLpeDBWrapper().
          isNewMeeting();
   }
   ...
   @Override
   protected boolean conditions() {
      return newMeeting;
   }

   @Override
   protected boolean actions() {
      meetings = engine.getLpeDBWrapper().
          getListOfPendingMeetings();
      ArrayList<Object> p; // paramsToSent

      for(Meeting m : meetings) {
         p = new ArrayList<Object>();
         p.add(m.getMembers());
         p.add(m.getDay());
         ...
         p.add(m.getLocationLongitude());
         p.add(engine.getContext().
             getResources().
             getString(R.string.mail));

         ArrayList<String> deviceIDs = new
             ArrayList<String>
             (Arrays.asList(m.getMembers()));
         try {
            if(!engine.getLpeDBWrapper().
                meetingRequestWasSent
                (m.getId())){
               engine.sendMessage("R021", p,
                   deviceIDs, 100);
               SentMeeting sentMeeting = new
                   SentMeeting(m.getId());
               engine.getLpeDBWrapper().
                   save(sentMeeting);
            }
         } catch (Exception e){
            Log.e("R011", "message was not
                sent");
         }
      }
      return true;
   }

   @Override
   protected boolean rulesGeneration() {
      createRule(this);
      return true;
   }
   ...
}
```

Figure 4. Proactive Rule R011 in Java

```
public class R024 extends AbstractRule{
    ...
    @Override
 protected boolean actions() {
      AudioManager am = (AudioManager)
          engine.
          getContext().getSystemService
          (Context.AUDIO_SERVICE);
        //For Silent mode
     am.setRingerMode
         (AudioManager.RINGER_MODE_SILENT);
      return true;
    }
    ...
}
```

Figure 5. Devices used for testing SilentMeet, in the process of receiving an invitation for a meeting

on that specific date and time and if this invitation has not already been accepted. If these conditions are satisfied, then this rule will trigger a pop-up dialogue on the mobile phone of this user to ask him/her if he/she accepts to attend this meeting, as seen in Figure 2. The operations are part of the **actions** phase of the rule. This rule does not generate other rules and does not clone itself. When receiving the invitation inside the pop-up, the user has 3 options: accepts the invitation, rejects the invitation or does not respond to the invitation by changing the application or by clicking on another part of the screen. In case he/she accepts the meeting, rule **R012** gets activated.

Even though **R012** is one of the rules which is executed by the PE at each iteration, it only gets activated when the conditions are true, i.e., the user accepts or rejects a meeting. The immediate effect, if the conditions are true, is to send the response to all the users invited to attend the meeting. If the answer of the user is positive and he/she accepts to join the meeting, then, at this particular moment, there are at least 2 persons that accepted to attend the meeting. In case the answer is negative, the device of the same user will register the meeting as refused and even if the meeting will still take place with the other participants, the devices of this user will not be switched into silent mode.

The receiving devices activate rule **R022** that gets as parameters the answer of a user with regard to a specific meeting invitation. If the answer is positive and the meeting is confirmed by at least 2 persons, the second GPaS will be activated. If the answer is negative, the device of the initiator of the meeting still waits until all the answers from the invited members will be received. Until then, the meeting will be in *pending* mode. If all the answers are negative or part negative and part unanswered before the meeting starts, the meeting will be considered as *canceled*.

E. Proactive Rules that compose the second GPaS

GPaS2 is composed of 3 Proactive Rules, i.e., **R013**, **R023** and **R024**. **R013** is only activated when a meeting has been created and accepted by at least 2 participants. It will check the current time on the device, and, if it is equal or less but not more than the meeting's start time minus 15 minutes, it will


```
{
  "PARAMETER_TYPES":[
    "String[]",
    "Integer",
    "Integer",
    "Integer",
    "Integer",
    "Integer",
    "Integer",
    "Integer",
    "Double",
    "Double",
    "String"
  ],
  "PARAMETER_VALUES":[
    [
      "user20@gmail.com",
      "user22@gmail.com"
    ],
    29,
    3,
    2016,
    19,
    6,
    20,
    6,
    49.6278694,
    6.153422,
    "user21@gmail.com"
  ]
}
```


Figure 6. An example of a JSON message that is passed between R011 and R021, when a meeting is created

start to check for the location of the device. If the location also corresponds to the location of the meeting, then the condition for executing the rule's **actions** are met. These actions include sending a message to the other participants to confirm the device's presence at the meeting's location. After sending the message, the device of this user that activated **R013** waits for receiving at least one message from another PE of a participant in order to activate the last rule, i.e., **R024**, which turns the smartphone into silent mode. Checking for the location of the user every 5 seconds consumes a lot of battery, so, this action is performed only when the current timestamp approximatively corresponds to the meeting's timestamp.

Upon receiving the message from one user that is close to the meeting's location, the PE of the other participants activate **R023**. This rule tells the local PE that there is at least 1 person attending the meeting and so, has permission to switch the smartphone into silent mode if the local PE is close to the meeting's location. If this last condition is carried out then the last rule is activated, i.e., rule **R024**.

The last rule of GPaS2 is in charge of finally silencing the mobile phone during that meeting. The only way this rule is executed by the PE is to get through all the previous collaboration steps of both GPaSs and to fulfill all the necessary conditions of each rule. The command for silencing the device is given in the **actions** phase of the rules, as seen in Figure 5. So, a user that did not reply with yes or no for attending

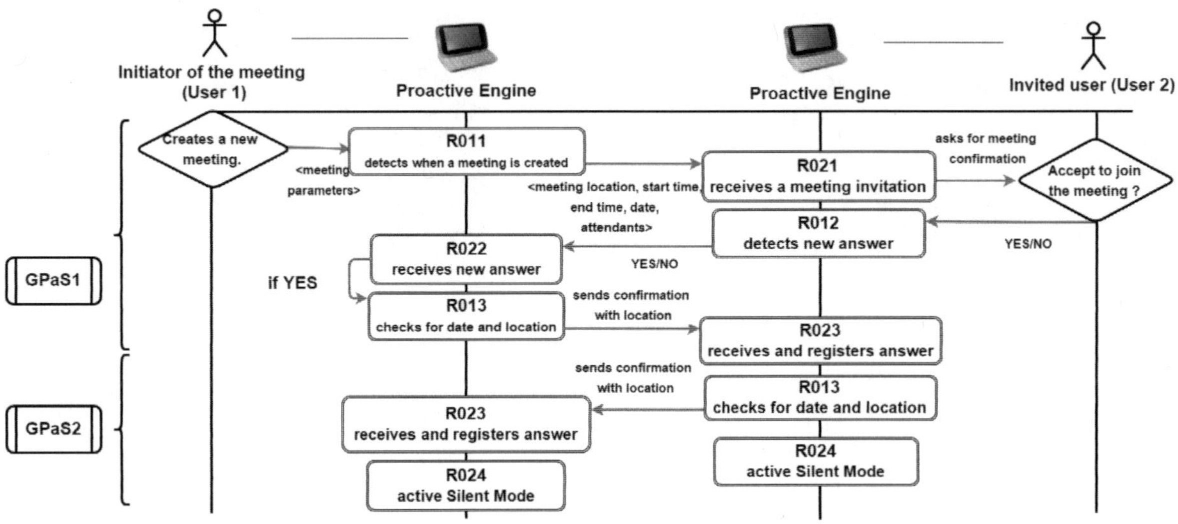

Figure 7. Sequence diagram with the collaboration steps of SilentMeet

the meeting, can have his/her mobile phone switch into silent mode if his/her device are close to the meeting's location, on the same date and same hour as the meeting. SilentMeet considers that by fulfilling these conditions the device is very likely to participate at that meeting, even though it did not provide a precise answer. This case includes a hybrid algorithm for establishing if a meeting will take place or not. The existing algorithms either check for an entry in the calendar or, more advanced applications, just check for the location of the current user but not the other users' location.

F. Cyclic Proactive Rules

A Proactive Rule can have the property of being *cyclic* if it continues to clone itself and gets executed by the PE at each iteration. For example, rules **R011**, **R012** and **R013** are *cyclic* because they need to continuously check for new meetings, for new answers from the users or for matching dates and locations of meetings. Cyclic rules can be generated by other rules and do not have to run from the beginning, when the PE starts.

G. Non-Cyclic Proactive Rules

Rules such as **R021**, **R022**, **R023** and **R024** are non-cyclic because they contain specific actions that need to be performed only once. They are usually triggered by other rules and are part of a chain of rules. Multiple examples of chains of rules are given in Figure 7. For instance, one chain starts with rule **R011** and ends with **R021**, which receives an invitation to attend a new meeting.

H. Message Exchange between Proactive Rules

Proactive Engines exchange information between each other with the help of JSON messages. The messages can contain commands to activate certain Proactive Scenarios or they can contain just simple context information. Figure 6 shows the content of a JSON message that is exchanged between Proactive Engines. More exactly, when a meeting is created on the device of the user with the email address *user21@gmail.com*, rule **R011** gets activated and sends a message to *user20@gmail.com* and to *user22@gmail.com*. The devices that get the invitation to the meeting activate rule **R021**, which receives precise data about the date, start time, end time, location, sender and list of invited members of the meeting.

I. Collaboration Process

For muting the mobile devices of the participants of a group, after a calendar event is detected, SilentMeet passes through a couple of rounds of collaboration. These rounds of collaborations are depicted in Figure 7 with the help of a sequence diagram. Moreover, it is shown how rules are activated by other rules. This example shows what will happen on the PE from the beginning of GPaS1, when a meeting is created on one smartphone, until the end of GPaS2, when the meeting is confirmed and the devices are silenced. The first GPaS can be activated, for example, 1 week before the meeting actually takes places but the second GPaS needs to wait until the same date and approximatively the same hour of the meeting to get activated. A user can receive multiple invitations in the same time and does not have to worry about how they will be handled. This is done automatically by the Proactive Engine. The collaboration process depends on the communication of PEs, which depends as well on the connectivity setting of each mobile device. The PE performs also error checking and handling in case a message is lost somewhere in the network and no answer is received from other PEs.

VI. TESTS

Tests were conducted locally at our university on 3 different devices: a Samsung Galaxy Note 3 and two Samsung Galaxy S6, as shown in Figure 8. All 3 devices use an Android

Figure 8. Devices used for testing SilentMeet, in the process of receiving an invitation for a meeting

operating system and have SilentMeet on top of the Proactive Engine middleware installed in order to be able to execute rules and collaborate with each other. The devices were part of a predefined group of 3 participants with the following email addresses used as unique identifiers: *user20@gmail.com*, *user21@gmail.com* and *user22@gmail.com*. During the tests, all 3 devices were connected via WiFi to the same network. Initially, all the devices had their sound turned on.

In the first series of tests, the user with the email address *user20@gmail.com* and using the Samsung Galaxy Note 3 was the initiator of a meeting and created it on SilentMeet's local calendar. The meeting was set to happen after 10 minutes of its creation time, on the same date, in the same location as all the devices, i.e., the campus at our university. The invitation was displayed on the screen of the 2 other mobile phones and, after the meeting was accepted by both guests, it was marked in the calendar of SilentMeet. The devices started immediately to check their locations, compared it to the meeting's location and shared it with the other guests, as the start time of the meeting was very close to the current time, i.e., less then 15 minutes difference. All 3 devices were silenced when the meeting started.

The second series of tests happened in the same conditions as the first tests except with one minor detail: one of the invited users did not accept or reject the meeting proposal. However, the minimum of 2 persons that accepted the invitation was reached and so, all the devices had activated GPaS2, which checked their locations before the start of the meeting. Because all the other conditions were accomplished, the 3 devices were silenced again when the meeting started.

For the third series of tests, the 3 users that were part of the meeting proposal accepted the invitation but only one user was at the same location as the location of the meeting, i.e., the user with the email *user20@gmail.com*. The device of this user did not get a location confirmation from the other 2 users so it did not switch into silent mode. Neither the 2 devices of the 2 other users.

A. *Measurements*

The main goal was to check if the application behaved as expected in the most common cases, e.g., when all the users confirmed their presence at a meeting and their location is the same as the meeting's location when it started, as well as the unusual situations. These unusual situations include not providing an answer of participating to a meeting but still attending that meeting, accepting the meeting invitation but not coming to the meeting or being the only one present at a confirmed meeting where nobody else is present.

B. *Results and discussions*

The tests showed that the application behaves as expected and that all three devices were muted after the negotiation process. In the given settings, it took around 10 seconds to reach a common agreement that the meeting will take place and to mute all three devices. However, this time is highly dependent on the frequency parameter of the Rule Engine, meaning that setting a lower time interval between two iterations will also lead to a faster execution of the GPaS.

VII. CONCLUSION AND FUTURE WORK

In this paper, we demonstrate that it is possible to easily design and implement a context-aware collaborative application on top of a rule-based middleware engine and with the help of Proactive Computing, more precisely, by using Global Proactive Scenarios. SilentMeet is able to detect and acquire relevant context-information about calendar events, to use a collective reasoning algorithm to establish if a meeting will take place or not and to take decisions of silencing the smartphone, based on the shared locations of the users. Furthermore, the location sharing process is handled very efficient in order to reduce the unnecessary battery consumption.

At the same time, several parts of the collaboration process were automated and the user's involvement reduced only to the most important operations. SilentMeet reduces the possibility of having meetings in the calendar that do not take place any more or which are canceled by the other participants. The smartphone turns into silent mode only when multiple conditions are met, reducing thus the risk of having the smartphone on mute when not attending any event. With only two GPaSs, composed of seven Proactive Rules, it is enough to achieve SilentMeet's goals.

Short term future work includes extending the application for checking for meetings not only in the calendar provided by the application but on the local calendar of the smartphone together with the calendar of other applications that are intensively used, such as Google's Calendar or the Outlook Calendar. Another point would be to enhance SilentMeet to allow the users to create, with the help of an additional GPaS, their own groups of people for meetings that happen more regularly. Long term developing more complex collaborative applications and other Global Proactive Scenarios on top of the Proactive Engine. These applications could have different application fields such as tele-medicine, transportation or e-Learning, where collaboration is a key aspect.

REFERENCES

[1] R.-A. Dobrican, G. Neyens, and D. Zampunieris, "Silentmeet-a prototype mobile application for real-time automated group-based collaboration," in Proceedings of the 5th International Conference on Advanced Collaborative Networks, Systems and Applications (COLLA 2015). IARIA, 2015, pp. 52–56.

[2] Kate Dreyer. Mobile Internet Usage Skyrockets in Past 4 Years to Overtake Desktop as Most Used Digital Platform. comScore. [Online]. Available: https://www.comscore.com/Insights/Blog/Mobile-Internet-Usage-Skyrockets-in-Past-4-Years-to-Overtake-Desktop-as-Most-Used-Digital-Platform (2015)

[3] Forrester. Latest IT Trends For Secure Mobile Collaboration. Forrester Consulting. [Online]. Available: http://www.connectedfuturesmag.com/docs/byod_forrester_tap_latest_it_trends_wp_en.pdf [retrieved: May, 2015]

[4] CISCO. VNI Mobile Forecast Highlights. CISCO Systems. [Online]. Available: http://www.cisco.com/c/dam/assets/sol/sp/vni/forecast_highlights_mobile/index.html [retrieved: May, 2015]

[5] V. Sacramento and et al., "MoCA: A Middleware for Developing Collaborative Applications for Mobile Users," Distributed Systems Online, IEEE, vol. 5, no. 10, Oct 2004, pp. 2–2.

[6] A. Salovaara and A. Oulasvirta, "Six modes of proactive resource management: a user-centric typology for proactive behaviors," in Proceedings of the third Nordic conference on Human-computer interaction. ACM, 2004, pp. 57–60.

[7] R.-A. Dobrican and D. Zampunieris, "Moving Towards Distributed Networks of Proactive, Self-Adaptive and Context-Aware Systems: a New Research Direction?" The International Journal on Advances in Networks and Services, vol. 7, 2014, pp. 262–272, ISSN: 1942-2644.

[8] G. I. F. Neyens, R.-A. Dobrican, and D. Zampunieris, "Enhancing Mobile Devices with Cooperative Proactive Computing," COLLA - The Fifth International Conference on Advanced Collaborative Networks, Systems and Applications, 2015, to be published.

[9] M. Slazynski, S. Bobek, and G. J. Nalepa, "Migration of Rule Inference Engine to Mobile Platform. Challenges and Case Study," in Proceedings of 10th Workshop on Knowledge Engineering and Software Engineering (KESE10) co-located with 21st European Conference on Artificial Intelligence (ECAI 2014), Prague, Czech Republic, August 19 2014., 2014. [Online]. Available: http://ceur-ws.org/Vol-1289/kese10-08_submission_4.pdf

[10] C. Choi, I. Park, S. J. Hyun, D. Lee, and D. H. Sim, "MiRE: A minimal rule engine for context-aware mobile devices," in Third IEEE International Conference on Digital Information Management (ICDIM), November 13-16, 2008, London, UK, Proceedings, 2008, pp. 172–177.

[11] R. Dobrican and D. Zampunieris, "A Proactive Approach for Information Sharing Strategies in an Environment of Multiple Connected Ubiquitous Devices," in Proceedings of the International Symposium on Ubiquitous Systems and Data Engineering (USDE 2014) in conjunction with 11th IEEE International Conference on Ubiquitous Intelligence and Computing (UIC 2014). IEEE, 2014, pp. 763–771.

[12] E. Benítez-Guerrero, C. Mezura-Godoy, and L. G. Montané-Jiménez, "Context-aware mobile collaborative systems: Conceptual modeling and case study," Sensors, vol. 12, no. 10, 2012, pp. 13 491–13 507.

[13] E. Williams and J. Gray, "Contextion: A framework for developing context-aware mobile applications," in Proceedings of the 2nd International Workshop on Mobile Development Lifecycle. ACM, 2014, pp. 27–31.

[14] S. Elmalaki, L. Wanner, and M. Srivastava, "Caredroid: Adaptation framework for android context-aware applications," in Proceedings of the 21st Annual International Conference on Mobile Computing and Networking. ACM, 2015, pp. 386–399.

[15] W. Wang, J. Gu, J. Yang, and P. Chen, "A group based context-aware strategy for mobile collaborative applications," in Advanced Technology in Teaching. Springer, 2012, pp. 541–549.

[16] L. Zavala, R. Dharurkar, P. Jagtap, T. Finin, and A. Joshi, "Mobile, collaborative, context-aware systems," in Proc. AAAI Workshop on Activity Context Representation: Techniques and Languages, AAAI. AAAI Press, 2011.

[17] J. Gabler, R. Klauck, M. Pink, and H. Konig, "uBeeMe - A platform to enable mobile collaborative applications," in Collaborative Computing: Networking, Applications and Worksharing (Collaboratecom), 2013 9th International Conference Conference on, Oct 2013, pp. 188–196.

[18] P. Coutinho and T. Rodden, "The FUSE Platform: Supporting Ubiquitous Collaboration Within Diverse Mobile Environments," Autom. Softw. Eng, vol. 9, 2002, pp. 167–186.

[19] D. Tennenhouse, "Proactive Computing," Communications of the ACM, vol. 43, no. 5, 2000, pp. 43–50.

[20] A. Gupta, A. Kalra, D. Boston, and C. Borcea, "Mobisoc: a middleware for mobile social computing applications," Mobile Networks and Applications, vol. 14, no. 1, 2009, pp. 35–52.

[21] S. Bendel and D. Schuster, "Watchmyphone - providing developer support for shared user interface objects in collaborative mobile applications," in Pervasive Computing and Communications Workshops (PERCOM Workshops), 2012 IEEE International Conference on, March 2012, pp. 166–171.

[22] R. Lübke, D. Schuster, and A. Schill, "A framework for the development of mobile social software on android," in Mobile Computing, Applications, and Services. Springer, 2011, pp. 207–225.

[23] F. Klompmaker and C. Reimann, "A service based framework for developing mobile, collaborative games," in Proceedings of the 2008 International Conference on Advances in Computer Entertainment Technology, ser. ACE '08. ACM, 2008, pp. 42–45.

[24] "Silence App," 2015, URL: https://play.google.com/store/apps/details?id=net.epsilonlabs.silence.ads [accessed: 2015-05-13].

[25] "Go Silent App," 2015, URL: https://play.google.com/store/apps/details?id=com.eventscheduler [accessed: 2015-05-13].

[26] "Advanced Silent Mode," 2015, URL: https://play.google.com/store/apps/details?id=com.joe.advancedsilentmode [accessed: 2015-05-13].

[27] "Silent Time," 2015, URL: https://play.google.com/store/apps/details?id=com.QuiteHypnotic.SilentTime&hl=en [accessed: 2015-05-13].

[28] "Auto Silent," 2015, URL: https://itunes.apple.com/us/app/autosilent/id474777148?mt=8 [accessed: 2015-05-13].

[29] Alastair Plumb. Slovakian Violist Lukas Kmit Interrupted By Nokia Ringtone, Incorporates It Into Recital. Huffington Post. [Online]. Available: http://www.huffingtonpost.co.uk/2012/01/23/slovakian-violinist-lukas-kmit-nokia-ringtone_n_1223086.html [retrieved: May, 2015]

[30] R. Dobrican and D. Zampunieris, "Supporting collaborative learning inside communities of practice through proactive computing," in Proceedings of the 5th annual International Conference on Education and New Learning Technologies. IATED, 2013, pp. 5824–5833.

[31] D. Shirnin, S. Reis, and D. Zampunieris, "Design of proactive scenarios and rules for enhanced e-learning," in Proceedings of the 4th International Conference on Computer Supported Education, Porto, Portugal 16-18 April, 2012. SciTePress–Science and Technology Publications, 2012, pp. 253–258.

[32] D. Zampunieris, "Implementation of a proactive learning management system," in Proceedings of" E-Learn-World Conference on E-Learning in Corporate, Government, Healthcare & Higher Education", 2006, pp. 3145–3151.

Smart Sensing Components in Advanced Manufacturing Systems

Rui Pinto*, João Reis*, Ricardo Silva*, Michael Peschl† and Gil Gonçalves*
*Department of Informatics, Faculty of Engineering, University of Porto
Rua Dr. Roberto Frias, s/n 4200-465, Porto, Portugal
{rpinto, jpcreis, rps, gil}@fe.up.pt
†Harms & Wende GmbH
Grossmoorkehre 9, Hamburg, Germany
michael.peschl@hwh-karlsruhe.de

Abstract—**The latest trends in Intelligent Manufacturing are related with shop-floor equipment virtualization, fostering the easy access to machine information, collaboration among shop-floor equipment and task execution on demand, paving the way for Flexible Manufacturing Systems. Therefore, it allows a high responsiveness to market changes and enables mixed model production. This concept was explored and further developed within an European project called Intelligent Reconfigurable Machines for Smart Plug&Produce Production (I-RAMP^3). The goal of I-RAMP^3 was to contribute to the improvement of European industry competitiveness, by shortening the ramp-up phase times and providing better tools to manage the scheduled and unscheduled maintenance phases. The main step forward on industrial systems was the development of the agent like concept named NETwork-enabled DEVice (NETDEV), which acts as a technological shell to all industrial equipment, both new and legacy. The present paper describes the NETDEV as a whole, applicable to a variety of contexts, but in particular to the virtualization of industrial Wireless Sensor Networks. This virtualization is named Sensor & Actuator NETDEV and extends the current sensor capabilities toward Smart Sensing, allowing for dynamic sensor location, collaboration, diagnostics and reconfiguration. As a technological background, the PlugThings Framework was used for rapid sensor integration of multiple manufacturers, along with UPnP as an enabler for standardized communication and device discovery in the network. The paper concludes by introducing future steps regarding the standardization of the I-RAMP^3 technology.**

Keywords–Smart Components; Wireless Sensor Networks; Intelligent Manufacturing Systems; Industry 4.0; I-RAMP^3.

I. Introduction

I-RAMP^3 is an European Project funded by the Seventh Framework Programme of the European Commission. This collaborative project involves both academic and industrial partners from Germany, Portugal, Netherlands, Hungary, France, and Greece. The vision of the project is to improve the European Industry competitiveness by developing technologies for smart manufacturing systems. To achieve it, the goal is to reduce the ramp-up phase of the shop-floor equipment and manage efficiently the scheduled and unscheduled maintenance phases, increasing at the same time the efficiency of the manufacturing process. By virtualizing all shop-floor equipment into an agent-like system, standardized communication skills and a layer of intelligence for collaboration between, e.g., machines and sensors are introduced, improving also the plug and produce concept towards flexible smart factories. In this context, each agent is represented as a NETDEV, which can represent both physical and logical devices in the shop-floor.

Physical devices deployed on the shop-floor can be both machines - such as a Robotic Arms or Linear Axis - handling systems - manipulators or gantries - buffers, sensors and other actuators. Specifically, sensors have the intent of monitoring the machines' conditions and the corresponding surrounding environment. In contrast, logical devices are virtual instances, which can be responsible for monitoring and diagnosing equipment condition, analysing the production flow or parameter optimization. NETDEVs have a standardized way to communicate using the Device Integration Language (DIL), which is a lightweight and task-driven XML-based language created in I-RAMP^3, in order to ease the quick delivery and reception of process information between all the virtualized shop-floor equipment. The transparency of discovering devices in the network and data exchange between them, using publish-subscribe services, is possible due to *UPnP* as a base technology.

Sensor data is extremely important to monitor machines at the shop-floor level and its environmental surrounding conditions for condition-based monitoring, machine diagnosis and process adaptation to new requirements. The I-RAMP^3 technology allows Wireless Sensor Networks (WSNs) to become more flexible and agile, acquiring new capabilities that can enhance shop-floor operations [1], [2], such as sensor collaboration, which aims for providing to the machine aggregated information instead of quantitative data, and sensor diagnosis and reconfiguration, which aims for detecting sensor malfunctions and correct them without jeopardizing the manufacturing process. Additionally, it allows for dynamic sensor node location used for sensor collaborations, to detect if sensor nodes are physically nearby other sensors and machines, and therefore data can be aggregated for process adaptation and ultimately use of proper instrumentation.

The present work is the result of integrating the solutions reported in [1] and [2] in a standalone technology and applying it in real industrial environment where different case scenarios were explored, not only for verification and validation purposes, but also to assess the usefulness of such approaches. Therefore, a more consistent solution is presented, where the sensor technology for WSN virtualization is integrated with other I-RAMP^3 compliant systems, such as welding machines and vision systems as NETDEVs. This ultimately results in an holistic perspective of the I-RAMP^3 advances in industry, not focusing solemnly on the main functionalities and capabilities, but also on the industrial dynamics of collaboration and the impact of using such a technology.

At the present stage, and based on the advances on WSN communication technologies such as *ZigBee*, 802.15.4 standards [3] and more reliable and long-lasting hardware, in the past few years WSNs became a hot topic for exploration and application in several domains. This is mainly due to its feasibility of installation, when it is difficult to use wired solutions, either by harsh location or high number of sensors used, and due to the easiness of maintenance and reduced costs of cabling [4]. Chen et al. [5] refer as advantages of WSNs their large coverage area, fast communication via Radio Frequency (RF), distributive organisation throughout a direct communication between entities and ubiquitous information. As Ruiz-Garcia et al. [6] pinpoint, some of the WSN advantages can be seen in concrete structures or in the transportation sector, where a controlled environment needs to be monitored in real-time. Additionally, Evans [7] presents enablers and challenges, along with some contextual applicability of WSN in a manufacturing environment and Gungor [8] presents challenges, design principles and technical approaches for industrial WSNs.

Specifically for the industrial domain, Ramamurthy et al. [4] developed a Smart Sensor Platform that applies the plug and play concept by means of hardware interface, payload, communication between sensors and actuators, and ultimately allows for software update using over-the-air programming (*OTAP*). Cao [9] explored a distributed approach to put closer sensors and actuators in a collaborative environment using WSNs. Chen et al. [5] push this approach forward considering the same approach, but taking into account all the industrial domain restrictions like real-timeliness, functional safety, security, energy efficiency, and so forth. All these industrial restrictions and an overview about the industrial domain was explored and presented by Neumann [10]. In the recent past, Chen et al. [11] tackled the Optimal Controller Location (OCL) in the context of industrial environment.

This paper is organized in seven more sections covering all the details about the present work. In Section II, the related work is revised, where several contributions regarding smart production systems are identified. In Section III, an overall description about NETDEVs is made, detailing the NETDEV classification, architecture and communication interface. Section IV depicts the sensor integration on industry and it's virtualization using the PlugThings Framework, detailing and all the capabilities associated with Sensor & Actuator (S&A) NETDEVs, such as collaboration, localization, diagnosis and reconfigurability. Section V talks about different industrial case scenarios used to validate a sensor implementation using the I-RAMP^3 technology, which serves as a proof of concept. In Section VI a discussion about the system and all the functionalities developed is made, Section VII talks about strategies for the future and the importance of standardization, and finally in Section VIII some conclusions are presented.

II. Related Work

In existing production environments, the 'smart factory' concept is still in its early stages. Commissioning is mainly a manual process, where machine parameters have to be found by the operator in a trial and error manner, sensors have to be regularly calibrated and communication between devices has to be established. This process is sometimes supported by software tools and discrete event simulation. This manual process still continues after commissioning, when re-adjustment and reconfiguration of the system needs to be made so the whole production line runs smoothly and efficiently. The same holds true when an industrial facility needs modifications or a production equipment has to be replaced. According to Barbosa [12], traditional manufacturing control systems focuses the processing of a shop-floor control in one central node, which is insufficient to meet current manufacturing requirements that demand flexibility, robustness, reconfigurability and responsiveness. Paradigms supported by decentralization and distribution of processing power are best suited to industrial requirements and constitute in principle a solution towards smart factories. Examples of such paradigms are Reconfigurable Manufacturing Systems (RMS) [13], Multi-agent Systems (MAS) [14] and Holonic Manufacturing Systems (HMS) [15].

Several approaches [16] based on these concepts were developed to support the manufacturing systems complexity, including real implementations in industry. These agent-based applications focused on flexible, reconfigurable and adaptive production at different levels and with different purposes, such as supply chain planning, business process management, production planning, scheduling and optimization, agile manufacturing, enterprise integration, warehouse planning and resource allocation. A very well known approach regarding HMS is the Product Resource Order Staff Architecture (PROSA) [17], which uses holons to represent products, resources, orders and logical activities. PROSA inspired many other approaches latter on, such as a control architecture for an AGV system [18] and an architecture for production control of semiconductor wafer fabrication facilities [19]. In fact, a real application of PROSA was conducted in a packaging cell for Gillete [20], by forming a collaboration between order and resources holons to accommodate changing demands. A more recent architecture called Adaptive Holonic Control Architecture (ADACOR) for distributed manufacturing systems [21] addresses the reaction to emergence and change in environments where frequent disturbances occur.

The industrial acceptance regarding HMS and MAS applications is still low, as pinpointed by Mcfarlane [22], mainly due to the lack of real proof about the applicability of these technologies on real scenarios, aspects related with the technology development process and consequence of the companies' business strategies. DaimlerChrysler applied successfully MAS concepts for both dynamic and flexible transportation and control systems on their production lines [23]. The prototype operated everyday for five years and resulted in a estimated 20% increase in productivity on average. DaimlerChrysler also co-operated with Schneider Electric GmbH to develop a control system for heterogeneous devices in environments with real-time constrains [24]. The US Navy incorporated in their ships a agent-based control system for the heating, ventilation and air-conditions systems [25]. Shen [26] presented a very nice compilation of the main agent-based projects and their achievements.

Before I-RAMP^3, there have been a couple of large projects to set up and improve the framework of HMS, namely the XPRESS project [27], GNOSIS project [28] and PABADIS project [29]. The most relevant aspect to XPRESS was the effort to set up a Scalable Flexible Manufacturing (SFM) architecture, a framework for organizing resources of hardware (machine tools, robots, etc.) and software (cell controllers, process planning, etc.) in computer automated environments, with an emphasis on autonomous decentralized scheduling.

In this approach, each unit in a factory was autonomous and manufacturing execution was the result of negotiations between the autonomous modules with a central 'black-board', containing order information and planning status information. Each resource makes a bid for the work and the best bid wins, leading to an autonomous distributed control.

The GNOSIS project concentrated on configuration systems for design and manufacturing. One part of GNOSIS dealt with 'soft products' and knowledge intensive engineering. In relation to XPRESS, a virtual factory was proposed, which provides reactivity and efficiency by the optimal use of distributed manufacturing resources. These resources are connected to form virtual manufacturing processes, which can be configured and operated as work cells based on product, process or production line principles according to changing demands from the market. The core idea is to have models that communicate with each other, providing both planning and coordination throughout the virtual factories. These GNOSIS concepts have been partly adopted by commercially available planning software. PABADIS demonstrated the advantages of mobile agents compared to classical Manufacturing Execution System (MES) and Supervisory Control and Acquisition (SCADA). Concerning the field level, only fundamental concepts were postulated. However, a flexible production is only possible if the integration of production units at the lowest level (machines, sensors, etc.) is taken into account. This was resolved by the XPRESS project and later, on I-RAMP^3.

In order to make the equipment more versatile, adaptive approaches to encapsulate process knowledge in agent-based production equipment are necessary. I-RAMP^3 incorporated this approach and extended it into a task-based production, where process equipment has expertise about a certain process domain and can execute any task of its domain, based on the description of the task, and can produce a quality result document. In I-RAMP^3, a framework to wrap existing equipment with a NETDEV shell was developed, which contains the required process intelligence and communication means, possible via the exchange of Device Integration Language (DIL) documents.

III. Network-Enabled Devices

NETDEVs are intelligent agent-based production devices that are responsible to equip the conventional manufacturing equipment - both complex machines, as industrial PCs or PLCs, and sensors & actuators - with standardized communication skills, along with intelligent functionalities for inter-device negotiation and process optimization. By wrapping equipment components with the NETDEV shell, they become equipped with built-in intelligence. This means that the NETDEV can incorporate an extensive set of internal models, which are executed on the NETDEV engine. The inherent functionalities include provision of a device self-description, conduction of conditioning monitoring and the provision of a device history, ability to interpret and execute tasks, ability to analyse and optimize a process and ability to perform additional analysis based on knowledge about itself. The NETDEV family is represented in Figure 1.

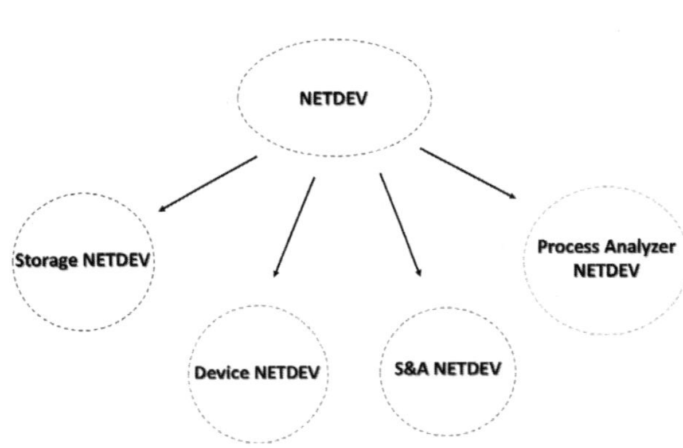

Figure 1. NETDEV Family.

A. NETDEV Classification

NETDEVs represent devices that can be categorized into logical and physical devices. Logical devices provide services for data transformation, storage, consumption or production. Physical devices provide physical object transformations or sensing. Therefore, physical devices will, in most of the cases, involve one or more physical objects. A partial NETDEV classification diagram is represented in Figure 2.

Among logical devices, Process and Data Storage can be found, which correspond respectively to Process Analyzer NETDEVs and Storage NETDEVs virtualizations. Process devices can do transformations on the production conditions, for instance the analysis (Analyzer) of production flow, scheduling (Scheduler) or optimization (Optimizer) of NETDEV parameters. The Analyzer provides production analysis of any kind, such as production flow, route optimization, etc. Scheduler correspond to devices that provide production scheduling services to the network, and consume data to feed the required calculations. The Optimizer provides external optimization services to NETDEVs that do not have built-in optimization modules for production parameters. The Process Analyzer NETDEV should be able to perform production parameter optimization for more than one NETDEV, assuming they are from the same type. Data storage devices provide storage means for NETDEVs without built-in storage facilities. NETDEVs should be able to find available Storage NETDEVs on the network and query the free space available, among other properties, to decide where a blob of data should be stored.

As seen in Figure 2, devices dealing with physical objects fit in categories for sensing, transportation or transformation purposes. Sensors correspond to devices that measure some physical property of an object or environment. Actuators correspond to smaller devices (mechanism) that performs some transformation on an object. Both Sensor and Actuators are virtualized into S&A NETDEVs. Stock/Buffer corresponds to devices that provides storage for physical objects. Moreover, Manufacturing corresponds to any device that performs some kind of physical property transformation to another object, such as weld and press. Finally, Handling corresponds to any device that performs some kind of spatial transformation (movement, orientation change, etc.) or holding of objects. Device NETDEVs are virtualizations of Manufacturing and Handling devices.

B. NETDEV Template

A model of a NETDEV and its components was developed in order to meet the industrial requirements. According to the

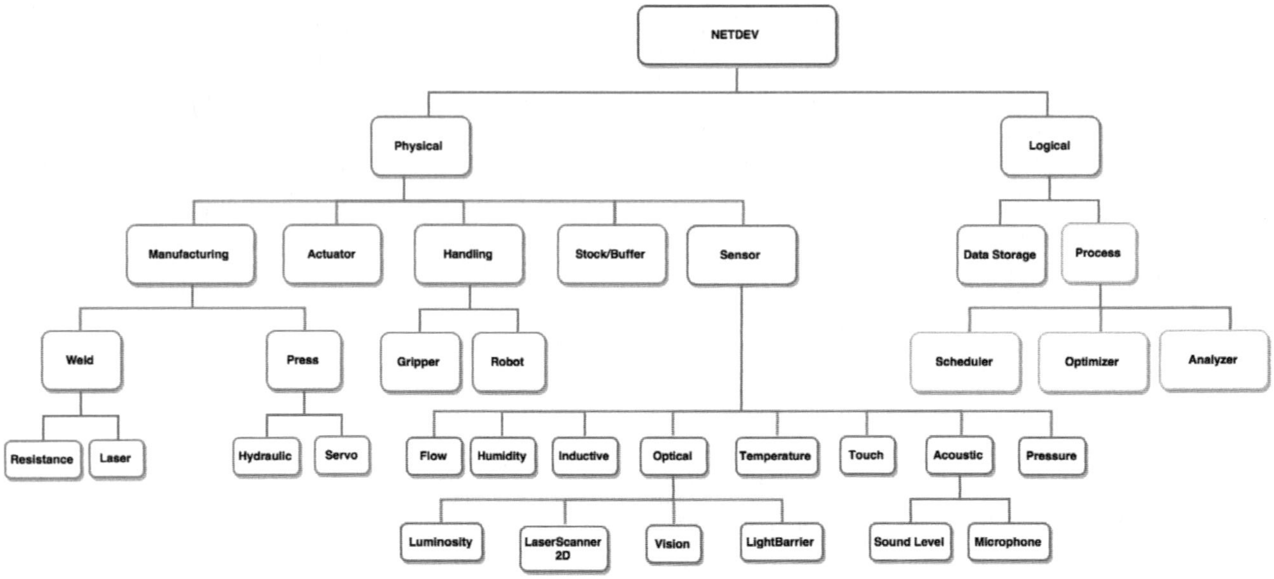

Figure 2. NETDEV Classification.

general I-RAMP[3] approach and architecture, several industrial requirements were derived: reduction of setup time and efforts during re-configuration; reliability of system operations; flexibility in component handling; information provision on device operation; capabilities and procedures classification; interfaces to enable the communication to all other equipment within the architecture; accessibility from "outside" in order to perform maintenance activities; flexible components in order to adapt for new products and variants; possibility to integrate new components; ability of switching tasks within minimal time; and adaptability to different processes and devices

This model was built in the form of a framework, which is used for the implementation of NETDEVs for specific processes. The template comprises both a collection of specifications for NETDEV implementation and a collection of software modules. The user can implement a NETDEV device in three different programming languages, because the NETDEV template is written in *C#*, *C/C++* and *Java*.

Based on the communication requirements, the template includes *UPnP* modules that allow the NETDEV discovery and service publishing. Since the *UPnP* is composed of tow main instances, UPnP Device (information provider) and a UPnP Control Point (information receiver), the developed template contemplates both instances. The UPnP Device is composed by a set of state variables and methods to access the information stored in those state variables. It includes the communication protocol implementation, namely the DIL, the main shop-floor capabilities of the device (represented by the corresponding state variables and methods) and an alive mechanism acting as a "ping" to know if the NETDEV is still in operation. The UPnP Control Point is responsible for recognizing other NETDEVs in the network and subscribe the information generated by the other components, by means of state variables and methods.

C. NETDEV Architecture

Based on the requirements of the developer and/or the equipment that it is intended to be virtualized, the NETDEV template can be used to implement several different types of NETDEVs. On the I-RAMP[3] project, four NETDEVs were implemented, according to the proposed industry requirements. These NETDEVs virtualize the main shop-floor components, both physical and logical. The NETDEV architecture is described in Figure 3.

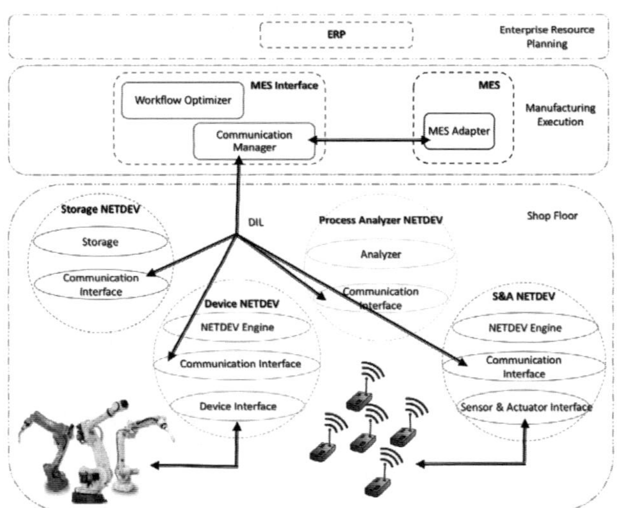

Figure 3. NETDEV Architecture.

The Device NETDEV is a virtual entity that represents any machine or machine component present on the shop-floor, such as manufacturing and handling devices.

The S&A NETDEV is a virtualization of every sensor

and actuator present on the WSN used on the shop-floor. Typical used sensors are the Liquid Flow, Luminosity and Temperature sensors. S&A NETDEVs have capabilities such as self-organization, when complex tasks require cooperation between sensors, self-awareness to automatically locate a sensor node, self-diagnosis for sensor malfunction detection and self-healing for automatic sensor reconfiguration.

The Storage NETDEV is a network storage that can either be implemented on a a single device or in separated software products. The goal is to easily extend a storage unit when a new device is plugged in the network. Different types of data can be stored, namely configuration values, counter values and firmware/program files. The system is resilient because one backup file can exist multiple times in the network, distributed over different storage NETDEVs, leading to data redundancy. Also, incremental backups are possible.

The Process Analyzer NETDEV is used for a production process analysis, such as welding or polishing of an equipment for condition monitoring, including sensor & actuators. This NETDEV allows the visualization of relevant Key Performance Indicators (KPI's). The analysis is dedicated to the condition monitoring and visualization of, first, a welding process quality, second, welding timer monitoring for equipment breakdown and, third, sensor group monitoring for sensor breakdown.

D. NETDEV Interfaces

NETDEVs are able to describe and optimize themselves towards their environment by providing knowledge and models about their properties, abilities, constraints and reuse abilities. Furthermore, they have the ability to perform condition monitoring and maintain a device history, interpret and execute tasks, optimize process, expose abilities and to predict its maintenance requirements.

A NETDEV has two main interfaces: the communication interface and the device interface. The communication interface handles all data exchange among NETDEVs and the Manufacturing Executing System (MES). It comprises the exchange of documents described in the DIL. The device interface is used to link physical devices and tools to the NETDEV. The NETDEVs are able to work with different tools and devices that have similar features, adapting themselves to the discovered unit.

The NETDEV communication is divided in three main steps. First, when the NETDEV enters the network it announces itself and gets knowledge about the existing NETDEVs already in the network. This discovery process of entities on the network is automatically done by the *UPnP* technology. Second, DIL is used exclusively for NETDEV communication, when tasks should be requested. It basically consists of document exchange between NETDEVs. Third, task content and data is specified and exchanged within the DIL documents. A simple case of NETDEV communication using DIL is presented in Figure 4.

DIL implements four different types of Extensible Markup Language *(XML)* documents and each one can be exchanged inside the environment between the NETDEVs. The four types are: NETDEV Self-Description (NSD); Task Description Document (TDD); Task Fulfilment Document (TFD); Quality Result Document (QRD).

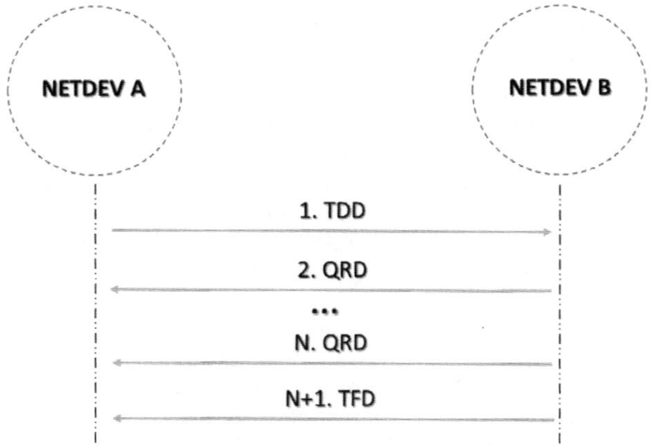

Figure 4. DIL Communication.

The NSD describes the capabilities of a NETDEV, which is basically a range of tasks that can be performed by the NETDEV. The tasks may be defined as goals and conditions, or as bare process parameter values. The task range gives the possible range of goals and conditions or parameter values, which can be realized and accepted by the NETDEV according to its physical capabilities. Additionally, NSD can be adapted, when self-diagnosis finds process restrictions.

The TDD describes the information defining a requested task as roughly specified on NSD. It determines one of the possible goals or parameter values, which have to be reached by the NETDEV. If it is a continuous task (for instance, detection of irregular signal values) or if it is a repetitive task, the period of the task execution or the number of task repetitions is given.

The TFD is a document-type acknowledge to the TDD, reflecting the settings with respect to the requested goals or parameters. The TFD also has a second purpose: It is used to inform other NETDEVs about the actual settings and let them decide if they can cooperate with the NETDEV under the present circumstances or if they have to wait until they can set them otherwise, via a new TDD.

The QRD describes the result achieved after process execution, which can be the description of the end state or the quality achieved after the process execution. In a continuous or repetitive process, the QRD is issued only at the end of all scheduled repetitions or time period and is giving a summary of the total repetitive or continuous process.

IV. Sensor & Actuator NETDEV

Sensor usage on industrial applications has become extremely important, since monitoring the behavior of a machine is crucial to adapt its operation due to regular changes on product demand. On a shop-floor environment, sensors should not be treated as an integral part of a machine, but a separated component, which like complex machines, should be flexible enough to change its operations according to process demands. In I-RAMP[3] were explored new concepts on WSNs applied in industry, aiming for the addition of an intelligence layer on sensors, which empower them to be as complex as machines, both sharing plug and produce features and both capable of communicating with each other on an agent-like system environment.

Intelligent WSNs rely on some features such as easy integration of sensor nodes from different manufacturers using, e.g., the PlugThings Framework [30], along with automatic calculation of the nodes' physical location, self-diagnosis capabilities using sensor data validation methods, and self-reconfiguration capabilities using *OTAP* technologies to re-program new sensor nodes on the network.

A. Sensor Integration

In the I-RAMP^3 project, the integration of multiple types of sensor nodes on the system is made using the PlugThings Framework [30], which contains a Universal Gateway (UG) to parse raw sensor data from the different sensor nodes. As can be seen in Figure 5, each sensor node of the network communicates directly to this gateway node, where the received measurements are processed and translated from raw data (stream of bytes) into readable form (measurement values). These data are compiled on *XML* based format files that are part of the Sensor & Actuator Abstraction Language (SAAL), which is used to communicate with Sensor & Actuator Abstraction Middleware (SAAM). All the intelligence related to the sensors is implemented in SAAM. When the SAAM receives a new message from a sensor node, it will collect the sensor board identification number (ID) and the communication module Media Access Control (MAC) Address. Both board ID and MAC Address are the unique identifier of a sensor node.

Joining a new sensor node to the network will imply the creation of a new S&A NETDEV corresponding to that sensor node, letting transparent to all the entities on the network what measuring tasks it can perform. Since a sensor node can have multiple sensors integrated, the corresponding S&A NETDEV will be able to perform different tasks related with the different sensor types of the sensor node. It will have one task per sensor integrated in the mote, being this way able to provide sensor information in a standardized way.

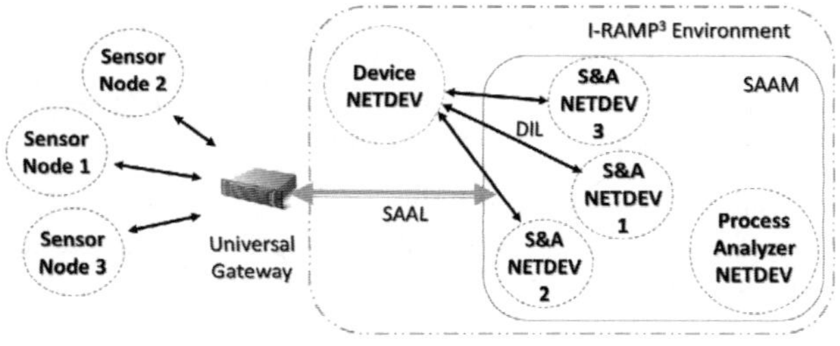

Figure 5. I-RAMP^3 Environment.

Basically, S&A NETDEVs have one functionality, namely task execution, to provide sensor information to other entities per integrated physical sensor in the sensor node. S&A NETDEVs can easily communicate with other NETDEVs on the network using DIL, such as Device NETDEVs and Process Analyzer NETDEV, which monitors sensor behavior while in a group collaboration. At this stage, S&A NETDEVs can execute two different tasks, both usually requested by a Device NETDEV: *Measurement* and *Group Formation* tasks.

1) Measurement task: Is used when the Device NETDEV needs the measurements of a single sensor node. Therefore, it should specify the desired type of sensor to receive the corresponding sensory data, the frequency of the readings, sensor accuracy, coverage radius of the sensor in spatial units (if applicable) and the number of cycles to execute the task.

2) Group Formation task: is requested when the Device NETDEV aims to collect several measurements at different locations, which means having multiple sensors executing the same task at the same time. In this specific task, the S&A NETDEV that receives the task is responsible for choosing possible S&A NETDEVs candidates to join the group, based on the task parameterization and the sensor location. This allows for a more distributed approach in terms of collaboration, rather than a peer-to-peer-like solution, implying a communication with all the S&A NETDEVs from a group instead of only one. In terms of parameterization, beside the desired type of sensor to receive the specific data, frequency of measurements, sensor accuracy and the number of cycles to perform the task, the *Group Formation* parameterization must also specify the number of sensors intended in the group.

B. S&A NETDEV Collaboration

S&A NETDEV *Group Formation* is a methodology used to improve the communication performance and reduce complexity between Device NETDEVs and S&A NETDEVs while executing tasks with a sensor collaboration nature. Thousands of sensors can exist on the shop-floor level, and therefore, the flow of information can be very high when requesting tasks. The *Group Formation* methodology is a more distributed approach that allows S&A NETDEVs to provide a more aggregated information when the task requested from a Device NETDEV requires measurements from more than one sensor node. Instead of establishing communication with every S&A NETDEV required, the Device NETDEV will have a single point of communication with one S&A NETDEV, which is responsible for forming and managing a S&A NETDEVs group.

The main premise for the *Group Formation* is that every S&A NETDEV is capable of forming a group. When a Device NETDEV requests a S&A NETDEV to form a group with a certain number of sensors, this S&A NETDEV is responsible for searching in the network, communicating via DIL, for available S&A NETDEVs that are capable of performing the same task as it and the corresponding sensor nodes must be physically located in the same production area. If the number of group members reaches the requested number of S&A NETDEVs in the beginning, the S&A NETDEV responsible to form it becomes the group leader, called Super S&A NETDEV, and the group is formed. Internally in the group, each S&A NETDEV will collect measurements during the requested number of cycles and the Super S&A NETDEV is responsible, not only to gather all sensor data, but also process it to a more meaningful value, to be sent afterwards to the Device NETDEV. When task execution ends, the Super S&A NETDEV will terminate the communication with the Device NETDEV and release the S&A NETDEVs from the group, which become available to execute other task requests from other NETDEVs. Figure 6 compares both peer-to-peer and sensor collaboration approaches.

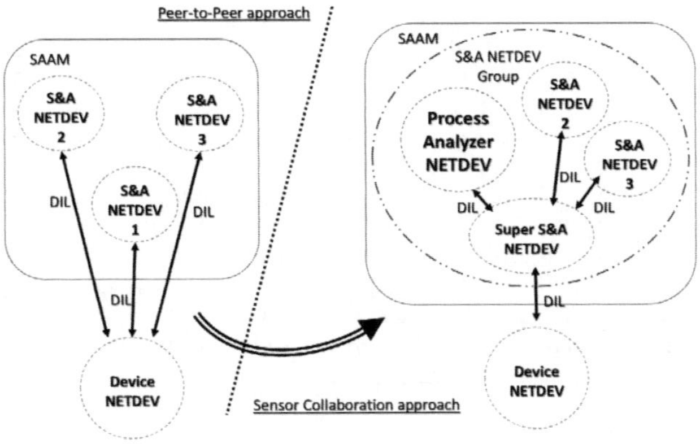

Figure 6. *Group Formation* Schema.

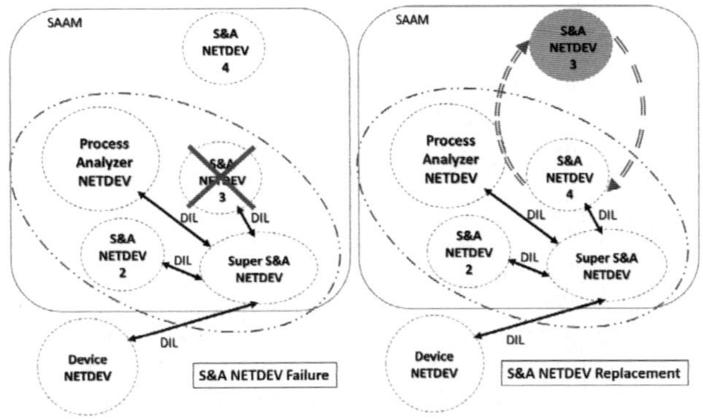

Figure 7. *Group Formation* - S&A NETDEV Failure.

An additional NETDEV entity represented in Figure 6 is the Process Analyzer NETDEV, which is created by the Super S&A NETDEV when the group is formed. This virtual entity is responsible for applying sensor validation techniques, such as the Spatial Correlation technique [31], [32], to assess the condition of the group based on the sensor data generated. The Process Analyzer NETDEV collects the sensor data from each element of the group and identifies the most devious data set by comparing the data sets from all group members. If the deviation is greater than a predefined threshold, then the sensor node is classified as probably malfunctioning. The Process Analyzer NETDEV reports to the Super S&A NETDEV, via DIL, the existing of a malfunctioning group member at that time, so it can make a decision about the faulty sensor node(s) and maintain the group functionality as consistent and reliable as possible.

With the *Group Formation* task, there are two main benefits from the task requester perspective. Assuming a Device NETDEV wants to collect and analyze data from multiple S&A NETDEVs: first, it avoids communicating with several S&A NETDEVs at the same time to collect data, since the responsibility to form a group is on the S&A NETDEV; second, the S&A NETDEVs can process all sensor data and provide a statistical description, passing the data analysis complexity to the group side. This means that the requester does not need to know any statistical technique to process the data from multiple sensor entities on the network. However, relying on one single point of communication, increases the vulnerability in case the task execution fails on that point. Hence, there are two failing scenarios on a group: 1) Failure of the Super S&A NETDEV or 2) one or more S&A NETDEVs from the group fail(s).

1) Failure of the Super S&A NETDEV: If the Super S&A NETDEV fails, the single point of communication supporting the interaction between the Device NETDEV and S&A NETDEVs from the group is lost. There will be no more conditions to continue with the task execution, so the task stops and the group is disaggregated. In the termination process, the Super S&A NETDEV is responsible for changing the process state of the remaining group members, so they can stop executing the *Measurement* tasks for the group, becoming available to perform new tasks upon request from other NETDEVs.

2) Failure of one or more S&A NETDEV(s) of the group: If a S&A NETDEV from the group is failing, the Super S&A NETDEV is still working correctly, so the group is not in danger of collapsing and the communication with the Device NETDEV is not affected. In this case, the Super S&A NETDEV is responsible for replacing the failing S&A NETDEV for a new one able to join in. While the replacement process occurs, the collected data from the group will be less accurate, because the results sent to the Device NETDEV do not contemplate all the requested NETDEVs, due to a temporary deficit of one S&A NETDEV (the malfunctioning one). Figure 7 depicts the process when a S&A NETDEV (in this case, S&A NETDEV 3) fails and is replaced by an available S&A NETDEV (in this case, S&A NETDEV 4).

C. S&A NETDEV Location

WSNs applied in industry are used to monitor different production cells on the shop-floor, consisting of spatially distributed sensor nodes, which are equipped with several sensors to monitor the environmental conditions surrounding the cells where they are located. If a machine, located in one of the production cells needs information about, e.g., the luminosity conditions surrounding the cell to execute a given task, the machine may require, from available sensor nodes placed in that production cell, valuable information for process parameterization.

In the I-RAMP[3] context, the Device NETDEV that is requesting the task should search on the network for available S&A NETDEVs with the required capabilities (described in the NSD), e.g., measuring luminosity conditions and, consequently can form a sensor group that measures luminosity. Facing a request for a *Group Formation* task from a Device NETDEV, the S&A NETDEV will only accept the task if the corresponding sensor node can fulfill the required parametrization and is physically located on the same area as the machine that requested the task in the first place.

Every NETDEV is characterized by its task execution capabilities (NSD) and the area on the shop-floor where the correspondent equipment is located. On contrary of machinery, the location of sensor nodes can be calculated dynamically by a S&A NETDEV location system, which uses the incoming RF signal strength of the sensor node on several beacons for position estimation. Beacons are physical entities located in known strategic positions of the shop-floor, mainly in the limits of shop-floor sections like cells or production lines and are responsible by receiving messages from sensor nodes, assess their signal strength and position in order to assign the current relative location to S&A NETDEVs. At this point in the implementations, only sensor nodes that are using *XBee* radio modules are acceptable to calculate dynamically the location.

Location systems on WSN is a very active research area and there is no universal solution for this topic. The main goal is to identify the physical location of a sensor node on the WSN. Each approach of node location is fitted to a specific operating environment, such as indoors or outdoors spaces like urban areas, forests or even underwater. In the industrial context, estimating the node positions in meters is not important, as the main goal is to find in which section on the shop floor the sensor nodes are located. The algorithms for node location are made of two main components: 1) Estimation of distance or angle between two nodes and 2) Calculation of the node position. First, the distance or angle between two nodes must be estimated to be used on the calculation of the node position related to one or more anchor nodes (nodes with a previously known location - beacon). Then, the information about the distance and the position is used by an algorithm to determine the node's location.

There are several methods [8] to estimate the distance or angle between two sensor nodes. Some are more precise than others, but on the other hand, they require more hardware resources, consume more energy and demand more computational power. Time delay based methods, such as Time Of Flight (TOF) [33], estimate the distance by measuring the time it takes for the RF signal to travel between them. Since the RF signal travels at speed of light, it could be extremely difficult to measure the signal time travel. So, time difference methods, such as Time Difference of Arrival (TDOA) [34], measure the difference on the time travel between the RF signal and an acoustic or ultra-sound signal, which, because it travels at the speed of sound, it must be easier to measure. This method requires extra hardware such as transmitters and receivers of ultra-sounds. Signal angle/direction estimation methods, such as the Angle of Arrival (AOA) / Direction of Arrival (DOA) [35], [36] is a method that uses the RF signal angle of arrival to determine the sensor node position. Again, the method requires extra hardware such as specific antennas in both transmitter and receiver. For last, the Received Strength Signal Indicator (RSSI) [34], [37], [38] estimates the distance based on the strength of the RF signal, which are theoretically inversely proportional, if perfect conditions existed. In comparison with the previous methods, this one has the advantage of no extra hardware is required, other then a simple antenna. The disadvantage is the lower precision of measurements when signal noise and interference exist.

In the I-RAMP[3], distance estimation is done between the sensor node and anchor nodes placed in know shop-floor locations, using the RSSI method. The considered propagation model is the Free Space model [39], [40]. Although having a lower precision (2m to 5m errors), the distance estimation is acceptable for the method applicability in the industrial scenario.

The radio signal is highly susceptible to noise [41] caused by reflection, refraction, diffraction, scattering, fading, inter-symbol interference and shadowing. Consequently, there will be distance deviations in the end. This can be minimized by filtering the signal using a moving average to better approximate the path loss logarithmic curve. The path loss coefficient is determined dynamically using path loss log-distance model using measurements of RSSI between beacons, using (1), where $P(d)$ is the RSSI in dBm, $P(d_0)$ is the RSSI at a fixed reference distance from the transmitter d_0, n is the path loss coefficient, X_σ is a normal random variable used to modulate, d is the distance in meters between transmitter and receiver, P_{TX} is the transmission power and A is the signal attenuation. Manipulating the formula, first the path loss coefficient is calculated using (2), where the RSSI and distance are between beacons. Then, (3) is used to calculate the distance between a sensor node and a blind node.

$$P(d) = P_{TX} + A - 10n \times log(\frac{d}{d_0}) + X_\sigma \quad (1)$$

$$n = \frac{|P(d_0) - P(d)|}{10log(d) \times 2} \quad (2)$$

$$d = d_0 \times 10^{\frac{|P(d_0)-P(d)|}{10n}} \quad (3)$$

The node position is calculated using the distance estimation of three anchor nodes closest to the sensor node with the Bounding Box method [38]. Bounding Box is a variation of the trilateration, which uses the position of three anchor nodes, with known positions and distances between them, to calculate the position of the sensor node, as shown in Figure 8.

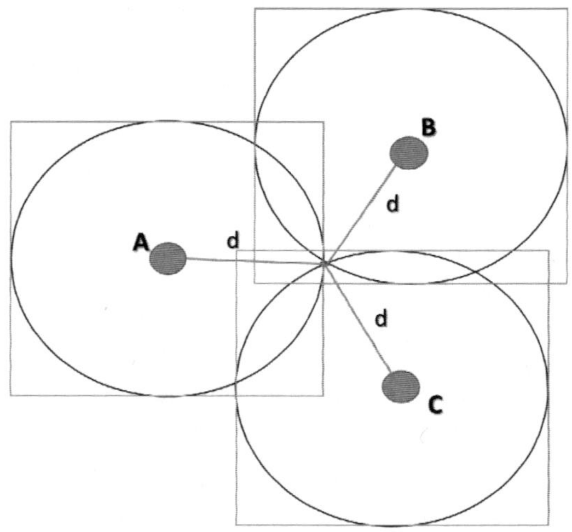

Figure 8. Trilateration and Bounding Box for node position estimation.

The position of the node is calculated by the intersection of three circles, each one is centred on the anchor node and with radius equal to the distance to the unknown position node. With Bounding Box, the calculation complexity is reduced by replacing the circles by squares. The intersection of the different squares results in a rectangle, where the centre is the estimated position of the node.

D. S&A NETDEV Diagnosis

Sensor data is used as an input for complex machines to control the manufacturing process and to adapt themselves according to external conditions. This adaptation allows the machine to be flexible enough to change its variable inputs and internal processing, controlling the production process to maintain product quality despite fluctuations. Machine's process depends on data measured from sensors, so it is very important that data stays the most reliable as possible when delivered to the machine. Data samples collected from sensors, especially from WSNs, are prone to be faulty due to internal and external influences, such as environmental effects, limitations of resources, energy problems, hardware malfunctions, software problems, network issues, among others, as shown in [42]–[45].

Sensor data validation consists of a set of methods applied to the data provided by the sensors with the main goal of detecting anomalies and malfunctions on these sensors and take action accordingly on the corresponding S&A NETDEVs. But, finding deviations from normal sensor readings do not necessarily mean that they occur due to a malfunction of the sensor node. Instead, they can occur due to an abnormal variation of the environmental conditions being measured. Despite being a sensor-based or an environment condition-based cause, each sensor node of the WSN is aware of its state and is capable of performing self-diagnosis during the task execution.

Anomaly detection methods generally classify data into correct or faulty. There is no right method that works better than all the others and no method guarantees success, because they all depend on several factors such as type of monitored variable, the overall measurement conditions, the sensor used and the characteristics of the environment being perceived [46], [47]. In [31], [46] is proven that anomaly detection should not rely on just one method, but instead on a number of methods applied successively for detecting different types of data faults. Furthermore, there are methods [46] suitable to be used online, and other more complex and demanding on the processing level, suitable to be used offline. Offline validation methods, such as Bayesian Networks (BNs), Artificial Neural Networks (ANNs), Regression Techniques like Partial-Least Squares Regression, etc., are used in many different contexts such as aerospace, energy, electric power systems, urban environment, among others [48]–[54]. Regarding S&A NETDEVs, techniques that provide a quick WSN diagnostics were used, such as Min/Max, Flat Line [31], [32], Modified Z-Score [55] and No Value detection.

The Min/Max approach is based on a heuristic rule, which defines upper and lower bounds that refer to hardware specifications or/and conditions that are not likely to occur in the current context. Therefore, if sensed data is within bounds, data are likely good, otherwise, the sensor may be faulty. The Flat Line technique is based on temporal correlation of a data set of the most recent collected measurements. If the difference between successive data samples remains zero, this means that the sensor is probably faulty. Modified Z-Score is a statistical-based technique used as an outlier detection mechanism. It takes into account averaged values and deviations to assess if a certain value do not follows the same behavior as others values in the data set. The No Value detection technique finds gaps in data sets. If the difference between the current time and the time stamp of the last measurement is unusually large, then probably the sensor has stopped the communication with the gateway.

On I-RAMP[3], the sensor data validation is characterized by four main steps, as shown in Figure 9: 1) First, raw data is acquired from the sensor nodes; 2) Raw data is converted into a readable form by the UG and sent to the SAAM; 3) While a S&A NETDEV executes a task, the received sensor data is validated by a sequence of internal methods to detect anomalies; 4) If anomalies on data are detected, the corresponding S&A NETDEV is marked as probably faulty, which results, depending on the severity of the error detected, in the inability of accepting future task requests or termination of the current task's execution.

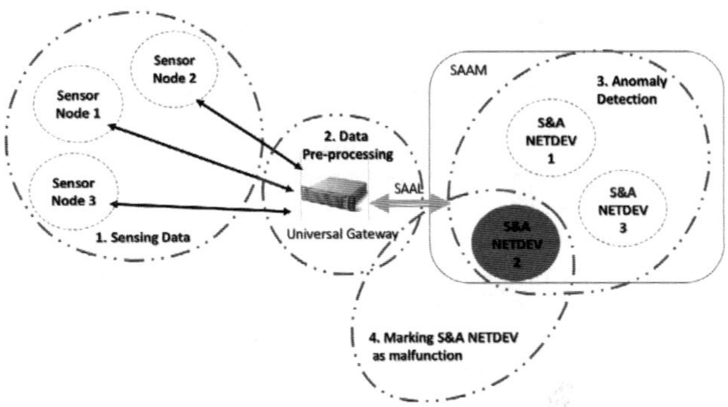

Figure 9. Sensor Data Validation approach on I-RAMP[3].

While the S&A NETDEV is executing a task, the data set of the corresponding sensor node will go through two validation modules: Module A, which is intended for detecting sensor malfunctions and Module B, which is intended for detecting abnormal behavior from the sensor node.

Module A validates the received sensor data using the Flat Line [31], [32], [56] and No Value detection methods, aiming to identify a malfunction sensor node. If the Flat Line method returns positive for error detection, it means that, on the sensor node, the board is reading the same electrical quantity for an unusual amount of time. This implies that the sensor is not detecting any variation on the environment quantity being measured or is failing to do so. Since electrical signals are time varying analog signals of voltage, current or frequency, usually associated with noise, it is very difficult to have sequence samples with no difference between them. Hence, when this occurs, it is most likely that the sensor is not correctly connected to the board. On the other hand, if the No Value method detects gaps in the data set, most likely the battery ran out of energy or the sensor node just broke down. Facing a malfunctioning sensor node, the corresponding S&A NETDEV is responsible for terminating prematurely the task execution, without any human interaction and making itself unavailable to take on other task requests.

Module B is intended for methods that detect outliers, such as the Min/Max detection [31], [32], [57], which detects readings out of system limit thresholds, and the Modified Z-Score [32], [58] that detects spikes and abnormal readings. This module returns a strong probability about the malfunctioning state of the sensor, despite lower than the one returned by Module A. This probability is based on the defective readings that, in this case, can be caused by sensor failing or abnormal behavior of the system itself. In such circumstances, the S&A NETDEV waits for the normal task termination, becoming unavailable regarding the acceptance of future task requests, while a maintenance process does not occur on the corresponding sensor node.

E. S&A NETDEV Reconfiguration

Over the Air Programming (*OTAP*) is a technology developed originally to update firmware for mobile devices. Since the use of this type of equipment greatly relies on wireless Internet access, *OTAP* has been used on the past years, from manufacturers to network operators, to deliver firmware updates to equipment with Internet access. However, because of the wide use of WSNs and their growing complexity, *OTAP* has been taken to a new direction towards WSNs [59]. A WSN could have thousands of sensor nodes and the maintenance of these nodes could be very time-consuming. Therefore, since they must all be re-programmed one by one, this is not a very cost-effective solution. Moreover, the WSN may have nodes located in difficult access places, so updating firmware in sensor nodes on site can be challenging. Several sensor nodes from different manufacturers are already embedded with the *OTAP* technology, which relies on updating firmware on sensor nodes from the gateway node, using the existing wireless communication between them, such as *XBee*, *Wi-Fi* or *3G*.

On I-RAMP^3, the WSN consists in different sensor nodes, gateway nodes connected to the UG and the communication topologies between them. The sensor node used in the I-RAMP^3 to proof of concept is the Libelium Waspmote PRO (v1.2) [60] sensor boards, equipped with the *XBee* radio module for the 802.15.4 communication protocol [3]. Updating firmware on the Waspmote PRO (v1.2) requires using the Libelium *OTAP* technology [6], which divides the OTAP process on two main steps: 1) node discovery on the network and 2) firmware upload. The OTA-Shell application [61] is used at the UG level to control the options available in *OTAP*, sending commands to the sensor nodes to be reprogrammed. A firmware upload occurs when the shop floor operator replaces sensor node hardware due to a severe malfunction detection on a sensor node (using the methods discussed previously). The logical representation of *OTAP* methodology in I-RAMP^3 is represented in Figure 10.

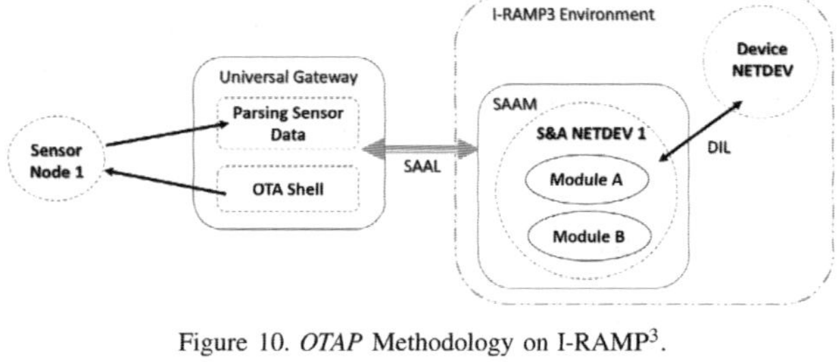

Figure 10. *OTAP* Methodology on I-RAMP^3.

When a S&A NETDEV is executing a task and a sensor node failure is detected, the malfunction could be caused by irreversible problems that require equipment replacement on the nodes, such as: 1) replacement of a bad sensor or communication module; 2) replacement of a bad sensor board; 3) replacement of the entire sensor node. Replace a bad sensor or communication module does not require firmware update of any kind, since these components are external to the sensor board that is running the firmware. On the other hand, when replacing a bad sensor board or the entire sensor node, a firmware update is required, which can be done traditionally or using the *OTAP* approach.

Traditionally, before a new sensor board is connected, it needs previously to be manually flashed with the right firmware. This approach may be counterproductive on a smart factory context, since the ramp-up time of replacing a sensor board could be very high. With the I-RAMP^3 *OTAP* approach, when a new sensor board is connected to the network, the sensor node is flashed automatically with the correct firmware using *OTAP*. The basic idea is to previously store on the UG the replaced sensor node's program in form of an automatic generated binary image after compiling the code and flash the new sensor node over the air with the stored binary image, replacing a malfunctioning one.

1) Faulty Sensor or Communication Module Replacement: Sensor node malfunctions may have its root cause on specific components of the node, leading to the replacement of only the bad component. A malfunctioning S&A NETDEV detected by, e.g., a Flat Line, could be possibly caused by a broken sensor that was used on the task execution requested. Therefore, the replacement process requires only the exchange of that specific sensor. On the other hand, if the malfunction is detected by, e.g., a No Value method, probably it is caused by problems on the communication module. The S&A NETDEV becomes temporarily unavailable, until the component exchange, by a shop-floor operator, is finished. When the replacement of the sensor or communication module is finished and the sensor node is connected again to the network, the UG will detect incoming readings from the same sensor board once again. Then, SAAM associates this new sensor node to the previously unavailable S&A NETDEV, making it available for task execution once again. If the communication module was replaced, the MAC Address associated with the S&A NETDEV is updated by the new one.

2) Sensor Board Replacement: In the I-RAMP^3 context, *OTAP* is used not for firmware update but for flashing a new sensor board for the first time it connects to the network, after replacing a failing sensor node. The process begins the moment a malfunction sensor node is detected during task execution and, a shop-floor operator diagnosis confirms the root cause being on the sensor board. This implies replacing the failing sensor board only, without exchanging good components connected to it, such as sensors and communication module. With the I-RAMP^3 *OTAP* approach, the shop-floor operator avoids flashing manually a new sensor board before it is connected to the system.

From the UG perspective, a sensor node can send two types of messages to a gateway node: sensor reading messages containing the sensor node information, as the actual measurement made, and "Alive" messages containing only information about the sensor node. The sensor node information required are the sensor board ID and MAC Address of the communication module. When the UG detects an "Alive" message, it means that the sender sensor node is not running any firmware yet and is waiting to receive instructions for an *OTAP* process. Because only the sensor board was replaced, the UG detects a MAC Address that was already associated with an existing S&A NETDEV but a different sensor board ID. This means that, despite a new sensor board, the sensor node is associated once again to the previously unavailable S&A NETDEV. Since "Alive" messages are received instead of sensor readings messages and the sensor node is associated with an existing S&A NETDEV (due to the matching MAC Address), a new *OTAP* process begins.

First, SAAM identifies which firmware is the right one to flash the sensor node via *OTAP*, based on the previously created S&A NETDEV capabilities. Hence, SAAM informs the UG to start a new instance of the OTA Shell, using the identified binary image to flash the specific sensor node. The UG runs the OTA-Shell, which starts by scanning the network to locate the new node to be flashed. When the sensor node is found, the UG sends the binary file to the identified node, which stores the file on the Secure Digital (SD) card. After receiving the program successfully, the sensor node reboots several times in order to start the execution of the new firmware. The firmware is copied from the SD card to the Flash Memory and the sensor node starts running the new binary file. After restoring its configuration, the sensor node is ready to operate again, by measuring again the environmental conditions and send the results to the gateway node. The UG will receive again sensor reading messages and the corresponding S&A NETDEV will change its internal state, becoming available for task execution once again.

3) Replace the Entire Sensor Node: The malfunctions detected may be severe to the point where none of the component on the sensor node can be saved, forcing the replacement of the entire sensor node. When this happens, a new sensor node is connected to the network, which will send to gateway node a sensor node ID and MAC Address that are new to the UG, resulting in the creation of a new S&A NETDEV by SAAM, available to take requests for task execution. The only way SAAM knows which tasks the new S&A NETDEV is able to perform, is by parsing the messages received from the sensor node and detect which are the sensor types connected to it. This occurs when the new sensor node is already flashed with the right firmware for the task intended. On the other hand, if "Alive" messages are received, SAAM can not possibly know which tasks the new sensor node is able to perform, because the messages received do not have any sensor readings to be identified and SAAM does not have a background to associate this sensor node to an existing S&A NETDEV with capabilities already identified.

V. I-RAMP^3 TECHNOLOGY VALIDATION

The results generated in I-RAMP^3 are relevant to the European manufacturing industries, specially in the field of fast ramp-up and commissioning of production lines. In order to ensure maximum impact, physical demonstrators were built in order to demonstrate and validate the I-RAMP^3 concept, which are described next. The aim of this section is to identify the demonstration goals of the project, according to the industrial requirements defined earlier, and to describe and discuss the demonstrators results, focusing on the sensor & actuators component implementations. The partners of the I-RAMP^3 consortium elaborated and compiled their current practises and problems into a number of quality goals, based on the results obtained on the I-RAMP^3 approaches. Some of these quality goals are shown on Table I.

TABLE I. I-RAMP^3 consortium current quality goals.

Quality Goals	Current Approach	I-RAMP^3 Approach
Time for component exchange	30 - 90 min	<5 min
Number of manual backup operations	10	0
Timeliness of backup data	Depending on the backup interval (e.g., daily or weekly)	Real-time
Configuring welding parameters	3 days	<2 hours
Adapting a welding process	1 day	<2 hours
Malfunction analysis time	Several hours	A few minutes
Level of setup personnel	High-skilled staff	Technician or novice engineer
Process parameter configuring	Several hours	A few minutes
Adapting to a new product	Several hours	A few minutes
Flexibility in use of standard subsystems	Manually configured	Self configuring subsystems

The demonstrators quality goals are classified into seven categories, namely reduction of process configuration time and efforts, faster and better local and remote trouble shooting capabilities, easy addition of sensors, actuators and production units to the production network, easy integrated management of the production network and proactive maintenance scheduling. Most of these goals were tested and validated in three main demonstrators, namely the demonstration towards 1) set-up and ramp-up of a new E-Vehicle assembly line, demonstration towards 2) enhancing device with re-use and predictive maintenance capabilities and finally the demonstration towards 3) component exchange in E-Vehicle subassembly unit. For the Sensor & Actuators components only the first two demonstrators were validated.

A. Demonstration towards set-up and ramp-up of a new E-Vehicle assembly line

This demonstrator consisted of validating equipment and sensor auto-detection in production environments, flexible and easy-configurable production using task-driven manufacturing and rapid ramp-up after device breakdown or configuration failure. Physically, the demonstrator used a welding machine cell, promoted by AWL. This cell consisted in a safe loading area where the parts to be welded are manually placed in a jig. Once loaded, the jig validates the parts, which are welded by one or more specific welding robots in a specific process (resistance or laser). The assembled product is subsequently manually processed or taken out by a handling robot for the next process step. The welding quality is monitored by a welding process controller. Moreover, the health state of the water cooling system of the cell was performed using liquid flow sensors. Figure 11 represents the AWL welding machine used in this demonstrator.

1) Rapid Ramp-Up After Device Breakdown: This use case aims to validate how a S&A NETDEV can detect malfunctions on the corresponding sensor node and, after replacement, how can the new sensor node learn how to perform the same task as the replaced sensor node did. In the welding cell there are two water flow sensors, which are compliant with the I-RAMP^3.

Figure 11. I-RAMP[3] demonstrator regarding set-up and ramp-up of a new E-Vehicle assembly line.

This allows other NETDEVs in the cell to quickly monitor the sensor's readings, unit of measurement, boundaries, etc., without worrying about the hardware specifications. In order to monitor the state of its cooling system, the Device NETDEV, which corresponds to the cell unit, requests a water flow *Measurement* task to the S&A NETDEVs. Figure 12 is a screenshot of the PlugThings Framework, which represents the water flow readings of one flow sensor used in the welding cell.

In this case, the maximum flow rate, expressed in liters per minute (l/min), of the sensors used is around 30 l/min and the minimum is 0 l/min. By the analysis of Figure 12, the normal flow rate of the welding cell is around 9 l/min and the maximum variation detected is +/-0.5 l/min. The flow rate of the welding cell could also be controlled manually, by opening or closing a water tap. One can observe this manual variation around the timestamps 01:54 pm until 01:55 pm. Regarding the perspective of the S&A NETDEV, Figure 13 represents the S&A NETDEV information before (process state is "Standby") and after (process state is "Productive") the water flow *Measurement* task execution. Besides the S&A NETDEV process state, other information is available, such as the type of the corresponding sensor, the most recent sensor reading, timestamp of each sample, cell or shop-floor area where the sensor node is located and the *OTAP* state.

To validate this use case, a malfunction on the sensor node was simulated, by disconnecting a wire on the sensor board during the *Measurement* task execution of the S&A NETDEV. This simulation results in misleading sensor readings (in this case 0) without any variation what so ever, as can be seen on timestamp 01:58pm in Figure 13. The S&A NETDEV quickly detects a Struck-at-fault type error and stops the task execution and change its own state to "Engineering". This process state means that the S&A NETDEV becomes unavailable to continue or accepting new task requests until maintenance is performed on the corresponding sensor node. In this case, this maintenance was in the form of replacing the sensor board by a new empty one, which results in the sensor node reconfiguration process, via *OTAP*. When the *OTAP* process is complete, the S&A NETDEV changes its process state to "Standby", waiting for new task requests from other NETDEVs. The described behavior of the S&A NETDEV is represented on Figure 14.

B. Demonstration towards enhancing device with re-use and predictive maintenance capabilities

This demonstration consisted of validating scenarios regarding a Device NETDEV optimization models, analysis models for predictive maintenance and the re-use of components based on condition monitoring. Physically, it was used a welding machine, developed by TECHNAX, based on resistance welding. This machine performs welding jobs on forks and electrical components on a brush-holder (used in alternators). First, a metal sheet is punched out and bent into a work piece. Then, two different forks are positioned on one work piece. Finally, both forks and work piece are assembled. Sensors were used in predictive maintenance, namely 1) detection of welding process disturbances based on the electrodes temperature values and 2) automatic calibration of exposure time on an optical metrology system, promoted by INOS Hellas. Figure 15 represents the TECHNAX welding machine used in this demonstrator.

1) Predictive Maintenance: This scenario intends to validate how monitoring the electrode's temperature variation on a welding cycle and finding patterns between welding cycles can provide additional information regarding the electrode's wear out. Monitoring welding parameters give additional information in order to predict bad components exchange and also to decrease the machine down time. Figure 16 illustrates the electrodes' temperature variation on different welding cycles.

In this scenario, each welding cycle lasted around 200ms and the temperature sensors had a measurement cycle of approximately 4ms (250Hz). The sensor starts collecting temperature measurements only when the electrode temperature surpasses the room temperature. The sensor saves this reading as initial temperature of the process and, for the next 200ms, it collects every temperature reading. In the end of the welding cycle, the sensor collected around 50 measurements, which are sent to the gateway node. Using the I-RAMP[3] technology, the welding machine corresponds to a Device NETDEV and the sensor node, which contains a thermocouple, corresponds to a S&A NETDEV. The S&A NETDEV stores the received temperature readings. The Device NETDEV requests, via TDD, a *Measurement* task from the S&A NETDEV, which sends, via QRD, the sensor readings. The Device NETDEV processes these results and restarts the welding process.

2) Automatic Calibration: This scenario intends to validate how sensors can improve a metrology process. In this case, the metrology system is composed by cameras and lasers. The system is used in the welding process, by detecting patterns on a captured image, analysing if the forks are well positioned regarding the work piece. There are several ways external sensors can be applied to assist this type of metrology systems. One of them takes into account the luminosity conditions in which the measurement is being made. It is evident that the light conditions in the region where the measurement is being made can negatively influence the results, leading to either false positives or false negatives. Therefore, luminosity sensors are used to provide a reliable and effective feedback regarding the variation of light conditions. Figure 17 represents a screenshot of the analysis of two image captures of a fork

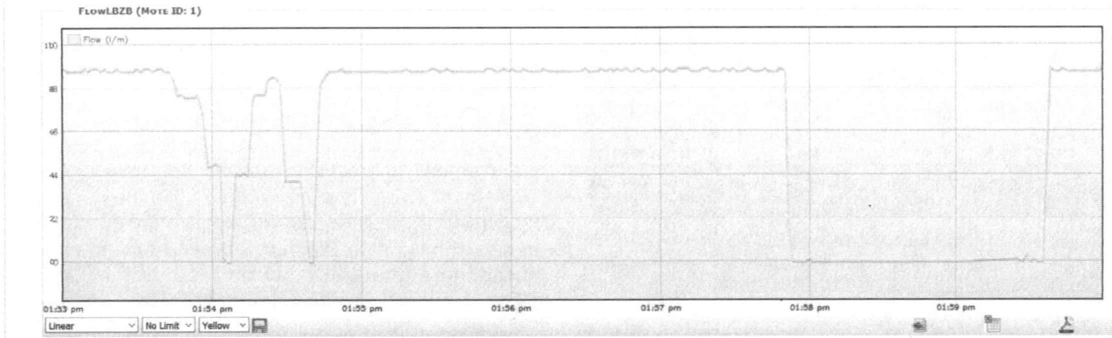

Figure 12. Water flow variation on PlugThings Framework.

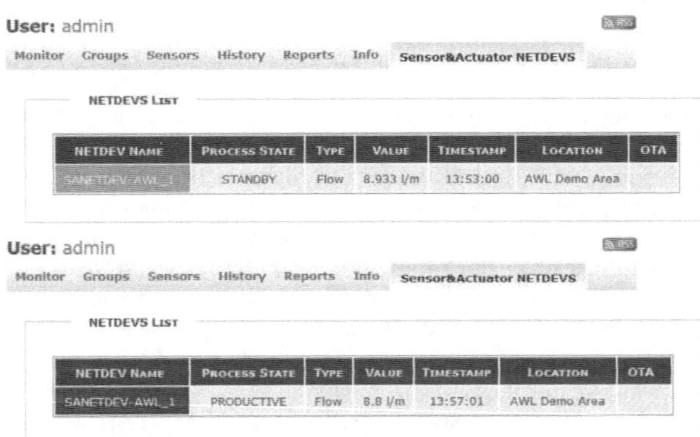

Figure 13. S&A NETDEV information on PlugThings Framework, before and after a *Measurement* task execution.

Figure 15. I-RAMP[3] demonstrator regarding enhancing device with re-use and predictive maintenance capabilities.

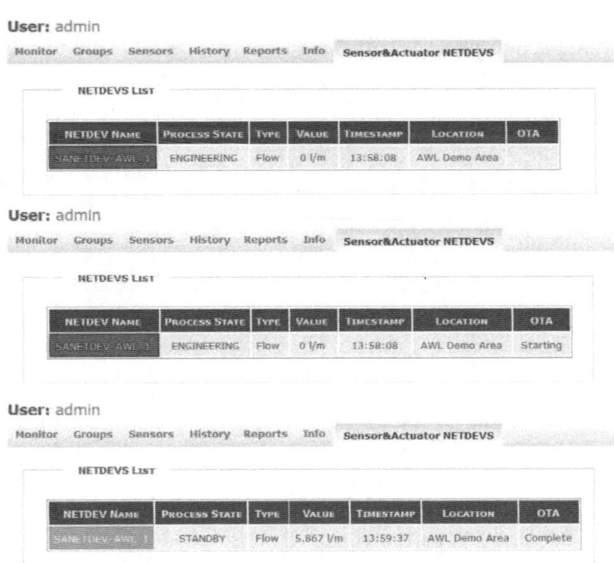

Figure 14. S&A NETDEV reconfiguration process when a sensor node malfunction is detected.

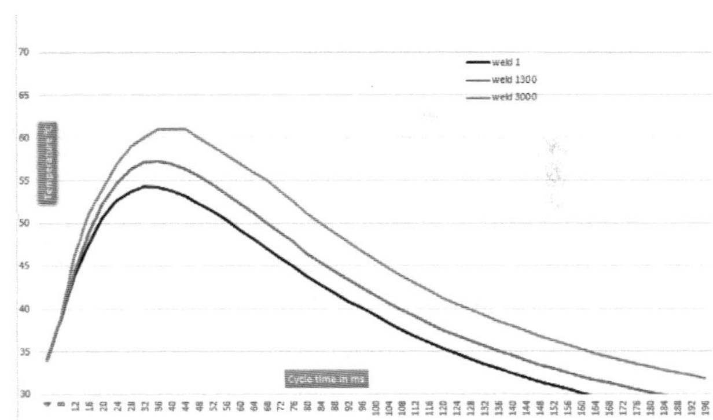

Figure 16. Electrodes' temperature variation on different welding cycles.

at the beginning of a welding process. The image on the left was taken without any exposure calibration, so detecting the fork is very difficult. On the other hand, the image on the right was taken with exposure calibration, so the fork was detected sucessfully.

The scenario is composed physically by a WSN, where each node is equipped with one luminosity sensor, a metrology system, composed by a camera and a laser and, the welding

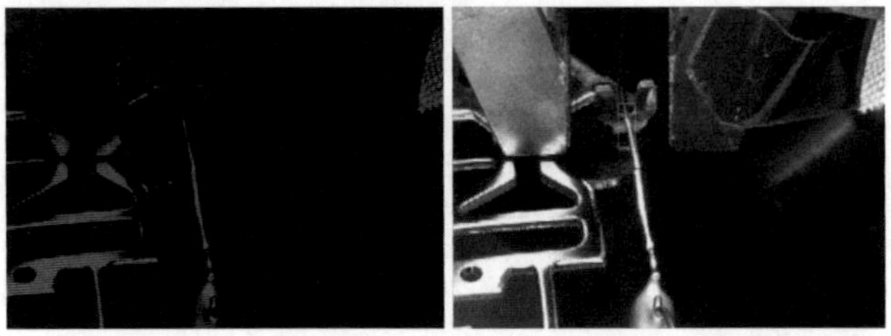

Figure 17. Metrology analysis of a non-calibrated and a calibrated camera image captures of a fork.

machine. The sensor nodes are distributed uniformly around the area to be monitored (the electrodes region). Using the I-RAMP³ technology, each sensor node corresponds to one S&A NETDEV, the welding machine and the metrology system correspond both to Device NETDEVs. For easiness on explaining, they will be called TNX NETDEV for the welding machine and INOS NETDEV for the metrology system.

In order to start a new welding cycle, the TNX NETDEV requests the INOS NETDEV for fork presence, which starts by capturing an image, analyse it and send the result back. The success of the image analysis depends greatly on the quality of the image. To maintain a high quality on the image, the exposure time of the camera must be adjusted before taking the picture, according to the luminosity conditions (The darker the luminosity conditions are, the higher should be the exposure time). Therefore, before capturing the image, the INOS NETDEV must request a *Group Formation* task to one of the available S&A NETDEVs on the network. The S&A NETDEV should have capabilities for luminosity measurement and the corresponding sensor node should be physically located on the same machine as the metrology system is. The S&A NETDEV form a "luminosity" group, which is constantly monitored by a Process Analyzer NETDEV. If one of these sensors is not working properly or is down, the Process Analyzer can detect it by means of the Spatial Correlation technique.

VI. Discussion

As discussed several times throughout the present paper, the use of WSNs is referred as a key element on the I-RAMP³ project. It has been explored as a benefit for the today's Manufacturing Systems by pushing forward the plug and produce concept and taking advantages of the latest technologies to do so. This plug and produce concept is achieved using the NETDEV concept on shop-floor equipment, which can readily describe and detail their own capabilities and announce themselves into the network to other NETDEV entities. The NETDEV technology allows collaboration between industrial equipments and execution of shop-floor tasks on demand. Therefore, the NETDEV technology delivers an easy and flexible solution for the industrial domain. Taking into account WSNs, all this flexibility and readiness is achieved making use of all the functionalities presented in previous sections, both at software and hardware level.

As described earlier, the collaboration between sensors, by means of *Group Formation* tasks is a way of reducing the communication entropy. This is important when several measurements from neighbor sensors need to be collected. Additionally, sensor collaboration aims for providing qualitative information (based on trend analysis) instead of quantitative (raw data). This means that the task requester does not need to have implemented any statistical techniques and doesn't make any extra sensor data processing, since this is done on the sensor side. Also, grouping sensors of different types and with different capabilities offers new sensing capabilities that are not available just with single sensors. Sensor collaboration is allied with the sensor location functionality, which allows to know, with a certain degree of precision, the location of sensors in a restricted area. Automatic sensor location influences and guides how sensors should organize and collaborate among themselves, ensuring the system reliability and effectiveness.

Sensor diagnosis capabilities provides feedback about the health conditions of the WSN, making use of sensor validation techniques already explored in the literature and tested in manufacturing environments. This diagnosis ensures a better monitoring of the manufacturing process and, therefore, is extremely beneficial in the prediction of maintenance phases. Also, the mechanism to detect malfunction sensors inside a sensor group is able to exclude a malfunction sensor node and replacing it by a new available one, without pausing the task execution. Maintenance can be done prior to the task execution. If redundancy on the number of sensors is not possible, sensor reconfiguration capabilities present a way to quickly react and resolve the diagnosed sensor malfunction, which may become a bottleneck on the production line. Recovery from failures offers more flexibility to the maintenance process, without requiring high-qualified technical personnel.

Another advantage of this approach is related with all the functionalities already available from a dedicated framework, releasing the user from being concerned about sensor collaboration and data processing. The only concern is the sensor integration, which is done using the S&A NETDEV template solution. From that point, information can be easily accessed, monitored and diagnosed. Thus, it is not required for the final user to know in detail how to implement a WSN diagnostics system. Instead, the focus should be on what to do when a certain malfunction has occurred and how to relate sensor group information with the product life-cycle in terms of process parameterization. This advantage is enhanced with the automatic process of forming, deforming and reacting to sudden changes in a sensor group, based on a certain task parameters and sensor location. Since the communication between NETDEV entities is based on a standardized task-driven XML language – DIL - it is very easy to implement a new system that encapsulates a machine, capable of communicating with these entities and easily interpret sensor information for process monitoring.

Additionally, this approach presents a self-reconfiguration capability when facing sudden sensor breakdown. In a real manufacturing environment situation, the shop-floor operator only needs to find the malfunctioning sensor node (information already provided by the Process Analyzer NETDEV) and replace its hardware by a new one. Automatically, the sensor node reconfigures itself by being re programed over the air, sparing the user to remove the sensor node, connects the board to a PC and writes or rewrites any lines of code.

In the perspective of the Manufacturing System Designer, there are benefits regarding the application of WSNs in industry. Based on the fact that most manufacturing environments are currently using wired sensors solutions instead of WSNs, the cabling complexity and savings in terms of installation time and cost can be reached, avoiding connecting and configuring sensors on PLCs or Machine Controllers. Wireless is a preferable solution, because of the amount of sensors used and their (sometimes) harsh locations on the shop-floor, and the effort associated with changing the code in the PLC to configure a new sensor. The easiness to integrate a new sensor into the system is achieved by only switching on a sensor node, using the plug and produce concept, which is automatically recognized as a S&A NETDEV, becoming ready for use. The plug and produce concept allows a rapid reaction to any foreseen and unforeseen events, such as sensor replacement, sensor addition for redundancy purposes in critical environments or in the case of sensor removal when disassembling a production line.

However, despite all the benefits that the plug and produce concept bring to the shop-floor, and based on the fact that most of the manufacturing systems nowadays have stable and functional production methods, there is mandatory to make, first, a risk assessment to evaluate how security issues associated with the new technology can threaten the company by making it venerable and, second, a coherent business plan to assess the impact of such a technology installation in the production line.

Security is a big issue in the industrial sector, specially nowadays, where networked infrastructures are used to connect several manufacturing systems. Companies are very concern to protect both their private data and know-how. Actually, methods for security can be in the form of entity identification and authentication for multi-level access control, network and communication protection, privacy, trust and management of information, and system fault tolerance. Regarding the use of industrial equipment, specially connected equipment such as WSNs, extended with the I-RAMP[3] technology, security concerns can be identified at the physical level, which includes equipment and communication, and cyber level, which includes the NETDEV infrastructure.

Zia and Jain [62], [63] pointed out that sensor networks pose unique security challenges because of their computing and communication limitations. Since security approaches require a certain amount of resources, such as data memory, storage space and energy to power the sensor node, it is difficult to implement such approaches in a WSN. It would be highly expose to remote tempering of it's sensor nodes, since the communication protocol may not be robust enough to guaranty a reliable communication. Moreover, WSNs may be deployed in environments where their sensor nodes would be prone to physical tempering, such as capture and vandalism. Sert [64] identified and described various attack types that are frequent in WSNs and corresponding defense mechanisms.

Regarding the NETDEV technology, security is directly associated with the network security level and the infrastructure that supports the NETDEVs, in this case, the UPnP protocol. Wong [65] identified many security threats on a MAS, such as corrupted naming and matchmaking services, insecure communication channel, insecure delegation and lack of accountability. Although many approaches [65], [66] tried to implement a security infrastructure for MAS, security itself should be a design characteristic in protocols and frameworks used for agent-oriented systems. In the case of the UPnP, this protocol was build on the assumption that the network is secure and only trusted devices have access to it. Selén [67] points out that the UPnP architecture currently provides one solution for security [68]. This solution proposes a relatively complex set of protocols and procedures, which make designing a secure UPnP-compliant device both expensive and time-consuming. Also, the plug and play capabilities of the protocol become jeopardized, since this scheme requires active human interaction, where the user must enter a password for entity authentication. More recently, Pehkonen [69] proposed and applied a patent for a secure UPnP network architecture.

A more business oriented perspective was taken in [70], where some aspects such as the impact of technology installation, human resources and training were discussed. The authors refer that such a technology would require an initial investment in human resources for machine adaptation and to fine tune the NETDEVs concept to be compliant with the overall manufacturing system, along with the required time for testing and validation. Additionally, training the system's end-users would also be required, along with a reformulation of the shop-floor action protocols. Nevertheless, the authors point out that not every equipment on a production line needs to be adapted. Possibly, only the more critical machines for maintenance or with high number of ramp-up phases should be shielded with the NETDEV, taking advantage of all inherent functionalities of the technology. This way, a previous analysis should be made, regarding the relation of the amount of machines that can be virtualized as a NETDEV against the long-term required investment. In that sense, this kind of system adaptation is more preferable to be applicable in machines with an expected long-term use, like several years, rather than a couple of months, due to the difficulty to overcome the CAPEX required to achieve the companies goals of performance and effectiveness. Although all these advantages could be achieved without the NETDEV concept, they would require a significantly higher effort for installation and maintenance. Therefore, to achieve the same level of efficiency and effectiveness, it would be necessary a considerably higher CAPEX and OPEX throughout a long time-span. For this reason, the NETDEV technology is more appealing and definitely a better cost-benefit approach.

VII. Roadmap for the Future

Flexibility is seen as one of the key aspects for bringing manufacturing back to Europe on a large scale basis. The tendency to more customized products and demand-driven manufacturing processes is seen as an opportunity for Europe's manufacturing industry – and in particular the Small and Medium-sized Enterprises (SMEs) – to respond to the nowadays leading roles, mainly of Asian companies in mass-oriented production. In order to meet the challenges that come up with rapid changing product portfolios, smaller lot sizes and continuously evolving process technologies, manufacturing systems are required to be easily upgradeable, into which new technologies and new functions can be readily integrated [71]. Demands for increasing productivity through highly optimized production processes create the need for novel manufacturing control systems, which are required to manage product and production variability and disturbances effectively and efficiently [17], and to implement agility, flexibility and reactivity.

In order to meet these challenges, high efforts have been made and are still to be done in research for flexible and agile manufacturing systems. Significant improvements in reconfiguration, performance or disturbance handling have been shown. However, the large-scale adoption in the industry is still missing. Among others, the major barriers are seen in proprietary tools, equipment and software systems as well as missing standards of usually heterogeneous manufacturing environments [16]. A coexistence of classical and advanced technologies as well as the stepwise approach is required in order to introduce new technology successfully [72].

Even more important for a broad take-up of new technology in industry is the technological feasibility and industrial readiness as well as a consequent cooperation of end users, system and components suppliers and research, in order to minimize the risks on investments and to gain acceptance at the end users side [73].

As a consequence, an integrated approach is required in order to tackle the challenges of wide technology uptake. Industrial leadership and the reflection of the complete added-value chain is needed. The requirements and opinions of big end users are very important as they finally use such flexible systems in their factories and thus, need to be taken into account in a very early stage. However, a very specific technological development for one or a very limited number of end users as a part of the I-RAMP^3 consortium is not efficient in order to guarantee a broad technology uptake. This would probably limit the technology development and deployment to the specific needs of the respective end users and hamper a wider penetration on the market. Much more promising is an approach in which the component and equipment suppliers as well as the system integrators play a leading role. This group is predesignated to overcome the limitations as they provide a huge technological basis for a huge number of application areas. They are usually in close contact to the end users and are often involved in the end users' strategic planning for innovation management [74]. SMEs are in particular important as they are the key driver of innovation in Europe [75]. Enabling the SMEs for the development and production of flexible systems for a broad number of applications, would therefore form the basis of a wide technology uptake in the industry.

Of essential importance is a widespread technology basis rather than only a punctual implementation and integration of technology. Several application areas and industrial sectors need to be address in parallel in order to achieve a critical mass of deployment. Standardization and harmonization needs to be taken into account and approaches for a smooth integration of legacy systems need to be developed. Several research studies demonstrated, based on concrete data and evidence, the benefits and role of standards in supporting and driving research and innovation. Standards play a multiple, catalytic role in the innovation system and in research projects by providing common terminologies, harmonised methodologies and comparability between research activities. At the same time, standards have a particular importance for market acceptance of technology-based innovation, by improving the marketability of research and innovation results.

VIII. Conclusions

Innovative intelligent systems have driven technology for years, and industry has followed this track. This enables manufacturing processes to improve their reliability and responsiveness when facing production changes or downtime, as well as time efficiency to minimize costs and effectiveness to increase production quality. These objectives guided the NETDEV development. Intelligent functionalities, such as information sharing by inter-device communication, device self-description, collaboration and negotiation, process optimization and condition monitoring are inherent capabilities of the NETDEVs. Applied to sensor & actuators, these capabilities are extended to self-organization, automatic device location, WSN health monitoring with diagnosis and automatic reconfiguration. Therefore, by taking advantage of these functionalities, one can greatly influence industrial processes regarding the decrease of ramp-up time, as well as the time needed to recover from scheduled and unscheduled maintenance. These results are a competitive advantage in demanding and fluctuating contexts. The main developments presented throughout the paper depict that, in terms of WSNs applicability in industry, there are open opportunities to explore new solutions and to improve the currently used systems. Despite the benefits of all functionalities presented in this paper, the boost of the deployment of smart components developed within I-RAMP^3 technology is needed, by unifying efforts towards the swift standardization of NETDEVs. The acceptance of NETDEVS and WSNs into industrial context needs to be pushed forward, by creating a developers' community and performing more pragmatic and real test-case demonstrators. The present work is a clear step forward into a reliable and flexible approach for industrial WSNs, aiming for paving the way into more intelligent manufacturing systems.

Acknowledgment

This research was supported by project I-RAMP^3 (FoF.NMP.2012-3) – Intelligent Network Devices for fast Ramp-up – funded by the European Commission under the Seventh Framework Programme for Research and Technological Development. We would like to show our gratitude to the whole I-RAMP3 consortium for all the support, assistance and fruitfull collaboration that resulted in the all the achievements and technological advances depicted in the present paper.

References

[1] R. Pinto, J. Reis, R. Silva, V. Sousa, and G. Gonçalves, "Self-organising smart components in advanced manufacturing systems," in INTELLI 2015, The Fourth International Conference on Intelligent Systems and Applications. IARIA, 2015, pp. 157–163.

[2] R. Pinto, J. Reis, V. Sousa, R. Silva, and G. Gonçalves, "Self-diagnosis and automatic configuration of smart components in advanced manufacturing systems," in INTELLI 2015, The Fourth International Conference on Intelligent Systems and Applications. IARIA, 2015, pp. 164–169.

[3] P. Baronti, P. Pillai, V. W. Chook, S. Chessa, A. Gotta, and Y. F. Hu, "Wireless sensor networks: A survey on the state of the art and the 802.15. 4 and zigbee standards," Computer communications, vol. 30, no. 7, 2007, pp. 1655–1695.

[4] H. Ramamurthy, B. Prabhu, R. Gadh, and A. M. Madni, "Wireless industrial monitoring and control using a smart sensor platform," Sensors Journal, IEEE, vol. 7, no. 5, 2007, pp. 611–618.

[5] J. Chen, X. Cao, P. Cheng, Y. Xiao, and Y. Sun, "Distributed collaborative control for industrial automation with wireless sensor and actuator networks," Industrial Electronics, IEEE Transactions on, vol. 57, no. 12, 2010, pp. 4219–4230.

[6] L. Ruiz-Garcia, L. Lunadei, P. Barreiro, and I. Robla, "A review of wireless sensor technologies and applications in agriculture and food industry: state of the art and current trends," sensors, vol. 9, no. 6, 2009, pp. 4728–4750.

[7] J. J. Evans, "Wireless sensor networks in electrical manufacturing," in Electrical Insulation Conference and Electrical Manufacturing Expo, 2005. Proceedings. IEEE, 2005, pp. 460–465.

[8] V. C. Gungor and G. P. Hancke, "Industrial wireless sensor networks: Challenges, design principles, and technical approaches," Industrial Electronics, IEEE Transactions on, vol. 56, no. 10, 2009, pp. 4258–4265.

[9] X. Cao, J. Chen, Y. Xiao, and Y. Sun, "Distributed collaborative control using wireless sensor and actuator networks," in Future Generation Communication and Networking, 2008. FGCN'08. Second International Conference on, vol. 1. IEEE, 2008, pp. 3–6.

[10] P. Neumann, "Communication in industrial automation—what is going on?" Control Engineering Practice, vol. 15, no. 11, 2007, pp. 1332–1347.

[11] K. Xin, X. Cao, J. Chen, P. Cheng, and L. Xie, "Optimal controller location in wireless networked control systems," International Journal of Robust and Nonlinear Control, vol. 25, no. 2, 2015, pp. 301–319.

[12] J. Barbosa, P. Leitão, E. Adam, and D. Trentesaux, "Dynamic self-organization in holonic multi-agent manufacturing systems: The adacor evolution," Computers in Industry, vol. 66, 2015, pp. 99–111.

[13] Y. Koren and M. Shpitalni, "Design of reconfigurable manufacturing systems," Journal of manufacturing systems, vol. 29, no. 4, 2010, pp. 130–141.

[14] J. Ferber, Multi-agent systems: an introduction to distributed artificial intelligence. Addison-Wesley Reading, 1999, vol. 1.

[15] S. Deen, "Agent-based manufacturing: Advances in the holonic approach, 2003."

[16] P. Leitão, "Agent-based distributed manufacturing control: A state-of-the-art survey," Engineering Applications of Artificial Intelligence, vol. 22, no. 7, 2009, pp. 979–991.

[17] H. Van Brussel, J. Wyns, P. Valckenaers, L. Bongaerts, and P. Peeters, "Reference architecture for holonic manufacturing systems: Prosa," Computers in industry, vol. 37, no. 3, 1998, pp. 255–274.

[18] S. Liu, W. A. Gruver, D. Kotak, and S. Bardi, "Holonic manufacturing system for distributed control of automated guided vehicles," in Systems, Man, and Cybernetics, 2000 IEEE International Conference on, vol. 3. IEEE, 2000, pp. 1727–1732.

[19] L. Mönch, M. Stehli, and J. Zimmermann, "Fabmas: An agent-based system for production control of semiconductor manufacturing processes," in Holonic and Multi-Agent Systems for Manufacturing. Springer, 2003, pp. 258–267.

[20] M. Fletcher, D. McFarlane, A. Lucas, J. Brusey, and D. Jarvis, "The cambridge packing cell—a holonic enterprise demonstrator," in Multi-Agent Systems and Applications III. Springer, 2003, pp. 533–543.

[21] P. Leitão and F. Restivo, "Adacor: A holonic architecture for agile and adaptive manufacturing control," Computers in industry, vol. 57, no. 2, 2006, pp. 121–130.

[22] D. McFarlane et al., "Industrial adoption of agent-based technologies," IEEE Intelligent Systems, no. 1, 2005, pp. 27–35.

[23] S. Bussmann and K. Schild, "Self-organizing manufacturing control: An industrial application of agent technology," in MultiAgent Systems, 2000. Proceedings. Fourth International Conference on. IEEE, 2000, pp. 87–94.

[24] A. W. Colombo, R. Schoop, and R. Neubert, "An agent-based intelligent control platform for industrial holonic manufacturing systems," Industrial Electronics, IEEE Transactions on, vol. 53, no. 1, 2006, pp. 322–337.

[25] F. P. Maturana, R. Staron, K. Hall, P. Tichý, P. Šlechta, and V. Mařík, "An intelligent agent validation architecture for distributed manufacturing organizations," in Emerging Solutions for Future Manufacturing Systems. Springer, 2005, pp. 81–90.

[26] W. Shen, Q. Hao, H. J. Yoon, and D. H. Norrie, "Applications of agent-based systems in intelligent manufacturing: An updated review," Advanced engineering INFORMATICS, vol. 20, no. 4, 2006, pp. 415–431.

[27] T. Ribeiro and G. Gonçalves, "Formal methods for reconfigurable assembly systems," in Emerging Technologies and Factory Automation (ETFA), 2010 IEEE Conference on. IEEE, 2010, pp. 1–6.

[28] GNOSIS Consortium, "Knowledge Systematization: Configuration Systems for Design and Manufacturing," p. 26, 2000. [Online]. Available: http://www.ims.org/wp-content/uploads/2011/11/2.4.12.2-Final-Report-GNOSIS.pdf

[29] J. Peschke, A. Lüder, and H. Kühnle, "The pabadis'promise architecture-a new approach for flexible manufacturing systems," in Emerging Technologies and Factory Automation, 2005. ETFA 2005. 10th IEEE Conference on, vol. 1. IEEE, 2005, pp. 6–pp.

[30] G. Gonçalves, J. Reis, R. Pinto, M. Alves, and J. Correia, "A step forward on intelligent factories: A smart sensor-oriented approach," in Emerging Technology and Factory Automation (ETFA), 2014 IEEE. IEEE, 2014, pp. 1–8.

[31] A. B. Sharma, L. Golubchik, and R. Govindan, "Sensor faults: Detection methods and prevalence in real-world datasets," ACM Transactions on Sensor Networks (TOSN), vol. 6, no. 3, 2010, p. 23.

[32] J. Ravichandran and A. I. Arulappan, "Data validation algorithm for wireless sensor networks," International Journal of Distributed Sensor Networks, vol. 2013, 2013.

[33] Y. Shang and W. Rum, "Improved mds-based localization," in INFOCOM 2004. Twenty-third AnnualJoint Conference of the IEEE Computer and Communications Societies, vol. 4. IEEE, 2004, pp. 2640–2651.

[34] A. Savvides, C.-C. Han, and M. B. Strivastava, "Dynamic fine-grained localization in ad-hoc networks of sensors," in Proceedings of the 7th annual international conference on Mobile computing and networking. ACM, 2001, pp. 166–179.

[35] D. Niculescu and B. Nath, "Ad hoc positioning system (aps)," in Global Telecommunications Conference, 2001. GLOBECOM'01. IEEE, vol. 5. IEEE, 2001, pp. 2926–2931.

[36] N. B. Priyantha, A. K. Miu, H. Balakrishnan, and S. Teller, "The cricket compass for context-aware mobile applications," in Proceedings of the 7th annual international conference on Mobile computing and networking. ACM, 2001, pp. 1–14.

[37] P. Bahl, V. N. Padmanabhan, and A. Balachandran, "Enhancements to the radar user location and tracking system," technical report, Microsoft Research, Tech. Rep., 2000.

[38] K. Vandenbussche et al., "Fine-grained indoor localisation using wireless sensor networks," Signal, vol. 75, 2005, p. 70.

[39] T. Singal, Wireless communications. Tata McGraw-Hill Education, 2010.

[40] C. Levis, J. T. Johnson, and F. L. Teixeira, Radiowave propagation: physics and applications. John Wiley & Sons, 2010.

[41] A. F. Molisch, Wireless communications. John Wiley & Sons, 2007.

[42] G. Tolle, J. Polastre, R. Szewczyk, D. Culler, N. Turner, K. Tu, S. Burgess, T. Dawson, P. Buonadonna, D. Gay et al., "A macroscope in the redwoods," in Proceedings of the 3rd international conference on Embedded networked sensor systems. ACM, 2005, pp. 51–63.

[43] G. Barrenetxea, F. Ingelrest, G. Schaefer, M. Vetterli, O. Couach, and M. Parlange, "Sensorscope: Out-of-the-box environmental monitoring," in Information Processing in Sensor Networks, 2008. IPSN'08. International Conference on. IEEE, 2008, pp. 332–343.

[44] N. Ramanathan, L. Balzano, M. Burt, D. Estrin, T. Harmon, C. Harvey, J. Jay, E. Kohler, S. Rothenberg, and M. Srivastava, "Rapid deployment with confidence: Calibration and fault detection in environmental sensor networks," Center for Embedded Network Sensing, 2006.

[45] R. Szewczyk, A. Mainwaring, J. Polastre, J. Anderson, and D. Culler, "An analysis of a large scale habitat monitoring application," in Proceedings of the 2nd international conference on Embedded networked sensor systems. ACM, 2004, pp. 214–226.

[46] N. Branisavljević, Z. Kapelan, and D. Prodanović, "Improved real-time data anomaly detection using context classification," Journal of Hydroinformatics, vol. 13, no. 3, 2011, pp. 307–323.

[47] J.-L. Bertrand-Krajewski, J.-P. Bardin, M. Mourad, and Y. Beranger, "Accounting for sensor calibration, concentration heterogeneity, measurement and sampling uncertainties in monitoring urban drainage systems," Water Science & Technology.

[48] O. J. Mengshoel, M. Chavira, K. Cascio, S. Poll, A. Darwiche, and S. Uckun, "Probabilistic model-based diagnosis: An electrical power system case study," Systems, Man and Cybernetics, Part A: Systems and Humans, IEEE Transactions on, vol. 40, no. 5, 2010, pp. 874–885.

[49] O. J. Mengshoel, A. Darwiche, and S. Uckun, "Sensor validation using bayesian networks," in Proc. 9th International Symposium on Artificial Intelligence, Robotics, and Automation in Space (iSAIRAS-08), 2008.

[50] J. Chen, H. Li, D. Sheng, and W. Li, "A hybrid data-driven modeling method on sensor condition monitoring and fault diagnosis for power plants," International Journal of Electrical Power & Energy Systems, vol. 71, 2015, pp. 274–284.

[51] A. Messai, A. Mellit, I. Abdellani, and A. M. Pavan, "On-line fault detection of a fuel rod temperature measurement sensor in a nuclear reactor core using anns," Progress in Nuclear Energy, vol. 79, 2015, pp. 8–21.

[52] S. Dauwe, D. Oldoni, B. De Baets, T. Van Renterghem, D. Botteldooren, and B. Dhoedt, "Multi-criteria anomaly detection in urban noise sensor networks," Environmental Science: Processes & Impacts, vol. 16, no. 10, 2014, pp. 2249–2258.

[53] K. Zhang, S. Shi, H. Gao, and J. Li, "Unsupervised outlier detection in sensor networks using aggregation tree," in Advanced data mining and applications. Springer, 2007, pp. 158–169.

[54] J. Rossiter and Z. Hensley, "Sensor data management, validation, correction, and provenance for building technologies," ASHRAE Transactions, vol. 120, 2014, p. 370.

[55] B. Iglewicz and D. C. Hoaglin, How to detect and handle outliers. Asq Press, 1993, vol. 16.

[56] G. Olsson, M. Nielsen, Z. Yuan, A. Lynggaard-Jensen, and J.-P. Steyer, "Instrumentation, control and automation in wastewater systems," Water Intelligence Online, vol. 4, 2005, p. 9781780402680.

[57] M. Mourad and J. Bertrand-Krajewski, "A method for automatic validation of long time series of data in urban hydrology," Water Science & Technology, vol. 45, no. 4-5, 2002, pp. 263–270.

[58] L. Jayashree, S. Arumugam, and A. Meenakshi, "A communication-efficient framework for outlier-free data reporting in data-gathering sensor networks," International Journal of Network Management, vol. 18, no. 5, 2008, pp. 437–445.

[59] I. Adly, H. Ragai, A. El-Hennawy, and K. Shehata, "Over-the-air programming of psoc sensor interface in wireless sensor networks," in MELECON 2010-2010 15th IEEE Mediterranean Electrotechnical Conference. IEEE, 2010, pp. 997–1002.

[60] Libelium, "Waspmote Technical Guide," p. 168, 2013. [Online]. Available: http://www.libelium.com/uploads/2013/02/waspmote-technical_guide_eng.pdf

[61] ——, "Over the Air Programming with 802.15.4 and ZigBee: Laying the groundwork," p. 40, 2013. [Online]. Available: http://www.libelium.com/uploads/2013/02/over_the_air_programming.pdf

[62] T. Zia and A. Zomaya, "Security issues in wireless sensor networks," in Systems and Networks Communications, 2006. ICSNC'06. International Conference on. IEEE, 2006, pp. 40–40.

[63] M. K. Jain, "Wireless sensor networks: Security issues and challenges," International Journal of Computer and Information Technology, vol. 2, no. 1, 2011, pp. 62–67.

[64] S. A. Sert, E. Onur, and A. Yazici, "Security attacks and countermeasures in surveillance wireless sensor networks," in Application of Information and Communication Technologies (AICT), 2015 9th International Conference on. IEEE, 2015, pp. 201–205.

[65] H. C. Wong and K. Sycara, "Adding security and trust to multiagent systems," Applied Artificial Intelligence, vol. 14, no. 9, 2000, pp. 927–941.

[66] G. Beydoun, G. Low, H. Mouratidis, and B. Henderson-Sellers, "A security-aware metamodel for multi-agent systems (mas)," Information and Software Technology, vol. 51, no. 5, 2009, pp. 832–845.

[67] K. Selén, "Upnp security in internet gateway devices," in TKK T-110.5190 Seminar on Internetworking, 2006.

[68] C. Ellison, "Upnp security ceremonies version 1.0," in UPnP Forum, 2003.

[69] V. Pehkonen and J. Koivisto, "Secure universal plug and play network," in Information Assurance and Security (IAS), 2010 Sixth International Conference on. IEEE, 2010, pp. 11–14.

[70] M. Kasperczyk and E. Ridders, "Efficient implementation of network-enabled devices into industrial environment," in INTELLI 2015, The Fourth International Conference on Intelligent Systems and Applications. IARIA, 2015, pp. 148–149.

[71] M. G. Mehrabi, A. G. Ulsoy, and Y. Koren, "Reconfigurable manufacturing systems: key to future manufacturing," Journal of Intelligent manufacturing, vol. 11, no. 4, 2000, pp. 403–419.

[72] C. Gerber, H.-M. Hanisch, and S. Ebbinghaus, "From iec 61131 to iec 61499 for distributed systems: a case study," EURASIP Journal on Embedded Systems, vol. 2008, 2008, p. 4.

[73] K. Sundermeyer and S. Bussmann, "Introduction of agent technology into a manufacturing company-experiences from on industrial project," Wirtschaftsinformatik, vol. 43, no. 2, 2001, pp. 135–+.

[74] Siemens PLM Software, "Leveraging suppliers for strategic innovation," 2009. [Online]. Available: http://www.plm.automation.siemens.com/

[75] EuroStat, "Industry and services statistics introduced," 2015. [Online]. Available: http://ec.europa.eu/eurostat/statistics-explained/index.php/Industry_and_services_statistics_introduced

Analysis of Collaborative Design through Action Research: Methodology and Tools

Samia Ben Rajeb
LUCID - University of Liège
Belgium
samia.benrajeb@ulg.ac.be

Pierre Leclercq
LUCID - University of Liège
Belgium
pierre.leclercq@ulg.ac.be

Abstract- **Analysing collective design activities is a complex task, especially in a context that involves the remote collaboration and/or multidisciplinarity. To support such an analysis, this article describes a dedicated process, instrumented by tools that can facilitate the data acquisition and visualization, and implemented in various contexts of higher education. The method presented here enables to cross-reference the two aspects of a collective activity: the process and the content treated by a group. The method offers the possibility to analyse different types of collective work configurations with a high level of flexibility that leaves the possibility to the researcher to update his/her analysis criteria even during the observed activity.**

***Keywords-* collaborative design; methodologies and tools for collaborative activity analysis; visualization of collaborative processes; collaborative action-research project.**

I. INTRODUCTION

Design and construction projects result from a complex collective activity involving several skills, starting at the earliest stages of the process [1]. These skills emerge from the fields of architecture and engineering, naturally, but also from the fields of ecology, sociology, and ergonomics, to name a few [2]. If all these skills need to be united, it is in response to strong competition, increasingly coercive qualitative and regulatory requirements, and short deadlines [3]. To address these real market conditions, design agencies and construction companies are looking for skills elsewhere, and adapt themselves as well as possible to this new context, without necessarily being prepared or equipped beforehand. This is why, today, it is important to fundamentally rethink training for careers in design (architecture, engineering, industrial design, etc.) to prepare future designers for this complex collective activity [1,4].

Indeed, this training is conducted, usually, over 3 to 5 years and is founded on project-based learning. This project-based learning is of course complemented by theoretical coursework that allows students to approach a range of areas necessary to master design. When these students work in teams, they need to manage their activity as a group, define each person's duties, coordinate, build agreements, and negotiate [5] Managing their project turns out to be complex to handle for novice designers as they continue to evolve in the context of ongoing learning and in one following an exploratory process. In this process, which is difficult to break down, they must specify both the functioning of the object to be designed and the means to be implemented. Faced with the difficulties of students working together, understanding a complex exploratory process, changing assumptions, and gaining perspective on their own design and collaboration activities, we ask ourselves the following question: could design be teachable in a format other than "project workshops"?

Without questioning the relevance of project-based learning, which is perfectly adequate for understanding design, we aim, in this article, to put forward a new training style created for design. Our approach, designed to be analytical and co-constructed, is to rethink collective activity in design and thus help the learner, whether Master's students or professionals, to gain perspective on their own activity in expression with others'.

In the aim of defining our own pedagogical approach, this article will first present a state of the art of commonly implemented approaches, to comprehend collective design activities. Then we will discuss our own approach in more detail and its general methods through the description of a training framework, called "workshop +". We follow by defining the four stages that this comprises, as well as the various methodological, theoretical and analytical tools put into play. We will subsequently list its assorted integrated applications, implemented for varied advanced design training sessions. Finally, experience feedback, contributions, limitations and perspectives of this teaching approach will be discussed, drawing conclusions from four years of its implementation in both academic and professional contexts.

II. BACKGROUND TO THE APPROACH

Group activities have been the subject of much research in psychology, ergonomics and cognitive science, for the purposes of modeling such activities [6]. These models are based on two synchronization modes: cognitive, referring to the construction of a context of shared knowledge; and operational, referring to the distribution of tasks among collaborators. These synchronizations are designed to build awareness that allows collaborators to interact with their environment and with the group of participants [7]. The role of common ground is crucial here because it enables each person to share their particular skills and to acquire new skills, to be able work with others [8]. Various studies have also highlighted the complexity of these activities, which varies according to the number of participants [9], the subject of the activity [10] or the time and space in which such interactions take place [11]).

Given this variety of configurations involving multiple participants, diverse methods of technical support have been proposed, which may target particular tool features as well as the organization of assigned workgroups. These forms of technical support come under the scientific framework of CSCW, "Computer Supported Cooperative Work" [12] and more specifically CSCD, "Computer Support for Cooperative Design", which focuses specifically on collective design activities [13].

Our alternative education proposal resides in this scientific field, focusing on instances when different present or remote participants work together around the same design subject. This phase is one of emerging ideas, choices and negotiations that ensue through interactions and artifacts shared among participants; it is even more difficult to understand, observe and analyze as it involves multidisciplinary skills. The original approach that we present in this article is driven by this perspective gained from stepping back from a complex collaborative activity.

Let us begin by contextualizing our approach in relation to others already destined for teaching design, then we will define the type of protocol that we have chosen and the analytical point of view that it is built upon.

A. Selecting an approach

Dedicated to advanced end-of-degree learners (second-year Master's or Research Master's students) or professionals questioning their collaborative design activity [14], the approach proposed here is complementary to that of the conventional workshop. It was elaborated to be collective, with the goal of focusing the attention of the learners on the process rather than on the object to be designed, leading them to a "meta" reflection on their own design process and collaboration.

Involving the active participation of learners in the specification of self-analysis activity, our approach lies in the scientific fields of participatory approaches.

Participatory approaches to research are multiple but strive for the same goal, that is, to associate an experience, an action, practice and analysis [15]. "Action research" is one such approach that breaks away from conventional scientific approaches, which systematically separate action from its analysis, collective practices from their theoretical elaboration [16]. Its main target is to manage the concerns of participants faced with a situation, by the intervention of research aimed at developing a shared understanding of the situation [17]. It is deemed "collaborative" when all participants (researchers and practitioners, observers and designers) attempt to co-construct new meaning relative to their activity [18]. This co-construction is created through the synergy of their views, but also through a reflection on one's own action with respect to others' [19]. According to Desgagné [20], this approach is based on a reciprocal relationship of self/co-reflection, self/co-criticism and, therefore, self/co-training, with oneself and with other collaborators. The implementation of "participatory action research" is mostly seen in the professional training of teachers, child welfare, specialized coaching, or territorial development but is still rarely used in the design field [21]. Integrating this into our approach encompasses a participatory protocol involving several participating designers, observers, and researchers. Its educational purpose is not to assess the value of the design project itself (as is the case for project workshops), but rather to describe the process that brought it about. It does not impose a method of design; instead, it investigates how it is possible to observe, analyze, or break the process down, in order to better perceive the collaborative activity and the complexity of interactions involved.

Our premise on design activity considers it to be one that is complex and difficult to break down, and one whose outcome is first contemplated, negotiated, valued, challenged and co-constructed before even coming into existence.

Two questions arise: How should we speak about the design process? Plus, how it is negotiated and co-deliberated by the group? To answer these questions, original tools have been created to query design and collaboration. They have been defined so that all designer/observer/researcher participants co-construct integrated meaning and decide all actions which result from it [22, p. 83]. They propose data harvesting protocols, processing and analysis of the observation data most appropriate to this analysis approach and help to collectively understand the complexity of the components of a collaborative design activity.

B. Defining the protocol

Since the 1990s, many studies have endeavoured to promote and assist collective activity. To summarize, we distinguish them as follows:

- those seeking to categorize and define collective activity [23];
- those focusing on the technical aspects of this activity [24];
- those concentrating on its social aspects [25];
- those concerned with developing human-machine interfaces, others with human-human interfaces, to assist collaboration [26];
- those developing methods and tools for the analysis of this complex activity in their real context or in a laboratory [27].

Focusing on the latter aspect to comprehend collective activity, one of the main data collection and processing methods for the analysis of collaborative situations is protocol analysis [28], which is generally intended for comments in controlled environments. This protocol analysis is based on two data collection methods: retrospective protocols and concurrent protocols. Each method can produce similar results for a coherent understanding of the problem-solving process, but they can also complete each other, according to research objectives [29].

Retrospective protocols. This protocol consists in asking the participant under observation, after (s)he has completed the activity, to choose elements representative of their activity, and then to describe them in order to better identify the specific features of their work, alone or in a group. It relates, therefore, to the study of design objects and their components as distinct from the situations in which the former evolve [28, 30]. This approach aids, we believe, in changing the point of view of the designers regarding their design object by asking them to conceptualize their activity and to utilize their memory. It has been shown elsewhere that, although the stored information may rely on short-term memory, this cumulative data can provide relevant details for the research question [27] and the origins of the decisions for the resolution of various problems [31]. Self-confrontation may also be another approach for analyzing an already completed task [32]. This consists in requesting a participant to perform a self-assessment of his or her own work processes (alone and/or with others) from footage of their activity [33]. However, we find this other method requires too substantial an investment by the participant in terms of time and research involvement.

Concurrent protocols. This protocol consists in asking the participant to verbalize his or her thoughts out loud while working on a specific task ("thinking aloud" [34]). These thoughts are then transcribed, coded and analyzed by the researcher. This approach rests on the assumption that the verbalization of thoughts during the problem-solving process does not affect the process [28]. Other researchers do not agree with this assumption, however, and consider "retrospective protocols" to be less intrusive in the process, as the protocol is put into practice following the completion of activity [35]. Yet, as part of a collective activity, the interlocutors are naturally found obliged to communicate and verbalize their thoughts to work together.

Thus, we consider that the "concurrent protocol" is meaningful since it better approaches real conditions of the activity and its context. Taking the activity's real context into account reinforces the ecological validity of our advanced training and does not exclude the social processes, teamwork and communication that constitute the reality of daily work.

C. *Application to a twofold analytical approach*

Analytical approaches are varied and may result in qualitative or quantitative results. As taking a step back seeks to be constructive and objectifiable for the learner, it is necessary to achieve a certain degree of precision in the processing and analysis of data observed. Analytical methods known in the literature are generally based on a segmentation system which, according to Nguyen et al. [31], can be oriented according to the process or content.

Process-oriented segmentation. This approach makes it possible to break the process down into several sequences related to the participants' intentions and to identify the time spent on each of these sequences, as well as the correlation between them. As proposed by Gronier [36], the COMET method [5] is used to describe the main phases of identification and argumentation of a problem. The coding grid, developed for the specific analysis of viewpoint confrontation processes in concurrent engineering [37], allows researchers in turn to draw up a tree of proposals and verbal interactions between collaborators' work. The analysis carried out by ALCESTE word processing software [38] also makes it possible to structure the information involved and shared by participants to solve a problem. Although all these methods complement each other, this "process-oriented segmentation" approach has nevertheless been criticized in some studies because it does not focus enough on content, i.e., on the problem addressed, on documents or even on annotations produced by the participants during the activity under observation (39).

Content-oriented segmentation. This approach makes it possible to complete the one above since it is specifically concerned with artifacts (e.g., pictures, notes, references, and models) and enables us to examine the cognitive interaction between designer and artifacts [40]. One of the best-known methods among these is that of Gero [41], which offers an encoding principle, named FBS, dependent on the functionality of the object ("Function"), the behaviour of participants ("Behaviour") and the collaborative structure ("Structure"). The author there considers design to be a series of transformations of the model's functions. Brassac and Gregori [42] proposed, for their part, a clinical approach which focuses on real activity and its various interactions by studying discursive productions, gestures, graphical representations and conversational sequences. This approach, according to their research [42], allows not only speech acts to be classified, by breaking them down into sequences and sub-sequences, but also the conversational dynamic between collaborators to be illustrated. In a similar vein, through the use of ethnographic studies, Boujut and Laureillard [43] immersed themselves directly into a real industrial environment and proposed a method of "action research", analyzing the framework and introducing new tools to aid in collaboration.

III. Definition of Advanced Training: Workshop+

Relative to the state of the art examined above, our approach lies clearly in "participatory action research". In the workshop proposed here, we group together supervising researchers and learners playing either the role of designer or of observer. All participants involved in this process are thus "engaged in a critical, dynamic reflection upon a situation that appeals to them" [22, p. 78]. So they are all active participants in the experiment. They participate together in data collection as well as in its processing and analysis by the co-construction of shared meaning around a collaborative design activity. In this context, the approach chosen was that of "concurrent protocols", focusing on the process and its evolution over time ("process-oriented segmentation") as well as on the design draft examined and on the interactions involved in building it ("Content-oriented segmentation").

By taking an interest in advanced university courses as well as in professional training, the challenge of our approach lies in the context concerned with our workshop+. It can take place either 1) in an educational context of project execution, possibly with large amounts of onerous data to be analyzed, or 2) in a professional context that, for privacy reasons, does not allow audio and/or video data to be recorded to process and analyze later, data being based on verbalization and transcription. This consists in confronting the participants with their (oral and graphic) interactions with the goal of self/co-analyzing and self/co-understanding negotiation and collective decision-making processes. This description is carried out qualitatively, in our approach, and also relies on quantitative data visualizations questioning various criteria involved in the specification of collective activity. It is therefore crucial to avoid the possible dichotomy often found in conventional research practices where researchers collect data by themselves, reframe their observations, analyze and then present them to the subject observed, once the entirety has been handled.

Rather, this co-construction of meaning regarding the activity and this moment of taking a step back to reflect are, as a result, performed here with the designer, not on the designer. While a traditional approach could ensure greater objectivity faced with the situation under observation, in the training contexts involved in this study, cross-feedback from that step back is given particular preference in our workshop+. Yet this does not prevent a scientific approach from being taken, so as to objectify some of the hindsight on the design and collaborative activity, both by designers and observers. Thus, thanks to specific methods of observation, note-taking, implementing a common coding grid, scientific analysis methods in the humanities, and analytical tools for data processing, our workshop+ seeks several objectives regarding the participants:

- to co-construct a reflection on their collaborative design activity,
- to develop their critical thinking by dealing with differing points of view,
- to structure and enrich mastery of their know-how and to support their conceptual strategy, and
- to start to take a step back thanks to an introduction to research practices in design.

The pedagogical approach proposed here in workshop+ is likewise divided into 4 stages:

- Step 1: experimentation via role-playing games, involving designers and observers with predefined missions and note-taking grids;
- Step 2: the transcription through the co-breakdown of the process and co-reporting of the actions observed and experienced by observers and designers;
- Step 3: data coding and processing via the co-construction of meaning for actions' specification;
- Step 4: analyzing and weighing up results through stepping back and co-defining negotiated knowledge, resulting in a co-modification of the action through mutual feedback.

For each of these steps, we will examine below the implementations and the targeted objectives, and will describe the different tools implemented to allow participants to begin reflecting upon their activity.

IV. FOUR STEPS OF WORKSHOP+

After a brief introduction regarding our training's objectives and motivations, the training begins immediately with experimentation, which consists of a two-hour collaborative design situation.

A. *Step1 - Experimentation*

Implementation. Learners apply an experimental protocol defined in advance according to a method dictated by the context (short vs long integration). The definition of this protocol is essential to ensuring the smooth running of the workshop+ and to guaranteeing its integration into a collaborative action research approach. Hence, each participant belonging to the same workgroup is given a role that he will keep throughout the workshop+: either as a designer (3 designers minimum per group), or as an observer (number defined by number of participants in the workshop+). Designers are arranged in a predetermined seating arrangement and face the design brief given to them. Observers take notes "on the fly," with respect to a common time reference given by a shared stopwatch. Each observer has a mission, precisely defined by a card dealt before the start of the experiment (Figure 1). This task may involve one of the following:

- a general observation, where the observation criteria are not dictated by the experimenter: the objective is to build a qualitative observation that takes into account the specificity of the situation observed;
- a detailed observation, structured according to a grid predefined by the experimenter: the aim here is to systematize their observations to make their data more explicit and more easily quantifiable.

The mission of each participant is only known by other observers after a minimum training time to overcome the main limitation of "concurrent protocols." This is why it is important that observers be perfectly well-prepared, capable and motivated, and that designers gradually forget their presence. To do so, the experiment was divided into 2 phases. During the first half hour, observers respond individually to specific missions, ignoring others' missions. After 30 minutes, the session is suspended: all observers are gathered in a room away from the observation site, to learn about each other's missions and to confront their difficulties in observing. This phase allows them to stabilize and coordinate their note-taking strategies to resume thereafter in a more coherent manner, adapted to the context observed. Then follows the second phase of the experiment, during which the observers continue their note-taking, whether general or specific. Designers, for their part, still do not know what the observers are scrutinizing. It is indeed essential that designers not know what observers are watching for. Otherwise, the risk of influence on the designers' working practices would increase and could make the observation meaningless.

Objectives. Enforcing the protocol makes it possible to set certain variables in advance, such as the seating of the designers around the table, reference documents given, the tools at their disposal, etc. This imposed setup also allows participants to better gauge, afterwards, the influence of the situation and the context of the design process and collaboration between designers (namely in that designers are not made aware of what must be notified by the observers, so as to keep influence on their work to a minimum).

Methodological tools. The protocol is proposed so as to describe the collective design activity. Thus, note-taking grids adapted to multi-collaborator interactions were defined according to 4 observatory themes identified through mission maps:

- Theme 1. Observe collaboration: each designer is assigned an observer whose mission is to focus on their actions while working (or not) with other designers. With respect to a single time, the observer describes the interactions of the designer under observation vis-à-vis others and the space in which the designer is working (RIN 2012). The observer also notes the documents used by "his/her" designer, and the types of performances used by the individual during the process;
- Theme 2. Observe design: one of the observers is specifically assigned to monitor the design process and artifacts that are created therein and/or shared by all designers. He or she must specify, among other things, part(s) of the project concerned by the designers' action (e.g., the building entrance) and the documents used and/or created to work on the project;
- Theme 3. Observe trends: one observer is assigned to list and describe the different analogies, specific manifestations of emotion, occasional use of tools, etc., implemented by the designers during the project design;
- Theme 4. Observe freely: this observer's mission is to meta-analyze collaborative activity overall in the design process observed, relative to key moments that seem important to him or her to emphasize.

Theoretical tools. The workshop+ is introduced by an introductory course regarding the scientific approach, supplemented by a course sensitizing the learner to "how to do" rather than simply "doing". Once the designers have been informed of the program for the project to be designed, observers privately undergo training on note-taking techniques and on the relevance of complying with the protocol in the context of a scientific approach.

Analytical tools. At this stage in the workshop+, no analytical tool, outside the note-taking grids, is given to observers yet (Figure 1). Everything is taken down "on the fly" using a stopwatch made available to them and displayed to all participants as the one and only reference, easily recognizable by observers, and which will subsequently allow them to synchronize their observations.

B. Step 2 - Transcription

Implementation. During the transcription phase, the time marker has a significant impact. All collected data is first synchronized according to the predefined criteria in the note-taking grids.

During this data synchronization step, designers and observers come together to discuss their views and chronologically transcribe their experiences and observations into a single account. This mutual account of the collaborative process is thus built, in the form of actions, through a consensus among the various participants. By putting every action into words, observers break down the activity into moments of interaction; they then transcribe these into distinct categories describing the collaborative

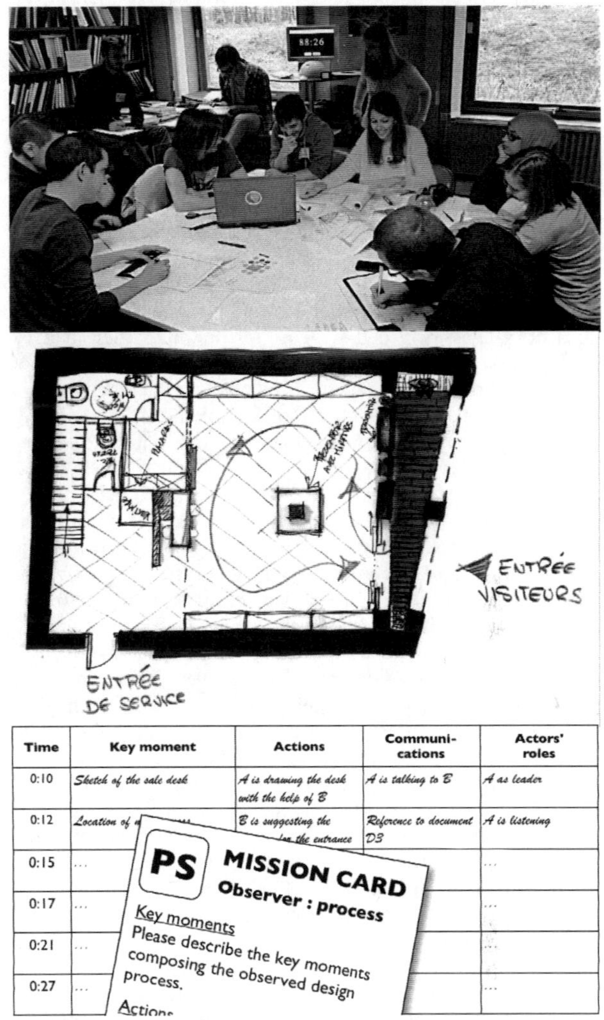

Figure 1. Protocol, design product, mission card and note-taking grid

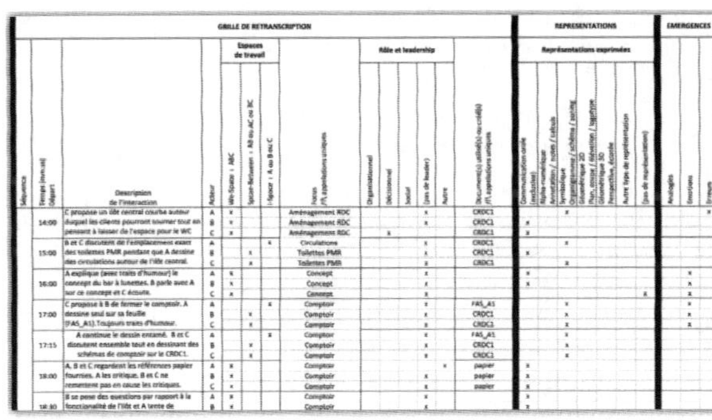

Figure 2. Notes taken converted to coded data

design process. The joint transcription process in words is already a first look back at the activity that took place. This transcript is carried out via a frame segmenting activity vertically according to a temporal reference to describe the process ("process-oriented segmentation"); and horizontally according to predefined criteria describing the content and specificity of each action ("content-oriented segmentation"): typology of action, workspace concerned, documents used, representations created, analogies observed, degree of object handling, degree of object abstraction, emotions expressed, etc. Each action is a testament to the design operations and collaboration implemented by each participant according to his or her viewpoint, relevancy and references. This action list is then segmented to split the process into several sequences. A sequence is thus a series of decisions, starting with the explicit expression of intent or of a problem that does not necessarily end with its resolution; rather, it may lead to the beginning of a new sequence that may or may not be directly dependent on the previous one. A sequence is composed of a succession of moments, these being composed of actions, representations and points of view (e.g., general layout > layout of ground-floor > layout of 1st floor > entry plan > etc.).

Objectives. This transcription step makes it possible to synchronize note taking and to set observers' viewpoints against designers' experience in a joint time description of the collaborative design activity (under the supervision of the researcher). In this step, each participant enters into dialogue with himself and with others so as to organize and specify the course of action for the activity observed. By setting each action into words, the participants negotiate and attempt to understand each other. This implies "leaving behind the implicit for the explicit", which sometimes involves a deconstruction/reconstruction of representations that participants had prior to their activity [44]. The transcript grid was defined well in advance by the researchers in order to provide a framework that will allow them, by a consensus, to collectively stop the main actions to be studied. It serves as a discussion framework for researchers/supervisors, for questioning certain defining criteria for the activity. This transcript grid later became a grid for reading and analyzing data for the whole group (designers/observers/researchers).

Methodological tools. The transcript grid (provided to observers with a structured observation mission) is composed of several categories (Figure 2). These categories are themselves divided into several exclusive criteria, as follows:

- description of the interaction between designers;
- identification of documents used or created by each participant;
- observation of trends: if an analogy, tool handling and/or a particular emotion was observed, for each participant;
- types of representation expressed by each participant (e.g., oral communication, notes, diagram, 2D drawing, 3D geometry, etc.);
- specification of workspaces for each designer: each designer working individually (I-space), two working apart (Space-between), or three working together in the same I-space (We-space).

Theoretical tools. A methodological manual is made available, defining all categories and criteria that make up the transcript grid.

Analytical tools. Automated formulas are inserted into the transcription file (.xls), helping participants to rapidly detect certain transcription errors.

C. Step 3 - Coding and data processing

Implementation. After synchronization, data is then transcribed collectively, to enable more accurate description of the evolution of the design project, the collective activity, and to enable increased accuracy of different analogies set forth by the designers. These criteria and categories stem from research and state-of-the-art presentations to students in theoretical courses associated with this workshop+ (see hereunder "Methodological tools"). Once encoded, the data is then processed by a tool called Common Tools (CT). CT is a web application initiated in the ARC COMMON research project [45] and developed by LUCID at the University of Liège. It allows all the encoded data to be viewed with respect to time, occurrences and specificities of each participant involved in the collective design process [1]. Visualizations proposed here concern the process as much as the content, by describing the temporal evolution of the participants' interactions and their implications on the mutual design object (Figure 3).

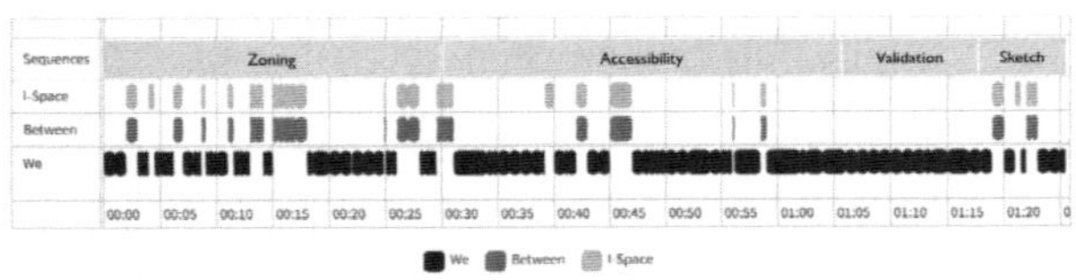

Figure 3. Example of visualization (timeline of workspaces) proposed by COMMON Tools

Objectives. This stage of coding and processing transcripts, by combining designers and observers, allows them to understand how to link their own observations with theoretical models, given in courses related to the description of collaborative design process. This approach therefore offers a second opportunity to step back and consider the process. Setting their acquired knowledge against what they observed during the experiment also gives learners the opportunity to challenge the transcription and coding grids provided by the supervising researcher. Learners can in fact redefine certain criteria or add new ones thanks to the flexibility of the grid and to the visualization facilitated by CT.

Methodological tools. For this third stage, new encodings complete the transcript grid: with respect to the design object (according to its degree of handling and of abstraction), to collective actions, and to types of analogies put into practice. Each encoding is divided into several criteria to detail the collaborative design activity more precisely. A methodological manual is provided, allowing learners to have the exact definition of each criterion.

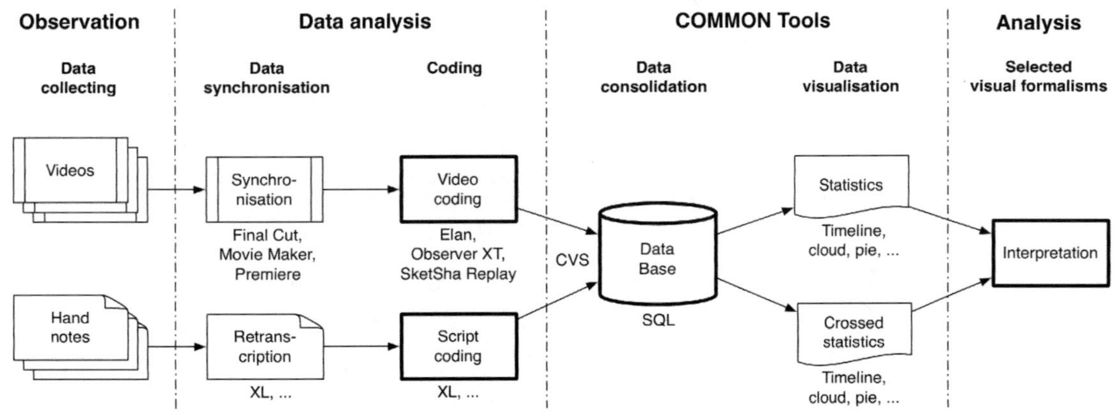

Figure 4. From data collection to processing by COMMON Tools for analysis purposes.

Theoretical tools. Based on this predefined experimental protocol, theoretical concepts to be called upon are introduced via course modules spread over the workshop+. Backed up by references from scientific design & cognition and CSCW communities, these modules present learners with the main concepts used in the workshop+: (1) design process models; (2) group activity specificities; and (3) the use of analogy in design.

Analytical tools. Provided to participants, the Common Tools platform performs data processing from the code frame (in .csv formats), transforming it into consolidated, quantified data (Figure 4). It then allows the user to view that data under an assortment of graphical representations (e.g, pie chart, stacked columns, timeline, crossing, clouds, etc.). This tool thus provides quantitative data visualization functions for different categories in the form of a panel of graphs (over 4000 graphs proposed by analysis). Each piece of data can be displayed by chart type, but also by participant or for all participants, by sequence or for all sequences, in occurrences or in duration. Trends, in turn, take the shape of dots in the timeline, to mark events occurring singly in the collective design process. The tool also allows two categories to be compared for advanced analysis of the complex collaborative design activity.

D. 4.4 Step 4 - Analysis and key results

Implementation. This final step marks the transition from description to interpretation. Here, all participants scrutinize the quantified data and choose the appropriate type of chart to affirm or reject comments made during the first instance of stepping back from the project. It allows them to integrate quantitative data, displayed via Common Tools, the relevant descriptive dimensions already having been identified qualitatively during transcription (e.g., communication strategies, types of sequences, forms of collaboration, body language, or interpersonal development).

Objectives. The objective of this stage is the mutual definition of the research questions specific to each experiment by observers and by designers, jointly. Here, all the participants also negotiate choosing the right graph style to give meaning to quantified results and to respond to questions. This step invites the group to query each other: what are our research questions? What do we want to put forward in relation to the collective activity and the design process we observed? How can we appraise our results? What can we take away with respect to what has been experienced/observed in the role of designer as well as of an observer? This step thus marks the third opportunity to step back, where the participants no longer focus solely on design analysis and collaboration, but also raise the question of the influence of the protocol on the functioning of the activity. This "metatheatrical" analysis concerns seating assignments designated by the protocol, the note taking grids and predefined analysis categories, as much as the approach itself to collaborative action research. In addition to the question, "How do designers collaborate and negotiate the project?" they examine, firstly, the negotiation process between observers for synchronizing their views and, secondly, their collaboration with the designers to set their observations against experiences within the same experiment.

Methodological tools. Introduced to the scientific process, learners apply social science analysis methods and learn to adapt the description of the facts to the interpretation of results, which they highlight by selecting relevant visual formalisms (graph styles) as visual data interpretation aids.

Theoretical tools. An additional course module presents learners with the typology of visual formalisms for the enhancement of scientific results (e.g., which to choose; how to read, describe and interpret them).

V. Implementation

Our approach was implemented in several advanced pedagogical frameworks for the analysis of and hindsight into design meetings in the form of workshop+. As discussed in the introduction, it acts as a complement to conventional project-based learning or to doctoral or professional training for teachers and/or design collaborators specifically interested in group activities.

TABLE I. CONTEXT OF IMPLEMENTATION

	Application context	Steps and analysis tools	Educational objectives
Short integration from 6 hours to 2 days	• 2nd Master in architecture, University of Liège • 1st Master Design, High School, Liège • International Design Research Workshop, Liège	• mission cards • qualitative analysis from note-taking • crossing observations and synthesis with pre-requisite knowledge	• construction of an experimental protocol • step back and on collective activity in design
Long integration from 4 to 8 days	• 2nd Master Architecture & Engineering, University of Liège • 2nd Master Architecture, University of Brussels • 2nd Master Architecture, University Ibn Khaldoun, Tunis • Master Research, in Ergonomics, University Paris 8 • Master Research in Design, High School, Tunis	• mission cards • qualitative analysis from freehand notes • crossing observations through a coding grid (xls file) • quantitative analysis and visual formalism with COMMON Tools • synthesis including theoretical coursework followed during the workshop	• introduction to scientific research • learning methods of collecting, processing and analyzing data • step back and on collective activity in design • considering the involvement of context in collaborative design activity

The fields of application involve architecture, engineering, design, ergonomics and project management.

Two workshop+ styles were proposed. These styles take into account the time allotted in the workshop+ depending on the context in which it is situated. Both styles were designed to train people to carry out a reflective, shared analysis of their design and collaboration process. However, they ranged from 4 hours to 8 days. Table I summarizes the characteristics of each, presenting their operational focus (regarding the time available for the workshop+), their pedagogical focus (regarding the learning objective targeted by teachers inviting us to employ this approach) and their theoretical, analytical and methodological tools, all complementary to each other.

At the end of each workshop+ each participant was asked to assess (anonymously) the activity's proceedings, its content and its interest relative to their academic and/or professional background. This assessment consisted of a questionnaire and 3 open questions. The questionnaire (imposing a scale of 1 to 5 on a criterion-based grid) included 12 questions concerning the modalities of the workshop, its relevance and the methodological, theoretical and analytical tools employed. The open comments were, in turn, related to the major contributions of the workshop+, the shortcomings raised and additional suggestions to consider. The following discussion will therefore be based on that assessment in addition to our qualitative observations made after four years' experience in implementing this activity.

VI. ADAPTABILITY OF THE COLLABORATIVE ACTION RESEARCH APPROACH

As outlined by G. Monceau [46, p.21], "not all participation in action research necessarily means collaboration, i.e., 'working together'." The approach proposed here was introduced to encourage progressive thinking, self-confronted, co-evaluated and co-constructed at the same time. Indeed, steps 2, 3 and 4 invite all of the participants (designers, observers, and supervising researchers) to describe their actions, through the transcript, collaborative encoding and analysis via imposed criteria. Trying to objectify all the activity into words by the interaction of various epistemological reflections, designers, researchers and observers converse, debate, look for evidence and challenge preconceptions. This progressive, fluid strategy maintains the co-construction of meaning as an active process, ensuring this triangulation between coding, analysis and interpretation of data. Although at first glance, these steps seem perfectly distinct (relative to the scientific approach described in the Section VII), they interfere with each other and also allow backtracking and a shared awareness of their activity's complexity. The keystone of collaborative action research is the participation of all collaborators (observers, designers and researchers) at every stage of the protocol: from the precise definition of the research question, to the collection, processing and analysis of data, up through the exploitation of results. Moreover, after having been implemented multiple times, the value of this type of approach is evident in a university curriculum for students learning their craft (Figure 5). More than 85% of them assigned a value greater than or equal to 4/5 for this criterion (1 = least important / 5 = most important). According to them, this work was not only the opportunity to study the activity of collaboration and design among multiple participants, but also to work together (as researchers, designers and collaborators) to find common ground on different concerted actions: "The challenge was at the time, above all, to agree on a single scenario at the start of transcription, to find compromises in order to construct a single reflection from many voices. Only this group reflection, based on consensus and the search for a common construction of what we could observe, has enabled us to comprehend and to be able to advance in our research." Thus emerges a dynamic way of thinking that promotes co-

construction of meaning in relation to both the situation studied and the activity examined.

However, to ensure such "thinking together", it is necessary up-front to query the purpose of this type of approach and its objectives for each participant. To begin with, participants' interests may diverge: the learners' primary goal is to question their practice, while for supervisors/researchers, the scientific investigation at hand is their core interest. Yet it is through the active relationship between learners and teachers, and the strong link with the world of practice, that the whole point of this type of approach emerges. One fosters the other through the development of a multi-referential framework. Indeed, all of the significance of this approach lies in this "metareflective" setting or *mise en abyme* ("observe a group activity to gain perspective on one's own activities" and "observe a group stepping back to co-construct meaning"). The product of stepping back from the activity here becomes co-constructed, without necessarily seeking to transform any one person's action, because it is not about differentiating identities or roles. Rather, it is necessary that the identities and roles of the participants remain distinct with a collective reflexivity and (new) knowledge and expertise that are co-shared/co-constructed in the work/research group. However, methodologically adopting a position on the border between "seeing the other as an object of study" (to maintain one's objectivity) and "identifying with the other" (to take into account the other's motivation) does not come easily to all.

Additionally, this point raises an ethical question, specifically in relation to the analysis and degree of validity. The description of the activity as actions, based on dialogue between researchers, observers and designers, can be questioned and its objectification challenged. Indeed, the collaborative nature of this action research promotes the establishment of a groupthink, capable of inducing an illusion of unanimous rationality and collective censorship (of oneself and others). This effect slows the emergence of collective intelligence and of a real step back from the activity.

This is why the role of the researcher and their supervising function are paramount here. Between "controlled activities" and "concerted actions", the supervisors/researchers must be fully aware of not only the contributions, but also the issues and limitations of this approach. They help to problematize the issue of "knowledge" and "expertise", to objectify it through the appropriate scientific approach and also to contextualize it in relation to a state of the art and theoretical courses prepared in advance. They not only serve the role of providing expertise in the analysis of complex activities; they also act as a partner, guiding reflection throughout the workshop. They strive to ensure that questioning should remain continuous and that hindsight be supported by co-defining questions and concerted actions. The researcher steps in here as a participant who cultivates self-learning and, by his or her point of view, enriches reflective, fluid thinking on the part of the whole group. Over 80% of participants also stressed the importance of this support in the group work mode, involving participants with different roles and courses alternating with well-equipped debriefing sessions.

However, this context creates an uncomfortable situation for the supervisor/researcher because they must develop their ability to support a group and to let go (as opposed to the test-tube effect of the laboratory, where the setting is completely under control), while taking into account both their theoretical and methodological expertise. As a result, the workshop+ serves to train both the professional researcher and the learner; consequently, it aids in rethinking what is typically a hierarchically-determined relationship, between learners in search of knowledge and teachers in possession of that knowledge. This hierarchical relationship has indeed proved its limitations in an advanced training context, where – from an educational perspective – reexamination, a forum for questioning and active thinking are favored, rather than mute listening and passive absorption of knowledge.

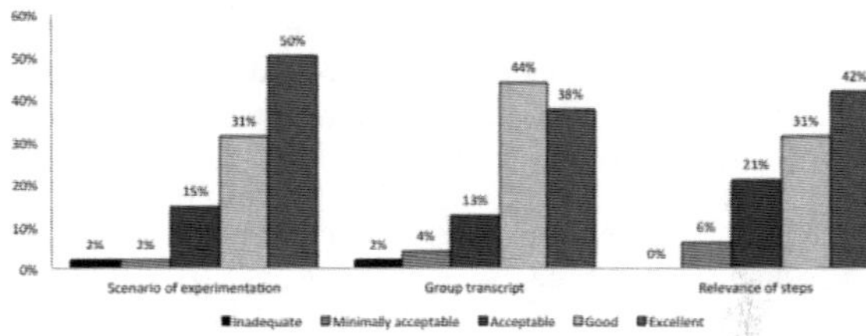

Figure 5. Value of workshop+ in the learner's overall education.

VII. Integration of a Scientific Approach into a "Professionalizing" Course of Study

- The primary interest of the workshop+ lies in heightening the awareness of a scientific approach in a professionalizing course. Indeed, the 4 steps that make up the workshop+ are highlighted in Figure 6 with respect to the main stages of a scientific approach. This figure illustrates the appropriateness of these steps with the demands expected of a classic scientific approach, while allowing different participants (researchers, designers and observers) to begin to step back to reflect and question prerequisites and theoretical courses taken, thanks to the following;
- the contemplation of similar studies that aim to model the complex activity of collective design: the research (supplemented data in the form of scientific articles) forms a theoretical reference frame that partially constitutes learners' state of the art;
- compliance with an objectified, rigorous and appropriate experimental protocol, based on the definition of operational working hypotheses and on the description of the facts in concerted actions (step 1, Figure 6): this first requirement makes it possible to see the impact of the situation and the context more clearly in the design and collaboration process among designers. Thanks to mission maps and note-taking grids, the student effectively takes in the

context under observation, but is also made aware of the complexity and difficulty in breaking it down in order to analyze and understand it;

- objectified description of actions, put together via a pre-constructed transcription and coding grid and (re)defined according to the theory and the state of the art given (step 2, Figure 6): by its synergetic nature, this second requirement allows participants' observations, knowledge and know-how to be weighed objectively, producing a cross-understanding and a common meaning, combining individual reflections with those of the group;
- the comparison of qualitative / quantitative analyses of the activity (step 3, Figure 6): this requirement ensures complementarity of the data analyzed, thereby facilitating the act of taking a step back;
- jointly highlighting the results (step 4, Figure 6): co-constructing (new) collectively negotiated knowledge aids in the emergence of a shared culture, which firstly concerns the problem defined, studied and questioned by the group; secondly, this concerns the approach that directly or indirectly affects how they act in their own activity and with respect to others. We believe that this type of irreversibility promotes hybridization of the perspective and the dialogue between the worlds of research and practice, often quite distinct from one another in university and/or "professionalizing" courses.

Even though collaborative action research may encounter some resistance, we find this approach to be scientific, albeit one which has unique qualities.

Its first singularity is of an epistemological nature. Indeed, it requires managing a dichotomy between data collection (which can only be achieved by the observers) and an action-research approach, which aims to be collaborative through the involvement of designers in the overall reflection (with these observers) on their design and collaboration activities. To avoid this dichotomy while respecting collaborative action research approaches, the workshop+ proposed puts forth several methodological, theoretical and analytical tools for the joint collection, processing and analysis of data harvested. These tools are defined so that, once the "experimental" phase has ended, all participants work together on the reflection phases. This approach seems to deviate from the classical conceptions of scientific work. Nevertheless, if the approach proposed here is paralleled with a conventional scientific approach, it is possible to show that one approach furthers the other, and that they do not contradict one another (Figure 6).

Its second singularity lies in its flexibility to adapt to the context being studied, i.e., its ability to take into account the specificity of each advanced training into which it is inserted (engineering, architecture, design, ergonomics, etc.). To do so, the protocol proposed enables course modules to be integrated, which provide the necessary theoretical knowledge, contextualized to fit the observed activity. Then, the protocol makes it possible to set the two aspects of the complex collective activity against one another: the process and the content addressed by the group. The focus of the research is as much to do with the specificity of each participant, as their workspace, documents, and interactions with other collaborators. The method of direct observation, without having recourse to recording video data, also serves to streamline the process of taking notes "on the fly." This process is less cumbersome than processing verbalization, but it does not exclusively produce qualitative observations. With COMMON Tools, the researcher also has rapid, easy access to graphs during the analysis phase with a variety of graph styles available, among which (s)he can choose those deemed most appropriate with respect to the research question at hand.

The ability to renew, to question and/or to add criteria and categories during transcription and coding is favoured by the flexibility of this approach, thereby making it possible to:

- analyze a corpus resulting from various configurations of collective activities involving multiple participants;
- leave the researcher free to update his/her grid and thus avoid preconceptions established prior to the activity, without any possibility of challenging them; but in addition,
- prevent the "hardening" of some concepts that might gradually stray from their initial purpose and context.

Within this dynamic position, between theoretical knowledge and practical knowledge, lies the third singularity of our collaborative action-research approach. Before examining this, a difficulty occurring at the data processing step should be highlighted (cf. Section IV.B). This problem concerns the analyst's choice of different criteria when coding for each action to be processed. It is sometimes difficult to categorize every action exclusively and definitively. However, the grid can split proposed actions (vertically, with respect to time) into sub-actions and also offers the analyst the possibility to cross two categories (horizontally encoded) and, therefore, to clearly specify the links between one test and another. This flexibility and crossover must be preserved so as not to place the data solely according to the prior interpretation of the analyst, who may quickly develop shortcuts or overly direct coding according to his or her own preconceptions. Questioning "given theoretical knowledge" thanks to "observed practice", collectively and objectively through a scientific approach, represents the second interest of workshop+, i.e., adopting a collaborative action-research project mirrored against what a scientific approach constitutes.

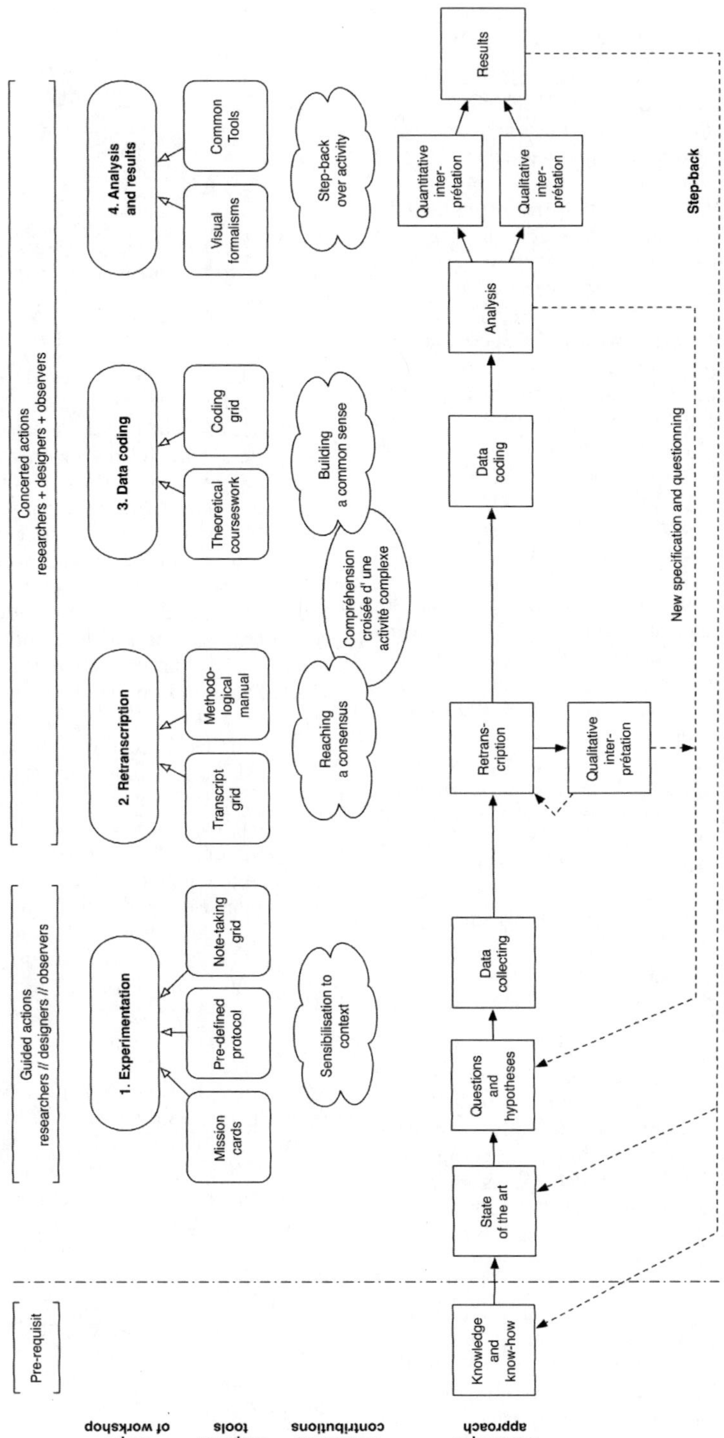

Figure 6. Scientific approach in the workshop+

VIII. Instrumentation of Taking a Step Back

In the notion of taking a step back and questioning activity, it is not a matter of tinkering with, adjusting or accommodating methodological, theoretical and analytical tools available to learners (Figure 7). It is more a question of degree of adaptability and taking into account the context studied. Accordingly, 85% of participants stressed the complementarity of support tools available to them in ensuring the establishment of a common reflective space and the construction of this constantly evolving collective intelligence.

The implementation of these tools was defined to address the activity, both qualitatively and quantitatively, promoting continuous distancing and joint interpretation of results highlighted, at every step of the workshop+. Via its predefined criteria, the grid (steps 2 and 3, Figure 4) tends to bring practice closer to experience, observation and analysis. By the quantitative illustration of data laid out according to various chosen criteria, Common Tools lets the user highlight the observed peculiarities of the design and collaboration process. It requires learners to rank the processed data and choose the appropriate visual formalism (step 4, Figure 4). This step encourages them to redefine their objectives and co-construct their research questions, as well as to identify what should be valued and highlighted in their results. The mediation offered by the tool allows them to step back, uncover points of view and shift meaning thanks to rapid access to graph styles helping to objectify and co-construct the interpretation. Over 70% of students highlighted the relevance of such a tool for interpreting data from coding grids. Some learners confirmed even that "perceiving my design and collaborative activity in a different way from this experience generates a step back and an awareness that lead us to question our actions and regulate them." In this way, they capture the complexity, as well as the involvement of the context, of participants' roles, of communication strategies used and of the design process itself in the way they work together.

However, the proliferation of graphs provided by COMMON Tools renders the work of analysis and interpretation of processed data difficult, especially for learners involved for the first time in a scientific approach. Indeed, so as not to make the tool too limiting, it is important to keep this flexibility in the choice of graph as well as in terms of the variety of criteria to represent. Nevertheless, it is contradictory to think that mere statistics alone, automatically performed by a tool, could construct meaning. The method put forward in this article, based on COMMON Tools, serves primarily to build a preliminary quantitative structuring of observations to navigate through the qualitative analysis of a complex collective activity. It does not then claim to attain condensed, definitive interpretations of the activity directly through a set of quantitative data. Subsequent interpretive work is needed, which would allow the researcher/analyst to quantitatively confirm or reject hypotheses proposed during observations and highlighted qualitatively in the corpus addressed.

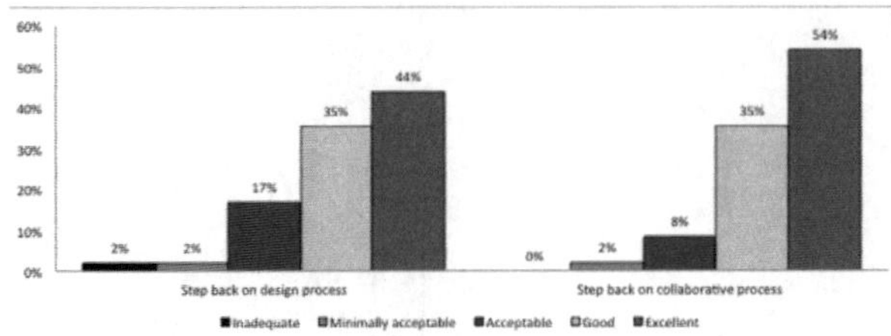

Figure 7. Use of workshop+ in taking a step back from design and collaborative activities

IX. Conclusion

What does such a workshop serve to do in an advanced design training course in a professionalizing context? This article seeks to shed light on this very question.

Indeed, comprehending ongoing design processes and providing new insights into collaboration by "doing-and-watching" rather than by simply "doing" (classic workshop approach) or "watching" (classical research approach) are the focuses when implementing collaborative action research. The approach we have chosen to adopt here attempts to bring the world of practice and the world of research. Applied to training during the final year of study in the field of design (i.e., in the Master's or the second year in a Research Master's) or in professional contexts, our goal is to promote the sharing of epistemological and educational space:

- for teachers, this enables them to tailor training on design in order to teach perspective;
- for learners, this offers tools to (1) co-construct a reflection on expertise (designing), (2) structure and enrich their mastery of this expertise, (3) communicate and work on communicating design, and (4) develop a critical mind by confronting points of view so as to start taking a step back, thanks to research practices in design;
- for researchers: it helps to explain the design and collaboration processes in various fields and to apply the approach to advance research in design.

Yet sharing points of view is not sufficient to produce knowledge. That is why this analytical approach introduces multiple (methodological, theoretical and analytical) tools promoting the act of taking a step back and questioning by the objectified co-construction of meaning (between researchers/supervisors, designers and observers) with a view to democratization of knowledge. But to what extent is this type of knowledge likely to be accepted, recognized and/or taken into account, both in the scientific and professional communities?

To promote this acceptance, it is necessary to develop an epistemological framework in line with the scientific requirements and the professional reality in which the collaborative action-research approach is placed. The aim here is to ensure a coherent, ethical and participatory partnership environment, where knowledge acquired from the academic world has no predominance on the knowledge gained from practice. Still, they must not ignore the theoretical production either, mirroring with other models constructed in advance, or processing in general. The conditions for co-construction of knowledge and meaning must be clarified well in advance.

Therefore, the definition of grids and criteria must be described thoroughly and put forward from theoretical research carried out by peers. The students' feedback shows that these grids help in characterization, precision, confrontation and distinction among different viewpoints. In this way, they participate in the process of objectification, continuous reflection and taking a step back, necessary to comprehend collaborative activity in design. Thus, coding concerted actions and comparing points of view promote deconstruction of know-how by the re-construction and co-construction of knowledge. One limitation of this tool, however, is the time spent transcribing (the result of reaching a consensus among all participants, which can consume a great deal of time). Nevertheless, this investment earns a quick return by the automated processing of data via Common Tools, the second major tool for this process.

The Common Tools web platform supports quantitative and graphical data processing. However, managing and interpreting a substantial number of graphs produced by Common Tools from co-encoded data remains difficult to handle. Over 10,000 potential graphs are provided by experience and little time is available for interpreting them. This complex analysis generally intimidates learners. Therefore, all participants are invited to (1) re-examine the whole issue on "the analysis of a collaborative design activity" by splitting it into co-defined sub-questions, (2) perform a preliminary qualitative, synthetic analysis on the whole activity and, (3) foster awareness of the relevance of a particular visual formalism in answering a particular question and/or promoting a particular hypothesis.

The result of such an approach should not be simplified or seen as the sum of participants' interests or interpretations, but rather as a dialogue co-constructed iteratively and continuously throughout the constituent stages of the workshop+. Moreover, the outcome may not match initial expectations, observations and preconceptions.

As already mentioned, the work of implementing this type of approach is feasible in the framework of a professional setting. What is more, we have participated in its initiation in several specialized architectural and engineering firms. Still, we have been faced with a certain reluctance brought about by several concerns. The first stems from the dreaded "pillage" of participants'/designers' expertise by researchers collaborating with them. The second concern relates to publishing results that are "discussed and, thus, valued far from the field where the data was collected and the first analyses performed" [46, p.28]. Added to this is the fact that publishing and communicating such results to other scientists outside of their own field does not seem to be a priority for practitioners. The real (but nonetheless legitimate) gap between the practitioner's priorities and those of the researcher can be a real barrier in the collaborative action research, especially in that "publishing", for a researcher, is a real need in his or her scientific practice. We believe that this fact should not hamper the application of this type of approach in a professional context, but must, on the contrary, find inspiration in aspects of real experiences. Its appraisal, both among scientific communities and practitioners, will encourage the production of academic knowledge in continuous connection with the reality on the ground: it requires cross-referencing "knowledge in support of know-how" and in return, "know-how in support of knowledge."

It is towards this action, alongside practitioners and in the field, that we aim to follow up this work. More than being merely interventionist, this entails driving and managing change in constant motion, which strives to be well-suited to its context and to all the participants involved in this type of activity.

ACKNOWLEDGMENT

This research is financed thanks to the grant Research Concerted Actions (ARC COMMON 2011-2015), the Scientific Research Direction of Education, French and Belgian Community, granted by the Wallonie-Europe Academy.

REFERENCES

[1] S. Ben Rajeb and P. Leclercq, "Instrumented analysis method for collaboration activities," Proceedings of COLLA 2015: Fifth International Conference on Advanced Collaborative Networks, Systems and Applications, IARIA, Lisbon, pp. 10-16, 2015.

[2] J. C. Hubers, "Collaborative Architectural Design In Virtual Reality," in PhD. diss. Delft University of Technology, Publikatiebureau Faculty of Architecture, Delft, 2008.

[3] L. L. Bucciarelli, "Between Thought and Object in Engineering Design," in Design studies, vol. 23(3), pp. 219-231, 2002.

[4] S. Ben Rajeb and P. Leclercq, "Co-construction of meaning via a collaborative action research approach," in Lecture Notes in Computer Sciences, Springer, LNCS 9320, pp. 205-215, 2015.

[5] F. Darses, P. Falzon, and C. Mondutéguy, "Paradigmes et modèles pour l'analyse cognitive des activités finalisées," in Ergonomie, Presses Universitaires de France, Paris, pp. 191-212, 2004.

[6] P. Chinowsky and J. E. Taylor, "Networks in Engineering: An Emerging Approach to Project Organization Studies," in Engineering Project Organization Journal, vol. 2(1-2), pp. 15-26, 2012.

[7] J. M. Carroll, D. C. Neale, P.L. Isenhour, M. B. Rosson, and D.S. McCrickard, "Notification and awareness: synchronizing task-oriented collaborative activity," in International Journal Of Human-Computer Studies, 58, pp. 605-632, 2003.

[8] C. Carmel-Gilfilen and M. Portillo, "Where what's in common mediates disciplinary diversity in design students: A shared pathway of intellectual development," in Design Studies, vol. 33(3), pp. 237-260, 2012.

[9] H. Demirkan and Y. Afacan, "Assessing creativity in design education: Analysis of creativity factors in the first-year design studio," in Design Studies, vol. 33(3), pp. 262-278, 2012.

[10] F. Détienne, G. Martin, and E. Lavigne, "Viewpoints in co-design: a field study in concurrent engineering," in Design Studies, 26, pp. 215-241, 2005.

[11] S. Ben Rajeb and P. Leclercq, "Using Spatial Augmented Reality in Synchronous Collaborative Design," in Lecture Notes in Computer Sciences, Springer, vol. 8091, pp. 6-15, 2013.

[12] S. Willaert, R. de Graaf, and S. Minderhoud, "Collaborative engineering: a case study of concurrent engineering in a wider context," in Journal of Engineering and Technology Management, vol. 15 (1), pp.87-109, 1998.

[13] S. A. R Scrivener, D. Harris, S. M. Clark, T. Rockoff, and M. Smyth, "Designing at a Distance via Real-time Designer-to-Designer Interaction," in S. Greenberg, S. Hayne & R. Rada (eds): Groupware for Real-time Drawing: A Designer Guide. London, UK, McGraw-Hill, pp. 6-23, 1995.

[14] S. Ben Rajeb and P. Leclercq, " Spatial augmented reality in collaborative design training: articulation between I-space, We-space and Space-between," in Lecture Notes in Computer Sciences, Springer, LNCS 8526, vol 2, pp. 343-353, 2015.

[15] P. Reason and H. Bradbury, Sage Handbook of Action Research: Participative inquiry and practice, London, Sage Publications, 2008.

[16] D. Greenwood and M. Levin, "Pragmatic action research and the struggle to transform universities into learning communities," in P. Reason & H. Bradbury (Eds.), Handbook of action research, London, Sage, pp. 103 -113, 2001.

[17] J. Bell, G. Cheney, C. Hoots, E. Kohrman, J. Schubert, L. Stidham, and S. Traynor, "Comparative similarities and differences between action research, participative research, and participatory action research," in http://www.arlecchino.org/ildottore/mwsd/group2final-comparison.pdf, 2004.

[18] S. Kemmis, "Exploring the relevance of critical theory for action research: Emancipatory action research in the footsteps of Jürgen Habermas," in Peter Reason & Hilary Bradbury (Eds.), Handbook of action research: Participative inquiry and practice, London, Sage, pp.91-102, 2001.

[19] C. Couture, N. Bednarz and S. Barry, "Multiples regards sur la recherche participative, une lecture transversale," in Anadòn, M., Savoie-Zajc, L. (eds.) La recherche participative. Multiples regards, pp. 205–221, PUQ, Québec, 2007.

[20] S. Desgagné, "Le défi de co production de «savoir» en recherche collaborative, analyse d'une démarche de reconstruction et d'analyse de récits de pratique enseignante," in Anadòn, M., Savoie-Zajc, L. (eds.) La recherche participative: Multiples regards, PUQ, Québec, pp. 89–121, 2007.

[21] H. Bradbury-Huang, "What is good action research? Why the resurgent interest ?," in Action Research, vol. 8(1), pp. 93-109, 2010.

[22] M. Bourassa, R. Philion, and L. Chevalier, "L'analyse de construits, une co-construction de groupe," in Education et Francophonie, vol. 35(2), pp. 78–117, 2007.

[23] P. Dillenbourg, "The socio-cognitive functions of community mirrors," in Proceedings of the 4th International Conference on New Educational Environments, Lugano, 2002.

[24] Y. E. Kalay, "Architecture's New Media. Principles, Theories, and Methods of Computer-Aided Design," in The MIT Press: Communication, MIT Press, Cambridge, pp. 83-198, 2004.

[25] E. L. Deci, J. P. Connell, and R. M. Ryan, "Self-determination in a work organization," in Journal of Applied Psychology, vol. 74(4), pp. 580-590, 1989.

[26] P. Leclercq, "Going collaborative," in Proceedings of 5th International conference CDVE Computer Aided Architectural Design: Experience Insight and Challenges, Calvià, Mallorca, 2008.

[27] J. S. Gero and H. H. Tang, "The differences between retrospective and concurrent protocols in revealing the process-oriented aspecs of the design process," in Design Studies, vol. 21, no. 3, pp. 283-95, 2001.

[28] K. A. Ericsson and H. A. Simon, "Protocol analysis: Verbal reports as data," in MIT Press, Cambridge, MA, 1993.

[29] H. Kuusela and P. Pallab, "A comparison of concurrent and retrospective verbal protocol analysis," in American Journal of Psychology, vol. 113, no. 3, pp. 387-404, 2000.

[30] S. C. Stumpf, and J. T. McDonnell, "Talking about team framing: Using argumentation to analyse and support experiential learning in early design episodes," in Design Studies, vol. 23, pp. 5-23, 2002.

[31] L. Nguyen and G. Shanks, "A framework for understanding creativity in requirements engineering," in Information and Software Technology 51, pp. 655–662, 2009.

[32] M. Suwa, T. Purcell, and J. Gero, "Macroscopic analysis of design processes based on a scheme for coding designers' cognitive actions," in Design Studies, vol. 19 pp. 455-83, 1998.

[33] V. Mollo and P. Falzon, "Auto-and allo-confrontation as tools for reflective activities," in Applied Ergonomics, vol. 35 (6), pp. 531-540, 2004.

[34] C. H. Lewis, "Using the "Thinking Aloud" Method In Cognitive Interface Design," in Technical report, IBM. RC-9265, 1982.

[35] P. Lloyd, B. Lawson, and P. Scott, "Can concurrent verbalisation reveal design cognition?," in Design Studies, vol. 16, pp. 237-59, 1995.

[36] G. Gronier, "Méthodes d'analyse des communications fonctionnelles en situation de travail collectif," in Recherches Qualitatives, 9, pp. 153-171, 2010.

[37] F. Détienne, G. Martin, and E. Lavigne, "Viewpoints in co-design: a field study in concurrent engineering," in Design Studies, 26, pp. 215-241, 2005.

[38] M. Reinert, "Alceste, une méthode statistique et sémiotique d'analyse de discours; application aux Rêveries du promeneur solitaire," in La Revue française de psychiatrie et de psychologie médicale, 49(5), pp. 32-46, 2001.

[39] K. Dorst and J. Dijkhuis, "Comparing paradigms for describing design activity," in Design Studies 16, pp. 261-274, 1995.

[40] L. Mondada, "Participants' online analysis and multimodal practices: projecting the end of the turn and the closing of the sequence," in Discourse Studies, vol. 8(1), pp. 117–129, 2006.

[41] J. S. Gero and T. M. Neill, "An approach to the analysis of design protocols," in Design Studies, vol. 19, pp. 21-61, 1998.

[42] C. Brassac and N. Gregori, "Co-construction de sens en situation de conception d'un outil didactique," in Studia Romanic Posnaniensia, no 25/26, pp. 55-66, 2000.

[43] J. F. Boujut and P. Laureillard, "A co-operation framework for product–process integration in engineering design," in Design Studies 23 (6), pp. 497–513, 2002.

[44] R. Legendre, Dictionnaire actuel de l'éducation, Montréal, Guérin, 2005.

[45] www.lucid.ulg.ac.be/www/research/common [retrieved: May, 2016].

[46] G. Monceau, "La recherche-action en France: histoire récente et usages actuels," in Les recherches-actions collaboratives, Presses de l'EHESP, pp 21-31, 2015.

Analysis of Impression in Exercise while Watching Avatar Movement

Taeko Tanaka and Hiroshi Hashimoto
Master Program of Innovation for Design and Engineering
Advanced Institute of Industrial Technology
Tokyo, JAPAN
Email:{b1315tt, hashimoto}@aiit.ac.jp

Sho Yokota
Department of Mechanical Engineering
Toyo University
Saitama, JAPAN
Email:s-yokota@toyo.jp

***Abstract*—This paper analyzes impression in an user exercise while watching an avatar movement that performs interaction where actions of human are imitated by using the skeleton model obtained from Kinect sensor. In the interaction, the perception of the level of delay, impression of delay and habituation to the delayed movement of the avatar are investigated through some exercising experiments where the human raises and lowers both arms. For changing the level of delay, we prepare parameter sets with five grades of filter of Kinect library, and also prepare the " precedent movement" and "synchronic movement" to extract the inherent impression for the delayed motion. From the results of the questionnaire for subjects who experience the delayed movement of the avatar, those visual impression are analyzed by One-Way Repeated-Measures ANOVA. The novel habituation based on a certain level in the experience was discussed as follows: For the perception of the level of delay, it became clear that at parameter 3 and above, about 40 % of subject sensed "delayed movement". For the impression of delay, it came to light that the subjects feel uncomfortable with the "delayed movement". For the habituation to the delayed, we found that while the "delayed movement" gave a different impression than the "synchronic movement" and the "precedent movement", it cannot be said that impression differed in the "synchronic movement" and the "precedent movement"**

Keywords–avatar movement; visual impression; exercise; delayed movement; post hoc analysis; habituation.

I. INTRODUCTION

This paper analyzes impression in an user exercise while watching an avatar movement that imitates the user movements, and is the extended version of the paper [1].

Avatar can be projected on a screen in real time by applying humanoid Computer Graphics (CG) on the skeleton model extracted from the human motion capture. By watching the avatar, the user can evaluate one's own motion in real time while moving.

However, in the real-time display of the avatar, in fact, time delay occurs during the process of extracting information from body motion and information process of applying it to humanoid CG. In other words, time delay occurs while the movement of user is reflected and displayed in the avatar.

Time delay is known to affect the human psychology. Many research works have been undertaken regarding this mainly focusing on the interaction between humans and artifacts. It was pointed out that the delay of the computer response time adversely affects psychology [2][3][4]. The psychological influence in the utterance delay was studied well [5][6] and it was found that delay of one second or more has adverse impact, and voice of the conversation tends to increase. The effect of appearance of an artificial agent and utterance time on psychology was studied [7][8][9] and it was shown that higher is the delay, worse are the psychological changes. In the conversation between humans and robots, it was investigated the effect of starting time of utterance by Robot and timing of nodding on the psychology, and revealed that delay gives bad feelings [10][11][12][13][14].

In these studies, it is stated that in the interaction between humans and artifacts, delayed reaction of artifacts to a stimulus from the outside world has a negative impact on the psychology of humans. This impact pertains to usability when a human uses the artifacts, and it must be treated as an important problem. However, these studies consider the cases while verbal communication is taking place, and they do not discuss the effect of time delay in the body motion interaction between humans and artifacts on the psychology.

In this paper, we will analyze impression of the delayed motion of the avatar as an artifact that performs interaction where actions of human are simulated. Motion considered in this paper is swing movement often seen in exercising, where the human raises and lowers both arms. We will have this discussion about perception of the level of delay, impression of delay, and habituation to delay. Here, the level of delay means a quantitative expression of how much the delay a human feels.

We will explain the details of the experiment conducted in this paper for psychological evaluation to analyze impression. Recent software systems of artifacts can adjust the delayed degree of movement with digital filter functions. In other words, it is possible to adjust the delay time in the process of displaying avatar with human motion capture.

Using this, in our experiment, we measured the stage from when the human clearly recognizes it as delay when the delay time is changed in a stepwise manner. Measuring this delayed degree should be useful in offering guidance for improving the avatar system. Here, we assumed that the impression for the delayed motion may be similar to ones for precedent or synchronic motion. So, we set up the both motion to extract the inherent impression for the delayed movement.

Next, we administered a questionnaire survey about the impression the subject got when seeing the avatar that moves according to the movement of the subject. We studied the impression the subject got when the he saw that movement of the avatar is slower than him (hereinafter referred to as the delayed movement) while the subject does the swing movement.

In Section III, in order to obtain the characteristics of this impression, we use different movements than the delayed movement. These are two types of movements, namely, state where movements of the subject and the avatar seem to be

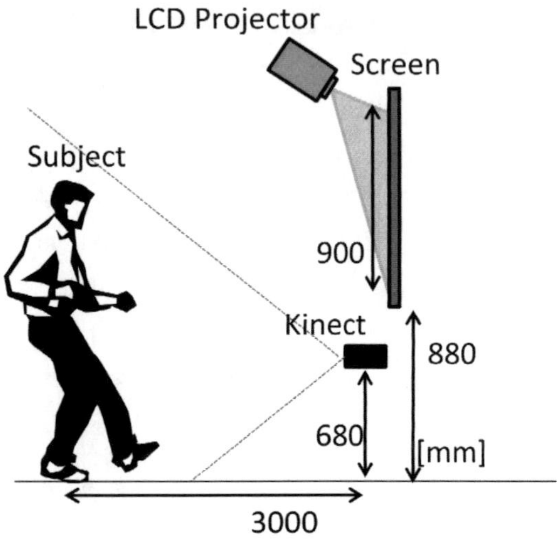

Figure 1. Outline drawing of the experiment setup

matching (hereinafter referred to as the synchronic movement) and the state where movement of the avatar seems to have progressed than that of the subject (hereinafter referred to as the precedent movement). The reason why these two movements are conducted is that the synchronic movement is used for the bench mark and the precedent movement is used to highlight the visual impression for the delay movement.

Then, we will compare impression evaluation and consider habituation to delay. In Section IV, we discuss the results of the comparison. In the last section, the paper is concluded.

II. Experimental Environment and Method

Hardware used in the experiment is comprised of "Microsoft Kinect for Windows sensor" for measuring the movement of the subject, PC that creates movement of the avatar based on the movement of the subject, and projector and screen for displaying the avatar to the subject.

Figure 1 shows the hardware configuration for measurement of the human motion and the avatar display system. The subject stands in front of the screen and Kinect with 3000 mm distance so that Kinect can detect whole body of the subject. As software, we used Kinect for windows SDK [15] which is the library for obtaining the human motion from the depth data photographed with Kinect and Microsoft XNA Game studio 10 [16] for drawing the avatar. With Kinect for Windows SDK, we can obtain the subject's movement data, and by transferring this data to Microsoft XNA, avatar can display identical movement as the subject.

Figure 2 shows an image of the avatar displayed to the subject during the experiment. The avatar moves to imitates the movement of an user. There are some types of figures of avatar, and we chose a man type as shown in Figure 2 because it is not the most uncomfortable feeling in our preliminary experiments. The skeleton model as shown in Figure 2 is to help the user recognize the movement expressly.

Figure 3 shows the experiment in progress where the subject is moving his body while watching the avatar. Strictly speaking, movements of the avatar and the subject are not synchronized. Rather, after measuring the movement of the subject with Kinect, movement is created in the avatar and after that the avatar will act. Therefore, irrespective of whether the subject realizes or not, movement of the avatar starts with delay. In Kinect, with the filter process, by delaying and advancing the subsequent movement, it is possible to control the delay time from the actual movement.

In this experiment, in the first place, we will measure the level of delay where the subject feels that delay has occurred while gradually increasing the delayed degree of the movement of the avatar. For implementing the delayed movement in the avatar, in this paper, we adjust the parameters of digital filter included in Kinect for Windows SDK v1.8. The filter is based on the Holt Double Exponential Smoothing method for joint position jitter. It is equipped with the smoothing and correcting functions, and it is used for removing the errors in the measurement data where such errors have occurred due to disturbance of measurement conditions and the like in Kinect.

By changing the parameters of this filter, it is possible to have smoothing and estimating effects and cause delay and look ahead in the movement data of the subject obtained with Kinect. Then, by implementing this movement data with delay on the avatar, movement of the avatar will be delayed than the actual movement of the subject.

A. Setting parameters

As the filter parameters, Prediction $[\geq 0.0]$ and Smoothing $[0.0, 1.0]$ are available. Although SDK provides "MaxDeviationRadius" and "JitterRadius", these two parameters are not adopted for changing avatar's motion, because these two parameters determine the region of compensation of jitter and these dimension is [m]. "Prediction" and "Smoothing" are adopted. The Value of Prediction is for estimating the movement, and its value is the number of frames that predicts the movement (Kinect's frame rate is 30 [fps]). Its default value is 0.0, and it tends to overshoot from around 0.5 (default value). So, we used the values in the range of 0.4 and below for delay movement. Value of Smoothing is the smoothing index. When it is 0.0, there is no delay, and when it is 1.0, delay is at the maximum. Default value is 0.5, and based on our experience, we selected values equal to or higher than this value.

Table I shows the perceived level of delay in five stages as the level of delay with respect to the delayed movement in this experiment.

TABLE I. Perceived level with respect to delay

Parameter set #	Prediction, Smoothing
1 (minimum delay)	Prediction=0.4, Smoothing=0.5
2	Prediction=0.3, Smoothing=0.6
3	Prediction=0.2, Smoothing=0.7
4	Prediction=0.1, Smoothing=0.8
5 (maximum delay)	Prediction=0.0, Smoothing=0.9

We will now explain about the method of creating this perceived level. During the course when the subject moves his body while watching the avatar displayed on the screen, we gradually changed the parameter value using the Smoothing function of Kinect. When increasing the parameter of Smoothing, the movement of the avatar will not be able to keep up with the movement of the subject, and movement will become sluggish. This state where the avatar hardly move is considered

Figure 2. Avatar (a man type) doing the swing movement and skeleton model (green colored), arm up (left figure) and arm down (right figure)

Figure 3. Experiment in progress

as maximum delay. Against this, the state where the movement of avatar appears to be synchronous with the subject himself is considered as minimum delay, and this interval was divided into 5 stages.

Subject's movement of raising and lowering arms while watching the avatar was aligned to the metronome of 100 BPM (Beat Per Minute) = 1.67 Hz, because the movement of subjects should be controlled in order to keep the frequency of the subject's movement, for the purpose of this paper. The sound of a metronome, therefore, was adopted as the standard sign for keeping the frequency of the movements.

Parameter set #1 through #5 shown in Table I was changed every 5 seconds. The subject would move his body for every parameter set. After that the subject was asked "Do you think that the avatar you just saw was delayed compared to your movement?" Subject's response was collected in Yes / No or Possibly as shown in Table II. This was repeated 5 times, and response data was collected and summarized.

TABLE II. Parameter set of percedence and synchronization

	Parameter set
Precedent	Prediction=0.5, Smoothing=0.5
Synchronization	Prediction=0.5, Smoothing=0.5

For verifying impression evaluation with respect to delayed movement, we thought that it is necessary to have another comparison target. Based on this, we designed "synchronic movement" and "precedent movement". The former one synchronizes with the movement of the subject, while the latter one advances the phase of movement using differential operation. This was also implemented by using the parameters of filter function of Kinect.

The parameters of "synchronic movement" adopted "Prediction = 0.5" (default value of the SDK). On the other hand, the parameters of "precedent movement" were determined by the preliminary experiment. "precedent movement" is the avatar's motion which is lead movement to the subject. The value of 1.0 is the highest prediction value and 0.5 is the default value of synchro motion. Here, there is a question: How step size of prediction parameter between maximum prediction and default prediction value should be determined and presented to subjects by being implemented to the avatar's motion? In this preliminary experiment, the value of 1.0 and 0.75 (the middle value between 1.0 and 0.5) were tentatively selected, and were implemented to avatar's motion to present their motions to subjects. If the subjects do not feel difference between two motions by two values, there is no need to select both values as the parameter for forming "precedent movement".

In order to verify this, we prepared two prediction values as 0.75 and 1.0, and verified the differences of the avatar's motions driven by two values. Here, 14 subjects participated in, and swung their arms with aligning to the metronome of 100 BPM while watching avatar's motion with above mentioned two values. Then they were asked "Did you feel difference between two avatar's movement? ".

As the results, 10 subject could not distinguish 0.75 from 1.0, and 1 subject distinguished the difference. Therefore, there is no distinct difference between two values from the binomial test: $p = 0.012 < 0.05$, null hypothesis which is human impressions of two movements are different was rejected.

Thus we adopted 1.0 being the maximum value of prediction for "precedent movement". These parameters are shown in Table III.

TABLE III. Responses where the subjects felt that the movement is delayed with respect to the parameter set in Table I

		delay	possibly delay	not delay	total
Parameter set 1 Prediction=0.4, Smoothing=0.5	number	0	0	14	14
	rate (%)	0.0	0.0	100.0	100
Parameter set 2 Prediction=0.3, Smoothing=0.6	number	0	8	6	14
	rate (%)	0.0	57.1	42.9	100
Parameter set 3 Prediction=0.2, Smoothing=0.7	number	6	6	2	14
	rate (%)	42.9	42.9	14.3	100
Parameter set 4 Prediction=0.1, Smoothing=0.8	number	6	6	2	14
	rate (%)	42.9	42.9	14.3	100
Parameter set 5 Prediction=0.0, Smoothing=0.9	number	10	4	0	14
	rate (%)	71.4	28.6	0.0	100

B. Experimental procedure

By using above mentioned parameters, we used three movements, namely, "delayed movement", "synchronic movement" and "precedent movement" in this experiment. The "synchronic movement" is placed as a bench mark to measure objectively, to compare, and to evaluate the difference of the impression. The following experiment was carried out for impression evaluation.

[Step 1] In the first place, in order to have the experience of the delayed movement of the avatar, while watching the avatar moving as per the settings of #3 in Table I, the subject moved his body for about 5 seconds along with the sounds of metronome and experienced the delayed movement of the avatar. Similarly, the subject moved his body for about 5 seconds for the precedent movement (Precedence in Table II) and the synchronic movement (Synchronization in Table II) and experienced these movements.

[Step 2] In order to find out perception of the level of delay, we changed the parameter set in Table I from #1 to #5 at every 5 seconds. Every time when changing the parameter, we asked the subject whether the movement is delayed or not.

[Step 3] Next, we find out how the impression regarding delayed differs from synchronic movement and precedent movement. For that, for each subject, we run the delay movement using the parameter sets in Table I for which the subjects felt the delay, and we changed the movements of avatar as per the following patterns.

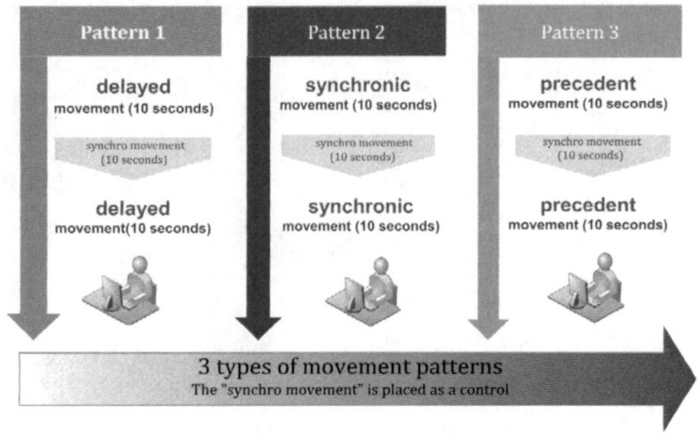

Figure 4. Outline drawing of the experiment setup

[Pattern 1] delayed movement (10 seconds) → synchronic movement (10 seconds) → delayed movement (10 seconds)

[Pattern 2] synchronic movement (10 seconds) → synchronic movement (10 seconds) → synchronic movement (10 seconds)

[Pattern 3] precedent movement (10 seconds) → synchronic movement (10 seconds) → precedent movement (10 seconds)

These patterns were created based on the concept of placing the synchronic movement at the middle position, and placing three types of movement patterns on both sides. Figure 4 shows an experiment flow.

In this experiment, there were 14 subjects, all males in their 20s. As for the sequence of the experiment, after completing [Step 1], subjects went to [Step 2], and after that they went to [Step 3]. [Step 1] is preparation for the experiment to be conducted here onwards.

III. ANALYSIS OF IMPRESSION EVALUATION

This section explains the analysis of the impression of the subjects. First, the evaluation items are explained.

A. Evaluation items

Restating the explanation given in Section II, the following are the evaluation items in impression evaluation.

P1: From what stage does the subject sense "delay" in the movement of the avatar? This leads to perceptual evaluation of the level of delay.

P2: What kind of the impression the subject forms regarding delayed movement of the avatar?

P3: Look into impression of each movement of the avatar, and see if there are any differences in the evaluation of each pattern. This leads to finding out habituation to delay.

For investigating P1, we conducted the experiment mentioned in [Step 2] in the preceding section. For investigating

P2 and P3, we conducted the experiment mentioned in [Step 3].

B. Analysis of P1

Response data for three perceptions, namely, the movement of the avatar is "delay", "possibly delay", and "not delay", was summarized for each parameter set. Table III shows the results of this.

From the results in Table III, for parameter set #3 and above, about 40% of the subjects responded that the movement of the avatar is "delayed". For parameter set #2 and above, about half of the subjects responded that the movement of the avatar is "possible delayed". Smoothing of parameter set #2 is set only slightly higher than the default value, and it resulted in somewhat ambiguous perception.

In the case of parameter set #4 and #5, the subjects are divided into two groups, namely, group that clearly recognized that the movement is "delayed" and the group that vaguely sensed the delay. However, this excludes a small number of subjects who responded that the movement is "not delayed". In the case of parameter set #5, about 70% of the subjects recognized that the movement of the avatar is clearly "delayed".

Based on these results, it came to light that the subjects sense the "delayed movement" of the avatar from parameter #3 onwards. At the stage of parameter set #2, the subjects may not sense that the movement is delayed.

C. Analysis of P2

In P2, we administered a questionnaire survey to find out the kind of impression with respect to the "delayed movement" of the avatar. Simultaneously, apart from the "delayed movement", we also studied the "synchronic movement" and the "precedent movement".

The method of data collection which was taken up in our questionnaire survey of experiment is "Semantic Differential Method" (SD method) [17]. The SD method aims at the evaluation of the object in the test that investigates the impression of the panel. It is the method which uses the pair of adjectives of the opposite meaning. In the SD method, the pair of adjective often results in three factors such as good-bad for evaluation, powerful-powerless for potency and fast-slow for activity [18]. We referred to the previous studies [19][20] related to impression evaluation of the movement of robot, we made the pair of adjective which applied the three basic factors of impressions (activity, potency, evaluation) defined for the SD method. Then we prepared 13 pairs of adjectives shown in Table IV and we conducted evaluation in 7 stages.

The impression questionnaire for Table IV was applied for three movements; delayed, synchronic and precedent.

The answers of the questionnaire were collected from 14 subjects. Next, we transformed the answeres by following procedure.

1) The seven stages of collected data for Table IV is classified into three categories (1-3/4/5-7) which are assigned to values of 1 or 0. For examples, the item no.1 includes two adjectives "fast" and "slow", they are assigned to values of 1 and 0 when the stages is within 1-3, respectively. The both are assigned to values of 0 and 1 when the stages be within 5-7. The both are 0 when the stages be 4. Here, there are 26 adjectives in 13 items. An illustrative example of classified result by this operating is shown in Figure 5.
2) The total amount of counting up the values for each adjective for three movements are used for the correspondence analysis [21]

TABLE IV. Impression questionnaire items for P2

No	factor	Evaluation Items		
1	activity	fast	⇔	slow
2	activity	smooth	⇔	awkward
3	evaluation	like myself	⇔	like others
4	activity	anticipated	⇔	unanticipated
5	evaluation	comfortable	⇔	uncomfortable
6	potency	soft	⇔	rigid
7	potency	sudden	⇔	not sudden
8	evaluation	favorable	⇔	disagreeable
9	evaluation	interesting	⇔	boring
10	potency	rough	⇔	calm
11	activity	sensitive	⇔	insensitive
12	evaluation	friendly	⇔	unfriendly
13	potency	natural	⇔	unnatural

Subject No.			1	2	3		14
questionnaire items	1	fast	1	0	1		0
		slow	0	0	0		1
	2	smooth	1	1	0		0
		awkward	0	0	0		0
	≈		≈	≈	≈	≈	≈
	13	natural	0	0	0		0
		unnatural	1	0	1		1

Figure 5. Illustrative example of classified result by operating with 1) for Table IV , each cell takes a value of 1 or 0

Here, the correspondence analysis is one of the methodologies that statistically analyze the frequency data. It is a useful method for the analysis of the data in the questionnaire survey. One of the goals of correspondence analysis is to describe the relationships between two nominal variables in a correspondence table in a low-dimensional space, while simultaneously describing the relationships between the categories for each variable. For each variable, the distances between category points in a plot reflect the relationships between the categories with similar categories plotted close to each other.

Figure 6 shows the results of the correspondence analysis. The following can be concluded from the results shown in Figure 6.

- Our finding is that the impression formed for "delayed movement" is different from that for "synchronic movement" and " precedent movement".
- On the other hand, it cannot be said that the impression

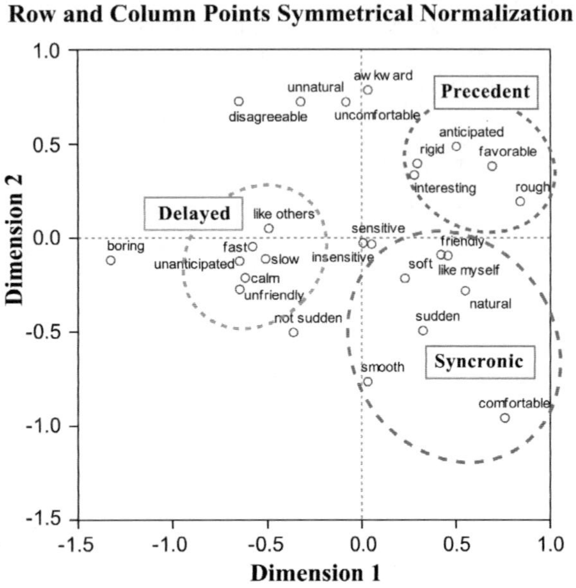

Figure 6. Results of correspondence analysis

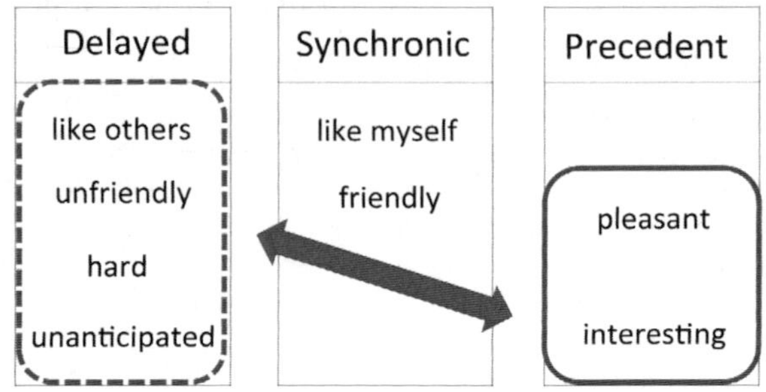

Figure 7. Typical impression of 3 types of movements

differs between "synchronic movement" and" precedent movement".

- For the "delayed movement", the subjects formed the impressions such as "like other human", "unexpected", and "unfriendly", and other impressions such as "fast and slow" and "moderate" based on the speed of movement.
- Figure 7 shows summary of findings by evaluation items. In precedent movement, even if movement was not synchronized, the result made a something good impression. Subjects felt it was pleasant and interesting. We found precedent movement made a better impression than delayed movement. This finding is in contrast with the impression of delayed movement.
- For "synchronic movement", the subjects formed the impressions such as "smooth", "natural", "like oneself", "enjoyable", "soft", and "comfortable".
- Subjects formed the impression that the "precedent movement" was "hard" and "intense". However, some of the subjects responded that they formed the impressions such as "interesting", "as expected", and "pleasant".
- As compared to the "synchronic movement", the subjects clearly realized the difference in the movement in the "delayed movement". The subjects felt uncomfortable that the movement of avatar did not match with their movement.
- There were some subjects who favorably treated the "delayed movement" as smooth movement. However, in terms of the overall trend, subjects had a negative impression of the "delayed movement".
- Impression became positive in the case of the "synchronic movement".
- In the "precedent movement", while there was negative impression, simultaneously, the subjects also found it "interesting" and "pleasant".
- In the settings of the "precedent movement", in the present Kinect, the avatar reacted acutely to the speed of exercising in the subjects, which formed the impression such as "hard" and "intense". However, there were opposite responses to this impression such as "interesting", "as expected" and "pleasant".
- We continuously examined whether there were any significant differences between the means of these three movement groups.

D. Analysis of P3

In the subsection C, we mentioned that apart from "hard" and "intense" that was the impression evaluation with respect to the "precedent movement", subjects formed the impression of "interesting", "as expected" and "pleasant" as in the case of "synchronic movement". Because it was found that the subjects formed similar impression in these two movement patterns, we will verify whether there are any differences in impression between the "synchronic movement" and the "precedent movement". From the point of view, P3 was designed.

The goal of this analysis was to compare means of the variable for the combinations of the three movements. We carried out impression evaluation for the experiment [Step 3] where three types of movements, namely, "delayed movement", "synchronic movement", and "precedent movement" are combined. Here, data group for each of three types of movements of avatar were named as data group of movements.

We set the hypothesis that "there is no difference between levels due to the data group of movement", and we carried out corresponding one-way analysis of variance (Repeated measures ANOVA)[22],. ANOVA is a "group comparison" that determines whether a statistically significant difference exists somewhere among the groups studied. If a significant difference is indicated, ANOVA is usually followed by a multiple comparison procedure that compares combinations of groups to examine further any differences among them.

Table V was made to be given to ANOVA in the next analysis and it shows the average value of response data obtained from 14 subjects for three movements.

TABLE V. Impression evaluation results using the SD method

Evaluation Items	Average Value of Response Data		
	Delayed	Synchronic	Precedent
1	4.86	3.57	3.57
2	4.00	3.14	4.00
3	4.57	3.43	3.29
4	4.57	4.00	3.71
5	4.14	3.00	3.71
6	4.14	3.71	4.43
7	4.86	4.14	4.00
8	4.14	3.29	2.71
9	3.86	3.29	3.00
10	4.86	3.71	3.71
11	4.00	4.14	4.00
12	4.71	3.43	3.14
13	4.71	3.43	3.57

Table VI shows the results of the one-way analysis of variance (Repeated measures ANOVA) which is used to determine whether there are any significant differences between the means of two or more groups.

Results in Table VI showed statistical significant in the group of movement from the significance level ($p < 0.05$). Accordingly, the hypothesis "There is not difference between the groups" was accepted, and it can be said that the impression formed in the subjects for three movements of the avatar are different. The effect of Evaluation items, by contrast, did not reach conventional levels of statistical significance.

Furthermore, in order to shed light on the difference between movements of different phase, we used the Turky's method [23], and conducted multiple comparison. Table VII shows the results of this comparison.

Based on these results, it is evident that in the movements of the avatar, "delayed movement" and "synchronic movement", and "delayed movement" and "precedent movement" are statistically significant ($p < 0.05$). In other words, the impression formed for "delayed movement" is different from that for "synchronic movement" and "precedent movement". On the other hand, it cannot be said that impression differs for "synchronic movement" and "precedent movement". Figure IV shows a plots with observed means of Data group in Table VI.

The two-way interaction between the Data group and the Evaluation items in Table VI had a non-significant effect, it probably does not make sense to look at the results. However, this is for amount of all adjective pairs, not for each adjective pair. So we thought further investigation for each adjective is needed.

We investigated the results in Table VI for each adjectives and for three movements. Figure 9 shows the observed means of the Evaluation items in Table VI. In this figure, a line shows a mean data of a prepared Evaluation items, and 13 polygonal lines corresponding to the adjective pair shows parallel each other.

Investigating the results in Figure 9, the evaluation items in Table VI were divided into two groups as shown in Table

TABLE VI. Test Results of Effect between Subjects

Dependent Variable:

Source		Type III Sum of Squares	Degree of freedom	Mean square	F value	Significance level
Intercept	Hypothesis	8138.579	1	8138.579	624.110	.000
	Error	169.524	13	13.040^a		
Data group	Hypothesis	84.806	2	42.403	17.757	.000
	Error	1179.619	494	2.388^b		
Evaluation items	Hypothesis	42.183	12	3.515	1.472	.131
	Error	1179.619	494	2.388^b		
Subject No.	Hypothesis	169.524	13	13.040	5.461	.000
	Error	1179.619	494	2.388^b		
Data group * Evaluation items	Hypothesis	41.289	24	1.720	.720	.832
	Error	1179.619	494	2.388^b		

a. Mean square(id), b. Mean square (Error)

TABLE VII. Results of Multiple Comparison

Dependent Variable: Tukey HSD

Movement (a)	Movement (b)	Difference in average value (a)-(b)	Standard error	Significance level	95% Confidence Interval Lower limit	95% Confidence Interval Upper limit
Deleyed	Syncronic	.86*	.162	.000	.48	1.24
	Precedent	.81*	.162	.000	.43	1.19
Syncronic	Deleyed	-.86*	.162	.000	-1.24	-.48
	Precedent	-.04	.162	0.960	-.42	.34
Precedent	Deleyed	-.81*	.162	.000	-1.19	-.43
	Syncronic	.04	.162	0.960	-.34	.42

Based on observed average value.Error value is mean squqre(error)=2.388

The error term is Mean Square(Error) = 2.388.

* Difference is averae value is significant at 0.05 level.

VIII. Group 1 is an evaluation word directly connected with a movement of the appearance and Group 2 is a stable impression words because the experiment was repeated. The chart was made using a mean of the data collected from our experiment, we could see the change pattern of the evaluation words.

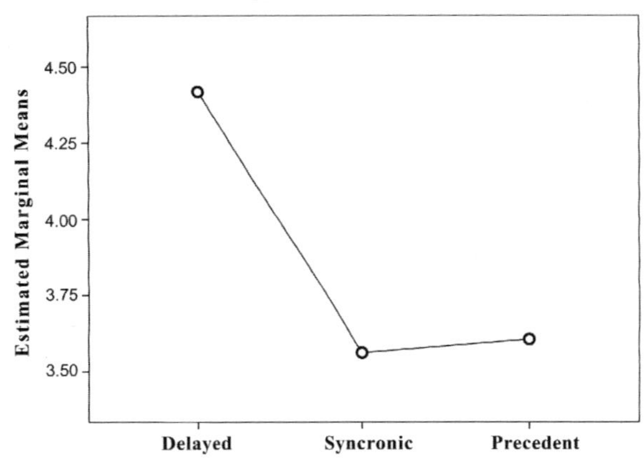

Figure 8. Estimated Marginal Means of score of Movement

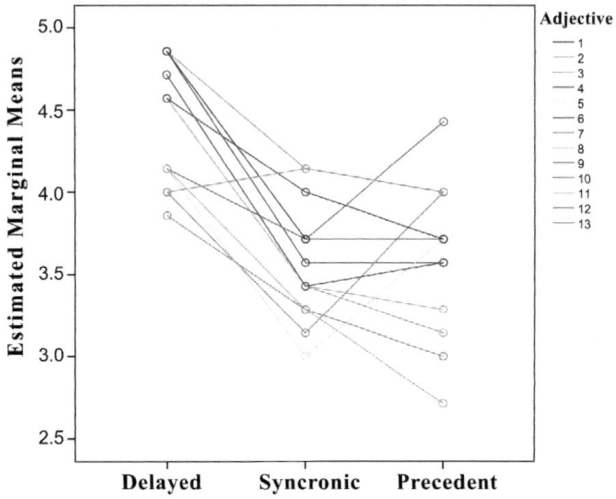

Figure 9. Estimated Marginal Means of score of Movement

TABLE VIII. Group of Evaluation Words

Group 1	Words of directly connected with movement Evaluation Items		
2	smooth	⇔	awkward
5	comfortable	⇔	uncomfortable
6	soft	⇔	rigid
Group 2	Words of stable impression Evaluation Items		
3	like myself	⇔	like others
4	anticipated	⇔	unanticipated
8	favorable	⇔	disagreeable
9	interesting	⇔	boring
12	friendly	⇔	unfriendly
13	natural	⇔	unnatural

Table VIII shows the group of evaluation words; "soft - rigid", "smoothly - awkward" and "comfortable - uncomfortable" and these are shown as the line in Figure 9. It is found that those shapes are forms as a V-shape and it is the same reaction at "delayed movement" and "precedent movement". This group have the pair of adjectives of activity or potency factor defined by the SD method.

On the other hand, "natural - unnatural ","anticipated - unanticipated ", "interesting - boring" and "like myself - like other" these pair of adjectives it is the same reaction at "synchronic movement" and "precedent movement". This group have almost the pair of adjectives of Evaluation factor; for example, good-bad for evaluation, defined by the SD method.

IV. Discussion

In this section, we discuss the results obtained in the experiments described in the previous section.

For the results of P1, the response data for three perceptions, namely, the movement of the avatar is "delayed", "possibly delayed", and "not delayed", was summarized for each parameter set. Table III shows the results of this. We conducted experiment and quantitatively define the level of delay where the subjects recognize that the movement of the avatar is "delayed" than their movement, and we ascertained the stage of this level. As a result, it became clear that at parameter set 3 and above, about 40% of subject sensed "delayed movement" where the movement in the avatar was delayed compared to the subjects' movement.

For the result for P2, some features are described by considering the results of the correspondence analysis in Figure 6. Figure 6 shows summary of findings by evaluation items. In precedent movement, even if movement was not synchronized, the result showed a something good impression. It is found that the precedent movement made a better impression than delayed movement. This finding is in contrast with the impression of delayed movement. Furthermore, it came to light that the subjects feel uncomfortable with the "delayed movement". In the "synchronic movement" experienced by the subjects after the delayed movement, they formed the impressions such as "natural", "like oneself", and "amiable", and in the "precedent movement", the subjects formed the impressions such as " hard" and "intense", as well as "interesting", "as expected", and "pleasant".

In the experiments for P3, we verified by using the repeated measures ANOVA whether there is any difference in the impression evaluation of each of three types of movements of the avatar confirmed in P2, namely, "delayed movement", "synchronic movement", and "precedent movement". From the results in Table VI and VII, it is evident that in the movements of the avatar, " delayed movement " and " synchronic movement", and "delayed movement" and "precedent movement" are statistically significant ($p < 0.05$). In other words, the impression formed for "delayed movement" is different from that for "synchronic movement" and "precedent movement".

Following these results and the results shown in Figure and Figure 9, we execute post hoc analysis. Here, we found that while the "delayed movement" gave a different impression than the "synchronic movement" and the "precedent movement", it cannot be said that impression differed in the "synchronic movement" and the "precedent movement". From our experiments, it is found that there was an interaction partially, not a whole of interaction. It is significant to check the pattern of data to judge whether there is an interaction.

As for the impression of the "precedent movement", the impression evaluation was "interesting", "as expected" and "pleasant", which was most likely because of habituation [24][25][26] in perception in terms of mitigation of the sense of discomfort to time delay and adverse psychological effect, becoming insensitive. From the interviews to subjects, some of them felt comfortable by watching the precedent movement of the avatar. They tried to follow the precedent movement at first, then as watching the repeated movement they had an illusion eventually as if the avatar would be a instructor and teach them an exercise to shaking up and down the arms. It is though that the reason why is some of peoples feel comfortable by following a certain instruction from the instructor.

This habituation differs from simple stimulation mentioned in the preceding studies [27][28][29][30] and reactive habituation [31][32][33][34] that occurs due to iterative presentation of irritation. Habituation showed by these results are similar to habituation explained by [35][36] in terms of order effect where after experiencing the "synchronic movement", the subjects become insensitive to the delay of the movement.

We think this effect based on the order is a new finding

that the order of movement patterns affects psychology. Now, we have not considered the mechanism of the effect precedent exactly, but we can say that the effect seems to be originated in the " Internal Clock " [37] of human beings. It is said that the Internal Clock sometimes varies caused by an extra disturbance such as the order effects and makes us misunderstand that two distances between the " delayed movement " and the " synchronic movement ", and between the " synchronic movement " and the " synchronic movement " are same.

However, we have used only three patterns of order in this experiment, and our next challenge is to study and discuss changes in impression and habituation for different order of movements. The aim of new experiment is to see whether the impression of three patterns of exercise with avatar change by another order under same conditions.

V. CONCLUSION

This paper analyzed impression in an user exercise while watching an avatar delayed movement that imitates the user movements. In our experiments, the avatar moves to imitates the movement of the subjects and the speed of the avatar's movement is changed by varying the parameters of the SDK which conducts and controls the avatar movement. We conducted the movement of the avatar as the "delayed movement", the "synchronic movement" and the "precedent movement"

To define the speed, we shed light on the numerical value of the level of delay based on the experiment where the subject recognizes that the movement of the avatar is "delayed" from his movement, and we verified its stage. Next, we conducted a survey about impression formed by the subject regarding the avatar that moves out of synchronization with the subject.

We set some novel assumptions to be tested by using the ordinary statistical methods, it is pointed out that the visual impression for the delayed movement of the avatar shows not only a usual situation but also varying situation under the conditions which is the context with the "precedent" and "synchronic" movement.

To test the importance of this factor, the new work need to be executed by some patterns with various orders. And in the future work, the authors will strive to increase the number of subject and the patterns with various movements to improve the accuracy of the analysis.

ACKNOWLEDGMENT

This work was in part supported by JST RISTEX Service Science, Solutions and Foundation Integrated Research Program and by JSPS KAKENHI Grant Numbers 25280125 and 26730139.

REFERENCES

[1] T. Tanaka, H. Hashimoto, and S. Yokota, "Evaluation of Visual Impression of Delayed Movement of Avatar while Exercising," International Conference on Intelligent Systems and Appications, pp. 10-15, 2015.

[2] J. Preece, Y. Rogers, H. Sharp, D. Beyon, S. Holland, and T. Carey, "Human-Computer Interaction," Addison-Wesley, New York, 1994.

[3] R. W. Picard, "Affective Computing," MIT Press, Cambridge, MA., 1997.

[4] J. Klein, Y. Moon, and R. W. Picard, "This computer responds to user frustration, Theory, design, and results," Interacting with Computers, ELSEVIER, vol. 14, Issue 2, pp. 119-140, 2002.

[5] A. R. Pearson, T. V. West, J. F. Dovidio, S. R. Powers, R. Buck, and R. Henning, "The fragility of intergroup relations: Divergent effects of delayed audiovisual feedback in intergroup and intragroup interaction," vol. 19, no. 2, pp. 1272-1279, 2008.

[6] S. R. Powersa, C. Rauhb, R. A. Henningc, R. W. Buckc, and T. V. Weste, "The effect of video feedback delay on frustration and emotion communication accuracy," Computers in Human Behavior, ELSEVIER, vol. 27, no. 5, pp. 1651-1657, 2011.

[7] J. Klein, Y. Moon, and R. Picard, "This computer responds to user frustration: Theory, design, and results," Interacting with Computers, vol. 14, pp. 119-140, 2002.

[8] H. Prendinger, J. Mori, and M. Ishizuka, "Recognizing, Modeling, and Responding to Users' Affective States," User Modeling, Lecture Notes in Computer Science, vol. 3538, pp. 60-69, 2005.

[9] N. C. Kramer, N. Simons, and S. Kopp, "The Effects of an Embodies Conversational Agent's Noverbal Behavior on User's Evaluation and Behavioral Mimicry," Intelligent Virtual Agents Lecture Notes in Computer Science, Springer Berlin Heidelberg, vol. 4722, pp. 238-251, 2007.

[10] Y. Yamamoto, Y. Kobayashi, Y. Muto, K. Takano, and Y. Miyake, "Hierardchical Timing Structure of Utterance in Human Dialogue," IEEE International Conference on Systems, Man and Cybernetics, pp. 810-813, 2008.

[11] T. Hashimoto, S. Hiramatsu, and H. Kobayashi, "Development of face robot for emotional communication between human and robot," IEEE International Conference on Mechatronics and Automation, pp. 25-30, 2006.

[12] T. Hashimoto, S. Hiramatsu, T. Tusji, and H. Kobayashi, "Realization and evaluation of realistic nod with receptionist robot SAYA," IEEE International Conference on Robot and Human Interactive Communication, pp. 326-331, 2007.

[13] S. Takasugi, S. Yoshida, K. Okitsu, M. Yokoyama, T. Yamamoto, and Y. Miyake, "Influence of Pause Duration and Nod Response Timing in Dialogue between Human and Communication Robot," Transaction of the Society of Instrument and Control Engineers, vol. 46, no. 1, pp. 72-81, 2011.

[14] M. Yamamoto and T. Watanabe, "Timing Control Effects of Utterance to Communicative Actions on Embodied Interaction with a Robot and CG Character," International Journal of Human-Computer Interaction, vol. 24, no. 1, pp. 87-107, 2008.

[15] Kinect for windows SDK v1.8, https://www.microsoft.com/en-us/download/details.aspx?id=40278, last accessed on May 20, 2016.

[16] XNA Game Studio 4.0, https://msdn.microsoft.com/ja-jp/library/bb200104(v=xnagamestudio.40).aspx, last accessed on May 20, 2016.

[17] C. E. Osgood, W. H. May, and M. S. Miron, "Cross-cultural Universals of Affective Meaning," University of Illinois Press, 1975.

[18] C. E. Osgood, "Studies on the generality of affective meaning system, ", American Psychologist, vol. 17, pp. 10-28, 1962.

[19] Y. Suzukiy and R. Ohmuray, "Impression Evaluation of Pointing Prediction Based on Minimum-Jerk Model," IPSJ Interaction 2013, pp. 249-254, 2013.

[20] T. Kanda, H. Ishiguro, T. Ono, M. Imai, and R. Nakatsu, "An evaluation on interaction between humans and an autonomous robot Robovie," Journal of the Robotics Society of Japan, vol. 20, no. 3, pp. 315-323, 2002.

[21] M. J. Greenacre, "Theory and Applications of Correspondence Analysis," Academic press, 1984.

[22] A. Field, "Repeated Measures ANOVA," Research Method of Psychology, 2008.

[23] R. E. Kirk, "Experimental Design: Procedures for the Behavioral Sciences," 3rd Edition. Brooks/Cole Publishing Company, 1995.

[24] R. B. Zajonc, "Attitudinal Effects of Mere Exposure," Journal of Personality and Social Psychology, vol. 9 (2, Pt.2), pp. 1-27, 1968.

[25] R. B. Zajonc, "Mere Exposure: A Gateway to the Subliminal," Current Directions in Psychological Science, vol. 10, no. 6, pp. 224-228, 2001.

[26] X. Fang, S. Singh, and R. Ahluwalia, "An Examination of Different Explanations for the Mere Exposure Effect," Journal of Consumer Research, vol. 34, pp. 97-103, 2007.

[27] R. L. Moreland and R. B. Zajonc, "A Strong Test of Exposure Effects," Journal of Experimental Social Psychology, vol. 12, pp. 170-179, 1976.

[28] A. Grimes and P. J. Kitchen, "Researching mere exposure effects to advertising: Theoretical foundations and methodological implications," International Journal of Market Research, vol. 49, no. 2, pp. 191-219, 2007.

[29] G. Toma, C. Nelsona, T. Srzentica, and R. Kinga, "Mere Exposure and the Endowment Effect on Consumer Decision Making," The Journal of Psychology: Interdisciplinary and Applied, vol. 141, Issue 2, 2007.

[30] A. Serenko and N. Bontils, "What's familiar is excellent: The impact of exposure effect on perceived journal quality," Journal of Informetrics, ELSEVIER, vol.5, Issue 1, pp. 219-223, 2011.

[31] E. H. Jones and J. J. B. Allen, "The role of affect in the mere exposure effect: Evidence from psychophysiological and individual differences approaches," Personality and Social Psychology Bulletin, vol. 27, pp. 889-898, 2001.

[32] C. H. Price, E. Burton, R. Hickinson, J. Inett, E. Moore, K. Salmon, and P. Shiba, "Picture book exposure elicits positive visual preferences in toddlers," Journal of Experimental Child Psychology, vol. 104, pp. 89-104, 2004.

[33] D. B. Verrier, "Evidence for the influence of the mere-exposure effect on voting in the Eurovision Song Contest," Judgment and Decision Making, vol. 7, no. 5, pp. 639-643, 2012.

[34] S. Delplanque, G. Coppin, L. Bloesch, I. Cayeux, and D. Sander, "The mere exposure effect depends on an odor's initial pleasantness," Frontiers in Psychology, doi:10.3389/fpsyg.2015.00920, 2015

[35] H. Schuman and S. Presser, "Questions & Answers in Attitude Surveys," Academic Press, 1981.

[36] D. W. Moore, "Measuring new types of question-order effects," Public Opinion Quarterly, no. 66, no. 1, pp. 80-91, 2002.

[37] T. Michel, "Temporal discrimination and the indifference interval, implications for a model of the 'internal clock'," Psychology Monographs, vol. 77, no. 13, pp. 1-31, 1963.

Stabilization of a Two-Wheeled Mobile Pendulum System using LQG and Fuzzy Control Techniques

Ákos Odry, Péter Odry
Dept. of Control Engineering and Information Technology
University of Dunaújváros
Dunaújváros, Hungary
E-mail: odrya@mail.duf.hu, podry@mail.duf.hu

János Fodor
Institute of Intelligent Engineering Systems
Óbuda University
Budapest, Hungary
E-mail: fodor@uni-obuda.hu

Abstract—**This paper studies the control performances of modern and soft-computing based control solutions. Namely, the stabilization of a naturally unstable mechatronic system will be elaborated using linear-quadratic-Gaussian and cascade-connected fuzzy control schemes. The mechatronic system is a special mobile robot (so called two-wheeled mobile pendulum system) that has only two contact points with the supporting surface and its center of mass is located under the wheel axis. Due to this mechanical structure, the inner body (which acts as a pendulum between the wheels) tends to oscillate during the translational motion of the robot, thus the application of feedback control is essential in order to stabilize the dynamical system. In the first part of the paper, the mechatronic system and the corresponding mathematical model are introduced, while in the second part the aforementioned control solutions are designed for the plant. The achieved control performances are analyzed both in simulation environment and on the real mechatronic system. At the end of the paper, a performance assessment of the elaborated control solutions is given based on transient response and error integral measurements.**

Keywords-Fuzzy control; LQG control; Kalman filter; mobile robot; self-balancing robot; future transportation system

I. INTRODUCTION

Nowadays, technological developments face dynamical systems that are getting more and more complex and complicated by the day. These complex systems are characterized by high order dynamics, uncertain parameters, and most often, their nonlinear mathematical model is only approximately known (such as the analyzed system in the INTELLI 2015 paper [1]). Over the last few decades, we have seen that conventional and modern linear control techniques have been extensively applied in control development and industrial automation, however, their performance is always questioned, when systems with uncertainty and unmodeled dynamics are controlled. In general, these linear controllers do not work well for nonlinear vague systems [2]. On the other hand, Zadeh's fuzzy logic and reasoning introduced a new control perspective, where imprecision and uncertainty form the basis of the inference mechanism [3]. Fuzzy logic control plays an important role in systems with unknown structure, and it has been widely used in automotive control applications. Thanks to its rapid progress, fuzzy reasoning is a fruitful research area for the Robotics and Control Community, where the achievable control performance and competitive control solutions are continuously investigated [4]. This paper studies the control performance of linear-quadratic-Gaussian and fuzzy control techniques.

The linear-quadratic-Gaussian (LQG) technique is a beloved method in the control of dynamical systems since it provides the optimal state feedback gain based on the well-developed mathematical algorithm [5]. Numerous researches have been dealt with its application and control performance in real embedded environments. Divelbiss and Wen [6] presented their experimental results of the tracking control of a car-trailer system, where linear quadratic regulator was used to track the trajectory. Ji and Sul [7] proposed an LQG-based speed control method for torsional vibration suppression in a 2-mass motor drive system, which gave satisfying performance and robust behavior against parameter variations. Recent efforts broaden further the set of experimental research results regarding the LQG control, including the control of inverted pendulum type assistant robot [8], self-balancing unicycle robot [9], unmanned helicopter in an uncertain environment [10], and quadrotor UAVs [11] as well.

On the parallel thread, fuzzy logic control has also proved its competitive performance. Due to the provided flexibility and smoothness in the control action, and the linguistic information based design technique as well, it is applied more and more in dynamical systems. McLean and Matsuda [12] designed a fuzzy logic controller, which provided acceptable station-keeping performance for a single main rotor helicopter even in severe turbulences. Das and Kar [13] proposed adaptive fuzzy controllers for the robust control of nonholonomic mobile robots that were characterized with uncertain parameters. Lee and Gonzalez [14] examined the achieved control performance of the conventional PID and fuzzy techniques for position control of a muscle-like actuated arm. Moreover, fuzzy control was successfully applied in the development area of walking robots as well. Kecskés and Odry [15] elaborated the optimized fuzzy control of a hexapod walking robot called Szabad(ka)-II. Finally, fuzzy logic based stabilization of two-wheeled inverted pendulum systems has also been investigated both in simulation environment and on the real plant [17]. Many applications have been proposed where fuzzy control showed superior performance (such as [12], [15]), however, the opposite outcome was often claimed as well (such as in [14]). Therefore, the effective and beneficial applicability of fuzzy control still remains an important issue to be further addressed.

The objective of this paper is to make an analysis, and give a comparative assessment regarding the achieved control performances of both control techniques. The robustness of the elaborated controllers will also be investigated using the simulation and measurement results. The controlled plant is a two wheeled mobile pendulum system [18] (hereinafter robot), whose dynamics is highly nonlinear, moreover, its mathematical model is characterized by uncertain parameters (the model has not been validated). It will be discussed what is the influence of the uncertain dynamics, and how it affects the achieved closed loop behavior of the real robot. The stabilization of the plant with the LQG technique has been investigated in [1], while in [19] a fuzzy control scheme has been designed. This paper summarizes the results of [1] and [19], and based on the evaluation of different step responses (where both the simulation and measurement results will be taken into account), the better control strategy will be identified. For the comparative assessment different error integrals (as quality measurement numbers) will be evaluated.

The remainder of this paper is organized as follows. In Section II, the mechatronic structure of the robot is introduced, while in Section III, the corresponding nonlinear mathematical model is derived. In Section IV, the control task and the LQG and fuzzy control techniques are reviewed. Section V deals with the elaboration of the LQG control strategy, while Section VI describes the applied fuzzy control scheme. The simulation and implementation results of the elaborated control strategies are given in Sections VII and VIII, respectively. Section IX describes the comparative assessment based on the simulation and measurement results, while Section X contains the conclusions and the future work recommendations.

II. The Fabricated Mechatronic System

The mechatronic system is a special mobile robot (so called two-wheeled mobile pendulum system) that consists of two wheels and a steel inner body (chassis). The wheels are actuated through DC motors attached to the body. As it can be seen in Figure 1, the diameter of the wheels is bigger than the diameter of the intermediate body, thus the robot has only two contact points with the supporting surface. Due to this mechanical structure, the inner body behaves as a pendulum between the stator and rotor of the applied DC motors, and tends to oscillate when the robot performs translational motion.

Figure 1. Photograph of the fabricated robot.

TABLE I. The Applied Sensors In The Embedded Electronics

Sensor	Manufacturer	Type
Accelerometer	STMicroelectronics	LIS331DL
Gyroscope	STMicroelectronics	L3G4200D
Current sensors	Texas Instruments	INA198
Incremental encoders	Faulhaber	PA2-100

Since the location of the center of mass of the robot can be under and above the wheel axis, two equilibrium points can be distinguished. Namely, the robot stays around its stable equilibrium point when the center of mass is located under the wheel axis. Therefore, around this state the translational motion of the robot is affected by the damped oscillation of its inner body. On the other hand, the robot is operated around its unstable equilibrium point when the center of mass is stabilized above the wheel axis. Around the unstable equilibrium point, the robot simultaneously performs translational motion and balances its inner body, which acts as an inverted pendulum. For video demonstration see the website [20].

The electronic construction is built around two 16-bit ultra-low-power Texas Instruments MSP430F2618 microcontrollers (hereinafter MCU1 and MCU2). The applied sensors are summarized in Table I. The actuators are 3V geared DC micromotors (type: 1024N003S) manufactured by Faulhaber. The motors are driven with pulse width modulation (PWM) signals through Texas Instruments DRV592 drivers. The electronic system is supplied from stabilized 3.3V, the source is a 1 cell lithium-polymer (Li-Po) battery. A 16 MHz quartz oscillator is used as the system clock.

Similar construction was built at the McGill University's Centre for Intelligent Machines [21]. It was proven that the two contact point construction is characterized by the so called quasiholonomic property that eases the control of nonholonomic systems. Another corresponding two contact point construction is the electric Diwheel built by the School of Mechanical Engineering at the University of Adelaide [22].

III. Mathematical Model

To be able to efficiently design the control algorithms of the system, its mathematical model has to be obtained first. Most of the electrical and mechanical parameters that characterize the robot dynamics (such as wheel radius or resistance of the motor) are quite accurately known from direct measurements, datasheets or from calculations performed by Solidworks, the rest of the parameters were experimentally tuned based on the measurements.

We indicate with θ_1 and θ_2 the angular displacements of the wheels, while with θ_3 the inclination angle of the pendulum (inner body). The parameters that characterize the robot are summarized in Table VI in the appendix. The following notations will also be used: $\sigma = \dot{\psi}$ as the yaw rate of the robot, and $v = \dot{s}$ as the linear speed of the robot, i.e., $\dot{\psi} = r(\dot{\theta}_2 - \dot{\theta}_1)/d$, and $\dot{s} = r(\dot{\theta}_1 + \dot{\theta}_2)/2$.

The motion of the system was determined by the help of the Lagrange equations [23], which lead us to the following equations of motion of the mechanical system [18]:

$$M(q)\ddot{q} + V(q,\dot{q}) = \tau_a - \tau_f, \quad (1)$$

where $M(q)$ denotes the 3-by 3 symmetric and positive definite inertia matrix, $V(q,\dot{q})$ denotes the 3-dimensional vector term including the Coriolis and centrifugal force terms and also the potential (gravity) force term. The Lagrange function and the exact elements of the matrices in (1) are described in the appendix. For the vector of generalized coordinates $q = (\theta_1, \theta_2, \theta_3)^T$ was chosen, since it contains the minimum number of independent coordinates that define the configuration of the system. The generalized external forces in (1) consist of the torques τ_a that are produced by the motors and the effect of friction τ_f that is modeled in the system [18]. The torques τ_a are described by the differential equation (2), where the input voltages and currents of the motors are denoted with $u = (u_1, u_2)^T$ and $I = (I_1, I_2)^T$.

$$\begin{aligned} \dot{I} &= \frac{1}{L}\left(u - k_E k \begin{bmatrix} 1 & 0 & -1 \\ 0 & 1 & -1 \end{bmatrix} \dot{q} - RI\right) \\ \tau_a &= k_M k \begin{bmatrix} 1 & 0 \\ 0 & 1 \\ -1 & -1 \end{bmatrix} I \end{aligned} \quad (2)$$

Regarding the effect of friction τ_f, only viscous frictions were assumed. Namely, viscous friction was modelled at the bearings and between the wheels and the supporting surface:

$$\tau_f = \begin{bmatrix} b + f_v & 0 & -b \\ 0 & b + f_v & -b \\ -b & -b & 2b \end{bmatrix} \dot{q}. \quad (3)$$

Based on (1) the state-space representation of the two-wheel inverted pendulum system is obtained. With the state vector $x = (q, \dot{q}, I)^T$ the state-space equation is [18]:

$$\begin{aligned} \dot{x}(t) &= h(x,u), \\ h(x,u) &= \begin{bmatrix} \dot{q} \\ M(q)^{-1}\left(\tau_a - \tau_f - V(q,\dot{q})\right) \\ \frac{1}{L}\left(u - k_E k \begin{bmatrix} 1 & 0 & -1 \\ 0 & 1 & -1 \end{bmatrix} \dot{q} - RI\right) \end{bmatrix}, \\ y(t) &= x(t). \end{aligned} \quad (4)$$

Remark: In the simulation environment the state-space equation (4) was implemented, however, during the design of the LQG controllers the 6-dimensional version defined by the state vector $x = (q, \dot{q})^T$ was used. This outcome was chosen because the current measurements were that noisy that the states $I = (I_1, I_2)^T$ could not be used in the feedback. The 6-dimensional model is derived by neglecting the inductance L of the motors.

IV. The Control Task

The anti-sway speed control of the robot was investigated in the analysis, e.g., such control strategies have been elaborated, which simultaneously minimize the oscillations (around the stable equilibrium point) of the inner body and ensures the translational motion of the robot:

- $\lim_{t\to\infty} \dot{s}(t) = v_d$ for the linear speed of the robot,
- $\lim_{t\to\infty} \dot{\psi}(t) = \sigma_d$ for the yaw rate of the robot,
- $\lim_{t\to\infty} \dot{\theta}_3(t) = 0$ for the oscillation of the inner body,

where v_d and σ_d denote the desired values of the linear speed and yaw rate of the robot, respectively. In the following subsections, the applied control techniques and the elaboration procedures are reviewed.

A. LQ control

The linear-quadratic control addresses the issue of achieving a balance between good system response and control effort [5]. It is based on a developed mathematical algorithm, which results the optimal state-feedback gain K. The feedback gain K minimizes the quadratic cost function

$$J(x,u) = \frac{1}{2}\sum_{k=0}^{N-1}(x_k^T Q x_k + u_k^T R u_k) + \frac{1}{2} x_N^T Q x_N, \quad (5)$$

where $x \in \mathbb{R}^n$ and $u \in \mathbb{R}^m$ are the state and input of the system described by its state-space equation, while $Q = Q^T \in \mathbb{R}^{n\times n}, Q \geq 0$ and $R \in \mathbb{R}^{m\times m}, R > 0$ are weighting matrixes. According to the LQ method, the state feedback matrix is given by $K = (R + B^T P B)^{-1} B^T P A$, where $P = P^T \geq 0$ is the unique solution of the Control Algebraic Riccati Equation (CARE). The optimal state-feedback $u_k = -Kx_k$ ensures the asymptotic stability of the closed loop system. The feedback matrix K is calculated by the built-in Matlab function lqrd(A,B,Q,R,Ts). Since the LQ control defined by the objective function (5) drives the system from the initial state x_0 to the state $x_d = 0$, the control structure shall be extended with the reference tracking matrices:

$$\begin{pmatrix} N_x \\ N_u \end{pmatrix} = \begin{bmatrix} A - I & B \\ C & 0 \end{bmatrix}^{-1} \begin{pmatrix} 0_{n\times m} \\ I_m \end{pmatrix}, \quad (6)$$

where 0 and I are the zero and identity matrices, respectively (the sizes are given in the subscript).

B. Kalman filtering

In the development of the optimal LQ control strategy it is assumed that the state variables are measurable, and the system is not disturbed by either internal or external noises.

However, in practice, the opposite situation is quite common, namely, that a part of the state vector is too noisy to be used directly in the feedback. The LQG strategy provides optimal control gain to stochastic, noisy systems by minimizing the expected value of the quadratic objective function (5).

Based on the separation principle the LQG control strategy is given by the state-feedback $u_k = -K\hat{x}_k$, where K is the optimal control gain determined by the LQ algorithm, while $\hat{x}_k$ state vector consists of the original states (those states of x_k that were not noisy) and the Kalman filter based estimation of the noisy states. Let us denote the unmeasurable or noisy states with ξ, than the corresponding noisy linear system can be given as:

$$\begin{aligned} \xi_{k+1} &= \Phi\xi_k + \Gamma\rho_k + w_k, \\ \gamma_k &= \mathrm{P}\xi_k + z_k, \end{aligned} \tag{7}$$

where the process and measurement noises are indicated with w and z, respectively, and according to the stochastic hypothesis these noises are uncorrelated and their mean value is zero. In this case the Kalman filter algorithm provides the optimal estimation $\hat{\xi}$ of the state ξ, i.e., $E\left[\xi_k - \hat{\xi}_k\right] = 0$ and $E\left[\left(\xi_k - \hat{\xi}_k\right)\left(\xi_k - \hat{\xi}_k\right)^T\right] \to \inf$. The estimation algorithm can be found in [24].

Therefore, the design steps of the LQG control strategy are the following: i.) Linearization of the mathematical model around an equilibrium point, ii.) Controllability analysis, iii.) Specification of the weighting matrices, iv.) Calculation of the optimal control gain K, v.) Identification of the noisy states, vi.) Specification of the noise covariance parameters of the filter, vii.) State estimation by Kalman filter and viii.) Application of the state feedback strategy $u_k = -K\hat{x}_k$.

C. *Fuzzy control*

Lofti A. Zadeh introduced the fuzzy sets [3] by extending the classical two-valued logic $\{0,1\}$ with the whole continuous interval $[0,1]$. Fuzzy reasoning is based on the application of these fuzzy sets, which result that the inference mechanism of a fuzzy logic controller is defined by simple IF-THEN linguistic rules. Hence, there is no need to define certain models, instead the empirical rules and the approximate reasoning lead to a heuristically defined control strategy. The algorithm is composed of the following parts [25].

- Fuzzification: Mapping the available crisp measurements to the fuzzy interval $[0,1]$. The fuzzy interval describes the membership of the fuzzy input variable. The membership function of a fuzzy set A is denoted with $\mu_A(x) \in [0,1]$, where x is the crisp measurement.
- Inference machine: The fuzzy IF-THEN rules define the implication relation between the antecedents and consequents. The inference mechanism consists of assigning the so-called firing level to the output fuzzy set defined in each rule. The firing level represents the result of the antecedent evaluation. The aggregation procedure is the last part of the inference machine, where the output fuzzy sets are combined into a single fuzzy set (overall fuzzy output is calculated).
- Defuzzification: Mapping back the output fuzzy set to crisp domain. The most popular defuzzification methods are the center of gravity and the weighted average method [25].

The concrete elaboration procedure (e.g., selecting the fuzzy sets and fuzzy rules, defining the inference mechanism, and applying the defuzzification method as well) will be described in Section VI.

V. Elaboration of the LQG Control Strategy

The goal of the elaboration is to calculate the optimal state feedback and reference tracking matrices that drive the motors such a way that both the speed control of the robot and the suppression of the inner body oscillations are ensured.

A. *Optimal state feedback*

The linear state space equation is given by the linearization of (4) around the equilibrium $(x_e, u_e) = (0,0)$:

$$\dot{x} = \underbrace{\left(\frac{\partial h}{\partial x}\right)_{(x_e,u_e)}}_{A_s} x(t) + \underbrace{\left(\frac{\partial h}{\partial u}\right)_{(x_e,u_e)}}_{B_s} u(t), \tag{8}$$

where the subscript s refers to the stable equilibrium point. In order to reduce the complexity of implementation the $\tilde{x} = Tx = \left(s, \theta_3, \dot{s}, \dot{\theta}_3, \psi, \dot{\psi}\right)$ coordinate transformation is applied. The resulting state-space representation is given as:

$$\begin{aligned} \dot{\tilde{x}} &= \begin{bmatrix} 0_{2\times2} & I_2 & 0_{2\times2} \\ \tilde{A}_{s,21} & \tilde{A}_{s,22} & 0_{2\times2} \\ 0_{2\times2} & 0_{2\times2} & \tilde{A}_{s,33} \end{bmatrix} \tilde{x} + \begin{bmatrix} 0_{2\times2} \\ \tilde{B}_{s,2} \\ \tilde{B}_{s,3} \end{bmatrix} u, \\ y &= \begin{bmatrix} 0_{2\times2} & \tilde{C}_{s,2} & \tilde{C}_{s,3} \end{bmatrix} \tilde{x}, \end{aligned} \tag{9}$$

where the block matrices are described in the appendix.

The controllability matrix [5] is given by $M_c = [B \quad AB \quad \dots \quad A^5B]_{(\tilde{A}_s,\tilde{B}_s)}$ and the evaluation of its rank results $\operatorname{rank} M_c = 4$. Therefore, according to the Kalman rank condition for controllability (KRCC) the system (9) is not controllable, since the dimension of the state vector is $\dim \tilde{x} = 6$. The non-controllable states of $\tilde{x}$ are the position s and the orientation ψ.

Thus, a new coordinate transformation $z = T_{C\bar{C}}\tilde{x}$ is defined, such that $T_{C\bar{C}} = (T_C, T_{\bar{C}})$ is a basis for $\mathbb{R}^6$, furthermore the columns of T_C form the basis for the controllable subspace, $\dim T_C = 6 \times 4$ and $\dim T_{\bar{C}} = 6 \times 2$. The state-space representation becomes

$$\begin{aligned} \dot{z} &= \begin{bmatrix} A_C & A_{C\bar{C}} \\ 0 & A_{\bar{C}} \end{bmatrix} z(t) + \begin{bmatrix} B_C \\ 0 \end{bmatrix} u(t), \\ y &= [C_C \quad C_{\bar{C}}] z(t), \end{aligned} \tag{10}$$

where, as a consequence of the definition, the state vector $z = (z_C, z_{\bar{C}})^T$ is clearly devided into two parts, namely $z_C =$

$(\theta_3, \dot{s}, \dot{\theta}_3, \dot{\psi})^T$ denotes the controllable states, while $z_{\bar{C}} = (s, \psi)^T$ contains the uncontrollable ones.

The LQ strategy is elaborated by using the controllable subsystem (A_C, B_C). The weighting matrices $Q = \mathrm{diag}(Q_{ii})$ and $R = \mathrm{diag}(R_{jj})$ were defined based on the Bryson's rule, where $Q_{11} = (15 \cdot \pi/180)^{-2}$, $Q_{22} = (0.08)^{-2}$, $Q_{33} = (50 \cdot \pi/180)^{-2}$, $Q_{44} = (50 \cdot \pi/180)^{-2}$ and $R_{11} = R_{22} = 3^{-2}$ were chosen. Solving the CARE the optimal control gain is

$$K^s = \begin{bmatrix} -1.75 & -1.26 & -0.2 & -0.61 \\ -1.75 & -1.26 & -0.2 & +0.61 \end{bmatrix}, \qquad (11)$$

while the reference tracking matrices are

$$N_x^s = \begin{bmatrix} -0.41 & 0 \\ 1 & 0 \\ 0 & 0 \\ 0 & 1 \end{bmatrix}, \quad N_u^s = \begin{bmatrix} 4.28 & -0.37 \\ 4.28 & +0.37 \end{bmatrix}. \qquad (12)$$

B. Kalman filtering

The Kalman filter is used to estimate the tilt angle θ_3 of the inner body (second element of $\tilde{x}$). Since the accelerometer measures the projection of gravity vector onto its axes, the angle is given by $\theta_{3,acc} = \mathrm{atan}\left(\frac{a_y}{a_x}\right)$ [26]. Unfortunately, $\theta_{3,acc}$ is very noisy, in the most control methods it cannot be considered as an accurate derived quantity at high frequency rates of rotation because the accelerometer measures both the static acceleration of the gravity and the dynamic acceleration of the robot as well. Thus, it is common to consider the gyroscope and accelerometer sensors as a noisy linear system and use the Kalman filter to estimate the state vector. The corresponding state-space equation is given as:

$$\begin{gathered} \xi_{k+1} = \begin{bmatrix} 1 & -1/f_s \\ 0 & 1 \end{bmatrix} \xi_k + \begin{bmatrix} 1/f_s \\ 0 \end{bmatrix} \rho_k + w_k \\ \gamma_k = \begin{bmatrix} 1 & 0 \end{bmatrix} \xi_k + z_k, \end{gathered} \qquad (13)$$

where the state vector $\xi = (\theta_3, \tilde{u})^T$ consists of the inclination angle $\theta_3[\mathrm{rad}]$, and the bias of the gyroscope $\tilde{u}[\mathrm{rad/s}]$. Furthermore, the input of the linear system is the angular velocity $\rho = \dot{\theta}_3[\mathrm{rad/s}]$ (measured by the gyroscope), while the output of the system is the derived angle $\gamma = \theta_{3,acc}[\mathrm{rad}]$ from the pure accelerometer measurements. The covariance matrices that characterize the measurement and state noises were defined based on offline measurements.

C. The LQG control strategy

According to the separation principle, the LQG control strategy is elaborated as follows. Around the stable equilibrium point the state feedback $u_k = -K(\hat{\theta}_3, \dot{s}, \dot{\theta}_3, \dot{\psi})$ ensures asymptotic stability of the closed loop system, where $\hat{\theta}_3$ denotes the Kalman filter based estimation of the tilt angle of the inner body and the optimal control gain K is defined by (11). The detailed control structure is depicted in Figure 2.

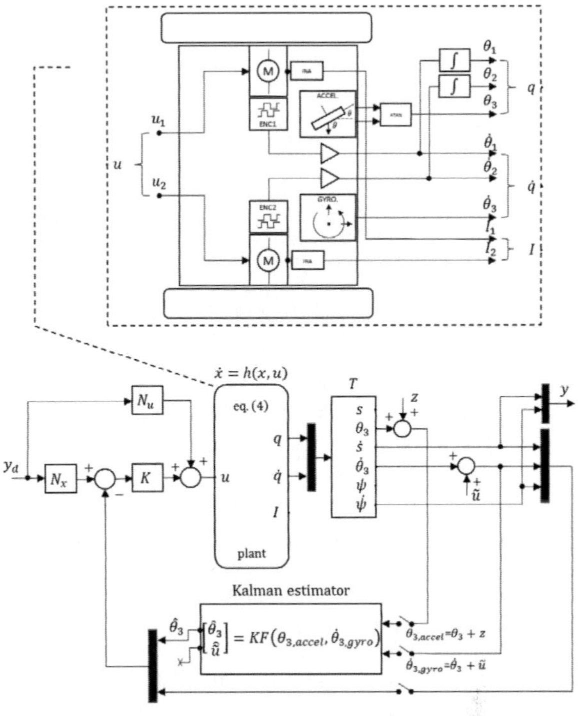

Figure 2. Detailed structure of the LQG control strategy.

VI. ELABORATION OF THE FUZZY CONTROL STRATEGY

The elaboration of the fuzzy control strategy consisted of defining the fuzzy logic controllers and a control scheme that satisfies the requirements of the anti-sway speed controller of the robot. This procedure was started by aggregating the deductions related to the behavior of the dynamical system using human common sense. The investigation resulted a control scheme that consists of three cascade-connected FLCs (hereinafter FLC1, FLC2, and FLC3). The control structure is depicted in Figure 3 [19].

FLC1 ensures the speed control of the robot. The input of the controller is the speed error $e_v(i) = v_d(i) - v(i)$, while the output is the variation $\Delta u_v(i)$ of the control voltage $u_v(i)$. An integrator is attached to the output of the controller, therefore, a PI-type FLC has been defined with the fuzzy rules defined in Table II, where the antecedent is e_v. Both the ranges of the input and output variables, and the membership functions are depicted in Figure 4. For the defuzzification of the output fuzzy set, the weighted average method has been chosen, therefore, the crisp control voltage u_v for the speed control of the robot is defined as:

$$u_v(i) = u_v(i-1) + \frac{\sum_{j=1}^{3} \mu^j(e_v(i)) \cdot \gamma^j}{\sum_{j=1}^{3} \mu^j(e_v(i))}, \qquad (14)$$

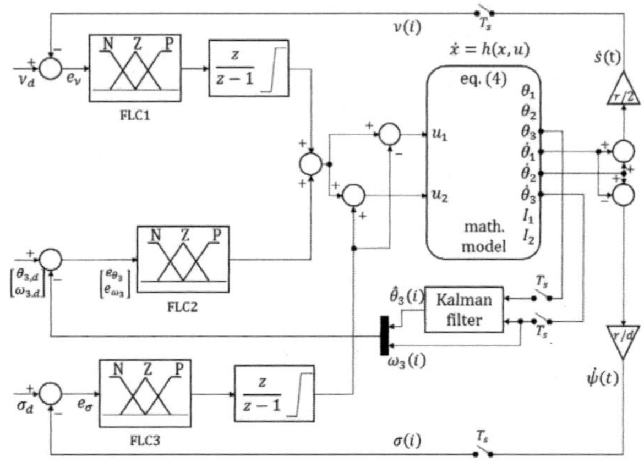

Figure 3. Block diagram of the fuzzy control scheme.

where $\mu^j(\cdot)$ returns the membership degree of the antecedent $e_v(i)$ related to the j th-rule, and γ^j is the singleton consequent.

FLC2 is responsible for the suppression of the resulting inner body oscillations. The inputs of the controller are the error of the oscillation angle $e_{\theta_3}(i)$ and its derivative $e_{\omega_3}(i)$, while the output is the control voltage u_{θ_3} that shall be applied in order to decrease the acceleration of the robot. By decreasing the acceleration, the inner body oscillation is suppressed. FLC2 works as a PD-type fuzzy controller, whose fuzzy rules are indicated in Table II (the antecedents are the errors e_{θ_3} and e_{ω_3}). The universes of discourse of the input variables are depicted in Figure 4. The crisp output of the controller is calculated using the weighted average method:

$$u_{\theta_3}(i) = \frac{\sum_{j=1}^{9} \min\left(\mu^j\left(e_{\theta_3}(i), e_{\omega_3}(i)\right)\right) \cdot \gamma^j}{\sum_{j=1}^{9} \min\left(\mu^j\left(e_{\theta_3}(i), e_{\omega_3}(i)\right)\right)}. \quad (15)$$

Finally, FLC3 ensures the yaw rate control of the robot. The input of the controller is the yaw rate error $e_\sigma(i) = \sigma_d(i) - \sigma(i)$, while the output is the variation $\Delta u_\sigma(i)$ of the compensation voltage $u_\sigma(i)$. Similarly to FLC1, a PI-type fuzzy logic controller has been defined, whose fuzzy rules and membership functions are given in Table II and Figure 4, respectively. The crisp output of FLC3 is given as:

$$u_\sigma(i) = u_\sigma(i-1) + \frac{\sum_{j=1}^{3} \mu^j(e_\sigma(i)) \cdot \gamma^j}{\sum_{j=1}^{3} \mu^j(e_\sigma(i))}. \quad (16)$$

The control voltages of the motors can be identified based on Figure 3.

$$u_1 = u_v + u_{\theta_3} - u_\sigma$$
$$u_2 = u_v + u_{\theta_3} + u_\sigma \quad (17)$$

The membership functions related to all control variables were chosen with triangular shapes. For the inputs and outputs of every FLC three membership functions were selected uniformly distributed across their universes of discourse (see Figure 4). Table III summarizes the inference mechanism of all the employed FLCs, while the fuzzy rules for the PD-type and PI-type FLCs are shown in Table II.

VII. SIMULATION RESULTS

The simulation of the proposed control strategies was done in MATLAB Simulink environment. The fuzzy logic controllers were designed by the help of the Fuzzy Logic Toolbox of MATLAB. The simulation results of the closed loop behavior is depicted in Figure 5.

From the top, the first is the linear speed $\dot{s}$ of the robot, the second is the yaw rate $\dot{\psi}$, the third is the resulting oscillation θ_3 of the inner body, while the last one is the applied voltage to the motors. The following reference signals were applied:

- $v_d = \{0.4, 0, -0.2, 0\}$ [m/s],
- $\sigma_d = \{0.5, 0, -1.2, 0\}$ [rad/s].

TABLE II. RULE BASE OF PD AND PI-TYPE FLCS

PD-type

Consequent		Antecedent₂ N	Z	P
Antecedent₁	N	P	P	Z
	Z	P	Z	N
	P	Z	N	N

PI-type (+integrator)

	Antecedent N	Z	P
Consequent	P	Z	N

TABLE III. PROPERTIES OF THE FLCS

AND method	OR method	Implication	Aggregation	Defuzification
MIN	MAX	MIN	MAX	Weighted average

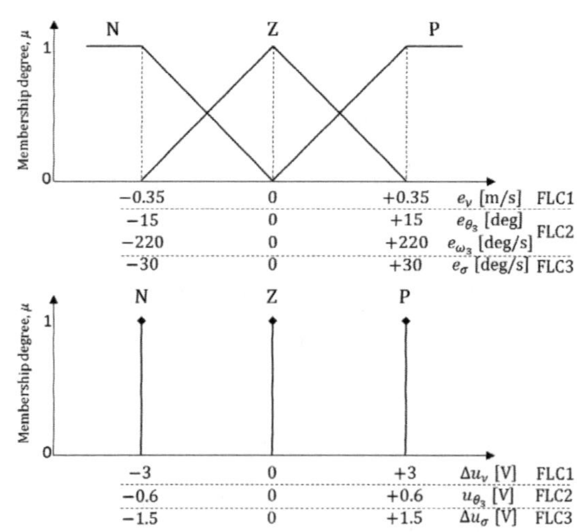

Figure 4. Membership functions of the employed FLCs.

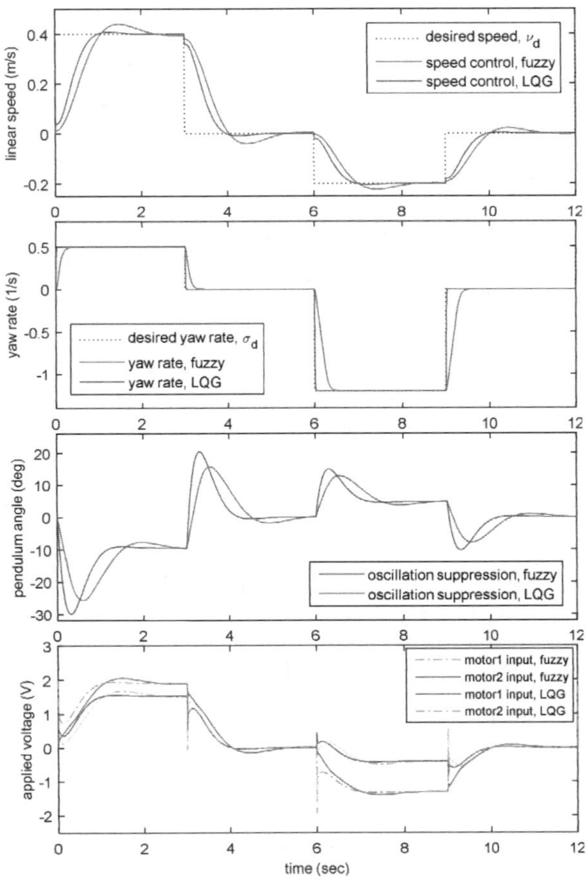

Figure 5. Closed loop behavior of the plant using the elaborated controllers (Simulation results).

The simulation results show that both the LQG control strategy and the cascade-connected fuzzy control scheme stabilized the dynamical system. It can be seen that the elaborated controllers simultaneously ensure the speed control (reference tracking performance is given in the first two subplots from the top of the figure) and the suppression of the inner body oscillations (third subplot). The dynamics of the plant was sampled at fixed $f_s = 100\ Hz$, which equals to the sampling frequency of the applied sensors.

VIII. Implementation Results

The control algorithm was coded in C language. MCU2 was programmed to work as an inertial measurement unit (IMU). Its main task is to read the sensor data (from accelerometer and gyroscope through SPI peripheral), and send a package consisting of $\theta_{3,acc}$, $\dot{\theta}_3$, and $\hat{\theta}_3$ to MCU1 continuously in every $T_s = 10\ ms$, where $\theta_{3,acc}$ indicates the inclination angle (determined based on the pure accelerations measured by the accelerometer), $\dot{\theta}_3$ denotes the angular velocity of the pendulum (measured by the gyroscope), while $\hat{\theta}_3$ indicates the Kalman estimation of the inclination angle. MCU1 executes the chosen control algorithm based on the collected measurements. It receives the package $(\theta_{3,acc}, \dot{\theta}_3, \hat{\theta}_3)$ from MCU2 and extends it with the instantaneous position and velocity of the robot $(s, \dot{s})$ based on the measurements collected from the incremental encoders. Once the measurements are updated, the chosen control algorithm updates the duty cycle of the PWM generator. Furthermore, the measurements are sent through a Bluetooth module with the frequency $f_s = 100Hz$. A GUI written in MATLAB records the measurements.

Regarding the LQG control, the calculated optimal feedback gains (11) and reference tracking matrices (12) have been directly used for the calculation of the control voltages by weighting the measurement results. The implementation of the FLCs was based on the fuzzy surfaces, which define the crisp output as a function of the input variables. Therefore, three look-up table has been stored in the flash memory of the MCU, and the control voltage has been defined by searching in these tables based on the instantaneous measurements.

The control performances are depicted in Figure 6. From the top, the first is the linear speed of the robot $\dot{s}$, the second is the yaw rate $\dot{\psi}$, the third is the angle θ_3 of the inner body, while the last one shows the applied voltages. It can be seen that both implemented control strategies successfully suppressed the oscillation of the inner body and ensured the speed control of the robot as well. In the experiment, the desired speed and yaw rate has been set to $0.4\ \mathrm{m/s}$ and $3\ \mathrm{rad/s}$, respectively (dotted lines in Figure 6). In the next section, the control performances will be qualified by defining different error integral formulas and a comparative assessment will be given based on the simulation and measurement results.

IX. Comparison of the Control Strategies

For the comparison of the elaborated control strategies both the transient responses and the overall control performance has been analyzed as well. The comparison was based on the closed loop behavior in time domain. For the quality measurement of reference tracking and suppression of inner body oscillations four different error integrals have been evaluated, namely these measures are the Sum of absolute errors (SAE), Sum of square errors (SSE), Sum of discrete time-weighted absolute errors (STAE), and the Sum of discrete time-weighted square errors defined by (18) and (19), respectively:

$$\mathrm{SAE}(e) = \sum_i^N |e(\mathrm{i})|, \quad \mathrm{SSE}(e) = \sum_i^N e(i)^2, \tag{18}$$

$$\mathrm{STAE}(e) = \sum_i^N t(i)|e(\mathrm{i})|, \quad \mathrm{STSE}(e) = \sum_i^N t(i)e(i)^2. \tag{19}$$

In (18) and (19), N denotes the length of the measurement, and e defines the error, which is the difference of the desired speeds and the actual speeds ($e = e_v$ or $e = e_\sigma$) in case of

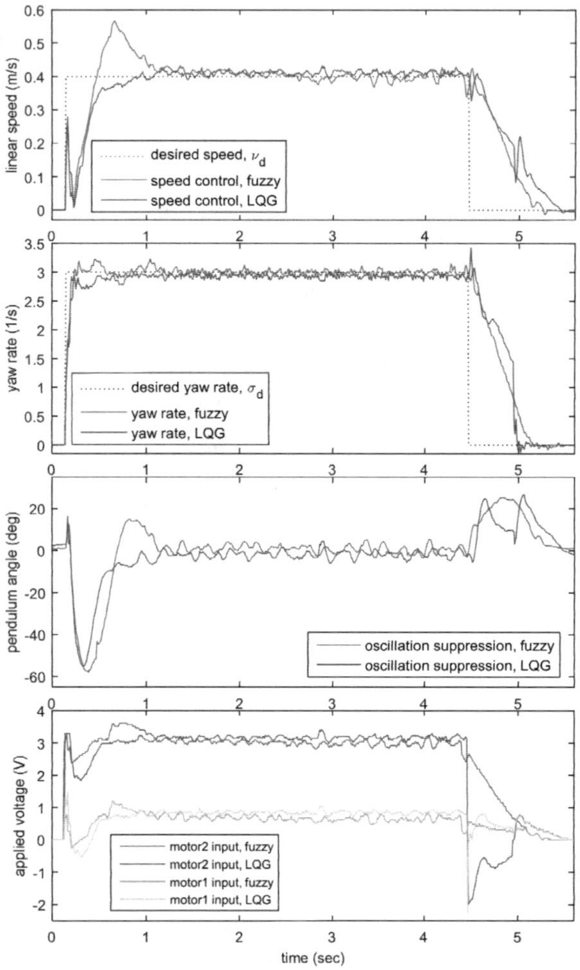

Figure 6. Control performances of the implemented LQG and fuzzy control strategies (Measurement results).

reference tracking, while in case of the suppression of the inner body oscillation $e = e_{\omega_3} = -\omega_3$ (since the desired rate of oscillation is zero, see Section IV). It was important to evaluate these quality-measuring expressions, because the results of the evaluation will form the initial fitness function values of the optimization of the fuzzy controllers in the next step of the investigation.

Based on the simulation and implementation results the qualitative characteristics of the elaborated controllers were summarized. The summary is given in Table IV, where T_{rise} indicates the rise time, $T_{5\%}$ denotes the settling time and ovs. is used for the abbreviation of overshoot. According to the simulation results, the LQG control strategy provided faster closed loop behavior with smaller reference tracking overshoot. From Table IV, it can also be read that the elaborated fuzzy scheme satisfies the control requirements with much bigger overshoot (0.036 m/s at 0.4 m/s reference speed), and due to the PI-type controllers it provides less

TABLE IV. CHARACTERISTICS OF THE CONTROLLERS

	Speed control of the robot			
	Simulation		Implementation	
	LQG	FUZZY	LQG	FUZZY
T_{rise} (s)	0.73	0.9	0.38	0.27
$T_{5\%}$ (s)	0.82	1.78	0.38	0.83
ovs. $\left(\frac{\mathrm{m}}{\mathrm{s}}\right)$	0.0083	0.036	0.018	0.14

	Suppression of the inner body oscillations			
	Simulation		Implementation	
	LQG	FUZZY	LQG	FUZZY
ovs. (°)	29.9	25.6	52.7	56.3
$T_{5°}$ (s)	0.85	1.19	0.71	0.91

aggressive closed loop behavior then the linear controller. Regarding the suppression of the inner body oscillations, both controllers performed the task similarly; the overshoot (e.g., maximum oscillation angle) was between 25-30 degrees.

These simulation results well predicted the outcome of the comparison related to the implemented controllers. The measurement results also proved that the LQG control strategy ensured faster system response and smaller overshoots. Regarding the fuzzy speed controller, the big overshoot is quite conspicuous (measurement results in Figure 6), and also, slower settling time characterizes the weaker performance of the fuzzy control scheme. Both realized controllers successfully suppressed the inner body oscillations with similar quality (e.g., the maximum overshoot was around 55 degrees).

According to the figures, it can be concluded that more satisfying control performance was achieved by the LQG control technique. The reason of the modest performance of the elaborated fuzzy control scheme could have different sources. It is important to mention that the realized controllers are the results of intuitive control design steps, meaning that the linear controller has been defined by selecting the Q and R weighting matrices (and taking into account the plant dynamics), while the inference mechanism of fuzzy control has been defined by the selected membership functions and rules. Moreover, it shall be kept in mind that the derived mathematical model (4) has not been validated, since the nominal (or calculated) values of inertia related (inertia matrix, center of mass) and electrical parameters (such as the resistance of inductance of the motor) that characterize the robot were used in the development procedure. The result of the not validated mathematical model can also be seen in Table IV, since we got significant differences between the simulation and implementation results. In fact, it was expected that the performance of the realized controllers will differ from the simulation results since the design procedure of the LQG control takes into account the mathematical model as a constraint equation (which is only approximately known), ultimately this difference led the system to a better closed loop behavior.

The evaluation of the quality measurement formulas (18) and (19) are summarized in Table V. The outcome of the evaluation results concludes controversy, since according to the calculated error integrals, the better overall control

TABLE V. QUALITY MEASUREMENT NUMBERS

	Fuzzy control			
	e_v	e_σ	e_{ω_3}	$\log_{10}\Pi$
SAE	30.4780	128.7299	$4.2689 \cdot 10^3$	7.2240
SSE	6.5300	218.3223	$1.1638 \cdot 10^5$	8.2199
STAE	85.6093	512.2402	$9.4892 \cdot 10^3$	8.6192
STSE	20.3829	955.1933	$1.6724 \cdot 10^5$	9.5127

	LQG control			
	e_v	e_σ	e_{ω_3}	$\log_{10}\Pi$
SAE	30.8451	150.3294	$3.7218 \cdot 10^3$	7.2370
SSE	6.9708	265.7726	$8.0833 \cdot 10^4$	8.1754
STAE	101.2168	581.9903	$9.1477 \cdot 10^3$	8.7315
STSE	23.8399	$1.169 \cdot 10^3$	$1.2966 \cdot 10^5$	9.5579

performance is provided by the fuzzy control scheme. The last column of Table V indicates that according to the SAE, STAE, and STSE quality measurement formulas the realized fuzzy control scheme results smaller aggregated error values. The rows of Table V define the chosen error integral formula, while the first three columns define the aggregated error value related to the errors e_v, e_σ and e_{ω_3}. The overall aggregated error value has been defined by multiplying the sub-aggregated error values, for example, in case of SAE:

$$\mathrm{SAE}_{\mathrm{overall}} = \log_{10} \prod_{e \in \{e_v, e_\sigma, e_{\omega_3}\}} \mathrm{SAE}(e). \quad (20)$$

Therefore, the ultimate outcome of the comparison is that the LQG control strategy provided better transient system responses, however, the better overall control performance was achieved by the cascade-connected fuzzy control scheme. Through this analysis, we could see that approximate reasoning and the heuristic knowledge oriented development gave satisfying control performances. This suboptimal control solution can be further investigated and improved by using the quality measurement formulas (18) and (19) in an optimization procedure. In this optimization procedure, both the shape of the membership functions and their ranges could be optimized for a better overall control performance.

X. CONCLUSION AND FUTURE WORK

In this paper, LQG and fuzzy control strategies were elaborated for a two-wheeled mobile pendulum system. The elaborated control strategies successfully ensured the speed control of the robot and the stabilization of the inner body oscillations as well. The control performances were tested both in simulation environment and on the real robot. The comparative assessment has been given based on real-time behavior of the system, where the LQG control strategy provided faster system responses, however, the elaborated fuzzy control scheme ensured better overall control performance. These experiments form our initial results in the investigation of the control performances of different optimized modern control methods. Future work will involve the identification of the unknown parameters of the robot, since it was seen that the approximately known mathematical model significantly influenced the final outcome of the investigation. Furthermore, the future research work will focus on the validation of optimized control strategies, where the defined quality measurement functions could lead the system to a better optimum.

ACKNOWLEDGMENT

We acknowledge the financial support of this work by the Hungarian State and the European Union under the TÁMOP-4.2.2.D-15/1/KONV-2015-0002 project entitled "Development of Smart technologies for High-tech industry".

APPENDIX

The Lagrange function of the system:

$$\begin{aligned}\mathcal{L} = &\sum_{i=1}^{2}\left(\frac{3}{4}m_w r^2 + \frac{1}{8}m_b r^2 + \frac{l^2 r^2}{2d^2} m_b \sin^2\theta_3 + \frac{1}{2}J_{\mathcal{B}}\frac{r^2}{d^2} + \frac{1}{2}k^2 J_r\right)\dot{\theta}_i^2 \\ &+ \sum_{i=1}^{2}\left(\frac{1}{2}m_b l r\cos\theta_3 - k^2 J_r\right)\dot{\theta}_3\dot{\theta}_i \\ &+ \left(\frac{1}{4}m_b r^2 - \frac{l^2 r^2}{d^2} m_b \sin^2\theta_3 - J_{\mathcal{B}}\frac{r^2}{d^2}\right)\dot{\theta}_1\dot{\theta}_2 \\ &+ \left(\frac{1}{2}m_b l^2 + \frac{1}{2}J_{\mathcal{A}} + k^2 J_r\right)\dot{\theta}_3^2 - 2m_w g r - m_b g(r - l\cos\theta_3).\end{aligned} \quad (A)$$

Elements of the inertia matrix $M(q) = (m_{ij})_{3\times 3}$:

$$\begin{aligned} m_{11} &= \frac{3}{2}m_w r^2 + \frac{1}{4}m_b r^2 + k^2 J_r + \frac{l^2 r^2}{d^2} m_b \sin^2\theta_3 + J_{\mathcal{B}}\frac{r^2}{d^2}, \\ m_{22} &= m_{11},\ m_{33} = m_b l^2 + J_{\mathcal{A}} + 2k^2 J_r, \\ m_{12} &= m_{21} = \frac{1}{4}m_b r^2 - \frac{l^2 r^2}{d^2} m_b \sin^2\theta_3 - J_{\mathcal{B}}\frac{r^2}{d^2}, \\ m_{13} &= m_{23} = m_{31} = m_{32} = \frac{1}{2}m_b l r\cos\theta_3 - k^2 J_r. \end{aligned} \quad (B)$$

TABLE VI. NOTATION OF THE ROBOT PARAMETERS

Symbol	Name	Value [SI Unit]
r	Wheel radius	$3.15 \cdot 10^{-2}$
m_w	Mass of the wheels	$31.6 \cdot 10^{-3}$
l	Distance between the COG and the wheel axle	$8.36 \cdot 10^{-3}$
m_b	Mass of the inner body	$360.4 \cdot 10^{-3}$
d	Distance between the wheels	$177 \cdot 10^{-3}$
$J_{\mathcal{A}}$	Moment of inertia of the inner body about the wheel axle $\mathcal{A}$	$81367 \cdot 10^{-9}$
$J_{\mathcal{B}}$	Moment of inertia of the inner body about the axis $\mathcal{B}$	$574620 \cdot 10^{-9}$
k	Gear ratio	64
J_r	Rotor inertia	$0.12 \cdot 10^{-7}$
R	Terminal resistance	2.3
L	Rotor inductance	$26 \cdot 10^{-6}$
k_M	Torque constant	$2.05 \cdot 10^{-3}$
k_E	Back-EMF constant	$2.05 \cdot 10^{-3}$
b	Viscous friction coefficient between body - motor	$2.1 \cdot 10^{-5}$
f_v	Viscous friction coefficient between wheels - ground	$1.8 \cdot 10^{-4}$

The elements of $V(q,\dot{q}) = (v_1, v_2, v_3)^T$:

$$\begin{aligned} v_1 &= 2\frac{l^2r^2}{d^2}m_b \sin\theta_3 \cos\theta_3 \dot{\theta}_3(\dot{\theta}_1 - \dot{\theta}_2) - \frac{1}{2}m_b lr \sin\theta_3 \dot{\theta}_3^2, \\ v_2 &= 2\frac{l^2r^2}{d^2}m_b \sin\theta_3 \cos\theta_3 \dot{\theta}_3(\dot{\theta}_2 - \dot{\theta}_1) - \frac{1}{2}m_b lr \sin\theta_3 \dot{\theta}_3^2, \\ v_3 &= -\frac{l^2r^2}{d^2}m_b \sin\theta_3 \cos\theta_3 \left(\dot{\theta}_1 - \dot{\theta}_2\right)^2 + m_b gl \sin\theta_3. \end{aligned} \tag{C}$$

The block matrices of equation (9):

$$\begin{aligned} &\tilde{A}_{s,21} = \begin{bmatrix} 0 & -0.08 \\ 0 & -136.5 \end{bmatrix}, \tilde{A}_{s,22} = \begin{bmatrix} -25.9 & 0.8 \\ 2338 & -73.6 \end{bmatrix}, \\ &\tilde{A}_{s,33} = \begin{bmatrix} 0 & 1 \\ 0 & -56 \end{bmatrix}, \tilde{B}_{s,2} = \begin{bmatrix} 3 & 3 \\ -279.6 & -279.6 \end{bmatrix}, \\ &\tilde{B}_{s,3} = \begin{bmatrix} 0 & 0 \\ -73.9 & 73.9 \end{bmatrix}, \tilde{C}_{s,2} = \begin{bmatrix} 1 & 0 \\ 0 & 0 \end{bmatrix}, \text{and } \tilde{C}_{s,3} = \begin{bmatrix} 0 & 0 \\ 0 & 1 \end{bmatrix}. \end{aligned} \tag{D}$$

REFERENCES

[1] Á. Odry, E. Burkus, and P. Odry, "LQG Control of a Two-Wheeled Mobile Pendulum System," The Fourth International Conference on Intelligent Systems and Applications (INTELLI 2015), 2015, pp. 105-112, ISBN: 978-1-61208-437-4.

[2] K. S. Tang, Kim Fung Man, Guanrong Chen, and Sam Kwong, "An optimal fuzzy PID controller," IEEE Transactions on Industrial Electronics, vol. 48, 2001, pp. 757 – 765, doi: 10.1109/41.937407.

[3] L. A. Zadeh, "Fuzzy sets," Information and Control, vol. 8, 1965, pp. 338 – 353, doi: 10.1016/S0019-9958(65)90241-X.

[4] H. B. Verbruggen and P. M. Bruijn, "Fuzzy control and conventional control: What is (and can be) the real contribution of Fuzzy Systems," Fuzzy sets and Systems, vol. 90, 1997, pp. 151 – 160, doi: 10.1016/S0165-0114(97)00081-X.

[5] G. F. Franklin, J. D. Powell, and A. Emami-Naeini, Feedback Control of Dynamic Systems. Pearson Prentice Hall, 2014, ISBN: 978-0-13349-659-8.

[6] A. Divelbiss and J. Wen, "Trajectory tracking control of a car-trailer system," IEEE Transactions on Control Systems Technology, vol. 5, 1997, pp. 269 - 278, doi: 10.1109/87.572125.

[7] J.-K. Ji and S.-K. Sul, "Kalman filter and LQ based speed controller for torsional vibration suppression in a 2-mass motor drive system," IEEE Transactions on Industrial Electronics, vol. 42, 2002, pp. 564 - 571, doi: 10.1109/41.475496.

[8] S. Jeong and T. Takahashi, "Wheeled inverted pendulum type assistant robot: inverted mobile, standing, and sitting motions," IEEE/RSJ International Conference on Intelligent Robots and Systems (IROS 2007), 2007, pp. 1932 - 1937, doi: 10.1109/IROS.2007.4398961.

[9] S. Zhiyu and L. Daliang, "Balancing control of a unicycle riding," 29th Chinese Control Conference (CCC), 2010, pp. 3250 - 3254, ISBN: 978-1-4244-6263-6.

[10] L. Yi-bo, L. Wan-zhu, and S. Qi, "Improved LQG control for small unmanned helicopter based on active model in uncertain environment," International Conference on Electronics, Communications and Control (ICECC), 2011, pp. 289 - 292, doi: 10.1109/ICECC.2011.6067810.

[11] O. Araar and N. Aouf, "Full linear control of a quadrotor UAV, LQ vs H∞," UKACC International Conference on Control (CONTROL), 2014, pp. 133 - 138, doi: 10.1109/CONTROL.2014.6915128.

[12] D. McLean and H. Matsuda, "Helicopter station-keeping: comparing LQR, fuzzy-logic and neural-net controllers," Engineering Applications of Artificial Intelligence, vol. 11, 1998, pp. 411–418, doi: 10.1016/S0952-1976(98)00005-0.

[13] T. Das and I. N. Kar, "Design and implementation of an adaptive fuzzy logic-based controller for wheeled mobile robots," IEEE Transactions on Control Systems Technology, vol. 14, 2006, pp. 501-510, doi: 10.1109/TCST.2006.872536.

[14] C. S. Lee and R. V. Gonzalez, "Fuzzy logic versus a PID controller for position control of a muscle-like actuated arm," Journal of Mechanical Science and Technology, vol. 22, 2008, pp. 1475-1482, doi: 10.1007/s12206-008-0424-7.

[15] I. Kecskés and P. Odry, "Optimization of PI and Fuzzy-PI Controllers on Simulation Model of Szabad(ka)-II Walking Robot," International Journal of Advanced Robotic Systems, 2014, doi: 10.5772/59102.

[16] M. Santos, V. López, and F. Morata, "Intelligent fuzzy controller of a quadrotor," International Conference on Intelligent Systems and Knowledge Engineering (ISKE 2010), 2010, pp. 141-146, doi: 10.1109/ISKE.2010.5680812.

[17] Cheng-Hao Huang, Wen-June Wang, and Chih-Hui Chiu, "Design and Implementation of Fuzzy Control on a Two-Wheel Inverted Pendulum," IEEE Transactions on Industrial Electronics, vol. 58, 2010, pp. 2988-3001, doi: 10.1109/TIE.2010.2069076.

[18] Á. Odry, I. Harmati, Z. Király, and P. Odry, "Design, realization and modeling of a two-wheeled mobile pendulum system," 14th International Conference on Instrumentation, Measurement, Circuits and Systems (IMCAS '15), 2015, pp. 75-79, ISBN: 978-1-61804-315-3.

[19] Á. Odry, E. Burkus, I. Kecskés, J. Fodor, and P. Odry, "Fuzzy Control of a Two-Wheeled Mobile Pendulum System," 11th IEEE International Symposium on Applied Computational Intelligence and Informatics (SACI 2016), 2016, pp. 99-104, ISBN: 978-1-5090-2380-6.

[20] AppL-DSP. Video demonstration of the robot. [Online]. Available from: http://appl-dsp.com/lqg-and-fuzzy-control-of-a-mobile-wheeled-pendulum [Accessed: 28 May 2016].

[21] A. Salerno and J. Angeles, "A New Family of Two-Wheeled Mobile Robots: Modeling and Controllability," IEEE Transactions on Robotics, vol. 23, 2007, pp. 169 - 173, doi: 10.1109/TRO.2006.886277.

[22] B. Cazzolato et al., "Modeling, simulation and control of an electric diwheel," Australasian Conference on Robotics and Automation (ACRA 2011), 2011, pp. 1-10, ISBN: 978-0-9807-4042-4.

[23] L. Sciavicco and B. Siciliano, Modelling and Control of Robot Manipulators. Springer-Verlag London, 2000, ISBN: 978-1-85233-221-1.

[24] G. Welch and G. Bishop, "An Introduction to the Kalman Filter," Tech. Rep. TR 95-041, Department of Computer Science, University of North Carolina, USA, 2001.

[25] Li-Xin Wang, A course in fuzzy systems and control. Prentice-Hall, 1997, ISBN: 0-13-540882-2.

[26] STMicroelectronics, "Tilt measurement using a low-g 3-axis accelerometer," Application note AN3182, 2010.

[27] T. E. Marlin, Process control: designing processes and control systems for dynamic performance. McGraw-Hill Companies, 1995, ISBN: 0-07-040491-7.

International Academy, Research, and Industry Association (IARIA)
412 Derby Way
Wilmington, DE 19810

ISBN 978-1-5108-5621-9

CURRAN ASSOCIATES INC.
proceedings.com